THE SUNFISH BIBLE

The Sunfish Bible contains just about everything important that has been written to date about this fabulous boat, other than in Class publications.

It started as a revision by Will White of his original *The Sunfish Book*. He first did a complete revision in the late '80s at the request of the second publisher, Hearst Marine Books, which had bought the rights from *SAIL* when that magazine went out of the book business. After the revision was finished, Hearst dropped the project (there was a recession) and the manuscript was lost. The revision in this book, therefore, is a completely new one. In addition to revision of the original to bring it up to date, it has a number of new passages — "stuff I forgot to include in the original", Will admits – as well as new information and a number of interviews with recent stars in the Class.

Someone suggested including Larry Lewis' *Sail It Flat*, which had long been out of print. When Derrick Fries' *Successful Sunfish Racing* also went out of print, it seemed sensible to include that, as well. Both Larry and Derrick gave Will permission to reprint their books, and they are included, as originally published, in this volume.

Paul Odegaard offered Will his collection of articles from *Sailing World* magazine and its predecessors, for which he had obtained reprint rights. Most are included in this book, and are reprinted with permission.

Finally, to make *The Sunfish Bible* complete, Will sought and received permission from *SAIL* and *Motor Boating & Sailing* magazines to include reprints of some watershed articles of theirs, as well.

At Peter Johnstone's suggestion, Will added *Kristi and the Fish Sun* from Gary Jobson's book *World Class Sailing*, written with Martin Luray, and an expanded article Will wrote for *Mid-Gulf Sailing* about the Luffing Lassies of Sarasota, Florida.

If you think all this is really more than you wanted to know about Sunfish, then browse through this book. It's astonishing how much affection this little boat has generated, and how little repetition there is.

Cover Photo: Onne van der Wal

THE Sunfish BIBLE

Including

THE SUNFISH BOOK
Revised 1996 edition
by ***Will White***

SUCCESSFUL SUNFISH RACING
(1984)
by ***Derrick Fries***

SAIL IT FLAT
(1971)
by ***Larry Lewis***

and

Sunfish Articles (1965-1995) *from:*

- ***Motor Boating & Sailing***
- ***Sailing World*** and its predecessors,
  Yacht Racing/Cruising
  One-Design & Offshore Yachtsman
  One-Design Yachtsman
- ***SAIL***
- ***Windward Leg*** –the Class newsletter

Inquiries may be addressed to:
Will White
7362 Palomino Lane
Sarasota, FL 34241.

Manufactured in the United States of America
Designed by Catherine Laur White, Laur White & White

White, Will W., 1930-
The Sunfish Bible

ISBN 0-9654005-0-6
Library of Congress Catalog Card Number: 96-92585

Contents

• Dedication

To all the camp followers, past and present, in the worldwide Sunfish fleet - husbands and wives, sons and daughters, mothers and fathers, girlfriends and boyfriends. They have made the Sunfish crowd the huge extended family it is. Bless 'em all.

• Acknowledgments

Gary Jobson, with thanks, for permission to reprint *Kristi and the Fish Sun* from *World Class Sailing* by Gary Jobson and Martin Luray, Hearst Marine Books, 1987.

Derrick Fries, with thanks, for permission to reprint *Successful Sunfish Racing.*
Photos: Bob Pool, Lee Parks, Steve Baker, Allan Broadribb, Bob Johnstone, Daniel Forster.

Larry Lewis, with thanks, for permission to reprint *Sail It Flat.*
Illustrations: Mark Smith.

Sailing World, with thanks, for permission to reprint the following articles.
Thanks, also, for the permissions of the authors, illustrators and photographers of each article.

- "A Boat is a Boat" by Bob Smith, *One-Design Yachtsman*, July 1965.
  Photos: Sue Cummings.
- "Tuning to Win: The Sunfish" by Robert Johnstone, *One-Design & Offshore Yachtsman*, January 1967.
  Photos: Severi.
- "Sunfish Worlds" by Jack Knights, *One-Design & Offshore Yachtsman*, April 1970.
- "Sunfish North Americans" by Major Hall, *Yacht Racing/Cruising*, November/December 1978.
  Photos: Jim Curwen
- "Sunfish Worlds" staff written from interviews, *Yacht Racing/Cruising*, October 1979.
  Photos: Daniel Forster
- "Frostbiting Barrington Style" by John Burnham, *Yacht Racing/Cruising*, April 1980.
  Photos: Paul Mello.
- "From the Experts – Sunfish" by Paul Odegaard, *Yacht Racing/Cruising*, August 1982.
  Illustrations: Brad Dellenbaugh.
- "From the Experts – Sunfish" by Scott Kyle, *Sailing World*, June 1992.
  Illustrations: Henry Hill.

Cruising World, with thanks, for reverting rights to Will White for the article

- "The Sunfish as Tender" by Will White, written March 1991.
  Photo: The author.

SAIL, with thanks, for permission to reprint the following articles.
Thanks, also, for the permissions of the authors and photographers of each article.

- "A Mighty Good Time" by Dom Degnon, *SAIL*, August 1987.
  Photos: Dan Nerney.
- "Masters Just Wanna Have Fun" by Tom Linskey, *SAIL*, May 1995.
  Photos: Peter McGowan.

Windward Leg, the Class newsletter, as well as the authors, with thanks, for permission to reprint the following articles.

- "The Workbench" – inspection ports – by Brian Weeks, *Windward Leg*, Spring 1991.
- "Handicapped Sunfishing" by Jim Uroda, *Windward Leg*, Spring 1991.
- "The Workbench" – transportation – by Brian Weeks, *Windward Leg*, Summer 1991.
- "Solutions for Rudder Problems" by Larry Cochran, *Windward Leg*, Summer 1991.

Motor Boating & Sailing, with thanks, for permission to reprint *Wet Ecstasy.*

Sunfish Laser, Inc., with thanks, for permission to reprint materials they own, including most of the photos in the body of *The Sunfish Book.*

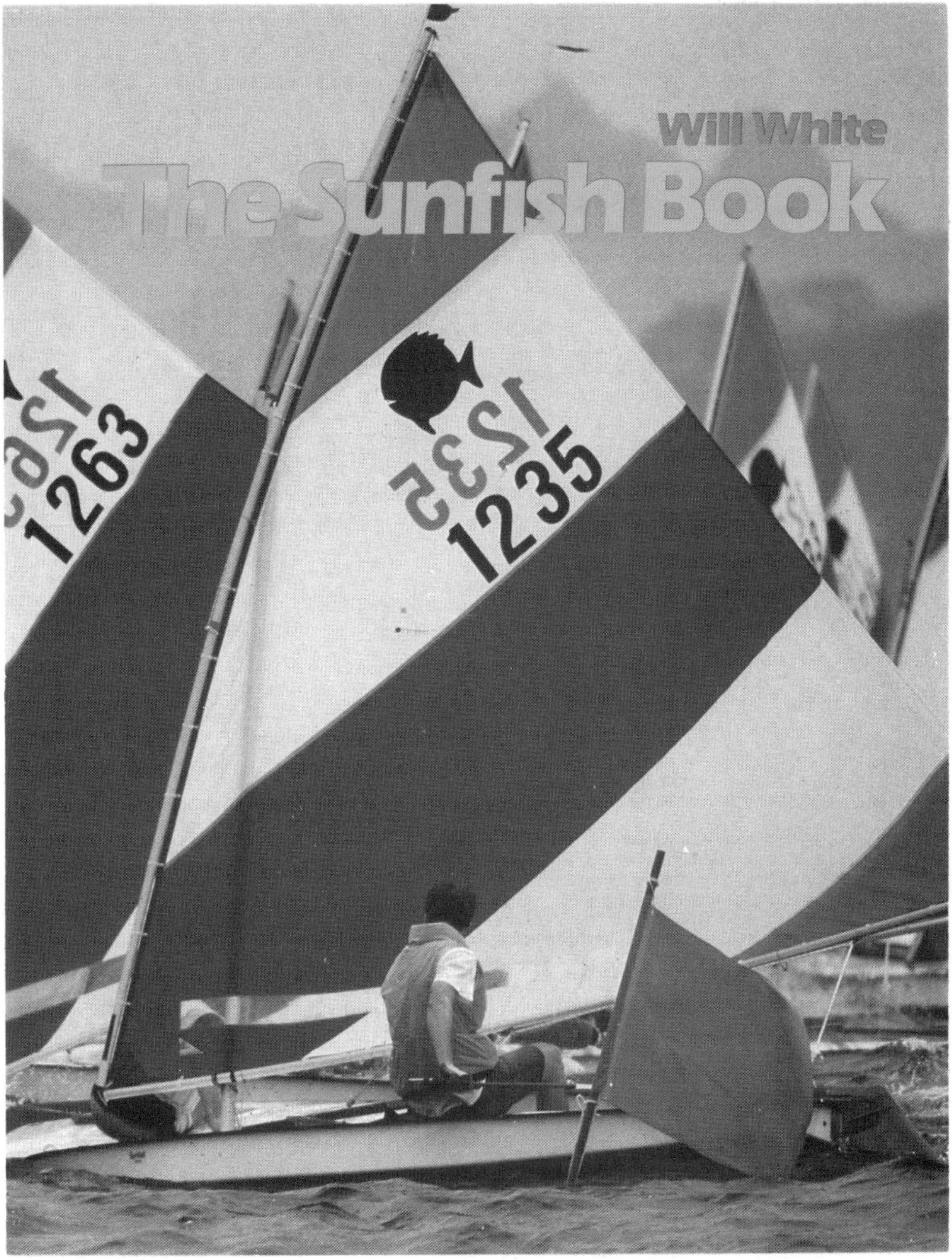

Will White

The Sunfish Book

Photo: *Daniel Forster*

New Edition
Revised 1996

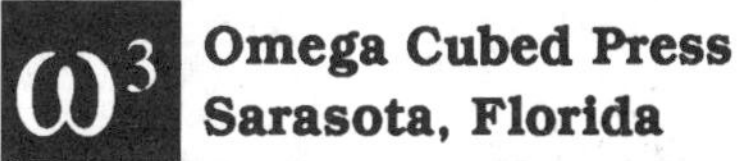

Omega Cubed Press
Sarasota, Florida

Inquiries may be addressed to:
Will White
7362 Palomino Lane
Sarasota, FL 34241.

Manufactured in the United States of America
Designed by Laur White & White

Original edition:
Manufactured in the United States of America
Designed by Design & Devices, Inc.

White, Will W., 1930-
The sunfish book

1.Sunfish (Sailboats) 2. Sailing. I Title.
GV811.63.S94W44 1982 797.1'24 82-10414

• Dedication

To my families, who put up with my Sunfish mania with enthusiasm or resignation (but they put up with it) — Alan, Christopher, Duncan, Elizabeth, Michael, Phyllis, Scott, Susan, Will IV .. and Catherine.

About the author

Will White learned to sail from books, and started to learn to race on Lake Winnipesaukee in 1944 under the tutelage of the son of the sailing master of the famous America's Cup J-boat *Ranger*. He went on to Tabor Academy on Buzzards Bay, where he became school champion and, when he was 17, won Brown University's regatta for prep schools. In the late '40s, he raced Rhodes 18s, Lightnings, and International 110s on Long Island Sound. He raced for Cornell University in the Naval Academy's 40-foot yawls in the intercollegiate MacMillen Cup, finishing second his senior year.

He didn't sail again until 1963, when he bought a used Sailfish. He traded that in for a used Sunfish in 1964 and won the first regatta he entered. In 1966 he won the Sunfish Nationals, the first year singles were sailed, and repeated in 1968, when the Nationals became the North Americans. He and Jack Evans invented the Great Sunfish Long-Distance Down-the-Connecticut-River Mixed Doubles Championship, which became the Connecticut River Sunfish Classic, still an annual event.

He was the first president of the United States Sunfish Class and then became Chief Measurer. He also served as the second chairman of the Super Sunfish Class.

Will retired from the advertising and public relations business in Hartford in 1990 and sailed his C&C 33 *Teysha* – single-handed, of course – to Sarasota, FL, where he now lives in the back woods with his wife Catherine, two cats, three dogs and four ducks. He still races Sunfish occasionally, as well as a Santana 20, *Flak*. He has been a contributing editor of *Mid-Gulf Sailing*, writes for *Cruising World* and *SAIL*, and is a vice-president of Boaters' Action & Information League (BAIL) and chairman of the Southwest Florida Regional Harbor Board.

• Acknowledgments

Champion sailors everywhere seem to delight in talking about their sport, and telling you, without reservation, why they think they are fast. I still owe all those with whom I spoke a big debt of thanks, from Carl Knight, the old master, to today's crop of outstanding Sunfish champions.

Others whose brains I've picked over the years include Gerrit Zeestraten, formerly of Curaçao, who was incredibly fast in big waves and wind, Paul Fendler, who is incredibly fast all the time and probably weighs 150 pounds soaking wet, and the champs I interviewed for the original book and this revision.

I would like to thank those at Alcort who were so helpful—Bruce Connolly, John Ray, Jack Evans, Warren Bowes, Rick Wonson, Bob Johnstone, Eric Skemp, Steve Baker, and Lee Parks. Lee has done more for the Class than any other person. Several years ago, Lee was elected a Life Member of the Class, at this writing still the one and only.

From Sunfish Laser, Inc., the current manufacturer, special thanks to its president, Peter Johnstone, and again Steve Baker, who left Alcort and went to work for another sailcraft company for a while but came back to his first love a couple of years ago. It was Steve who suggested the title for this book. Special thanks , too, to Peg and Terry Beadle of the Class office; Brian Weeks, president of the U.S. Sunfish Class Association, and Larry Cochran and Paul Odegaard, long-time members of the Class Advisory Council.

I have to thank the old-timers with whom I raced at the Darien (Connecticut) Sunfish Yacht Racing Association, whose sailors dominated the class in the late '60s, and the Barrington (Rhode Island) Frostbite Racing Association. Both helped develop a number of champions. And, of course many thanks to all the Sunfish sailors who are quoted here, all whose brains I picked without attribution and all who pushed me to finish this five-year project.

Much of the original book was dictated while I traveled to and from regattas. My thanks still to Jeannie Marshall, one of the world's nicest people and a magician on the IBM System 6 Word Processor, who typed it. Huge thanks also to Michael Brandow, who keyboarded an enormous chunk of this edition. Thanks to Peter Johnstone, Paul Odegaard (he recently reverted to the original Norwegian spelling of his name), Lee Parks, and Barbara Stilley, who proofread the first draft and offered helpful comments. And most especially I thank Catherine Laur White, designer, desktop publishing maven, genius on the Macintosh, and my wife. She can hardly be blamed if she never wants to hear about Sunfish again.

Contents

Will White at the 1977 National Team Race Championship in Bristol, Rhode Island. The sail was an experimental version built by Ratsey. In the background, with sail 13185, is second World Champion Ted Moore.

Introduction

The Sunfish is pure sailing, the essence of sailing. Practically no upkeep. No worries about moorings and boat yards. Five minutes from arriving at the water's edge, you can be off and sailing. It was the first off-the-beach boat and it introduced thousands of people to the sport.

The Sunfish was designed with no preconceptions. It is doubtful that a naval architect, thoroughly indoctrinated in fine bow entries for speed to windward and high-aspect-ratio marconi sails for aerodynamic efficiency, would have come up with a mackerel's-head-and-cod's-tail hull, or the absurd equilateral triangle sail. But these two features are among those that give the Sunfish its character.

The shallow vee-bottom of the hull and hard chine,together with its rather generous beam, make the Sunfish comparatively stable and forgiving. It's an ideal boat for children or those learning to sail. It can be righted easily if it capsizes. Most small sailboats capsize quite regularly. But a Sunfish was the first one you could right, climb back aboard, and sail off without worrying about whether you could get the water out before you capsized again. In fact, it is quite possible to anticipate the capsize, roll over on the daggerboard as the mast hits the water, pop it back upright with the same rolling motion, and hardly get your socks wet.

The crazy lateen rig is another benefit. Drop the sail, lift out the mast, and roll everything together in one simple package the same length as the boat. While others are still fussing with sleeves and tracks, multisection masts and booms, and sail battens, you are on the road home or relaxing on the beach.

Just as the Sunfish represents pure sailing, it offers pure sailboat racing. No need for a new set of sails every year. Your one triangular sail, properly set on the spars, will last for years and still be competitive. No need to keep buying or changing expensive hardware to keep up with the latest sailing theory. Even if you attach the best of everything allowed by the Class rules, you'll have a hard time spending more than $200, assuming your boat already has a racing sail and daggerboard.

It is important to know something about the people who race Sunfish, too. Each major racing class has a personality of its own, and I think the Sunfish crowd has a very special mystique. They are not particularly clannish and they are happy to welcome new people. They tend to be family-oriented, and attend regattas with wives or husbands and children. The racing tends to be fierce, but joyfully so, and the abrasions are usually left out on the water. Most of the young champions grew up with Sunfish, learning to sail from their parents or older siblings, who may have been champions in their day. Each new regatta is like a family reunion. So if you want competition with a sense of fun, Sunfish racing is probably for you.

Your Sunfish should remain competitive for a lifetime, if properly maintained. It is, by some people's reckoning, overbuilt. It can withstand abuse that would crack most racing dinghies like an egg shell. Of course, nothing in this world is perfect. The Sunfish is mass produced and occasionally a lemon will slip by. This almost always used to take the form of a leaker, exceedingly annoying but usually easy to fix with a little resin and filler. Today, the consensus is that quality control is better than it's ever been, so leakers are almost non-existent in new boats, and Sunfish Laser, Inc., will correct any problems during the warranty period. Another flaw I used to find a little maddening in an otherwise well-made boat was the finish on the wood parts. Of course, fine varnished mahogany is almost as rare in small boat building today as silver-plated hardware, so perhaps I am overcritical. Otherwise, the Sunfish is a yacht-quality boat.

In all, I must admit I am crazy about the Sunfish. It is pure sailing, and sailing is the most fun you can have with your clothes on. (My apologies to Jerry DeLaFemina, a fellow toiler in the advertising vineyards, who thinks advertising fits that definition. Advertising sure is fun, but not as much fun as sailing!)

Will White
Sarasota, Florida,
July 1996

1 Background on the Boat

"LIFE'S OUT STOP WE'RE IN STOP ALL'S FORGIVEN STOP COME HOME"

Cortland "Bud" Heyniger was on holiday in the Southwest when he got that telegram from his partner, Alex "Red" Bryant. (They preferred their Alcort names, "Cort" and "Alex", in business; "Red" and "Bud" were for personal friends. Many of their business friends, however, quickly became personal friends.) It brought Cort home to Waterbury, Connecticut, by the next available means of transportation. The telegram referred to a spread in LIFE about a funny looking sailing machine called the Sailfish. It was August, 1948, and the fledgling firm of Alcort, Inc. was 2½ years old. (They named their company Alcort instead of Cortal so it would be up front in the Yellow Pages.)

Alex and Cort had been friends since they were in kindergarten together. "We were house builders at an early age," according to Alex. They formed the Prospect Street Hut Society, and rebuilt the hut several times. That was followed by a glider ("Fortunately, it didn't fly.") and their first commercial venture, a gadget called the "Klickety-Klack-Marble-Track." They had no formal training in woodworking; "we simply taught each other."

"We were still in school, and we made some iceboats. That's what started the whole thing," Cort told me in 1980. They were basically Skeeter class iceboats, with 75 square feet of sail. Most Skeeters are one-man boats, but the partners built a one-design version that sat two and called it the Yankee class. It was mainly a venture for fun. "The winter before the war we only had one weekend we couldn't sail, and we never had so much fun in our lives," Cort said. It was 1941, and they did not return home from war for four years. When they got home, they found that the barn in which their Skeeters were stored was burned to the ground, but fortunately the owner had insured the building's contents. They

Al and Cort of Alcort, who parlayed a surfboard with a sail into the most popular racing sailboat and family fun boat in the world – the Sunfish. Alex "Red" Bryan on the left, with Cortland "Bud" Heyniger and a mess of Sunfish.

returned to a pile of ashes but there were also orders for more Skeeters. That was enough to put Alcort into business.

Cort again: "We made ice boats and then we needed something for the summertime. We tried row boats and we put together a few hobby kits, and then this fellow came in and wanted us to make a paddle board for the Red Cross. We told him how much it would cost. He threw up his hands and said the Red Cross couldn't afford it. But he made the mistake of leaving the plans there, which were not much, and we made one

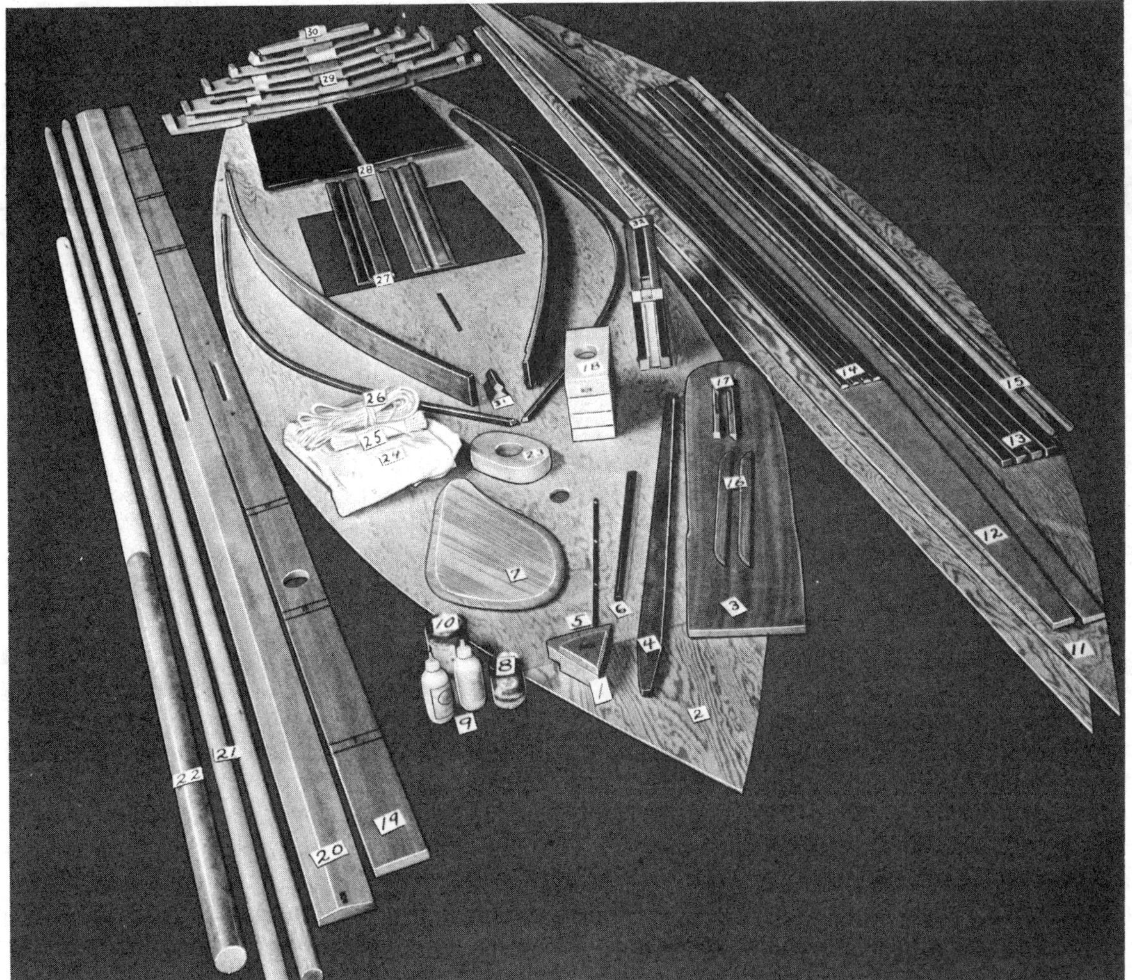

This is the way your Sunfish came if you bought it in the early '50s.

anyway. Alex put a canoe sail on it and that's what started the Sailfish.

"That was the first one. The thing was only 22 inches wide and we were trying to figure a way to keep it upright. Obviously we needed more beam, which we put on the next one. It was like trying to sail a log, that first one.

"We went through a couple more models. The first Sailfish was 14 feet long and then we couldn't get any more 14-foot plywood. So we made some 12-footers. That's the one that got into LIFE. That really was the first Sailfish - the 12-footer."

The first few dozen Sailfish were sold to friends on various small lakes around Connecticut and central Massachusetts and on Long Island Sound. The Waterbury paper heard about it and wrote it

Background on the Boat

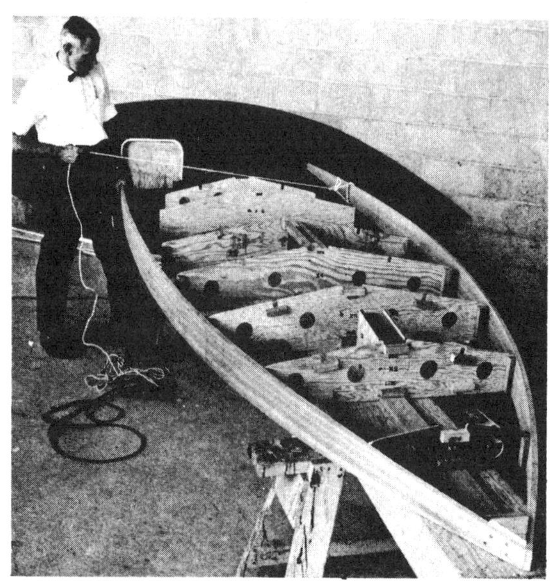

Cort Heyniger demonstrates how the topside strakes were bent to the ribs in building a Sunfish from a kit. Kits have not been marketed by Alcort since the mid-60s.

up. At that point, they were still calling it the Sailboard. A marketing friend told them that "Sailboard" would never do. He had a mounted sailfish trophy in his office, and somebody said, "That's it!" or "Eureka!" or something, and the Sailfish was christened.

The first plant was in the loft of a lumber yard, a two-story brick warehouse building. After the LIFE article, Alcort outgrew the loft, and then two more buildings in the north end of Waterbury.

How did the LIFE article come about? A clever publicity man? "No," Cort Said. "A friend of ours brought a date up from New York. She could sail the Sailfish better than he could, and she had never seen it before. It turned out she was one of the music editors for LIFE. She went back to New York and said, "Hey, fellows, here's something that would make a good story." We didn't know anything about it until they called up and wondered if we could get something together, and where. We suggested Madison, Connecticut.

"We went down there for the weekend, and Saturday we had 15 boats there. We had a lot of friends and they helped us a lot. They came from all over Connecticut. The only trouble was, it rained Saturday and it was foggy all day Sunday, so they couldn't get any pictures. And there was no wind. The LIFE people went back to New York.

"On the next Monday, we got word from the weather people up in Hartford that it was going to be a good day. They had told us in New York, 'When you get some good weather going, we'll come back.'

"Alex had been in the Air Corps, and he knew about weather reports. So we told the LIFE people to come back at noon on Monday, because that's when it was going to start.

"Well, they came back up and took pictures all Monday afternoon and some on Tuesday. They went away, and later we called them, and they said, 'Well, we've got all these pictures and a story written up, but we don't know whether it will get in the magazine or not.'"

The story did appear, and a whole new kind of yachting was born.

Almost from the beginning, Alcort sold kits as well as finished boats. I asked Cort how long it would take an average handy person to build a Sunfish from a kit. "It said in the catalog a few dozen hours. The handier a person the more time he or she spends on it, and it's awfully hard to guess how long it will take. A real perfectionist could spend a whole winter on it and enjoy it. Some people slapped them together in no time and then they had leak problems for the rest of their lives." Later, he said in disbelief, "We found that some people were installing screws with a hammer instead of a screwdriver."

There is an apocryphal story that the Sunfish was designed so that Aileen, Alex Bryan's wife, would have a place to put her feet and sail comfortably after she became pregnant. Actually,

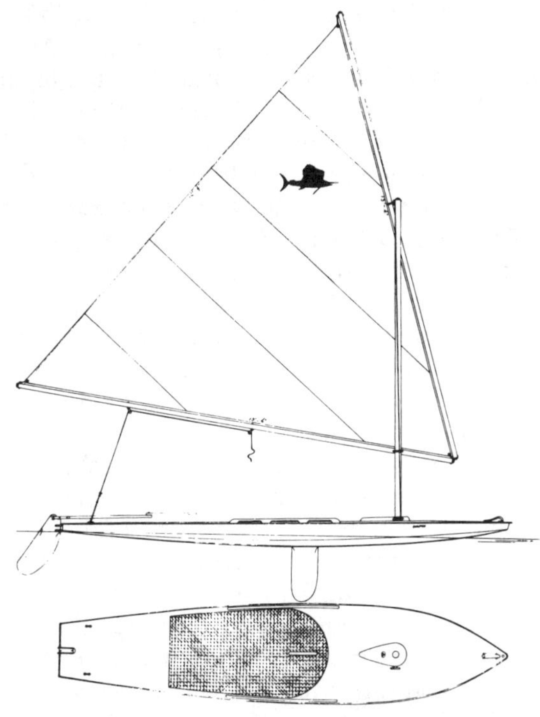

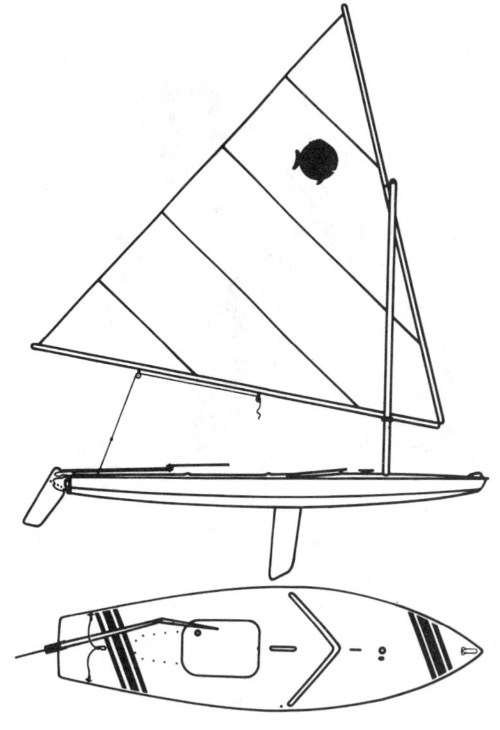

Super Sailfish specifications:

Length	*13ft. 7 in.*
Beam	*35 1/2 in.*
Sail area	*75 sq. ft.*
Hull weight	*98 lbs.*

Sunfish specifications:

Length	*13ft. 10 in.*
Beam	*48 1/2 in.*
Sail area	*75 sq. ft.*
Hull weight	*139 lbs.*

Cort told me, the Sunfish was designed because both his wife and Aileen, who was the daughter of sailing legend Cornelius Shields, were uncomfortable sailing the Sailfish. "I didn't like it myself."

Even in 1981, nobody seemed to remember whether the first Sunfish was built in 1952, '53 or '54. Cort did remember that the lines were lofted by the little company's first employee, Carl Meinert, right on the shop floor.

"They looked pretty good, and that was it," Cort said.

The original wooden Sunfish was 13 feet 7 1/2 inches long with a beam 1/2 inch shy of 4 feet. The sail area, like that of the Super Sailfish, was 75 square feet. The hull weighed 130 pounds. The original Sunfish had a lot of parts in common with the Super Sailfish, which was the same

Background on the Boat

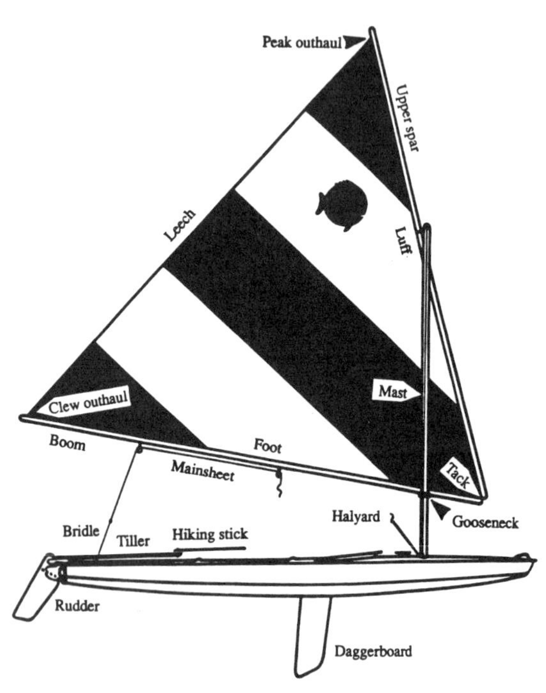

Sunfish nomenclature

length and had supplanted the 12-foot Sailfish. The transom, rudder and spars were identical although the daggerboard was longer to compensate for the deeper hull.

The original Sunfish flyer lists the following specifications: "The best marine plywood and Philippine mahogany. Rudder, tiller, daggerboard, coamings, and rubbing strips are also mahogany. Mast and spars are selected Sitka spruce. Fittings are brass, bronze, and aluminum. Sail is specially treated mildew-resistant white sailcloth." In those days, sailcloth meant cotton. The picture shows a beautifully setting 10-panel cotton sail. It also shows a wrap-around coaming like a wishbone, starting where the present splashrail starts, and wrapping clean around the cockpit at the rails.

Heyniger designed the original flip-up rudder mechanism, which was made of bronze. Alcort switched to a different aluminum design in the late '60s because the original fitting had a tendency to pop out when subjected to considerable side pressure in heavy air, causing you to lose control, an infuriating business. Many people modified their old hulls at considerable expense and effort to take the new, more satisfactory mount. The rudder cheeks have been made of plastic instead of cast aluminum since the early '90s. The early plastic ones were known to break in heavy air, but they have since been beefed up.

Heyniger also designed the gooseneck, called the yoke in company literature until very recently, with some help from Wilcox-Crittenden. "We didn't know about the shrinkage of bronze," remembered Heyniger, "so the cast part was actually smaller than the pattern, but that was all right. It was already heavier than it needed to be. The casting shop jumped with glee every time we ordered another 100. You buy castings by the pound!"

Who designed the famous logo? "I guess I did," said Cort. "I took a nickel and drew a circle around it, drew a tail on, and a mouth and eye...and that's how it developed."

The original sails were white; later the partners offered blue and red cotton.

Along about the time the first Sunfish was developed, Alcort acquired an advertising agency named Gotham. The account executive was Duncan Sutphen. He turned out the first few flyers and brochures. Shortly after that, Cort and Alex decided to look for an agency closer to Waterbury, and called the Graceman agency in Hartford. John Brotherhood, later to be one of my partners, was an account executive there. The day of the call, Ed Graceman called his staff together and asked, "Does anyone know anything about sailboats?" John was the only one who did, so he became Alcort's second advertising man.

"There were two nice guys sitting in the middle of a pile of shavings," John said of his first visit to Alcort. "I can remember two major marketing pronouncements I made to Bud and Alex. The first was that they should establish a network of dealers, and stop trying to be just a mail-order operation. It took awhile, but they finally agreed, and I was right. The second pronouncement was that the Sunfish would never sell. I thought the Sailfish was unique, but that the Sunfish was trying too much to be a real boat. Oh well, .500 isn't too bad."

The Sailfish was phased out by 1962, but the Super Sailfish lived on for quite a while, in and out of production at some 100 to 200 boats per year. Now it has been out of production for close to 20 years, although just before it was sold Alcort was playing with the idea of a revival, including wooden kits.

The next big step Alex and Cort took was to hire a young MBA from the University of Michigan, who wanted to be in the sailboat business. "He was the one who kind of drove us along," Cort said. "He was a big help to us." His name was Bruce Connolly, and the date was June, 1956.

In 1958, having outgrown the third plant it had taken over, Alcort designed and built its own plant. They were still building wooden boats. "Then, in 1959, Joe Schmidt of Naugatuck Chemical convinced us to try fiberglass," Bruce said. "Their technicians came in and taught us how to build with it. We started with the Super Sailfish, and built that for a year. In 1960 we started building the Sunfish in fiberglass."

A number of changes were made in the Sunfish for the shift to fiberglass. The hull was made deeper, and the boat was given a little more freeboard forward to help reduce the original boat's tendency to submarine before the wind.

The front page of the second Sunfish brochure pictures Alex Bryan heading for the dock after a test sail. The first brochure was a simple one-page bulletin.

Background on the Boat

The deck was given a little crown, and the chines were rounded to make them stronger and more easily removed from the molds. It was also an inch wider, because of the flanges where hull and deck were joined. It also became 2 1/2 inches longer, with a bigger transom."

The glass and wood Super Sailfish, being almost identical in shape and weight, were competitive. But the fiberglass Sunfish was a faster boat in almost all conditions than the wood one. I had a wooden Sunfish for a couple of years, and actually managed to win a regatta with it. It had absorbed a lot of water, and was much heavier than the average glass boat. The extra weight proved an advantage in light, puffy conditions; the momentum carried you through the lulls, while the lighter boats stopped dead. Bob Bowles, the third World Champion, was another who started with a wooden Sunfish - he built it himself - but after a year or so he switched to glass.

The boats are built by the hand lay-up method, inside female molds. This is a quality way to build a boat, and is still used, even though newer - and cheaper - chopper gun methods of building small boats are available.

First a layer of gelcoat is sprayed in the mold. After the gelcoat comes a layer of resin. Fiberglass mat is squeegeed into it, and more resin applied. A woven roving is next, giving the Sunfish its long-lasting strength, followed by more resin. The molds hang from an overhead track on bars fore and aft, so they can be flipped upside down and the raw hull, cockpit tub, or deck can be shaken out.

Styrofoam blocks are glued in with foam-in-place polystyrene and then the decks are glued on the same way. Then comes a Rube Goldberg step. About a hundred heavy spring-loaded clamps are snapped into place around the circumference to bond the joint until it is dry. The workers who do that must be strong enough to pop tennis balls with their bare hands! Before the deck is placed on the hull, of course, the cockpit tub, daggerboard well and mast well have been properly positioned.

The old-style fiberglass Sunfish had a deck with just a slight crown. It was joined to the hull with a molded-in flange that stuck out from the hull at the same angle as the deck. After deck and hull were joined and the mating flanges glued, the joint was routed to the proper dimension and an aluminum rub-rail was pop-riveted around the whole boat in three sections. The new Sunfish has a rolled deck edge with a matching flange on the hull, and no rub-rail is used. It makes a stronger bond, and is much more comfortable for hiking. On the old-style boat, the fittings were then screwed into oak blocks that had previously been glued to the inside of the hull and deck. On the new boat, fittings are fastened with bolts to threaded aluminum backing plates. A hole is drilled in the deck for the drainage hole, another through the bottom of the cockpit tub and hull for the DePersia bailer, and a third in the forward face of the cockpit tub to equalize pressure in the hull with the atmospheric pressure outside (without it, the boat might pop a seam when the barometer is way down.) The hull is then tested for leaks by applying a little air pressure through the equalizing hole and coating all seams with soapy water. If any bubbles show up, there's a leak there, which is plugged with plastic putty.

For much of Sunfish history, the weights of the boats varied considerably, depending on how careful the workers were in applying the resin to the fiberglass. I know from personal observation that Alcort tried to improve its quality control in this area. After Alcort, through a succession of manufacturers, quality control had its ups and downs, and hull weights could vary considerably. At this writing, quality control seems to be well in hand at Sunfish Laser, Inc., and hulls weigh within five or six pounds of each other.

The gelcoat for the deck stripes, now long gone, was applied between strips of masking tape.

For many years Sunfish decks were unique for their "bar sinister" stripes. When did the deck striping come in? "That was about '65 or '66," said Bruce Connolly. "They said it could not be done, so I forget what show I went to but I started striping the boats myself with a shiny-faced tape. It was so successful at the show that I was selling rolls of tape for a short time, until Carl Meinert discovered how to stripe the foredecks. That went along for a couple of years until we needed something new, and then we started to stripe the afterdeck as well. Now, they can't build a boat without striping because of the burning of the molds."

With the switch to the rounded deck edges, the stripes were eliminated. I never heard anyone complain.

A lot of things were done over the years to jazz up the Sunfish, primarily because dealers wanted "something new." The "Daisy" sail shown on Page 12 was a suggestion by Ratsey, the original sailmaker, but Alcort thought that was too much. They did try a version of the boat with red hull and yellow deck and sails striped in the same colors.

Over the last few years various models have been brought out with fancy plastic sheet appliqués which fortunately (to my mind, anyway) can be peeled off. One year, the second manufacturer had two models, each with plastic appliqués on the foredeck and matching graphics silk-screened on white sails. The silk-screening started to peel off after about a year of sailing. The '95 model had a foredeck covered with freehand slashes in every color of the rainbow. Some people liked them; others peeled them off.

With the introduction of fiberglass came other new materials. The spars became aluminum, and the sails were offered in nylon and then in dacron. Alcort did not make fittings, or mold its own plastic or aluminum parts, but almost everything else was made at the Alcort plant in Waterbury, Connecticut.

Looking back on the boat's development, Bruce Connolly said that a major innovation, from a marketing viewpoint, was "the discovery of the DePersia bailer. It went into both the wooden kit and the fiberglass boat. Up until then, you had to carry a bailing can. I remember having to tell people that and being very embarrassed about it." It was originally made of bronze, with a screw-on cap that could gall and become frozen. For years now it has been made of nylon plastic, with a pop-off plug like a cork.

The first major change in the Sunfish design was the inclusion of a storage well molded as part of the cockpit tub, under the afterdeck. This is undoubtedly very handy for day sailing, and even for racing if you want to carry along a lunch or a bottle of water or stow your life jacket out of the way. But in heavy air, it becomes a big water trap, and was, at first, rather resented by the

Background on the Boat

serious racers for a few years. Now, most of us are sailing newer Sunfish, so we all have the same handicap. Nevertheless, some people still inflate a beach ball inside the storage well to reduce its capacity for water. I once drew a design on paper for a drawer with a gasket around the forward edge to fit snugly into the well. Alcort considered it for a while, but as far as I know they never went as far as to try out the design in practice. For a while they provided a nifty soft-side storage cooler as standard equipment, which did the same job as the beach ball.

Nobody could remember, even in 1979, just how much the first Sunfish cost. Neither Cort nor Alex kept many records during the early days. "We'd get so cluttered up with stuff that we'd throw a bunch away," they say. "And you forget to save one of everything." They think the first Sailfish cost $128.50 and that the first Sunfish was priced at $195, so that it was under the $200 mark.

I think they may be over-compensating for inflation. The first Sunfish flyer, of which I think I possessed the only surviving copy (now in the Class archives), boasts a price of $386 F.O.B. Waterbury. And I have another flyer, dated 1963, that lists the Sunfish kit at $297, and the fiberglass Sunfish at $476. In the same flyer, the standard Sailfish kit is $209, the Super Sailfish kit $239, and the fiberglass Super Sailfish $394. As I remember, I bought a used Super Sailfish in '63 for $100, and traded it in for my first, used Sunfish in '64 for another $100.

At one time, the price of Alcort's boats was rigidly maintained by the dealers. Then, for a while, thanks to the Robinson Patman Act and similar laws, retail prices were not even suggested. Even without controlling pricing, however, Sunfish now cost about four times what they did when I first started sailing them. Nevertheless, a Sunfish is probably one of the best-built toys around. A lot of years ago, FORTUNE named it one the best American-made products. I have owned more of them than I can remember, and I never sold one for less than I paid for it.

The Alcort story is an exception to the old rule that nice guys finish last. As Bruce Connolly said of Alex and Cort, "They were great people to work for, absolutely the best. They were like a father image to me. Alex and Cort were literally two of the nicest guys I've ever known."

By the mid-'60s, the business was growing ever-larger and the partners decided it was time to sell. "We were growing so rapidly that we felt we either had to go public, which we didn't particularly want to do, or find a larger financial partner. We picked AMF for a certain amount of synergism with the other AMF sports and leisure products. We needed greater financial backing."

In 1969, the partners sold Alcort to AMF. They believed the decision was a good one. The Sunfish, which had always been their mainstay, continued in production and, by 1982, over 200,000 had been built and sold. By now, in 1996, the figure is more than 300,000.

In 1985, at the height of the unfriendly takeover binge of those years; AMF became the target of takeover artist Irwin Jacobs. His objective was to sell off many AMF divisions, including Alcort. He won.

Alcort was sold to two men who had made Boston Whaler a success story, David Loveless and Jerry DeGarmo. They also bought Aquasport, a motorboat maker in Florida, and the two traded off running the two divisions. It was under their direction that the new rolled deck edges and the larger cockpit were introduced, with the concurrence of the Class officers. They also experimented with radial-cut sails and Mylar sails, neither of which were Class-approved for racing, and several offshore sailmakers. For a while, it was difficult to find a competitive sail, a fact that led the Class officers to start development of a truly one-design racing sail.

In 1988, Loveless and DeGarmo sold out to Pearson Yachts of Portsmouth, Rhode Island, a successful builder of cruising boats. Pearson moved manufacturing to its Rhode Island plant, and also bought the U.S. manufacturing rights to the Laser. Things seemed to pick up for both classes, but the fierce shake-out in large-boat manufacturing pulled Pearson down in 1991.

Peter Johnstone, son of Bob Johnstone, three-time South American Sunfish Champion and former Alcort V.P., formed Sunfish Laser, Inc., and is president. North Sails, whose president Tom Whidden had worked at Alcort in the early '70s, became majority shareholder. They bought the world-wide Sunfish and North American Laser rights and molds. All of them are world-class sailors. It appears to have been a successful venture for both the backers and the two Classes.

• Class Development

The early Sunfish racing was all doubles. Bruce Connolly wanted to promote the Sunfish as a family boat, and most of the early sailors seemed to like it that way. However, the serious sailors agitated for single-handed racing, and in 1966 Sunfish singles were added at the National Championships. Even in that first year, the singles fleet, at 95 boats I believe, was approximately three times the size of the doubles fleet. After a couple of years, Alcort decided to hold Singles and Doubles Championships at the same time in two different places. They preserved doubles racing for a year or two more, but now about the only doubles race left is the Connecticut River Race.

The Sunfish introduced sailing to a whole new group of people - younger people mostly, who could not afford the bigger boats of the time or membership in a yacht club. For the Sunfish you didn't need a club, or a mooring, or a boatyard, or all the other expenses associated with those upper class symbols. You carried the boat on top of your car, launched it from a beach, and never needed a boatyard because the boat never needed maintenance. Those were the qualities that made the Sunfish the largest fiberglass one-design class in the world.

One of the first fiberglass Super Sailfish, with first sales manager Bruce Connolly aboard. Bruce is credited by most Sunfish old-timers with building the Sunfish class to its present pre-eminence.

What made it the largest fiberglass one-design *racing* class in the world was the fierceness with which its one-design nature was protected. In the first place, it was the first manufacturer-owned class to achieve popularity. The class organization was a benevolent dictatorship, and while there had been a few attempts to take over the class on

Background on the Boat

a more democratic basis, most Sunfish sailors would just as soon have left things to Alcort. Their wishes were well represented by an advisory committee, which was usually consulted before any major changes were made.

Bruce Connolly felt that the most important contribution the Sunfish made to yacht racing was the concept of manufacturer control. Only in that way, he felt, was the unique one-design nature of the boat maintained. He pointed to the Laser and the J-24 (which were manufacturer-controlled in the early days) as proof. It's a point well taken, I think. Those sailors who were dissatisfied with Alcort control wanted the class to allow sailors more leeway, including opening up the sails to all sailmakers. Alcort resisted.

What changes and additions have been permitted over the years have been permitted primarily to improve convenience and safety. It is still quite possible to take a boat right out of the box and win races against boats that have been completely equipped with all of the gadgetry permitted.

Because the Sunfish was controlled completely by the manufacturer, it remained as one-design a boat as possible. Well, almost. Both before and since the company's purchase by AMF, Alcort resisted the temptation to play the planned obsolescence game. It made some changes over the years, a couple of which have been allowed to make the boat a little faster, but they were made primarily for competitive market reasons, usually with the concurrence of the racers.

Even if you do not intend to race, the changes and additions permitted by Class rules should be of interest to you. First, the success of the Class has, in large part, been because its one-design nature has been fiercely defended. That increases its desirability and therefore its resale value. Second, many of the permitted changes make the boat safer and more convenient to sail, increasing your potential enjoyment. The non-racer will also get benefits from joining the Class association. Many of the articles in the Class newsletter, the *Windward Leg*, are helpful to the casual Sunfisher, including repair tips, ideas to make you a better or safer sailor, and profiles of Sunfish sailors, quite a few of whom race to make new friendships and renew old ones.

Lee Parks, elected first Class Secretary, first Chief Measurer, first and only Life Member, and current IYRU coordinator for the Class.

Shortly before AMF was taken over, Alcort was under intense pressure to cut costs, and decided it could no longer function as the Class organization. The overhead was too great. A subsidiary benefit was that the Class, once it was under the control of the sailors, would be accepted by the International Yacht Racing Union for sanction as an International Class.

At a meeting at the 1983 North American Championship in Wilmette, Illinois, Lee Parks, the last Alcort-employed Class Secretary, announced the decision. She held an election of those present. The officers elected would be the nucleus of the new Class organization and develop its Rules and By-Laws. Ernie Kervel, who has organized three stellar World Championships in his island of Aruba, was elected President of the

International Sunfish Class Association (ISCA), and I was elected President of the United States Sunfish Class Association (USSCA.) Lee Parks was elected Secretary of both.

Thank heavens she was. Without her guidance and hours of work, Paul Odegaard (second ISCA President) and I and the other officers could not have made the transition nearly as smoothly as we did. She has been elected a Life Member of the Class - the only one, as of this writing.

• The Sail

The first major change to the sail, made towards the end of 1967, was a better shape. The sail of the very first Sailfish was made by Ratsey and Lapthorn, although Alcort bought them from Old Town - the canoe company - for a couple of years before they discovered they could buy them directly from Ratsey. Every Sailfish, Super Sailfish, and Sunfish sail until 1979 was made by Ratsey. The original sails were cut very flat, and lacked power under many conditions. So, in 1967, the decision was made to change the pattern, and produce a fuller sail. Alcort made one of the few tactical errors in its marketing history when it tried to keep the change secret. Sailors soon discovered that the new sail was faster, however, and within a year or year and a half, anyone with serious competitive ambitions had to switch to the new sail. For a while, there was a certain mystique about those Ratsey sails, and suspicion of Alcort. In certain fleets, sailors became convinced that only sails with a serial number ending in M on the Ratsey label were really competitive, but that conviction did not prove out in major competition.

In 1979, Bruce Connolly told me the reason for that change. The Sunfish had spawned a number of competitors, and finally one of them, the Scorpion, came through with a sail with a little bit more draft. "It took a fleet away - it knocked over our fleet out in one of the lakes in Mississippi, a very fine Sunfish fleet. We just took care of that by having Ratsey make a decent dacron sail and shipped it down to the dealer, who happened to be the best sailor in the fleet. Literally, once he put this thing on the water, that was the end of the Scorpion." The 1967 sail was a copy of that winner, and the pattern for all sails until 1978.

In 1978 and 1979, Hans Fogh of Canada, a transplanted Dane who had learned his sailing and sailmaking from the greatest one-design sailor of all time, four-time Olympic Champion Paul Elvstrom, was asked by Alcort to design the ultimate Sunfish sail. After much testing, the design was fixed, and manufacture of Sunfish sails was transferred to Fogh's plant in Canada (now part of North Sails.)

The only other exception to Ratsey's unbroken monopoly on Sunfish sailmaking was during the late '60s and early '70s, when Sunfish were manufactured in Canada, and Fogh produced some sails to the Ratsey design. These were sold only in Canada, except for a final batch of 50 that were left over when manufacture in Canada ended. The 50 were sold to summer camps and resorts, so that the chance they would be used for anything but intramural competition would be very slim. As far as I know, none ever showed up at a major regatta. They were beautifully made sails, with leather patches at the corners, and stronger grommets on the foot and luff. The first Fogh sails were also better made than the Ratsey sails.

In the late 1960s, Jack Evans proved that carrying the sail low was fast. Jack, three-time Sailfish National Champ and an aeronautical engineering student, switched to Sunfish - Sailfish racing was dying out. Most Sailfishers switched. He introduced us to the end-plate effect. By carrying the sail low, he explained, you let the deck serve as an end plate, reducing turbulence around the boom. Sailors in other

Background on the Boat

classes and offshore racing boats were learning the same thing, and deck-sweeping jibs became de rigueur. Jack was 1970 North American champ. Later, he worked for a number of years for Alcort as Class racing manager. He helped design the Force 5 and Super Sunfish.

On a Sunfish, carrying the sail low to the deck blocked the view to leeward, and port-starboard collisions became frequent. Bruce Connolly decided to OK sail windows, limited to a 12-inch by 24-inch rectangle. The window helped, but the view through the short rectangle was too narrow. Finally, at the first World Championship, Bruce decreed that any rectangle was OK, as long as the area did not exceed the area of the original rectangle, 288 square inches. The local St. Thomas sailmaker was kept busy for a few days sewing in long, thin windows, about 3 ½ inches high, and these became the Class standard for many years. You had to bob and weave to see through them, but they served the purpose. They became indispensable for racing.

You could buy a sail with the new window, parallel to the boom, from an Alcort dealer, but many racers had a window installed in windowless sails with dimensions and angles they considered gave them a better view. At some major regattas, measurers found windows larger than the 288 square inches allowed, and made the offending competitors bring them down to the maximum area with duct tape.

In 1986, the rule on size was changed to permit windows up to 600 square inches for increased safety. The narrow window, on a beat in really heavy air, dropped too low to see through when the boat heeled.

Because of the inconsistent shape and quality of sails that crept in after Alcort was sold, and the phasing out of the Fleetcloth from which Sunfish sails had been made for years, the Class officers started to work with Hans Fogh on a racing sail. We knew it would be more costly, because a better grade of sailcloth would have to be used, but it seemed to be the only way we could keep Sunfish one-design. While we were at it, we asked Hans to make it as fast as possible under all conditions, drawing on his experience as the Class sailmaker to improve on his original design.

The first two new sails, the result of almost a year's testing of different designs by Hans and some other top sailors, were first test sailed against that year's Worlds sails by Class officers at the 1988 World Championship in the Bahamas during the lay day. Hans promised that extra quality control would be used to insure that the sails were as one-design as possible, and ISCA adopted the new design at its annual meeting, held in conjunction with the Worlds.

The racing sail has lived up to its promise, and as this is written has proved long-lived - and necessary for success in the top echelons of racing. While it costs more, its long life probably makes the cost per regatta a bargain. All the sails are white, because, as Hans explained, different colors of cloth stretch at different rates, shortening the competitive life of sails. Not all white sails are racing sails, and there have been racing sails with colored panels made for World Championships, which are then sold on the open market.

The easiest way to tell a racing sail is by the triangular strengthening patches on the leech at each seam. Hans found that a Sunfish sail first starts to stretch in those areas. Just to be sure, check the identification patch at the tack. It carries the legend "Racing Sail."

There was an interesting phenomenon each time new sails were introduced. Even though the new sails proved in time to be faster than the old, it took a while for the top sailors to get used to the differences. Even though the new "secret" sails had been in use all summer in 1968, I managed to win the North Americans with the old-style sail, primarily, I think, because I was attuned to it. Early in 1969, it became apparent that I was outclassed with the old sail, and I switched to the new one.

A similar phenomenon occurred in 1979, the first full season with the new Fogh sail. Alan Beckwith won the North Americans with his old, well-blown-out Ratsey sail, as did Joe Blouin in 1980. But at the 1981 North Americans, Paul Odegaard won with a Fogh sail, having reluctantly abandoned his old favorite Ratsey early in the season. Mike Catalano, who was still convinced that the Fogh sail was no improvement on his Ratsey, wound up a dismal - for him - sixth.

The new racing sail didn't take that long to adjust to, and most serious competitors switched to it almost immediately.

• The Daggerboard

The other big Sunfish changes have been in daggerboard design. The first change, in the early '70s, replaced the original round-bottom board with what Alcort called the "Shadow Shape" board. It was a disaster, because it had less surface area than the old. Every serious competitor soon found he had to have an old board if he wanted to have a chance at winning. In the World Championships, competitors were all issued the new boards, so everything was supposed to be even. But a number of Americans felt they were handicapped, because they were used to the old board. The Caribbean sailors, however, were accustomed to competing against each other year-round with the Shadow Shape board, since they adopted Sunfishing after it came in. As a matter of fact, in 1973 and 1974, Caribbean sailors won the Worlds.

What was the reason for the change? "Don't blame me; blame yourselves," Bruce told me. "You're the guys who made so much of a fuss about the shape of the board. The whole racing class kept saying it wasn't right, it didn't do this,

Four daggerboards are permissible on a Sunfish but all must have been made by the Sunfish manufacturer. Illustrated (top, left to right) are the three wooden boards supplied over the years. The new plastic racing board is shown at bottom.

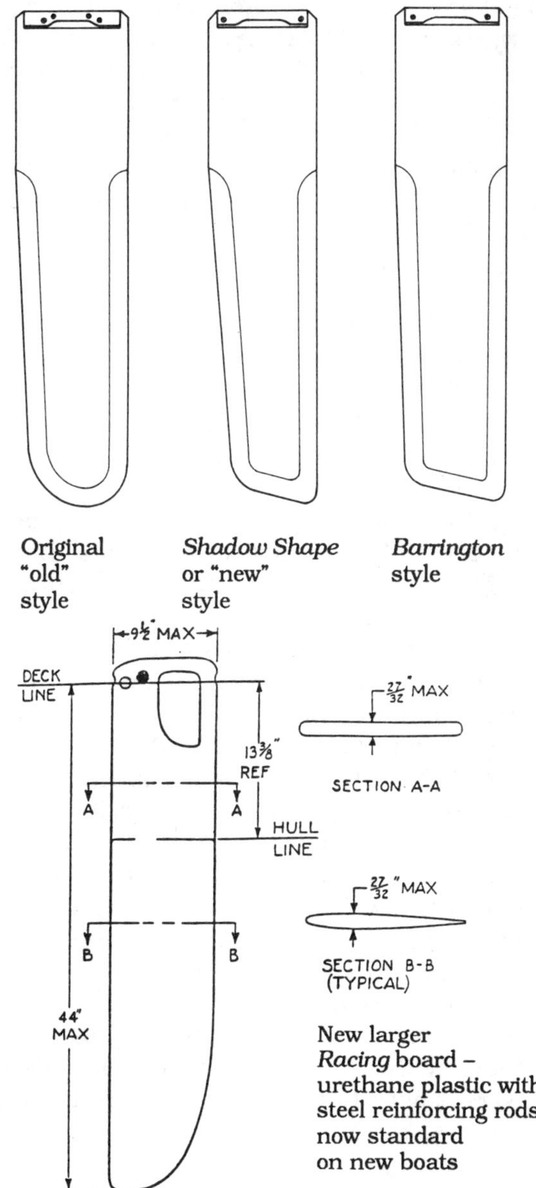

Background on the Boat

it didn't do that. Don't forget that it was about the time the Laser was coming along and the Laser had the shaved board. So I went to Fred Scott (the Alcort designer at the time and responsible for the Force 5) and said, 'Okay, go ahead and do it equal to or better.' So he came up with a thing that was equal to or better. I didn't know anything about airfoil sections and all that, so he gave them a shape that looked more modern."

Finally, in 1980, AMF Alcort came out with a third board, after testing it among several top sailors during the 1979-1980 frostbite season of the Barrington, Rhode Island, fleet. The Barrington board, as it became known, has approximately the same area as the very first board, but also has an angled bottom tip like the newer "Shadow Shape" design. It seemed to be as fast as the old board, but many sailors were for many years convinced that the original board was best.

All that changed in 1993, when, after many years of testing different board concepts, the new racing board was approved. Larry Cochran, a retired aerospace engineer, probably did more work on it than anyone. Harry League and Rod Koch worked on it, too, and kept the momentum going. Many others, including former Sunfish World Champ Bruce Sutphen, who was working on the AMERICA^3 design team, and second ISCA president Paul Odegaard, also an engineer in the aerospace field, contributed much to it, too. So did Mark Lindsey, a well-known builder of blades for one-design boats of all kinds, and Glenn Henderson, a naval architect whose designs push the frontiers of sailboat speed.

Although I don't race much at the top levels anymore, my first race with the new board was a revelation. It was against a motley assemblage of Lasers, Laser Radials, and sailboards at the Wednesday evening races at my local club. The conditions were, to be sure, my favorite combination - flat water and a strong, shifty breeze. As we popped off the line I immediately realized that I could point higher and tack more quickly than with the old board, without stalling out, which was easy to do with the old boards. I led until the last leg, when former Laser champ Dave Olsen, one of the best Master sailors around, finally passed me in his Laser. It was exhilarating.

The new board has 22 percent more area than the old boards, its major advantage, and a better hydrodynamic shape. And it's made of structural foam plastic with a tough urethane skin, with steel strengthening rods to keep it stiff. It costs extra, but like the racing sail probably paid for itself over many regattas. Now, new Sunfish come with the plastic board as standard, and you don't have to struggle to get the right shape to the leading and trailing edges, and constantly sand and varnish to preserve a racing finish, both of which were necessary to keep the old wood boards competitive. Now the Sunfish is truly a one-design racing machine again. Hooray!

The Class, as this is written, is contemplating a new rudder. It will probably also be plastic, and may become larger, with a more vertical orientation and a better airfoil shape for more precise steering.

Alcort has made a number of other changes over the years, some of which made the racing sailors nervous, but in time the new boats were shown to be just as fast as the old ones. Some of the earliest changes were made before serious competition started in the class - the switch from wood to fiberglass, the switch from cotton to nylon and then finally to dacron. To be competitive, you had to have a fiberglass boat with dacron sail. I never came across a wooden mast in competition, although the original Sunfish masts were wood.

• The Mast

The first significant change made in the fiberglass Sunfish - at least the first one of which I was aware - was the switch from a tapered aluminum mast to a straight round section. For a very short time, some sailors were convinced that the tapered mast had to be faster, because it had to be lighter at the head. However, in spite of the logic of this position, it became evident that there was no difference. We balanced the masts on a fulcrum to see if the head was, indeed, lighter, and proved to ourselves that it wasn't. We then learned that the masts had been tapered by thickening the wall section, which explained the apparent anomaly.

• The Boom

The foreward block on the boom, as installed by the factory, is too far aft for the low deck-sweeper position used universally today by racing sailors. Some time ago, a rule was added to permit sailors to move the block forward. Now the rules permit attachment of the boom blocks anywhere.

Some sailors found that the sheet could jam in the boom blocks, especially with sheets as thick as $^3/_8$ inch, and asked that a rule be added permitting swiveling blocks. This was voted down, but then Larry Cochran remembered that for a time Alcort sold boats with swiveling boom blocks by Racelite, which automatically made them legal, since they were supplied by the manufacturer. Their model number is RL221, and they are still available. Another rule was added recently that permits any boom block eye strap, so many sailors have replaced the rather flimsy stock straps with bigger ones. Larry recommends Ronstan eye straps, model RF-498. It is permissible to bolt them through the boom, which is a good idea. The factory installs them with rivets, and occasionally they let go.

• Eyebolts

Years ago, Alcort switched from using an eyebolt and pulley at the head of the mast to the simple plastic fitting used today, with a hole for the halyard. This change caused some consternation with at least one of the top competitors, who felt that the inherent looseness of the block system allowed the rig to "breathe." We pointed out to him that the rig could "breathe" just as well if he left an inch or two of slack in the halyard. At the same time, Alcort switched to one-piece plastic caps for the outer ends of the spars, eliminating the need for eyebolts there. Since this lightened up the rig a trifle, no one objected. There was some worry that the flimsy looking plastic would break easily, but that has produced fewer problems than the old eyebolts, which used to come loose from their nuts because of road vibration when traveling.

Those pesky eyebolts are still used at the forward end of the spars, to hook them together. Because the eyebolt and the boom thrust down towards the deck, more than one Sunfish has had a half-moon scratch dug into its foredeck, when the sail dropped low because of a loose halyard. Alcort wrestled with a better system, and produced a plastic acorn nut that reduced the problem. Another way to protect the deck from the eyebolt is to slip two-thirds of a sailset around the boom over the nut and fasten it with machine screws or pop rivets, to act as a skid. This fix, strictly speaking, is illegal, because it is not specifically approved in the rules.

Just about the time I finished writing the first version of this book, Alcort came up with the simplest solution of all. Instead of the round cap that was installed at the tack end of the boom, they substituted the cap used at the peak and clew, which has the extended eye lip for the outhauls. The lip on the boom faces down towards the deck and hits the deck before the eyebolt does. Since the cap is plastic, it does less damage. You

Background on the Boat

can still scratch your deck if the rig drops too low, but a light scrape won't make a gouge.

• The Hiking Strap

Another important change since the publication of the original book was an addition to the rules to permit a hiking strap. The new boats now come with one, stretching from a padeye about midway up the cockpit well forward to another padeye fastened to the lip at the bottom of the storage cubby. It's great for short people, and, in really heavy air, even for tall people. But wear stiff padding under your thighs, or you won't be able to hold a super-hiking position for long.

All these changes bring the Sunfish Class up to date as of 1996. Additional material about how to set up each of the boat's hull and rig components will be found in later chapters.

• The Super Sunfish

The Super Sunfish grew out of an idea first proposed in the early '60s by one of the real Sunfish Class stalwarts, John Black Lee of New Canaan, Connecticut. Like many other sailors, he was bothered by the aerodynamic inefficiency of the lateen rig, and started playing around with ways to put a more conventional high-aspect-ratio rig on the Sunfish hull. He experimented with spars and sails from other one-design classes, and tried to get Alcort interested in the idea. Alcort, with what may have been good marketing judgment at the time, decided not to mess around with a good thing. On the other hand, it may have opened the way for the Laser.

In 1972, John decided to launch a more sophisticated version of the Sunfish on his own. With Alcort's help, he put together a high-performance rig using a single-piece, tapered spar, midboom sheeting and a traveler inside the forward edge of the cockpit. The rig also included an outhaul, a Cunningham, and a vang, all adjustable on either tack through clam cleats

The Super Sunfish: a high-aspect-ratio rig on a Sunfish hull with a traveler in the forward end of the cockpit and cleats in the splash rail.

mounted on the splash rail.

The point of all the added controls is to enable a racer to change aerodynamics of the sail. With various combinations of line tension, the draft can be moved forward or aft, the leech tightened or loosened, the sail's depth in cross-section flattened or deepened. The midboom sheeting permits the sail shape to be retained while changing the sail's angle to the center line of the boat, easing out the traveler in the puffs and trimming in as the boat picks up speed.

John christened his new Sunfish version the Formula S. In two or three years, more than 200 were being raced and there was a North American Championship and a Grand Prix circuit. Things were going swimmingly and the boat was chosen for the Interclass Solo Championship, sailed singlehanded each year in three different classes.

By the time the Formula S had established itself, Alcort - now AMF - tacitly acknowledged the error of its original decision. It was also looking for another way to combat the then-new Laser. Under the guidance of Jack Evans, the company began development of its own high-performance rig. The new version was introduced at the New York Boat Show in 1974 and was labeled the Super Sunfish. Formula S owners were given a price break to convert to the new Alcort rig.

The Super Sunfish had a good run for about 10 years. It wasn't better than a Sunfish; it was just different. To my mind, it was like owning two boats for less than the price of a boat and a half. For the sailor who had ambitions to move up into higher performance sailing, such as the Olympic classes, a Super rig provided a lot of teaching before he or she invested in a more delicate, expensive machine. Too bad it died.

The Super Sunfish.

Background on the Boat

Alcort Sailboats Inc.'s 1988 Sail Designs.

• The 1996 Sunfish

As this is written in 1996, a new Sunfish comes with:

- a 31-inch coated wire bridle with no loop,
- a new set of boom blocks with wider sheaves that can take a 7/16-inch sheet,
- a swivel block mounted on the foredeck in place of the sheet hook that for years was mounted on the forward lip of the cockpit,
- hiking straps, affixed lower on the forward wall of the cockpit,
- an aluminum hiking stick with rubber universal,
- a soft polypropylene sheet that floats,
- pre-stretched dacron halyard,
- and the racing board as standard. No more wood daggerboards – good riddance.

Many dealers are offering a racing package option that includes the racing sail, a ratchet block and clam cleats on the foredeck for the sheet, and adjustable outhaul and Cunningham with clam cleats on the boom.

Ashore and Afloat 2

Nine out of 10 Sunfish owners do not race. They just sail casually and have a lot of fun. But, whether you intend to race or not, you should master the basics of launching, sailing, and, in general, handling the boat. That is what this chapter is all about.

• Transportation

There are many ways to transport Sunfish. The boats are comparatively easy to move about and people who don't have to travel far to the water often slip a Sunfish into the back of a station wagon. Perhaps the most popular method of carrying the boat, however, is on top of a car.

Most any kind of luggage rack will do, although wooden bars shaped to the crown of the deck and padded with carpet provide the best protection. In an emergency, a couple of old tires wrapped in some kind of cloth provide just enough stability and protection for both car and boat, assuming the boat is well tied down. That's a very important point no matter how you transport your Sunfish. I know of at least a dozen boats that have required extensive repairs after flying off alone down the highway. It is a testimonial to the boat's ruggedness that I've never heard of one being completely demolished in this way. But it's not something you want to do just for the fun of spending your money.

I once made a rack of galvanized water pipe to fit on a convertible. It looked rather like a giant iron bedstead, but it served its purpose well. It fit over the car top, the legs supported on the four fenders. Each leg ended in a large suction cup. It was even possible to raise and lower the top with a Sunfish in place on the carrier. I fastened the boat down with specially adjustable lines, each with a hook to grab the bumper, a tent line toggle to snug the line down, and a spring to absorb road shocks. I had this rig for quite a while and used it on three different convertibles. Finally, I got tired of lifting the boat on and off the carrier and bought a trailer.

Roof rack with ramp.

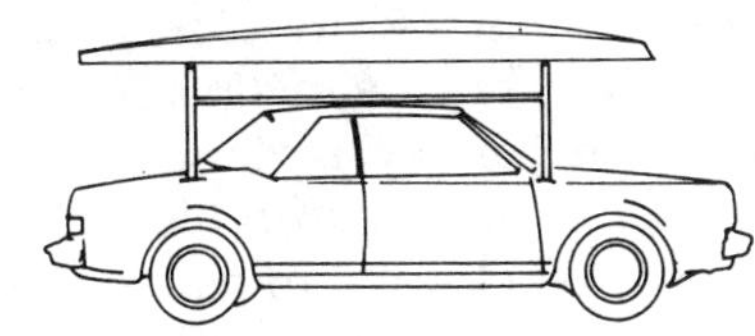

Pipe rack.

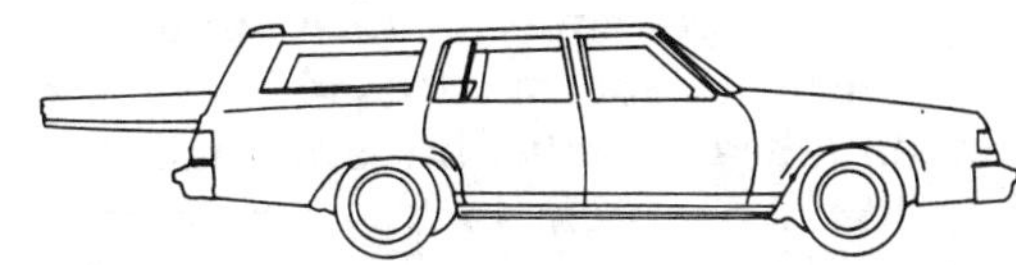

Back of station wagon

Sunfish can be carried on a roof rack, on specially made pipe racks if you own a convertible, or even nestled in the back of a station wagon.

A trailer is certainly a convenient way of getting your Sunfish to the water and almost any sort of trailer will do. Most people have trailers that carry their boats right side up, but some carry them upside down so that the bottom doesn't get gunked up with road tar and scratches. A full boat cover can be used to protect the entire hull from road dirt.

The Sunfish is a rugged boat but it should be well supported on its trailer. If you let the hull rest on fore-and-aft supports between the chine and keel, especially under the cockpit tub, flexing will occur and this will eventually cause cracks.

Ashore and Afloat

I had one Sunfish that eventually split right along the chine. (I did learn, however, that this boat had been made by a Texas firm under subcontract to Alcort and that it and others suffered from a lack of adequate resin. At the time, in the early '60s, Alcort had outrun its own production capacity.)

I have seen as many as four Sunfish carried on the standard Sunfish-style trailer, and even more on special heavy-duty rigs. Racer Tom Ehman had the misfortune to flip a four-boat rig on his way to the North Americans in the mid-'70s. The center of gravity was too high. Alcort used to supply extra bunks to make a two-boat rig out of the standard trailer, which is no longer sold. This worked very well. Some owners build racks that sit between two Sunfish and put all the weight on the bottom boat. Most Sunfish thus burdened seem to survive. I used to carry two boats on an Alligator trailer but eventually broke both springs. A truck-spring-repair garage installed new heavy-duty springs and there hasn't been a problem since.

The biggest problem with trailers is that the electrical systems go bad very easily. It is important to make sure that the wiring is fastened to the frame at many points. Otherwise, the constant flexing will work-harden the wire and eventually break it. Fittings of all kinds seem to rust easily on lights and connectors. I finally made a lighting rig that attaches to the rudder fitting of the boat itself. This rides nice and high and is easily seen by following motorists. When the trip is complete, the lights ride in the trunk of the car, protected from the elements. Even with a cover over boat and trailer, the lighting system still seems to deteriorate. It is a problem you have to keep up with.

How best to carry spars? A couple of companies make spar carriers. These are usually two-piece affairs, one attaching to the rudder fitting, the other sitting in the mast hole. They seem to work very well. I carry my spars on H-shaped wooden bunks that are well-padded with carpeting. One sits over the halyard cleat on deck, the other just behind the cockpit. The spars are secured with shock cord. Larry Lewis used to do just fine with a couple of old 12-inch tires, resting the spars atop them. Now, some Sunfishers attach 14-foot lengths of 8-inch diameter PVC pipe to their trailers, capped at both ends. They just slide in the spars, with the sails still attached to them, and they're protected from the elements.

• From Shore to Water

Having arrived at the beach, how do you get the boat from car to water? At most regattas, there are plenty of people around, and most boats are simply carried down to the water. But a number of commercial dollies are available, and many sailors have fashioned their own. These seem to fall into three categories.

First, there is the miniature trailer, which is a set of wheels with a long handle and bunks to drop the boat on. These are easy to use but are relatively expensive. Second, and for many years the most popular, is a rig that slips up into the daggerboard well, leaving two wheels under the hull to roll on. Third, there are dollies that attach to the transom, either clipping to the bridle eyes or the rudder mount.

All these methods are better than dragging the boat over a rocky beach. Whatever kind of dolly you use, you will want relatively large wheels, both in diameter and tread width. Otherwise, the dolly will be hard to hustle through sand. One of the neatest rigs I've seen was homemade. It attached to the transom and used an inflatable yacht fender as a roller - the kind with the hole through the middle. A piece of pipe was slipped through the hole as an axle. Another rig used what looked like a light airplane tire inner tube, barely inflated, to support the boat and glide over the sand. I once made a dolly out of bicycle

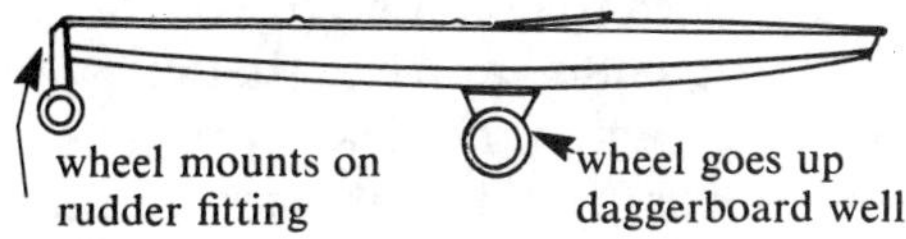

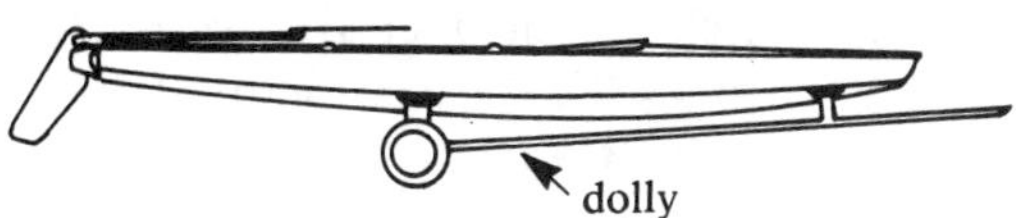

A Sunfish can be moved to the water with the aid of wheels that mount on either the rudder fitting or in the daggergoard slot, or on a dolly.

wheels. They made up in diameter what they lacked in tread width. The sheer size of the thing, however, made me abandon it.

One commercially made gadget that didn't last long on the market combined a roof rack and dolly. The problem was that the wheels were too small. You had to trundle the Sunfish along sideways, which meant you needed a wide swath of beach all to yourself. When you got to the car, you hooked the handles of this wheelbarrow-like contraption to the racks on top of the roof, walked around and lifted. The whole rig telescoped into the roof racks and, if you were patient and didn't rush things so the mechanism jammed, you were ready to go. I've also seen some homemade rigs that provided ramps up the trunk of the car to the roof. There have been ads recently in the Class newsletter, *Windward Leg*, for a roof rack that makes loading the boat on top of the car a one-person job.

The most difficult transfer I can remember involved a rented pick-up camper in which we attended the North Americans at Gananoque, Quebec. We carried the boat on top of the camper. Getting the boat on top was no problem because our driveway had high banks on either side. But when we reached the yacht club at Gananoque, it took a crew of about six friends on the ground and two or three atop the camper to get the boat down, and even then we almost dropped it. As it happened, another contestant had a pick-up truck camper, too, but he planned ahead. He had a most ingenious derrick welded up of pipe. With it, he could load and unload by himself, with his wife just lending a hand - just like a yacht taking aboard its tender.

Chris Urfer had the simplest solution. Chris was not that big, but what there was of him was all muscle. He simply flipped his boat up over his head and portaged it, his head in the cockpit - a strange shell-bearing sea creature. When he got to the car, he pressed the Sunfish over his head and slid it onto the racks. At the first Worlds, Jeorge Bruder of Brazil carried his boat to the water, fully rigged. Later, after a full day of trade-winds racing, he carried it back up the beach. But he was a legend even in the Finn class, which has more than its share of muscular gorillas!

• Launching from the Beach

Most Sunfish are sailed off the beach. This presents three possible scenarios: the wind may be blowing onto the beach; it may be blowing across the beach; it may be blowing off the beach. No matter which direction the wind blows from, there are a number of things to do before you think of actually pushing off into the water.

Get organized. Be sure the tiller is under the bridle, that the halyard is coiled out of the way, and that the end of the mainsheet is knotted - so that the sheet cannot run out of the block - and reachable from the cockpit. The daggerboard should be in the cockpit, with the top propped on the foredeck, so that you can slip it easily into the slot once you launch the boat. The rudder, too, must be in the up position, for reasons that will soon be apparent.

Ashore and Afloat

If the wind is blowing up or down the beach, you can raise the sail with the boat heading straight down into the water. The sail will swing out to one side or the other, "weather-vaning" to the wind. If possible, keep the bow into the wind before raising sail. Otherwise, if the sail fills before the boom lifts off the deck, the boom will swing around and the tack fitting may gouge a curved track in the foredeck.

When launching, especially into a swell, the board and rudder are especially vulnerable. The swell can lift the hull clear of the bottom, letting the board or rudder drop down. Then the swell races back out and the boat drops down onto the bottom. If the boat has heeled at all, the board and rudder will hit with a sideways impact. The Sunfish's weight alone can now break them. If you have already jumped aboard, the daggerboard and rudder will surely break.

The second type of launch, when the wind is blowing onto the beach, is more difficult than when the wind is blowing parallel to the shoreline, especially if the wind is strong.

The reason for this is that you will have to have the daggerboard down. You will be beating to windward off the shore, and that means you have to have the board down to prevent side-slip. If there are swells, you had better plan to wade out from shore, because the boat will slip back toward shore as you jump aboard, and you have to allow room to get that board down and time to get it biting into the water.

In such conditions, wade out up to your armpits, keeping the boat headed into the wind. Drop in the daggerboard, twist the boat so that you can climb in from the windward side - that is, push the bow away from you - and make sure the sheet is loose, so the boat won't try to sail away from you. Jump aboard, drop the rudder down quickly, pull in the sheet, and sail off. Make sure the sheet is free before you ever leave the beach! Once aboard, remain on the windward rail, or you may find yourself flat on your back in shallow water with the boat on top of you, a very uncomfortable position and one that can damage you or the spars when the next wave hits.

Obviously, it is best to get used to into-the-wind beach launching in light air, before you tackle big waves and stronger breezes.

The third launching condition is having the wind at your back as you face the water. If you try to raise the sail with the bow pointed towards the water, it will "weather-vane" a full 180 degrees, streaming out ahead of the boat. If your mainsheet has been reeved through a block on deck, the stopper knot in the sheet's end will stop the sail's outward swing and the boat can - if the wind is strong enough - be spun completely around.

There are two good methods for launching when the wind is off the beach. One is to launch the boat before hoisting the sail, swing the bow into the wind, raise the sail and then jump aboard. You can take your time about lowering the rudder and slipping in the daggerboard since the wind will be pushing you offshore. The problem with this approach is that you have little or no steerageway. The boat may swing around so that the sail will fill as you hoist it. Once again, the danger arises of gouging the deck with the tack fitting, where the boom joins the upper spar.

The second way to launch with the wind is to point the bow up the beach and raise the sail. You can then launch the boat backwards into the water, jump aboard while the sail is still luffing, drop the rudder before you try to put in the board, then let the boat swing around until the sail fills. In this situation, you don't need to lower the board until the boat is sailing, since leeway is not a worry when you are sailing downwind.

It is quite possible, by the way, to sail a Sunfish backwards, a useful maneuver at times. Sometimes, people do it just for fun. The trick is to let the boat get some sternway with the sail luffing just enough so that the rudder will bite in. Steering a boat backwards is just like riding a coaster wagon. You turn the tiller so that the rudder end is pointing in the direction you want to go. Once you have learned to steer this way, with the sail luffing, you can then push the sail out to catch some wind on the "wrong" side, and away you go.

• Launching from a Dock

The principles involved in launching from a dock are similar to those in launching from a beach. Whenever possible, you want to be able to point the bow into the wind when you raise the sail. If you are on the windward side of a dock, and the dock is too high for the sail to swing out over it, you have a problem. The sail will fill before the boat has a chance to get some headway, and you will be plastered up against the dock. Any sharp projections on the dock will probably rip the sail.

Fortunately, it is not very difficult to paddle a Sunfish. Just paddle out away from the dock far enough to permit you to raise the sail, drop the rudder and daggerboard, and sail away before you drift back into the dock. Allow plenty of drifting room.

However, if you must raise the sail from the windward side of a dock, you may be able to do so with the help of a second person. Lift the boom up and hand it to your friend on the dock, and have him hold it so that the boom is pointing dead into the wind. Raise the sail quickly and hope that the wind does not shift too much for your friend to keep up with it. If he stands right on the edge of the dock, of course, your boat itself can be pointing right into the wind, since the boom extends over the transom. If the wind does shift before he can shove you off, you will "weather-vane" around and be plastered helplessly against the dock. Before raising sail, have the rudder and daggerboard down. Then, have your friend give a good shove from the end of the boom, and you will shoot out with some steerageway and be able to bear off and sail away. Leaving a dock like this, however, is a tricky maneuver at best.

• How to Sit in a Sunfish

Obviously, if you are just sailing for fun, you will sit any way that feels comfortable. You should, however, know the most efficient way to sit in the boat, just in case you want to get someplace fast someday. The Sunfish wants to sail flat on the water under most conditions. That means fore-and-aft as well as side-to-side.

Under most conditions, you should sit with your weight at the forward edge of the cockpit. The neophyte sailor wants to face forward, with the tiller right alongside his hip. This yields poor control and makes the stern drag in the water. Sit sideways on the windward side of the boat. It may feel awkward at first, but it gives you full control of the boat. Your aft hand controls the tiller - get used to using the tiller extension instead of the tiller itself - and your forward hand controls the mainsheet. Sitting sideways, you can control the side-to-side trim of the boat easily by moving in and out.

A word about the tiller extension, often called the hiking stick. For many years it was a short wooden stick attached to the forward end of the tiller with a bolt, but in the '80s any sort of stick, with a universal joint or flexible connection, was permitted. Today, a length of 36 to 39 inches seems favored by almost all the top racers. The stick is carried across the body, with steering mostly a matter of twisting the wrist. It used to be axiomatic that you had to use your teeth as a cleat when hauling in that long sheet, but now, with the long stick and the flexible joint, it is possible to feed the sheet from the forward hand to the tiller hand in big sweeps, just as fast as

Ashore and Afloat

A rather awkward way to sail a Sunfish. If both sailors would slide their bottoms out over the water, they would be more confortable and the boat would flatten out, relieving the heavy weather helm (note the angle of the rudder). It would also help to slip the sheet through the deck block, which would flatten the sail. Steering by foot is one way to free up a hand, but it's not comfortable for long.

pulling it in across your face and grabbing it with your teeth. I must admit it took a long time for me to become convinced, but at one regatta not so long ago I bit my cheek for the hundredth time and then broke a tooth, for the second time. I surrendered and bought a long stick, shaped like the grip and shank of a golf club, with a flexible connector, and am learning to use it. An added advantage of the long stick is that, as you tack, you can pass it behind your back to your other hand, which is holding the sheet, and never let go of either. Once you've mastered that technique, along with the roll tack (we'll get to that later in the book,) you'll look like an expert.

Because the wind is often puffy, and you will be moving in and out fairly often, you will want to be able to slide. That is why few serious Sunfish sailors put antislip strips on the deck. You may, however, want them in the bottom of the cockpit.

On a warm, lazy day, you may want to drop into the cockpit, sitting forward in the well with your legs curled up beside you. It may sound uncomfortable, but it soon becomes second nature. Or you can just flop down into the cockpit in a sitting position, with your legs spread out on the foredeck and your back leaning against the after edge of the cockpit. That's when a urethane life jacket becomes not only a safety feature but a cushion as well. Use it as a backrest. Just remember that a sudden puff can conceivably dump you over before you can climb out.

• Safety on the Water

Unless I am sailing on a very small lake in mild weather, I almost always wear a racing life vest. I am, perhaps, overcautious, but I have seen summer squalls come out of nowhere on the nicest of days, capsizing whole fleets of sailboats. Usually, there is some warning, but some squalls come in from a totally unexpected direction, catch the sail aback, and flip a boat over before the sailor knows what's happening. In one instance I

Light air sailing style, with the skipper hunkered down in the cockpit. Surprisingly, it's not at all uncomfortable, even for a six-footer.

Ashore and Afloat

know of, the boom cracked the sailor's head, knocking him overboard and stunning him long enough so that he became separated from the boat, which drifted off. Fortunately, he was wearing a life jacket. There was another boat nearby and he was rescued.

Even if you don't wear a life jacket, at least have one aboard. The Coast Guard requires one for each person on the boat.

Whether or not you're wearing a life jacket, remember that a Sunfish will not sink, even if it is punctured and filled with water. The boat is equipped with foam flotation and, as long as you stay with your Sunfish, you are all right. If the boat turns turtle and remains that way, with the mast pointing downwards, you may have trouble getting aboard, especially if the daggerboard has slipped out. (For this reason, you should tie the board to the deck. The boat is now supplied with a padeye on deck and a hole in the daggerboard handle for just this purpose. A length of line is even included.) If the daggerboard floats away from you, a Sunfish is practically impossible to right. However, if the board falls out of the slot and you have it attached to the boat, you can swim beneath the hull, shove the board in, and prepare to right the boat.

Almost everyone who has sailed a Sunfish for any length of time has capsized it. Compared to a Finn or a Laser, the Sunfish is a very stable boat, but stable is a relative term. When you are racing hard, trying to get the most out of the boat in a stiff breeze, you will eventually find yourself in the water. For this reason, it is a good idea to practice capsizing on purpose.

If you are sitting to windward and capsize to leeward, and your reflexes are fast enough, it is quite possible to lean forward over the windward side of the boat, swing your legs up and over, and land on the daggerboard just as the sail hits the water. While on the board, hold on to the windward edge of the hull, lean your tail out over

Sunfish can carry a surprising number of people, although four heavies like these shouldn't venture out in open water. This was part of a relay race at the sixth Worlds; another sailor was added at each leg of the race. (Bow to stern: the legendary Arthur Knapp, who raced America's J-boats in the '30s, and Sunfishers Bob Knapp – no relation – Henry De Wolfe, and former World Champion Bob Bowles.)

the water, and the boat will pop right back up. Again, if your reflexes are fast enough, you can pull yourself back into the boat with that same pivot-on-your-stomach movement, and never get anything but your socks wet. I used to do this before the start of every light-air race, having convinced myself that a wet sail was faster than a dry one.

Should you find yourself in the water alongside your Sunfish, shake the water out of your eyes, make sure the daggerboard is in the trunk all the way, and swim around the boat until you're at the place where the board emerges. Do not let the boat get away from you. Now reach up and pull yourself onto the daggerboard. This may be enough to right the boat. If it isn't, because you are too light, stand up on the board and back out to its very end, holding on to the side of the hull. You may have to lean out rather far in order to get this started, especially if the sail has filled with water. Watch the sail carefully. When it starts to lift, time things so that you can dive into the boat quickly, because it will suddenly jerk upright as it shakes the water loose from the sail.

If the boat doesn't want to right, it may be because the sheet is still cleated in a close-hauled position. Just reach over into the cockpit and free it. This should bring the boat upright, even if you weigh only 85 pounds.

Sometimes, especially if you fall to leeward into the cockpit as the boat capsizes, it will keep right on going and turn completely upside down, turn "turtle." When this happens, you should probably work your way around to the windward side of the boat without letting go and, using the daggerboard, pull yourself onto the bottom. Make sure the board remains fully lowered; that is, with the boat upside down, extended all the way up. Then kneel facing the board and slip your feet over the side until your toes are on the rub rail or lip. Holding on to the tip of the daggerboard, lean backwards as far out as you can. The boat should slowly come up. It if does not, the peak is probably stuck in the mud.

In this case, you will have to go around to the other side of the boat - the lee side - and hope that the wind will help you slip the mast out of the mud as the boat comes up. If you try to right an inverted boat from the leeward side, the wind will catch under the sail as it comes up from the water, and probably capsize the boat back on top of you again, especially if you try to pull yourself in before the boat has steadied. For this reason, you should try to right the boat from the windward side if you possibly can. Then, when the sail comes up, you will be on the weather side, balancing the pressure on the sail. Once the boat has settled down, you should be able to pull yourself into the cockpit.

Capsizing can be frightening when it first happens. For this reason, it really makes sense to practice on a nice calm, sunny day. Do it a few times until you have the feel of it. Then, if you capsize on a day when the wind is blowing and the waves are trying to wash your breath away, you'll have some confidence in what you are doing. Like anything else, once you know how, righting a capsized Sunfish is easy.

Once you have righted the boat in a heavy wind, it is probably a good idea to let the sail luff a bit to shake off some water and let you get your breath back. The sudden exertion of the capsize and righting, especially if the water is cold, can take a lot out of you. When you have your breath back, sail off.

• Staying Upright in Heavy Wind

Even in 50 or 60 knots of wind, it is possible to sail on a reach in a Sunfish. You want to keep only the aft corner of the sail drawing. You'll have to hike hard and may not be able to go in the direction you want, but you can get the feel of the boat.

It may be difficult or impossible to progress to windward in such strong breezes. Just by reaching back and forth, however, you can stay off a lee shore. If all else fails, and you are worn out, drop the sail, roll it up and wrap the sheet around it a couple of times. Then flop into the cockpit. You will survive until somebody finds you or until you drift to shore. Remember, the Sunfish evolved from a lifesaver's surfboard. It makes a

Ashore and Afloat

A relatively small sailor demonstrating beautiful heavy-air form. His feet are hooked about at the midpoint of the forward and aft lips of the cockpit, putting his center of gravity, about at his waist, well out over the water. Today, hiking straps are allowed.

pretty good life boat.

If you want to go downwind in really heavy air, consider dropping the sail and sailing on under bare pole. You will find that you have plenty of steerage way.

• Clothing

Shorts and bare feet are the order of the day for most Sunfish sailing. You may as well get accustomed to getting wet. As it gets cooler - and even a hot day can be cool if you are wet and the wind is blowing - add clothing from the waist up. Wear a shirt over the life jacket. This keeps the jacket from snagging on the boom. If necessary, a foul-weather jacket comes next, covered by another tee shirt. If it is really cool, wear a sweater beneath the foul-weather gear. Choose a wool or polypropylene sweater. It will keep you warm when it is wet.

If, at the point you need a sweater, and are starting to get cold from the waist down, add foul-weather trousers to the costume. You will want the bib-type high-waisted trousers or your back will be exposed when you are hiking out. Some sailors reverse the process, wearing bib-type foul-weather trousers before adding anything above the waist. This protects them from the wind, up to their armpits, at least - and, together with a life jacket, keeps most of the body warm. The arms are free to work the sheet and tiller. Whichever method suits you best, the important thing is to keep your trunk warm. If you do that, your arms and legs won't feel cold right away, and you'll be able to keep up your strength.

There are many items of clothing designed just for dinghy racing - specialized wet suits, waterproof coveralls, dry suits, gloves, shoes and boots, hiking pants - but we'll get to them later when we talk about racing.

On a hot summer day, remember that you may be out on the water long enough to get quite a sunburn. If you are wearing a bathing suit or are shirtless, always take along a long-sleeved shirt and a bottle of suntan lotion. If you want to keep these items, or anything else, dry, put them in a really waterproof bag.

Tuning the Boat 3

The concept of the Sunfish is to maintain a class that is as totally one-design as possible. Most of us believe that you can take a racing Sunfish - one with a racing sail and racing daggerboard - out of its box, tune it up, and go out and win races. Tuning can mean as little as proper position of the gooseneck and tension of the outhauls for the day's sailing conditions.

On the other hand, there are a lot of things you can do to your Sunfish that will, presumably, increase the odds in your favor. The Class philosophy is to permit modifications that increase safety or ease of handling, but not boatspeed. Whether or not all permitted modifications also give a slight racing edge, most top Sunfish sailors take advantage of them. Ease of handling will often translate into fractions of seconds that the sailor can use to concentrate on making constant adjustments for better boatspeed...watching the wind to take advantage of small changes in direction or strength...and analyzing the developing situation on the water to make the right tactical decisions. On the other hand, as you add modifications, you may add complexity, which can distract you from all those more important things. Just remember the primary Class rule: If it's not specifically permitted in the rules, it is forbidden.

• The Rudder

Two things can be done to the rudder blade. You can put on any kind of finish you want, including a layer of fiberglass and resin. And you can do anything you want to the profile of the

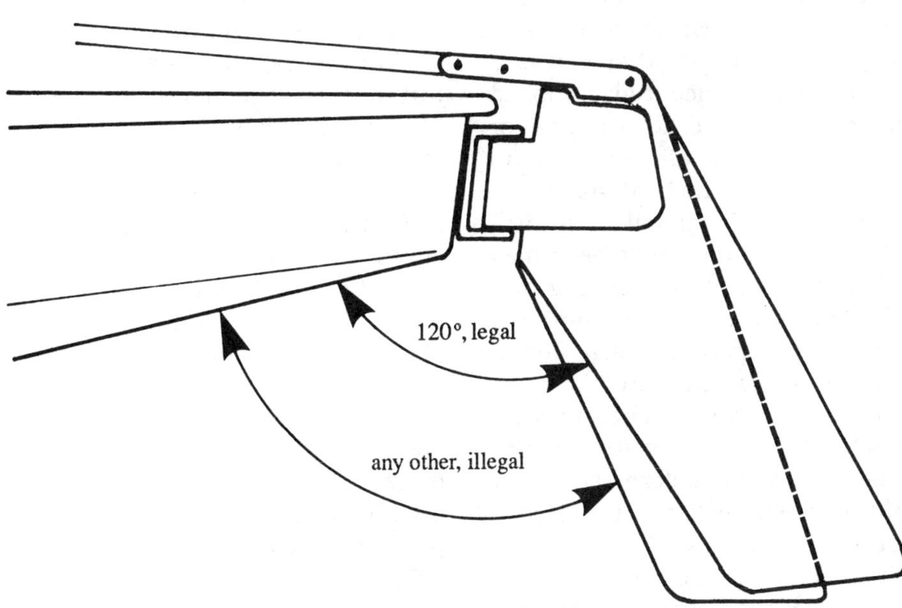

According to Class rules, the Sunfish rudder is legal if swept back at a 120-degree angle, but is illegal at anything less.

Tuning the Boat

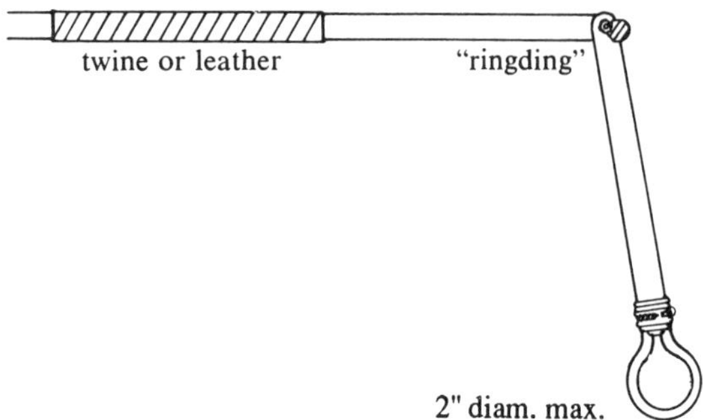

To protect it from the bridle, wrap the tiller with twine or cover with leather. Be sure to cover the "ringding" with tape so it won't snag. Racing models now have a longer hiking stick with a flexible universal joint.

3/4"
1¼"

To shape the rudder or the old-style wood boards, make a tracing of this full size template for the leading edge. (Courtesy Larry Cochran and Paul Odegaard.)

leading and trailing edge, so long as you don't go more than 1¼ inches in from the edges. The latter change was instituted by Bob Johnstone when he was Marketing Vice President for Alcort, and frankly, I thought, and still do, that it was a terrible mistake, especially since it also applied to the daggerboard. More on that in a page or two. It didn't make the boat safer or easier to handle; it was done to make the boat faster.

And it's a lot of work. A lot of sailors studied the best possible foil section that could be formed on an inch and a quarter of the leading and trailing edges. Engineers like Paul Odegaard and Larry Cochran pored through NACA airfoil studies. The usual technique is to sand down the trailing edge to make it sharper and build up the leading edge with auto body putty to the maximum profile dimensions before sanding it down to a roughly elliptical section. The objective is twofold: to provide the fastest shape through the water, and to resist stalling out or cavitation as the rudder is angled to the water when steering. Some sailors opt for the elliptical section, considering it the fastest shape. Others chose a more rounded leading edge on the theory that this resists stalling better. In terms of finish, the consensus is that a fine, sanded surface is better than a glossy one. I believe some test-tank work has been done that proves it. The factory finish on the wood parts of the Sunfish is glossy smooth, but follows the deep grain of the unfilled Philippine mahogany, leaving a slightly ridged effect. Sanding this finish down smooth will usually expose raw wood, so refinishing is probably a good idea, even if you don't doctor the edges.

Most sailors feel that rudder and tiller should be an almost rigid unit, with as little slop and sideplay as possible. In time, the bolt holes in the rudder and rudder head widen as the pivot and tiller bolts work on them, and a certain amount of play results. The rules permit insertion of metal bushings in these holes, and a few sailors install them even on new equipment, just as preventive maintenance.

The original Sunfish came with a complex 10-piece bronze and brass arrangement for connecting the rudder to the boat in a manner that permits the rudder to kick up if it hits something. It's a hinge and latch arrangement that depends on a brass spring to keep enough tension in the system to keep the rudder down, but not so much that it won't release when the rudder strikes an obstacle. You adjust the tension with a thumb screw. In practice, you screw down the tension as tight as your fingers can stand, but even then, the rudder might pop up in very heavy air. The result is usually a death roll to windward as the boat rounds up.

Alcort solved the problem with a unit originally developed for the Minifish, a 12-foot version of the Sunfish that never quite caught on. This was, for many years, an aluminum casting with spring-loaded wood blade. The design is still the same, although the cheeks are now made of a tough plastic instead of aluminum. The first plastic units had a tendency to break; at this writing the unit has been beefed up, and seems to be holding up fine.

In 1995, Sunfish Laser offered the Class a new design with a plastic blade, like the latest daggerboard. It is still being evaluated by the Class Advisory Committee, which is responsible for recommending rule changes.

• The Tiller

When you buy a boat, one of the most important things to check is the straightness of the grain in the tiller. If it isn't straight from one end to the other, there is a weak spot where the grain curves off to one side. It will, you can bet on it, break at the most inopportune time.

Many sailors use some kind of anti-chafe material around the tiller where it rubs against the bridle. This can range from leather or tightly wrapped cord to a few turns of duct tape. Without it, the finish is soon rubbed off, then the edges of the tiller itself, and in time rot can set in. Take the time to add the chafing gear.

Until fairly recently, the Sunfish came with a short wooden hiking stick or tiller extension, which bolted to the end of the tiller. Today, almost everyone has substituted a longer metal or plastic extension with a universal joint or flexible urethane connector, and the boat is now supplied that way.

If you are going to sail with the old wooden extension, make sure to keep it in good repair. The bolt will quickly wear away at the holes in both the tiller and extension, increasing the strain as the bolt works and opening up the possibility of dry rot. Keep the bolt tight, and make sure varnish gets down into the holes when you refinish. More than one sailor has lost the old stick when either it or the tiller end broke off. If that doesn't dump you in the drink (you're usually hiking hard when it happens) you'll find it hard to steer with a broken tiller, or even with a good tiller but no hiking stick.

It is Class-legal to install a ring or some other kind of handle on the end of the hiking stick. Most commercial ones come that way, with a rubber ball, or a golf grip, or some other method to keep the stick from slipping through your fingers. With the wooden stick, the most common handle used is a standard Sunfish sail clip (See sketch.) To install a sail clip, drill a hole on one side of the end of the tiller extension for the prong and fasten it firmly on the other side with a round- or combination-head stainless steel screw. Number 6 or 8, ½" long, seems about right. It's better to install it in a horizontal rather than a vertical position. In the vertical position, the clip will prevent the extension from riding over the top of the tiller when you tack or gybe. Glue the prong of the clip into the hole you have drilled for it, and then lash or tape the whole connection.

• The Daggerboard

With the new racing daggerboard, there is little you can do within the rules except refinish it, and there's not much point to doing that until it needs to be repaired or has gotten scratched.

An interesting argument was pretty much

Tuning the Boat

Daggerboard sections: 1. The ideal airfoil section won't fit in the well (dotted line.) However, the wooden board's cross-section (2.) may be built up with auto body putty or Marinetex and then rounded to an elliptical shape on the leading edge (3.) The completed board may be covered with fiberglass cloth and resin. These rules apply to the rudder as well.

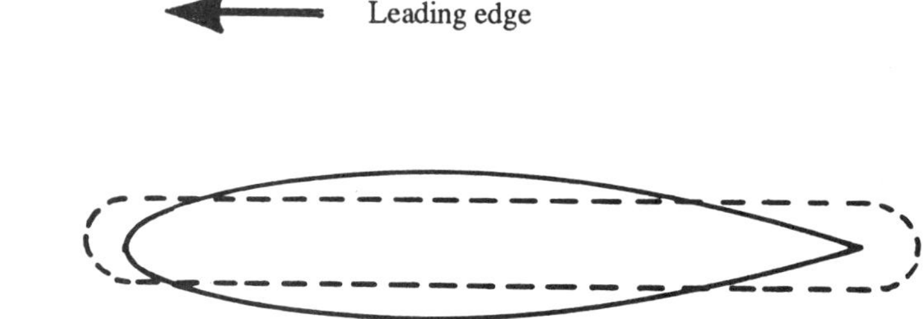

1. Ideal airfoil.

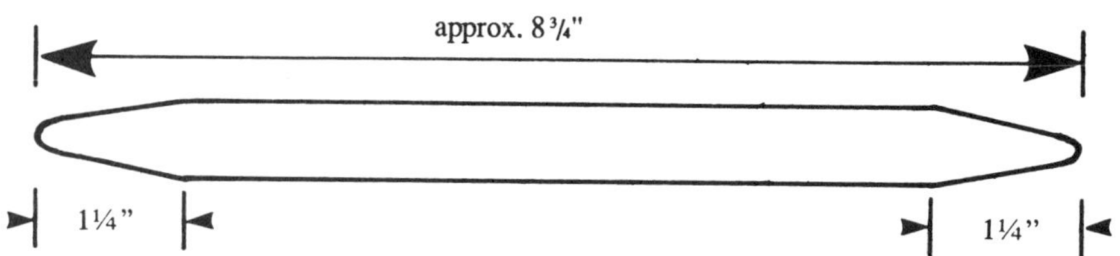

2. Standard wood board cross-section.

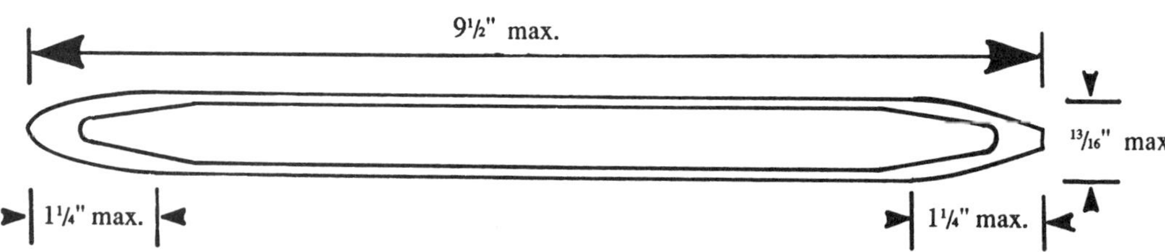

3. Improved cross-section.

settled during the several years of experimentation to develop the racing board. For a number of years, just about everyone who used the Barrington board used it with the long edge aft. Then Bruce Sutphen won the Worlds in 1987, sailing with the long edge forward. Others, of course, immediately tried it. Some found it was more efficient...if you could keep the boat in the groove (the fastest combination between pinching and footing.) In the final design of the racing board, the long edge must go forward, or the hydrodynamic shape won't work. Perhaps because it is larger, finding the groove with the racing board is relatively easy.

The old wood boards, like the rudder, can be reshaped for 1 ¼ inches at the leading and trailing edges. Some people spent hours on their boards, filling, shaping, fiberglassing and sanding, until they thought they had the ideal hydrodynamic shape possible within those limits. One enterprising sailor went into business building such an "ideal" board from scratch, until Steve Baker, then Alcort's Class manager, rewrote the ambiguous rule to prevent boards made by anyone but the Sunfish manufacturer. Since the new plastic board is far superior - and larger - than the old wood ones, this frustrating work, and the arguments with the Class measurers that arose at Class championships, have disappeared.

If you use a wood board, however, be aware that the two strips of wood across the top called handles, which serve as stops to prevent the board from falling through the hull, almost always tear loose by splitting slivers out of the top of the board where the screws are fastened. This happens when you slam the board down harder than you mean to, as when you are coming down on the leeward mark. The adrenaline is pumping and you have to gybe NOW and...wham! For years I installed small brass angle irons under the handles, and extended the life of a board to 10 years or more. It also helps to remove the screws and apply a little epoxy glue under the handles and into the screw holes before screwing them back down again.

Under the Class rules, installation of an extra handle or eye on top of the wooden daggerboard is permitted. This helps you raise the board and also permits a line to be fastened to a point on the boat so the board won't be lost overboard. The Sunfish now comes with an extra line and a padeye on the deck for this purpose. In 30-odd years of Sunfish racing I have managed to flip a board over the side only once, so I don't bother with the retaining line. To me, it is just one more line to get tangled in something. However, when I'm off sailing by myself, I use it. If the only way home is to windward, you'll be in deep doodoo without a board.

Another item specifically permitted by the rules is a daggerboard-retaining device. This is different from the safety line, and is used to keep the board up off the wind. We used to have to keep the board up by leaning on it, or jamming a foot against it, until the retainer was permitted. It is usually a piece of shock cord in a long loop around the board, held taught with hooks over the edges of the deck, centered on the daggerboard well. This design provides a snubbing action on both edges of the board, and keeps it centered so there is little chafe against the edges of the well, which in older boats were often sharp. If the wooden board scraped up and down often against these rough edges, little feathers of mahogany would be peeled out. Feathers on the leading and trailing edge are real slow.

Another type of retaining device also serves as a JC strap. It was used in the early '60s, then outlawed, then reinstated in the '80s. It is a long shock cord fastened at the tack to the eye bolts joining boom and upper spar, led around the mast and halyard, and back to the tack. After you drop the daggerboard into its well, you pull the loop of shock cord back around the daggerboard as well.

Tuning the Boat

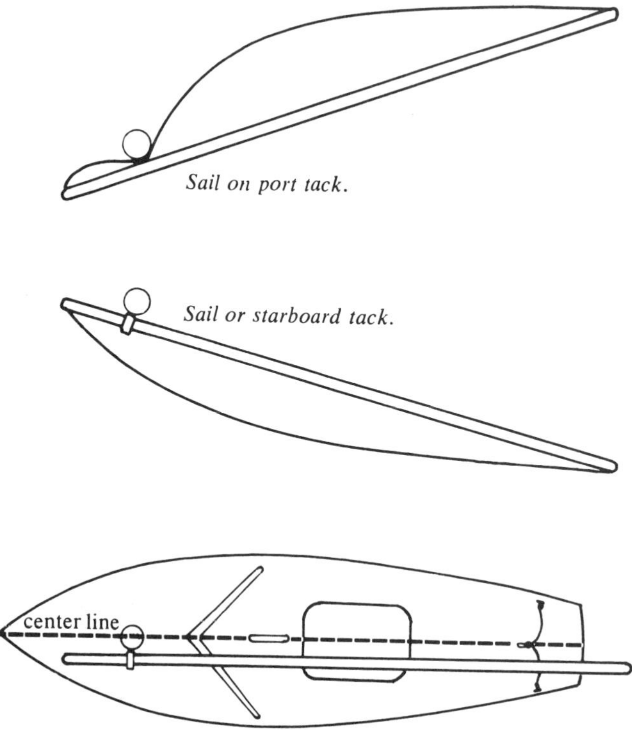

The shape of the Sunfish sail is affected by the boat's off-center boom and, on port tack, by the mast.

The tension holds the board up, and also (this is the JC strap part) pulls the boom outboard automatically when you let out on the sheet—very handy when you are rounding the windward mark in light air that isn't strong enough to push the sail out. During critical roundings, it is nice to be able to use your hands for steering the boat, raising the daggerboard, and handling the sheet. This rig has the drawback of pulling the board forward, increasing the danger of wear on its edges. But a piece of shock cord tight across the front of the board, from one side of the deck to the other, and a little care in raising and lowering the board help preserve the edges.

Class rules permit lining the daggerboard well with material - thin wet-suit material is usually used - so long as there is a two-inch gap on both sides. This fix reduces wear on the board and keeps it firm in the well. Many sailors believe a sloppy board is slow.

• The Bridle

A lot of thought went into various methods of overriding the function of the original bridle, which had a loop in the center to hold the end of the sheet centered over the tiller. Why the interest? Because the Sunfish sail sets differently on starboard and port tacks. First, the mast cuts into the sail on port tack. Second, the whole rig is not centered, but is offset on the port side by about six inches from the centerline of the boat. For both these reasons, the sail is fuller on starboard tack. The mast does not interfere, and the sheet does not exert as strong a downward pull because the angle from the centerline is more acute - it pulls the sail in more than down.

Garry Hoyt, the first Sunfish World Champion, and other Caribbean sailors figured out that they could increase the downward pull on starboard tack, tighten the leach, and flatten the sail, if they clipped the end of the sheet on the port side of the bridle rather than to the eye in the middle. This proved to be an important advantage in heavy air.

Soon after Garry's Worlds victory, Caribbean sailors started to loop the sheet under the bridle, so it could slide past the eye and exert a more downward pull on both tacks. Enough sailors started to use this system that it was made legal in 1978 to tape the loop so the sheet wouldn't get hung up on it. Then, in 1980, the rules were further relaxed to permit a piece of line to be substituted for the wire bridle. It can be knotted to curtail the sheet's travel as much as desired on either tack but must be between 30 and 32 inches long.

With the older sails, some racers found they were faster in light or medium air when they used the eye. Others preferred the original Hoyt system, even in heavy air. But with the new racing sail introduced in '88, there is almost universal agreement that a rope bridle, allowing full travel from side to side, works best in all winds. Now,

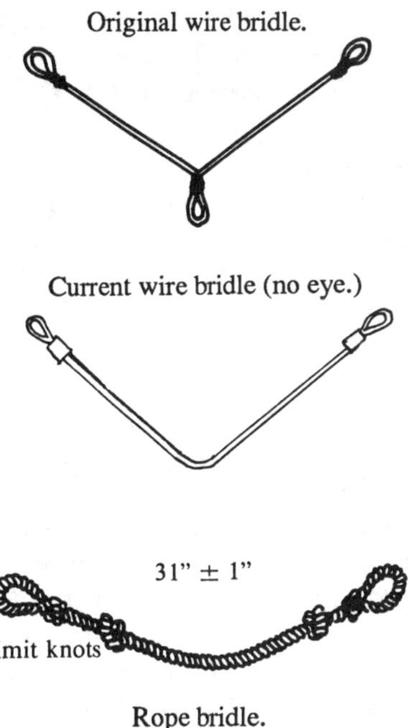

The rope bridle is best because it's adjustable.

Sunfish Laser supplies the boat with a wire bridle without the eye.

It is also legal to use any length sheet, and to tie the sheet's end to a small block riding on the bridle (also now supplied by Sunfish Laser.)

When the Sunfish gybes, it is not unusual for the sheet to droop down between the two boom blocks and catch an ear or life jacket. Attach a couple of loops of tape, line or garden hose to the boom between the blocks, and pass the sheet through them. The rules say it must be something soft or something that will swing out of the way. You might not mind losing an ear, but you sure don't want to capsize!

Another annoyance when making a flying gybe

Tuning the Boat

is that the aft end of the sheet, between the boom and the bridle, can droop down and snag a corner of the transom at the lip between deck and hull. A snap pull on the sheet just before the boom flies over will help. Just be aware it can happen, and glance back to check after every gybe.

• The Cockpit

Some people put antiskid stripes on the deck alongside the cockpit and on the bottom of the cockpit well. Most racers, however, find they want to slide back and forth, in and out, to help steer the boat, rather than anchor themselves in one position.

If you have an older Sunfish, the inside lip of the cockpit may have an aluminum protective strip. This strip, which was installed for 10 years or so, is a mixed blessing. It protects the raw fiberglass edge from your shoes and you from any sharp edges that may be left on the fiberglass, but on occasion the rivets that hold the strip work loose, leaving sharp projections to snag your clothing or skin. Some owners tape this edge all the way around the cockpit, or install a split piece of rubber hose or surgical tubing for protection. This addition is still not specifically approved in the 1995 version of the Class rules, even though a great deal of effort was made to include such often-used fixes when the rules were updated, but it is not likely to be protested by anyone. Today, the cockpit lip is protected by a plastic U-shaped strip that is glued on. It can be kicked loose, but it's the best solution yet. You can buy it through a dealer.

In heavy weather, a lot of water sweeps across the deck. The fewer obstructions, the better. A coaming or splash rail really acts as a brake when you take a lot of water over the bow, but it is illegal to remove the Sunfish coaming. It does deflect water from you and the cockpit, which, by the way, is a most effective water brake itself, not to mention a water trap. If your bailer isn't working - or even if it is - you're likely to be sailing with three or four inches of water in the cockpit going to weather in heavy air. The bailer gets rid of most of it off the wind.

There might be an advantage to decking over the cockpit completely but that would be disallowed. In one Connecticut River Race, I stowed all our gear in the cockpit, covered with a tarpaulin. The idea was not so much to avoid shipping water as to provide better weight distribution and allow me to carry the sail closer to the deck. Whatever I gained that way, however, I lost in ease of handling. We also shipped a bit of water, which made for wet sleeping bags. After that, I went back to the original system of carrying the camping gear in several heavy-duty plastic garbage bags strapped to the deck behind the mast.

For racing, the storage cubby aft of the cockpit is big enough to stow foul weather gear, lunch, and a small sack of tools. Stowing them in heavy waterproof bags keeps them dry, and helps keep the cubby from trapping water.

• Sheet Blocks

If the boat isn't already equipped with them, the first pieces of additional equipment a sailor will install on a Sunfish are a deck-mounted mainsheet block and mainsheet cleats. The simplest rig is just a swiveling block or padeye with an integral cam cleat, but most racers find this unsatisfactory. When hiking out hard, you cannot always release the sheet from the cam cleat without pulling yourself part way back into the boat to get the right angle to lift the sheet far enough to release it. Since you are normally trying to release the sheet when a puff hits, you also want to be hiked out as far as you can. Coming back into the boat allows it to heel and, in extreme circumstances, can cause you to capsize.

Most sailors prefer a block centered on deck right in front of the cockpit lip, with vertical clam cleats as far outboard as the configuration of the deck over the cockpit well will permit. The preferred block is a big Harken Hexaratchet. The sheave of this block is big enough to grip the line strongly, relieving the strain on your hand when the ratchet locks. Smaller ratchet blocks, including Harken's baby Hexaratchet, don't grip as well.

Depending on the block used, you may have to raise the cleats on spacers of wood, plastic or some other material to give them the proper bite on the sheet as it comes out of the block. Lately, many of the top racers have dispensed with cleats altogether. They feel the cleats interfere with sliding forward, as when steering over waves, and make them lazy when they should be adjusting the sail. I see more cam cleats than clam cleats these days, but I suspect that may be because they cost more and are touted by dealers. Instead of vertical clam cleats, I have switched to horizontal ones with the opening facing forward. It's easier to slide over them, and easier to find the opening with the sheet without looking down.

On the other hand, some owners, especially those who race in heavy air a lot, like to raise the cleats on blocks two or three inches high, to provide a hand-hold. On long windward legs like those of the Worlds in trade-wind venues, the hand-hold offers the opportunity to rest a little while hiking hard, by taking some of the strain off your legs. I have accomplished the same thing at such Worlds by using long bolts and stacks of big washers beneath the cleats. Comfortable and easy to hold.

Unless you are in super shape with strong arms and endless endurance, I would advise using cleats, if only to give your sheet hand a rest once in a while, and for those occasions when you need it for something else.

• The Compass

Many Sunfish racers mount a compass on the foredeck, in front of the daggerboard. Be aware that the steel rods in the racing daggerboard can throw a compass off. Test the compass position with the daggerboard out of the slot, then drop the board in slowly and see if the magnetic card moves. If it does, you may have to move the compass off-center, forward of the splashrails. Most racers mount the compass temporarily, in a wooden box that can be strapped to the deck with shock cord or taped down with that most important item in the sailor's ditty bag - duct tape. (Duct tape can patch a sail, protect the gooseneck from the boom, whip a line, hold racing instructions or chart to the deck beneath clear plastic, even make a temporary patch over a hole in the hull after a collision - I once was able to finish a regatta that way.)

A compass is important to help you detect wind shifts when there is no good reference point like a buoy or shoreline landmark. It can also help you find the next mark on long courses. Many sailors who race only on small lakes or protected harbors find the compass unnecessary, but if you travel to major regattas on large bodies of water, you will probably need one. A few sailors find they can detect wind shifts by watching the water and the other boats, but most of the good ones train themselves to watch the compass.

The quality of the compass is important. I have made do with a simple internally gimballed deck-mounted compass. Alcort used to sell one for just over $10. They are now available, for about $30, with colored quadrants to help reduce confusion when you are trying to detect windshifts and the course to the next mark.

It is not unheard of for a sailor to spend more than $100 for a good Suunto or Ritchie compass, which holds its direction better on a bouncy deck. Paul Fendler gave credit to his compass for his victory at the 1975 Worlds in Venezuela. He said

Tuning the Boat

it allowed him to detect five-degree wind shifts, which he played on every leg.

• Other Stuff on the Foredeck

Some people tape a pencil or grease pencil to their decks, so they can jot down compass courses to each of the marks, sail numbers of key competitors or a competitor who has fouled them, or other hard-to-remember things. Another handy item is a clear plastic bag or acetate sheet taped to the deck, as mentioned above.

Other sailors have some sort of arrangement for fastening a stopwatch to the deck or splash rail. It is possible to get along without a stopwatch if all the starting sequences are dinghy starts, where the race committee calls out signals every minute until the final one, when they give signals at 10-second intervals with a five-second final countdown. But at major regattas like the North Americans and Worlds, the official IYRU sequence is used, with five minutes between signals. Even under these conditions, you can get by without a stopwatch if you can train yourself to keep track of a sweep-second hand on an ordinary watch. I did that until digital watches came along; now the cheapest Casio keeps perfect time and is more water resistant than most of the old-time mechanical "waterproof" watches. I went through three of those mechanical stop-watches before I gave up on them; none ever proved waterproof. So get one of the cheap, water-resistant digital watches with a built-in stopwatch. They work very well, and are often more accurate than the race committee's, which may be an old mechanical one handed down for generations.

Another word about stop watches - Jumper Lee, son of John Black Lee, the father of the Super Sunfish, developed a stopwatch you listen to rather than look at. Its series of beeps are easily decoded, once you get the hang of it. With that watch, you can know the time almost continuously, and you don't have to take your eyes off the competition and the starting line. I like the idea. In fact, I once called out the time into a little pocket dictating machine, rewound it, and then timed it as it played back. Unfortunately, it was off by four or five seconds on a five-minute replay, and that is much too much of an error. Jumper's gadget was accurate to the microsecond, or close enough. He sold a few through an ad in *Yacht Racing*, years ago, but not enough to make production worthwhile. I saw an ad for a similar device a few years later, but it apparently didn't fly, either.

• The Hull

The biggest problem with Sunfish is that sooner or later they spring a leak. It might be around the daggerboard trunk, it might be around the mast step, it might be around the bailer, or it might be at the deck/hull joint. You even get a wicking effect through the fiberglass from minor cracks in the gelcoat. As soon as that happens, you will probably get an added five or 10 pounds of weight to your boat, just from water absorbed through the hull. Of course, the longer you are on the water during a race, the more that leak will fill you up. It's not just the weight of the water. It's more the sloshing of the water back and forth, creating oscillations that will slow you down, especially as you try to work your way through waves. At this point, if you have not already done so as a matter of convenience, you will probably want to install one or more hatches. That way, you can get into the hull with a sponge and get out the loose water. Transom-mounted plugs on either side of the rudder can also be used to drain the boat on land. The tiny plug the manufacturer installs on the starboard edge of the deck, near the splash rail, does not do the job very effectively.

A number of Sunfish owners have installed round, waterproof hatches fore and aft on the deck. They can then blow warm air through the hull using the blowing end of a cannister vacuum cleaner. After a few hours, the hull will be considerably lighter, as the warm air hauls the moisture out of the fiberglass. Class rules permit water-tight ports on deck or in the cockpit. They must remain closed from start to finish of individual races, but you can open them between races to sponge out - or pull out a beer you've stored there.

Serious racers will debate the subject of hull stiffness versus lightness. Sometimes a light hull is important but, given the choice, I prefer a stiff hull, even if it means a slightly heavier one. A light hull means that you will get on a plane a little sooner, and in lighter wind. But stiffness, in my experience, will help your boatspeed both on and off the wind. Furthermore, it is the consensus among dinghy racers that a hull so light it "works" as it goes through the waves slows you down.

I suppose the ideal is as light a hull as possible without compromising stiffness. I don't know anything that can be done to stiffen a hull, unless it is to apply another layer of fiberglass to the outside of the hull. That might have been considered legal at one time, but when Dennis Connor applied sheets of material to his 12-Meter when he won back the America's Cup in Australia, we added to the rule that any finish to the hull is allowed as long as it is applied in liquid form.

We'll talk more about this matter of weight versus stiffness in conversations with some of the champions.

• Repairs

As I've said, the Sunfish is beautifully built. It's one tough boat. But in time, or through an accident, it may need repairs.

Most often with older boats the repair is to fix a leak. Usually, you won't know where the leak is. You just know that water is finding its way into the hull. Not a big problem.

Tape over the vent hole in the forward wall of the cockpit tub. Blow air into the drain hole, and then tape it over quickly before too much air blows out again. Not too much air pressure; you don't want to open up extra leaks. A foot or hand pump, or the blowing end of a canister vacuum cleaner, provide more than enough. Then, with a paint brush, spread a 50/50 mixture of soapy water around in the mast step and the daggerboard well where you see seams. Also spread the soapy water all around the boat where deck joins hull, and where the splash rail and fittings are fastened. The soapy water will bubble wherever there's a leak.

Mark the bubble spots, rinse, and dry well. Mix up some MarineTex, or an epoxy resin mixture with fine-chopped fiberglass or sawdust, about the consistency of peanut butter. Spread it around where the bubbles were, let dry, sand smooth. If the leak is under the splash rail or a fitting, a seam of 3M 5200 bedding compound should be enough. That should do it, but test again with pump and soapy water to make sure.

Sunfish Laser, Inc., has an eight-page repair manual that covers just about any repair you may have to make. Their address is on the inside back cover.

4 Tuning the Rig

The most important part of tuning, even more than modifications to the board and rudder, involves the sail and spars. When set up as recommended in the literature that comes with the boat, the rig is not very efficient for racing. The first thing you must do is to tie the halyard at least one full sail clip higher on the upper spar than recommended. This will bring the boom close down to the deck for that end-plate effect discussed earlier. Adjust the tie-off point so that the tack, where boom and upper spar meet, is just two inches off the deck. Don't carry it much lower than that; halyards can stretch or slip, and the tack can make an ugly gouge on the deck.

• The Mast

Another tuning step most racers have adopted is to wrap the mast with duct tape at the bottom and again just below the point where the mast exits the deck. This step makes the rig more rigid in the boat. It also prevents the mast from rotating easily, which may be bad or good. It's bad if that makes the upper spar ride up over the mast cap on a port-tack run; it's good in that, if you have sand in the bottom of your mast well, the rotation won't grind down the mast step and cause a leak.

To increase rigidity even more, some sailors use a trucker's hitch in the halyard to give it a double purchase. After they hoist the sail, they tie a loop in the halyard a foot or two above the deck. They then pass the halyard through the deck eye, back up through the loop, back down through the eye again, and belay it off tight on the deck cleat.

• The Gooseneck

The gooseneck can slide on the boom when it's loose. The factory-suggested position is too far aft when the boom is carried low. Most like to adjust it according to wind conditions, moving it forward in light air - as close as 12 inches from the tack with the older sails - and aft as the wind picks up. Today, 14 to 14 1/2 inches from the front of the boom is considered pretty extreme, with the consensus about 16 inches. With the gooseneck forward, the boom is cocked well up above the transom. In really heavy stuff, the boom will be carried practically parallel to the deck. The lower the rig, the less heeling moment there is. With the gooseneck forward, the boat can be pointed higher, but it's harder to keep the boat "in the groove" - moving well without stalling. The heavier the air, the harder it is to keep from stalling. Stalling happens when the daggerboard loses its hydrodynamic flow, or lift, and the boat starts to crab to leeward - a very slow way to go to windward. As the wind picks up and the waves get bigger, you need more drive to punch your

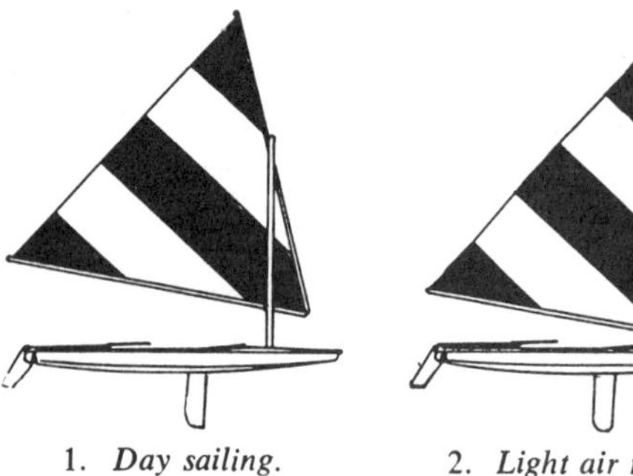

1. *Day sailing.* 2. *Light air racing.*

3. *Heavy air racing.*

4. *Jens heavy air racing.*

way through, so really close pinching is less important. Moving the gooseneck back in heavy air also reduces weather helm. Weather helm drags the rudder through the water at an angle. That's slow, and it's also tiring for your tiller arm.

Constant adjustment of the gooseneck eventually stripped the threads of the bronze machine screw that came with the original gooseneck. Carl Knight started a trend by substituting a stainless steel screw for the bronze one, and in time the builder switched to stainless with a hex head instead of the slotted screw head that was originally used. Since the early '80s, several cam action devices have been offered for the Sunfish gooseneck, all of which work well. One of them is still advertised in the Class newsletter, *Windward Leg*, and is available from Peg Beadle, who runs a mail-order business for sailboat equipment and also runs the Class office with husband Terry. A lot of top competitors use the devices, because they allow adjustment of the gooseneck without tools.

• The Jens Rig

Jens Hookanson of St. Croix in the Virgin Islands won the 1976 North Americans at Association Island, NY, using a complicated rig developed in his home waters to handle the heavy air of the trade wind belt. It was dubbed the Jens or Hookanson rig by the competitors, and the name stuck. It was created by tying the halyard to the upper spar at roughly the factory position - lower on the spar than the normal racing position - and then lashing the spar to the mast about a foot down from the masthead before bringing the halyard up through the mast cap. This rig kept the sail low, but made the free end of the upper spar longer, and therefore bendier. The bending in heavy air spills wind, making it easier to hold the boat flat. With the Jens rig, a light sailor can sail faster that way, even though the sail is now less efficient. Even the Sunfish sail can overpower the boat when the wind gets strong enough. The Jens rig helps lighter sailors compete with the heavyweights in strong winds.

For a number of years after Jens introduced it, only lightweights used it. Then some of the best sailors learned it improved their performance, even though they could hold the boat down pretty well without it. Since they didn't have to work so hard, they were able to concentrate better on tactics and technique. Today, however, use of the Jens has dropped a bit. It may be a macho thing, or sailors are spending more time building up their endurance, or the new racing sail, as some believe, isn't as overpowering, when it is pulled out tight on the spars, as the old ones were.

The problem with the Jens rig as originally tied is that it is almost impossible to drop when the boat is out on the water, and that is a hazard, especially for a less experienced sailor caught in a sudden squall. The best solution, one that was allowed shortly after Jens popularized the rig, was to use a separate line to tie it in. Just recently, the rule was changed to make it the *only* way allowed, and the extra line must be rigged in such a way that the sail can be lowered from the cockpit. It has even been made legal to mount a cleat on the mast, which may be used either for the Jens line or the halyard. However, some way of keeping the mast in its step with the halyard must be provided, so the rig won't fall out if the boat turtles in a capsize. Three cheers for safety.

Another safety consideration is to make sure the Jens is not tied too low. About 18 inches from the top of the mast is close to maximum. Tie it lower than that and you stand a chance of bending the upper spar, because so much of it is then unsupported.

The best way to tie in a Jens, I believe, is to tie a loose bowline around the mast with one end of the Jens line, then bring the other end up through the halyard hole at the top of the mast and down

Tuning the Rig

Jens Hookanson of St. Croix (40) the year he won the North Americans in heavy air with his now-famous "Jens Rig" – the upper spar tied low on the mast. Note, also, his hiking technique. His right foot is under the cockpit lip, with his left crossed over it and hooked under the boom. He claimed it was comfortable! Today, a hiking strap is permitted.

to a cleat on the mast. The halyard is then tied lower on the upper spar and led over the bowline loop, back down through the deck padeye, and cleated to the halyard cleat in the usual way. With this rig, the depth of the Jens can be adjusted on the water. See the sketch in Scott Kyle's article from *Sailing World* among the reprints later in this book. Scott tied the Jens line off at the mast cap, but that was before the rules permitted the extra cleat on the mast.

• Bending on the Sail

Before the racing sail came along, setting the sails on the spars was an important aspect of tuning. After 1967, when the first fuller cut sail was introduced, it was important to set it very loosely on the spars. Bending on sail this way produces a pronounced scallop along the foot, and often a bit of scallop along the luff as well. I couldn't stand a sail with a scalloped luff, because the scalloping starts to flutter a little bit before normal luffing as you feather up to the wind. I was convinced that the scalloped luff meant you had to foot off a hair more than with a sail that could be set with a little tautness in the luff. Others seemed to be perfectly happy with a scalloped luff. The problem became less when the first Fogh sail was introduced. Now the racing sail is almost universally set without scallops on the luff, and few sailors carry scallops on the foot, either.

Many sailors experiment with foot and luff tension, to get different shapes for different wind and wave conditions. Others experiment until they find "the best" set, the one that suits them best, and leave it there. However, as competition increased over the years, fiddling with outhauls became the rule rather than the exception, and the Class permitted adjustable ones in 1978. It was then made permissible to install cleats on the spars, with long adjustment lines out to peak and clew. Now, the rules allow both cleats on the boom. Most top competitors create an extra purchase by tying loops in the line to serve as turning blocks - trucker's hitches, as described above for the halyard. Instead of tightening the luff with a line all the way up to the peak and back, they tighten it from the first grommet from the tack, pulling down on this line to tighten the rest of the luff. It's so popular that North now supplies the racing sail with this grommet reinforced. With this system (again, see Scott Kyle's article) both luff and foot can be adjusted from the cockpit under sail.

Nowadays, the adjustment for the foot is called the outhaul, and for the luff the Cunningham or inhaul. Jeff Linton says he adjusts the Cunningham several times each windward leg in puffy conditions or waves, letting it out for fullness when he needs power and tightening it when he wants to point higher.

The subject of lace lines versus sail clips was a hot one years ago. The sail was very flat, and sailors went to great lengths to try to get extra draft. With lace lines, they could try to induce draft by tying the sail close at the three corners, and progressively looser where they wanted the greatest draft. It didn't seem to help. It is still permissible to use lace line or individual ties of line in place of the clips. The rule was that the sail could be no more than 2 inches from the spar. Today, with the new racing sail, just about everyone uses the sail clips.

Two exceptions: at the two grommets below the halyard on the upper spar, and at the peak and clew grommets. The first is most important. Tie short pieces of line around the spar through those two or three grommets below the spot where the halyard is tied to the spar. That way, even if the line gets jammed between the spar and the mast, the sail can slide around into its natural position when you tack or gybe. Sail clips do get jammed at the mast, and because they don't allow the grommets to slide, the sail takes on a hard spot.

Tuning the Rig

The other exception - at the peak and clew - is subject to debate. Some sailors use neither sail set nor line to fasten the clew and peak grommets to the spars, feeling that this opens up the leach and "lets it breathe," whatever that means. Others compromise by tying them loosely with line. And still others use sail clips there, as with the rest of the grommets. There probably is no universal rule for everyone; each sailor's style varies, and what works best for one is a go-slow for another. And what works in light air and flat water may not in a blow and steep chop. Experiment and try to determine what works best for you in what conditions.

• The Free End of the Halyard

The free end of the halyard is used for a number of things, most of them considered legal. It can be tied to the tack, and then looped on deck around the mast with one loop on either side of it. On reaches and runs the line can be held taught, acting as a JC strap to hold the sail out. Most sailors now use the end of the halyard as a downhaul on the gooseneck, to prevent the boom from riding up on reaches and runs and developing too much twist. Sunfish sailors call this a vang, although a few rig a true vang with the halyard end, tying a clove hitch to the boom about 18 inches aft of the gooseneck and then at the base of the mast. I used the halyard as a JC strap until the shock cord/daggerboard retainer/ JC strap was legalized. Now I just use it to tie down the gooseneck, and wrap the rest into a tight coil, which I slide under the taught halyard between deck padeye and cleat.

• Telltales

In my opinion, you practically have to have telltales - not only a fly at the peak, but a couple of yarns or feathers sticking out in front of the upper spar. Some very good sailors pride themselves on being able to sense the wind without any telltales at all, but, especially in light shifty air, I think they are indispensable.

A few people use only one telltale, on a wire sticking straight out in front of the upper spar, parallel to the boom. Others carry two, on a straight piece of wire fastened at 90 degrees to the boom. I prefer telltales on wires at 90 degrees to each other, each at a 45 degree angle to the boom. Such a telltale unit is available as the Feathermate, designed and sold by Paul Odegaard through the *Windward Leg*. It is installed on the upper spar with a plastic clip and comes with both feathers and yarn, to suit your preference. I make mine from the aluminum ground wire used to ground TV antennas. It can be bent and adjusted easily, and then folded out of the way when you roll up the sail. They're easy to make and cheap, so when they break, it's no problem to replace them. I fold the ends down at 90 degrees, and tape synthetic knitting yarn at the tips. Why synthetic? It dries faster.

There are dozens of commercial masthead flies available that can be attached to the peak. But again, I prefer a piece of aluminum groundwire with a piece of yarn on the end, taped to the peak and sticking straight out like an extension of the upper spar. The main value of the peak fly is for downwind work, but, under shifty conditions, especially in light air, it can help you deduce an average of winds coming in at different angles. Yes, it is quite possible to have the wind abeam down at deck level and coming from straight ahead up at the fly, or vice versa, especially on small lakes or rivers. Knowing this, and adjusting your sail to the best average, can keep you moving when the rest of the boats are stalled out, and that can mean the difference between being in the pack or way out ahead. I know few sailors who can do that without telltales, and while such conditions are the exception, I use my telltales most of the time, just in case. The exception is in heavy air, when your concentration should be in working your way through the waves.

In very heavy air, I find that the fly at the peak is a better indicator than eye-level telltales, probably because the waves break up the smooth air flow. In very light air, I find myself concentrating almost exclusively on those forward, eye-level yarns, to take advantage of every little shift to feather my way to windward. This is especially true if the wind is fairly even over the course. Much of the time in really fluky stuff, there will be puffs and holes, and it is more important some of the time to keep your eyes on the water and try to sail where the puffs are, rather than concentrate on shifts. Knowing when to do one and when the other is one of those imponderable instincts it is almost impossible to teach.

In addition to telltales at the peak and at eye level, some sailors use telltales on the sail itself. These are often called "woollies" to differentiate them from the ones out in clear air. The idea is to fasten them on the sail a bit aft of the luff, or the mast, one on each side, in pairs. When airflow is optimum, the leeward woollies should stream aft and the windward ones should actually lift above the horizontal occasionally. Because the Sunfish sail sets differently on each tack, the woollies react differently, too. A few Sunfish sailors have learned to use woollies in spite of the differences, but most have given up on them. If you find it hard to keep in the groove you might experiment with them. They might help you.

Finally, some sailors use telltales on the leach of the sail. They are supposed to stream aft when the airflow is optimum. My original Fogh sail came with them attached, but I found that, going to windward, if they streamed aft I was footing too much - going faster through the water but slower towards the windward mark. Like woollies, you might want to test them. They might be useful for your style of sailing.

Various types of telltales have been tried, but those at eye level, attached to wires in a V configuration from the upper spar, seem best. A peak fly is useful off the wind. Masthead fly and sail woollies have been found useful by a few Sunfish sailors, as have leech or trailing-edge telltales.

Sunfish telltales.

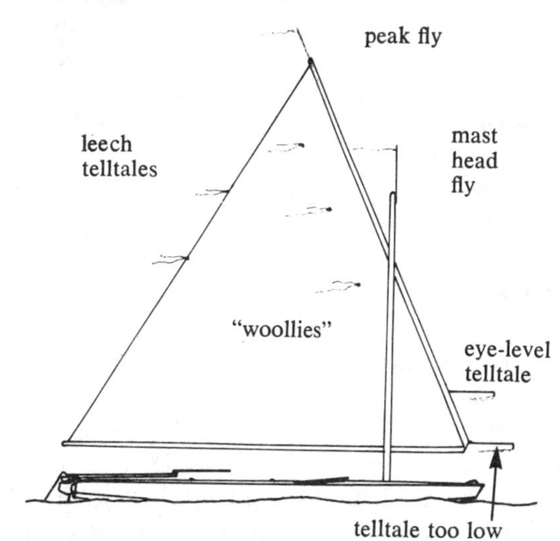

Bird's-eye view of telltales.

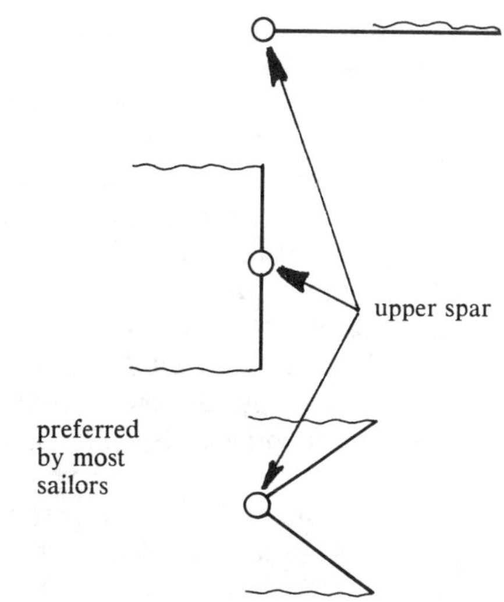

5 Tuning You

We've talked about tuning your boat. Today more than ever, if you really want to be in the top ranks of competition, you have to be in tune yourself. Most Olympic yachtsmen train for their sport as intensively as any track star. They run. They lift weights. They do aerobics. They even study ballet. So do many of the top Sunfish competitors. Some of them are good enough to have legitimate Olympic aspirations.

For Sunfish racing, the two most important sets of muscles are your hiking muscles and your sheet-pulling muscles. I can't give you their biological names. Obviously, though, if you sail a lot in heavy air, those are the muscles you'll exercise, whatever they're called. Sailing is the best exercise for tuning your body for sailing.

• Hiking muscles

Your hiking muscles are mostly back and leg muscles. For a while, way back when, some Sunfish sailors concentrated on their stomach muscles. In fact, these are not vital for hiking. In a proper hiking position, you are sitting fairly upright, with your tail out over the water. Your weight is supported by your leg muscles, with lots of pressure under your thighs, somewhere between your bottom and your knees. Since your center of gravity is somewhere around your waist, leaning back adds relatively little righting moment. You will lean way back for momentary surges of wind, but it is impossible, I bet, for even the best-trained athlete to sail a half-hour windward leg in a supine hiked-out position. Some competitors sail light-air races with their backs on the side deck, so they can keep their eyes on the sail and their profile low to reduce windage. There is no strain on your leg or stomach muscles in that position, but your neck will get stiff. I've tried that position, but I could never make it work for me. Very few people use it any more.

Training muscles to hold a tense position, resisting considerable force, requires somewhat different conditioning than is required for repetitive movements. Paul Elvstrom, who invented many of today's dinghy-racing techniques, had a special bench from which he could hike out while sitting at his desk. The best exercise for hiking out, he figured, was hiking out.

You can get much the same effect with an exercise suggested by Larry Lewis. I've been told it was invented by skiers. Stand with your back about a foot or two from a wall. Then lean back against it, bending your knees so that your thighs are roughly parallel to the floor. If you are not used to it, this exercise will bring tears to your eyes in a few minutes. But, after a while, you should be able to hold it for 30 minutes or so and catch up on your reading at the same time. I would suggest shifting your position a little once in a while when you do this, or you may cut off circulation somewhere.

As many a sufferer knows, the back is one of the most vulnerable parts of the human anatomy. Long periods of hiking out while straining against the sheet and tiller can put a lot of kinks in your back. So, back-limbering exercises are a good idea. The old stand-by, touching your toes, is good. Lying on your back and pulling your knees up to your chest - one at a time and then both together - is also good. When you have done that for a while, clasp your knees with your arms and rock back and forth. Start these exercises slowly, working up your intensity of execution carefully, since the back muscles need to be limbered up before they can safely do their best work.

• Sheeting Muscles

To get your arm and shoulder muscles in correct shape, you can use various hand weights and pulling machines. The motion you will be using most consistently while sailing is pulling the sheet from well inboard to shoulder height,

Joel Furman, North American Champion of 1975, demonstrates the spread-eagle hiking style favored by short people until hiking straps became legal.

or even over your head if you are trying to get the boat on a plane. So, simulating the same sort of motion with a weight or weighted line on a pulley arrangement is good exercise.

I have considered setting up a Sunfish or a simulation of its deck area on some sort of motorized gadget that will simulate a stiff chop, something like the bucking bronco machines that used to be popular in "Western" bars. There would be a block on deck with a 5/16th-inch line reeved through it to a pair of overhead pulleys. At the end of the line would be a 10 or 15-pound weight to simulate the pull of the sail. Even without the bucking arrangement, such a rig would be a step up from the hiking bench. Hike out and pump the sheet for an hour or so every other day, in sets of 20 minutes or so, and you should be able to survive any regatta without tiring. Tired sailors don't sail fast.

• Pads

Hiking out hard on a Sunfish can cause pain. If you hike with the natural crease between your buttocks and thighs at the edge of the boat, you're not hiking hard enough in heavy air. You have to go beyond that. And for every inch beyond, the leverage of your body increases, squeezing the backs of your legs against hard fiberglass.

To spread out the pressure a little, many sailors sew pieces of heavy carpet to the backs of their sailing pants. Others wear two or three pairs of sweat pants. I tried the foam pads from an old life jacket slipped into special pockets on the legs of some coveralls. Very comfortable, but it made ducking under the boom when tacking chancy at best. After a couple of capsizes, I took out the pads and accepted the discomfort. Upside down is slow, too!

Today, there are many designs for hiking shorts that have heavy plastic batten material sewn in under the thighs. These are great, although I have found I need suspenders to keep them up. Otherwise, they tend to work down around my knees, where they are definitely an impediment. Many sailmakers and boating supply outlets that cater to dinghy racers have them in stock in several sizes.

• Shoes

I used to sail barefoot, and my toes paid for it over the years. Some sailors wear Topsiders, others wear tennis or basketball sneakers, and still others sea boots or special hiking shoes. If you have cleats bolted through the foredeck into the cockpit, you'll be especially smart to protect your feet. Even more dangerous than cleat bolts

Tuning You

in the cockpit are hazards on shore: broken bottles and the ring-dings from pop-open cans, or clam shells, broken bits of concrete or more exotic hazards like coral. All those and more have bitten friends of mine who were launching Sunfish in bare feet.

Other things to guard or pad yourself against: the boom block that grabs your hair; the many hard corners that can smack your knees or elbows. Some competitors wear a sweatband or hat, together with basketball kneepads and elbow pads. Unless you have a thick head of hair, a hat is a necessity in bright sun, and a visor reduces eyestrain. Ophthalmologists recommend good sunglasses, too. Some sailors swear by polarized glasses, which are supposed to reduce glare off the water so you can see waves and wind signs better. Just be sure that, even if your lenses are clear, they have a good coating that screens out UV (ultraviolet) rays.

• Carrying Weight

The ideal Sunfish sailor would be about seven feet tall and weigh 145 pounds. He would have massive shoulders and most of his weight in the chest area, and would never tire. As far as I know, there is no Sunfish sailor who meets this description, and that is just as well. He would probably be unbeatable, if his sailing skills were really good. An individual with such a physique would be light enough to get his boat on a plane quickly even in marginal conditions, and could get his weight outboard to hold the boat down in very strong puffs. With the weight high, he would also be able to get his body moving with the pendulum effect used by many top sailors to torque their boats over the waves to windward, or to help steer the boat.

There are no Sunfish sailors of quite this description, but most of the top ones come close, either naturally or with the help of extra weight. Derrick Fries, for instance, was a little heavier than the ideal, but he has a long limber body and great strength.

It used to be that you could carry water as weight. This was carried either in the form of clothing or rubber bottles on chest or back. The reasoning was that, if you fell overboard, the water would not pull you down, since it weighs no more than the stuff you're floating in. If you are wearing a life jacket when carrying extra weight, you won't drown. However, the wet clothing or the water bottles were usually easily removable. Otherwise you would find it very difficult to climb back into the boat.

You could buy special water jackets or wear cotton sweat shirts and soak them up. Most people who used sweats tore off the sleeves and slit them down the front, cardigan fashion, with some kind of simple release arrangement to hold them together. Then, if you fell in, you could take them off easily.

Carried high on the chest and back, weight could be leveraged fully for hiking out and for torquing. You didn't need very much. Ten or 15 pounds was plenty for even the well-conditioned athlete. If you did wear extra weight, the Sunfish Class limit was 10 kilos, or 22 pounds, as of the 1980 Class rules. (The IYRU permitted up to 22 kilos - almost 50 pounds - of wet clothing, and some of the early Finn sailors tried to carry that much to match the muscular gorillas who seem to gravitate to that man-killing class. As a result, not a few Finn sailors got bad backs. A bad back, as everyone who has ever had even a touch of back problem will tell you, is no fun.)

IYRU has just, as this is written, outlawed "clothing or equipment for the purpose of increasing his weight." How they plan to eliminate fluffy, absorbent clothing has some people baffled. The 1996 Sunfish rules had to conform to the IYRU rule, so extra weight is no longer allowed.

The Start and the Windward Leg 6

It is impossible to reach the top ranks of racing without knowing instinctively the International Yacht Racing Union Rules under which you will be competing. Most of the rules are quickly and easily understood and, for convenience, can be abbreviated on 4x5-inch cards. U.S. Sailing (formerly the United States Yacht Racing Union) publishes a fine capsule summary of the rules that was originally prepared by Tom Ehman, three-time runner-up at the Sunfish North Americans. The rulebook itself is also available from U.S. Sailing as are a number of books and videos explaining and picturing how the rules work in practice. Make sure you get the current rules - they are revised every three years.

Scattered among the race situations described in the following pages are tactical situations involving the rules. Study these together with the rules so that you understand how they apply. Expect to get lots of education from race postmortems, too. Unless you are very cautious, you are certain to become personally involved in a few protest hearings as well. When you do, it's important to your success to keep your emotions under control.

I think a word about the spirit of the rules is in order here. Until recently, and even then only in major regattas, there were no umpires or judges on the course. Every sailor is considered to be honest and willing voluntarily to take his medicine if he causes a foul. When there is a legitimate disagreement, a protest is in order.

One final point on the rules: Until you are confident about the rules, play it safe and stay out of the way. The sailor who causes a flagrant foul at a multiboat mark rounding can ruin a regatta for several others who might otherwise have been in contention. Of course, if you foul someone and damage his boat, the honest thing to do is pay for repairs. Occasionally, a new sailor will crash into another competitor, holing the other's hull or tearing a sail, and then slip off never to be seen again. I assume they do this out of shame, not dishonesty, but the effect is the same.

• The Start

Almost all sailboat races begin with a timed start. The official IYRU starting sequence begins with a Warning signal and a white or yellow flag 10 minutes before the start, accompanied by a sound signal - a gun or horn, usually. At six minutes the flag goes down - no sound signal. At five minutes, a blue Preparatory flag and a sound signal. At one minute, the blue flag goes down. The Start is signalled be a red flag and a sound signal.

There are a couple of peculiarities about this system. First, it's the flags that count - the sound signal is just to call attention to the flag. Most committees are practiced enough to have the sound and the flag practically simultaneous, but it's good to know that the flag rules. Second, there is often no alert to exactly when that 10-minute Warning is going to happen. Unless the race committee starts the sequence at precisely the pre-announced time, and your watch is in sync with theirs, you may be caught off guard, and not get your watch started on time. If that happens to you, wait for the Preparatory signal. There are still five minutes to go - plenty of time before your start.

Each sailor's objective is to be just a foot or so downwind of the line at the start, with clear air, going full steam to windward. It takes a lot of practice to get all the variables right - the timing, the clear air, and the speed - without fouling anybody. And there are more variables than those three, as you will see.

Theoretically, the perfect starting line for a windward start is at a right angle to the wind direction. I say theoretically, because the wind is almost never that steady. Many times the line is at a right angle to the average wind direction.

The Start and the Windward Leg

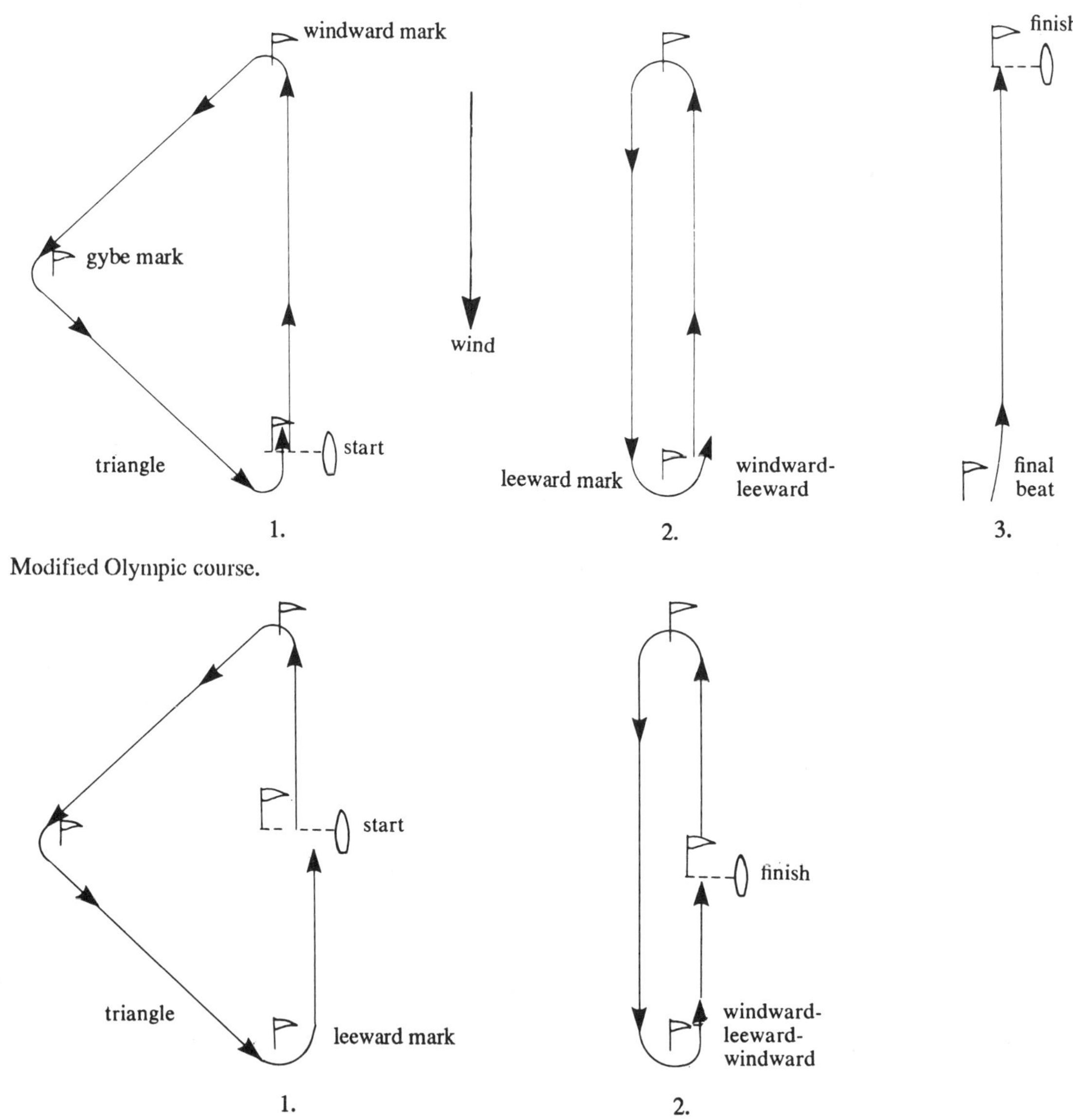

The "Olympic" and "modified Olympic" courses. There is actually one less windward leg to a "modified Olympic." There are now several other courses specified at the Olympics...and at Sunfish regattas.

The Start and the Windward Leg

Shortly after a start at the 1979 Worlds in Medemblik, Holland. Beyond the shoreline dyke, the land stretches off for miles, below sea level. No. 132 seems to be in good shape, unless 133 to leeward can squeeze up and dose him with backwind. No. 139 checks over his shoulder to see if there's room to tack out of there: if the right side of the course is favored he may be the first one over there and recoup a mediocre start. No. 147 is thoroughly blanketed and has just hit a wave; he'd be smart to tack and take the stern of 112 just to clear his air. Note the midline sag.

The committee boat will almost always be placed on the starboard end of the line as you face the first mark from the start and the port end will have a buoy or marker. Since almost all boats will start on starboard tack - the right-of-way tack - the port end has come to be known as the leeward or pin end and the starboard end has become known as the windward or committee boat end.

One thing that the new competitor may not realize is that any point on the line is the same sailing distance from the windward mark as any other, as long as the line is square to the wind. Most experienced sailors will try to determine which end of the line is favored - that is, slightly further upwind. If an end is slightly favored many will congregate there and you may find yourself with the middle of the line to yourself. This could be an advantage if the line is almost square and the boats gathered at the favored end slow each other down.

The classic starting method, used for years by most racing sailors, was to sail away from that point on the line you wish to cross on the start,

The Start and the Windward Leg

The leeward end is slightly favored at the start of this race for the Inter-Class Solo Championships. Note that three boats were late (5, 8, and hidden) trying to find a hole. The three that opted not to fight it out down there seem to be doing all right, especially No. 1. It's better to get a fast start in clear air than to be at the favored end and buried.

on a port-tack broad reach at a 45-degree angle from the line. If you crossed the line heading downwind at exactly one minute before the start, you would head up and tack on to starboard, close-hauled, starting about 35 seconds before the start. If the 180-degree-turning maneuver took you 10 seconds, you would then be sailing close-hauled back to the point on the line right on the gun. Obviously, this method takes very accurate timing. It also assumes that the boat travels the same speed on a broad reach as it does close-hauled. Most boats don't, so you have to factor in the speed differences on the two points of sail.

Nowadays, most Sunfish sailors use what is known as the dinghy start. Like so many "modern" innovations, its invention is credited to Paul Elvstrom of Denmark. Under this system, the boats hover just below the line, with the sails drawing just enough to give them steerage, and try to maneuver so that they have a clear space to leeward five to three seconds before the start. At about three seconds, you sheet in, get the boat moving, and cross the line with the gun.

With this system, the timing is not so exquisite, but the maneuvering is intense, since you really have to get that clear space to leeward without fouling anybody. The idea is to try to get the boats

The Start and the Windward Leg

Left: *A typical shifty-wind start. Some skippers think the windward end is favored, others are driving for the leeward end, and the boats in the middle have sagged off the line. The North Americans, Indian Lake, Ohio, 1975. Will White won the pin end (31582.)*

Below: *Paul Odegaard pulls off a perfect port tack start at the Worlds in Puerto Rico in 1974. He was one of the few to notice that the wind had backed just before the starting gun, suddenly favoring the pin end.*

to leeward to sail a little faster than they need to, so that you can then slow up for those last few seconds before you sheet in, leaving a gap between you and the leeward boat.

If you are just starting out racing, you should probably plan to start somewhere in the middle of the line, until you have the timing down pat. Get up close to the line within the last 30 seconds of the countdown and try to keep your air clear. If a boat tries to ride over you to windward, let him do so as long as you will have clean air for about 10 seconds before the start. However, if

The Start and the Windward Leg

there are only a few seconds to go before the start, pick up speed and force him right up to or over the line. But don't go higher than close-hauled - that's a rule.

If he still manages to get ahead of you, try to bear off and pick up speed, sailing straight down the line until the gun, and then head up to close-hauled. If you have timed it right, you will not be over early and you will be moving in clear air. Depending on how long a line the committee has allowed for the size of the fleet, you may find this a little risky, even in the middle of the line, but it is duck soup compared to the favored end. There, the boats are really jockeying for position and many of them are getting buried.

However, sooner or later you will get good enough at starting in the middle of the line that you can start to try your hand at the favored end. Just make sure it *is* the favored end and not an illusion.

A good approach to the windward (committee boat) end start is to come up on port, tack just under the pack and then bear off the line a little with a full head of steam. If you hit the line right on the gun, you will be backwinding the rest of the fleet. If you can sail higher than most of them, they will eventually have to tack away from you.

When the leeward (pin) end of the line is favored, one way to approach the start is to sail down the line, trying to stay ahead of the fleet. As long as the fleet is overtaking you to windward, you can luff up to the line,

A typical jam-up at the leeward end of the start – Aruba Worlds, 1974. Numbers 549 and 542 are too early, but peeled off in time.

577 trying to stall before the gun, loses steerage ...

...and hangs up on the leeward pin.On the other hand, farther up the line, 599 has cleared a nice hole to leeward, and may have the best strart of all, unless 620 clears the pin with a full head of steam.

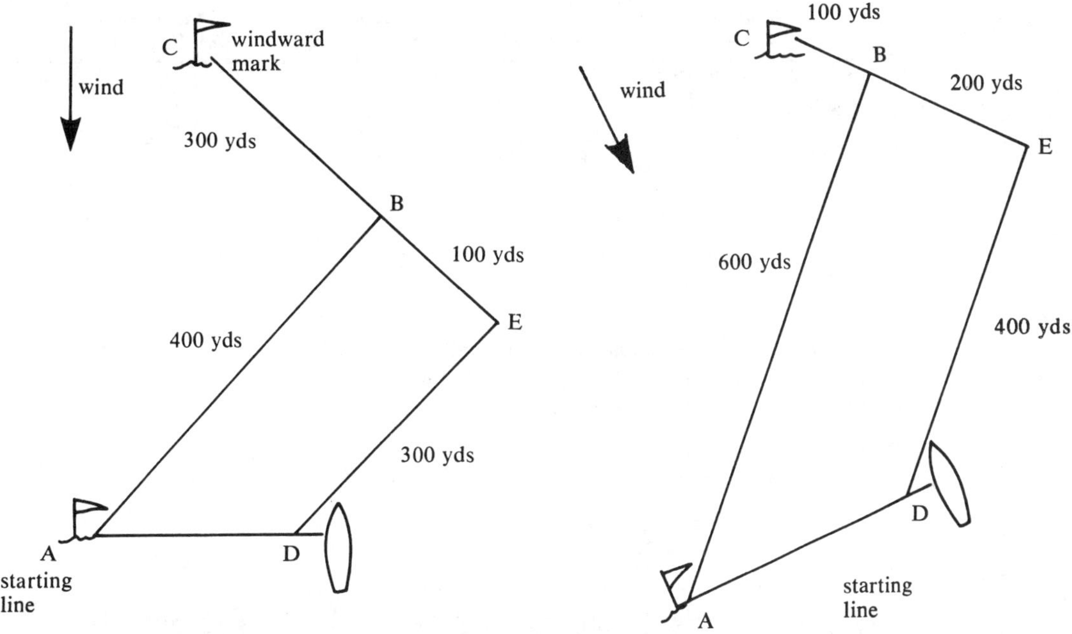

Why the starting line is set square to the wind. In both courses, ABC is the same distance as DEC.

slowing the whole parade down, until you feel it is safe to sheet in and head for the pin. If your timing is absolutely correct, you will hit the leeward end of the line right at the gun and have the whole fleet in your backwind.

To get the position at the head of the parade, it is often best to come in on port tack, flip over to starboard in front of the fleet a few dozen boat lengths from the port end of the line, and then lead the parade. However, if two or three other boats have done that ahead of you, only one of you can be right. Often, the boats will start stacking up at the leeward end several seconds before the gun and hover there before they hit the line. Even if they do manage to stall this way, they have lost their headway and the windward boats can often steam right over them. So whichever way you approach it, leading the parade is chancy at best.

In large fleets there must be a long starting line. The committee should make the line long enough so that every boat in the fleet can have a position right on the line rather than getting itself buried in a second or third tier. Even with the longest line in the world, enough boats will try for the favored end that the middle of the line is almost never cluttered. That gives you an opportunity to take advantage of midline sag, a phenomenon that almost always takes place on long starting lines. Boats sailing two or three boat

The Start and the Windward Leg

hole to leeward
starting line
you

The dinghy start; try to maneuver so you have a hole to leeward three to five seconds before the start.

30 seconds to go
gun! perfect start with full speed
starting line
in mid-tack at 15 seconds

Classic timed start has been used for years, but takes very accurate timing.

Typical midline sag at the start of a world championship race, Holland, 1979. No. 123 seems to be in good shape, but from the angle at which all the boats are sailing, it would seem the leeward end is quite favored.

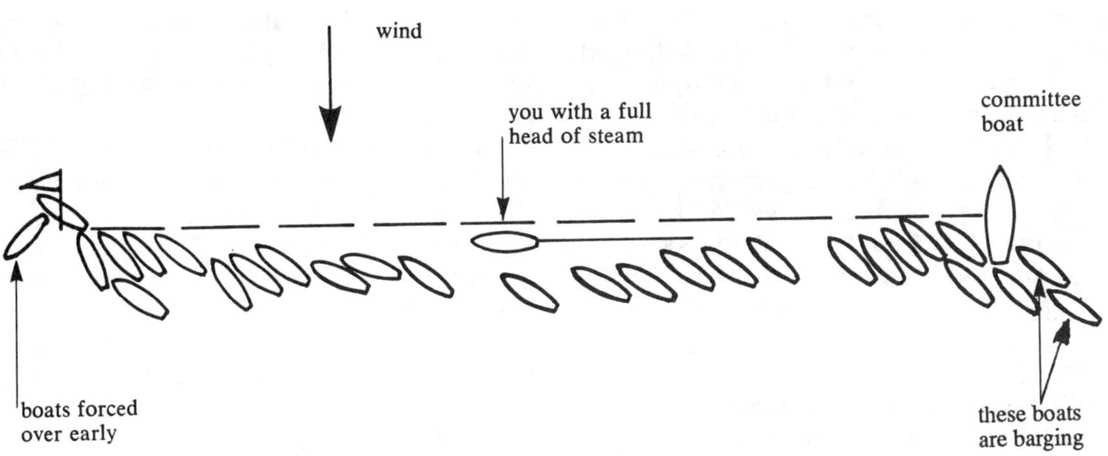

Big fleet start with midline sag (2 seconds to gun.) Note the boats that are barging on the right, and the boats forced over the line early on the left.

lengths below the line, planning to get up on the line shortly before starting, will almost always play it safe and misjudge where the line is towards the middle. They *should* be cautious because being over early means either having to struggle back to the starting line and restart after the gun, if you hear the hail that you are over, or it means disqualification if you don't hear the hail and don't go back.

However, if you start at the committee boat end and sail down the line straight toward the leeward pin, you can judge your position with greater accuracy, especially if you can line up the pin with a fixed point, usually a landmark on shore. You can sail along on a beam reach until you hear the gun, then harden up and go full tilt. Meanwhile, the others who have decided to start in the middle but have approached it from below the line will see you coming and be certain that you are over the line to windward. Nine times out of 10 they will all be a full length or more downwind of you and you will have the starting line all to yourself! In a big regatta, with 60 boats or more, this is my favorite start, unless one end or the other is drastically favored.

A word of caution - if the current is sweeping you towards the windward mark, you may easily be swept over early. Under these conditions half the fleet may misjudge and you will get midline bulge instead of midline sag. Then you're better off at an end rather than the middle, especially since there will probably be at least one general recall.

The rules of the regatta may make a dip start from above the line a problem. Sometimes, in very large fleets, the race committee will try to forestall general recalls by enforcing the "around-the-ends" rule for every start. That rule, usually enforced only after a general recall, says that if you are over early in the last minute before the start, you must sail around one of the ends of the line before re-starting. You can't just dip down

The Start and the Windward Leg

below the line and start again. An even more onerous rule is the "black flag" rule, which says that, within one minute of the starting gun, anyone over the line and inside a triangle formed by the line and the windward mark is disqualified! Most race committees won't fly the black flag until after several general recalls, but occasionally a committee will institute it throughout the regatta. Look for these possible rules in the race instructions, listen for them at the skippers meeting, and watch the committee boat for the black flag.

• Offwind Starts

Sunfish races are not always started to windward. Some clubs traditionally have a fixed starting line, usually off the clubhouse dock, so that non-racing members can watch the starts and finishes. This means that as often as not, the start will be a reach or a run. Years ago there were some major Sunfish championships run under such conditions. Awful.

A reaching start is feeding time at the zoo. Obviously, the windward end is hopelessly favored, if the reach is anywhere from a beam to a broad reach. Everybody except the windward boat will be blanketed.

The alternative is just to figure out the angles the best way you can and hit that line right on the gun at the windward end before anyone else. Your odds are very bad. The thing to remember is that with a reaching start it is better to be the second or third boat in line at the windward end than to be the second or third boat to leeward. The others may be on the line at the gun, but you will be sailing a whole lot faster in clear air and should be able to pass them just 100 yards or so from the start.

Finally, there is the dead downwind start. Here, the end of the line to start on will probably depend on which way you will round the first mark. You want to be on the inside because what is probably going to happen is that the fleet will spread out in a long flank, everyone abeam of everyone else, and the inside boat at the mark will be like the inside skater of a game of crack-the-whip. Everyone else will have to "cartwheel" around him around the mark.

The downwind start is also one where being a little late across the line may be an advantage. Even if you manage to get the best start on the favored end - the one that will give you that inside crack-the-whip position - you are in trouble if there is a boat behind you. He can just blanket you and them come up and take an overlap on you so that *he* winds up with the inside position. For this reason, you may want to be on the favored end, but the last one to cross there.

There are endless ways to begin a race and no one could ever cover them all. Everyone has different preferences, as you will see in the interviews later in this book. No matter how well planned your start is, you must always be ready to change your plans quickly and deal with the unexpected. This is why you should have a good knowledge of the International Yacht Racing Rules. They are a necessary tool for determining your options on any start. The ideas set forth here are just a beginning to get you thinking of the variety of tactics available.

Though I have touched on reaching and downwind starts, happily they are rare. The majority of starts are to windward from a line that is square to the wind, so the first leg will be to windward.

• The Windward Leg

Once you've made your start, you'll be concentrating on making your Sunfish go just as fast as possible. Other things being equal, the fastest way to sail is to have the sail itself working as closely as possible as a perfect airfoil. The simple rule to remember on all points of sailing is that the sail should be out as far as it will go

Coming into the windward mark, most of the boats seem to have over-stood – they are bearing off, compared to the two boats in the background. The sailor on the right, Mike Kerman, is mini-hiking. No. 752, Dennis Parsons, could probably bear off considerably and blanket him, squirt out ahead, and round first. If he doesn't, Mike will have an overlap. Venezuela Worlds, 1976.

without luffing, until it is 90 degrees from the center line, under most conditions. Then you have to stop. If a sail is pulled in too far, it will stall. Stalled, a sail feels like it's pulling you sideways. When beating to windward in light and medium air, you want to test the wind continually by letting the sail get just a little soft along the luff - just a slight dimple. React to that immediately by bearing off just a hair, until the dimple fills in again.

Just as a bowler tries to find his groove on the alley, the sailor tries to find just the right groove going to windward. The groove will always be a little different, depending on the combination of waves and wind. But it is always there - the right combination of pinching and footing. Pinching is sailing as close to the wind as possible. Footing is cracking off from that pinched position by a few degrees, or even a fraction of a degree, to gain a little speed. I've always found that the best sailors are the ones who can snuggle up as close to the wind as possible and still keep their boats moving well.

The key to effective pinching is avoiding either a stalled sail or a stalled board. On boats like the Sunfish, with too little board or keel, one can sail

The Start and the Windward Leg

so close to the wind that the board stalls and the boat starts sliding to leeward. That's especially true of the Sunfish, even with the new board. To pinch effectively in a Sunfish, you must learn to sail on a razor's edge. Footing, although usually not as fast a way to get to the windward mark, allows a greater margin for error. The new racing daggerboard lets you pinch a little closer than the old one did, although the perfect groove is still quite narrow.

There's another trick to handling puffs that I learned years ago: when a puff hits, wait a couple of moments until your Sunfish has picked up speed, then sheet in and pinch a little closer to the wind. But be aware that when you do this, you are likely to flatten the sail, because the boom will bend down. Depending on conditions, you may not want the sail flatter. So trim in a bit more than you need, then let the sheet out an inch or two. The sheet will run out most of that two inches in the forward boom block, but almost none in the aft boom block. Your sail will still be sheeted in, but you have relaxed the bend in the boom, allowing the sail to fill out a little. You'll be able to pinch up still, but you'll have more power. This seems to work best in relatively smooth water and winds of six or eight knots - when you're sitting near the edge of the deck, but don't have to hike out. Try this a few times, watching the sheet and the boom between the two blocks. You'll see what I mean.

There are many times when a pincher has to foot off, however. A Sunfish is not exactly designed for slicing through the waves like a 12-Meter. Its broad, flat bottom pounds; its blunt bow pushes too much water. When the waves get so big or steep and close together that your forward way is appreciably slowed, it's time to crack off a little bit, let the boom out some, and get the boat moving again.

Conditions are never the same for even one second in sailing a boat. In waves, you are constantly either sailing uphill or down, and as the waves get larger, you have to pay more and more attention to them and less and less to the direction of the wind. Usually it is best to take a rather zigzag course through the waves, trying always to go through the low spots.

It might seem logical to bear off and gain speed going up the wave and pinch up as gravity helps you down a wave. As a matter of fact, however, the opposite is usually best. In other words, you pinch up a little going uphill, and foot off and gain speed downhill. One of the reasons is that, as you go up the hill, you slow down, and the wind's strength is translated into greater heel and less forward movement. And heeling is one thing you don't want to do much going to windward. Moreover, you want to spend as little time on the uphill side of the wave as possible. So the best technique seems to be to get up as much speed as possible going downhill and head up going up the wave, when everything works against you.

That's the steering part of going to windward in waves. There are additional techniques - part of kinetic sailing - that you can use. As the boat is going down the wave, you don't have to hike as hard. The wind is translated into forward motion instead of heel. As the boat reaches the bottom of the wave, let it heel a little on purpose and hike hard as you go up the wave, resisting the heeling force, sweeping the sail a little to windward, and getting a little squirt of speed as you go over the crest of the wave, then landing your weight back in the boat with most of it on the forward leg, giving a little push down the wave. This use of the body to steer over waves has been named "torquing." Note that this may be illegal under strict interpretation of the rules. The rationalization is that this series of exercises is really a form of steering with the body, not a way to push the boat faster.

Much Sunfish racing takes placed on sheltered bodies of water, where waves have little

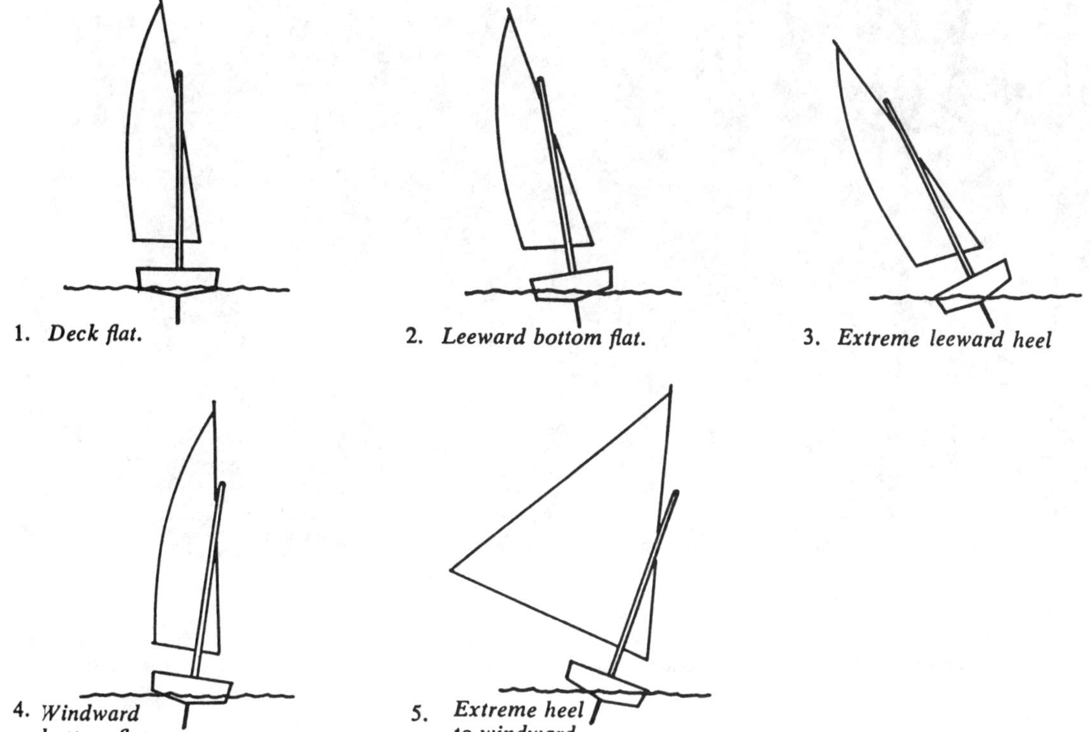

Angles of heel: when beating to windward (1.) keep the boat really flat when pinching to windward in smooth water. This provides maximum lateral resistance. (2.) Keep the leeward bottom flat under most other conditions when going to windward. (3.) In drifting conditions, heel the boat so that the deck is nearly in the water. This keeps the sail aerodynamically effective and reduces wetted surface. (4.) In light air, champion Joel Furman often heels to weather (see interview page 127.) (5.) Downwind, heel the boat to windward to reduce weather helm.

opportunity to build up. Under such conditions, pay more attention to the wind than the water. Not only are the waves less important, but the wind is apt to be much more puffy and much more shifty. Under such conditions, most of your concentration will be on maintaining that groove - keeping the boat as close to the wind as possible without stalling.

Even in strong steady winds, the wind will change direction from time to time, and within the short space of a minute, there may be two or three perceptible little shifts that the really sharp sailor can detect and use to make better speed to windward. I dare say many good sailors are not even conscious of doing it. If you want to get that kind of rhythm and instinct to your sailing, try keeping your eyes glued on the telltales or masthead fly, as well as on the luff.

The idea is to feather your way to windward, and it works best in light to medium air with flat

The Start and the Windward Leg

Big swells on the way to the windward mark, Venezuela Worlds, 1976. If 780 is on the lay line, 772 will probably be able to tack right under him with a safe leeward position, squeeze up, and round just ahead. But 709, which is crossing in front now, will have to make two quick tacks in that bouncy water, slowing down considerably. He may have to take the sterns of 772, 780, and the boat to windward of 780. Position is very important coming in to the windward mark in a crowd.

water. Under those conditions, you can concentrate almost exclusively on feathering - that is, heading up with every little lift and bearing off with every little header, just shy of stalling. A sailor with lesser skills will steer a straight average course, adjusting only to the gross wind shifts, and be totally baffled that another boat, seemingly steering exactly the same course, will slowly eat up to windward with better boatspeed. So it's a technique worth cultivating. In its own way, this can be more exhausting that hiking out in heavy air and a steep chop, because of the constant concentration required.

As the wind picks up, a gradual change in technique is required because of increased wave action. Then, the first injunction you'll hear from practically any sailor is, "Sail it flat!" Flat doesn't mean with the mast straight up, however. Most Sunfish sailors allow enough heel so that the leeward half of the bottom is flat, allowing the chine to dig in for more lateral resistance.

About the only exception to that is when you're coming into a really big breaking wave, and there's no way around it. In that situation, some sailors let the Sunfish heel as much as 45 degrees, letting the boat slice through the wave. If you take such a wave flat, it may smack the bottom at such an angle that it will stop you practically dead in the water. Whether you take that wave flat or heeled, you want to throw your body out hard, and give a tug on the tiller, just as the wave hits.

In heavy air or trade wind conditions, when only the strongest can keep the boat flat and the sail drawing full at all times, it becomes necessary to learn to spill air by an almost constant pumping of the sheet. This is quite different from

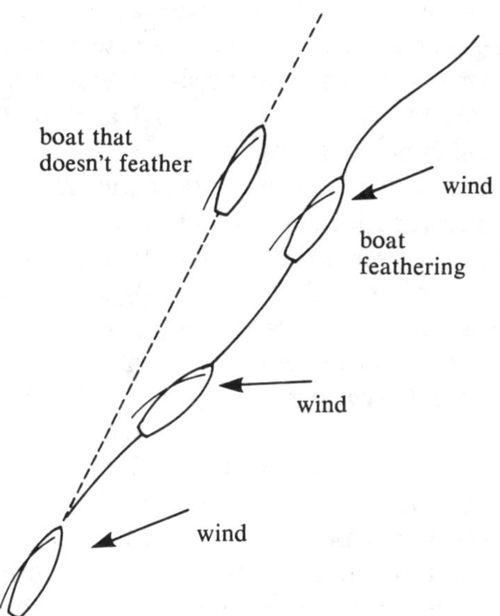

Feathering your way to windward.

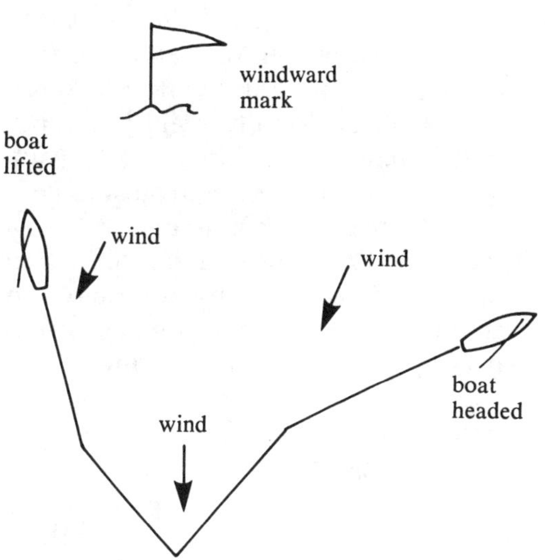

Lifts and headers.

pumping the sheet to enhance flow over the sail, in effect rowing the boat to windward, an illegal technique perfected by the real kinetics experts. The problem, of course, is that practically no one can tell where one ends and the other begins. The best trade wind sailor of the mid-70s, Gerrit Zeestraten of Curaçao, used a Harken block - with the ratchet *off*, so the sail could be let out as fast as it could be brought in.

All of these techniques should help you with boatspeed. But boatspeed is only part of the equation. You have to keep your eye on the other boats, and on what the wind and waves are doing. People who spend too much time concentrating only on boatspeed soon learn the reason for one of the most important axioms of sailboat racing: "Keep your head out of the boat!"

• Lifts and Headers

When the wind shifts so that you can sail closer to the mark, you've sailed into a lift. A header is the opposite - it forces you away from the mark. By and large, the right thing to do is to tack whenever you are headed. But you have to figure out if the shift is for real. In some conditions, the wind will shift in fairly predictable patterns - every 30 seconds or as much as every 30 minutes. In other situations, the wind will shift sharply for a second or two, and then slip back to its original direction or beyond. When that happens, you may tack through as much as 180 degrees, instead of 90 degrees. In other words, you have tacked into a header - a very frustrating and costly maneuver. So it pays to study the wind, and decide how long you should wait, after being headed, before tacking. Obviously, under some conditions, this will be only a second or two. In other conditions, it may be smart to wait ten seconds or so to make sure the shift is for real.

There are some generally accepted tactics to handling wind shifts, besides the obvious one of tacking on headers, and that is the obvious but often overlooked strategy of timing your tacks to stay between the rest of the fleet and the

The Start and the Windward Leg

windward mark, and taking every advantage of wind shifts to cross in front of a boat with which you might have been even or even been trailing.

Obviously, if everyone in the fleet is following these tactics, and is equally adept at timing the wind shifts, nobody is really going to gain an advantage. No one would gain an advantage, that is, if the shifts were the same, and at the same strength, clear across the course. But of course they never are. In really shifty and fluky winds, it is even possible to see two boats, no more than 100 yards apart, sailing in the same direction but on opposite tacks. So the advantage will go to boats that best play the shifts in their particular areas of the course...or, given equal speed among the fleet, the advantage will go to those who go to the right parts of the course to pick up the best combination of shifts and wind strength. That's what sailors mean when they say they are "in sync" or "in phase."

It is the ability to be where the wind shifts are best and wind strengths are strongest that separates the really outstanding sailor from the highly competent one. It's an uncanny thing called wind sense, and like any other natural ability, it can be developed through careful observation and reasoning. It is also a matter of keeping your eyes open - you can often see what the wind is doing by watching the way the other boats are sailing on the course, and, more important, by watching the action of the wind on the water. This wind action is most obvious on light, shifty days, when little cat's paws of wind make ripples on the water and are obvious for all to see. Starting with these more obvious observations, a careful watcher can learn to find wind under almost any conditions, often without even being conscious that he's doing it. This ability can reach even into the high wind conditions, when you can observe a heavier concentration of spindrift blowing off the tops of waves in one area than in another, and avoid the too-powerful winds that can lay you flat (on the other hand, those sharp gusts of wind may flatten the waves, and actually make it easier to control the boat. There are no hard and fast rules). Occasionally, in light air, you'll see an experienced sailor stand up in the boat, scanning the water to windward for signs of wind.

Almost every top-caliber sailor will tell you to get out to the course early to figure out the wind shifts and the currents. On some courses, one side or the other will be heavily favored, either because the wind is stronger there or the current more favorable. On others, it makes most sense to work your way up the middle, tacking on the headers. And on some courses, the middle is the worst place to be - either side will do. This is often true on harbors or lakes that are roughly round, because the wind seems to sweep around the shores. On other courses, a point of land or tall hill will bend the wind in such a way that one side or the other is favored.

Another consideration in figuring out shifts is to decide whether the shifts are oscillating or persistent. An oscillating wind shifts back and forth on a fairly consistent basis five or 10 degrees to one side and then five or 10 degrees back. A persistently shifting wind will shift five or 10 degrees one way and not come back quite full swing. With each pair of shifts, the wind changes its average direction, moving clockwise or counterclockwise. When the wind persistently shifts towards the clockwise direction, it is called a clocking or veering wind. When it is shifting the other way, it is called a backing wind.

In a persistent shift, unless you expect the wind to lift you right up to the mark, it is better to start on the tack on which you expect to be headed. Then you can tack early, and be lifted up to the mark. If you try to take advantage of a lift initially, you will be headed on the last half of your course, and sail what is known as the great circle route. You don't want to sail the great circle route.

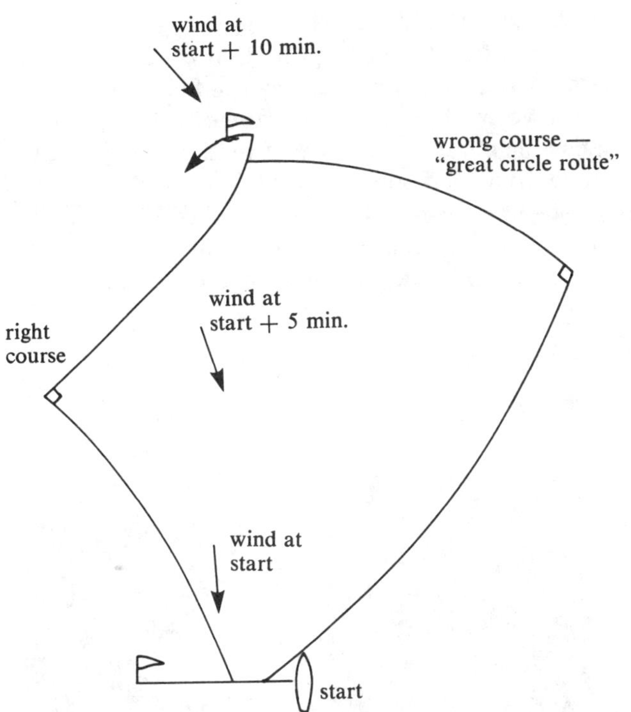

Handling a persistent wind shift. You should try to figure out whether the shifts are oscillating or persistent.

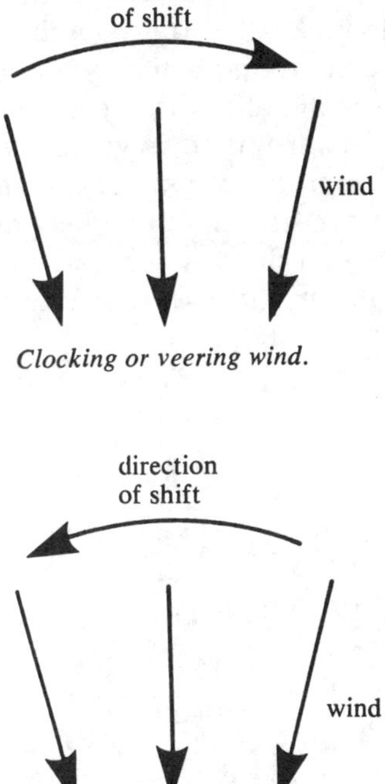

Clocking or veering winds, and backing winds.

• Tacking

In tacking a Sunfish, it almost never pays to tack slowly. The boat spins on its daggerboard like the proverbial dime. Don't rely on the boat's momentum to carry you through the wind, as with a heavy displacement keel boat. It will stop you dead in your tracks. It is, however, extremely important to tack in a lull between waves, or to spin it over right on the crest of a wave if you have taken it well.

Roll tacking works well with a Sunfish. Roll tacking consists of hiking hard as you start your turn into the eye of the wind, so that the boat heels to windward, and then diving to the other side of the boat with a 180-degree pirouette, bringing it back flat as you come up on the new tack. This technique provides a double-fanning effect of the sail that pushes you to windward an extra few feet and can give a little extra squirt of speed. It is possible to work your way to the windward mark this way in a flat calm. But it's illegal. The test is whether you increase your progress to windward. If you do, your tacking is illegal. And don't let your mast come up beyond the vertical as you bring it up on the new tack. That, too, is illegal.

Since the longer tiller extension (hiking stick) with universal joint was legalized, the accepted

The Start and the Windward Leg

practice has been to hold on to stick and sheet at all times while tacking. You accomplish this by bringing the stick around behind your back with your aft hand while allowing the sheet to slide through your forward hand as you bring it back to switch hands on the stick. For a moment, as you pivot, you are holding both sheet and stick in one hand. As you sit back down after the pivot, you transfer the sheet to your new forward hand.

• Windward Tactics

Assuming you have pulled off a fairly decent start - right on the line, moving fast, with clear air - your objective is to move out with best possible boatspeed, in the direction you want to go, with a good opportunity to control the rest of the fleet. If the fleet is sizable, you will be meeting a lot of other boats, each concentrating on keeping clear air and trying to get ahead of the fleet.

A Good Tack

1. In about 10 knots of wind, Chipper Clifton of Sarasota begins his tack by sliding in a bit to heel the boat...

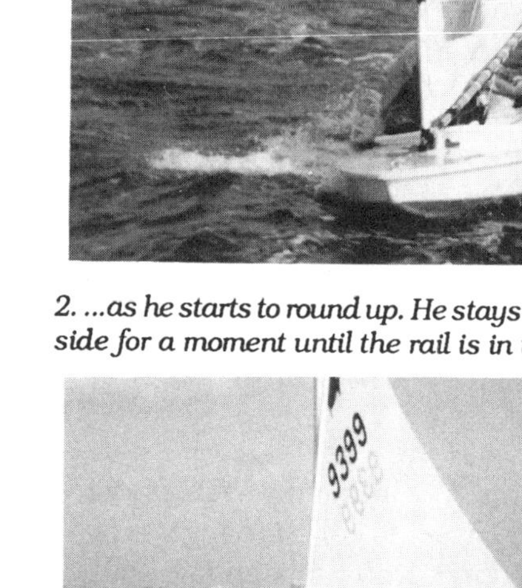

2. ...as he starts to round up. He stays on the old windward side for a moment until the rail is in the water...

3. ...then comes across smoothly to the new windward side, still holding the hiking stick with his left hand...

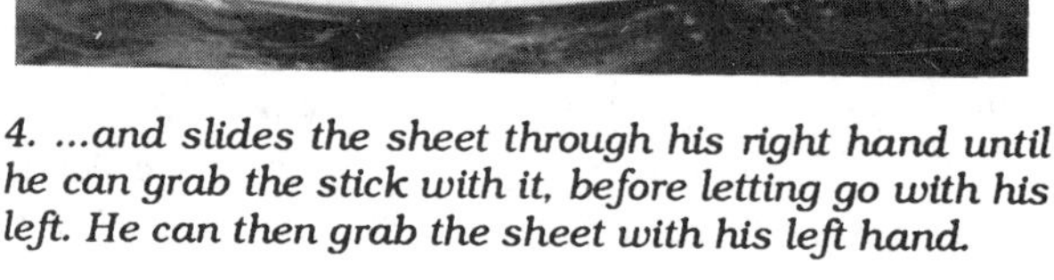

4. ...and slides the sheet through his right hand until he can grab the stick with it, before letting go with his left. He can then grab the sheet with his left hand.

It is generally advisable to stay between the bulk of the fleet and the mark and to tack when you can cross in front of a significant number of boats. Later in a regatta, when the leaders are identified, it is best to consider them "the fleet" and ignore the also-rans, even if the also-rans are a larger clump of boats.

This general strategy holds even if you believe the leaders are heading for the wrong side of the course, depending on your reading of the odds.

Roll tack: (1.) Sailing flat. (2.) Let her heel. (3.) Hike to windward as you turn through the eye of the wind. (4.) Bring her back up. (5.) Hike her flat again.

The Start and the Windward Leg

In other words, it is better to catch a few boats on the wrong side of the course than take a flyer on the "right" side and then get skunked when it turns out to be the wrong side after all. There will be occasions when one side of the course or the other is heavily favored. And sometimes both sides of the course are heavily favored over the center, especially on bodies of water that are roughly round in shape. In these situations, you may have to take a short hitch in the wrong direction just to free your air. But try to avoid those situations. If the lay line is heavily favored, it may be necessary to eat a little bad air to get over there, especially if you are among the leaders. It is usually better to consolidate a 10th in a large fleet than take a flyer for a first and wind up 36th.

Your strategy will also vary depending on whether you are willing to settle for the best possible place in a regatta or whether you subscribe to the philosophy that second place is no place at all and decide to go for broke and win all the marbles. In a club season championship, or a multi-race regatta, a string of seconds and thirds will probably do a lot more for you than an occasional brilliant first and out of the money the rest of the time.

Out on the course, when you are on starboard tack, you have the upper hand - to a point. What you don't want to happen is to have a port-tack boat tack right after crossing you, so that he is sitting on your wind - that is, his sail is stealing the wind from your sail. The next worst thing that can happen is to have a boat tack just before he crosses you in a position to stay ahead of you - that is, the wind is thrown off his sail into the back of your sail, causing turbulence and slowing you down.

If a boat tacks on top of your wind - unless your present course is highly favored - it is probably best to tack and clear your air, tacking back as soon as you have re-established your boatspeed. Failing that, you may be able to bear off as the other boat tacks, gain speed, sail through the wind shadow and clear your air. You will have dropped a boat length or two to leeward, but you will have been able to maintain your course with clear air. Note that a boat to leeward and only slightly behind will still usually have clear air. To really blanket you, the other boat must be at roughly a 45-degree angle forward of your bow, right between you and the wind.

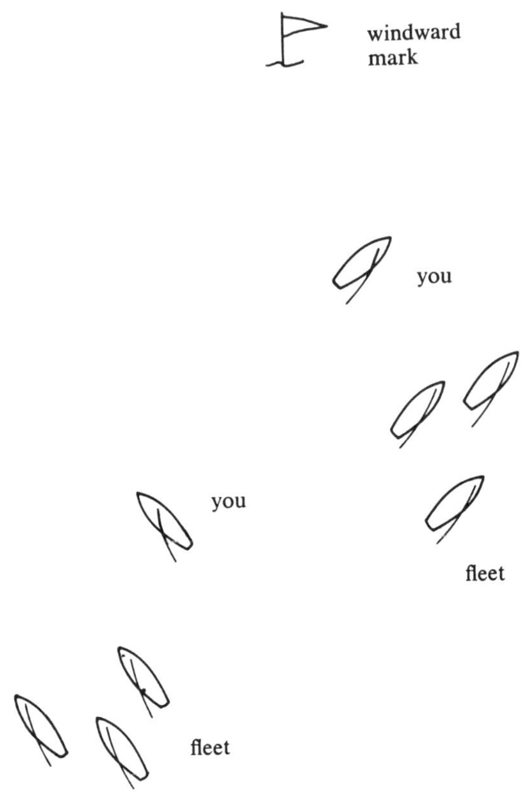

If a boat tacks on your lee bow and backwinds you, you have the choice of tacking, pinching up

Time your tacks to stay between the rest of the fleet and the windward mark.

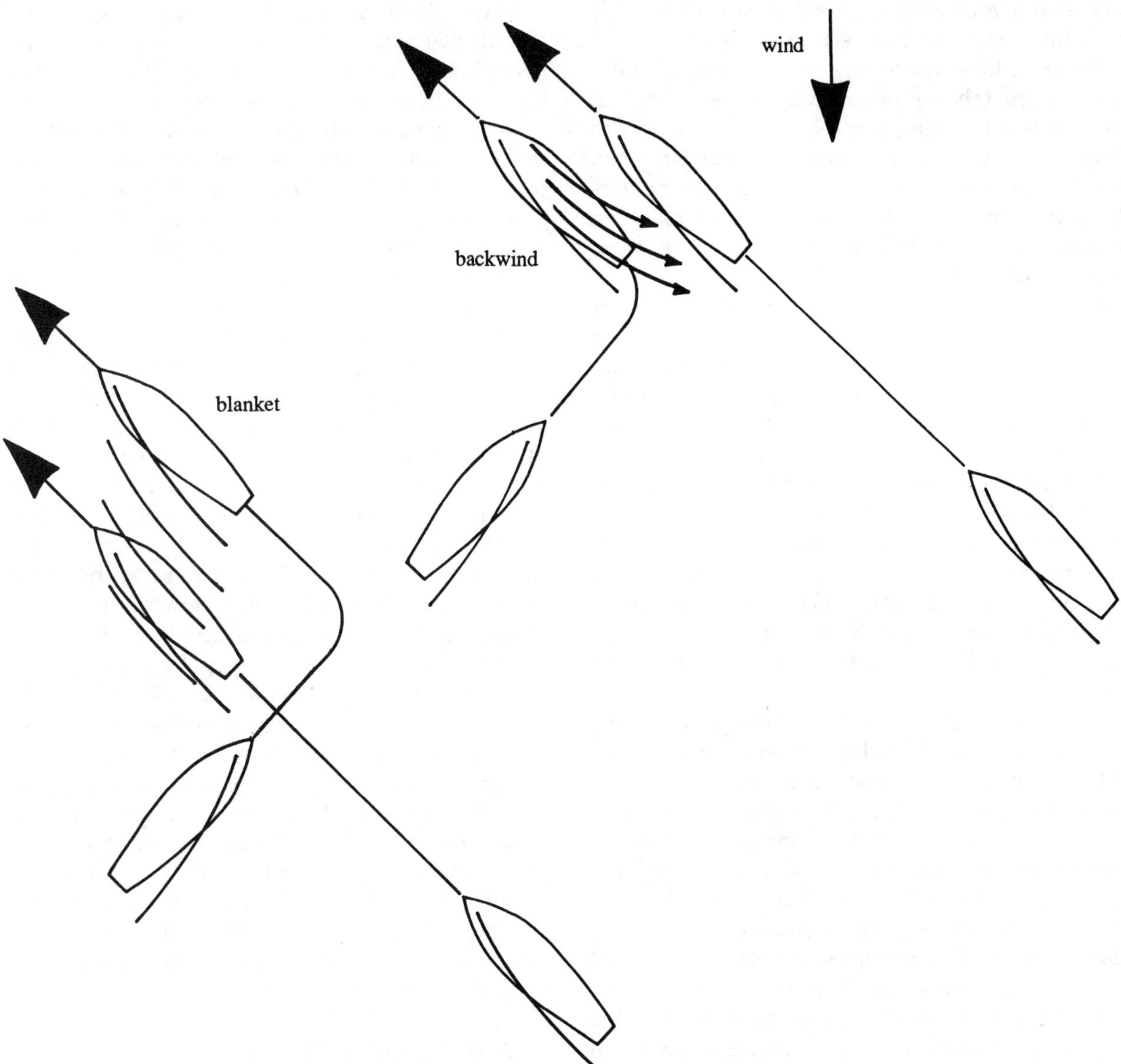

Tacking to blanket and tacking to backwind. You don't want to have a port-tack boat tack right after crossing you, stealing the wind from your sail. And you don't want a boat to tack just before crossing you; that will backwind you, spoiling the air flow over your sail.

The Start and the Windward Leg

to get up out of his backwind, or bearing off in hopes that you can gain enough boatspeed to ride over him before he has regained full way.

When a boat tacks in your vicinity, he must stay completely out of your way while tacking. If at any point during his tack, he forces you to change course, he has committed a foul. However, the minute his hull is headed on its proper close-hauled course, he has completed his tack, even if his sail is not drawing yet, and the regular racing rules apply. If he is clear ahead or to leeward, he has the right of way. On the other hand, if he is to windward, and you gain an overlap, you have the right of way, although you have to allow ample time and opportunity for him to keep clear after you have established the overlap.

In general, having another boat tack close to you is trouble. So your tactics, whenever possible, should encourage the other boat to stay on the other tack. A hail of "go ahead, you're clear" may do the trick, even if you have to bear off a little bit. One thing you cannot do to discourage a boat from tacking near you is to alter your course so as to confuse him, especially if you have the right of way.

Most of the time when you are racing, you really want to keep your air clear and not mess around with other boats. But towards the end of a regatta, or at the beginning, if you know that the real competition is going to be between you and one or two others, you may want to get tricky and play aggressive tactics. This really has to happen at the start, with you in a commanding position over your chief competitors. But if you don't do it there, maybe you can do it somewhere out on that first windward leg during one of those crossing situations we have just discussed. In this case, you want to be able to tack on top of him and take his wind. Or maybe you want to tack just ahead of him, so that you do not have his wind, but you have him in a position where he can't get away. Or you may just tack under his lee bow and slowly squeeze up under him, slowing him down with your backwind. Sometimes you do that just to psych him out, sometimes because you want to make sure you beat him in as many races as possible.

When you do this, most of the time your opponent can usually just tack away. So you have to think two or three tacks ahead, to be sure you can maintain your dominant position. If you are close on his wind, and he tacks just a fraction of a second before you, he may be able to shake you off. So in the early stages of a race, it is usually better to keep a loose cover on that opponent - just making sure that you stay ahead but not disturbing his wind too much. Otherwise, you will force him into a tacking duel, and both of you will lose other boats. Remember, such aggressive tactics only make sense for a thoroughly experienced sailor working against another of equal ability or slightly greater boatspeed. Since the risks of fouling the other boat are great, try such tactics only when a major championship is at stake. In the first place, it is of questionable sportsmanship, I believe - living within the letter of the law but bending the spirit. Such tactics have seldom been used in Sunfish competition and when they have, there is usually a legacy of bad feeling. Most of us would prefer just to sail the best race we can, and may the best man win. If you would rather beat your competitor than be his friend, then by all means clamp a tight cover on him and sail him off the course. But if you sail as much for good fellowship as the thrill of victory, think twice before using the rules too aggressively.

• The Windward Mark

Many experienced sailors think of the windward leg as three separate parts. First, there are the few minutes after the start, when you are sorting things out, trying to get your air cleared, and trying to get to the favored side of the course.

The Start and the Windward Leg

Right: *Rounding the windward mark at the 1976 Worlds in Venezuela. Eventual winner Paul Fendler is out front. No. 729 has just barely cleared the mark, but already his board is up and his sail out. However, he's on the uphill side of the wave, and Paul is pointing to a low spot, going downhill. So he's probably going a lot faster, and can take his time getting the board up. First things first.*

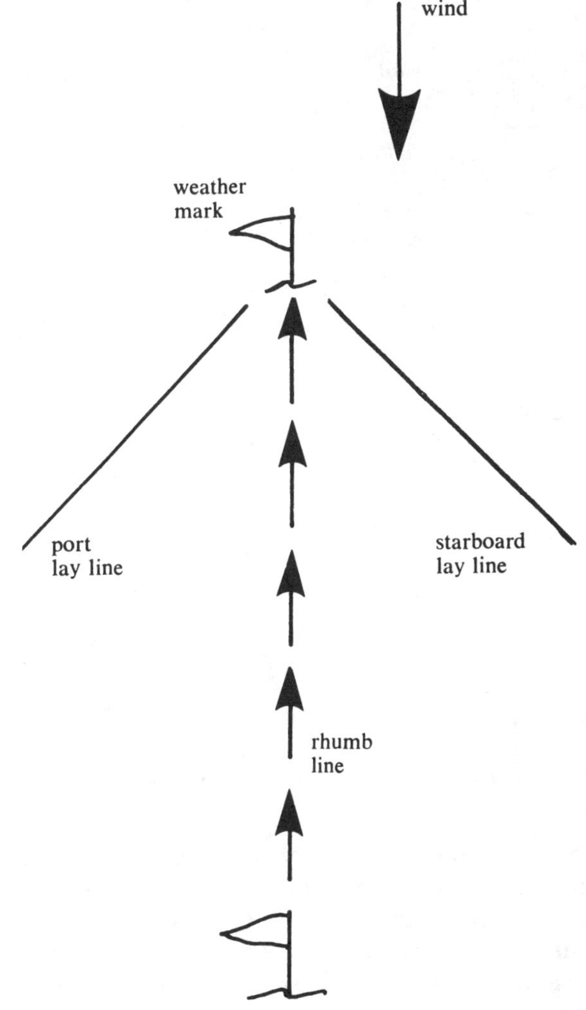

You almost always want to avoid the starboard lay line until the last few boat lengths.

Second is the middle part of the leg, when you can concentrate on boatspeed and what the wind and waves are doing, and on tacking on the headers. The last few hundred yards to the windward mark are often the most important part, when the way you approach it can mean the gain or loss of dozens of places in a tightly bunched fleet.

As with almost any other part of the course, the important thing is to be in the right position with your wind as clear as possible. The right position is usually inside - that is, closer to the mark than anybody else. Ideally, you can round the mark close aboard as you approach it on the end of the windward leg, and then make a nice smooth turn on to the reach, lined up with the next mark and nobody on your wind on the starboard quarter, assuming that you are rounding the mark to port, which you always are in Olympic competition or in Sunfish World Championships.

On the other hand, if you are inside as you

The Start and the Windward Leg

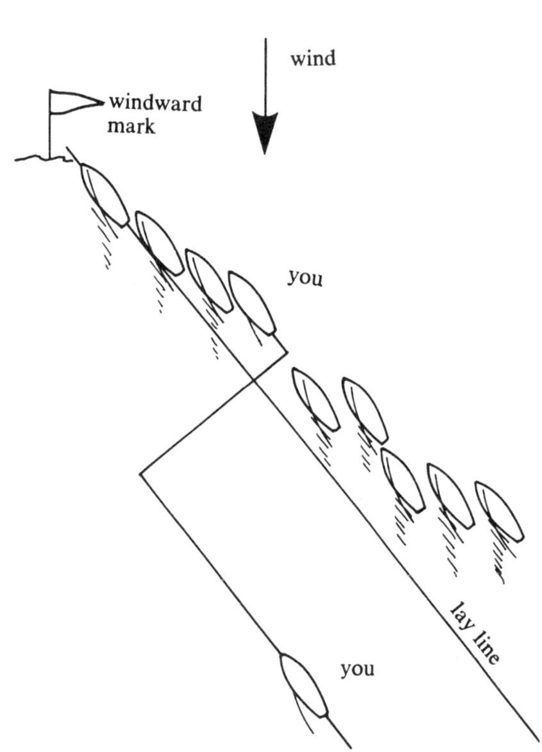

A good approach to the windward mark in a big fleet.

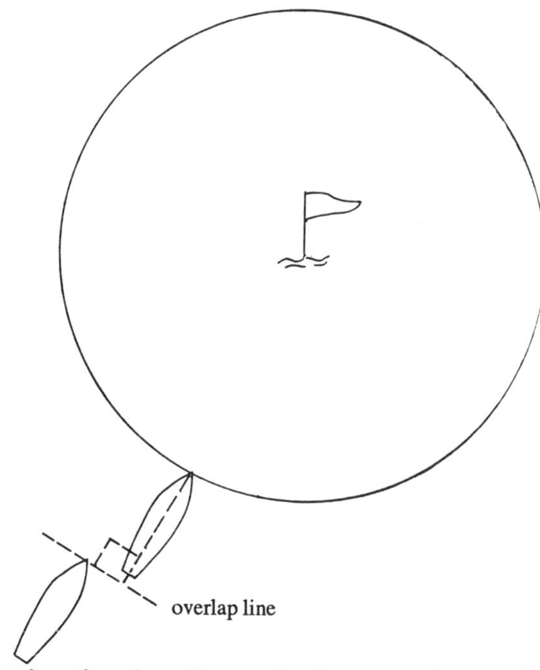

Two-boat-length circle. Overlap line is 90 degrees from center line at aftermost point (on a Sunfish, it's the rudder.) An overlap must be gained before lead boat reaches the two-boat length circle.

round on to the reach, the boat just outside you may have a little more way, or can force you to make a tight turn and slow you down. If he can ride over you and sit on your wind, then the inside position isn't so hot. Usually, however, the outside boat cannot force you to make a sharp turn, since you have the right of way as leeward boat after you leave the mark.

So how do you get that inside position? Almost always, the best way is to approach the last few hundred yards on port tack, about six boat lengths downwind from the mark. This gives you a little bit of maneuvering room to find a hole into which to tack, assuming a lot of other boats are coming down on the starboard lay line. Almost always, you want to avoid the starboard lay line, because as more and more boats join it, they have to tack farther and farther to windward - beyond the lay line - in order to keep their wind clear. As a result, they sail a number of boat lengths further than they really have to. And in a hot fleet, that can mean the loss of several boats. However, there will be times when the tactic of coming in on port is just too dangerous - there are just too many boats in that starboard lay line parade. They may be coming all in a row, with scarcely a boat length between them, and all aiming right at that pin. If you tack under them, you will be hopelessly blanketed, and you will probably drift down below the mark, if you don't hit it. If you are coming in from six or eight boat lengths downwind, however, you will almost always be able to find a hole. But your timing must be near perfect.

As with almost any other section of the course,

being all alone eliminates a lot of problems. Of course, you don't want to be all alone at the tail end. The nicest place to be is all alone out in front. In small fleets, mark roundings are seldom the mass hysteria they are in a fleet of 50 or 100 boats. But at major Sunfish regattas, there will almost always be a good-sized fleet. So it is best to learn to handle yourself in a pack. Then the solo stuff will be easy.

Since more fouls probably happen at mark roundings than anywhere else, a review of some of the rules is in order. If you tack too soon and can't quite pinch up, or if the current against you is stronger than you expected and you find yourself hitting the mark, you'll have to go off by yourself and do a 360 degree turn without getting in anyone's way.

If you are all alone, it's easy. But if you're in a pack, remember that all the other boats have right of way over you while you are making your circle to exonerate yourself.

If you have the inside overlap going into the mark, you have the right of way. If you see that another boat is going to force you into the mark, the usual advice is to make sure that you hit the offending boat before you hit the mark. This advice is somewhat in conflict with the rule to avoid contact whenever possible, but I suppose the idea is that, if contact is unavoidable, it might as well be with the boat, before the mark. That establishes that you were forced into the mark by the offender, absolving you from the necessity to do a penalty circle.

What if you are coming in on the mark on port, tack right under another boat, and force your way in that way? The answer is that, if you can tack and get on your proper close-hauled course before the other boat has to alter course in any way, you can then force him up, even within the two-boat-length circle that establishes an overlap. The delicate part of such a maneuver is to make sure that you complete your tack before the other boat has to alter course, because the burden of proof that you did so is on you.

Rounding the windward mark outside of a boat or two is not necessarily bad. You keep your air clean and you may be able to ride over a couple of boats as you bear off on the reach, particularly if they are preoccupied with each other or aren't too aware that you are there. Then, depending on how close the boats behind you are, you have the choice of which way to head for the gybe mark. What you don't want to happen, of course, is to get caught up in somebody else's luffing match, giving the boats behind you an opportunity to sail straight for the gybe mark with clear air. That's the spot you want to be in. Which brings us to the next leg of the course, the reach.

7 Off the Wind

First, let's look at how to get the most boat speed on a broad reach. That's what your course will be on an Olympic course, assuming it has been properly laid out and the wind has not shifted. In the real world, of course, that leg can be anything from a beam reach to a run. But we will concentrate here on the most likely situation - some form of a broad reach, with the wind coming in at roughly a 45-degree angle over the corner of your transom.

• Reaching Speed

The first thing you want to do is let your sail out as far as it will go without luffing and then pull the board up as far as you can without allowing leeway or "crabbing." Then you want to heel your boat so that it practically steers itself, which probably means heeling to windward somewhat. Your position in the cockpit will vary with the strength of the wind, but generally, short of burying the bow, you want to be quite forward.

If the breeze is five knots or so and the water quite flat, your best bet will probably be to freeze in this position, steering as smooth and straight a course as you can. If the winds are in this speed range, but shifty and puffy, you should bear up in the lulls to maintain your speed and then bear off as the wind picks up to take you closer to the mark. Generally, we are talking about relatively small changes in course direction, between five and 10 degrees in most cases. It pays to keep your eye on the telltales and to keep the sail at the optimum angle to the wind. Whether you are sailing an arrow-straight course or playing the puffs, keep that sail just shy of luffing or, if you are using "woollies" or telltales on the sail, concentrate on keeping them both streaming correctly, the outboard ones streaming aft, and the inboard ones occasionally taking a flick up.

As the waves become larger, you will note that going downhill is considerably faster than going uphill. At a certain combination of wind strength

At the Worlds in Venezuela, 1976, 715 has a chance to stay on his wave if he bears off sharply. Check the other boats. Who's surfing and who's climbing?

Diane Harrison pumps hard to get her boat planing in marginal conditions at the 1976 Worlds, Venezuela. Note the lace lines progressively looser along the boom toward the clew, to free up the leech. Diane was probably anticipating heavy air.

and waves, the boat will jump up on a plane - instead of pushing through the water, it will lift up over the surface and will skip along, like a flat rock skimmed across a pond. If your boat does this before your neighbors', you will notice you're going maybe twice as fast as they are. In recognition of this, the IYRU rule-makers have left us one kinetic loophole. It is perfectly legal to pump the sail once on the face of the wave, to help the boat get up on that lovely plane. It is an ability that you will have to learn if you want to be competitive in a Sunfish.

That is not to say that the only way to get on a plane and stay there is to use a lot of acrobatics. Steering the right course over and through the waves can be even more important than kinetics. Most of the top downwind sailors I know are unanimous in expressing one idea: "Keep her pointing downhill" or "Head for the low spots." The technique is similar to that of a surfer's. Once he's on that comber, every fiber of his being is concentrated on staying on the forward face, making the ride last as long as possible. In point of fact, the good downwind racer wants to go one better. He wants to go down the face so fast that momentum will shoot him up over the back of another wave, so he can go down the face of the wave ahead. By being conscious of the way the waves are forming, a good sailor can actually do that, if the wind is strong enough.

Even in steady, light-to-medium breezes, there can be quite a difference between your boatspeed and the other boats'. But as the wind picks up to planing conditions, the ball game changes drastically. The lighter sailors will usually pop up on a plane sooner than the heavier ones. Since planing speed can be twice as fast as through-the-water speed, this can make for some highly frustrated heavyweights.

All is not lost, however, for the talented sailor who can pop his boat on to a plane faster than the majority of his competitors. There are a number of techniques for bringing that boat on to a plane. The most common is to give a sharp tug on the sheet - a "pump" - to provide a little extra surge of power. It used to be OK to pump three times, and add an ooch and a scull, for each wave. No more. An ooch is a sharp body movement forward against the boat that breaks it free of the water and on to a plane. A scull is a tug on the tiller that provides a forward thrust against the water, like the tail of a fish. These three movements together, as the stern of the boat is lifted by a wave, can help you surf down the front of a wave for quite a while. It used to be quite legal to do so to promote surfing. Now only pumping - and only once per wave - is permitted.

This technique is not quite as effective in a Sunfish as it is in a broad flat-sterned boat like the Laser or Force 5. The tug on the wide lateen

Off the Wind

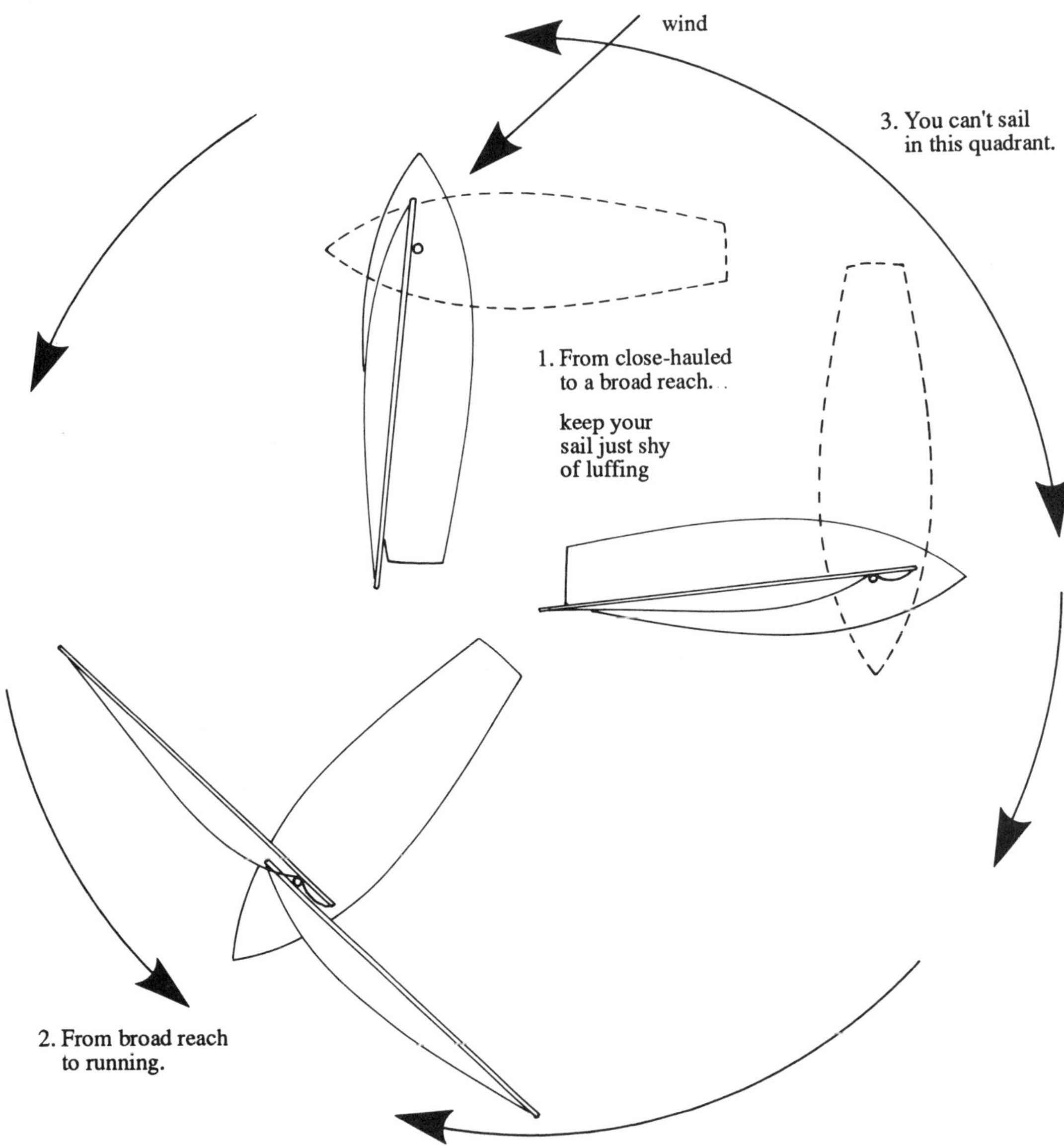

First secret of sailing fast:

1. From close-hauled to a broad reach – keep your sail just shy of luffing.
2. From broad reach to running, keep sail at 90 degrees to center line (on either tack.)
3. You can't sail in this quadrant: the sail luffs.

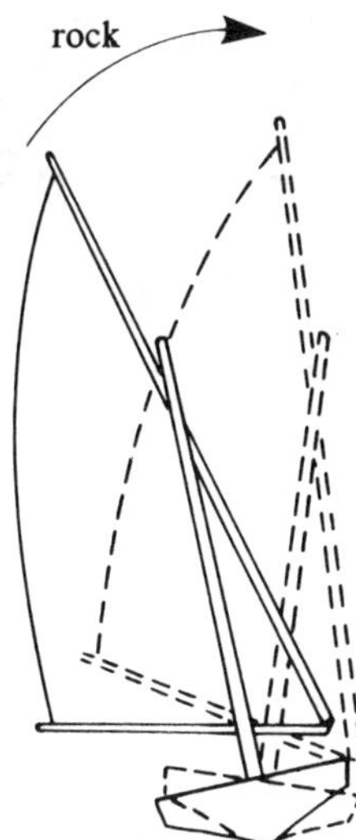

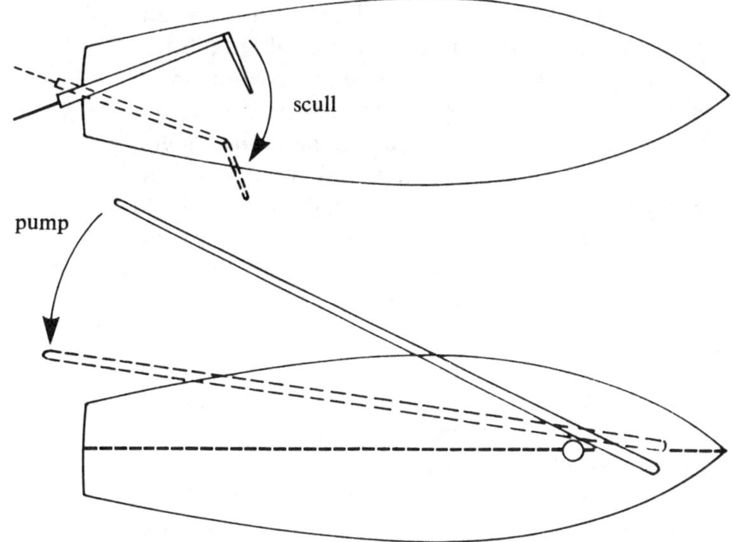

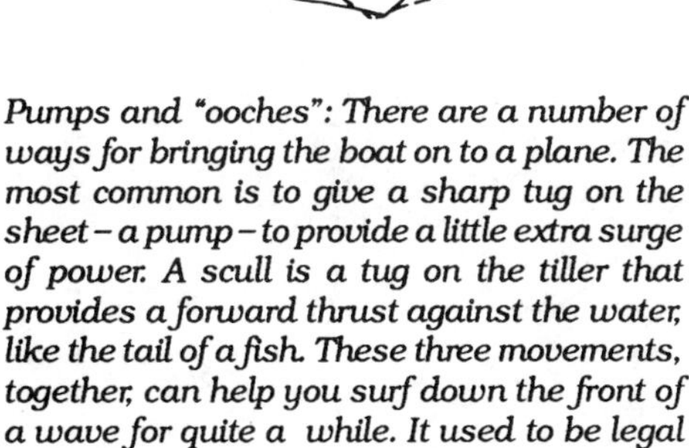
Pumps and "ooches": There are a number of ways for bringing the boat on to a plane. The most common is to give a sharp tug on the sheet – a pump – to provide a little extra surge of power. A scull is a tug on the tiller that provides a forward thrust against the water, like the tail of a fish. These three movements, together, can help you surf down the front of a wave for quite a while. It used to be legal to do all this to promote surfing.
Now only pumping once per wave is permitted.
Sometimes pumping is over-used. Many people waste time trying to make it work when they should be concentrating on sailing downhill on the waves.

sail is not as effective as the tug on a high-aspect sail, either. However, because it is not as effective, it is harder to learn on a Sunfish, and the advantage to those who *do* learn is even greater.

In a Sunfish, many people waste time trying to make this kinetic technique work, when they should be concentrating on sailing downhill on the waves.

Off the Wind

• Reach Tactics

The big question on either reach is whether to go high or go low. A lot has been written about this, because there are a lot of variable factors.

One general rule - and there are a whole lot of exceptions to it - is to go low on the first reach and high on the second. The reason is that, going low on the first reach, you will likely be inside at the gybe mark. Likewise, going high on the second reach you'll be inside at the leeward mark, permitting you to round up on to the beat to windward of anybody rounding with you.

Now the exceptions.

On rounding the weather mark, your decision may very well be made for you by your position relative to the boats immediately around you. If you have rounded inside, and there are other boats immediately on top of you, you may want to go quite high to keep your air clear. Here you are in double jeopardy. If the boat or boats behind you elect to go high with you, you may have to sail a considerable distance off-course to stay ahead and clear. Sometimes, the nearest boat may be so close that he cannot bear off without fouling you - you have the right of way, since you are the leeward boat. If you suddenly find yourself in this position, you will probably lose a lot of boats unless you come back down close to the course to the next mark. Probably the best thing to do is to bear off sharply, try to break through on the other side of your pursuer's wind shadow and hope that he'd rather sail his own race instead of chase you all over the course.

On the other hand, as you round you may be able to duck down to leeward of the rhumb line to the next mark, so that you are far enough to leeward that any other boats rounding with you will not take your wind by much. That can mean that you need a lead of six to 20 boat lengths, depending on the wind speed and the number of boats to windward. Generally speaking, a strong, steady wind will cast the longest wind shadow.

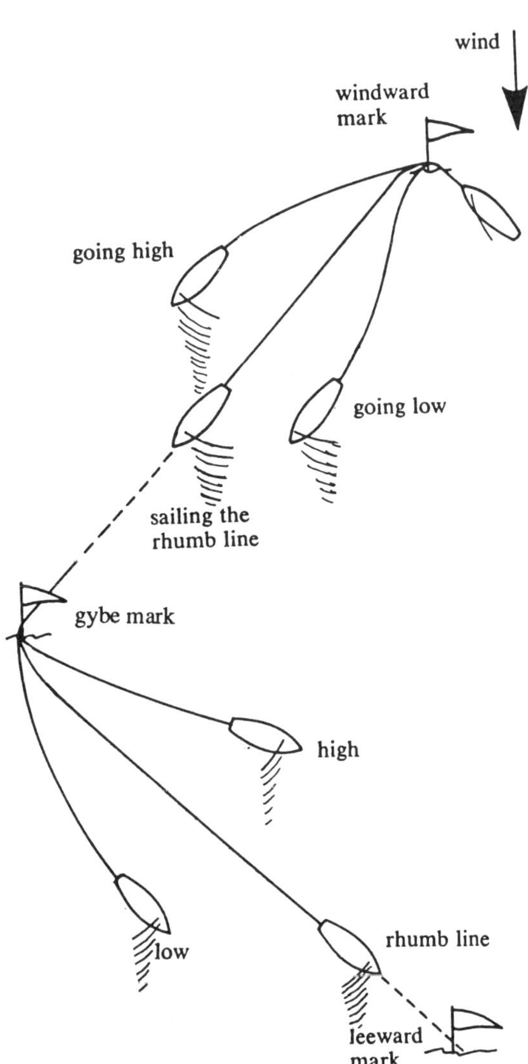

The reach: a general rule is to go low on the first reach and high on the second.

In a softer, shifty wind, the wind shadow will shift around and be broken up, making the wind shadow less of a problem once you have escaped the turbulence.

The advantages of coming in on the mark from below the rest of the fleet are that you will be inside with buoy room, traveling a little faster than the rest of the fleet, which is sailing with the wind further aft. On a reach, other things being equal, the farther aft the wind is, the slower the boat goes.

Another important factor in deciding whether to go high or low on the first reaching leg is the size of the fleet, or more particularly the size of the fleet around you. If you round the windward mark with many boats close behind you, most of them will go high and build a wall to windward. In that situation, the wind will be disturbed for many boat lengths to leeward, and you will lose the advantage of sailing low.

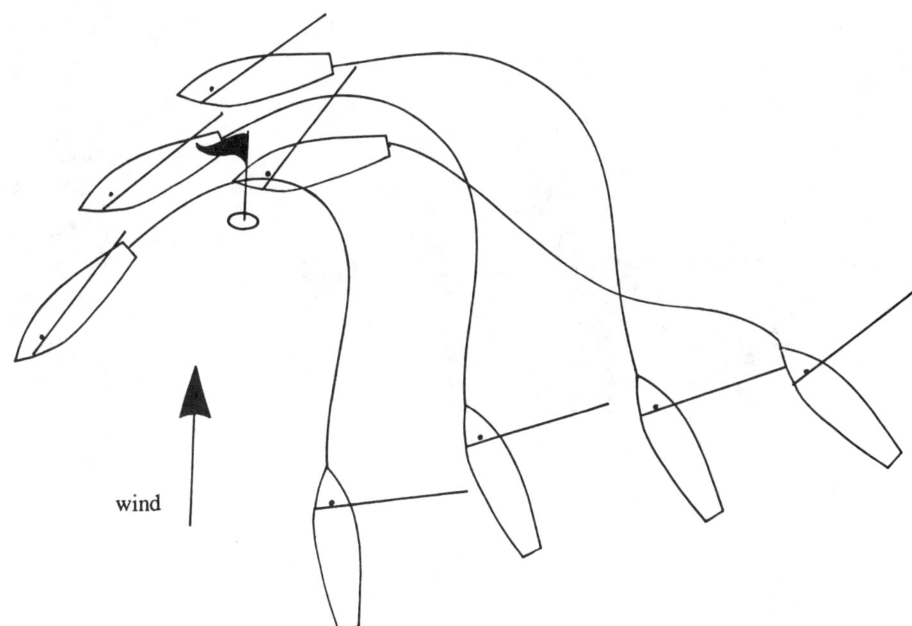

Go slow and win – coming up behind a clump of boats to gain an inside overlap. It's a difficult maneuver.

But if there are good gaps between clumps of two or three boats, you may find it advantageous to go low, because there will be clear air to leeward of those gaps. The clumps are probably battling to keep their air clear and working considerably to windward of the rhumb line. You will be sailing the rhumb line, in which case you will get there faster and perhaps gain an advantage on several boats.

But if there are gaps between individual boats, they will likely sail only a little above the rhumb line, making it more difficult to make up the difference in distance if you sail a loop to leeward. However, if you think you are a little faster than most on the reach, it will pay off, if only to get that inside position at the mark.

All of these tactical considerations assume pretty much equal boatspeed with others on that leg with you. In planing conditions, however, especially marginal planing conditions when you can make big gains on less skillful competitors, the first priority is boatspeed and keeping your air clean. In these conditions, most of the top sailors go high - they call it "the passing lane" - and blow by boat after boat. Then, on the last few hundred yards of the course, they try to pick their best angle on the mark to permit them to gybe cleanly around while perhaps gaining another boat or two. This could mean shooting for an inside overlap before the two-boat-length circle is reached, or rounding quite wide, letting others get tangled up with each other on the inside. In the latter situation, even though you sail a slightly longer course, you may gain because the other boats will interfere with each other. The other boats will make the air turbulent, disturbing the pressure on each others' sails, and they also stir up a lot of turbulent water.

On the second reaching leg, it is much harder to benefit from sailing low, especially in big fleets. Because the inside position is so critical at the leeward mark, almost everyone sails high, making that wind-stealing wall of sails even more

Off the Wind

The leeward boat (right) is luffing up the windward boat. That's permitted, as long as the mast of the leeward boat is ahead of the helmsman of the windward one.

Dave Chapin in midgybe, with Cor van Aanholt outside. If Dave's sail hits Cor's, Dave will foul. Joel Furman is hot on their heels. Super Sunfish Champion Bill Boll (152) watches warily as he comes up close-hauled to round the mark. Cor and Joel have right of way as long as they stay on starboard. Note that Cor (150) has a Jens tied on, even though the air is quite light.

At the North Americans, Indian Lake, Ohio, 1975. Rounding the gybe mark, five boats engage in a luffing match, heading way above the rhumb line to the leeward mark. Not too bright. Will White is out ahead and out of trouble. Tom Ehman bears off and avoids the nonsense. Tom was runner-up; Will third.

Three of the top Americans round the gybe mark at the 1979 Worlds in Holland – Alan Scharfe (128), Don Bergman (180), and Alan Beckwith (165). Note that Alan Beckwith has grabbed his sheet directly off the boom to make it a little easier to pump. Note, too, that all the boats have Jens rigs tied on – the first Worlds where the practice was almost universal.

impenetrable. Moreover, it is very difficult to come up high in the last 200 yards and gain an overlap by slipping into the line of boats coming down on the mark.

As in all sailing tactics, however, there are exceptions. It is not at all unknown for the boats in the windward parade to get so intrigued with keeping their air clear that they sail a considerable distance above the rhumb line - so much higher that when they finally fall off for the mark, they are practically running before the wind and piling up into a big mob as they take each other's wind.

Off the Wind

A crowd at the gybe mark at the 1976 Worlds, Venezuela. The boats on the left are going high of the rhumb line. No. 703 is probably smart to head low to free his air but there are so many boats close behind him that it may not work.

The leeward mark at the 1978 Worlds in Puerto Rico shows how far the fleet can spread on a downwind leg. No. 960 has made a good rounding, if he can avoid the capsized boat.

Boats seem to leap out of the water at the gybe mark – Venezuela Worlds, 1976. If there's a nice gap behind these boats, the boat outside on the turn isn't hurting .

Off the Wind

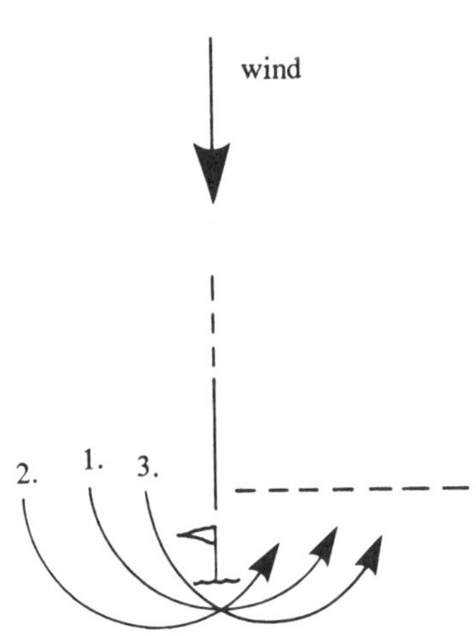

Rounding the leeward mark. (1.) Close to mark at middle on rounding (best when you're alone.) (2.) Close to mark at end of rounding (best in a crowd.) (3.) Close to mark at start of rounding (don't do it.)

The boats that have gone the highest may even have to gybe twice in fairly quick succession to round the mark.

While all this is going on, you may be able to gain enough speed coming high to the mark to break through to the head of the clump that has formed and gain quite a few boats in the process. But it is a delicate maneuver, requiring a considerable amount of finesse and luck.

Almost as good is to come up high behind such a clump of boats, take the wind of all of them as they run down on the mark, and gain an inside overlap. This is an even more difficult maneuver, because you have to get that overlap before the boat or boats ahead of you have reached the two-boat-length circle described in the rules. If all those boats ahead of you have to do a double gybe around the mark, you may find yourself in a real pile-up, and it may be a lengthy protest session when you get back to shore.

It's all very exciting, but most of the time you will be better off sailing a more conservative leg, either following the parade sailing high of the rhumb line or sailing low and hoping for a nice fat break in the line of boats that you can sail into as you round the mark, coming up close at the end of your rounding maneuver so you will be as much to windward as possible as you sheet in for the weather leg. And sometimes it can even pay to slow down and let a clump round ahead of you. They'll often come in very tight to the mark and have to round wide, leaving a gap for you to slip into close to the mark as you sheet in. You'll be behind, but to windward, so you will have pulled up even with them. That's a tactic called "Slow down and win."

• Rounding the Leeward Mark - 1

At the leeward mark, the rounding maneuver itself can save or lose you a couple of boat lengths, even if you are all alone. If you round it too sharply, your rudder acts as a brake and you actually slow down. If you come close to the mark as you begin to round, you will complete your rounding farther away from the mark. Other boats may round closer as they finish rounding, pinning you to leeward so you can't tack if you want to.

When you are several boat lengths ahead of the next boat, make a wide rounding so that you don't slow down, and cut the mark closest at the bottom of the turn, leaving roughly an equal amount of water on the downwind and upwind sides. That way, the bottom of the loop will take you the least distance from the windward mark.

If there are other boats close behind, the best way to round is a nice even turn, starting wide and coming up close to the mark as you reach the close-hauled position. This way, you pin boats in your wake and have freedom to tack if you want.

Because you end up to windward when you

make the first part of your turn wide, you can sometimes come out ahead of a boat that has the inside position at the mark. If you can force him to take the mark close at the start of the turn, he will either have to sweep wide, permitting you to come up inside and to windward, or he will cut the turn so tight that he slows down, giving you an opportunity to tack under his transom with better speed and so break away on starboard tack.

One tactic on approaching the leeward mark that can often gain you an inside overlap if you are behind, and is difficult to defend against if you are ahead, is this: if you are close on another boat coming into the mark, hang back a little to starboard of the boat you are going to attack until you are about five or six boat lengths from the mark. Then swoop up sharply, sailing across your opponent's stern. You will go faster because you will be on a closer reach and you will take your opponent's air. As soon as you have an overlap, hail for room, and you have put another boat behind you. Just make sure you have gained your overlap before your opponent reaches the two-boat-length circle.

If you are defending against this maneuver, keep a close watch on your pursuer. Occasionally take a little sharp jig up to windward, letting him know that you know what is on his mind. Make those jigs sharp and even do things to slow your boat down, so that he is forced into a position where he overlaps you to leeward. In that position, he cannot swoop up without fouling you. That forces him to go outside you around the mark.

If you can't possibly force him to leeward, at least you may be able to keep him from making that swing to windward until you have reached the two-boat-length circle. Immediately hail, "No room"; the burden of proof if he does force his way in will be on him, and he will then be in a very tough defensive position if you protest him. Just to be on the safe side, you might swing your stern around by bearing off sharply, so that the overlap line from your stern eludes him.

If all else fails, try to swing wide so that you round just astern of him, but with the ability to cut inside him at the end of the turn, which will put you out of the worst of his bad air on the beat to windward, and at least as close to the windward mark as he is. He will be backwinding you, but that is a lot better than having him sit on your wind. Unless there are compelling strategic reasons to stay on port over to the right side of the course, you will soon be able to tack clear.

• The Second Windward Leg

If you have been able to round the leeward mark with a nice smooth circle, inside and to windward of the crowd around you, you may well have experienced the thrill of catching two or three or more boats through your astute tactical maneuver, especially if you have managed it without hitting a boat or a mark. Now you have to settle down and race that second windward leg. As mentioned before, we are assuming an Olympic course, with three full-length windward legs.

Many Sunfish regattas will be held on a modified Olympic course, which means that the start is in the middle of the windward leg. If you draw such a course out on a piece of paper, you will see that there are really only two full-length windward legs, since you sailed the first half of one of those legs at the start and the last half on the final beat to the finish. (See diagram on page 64.)

On a true Olympic course, the start is at the leeward mark, and the finish is at the windward mark. This means that the race committee must either arrange for two committee boats, or the committee boat must be moved from the leeward position to the windward position during the course of the race. It is much more satisfactory for the committee if they can leave the boat on station in the middle of the leg and avoid the

Off the Wind

sometimes frustrating necessity to up anchor, then drop it and try to create a nice square finish or starting line.

Whether the course is Olympic or modified Olympic, the second leg will always be a full-length one, from leeward mark to windward mark. The strategic decision is whether to sail up the middle and play the shifts, or shoot for the corners because one side or the other is favored - or because both sides are favored over the middle. This decision becomes a more critical one when you are sailing a modified Olympic. In this case, that second windward leg is twice as long as the first or last one, and you therefore can sail twice as far from the competition. That makes things harder to control, and can make for major differences in the conditions from one side of the course to the other. If you round early, and try to cover the competition, the best thing to do is try to stay in the middle, until you can tell which way the competitors are going. If they split up, some going to port and some to starboard, you at least have the opportunity to gauge which side of the course seems to be favored - on which side the boats seem to be sailing faster, not only through the water, but also to windward. Which side has a favored wind slant, and is being lifted to the mark? Which seems to be in more favorable current?

By the second beat, the fleet has spread out even more. You can concentrate on covering the fleet, wind-hunting, tacking on the headers, or just on boatspeed. Of course, you really have to do all that, but the priorities may change from race to race, or leg to leg, or even moment to moment. In the early part of the race, you will be trying to get your air clear. Or, if you have managed to get a fairly good start, you will be concentrating on consolidating your position and staying in front of the majority of the fleet.

Those will probably be your priorities, unless you are convinced that one side of the course or the other is the place to be. Then, you may sacrifice those objectives to getting out on the favored side of the course. You may even be willing to take a little bad air to get there. As mentioned earlier, there are times when it pays to shoot the corners - sail all the way out to the lay line or even beyond - to stay in good air or favorable current as long as possible. This tactic can be especially important on small lakes or roughly round harbors. In other cases, you may be racing along a straight shoreline, with more wind and less adverse current along the beach. Or there may be a channel out towards the edge of the course where the current is strong and favorable.

But usually, if conditions are roughly equal across the course, it pays to keep your air clear and tack on the headers. By the second windward leg, you should be able to determine the best course, if you have kept track of which boats came out ahead on the first beat, and where they went. Of course, in unstable conditions, one side can be favored on the first beat and the other on the next.

On a long leg, like the middle windward leg of a modified Olympic course (triangle-windward-leeward-windward, with the start/finish line in the middle of the windward leg) it is not at all unusual to find that one side of the course is favored on the first half of the beat, and the other on the second half. If you can get in phase with such shifty conditions, you can really get out ahead of the rest of the fleet, unless a lot of them are as lucky or as perspicacious as you are. On the other hand, you can get completely out of phase and get tanked. When conditions are as variable as this, there will usually be quite noticeable wind cells or streaks - puffs or lines of wind traveling across the water making ripples - and agonizing dead spots in between.

I have read two theories on how to maximize the effects of these puffs - how to stay in them, and get the best angle to the next mark. One theory says that each of these puffs is roughly fan-shaped, so that if you are on starboard tack and you hit one along its right side (as it comes toward you) you will be headed. The trick then is to stay in the puff even though you are headed, on the theory that the extra speed from the extra wind will outweigh the longer course to the mark, and that you will get a lift anyway as you sail through it. On the other hand, if the puff reaches you and you are toward its far left side, you will get an immediate lift, but should tack anyway to stay in it, even though it is contrary to the rule of tacking on headers. On a day with only occasional puffs, but strong ones, this tactic makes a great deal of sense.

The second theory is that puffs are affected by the cyclonic nature of wind formations - that is, in the Northern Hemisphere, they tend to swirl in a counter-clockwise direction. According to this theory, the left side of this cyclonic trend is a puff; the right side is a lull. If you meet a puff low and to the left on port tack, you will get a lift; high and to the left, you will be headed. The trick is to know whether you're high or low. Then the trick is to stay with the lift if you're low, until you hit the center, then tack out, when you'll be lifted again. If you hit it high, you're headed, so you tack out of there. Whether this theory has any validity I don't know, but since you normally tack on the headers, it works.

I have seen plenty of fanshaped puffs, and the cyclonic theory may explain why there are wind shifts that oscillate fairly constantly. But it seems to me most puffs just come across in flat sheets, sometimes heading you, sometimes lifting you. Stick with the tack-on-the-headers approach unless you keep finding yourself in a dead spot. Then, shift your tactics to scanning the water for puffs, and try to be in them a lot more of the time than you are out of them.

If you are beating to windward and see a puff straight ahead of you, by the time you reach it,

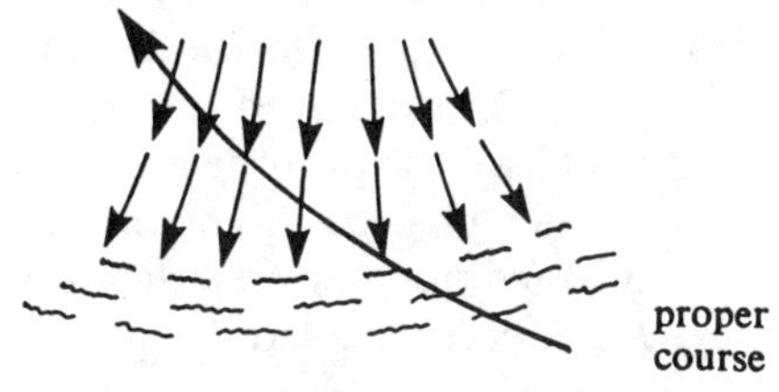

1. *Fan-shaped puff.*

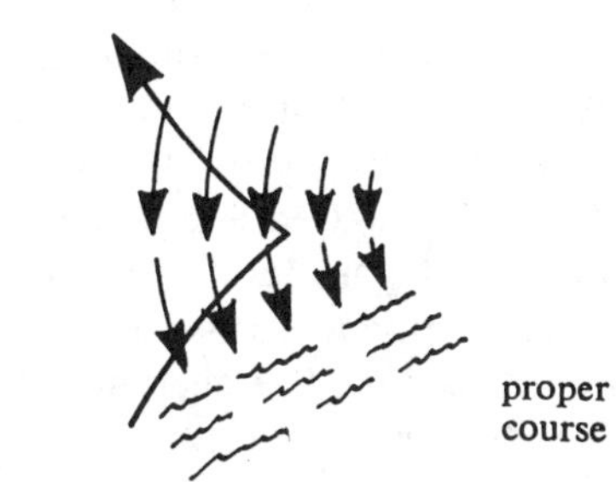

2. *Cyclonic puff.*

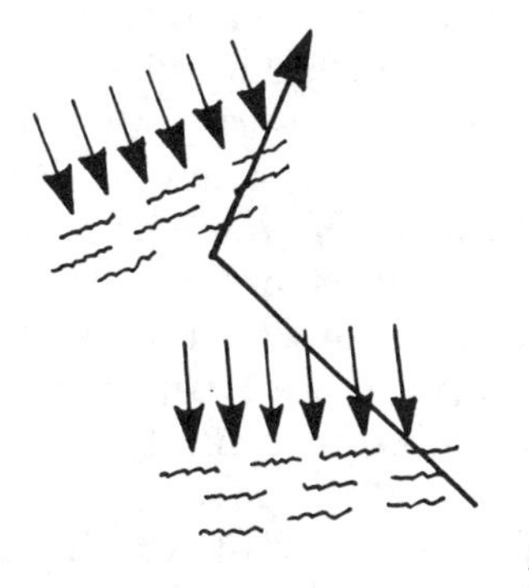

3. *Sheet puff.*

Puffs: (1.) Fan-shaped puff. (2.) Cyclonic puff (Northern hemisphere.) – stronger on left. (3.) Sheet puff – tack on header!

Off the Wind

more often than not, it will have moved on or died out. The trick is to gauge the speed at which you are moving, the speed at which the puff is moving, and lead the puff the way a skeet shooter leads the clay pigeon. It can be discouraging, especially since puffs often fade away as you get there, even if you have led them properly.

A bugaboo to watch out for is what has recently been termed a velocity shift. This kind of shift happens when the wind drops suddenly. Your forward momentum, even in a Sunfish, creates a wind of its own, which combines with the actual wind to create what is known as the apparent wind. When the actual wind, termed the true wind, dies, most of the wind felt by the sails comes from forward, and your apparent wind moves forward too, heading you. With this kind of header, the velocity header, you usually don't want to tack. First, your tack will be slow, because the wind has dropped, and second, you may well be tacking into a hole, the dead spot that caused the velocity header in the first place. When you feel the wind drop, and you are headed, look at the water close upwind and try to determine, from the ripples on the water, where the wind is and where it isn't. Stay with the ripples, or on the tack that will bring ripples down to you soonest.

It's a rewarding feeling when you get in phase with the puffs, and work your way out ahead of the fleet. It is under such conditions that you will find that strange anomaly, the fastest sailor on the course finishing mid-fleet. He has been concentrating so much on boatspeed that he has neglected to wind hunt. Under these conditions, smart sailors keep reminding themselves, "Get your head out of the boat!"

Another anomaly to watch out for is the occasional condition where one corner of the course is so much more favored that it pays to overshoot the lay line. You may have shot the corner perfectly, tacked right on the lay line, and be coming in on the mark with clear air, only to discover a boat that was safely tucked behind you now bearing down from above and passing you before you reach the mark. He has overstood, but found so much better air or more favorable current that it has paid off for him to sail the longer course. If he is a good sailor, you can assume that he figured it out. If he is a mediocre sailor, perhaps he has just lucked out. Either way, you have learned something, something that may be worth a try on the next windward leg or in the next race.

One final but very important point about the second windward leg. If it is the classic modified Olympic course, the regatta rules may state that you cannot sail through the start/finish line on your way to the next mark. "The gate is closed" in the jargon of the guild. This is a precaution often instituted by race committees to avoid confusion if there is more than one fleet racing, with more than one start. Consider the situation on a short course. There are four fleets - a championship fleet, a consolation fleet, doubles, and juniors. The first fleet gets off just fine, but the consolation fleet has several general recalls. By the time the juniors get off the first fleet is already finishing, and the second fleet is on the second windward leg. If all three were permitted to sail through the line, the committee would have a terrible time keeping track of who is over early at the start, who is finishing, and who is just sailing through. In almost every regatta I attended in the early days of the modified Olympic course, where the line was off limits except for starts and finishes, someone forgot, sailed through, and was disqualified. Experienced racers are used to it now, but keep it in mind. It's a lousy way to lose a race.

• The Leeward or Downwind Leg

Tactics in rounding the windward mark after the second beat are much the same as for the first. Here again you want to have your air clear as you head for the leeward mark and to be on the correct side of the course, if there is one.

Keeping your air clear as you round for the run is a little simpler than rounding onto a reach. You can sail off to the right or left for a considerable distance on either tack to avoid being blanketed. On the other hand, there is often a new complication - the boats that are still beating to the windward mark. On the first reach, you were sailing parallel to the port-tack boats on the windward lay line. Now, you have to sail down through the boats still on a beat. It often makes sense to stay on starboard tack during the first part of the run, so you keep your rights over the port tack beaters. You still have to worry about those on starboard. Since they are to leeward on the same tack, they have right of way. Even the port tack boats are a problem, however, since they are often more intent on their sails and the other boats that are still beating. If you have a collision, you will be in the right, but you will have been slowed down and may lose boats. The problem is that you will find it hard to see through your sail when you go downwind. Even with the window in the sail, you will have to bob and weave quite a bit under most conditions to check for boats hidden by the sail. If you heel your boat to windward, your visibility will be improved.

Heeling the boat to windward is the right thing to do, anyway, to improve boatspeed. Heel almost to the point of capsizing, with the seat of your pants often dragging in the water. There are two reasons for doing this. First, the center of effort is kept over the boat. That way, the sail is not a huge lever trying to make the boat round up to windward. If the boat is flat, you have to resist this rounding-up effect with the rudder. Dragging your rudder through the water at an angle slows you down. Heeled to windward may seem an unstable position...and it gets more so as the wind and waves pick up...but it actually is more stable once you get used to it. The second reason for heeling the boat is that it reduces wetted surface, reducing hull drag and increasing your speed.

You can actually steer the Sunfish downwind without the rudder if you have the balance of a tightrope walker. Heel the boat hard to windward with the sail over on top of you and the boat will turn to leeward. Let the boat flatten out and it will head up. Theoretically, you could pull your rudder out of the water as well as your daggerboard, further reducing friction drag. With the old style rudder, some sailors did lift most of the rudder out, but with the new spring-loaded design, it's practically impossible to do that. But the more you can steer with your body, using boat heel to change direction, the straighter you can keep your rudder and avoid dragging it at an angle through the water.

There is a theory that it pays to gybe on the headers, just as it pays to tack on the headers going upwind. The idea is to try to stay on a broad reach rather than a dead run, which should improve your speed through the water enough to make it worthwhile to sail the longer course. It works great on iceboats and catamarans and many other boats, but it doesn't seem to work with Sunfish. It works if you do it to stay in stronger wind or to stay on a big wave, but not in steady wind and water. In very light air, a well executed roll gybe may actually squirt you out ahead a little bit, but if you do it only for that reason, you are cheating. By and large, steer a straight course downwind as long as you can keep your air clear and wind and current are fairly even across the course.

Another peculiarity of the Sunfish is that it often sails fastest downwind a little by the lee - that is, with the wind coming over the lee quarter a bit, probably no more than five or eight degrees, depending on conditions. A few of the best sailors dispute this theory, but it seems to work for the majority. For one thing, it seems to help steady

Off the Wind

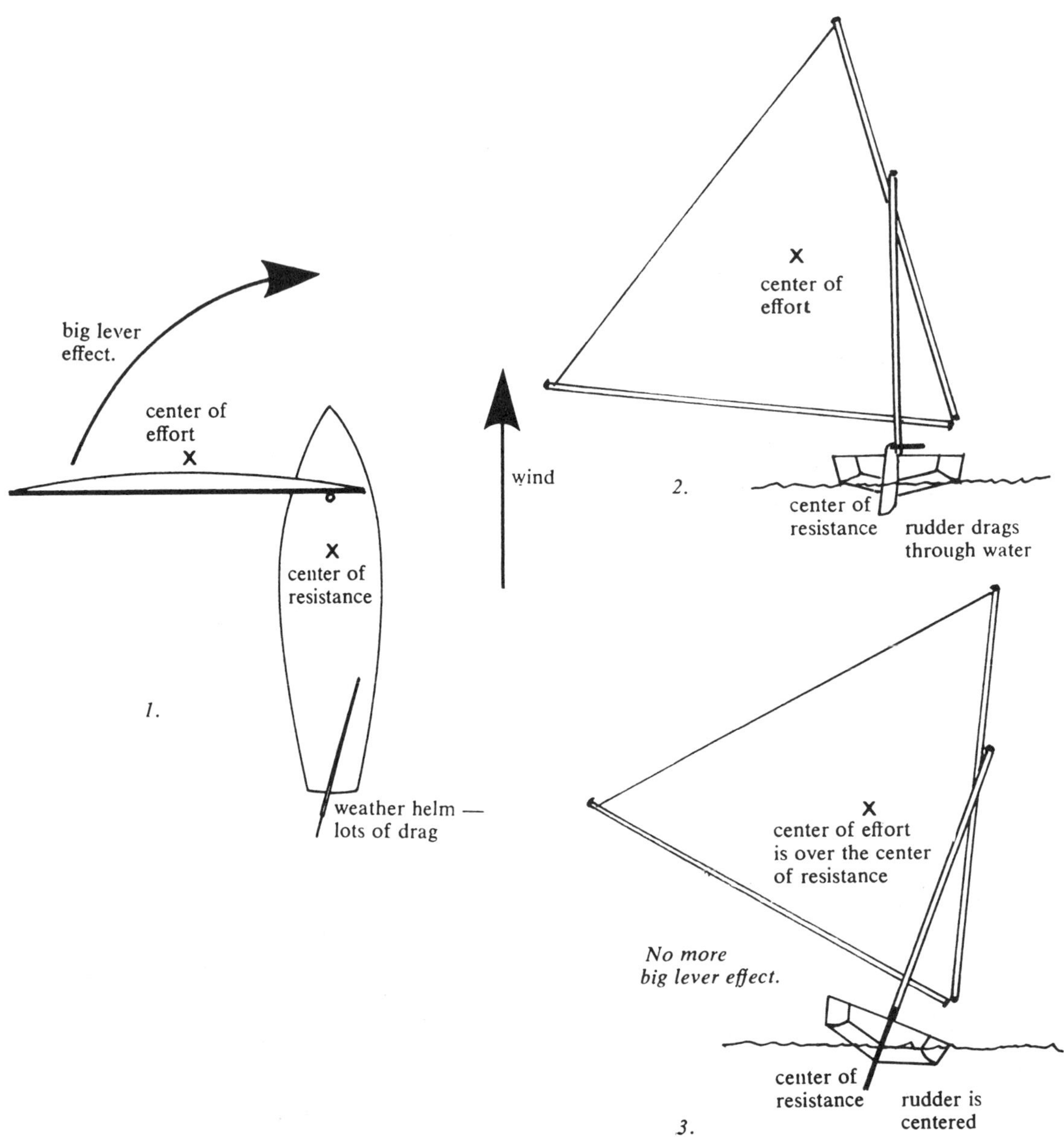

These drawings show why it is advantageous to heel your boat to windward when sailing downwind. (1.) A big lever effect, indicated by the curved arrow, is created by the sail. Weather helm is the result and the tiller must be moved to counteract it, causing drag. (2.) The same situation shown from astern. The turned rudder slows the boat. In (3.), the boat has been heeled to windward. Now the center of effort is over the center of resistance and the rudder can be centered, reducing drag. The lever effect has been eliminated, and the wetted surface has been reduced. The lower the wetted surface, the lower the friction drag between water and hull.

Off the Wind

the boat a bit when you are heeled to windward, and the boat seems to track a little straighter. The opposite peculiarity of the Sunfish is that, on a broad reach with the board all the way up and the sail all the way out, the boat is drawn to windward, because the sail begins to develop some lift. The boat is slowed when that happens - it is going at an angle rather tracking true. The fix is to drop the board until the crabbing stops, or bear off a little.

Figuring out where the wind and current are best downwind is pretty much the same as figuring it out upwind. I find keeping track of wind streaks is easier downwind. Keep looking back for those tell-tale ripples, and to make sure your wind is clear of the wind shadows of following boats. This is where the mast-head fly is a big help. If the fly is pointing at a nearby boat astern of you, you can be sure he is sitting on your wind. Get out of there!

Just remember that favorable wind is favorable wind either way, but favorable current upwind is unfavorable current down. Beside watching the wind ripples on the water, clues come from flags and smoke, and especially from other boats. A little harder to fathom is the current, since you not only want to be in it if it's favorable, you want to be in the strongest part of it, unless that takes you too far off course. If the current is against you, naturally, use the opposite strategy - get in the weakest part of the current. If the current is across the course, compensate for it by sailing slightly into it, so your track over the bottom is as straight as possible towards the leeward mark, other tactical considerations aside. Line up the mark with a point on shore if possible. You can catch sailors who are not conscious of the cross-current. They'll point their bows at the mark and, because the current is sweeping them sideways, wind up taking a great circle route to the mark.

Besides heeling the boat to windward, you will want to have the board all the way out of the

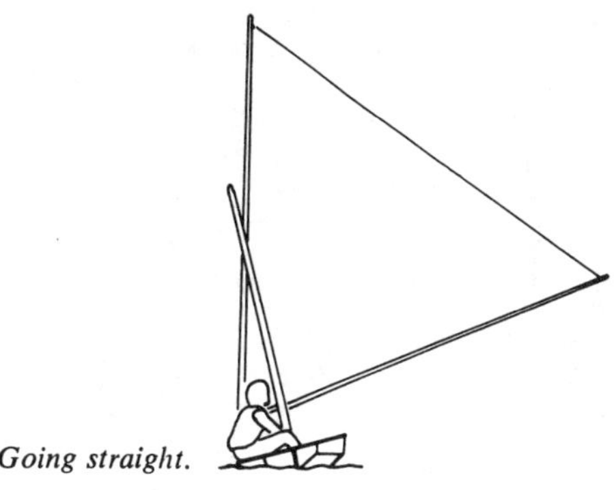

Going straight.

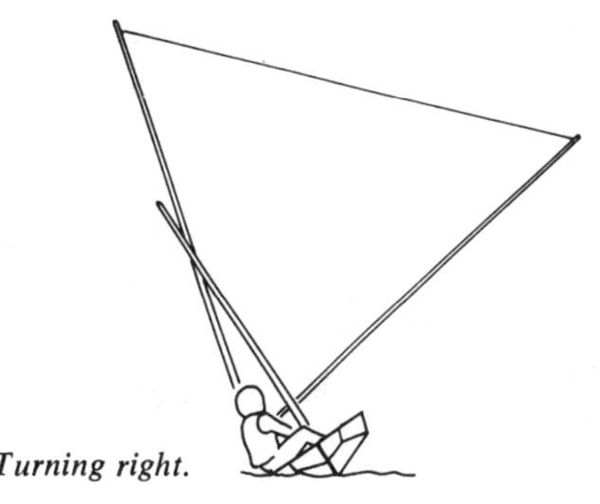

Turning right.

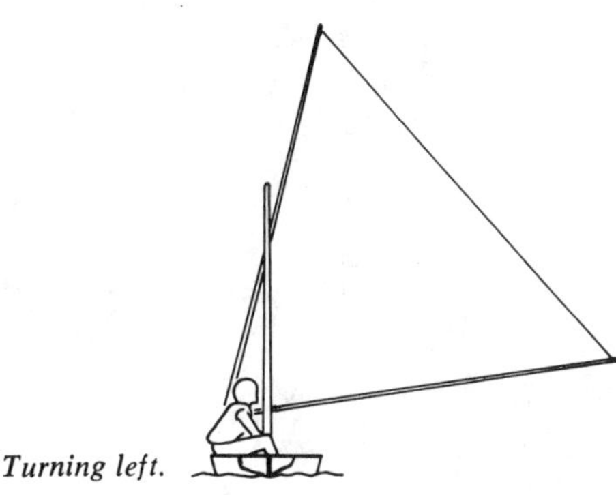

Turning left.

Steering downwind with your body. It's theoretically possible to steer downwind without the rudder if your balance is good.

Off the Wind

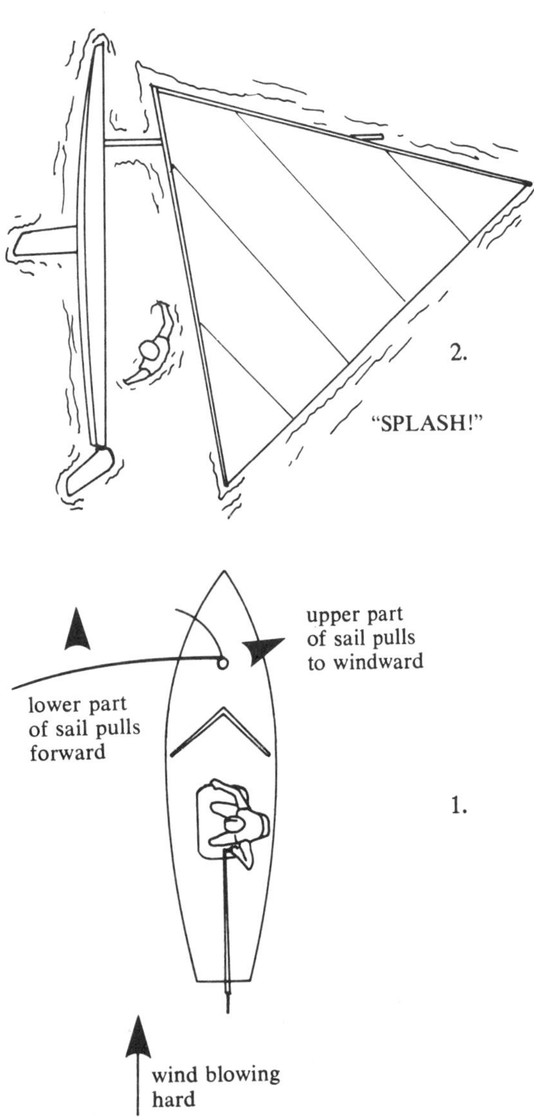

Death roll: Upper part of sail pulls to windward; lower part of sail pulls forward.

water. That means flush with the bottom of the keel, not all the way out sitting on the deck or in the cockpit. If you take it all the way out, water flushing up through the trunk acts as a brake. For the same reason, the new board with its cutaway aft edge may be better left with three inches or so still sticking below the keel.

Under all but the heaviest conditions you will want to have the sail out at a 90-degree angle from the centerline of the boat, presenting as much area as possible to the wind. The conventional wisdom is that when you are running, the sail acts purely as a parachute and you get very little benefit from aerodynamic lift. Under this theory, the objective is to present as much sail area to the wind as possible. To increase projected sail area, you tighten the outhauls.

Currently, however, some of the top sailors find they sail faster by relaxing the outhauls, putting more belly in the sail. If you find that works for you, just remember to tighten the outhauls again at the leeward mark for the last beat to windward.

In very heavy air, the sail may develop enough twist so that, if the boom is at 90 degrees to the centerline, the top of the sail is twisted around so it presents an airfoil shape to the wind. But instead of pulling the boat forward, its effect is to pull the boat over to windward. That can start you on a death roll - a capsize to windward. The solution is to pull the sail in as violently as possible - exactly opposite to the sailor's instinct to let the sail out whenever he is in trouble - and throw your weight to leeward. This deathroll effect is less severe in a Sunfish, because the rig is low and the upper spar prevents the more extreme twist possible in a marconi rig. But it can still happen.

So in very heavy air, it is probably wise to pull the boom in to a 75- or 80-degree angle. In real survival conditions, you can usually stay on a solid plane with your sail sheeted in even further.

Off the Wind

If the sail is too far out, it can start the boat oscillating - rocking violently from side to side - or even lift the stern as a wave comes up under it and pitchpole you. The bow digs in, the stern flies up, and you can be flipped forward like a pea being flipped off the blade of a knife.

The problem of burying the bow can start to plague you even in medium winds, depending on the waves. In medium air with a steep, close chop, the boat has a tendency to race down the face of a wave and into the one in front of it. Since there is little freeboard on a Sunfish, it's like burying a shovel in the snow, and the boat tends to submarine. This is a very slow way to move through the water at a time when you should be skipping over the top of it. Moreover, the rudder has a way of popping up out of the water as the bow digs in, and you lose control. You will usually round up to windward sharply, and that considerably delays your progress to the next mark. But rounding up to windward is not as bad as the alternative. The bow might round off sharply to leeward, causing a flying gybe. Suddenly you are on the lee side, and you will be lucky if you don't go swimming, with the boat capsized on top of you.

So one of the first things you have to learn in sailing downwind in a Sunfish is how to keep the bow out of the water. Be ready to move your weight aft—quickly! That will help bring the bow up. However, if you move too far aft, the boat will have a tendency to sit down in the water and drag its stern. Dragging your stern slows you down.

So watch your steering and try to find a depression in the waves ahead through which you can slip your bow. Unfortunately, the fastest planing angle down the wave may not be the safest, so you have to keep making split-second compromises between sailing fast and sailing into a wall of water. Under such conditions, don't try to be gentle with the boat. Sharp swings of the

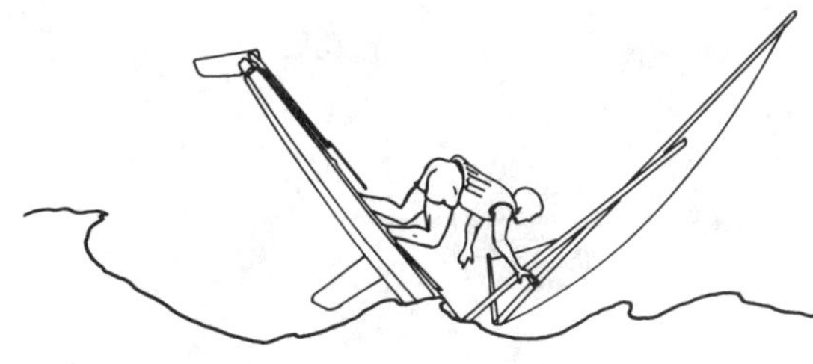

Pitchpole!

rudder are often necessary to flick the bow out of the way of a big wave ahead. You get the feeling that the waves are rushing at you, instead of the other way around, but the effect is just the same. Keep that bow clear!

In big swells in open oceans, you can use surfing techniques that will really move you out ahead of the competition. Paul Fendler and Mike Catalano were the first to develop these techniques in Sunfish, and they seem to work best for such relative lightweights. From far astern at the Worlds in 1976 in Venezuela, it looked to me as if they were practically throwing the boat sideways up the waves. They would give a strong flick of the rudder as they came to the bottom of a wave, heel sharply to windward, pull the sail in to about a 45 degree angle, with the result that the sail became practically a parawing, seeming to lift the boat as well as pushing it forward. The technique was extremely successful for Paul and Mike (they finished 1-2) but the best downwind sailors now seem to be able to roar downhill fast without such extreme maneuvers.

This sideslipping technique seems to work well in other classes as well. I once raced an Apollo (another short-lived Alcort class) at their North Americans against such top-flight international sailors as Gary Jobson and Hans Fogh. Hans went

Off the Wind

World Champion (1976) Paul Fendler demonstrates his way to make time up the face of a wave on the run – extreme windward heel as you reach across, sideslipping uphill. He has the board all the way out, in the cockpit!

into some detail at the regatta post-mortems on how important it was to get the centerboard completely out of the water - the boat had rubber flaps that closed up the slot when the board was fully retracted - so the boat could be slipped at a yaw through the water to get that parawing effect, or at least to get some air flow over the sail so that it would act as a wing a little bit, instead of a barn door.

Most of the top sailors agree, however, that the single most important technique to learn is to keep the boat moving downhill as much of the time as you can. In time, you will learn what the waves are doing behind you from the action of the waves on either side and ahead. Like riding a bicycle, it is a matter of instinct, reacting to feedback from the vehicle you are riding.

Downwind, all other factors being equal, the most important rule to remember is, "Sail downhill!"

• Rounding the Leeward Mark – 2

Rounding the leeward mark after the run is very similar to rounding it after the reaching legs. In fact, the last couple of hundred yards are often the same, when the whole fleet will have sailed to weather of the rhumb line on the reach and they are actually running down to the mark. All the options mentioned in the section on rounding the leeward mark after the reach apply here. As in that situation, when there are lots of boats with you the most important thing is to try to be inside at the mark, and round up close to the mark at the end of the turn, so you are close-hauled as you pass the mark close aboard.

Sometimes, when boats have been running down on starboard tack and are fighting for an overlap, they wind up so far to the left of the rhumb line that they have to gybe over onto port to get to the mark. Several boats making two quick gybes at the leeward mark can easily get tangled up with each other. If other boats are managing to make it to the mark while still on starboard, they have right of way before the port-tackers reach the two-boat-length circle, compounding the confusion. If you see a situation like that developing, you may be able to slow down and slip through close to the mark even though you didn't gain an overlap, because the boats ahead of you are so preoccupied with each other that they are carried off to leeward and none of them can close the door on you. That's tricky and dangerous. A safer tactic may be to keep up your speed, round behind the pack but close aboard the mark as you come up close-hauled, and trust that your greater speed will help lift you above the pack long enough for you to find a chance to tack away. Just be aware that a lot of boats may still be running down to the leeward mark. If you tack and sail through them, you will have right of way once you have completed your tack, but they'll be taking your wind and causing a lot of turbulence.

• The Last Beat

You are now on the last beat to the finish. You should have the windward leg pretty well figured out by now. But don't bet on it. Don't get complacent. Watch what is going on around you just as carefully as you did the first two times around, because conditions will probably have changed a bit. Has the tide turned? Has the wind shifted? Has the favored side changed?

If you are sailing in a steady oscillating wind, you may have rounded in the same part of the cycle the first two times, but be in the opposite phase this time. In other words, the starboard tack may have been the lifted tack the first two times, but this time the port tack is the lifted tack. If there is shoreline in view ahead, or if you have a compass on deck, remember what your course was as you headed up close-hauled the first two times. If, as you round up on port tack, you are sailing higher this time, you'll want to stay on port until you are headed. If you are sailing lower, you'll probably want to tack...all other things being equal, that is. As always.

A land reference is usually more accurate if there is one, but it pays to have a compass and use it, especially if you will be sailing in open water, where the water meets the sky and there are no fixed reference points. Many sailors are successful without a compass, just as many are successful without telltales, but they can both give you a little extra edge, so long as you don't fixate on them to the exclusion of more important signs. Learn to use them, but remember to keep your head out of the boat!

If you are sailing a modified Olympic or some other course with the start/finish line in the middle of the weather leg, that last windward leg will be short. For some reason, many sailors seem to let down on this leg. They seem to feel that, because it is short, they are pretty much frozen in the position they hold at the leeward mark. Not so! If most of the others are letting down, and you give it a last fierce burst of concentration, you can often pick up quite a few boats on this leg.

Because all the boats are sailing into a funnel, with the finish line at the neck, it becomes clearer and clearer which boats are favored and which are not. If you concentrate on covering the boats behind you and try to overtake the boats ahead, taking advantage of every small shift and puff, and if the others feel they are in a parade, you have a tremendous advantage. It's a final charge at the end of a tournament, the kind for which Arnold Palmer was famous in golf.

So bear down and don't let up on that last leg. Next to the first few hundred yards at the start, it is the most important part of the race.

8 The Finish

Before you get to the point where you have to commit yourself to one end of the finish line or the other, try to figure out which end of the line is closer to you. Finish lines are seldom square to the wind, any more than starting lines are. However, the finish line will usually be considerably shorter than the starting line, since the whole fleet doesn't finish at once. Nevertheless, you can lose a boat or two - or considerably more, in a tightly packed fleet - by finishing at the wrong end of the line.

On a course where you can pass the finish line close aboard on an early leg, try to judge which end will be favored on the last leg to the finish. Don't assume it will be favored on the last leg, however. The wind is always shifting. Factor in the latest wind direction when you plan your last leg.

• Windward Finishes

When you are beating to the finish, the important thing is still to keep your air clear and work that magic combination of the favored side of the course, if there is one, the wind shifts, and the puffs. But keep track of the shifts in relation to the finish line. At some point, you have to commit to one end or the other. If there are boats ahead of you, you can usually determine the favored end by watching them finish.

If the line is square to the wind, it doesn't matter; plan your last tack so you're in clear air. But if one end or the other is favored, tack for it. Try to come in on port if the left side of the line is favored; come in on starboard if the right end is favored. That way, you are more likely to keep your air clear.

The committee boat will usually be on the right side of the line. If it's a big one, it can blanket you if you come in close on starboard tack. If the committee boat side is so much favored that you can chance slowing a bit in its shadow, it may pay to overstand a bit, so that you can bear off as you reach it, swoop through, and then head back up to close-hauled as soon as your wind is clear.

You may have trouble coming in close on port tack because boats that have finished often have a bad habit of congregating just off the left side of the line. Their blanketing effect can be much worse than the committee boat's. Yell at them. But allow for those conditions when you plan your finish.

If you are in the lead, or ahead of a competitor you have to beat, it makes sense to cover even if it means crossing at the wrong end of the line. The favored end can change in the last few seconds of the race with a sudden wind shift. The important thing is to cross ahead of the competition, not to cross a second or two earlier than you otherwise would.

If you have a good view of the line, and are practically even with another boat or boats, you may be able to tack half a boat-length before you reach it, so that you are rounding up with full speed. Your bow will shoot across the line a fraction of a second earlier, and you may cross ahead by a nose. If there's not room to tack, bear off again after shooting the line. Obviously, your timing must be perfect, because the Sunfish doesn't shoot very far to windward.

If it looks as if you will be crossing with a clump of boats, it may be important to get the berth closest to the committee boat. That way, you can be sure the person calling the finishes will see your sail number. In a near-dead-heat situation, your number has the better chance of being called first. In large regattas, it's not unusual for a half-dozen boats to cross in an interval of a second or two.

Obviously, such finishes are a matter of inches. Sailors who keep their wits about them and can take split-second advantage of what's going on for the last few boat-lengths before the finish can sometimes gain two or three boats literally at the last second.

The Finish

One last word. Before trying any breath-taking maneuvers, be sure it is worth the risk. If the trick is not likely to have much bearing on your finish in the regatta, why chance committing a foul?

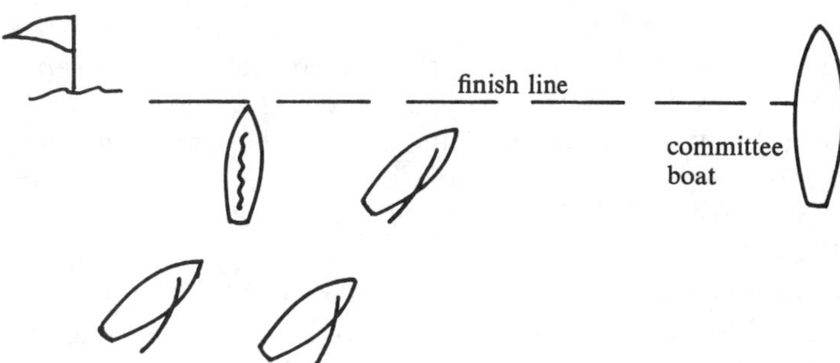

The finish: Luff up and win!

• Downwind Finishes

Not all finishes are to windward. A simple triangular course or a windward/leeward course ends with the boats reaching or running back down to the starting line, which becomes the finish line. Normally a committee will avoid such courses, because with the sails out parallel to the starting line, the numbers are difficult to read. However, some clubs traditionally use a line off their dock so that spectators can watch starts and finishes. Or a course may be shortened for lack of wind. At any rate, you may occasionally finish on a reach or run.

When the course is a simple triangle, the line often stays the same as at the start, although it should be swung around to be perpendicular to the course from the last mark. Imagine a triangular course with marks to port. If the line is set perpendicular to the wind for the start, and not moved for the finish, the starboard end as you reach to the finish will be heavily favored. Try to find out before the race if the committee plans to swing the line so that it is perpendicular to the last leg for the finish. The middle of the line will then be closest to the last mark. But it may pay to aim for the left end of the line, because the Sunfish sails a hair faster, under most conditions, as the wind moves forward on the beam, up to some point between a beam reach and close hauled. A lot of competitors will instinctively aim for the right end, because it was closer at the start. Aim for the left end and you'll be sailing faster and probably in clear air.

If the last leg is dead downwind, as in a simple windward/leeward course, the tactics are almost identical to those for the run to the leeward mark in the traditional Olympic course. The most important thing is to keep your wind clear, but it's also important to figure out if one end of the line or the other is favored. Head for it, or as close as you can get to it without dropping into someone's wind shadow. If, when you figure out the favored end, you find yourself on the wrong side of the course, it may pay to reach over near the end of the leg, gaining enough speed to slip in front of a competitor just before the line. Alternatively, if you know that move won't work, it's sometimes possible to reach over behind him, take his wind for just long enough to slow him down, and then sweep over him to windward to edge him out at the line.

Watch out. He may slam his board down and give you a sharp luff, which he has a right to do under the rules. Even if he doesn't tag you, he may force you to the wrong side of the line before you can recover. He has to do this before the two-boat-length circle, and break your overlap if you've gained one, at which point the onus of proof is on him...but you may make him mad enough to try it.

Another important thing to remember about the finish is that the moment of finishing is when

The Finish

the first part of your boat crosses the line - normally your bow. But you haven't *finished* finishing until the last part of your boat clears the line. In other words, if you are going much more slowly than another boat, but your bow gets to the line ahead of hers, you beat her even if your stern clears the line after hers. (We're talking about the boat here, people.) But you are both racing and subject to the racing rules until both of you have cleared. So if you cross the line on port, and your bow crosses before that of a starboard tack boat, you have won until the point she must bear away to avoid hitting you - and then you have lost because you have been disqualified or must accept an alternative penalty, depending on the rules of the regatta. Technically, if you both have cleared before she has to change course, you are in the clear, but you might get thrown out on the basis of poor sportsmanship. Even when you are not racing, starboard tack has right of way.

As implied earlier, it is also bad sportsmanship, or at best just plain rude, to hover close to the finish line or the lay lines after finishing. Especially if several boats do so to rehash the race, the wind of the boats still finishing will be badly disturbed, and that's not fair to them. After you have finished, keep sailing until you are well clear of those still racing, and urge others who have finished to do the same. This problem is not as bad as it was a few years ago, but some sailors still don't realize the havoc they can create by hanging around close to the finish.

• After the Race

Some of the most valuable hours at a regatta, especially for the novice, are spent not on the course, but in discussions afterwards. The post-mortems can be invaluable. Why did winners sail the courses they did? How did they manage to avoid the holes or stay out of the bad current? How did they know that the wind was going to shift? How did they pick their way through that steep chop? How did they manage to stay clear of that mess at the leeward mark? Why did they start in the middle of the line, even though the leeward end seemed favored? Get involved in those discussions. At first, you won't even know the question to ask. By listening closely, you will learn a lot. And don't be shy about it. Sunfish sailors are a friendly lot and like nothing better than to discuss the strategies and tactics that helped them win or the mistakes that helped them lose.

Then, if you are serious, go one step further. Keep a journal. For several years, when the Darien Sunfish Yacht Racing Association was breeding regatta winners by the dozens, Larry Lewis used to write a report of every Sunday's racing. He would have it mimeographed and hand out copies to the rest of the sailors the following week. He seemed to have total recall and was a keen observer. I am convinced that Larry did more to turn Bob Bowles, Bob Bushnell, Carl Knight and myself into champions of the late '60s and early '70s than we did ourselves.

The champion of champions in those days, Carl Knight, also kept his own journal. He would review it before every regatta, which not only helped him to psych himself up but also reminded him of past mistakes or techniques that worked. Derrick Fries, the winningest sailor of all, also kept a diary.

I don't know if Paul Fendler kept a diary. He did have a corollary practice. He was one of the first to practice psychic sailing - going over and over again in his mind past races and imaginary races with situations he extrapolated from his memory bank. Then, when faced with a similar situation, he would react instinctively, doing the right thing more often than not before he even had a chance to think.

Interviews with the Champions • 1981-1982 9

I once made a survey of the competitors returning on a plane to New York from the World Championships in Venezuela in 1976. I asked them if they ever sailed their Sunfish just for the fun of it, or only when they were racing. The winners, the consistent champions, got downright poetic about the pleasure they get from sailing. Many of them jump into their boats whenever they can, just to sail. They love to hang out in the hot sun when barely a zephyr is stirring. And they love to get out in gales that would blow your breath back down your throat (the kind of weather that makes race committees cancel races) just to pit themselves against the storm.

When you think about it, that's not surprising. Given two individuals of equal talent, which one is most likely to win? The one who sails every chance he gets, and puts time in on the water just for the fun of it, or the one who only races? In terms of hours of practice alone, the one who just loves sailing is bound to come out on top more often. But I think it is more than that. I think it comes from a sense of unity with wind and water and boat. Once in love with sailing, you don't fall out of love. And that's what probably separates the true champion from the also-rans or the occasional flash-in-the-pans.

As a former columnist of *Motor Boating & Sailing* said in print a few years ago, after his first sail in a Sunfish, "Nothing, but nothing, should be that good the first time; not the first beer, first dish of yogurt, first love." Following are interviews with Sunfish sailors who sail for the fun of it but who have also become champion racers.

The first seven interviews, the ones in this chapter, are reprinted almost verbatim from *The Sunfish Book* as it was published in 1983. They were presented in alphabetical order of their last names, and remain that way. Some of these champs have moved on to other boats, some still show up occasionally at Sunfish regattas, and two — Paul Odegaard and Joel Furman — are still very active in the Class.

Some of the terms these champs use in this chapter were current at the time of the interviews, but may be confusing now.

For instance, the "new" sail refers to the third sail shape sold by Alcort, Hans Fogh's original design when he first started building sails for Sunfish in 1978. Today's "new" sail is the special racing sail, also by Fogh (now North Sails Canada), introduced in 1988.

The "new daggerboard" refers to what is now known as the Barrington board, the third board shape developed by Alcort, introduced in the mid-'70s. Today's "new" daggerboard is much longer, a special racing daggerboard made of structural urethane foam plastic reinforced by metal rods, introduced in 1993. These two changes brought the boat back to its original intended status as a true one-design boat, while correcting drawbacks in the original designs.

A new chapter has been added after this one, containing interviews in late 1995 and early 1996 with some of the newer champs - again in alphabetical order of their last names.

Interviews with the Champions • 1981-1982

● Mike Catalano

Mike Catalano started sailing in Connecticut, dominated Sunfish fleets a couple of summers in Wisconsin and Minnesota, and now lives in Florida. The one-time "enfant terrible" of Sunfish sailing, he competed in his first Worlds at the age of 16. He has won innumerable Midwinter and Regional titles in both Sunfish and Force 5s, but the North American and World titles have managed to elude him, even though he was often clearly the fastest man on the course.

Will: Let's talk about sailing upwind. What about kinetics?

Mike: Upwind, I don't even know what I do with my body. I don't pump and rock the way a lot of people do in waves upwind. I do that a lot downwind, but upwind I think I am more conscious of heeling than I am of back-and-fourth movement. If I see a puff coming, I hike out before it gets there. That works.

W: *Do you use woollies on the sail?*

M: No, because I feel they're very deceptive. All they do is keep you from pointing high enough. I think other kinds of telltales, out front at eye level, are important upwind. I'm always on the verge of luffing with my main and the way to do that is to use telltales that are in your line of vision, so you're constantly looking at them.

W: *What is the important thing off the wind?*

M: If there are waves, sail the waves. You may be way off course a lot of the time, but who cares? Don't worry about the course. Sometimes, it's good to get in the wake of another Sunfish. That is the best tactic in the world for getting an overlap at the mark, but you have to plan it and time it right. I go for the big splashy ending at the buoy. I get seven boat lengths behind a guy with a wake and when I think it's the right time, I jump on the wake, pump down the wave and stick my bow just inside his stern before the two-boat-length circle at the mark. I've done it a million times. I think it's a great tactic, but timing when to get on the guy's wake is most important.

W: *How about your outhaul? Do you play with that?*

M: No, I don't have an adjustable outhaul. I believe in keeping the boat so simple, it's sickening. My boat has none of that stuff. The only time I ever adjust is if the wind goes from real strong to real light between races. Then I drop the sail and slack off the outhauls.

W: *Let's switch to the start. What's your favorite start?*

M: You'll always see me in on top of the starting line. I make my decision about where I'm going to start at the last possible moment. I like to start in the middle and take advantage of midline sag. Many times people yell that I'm over the line, but I don't listen to them. I cannot remember a time when I have been early. I just keep going and then I'm free.

W: *Suppose you get a bad start and you're kind of buried. What do you do?*

M: You have two choices. You can sail through the fleet or around it. You have to evaluate the situation. There are times when the fleet is sailing so poorly - they're all on the wrong tack - that you can sail right through the middle of them on the opposite tack with better boatspeed. If the fleet is sailing pretty well and there are wild wind shifts to the side, go for the corner. You could end up in the top 10 or 80th, but generally if you're a good sailor and go to the corner intelligently, you will gain. People who go into the corner blindly never win, except maybe once a year — because they get real lucky.

Going for a corner means going way over and going there in style. In other words, getting a lift to get you over there and then skipping only one shift. Let's say people are tacking back and forth on the oscillations, but are generally favoring the right side of the course because there is a persistent lift to the right. What I do is skip one set of oscillations and get away from the fleet. I keep sailing through a header until the next lift, when I get headed. By then the entire fleet is one whole tack to the left of me and all I've lost is one oscillation. It's a small price to pay to get around a whole mess of boats, if you're faster than they are. There has to be a persistent trend to the shifts and you have to know you're going to get something good over there. Then you get right back up to the top of the fleet again and start sailing like a champ. Simple strategies work very well.

W: *Let's get to the boat itself - the tuning. What do you do to your rudder and board?*

M: My rudder and board are very simple. Unfortunately, Bob Johnstone completely ruined the one-design board by allowing all the shaping - which I was very much against - but I went out just like the rest of them and bought some Bondo auto body putty. My rudder is blunted and painted with epoxy. I also blunted the leading edge on my centerboard. I painted them both white because it helps show up any weed I pick up.

W: *How about the tiller and the hiking stick?*

M: I don't use the universal joint on the tiller extension. After 20 years, I'm not going to change now.

W: *What kind of handle do you put on the extension?*

M: I don't. I found that if I used a ring, every time it broke I would end up falling in the water, hitting someone or getting buried. So now I have a big ball of tape on the end and a bunch of rings of tape down to the tiller for a

Interviews with the Champions • 1981-1982

better grip. I grip the extension palm up because my biceps are stronger. I've been lifting weights and I'm getting to the point where I am strong enough to horse the boat any way I want to. I've been working out every day and my arms are so strong, they never get tired any more. I'm improving my upwind sailing.

W: *What kind of daggerboard retainer do you use?*

M: A piece of shock cord that goes forward to the mast. Real simple. It also has a much more important job: it holds the spars on the trailer.

W: *About the hull: do you worry about weight and stiffness?*

M: No, the Sunfish I have now has a little bit of "oilcanning" somewhere, but that doesn't seem to bother it. It goes pretty fast. I've never weighed any of my Sunfish. All I know is if I worry about that, I can't sail well. I just don't care.

Years ago when I worked for Alcort, I got accused of having a specially made boat. So I got rid of that boat and bought one right off the line. I had it picked up from a dealer and I carried the invoice around with me. The Sunfish I have now is just a regular old Sunfish I picked up two years ago, and it's just fine. I didn't get a chance to weigh it. My main criterion was price, not weight.

W: *How about sail shape?*

M: I'm still using the old sail, for two reasons. One, I have no money to buy a new one, and two, I had a chance to sail that new Fogh sail when it was designed and I didn't think it was any better. I think it has two or three points of sail when it's better, but I still sail fast with my old sail. In anything up to about three knots - I'm talking about drifters - I think the Fogh is better. From three knots to about 16 knots, when I am hiking out hard, the Ratsey is better. Above 16 knots, the Fogh is better if you use a Jens rig. I think the Fogh can also be fast off the wind, on a reach.

W: *Talk about the Jens rig.*

M: I'm not an expert. I've used it four times in very heavy air and liked it. It's very rough on the upper spar, but it works well.

W: *Do you get out on the course early and check out the weather and the wind and the tide and all that?*

M: No, I like to be the last guy out. Being a pilot, I call flight service the night before or in the morning, so I know the overall weather pattern. I like to know what the upper air masses are doing and what the wind is at 20,000 feet and all that, just to get an idea of what could happen. In Florida, we have to watch the heat, because that changes the wind. Even though I check the overall weather, all I have to do is look at the course - because in small boat sailing, the weather mark is only a mile away. You can turn around and look over your shoulder and see what the wind is going to do. Everything is so local, you don't need to be an expert.

I do check the starting line very carefully to see if the windward mark is directly to weather, on average, because the wind is always back and forth. This tells you if you are going to be on port or starboard tack a lot and keeps you from committing the ultimate sin: overstanding. One little tack at the mark, instead of sailing six miles and overstanding, is worth it.

W: *Good to talk with you again, Mike.*

Interviews with the Champions • 1981-1982

Dave Chapin

Dave Chapin of Springfield, Illinois, completely dominated the Sunfish Class from 1977 to the 1980s, especially in terms of boatspeed. Nevertheless, he was second at the North Americans in 1977 and fifth in 1978, despite five firsts in individual races. In 1978, he was second in the Worlds. It was not until the 1979 Worlds that he became a champion. He slipped to second in the Worlds in 1980, but regained the World crown in 1981. Meanwhile, he won the U.S. single-handed title (the O'Day Cup) and the Snipe Class Nationals, North Americans and Worlds. *Sailing World* named him dinghy sailor of the year in 1980. Dave's brother Steve also did well. He finished 11th in the 1981 Sunfish North Americans.

Will: How do you make a Sunfish go to windward? Do you use telltales?

Dave: No, I don't use telltales. I feel confident about looking at the water to see what the wind is doing.

W: *Do you consider yourself a pointer or a footer?*

D: I don't consider myself a pointer, because if you are in phase, you should be footing to go to the next header. If you're pointing every time the wind shifts you're going to lose. There are times when it is good to point if you can keep your speed up. One example is when you come off the starting line and want to squeeze off the boats below you. You squeeze up for a while - if you don't want to tack - to get out of their bad air, and then drive over them.

W: *How do you carry your bridle in light air?*

D: I carry the mainsheet in the middle all the time, until it starts to pull the boat too far sideways. Then I let it go to both sides.

W: *How about the new sail versus the old?*

D: I like the new sail better, I guess. It seems fuller.

Interviews with the Champions • 1981-1982

W: *Do you have any problem with it puckering along the luff in light air?*

D: No, I've only used the new sail at the Worlds. But you don't want it puckering along the luff - that's for sure. You should ease up the outhauls enough to relax the sail.

W: *What about tacking? How do you tack in various kinds of water?*

D: If the waves are not too big, I try to tack right on top of a wave. Then I can get around before the next wave hits. I tack just as the wave is passing under me.

W: *How do you handle the sheet as you go through waves?*

D: If a wave really stops me, I ease the sheet out a bit to get my speed back up. I'm always working the sheet a little bit. When I slow down, I ease it out and then when I get to a smooth spot, I trim it in, and go a little faster. I don't hold the sheet in one position - that's for sure.

In general I don't think pointing pays. You have to be aware of what boatspeed you're losing. Some guy may go higher than you, but if there is no wind shift you could end up in the same relative position because you have had better boatspeed. You would tack and come together. But you want to be the lower guy because if you get a header, it will hit you first. Of course, if you get a lift, you would have gone the wrong way. You have to foot to the header.

I think it's really good to get your outhauls tight going upwind in really heavy air. On a reach, it's not so good, so it's a trade-off there. If it's light, it's good to have your sail really flat. Trim in the mainsheet really hard, get it down on the corner and really whale it in. I tie a rope on for a bridle so the sheet will go from side to side. I like to be able to adjust things while I'm sailing. If I hit a lull, I pull the boom up to the center for power. If I get a big puff, I kick it back down with my foot.

W: *So what you're saying is that in medium winds you keep the sheet centered on the bridle eye?*

D: Yes. Until I hike out, I keep it centered. Then if it starts blowing harder, I pull really hard on the mainsheet and it flattens out the sail a lot. If it's wavy, I keep it in. If there are a lot of waves, I try to steer around them.

W: *Talking about catching waves off the wind...how do you know when one is coming? You probably don't look back. Can you tell from the water around you?*

D: Yes. I look forward at the bow of the boat. I definitely don't look back. When I see the tall part of the wave going by my bow, I know it's time to look for another hole to sail down into.

W: *You just want to steer downhill all the way?*

D: Yes, but you don't want to sail all the way to the bottom of a wave and stop and wait for the next one. You have to reach up a lot sooner than that to keep your speed.

W: *What happens when your speed dies?*

D: Just remember that when you get on a wave, you should go radically down it. You'll work your way to leeward and then when there's not much more room on the wave, you should start heading up. Your apparent wind will be such that your speed will be a lot better. This way you can keep your boat going at top speed the whole time. To catch a wave, you often have to pump. "Ooching" doesn't help that much except when sailing dead downwind in really big seas.

You can learn to steer the boat by moving your weight from side to side. When you want to go down a wave, rock the boat to weather, trim the mainsheet and steer down a little. Kind of kick the boat down the wave. When you want to head up, sit in and roll the boat back over. As the chine digs in, the boat heads up. Then you flatten it back down again. If you get a couple of rocks in, it won't hurt.

W: *Do you tie a vang on?*

D: Yes, I tie a vang around the gooseneck, using the halyard end.

W: *How about gybing on the downwind leg? Do you do much of that to try to get the lifts right?*

D: Yes, I think it's pretty important. In Aruba, I didn't gybe on one shift and I lost the regatta. I don't think Sunfish sail by the lee as well as some people think they do. It's better to keep gybing on the shifts.

W: *How about moving your weight fore and aft? Do you do much of that, or is it mostly side to side?*

D: I don't "ooch" very much. I find that moving from side to side is more important. When you get on a wave, you have to go straight down it, even if that is 45 degrees off your course. The lower you get, the more you're going to be able to reach up. So if you're looking to gain, take your gains as far to leeward as you have to. Even if you get five waves in a row, just work straight to leeward and you'll be able to reach up in front of the fleet in flat water. You should go high when there are no waves in light air and low when it's windy or there are good waves to ride.

W: *Do you have any tricks or secrets about keeping the bow from burying?*

D: Jump back. Usually, if you jump back hard, you can pop the bow out. You have to anticipate because as soon as your bow buries, it's too late. The bow goes under when you don't get out of the wave soon enough, when you ride it all the way to the end. You stick your nose in the wave and that's it.

W: *How do you like to start?*

D: Well, I usually have pretty good boatspeed, so I like to start conservatively. I stay away from the ends of the line, especially at the Worlds, so it's hard for people to call me back. I like to squeeze up to the guy to weather of me and then drive off into the hole. Everyone knows what he would like to do, but sometimes it's hard to execute it. When you get into a good fleet, you may find that when you make your hole, someone is going to take it.

W: *If the leeward end of the line is favored - which it seems to be most of the time - why don't you fight it out down there?*

D: The only time I would consider it is if someone really good is down there and that's someone I have to beat in that race. It just depends on the series. It's risky down there. It's risky at both ends, and I stay away from them if it's going to be a long race. I prefer just to hang back and not risk everything at the start.

W: *Let's talk a bit about tuning a boat. What do you do to your boat?*

D: I think outhaul tension is very important. I try to go out for a spin before a race and test a few things. If the boat seems to be sliding a bit too much to leeward or seems to have plenty of power but might go a little faster, I tighten the outhauls. Then if I start going upwind and the boat stops when I hit the wave and then doesn't accelerate very fast, I ease out the outhauls. I tend to adjust the outhauls a lot. I think the sail must set right. That's the key to going fast.

W: *You're the first person I've ever heard say that. That's interesting. How important do you think the rudder and board are?*

D: As long as they are in fairly decent shape, I don't think they really matter. I think the sail is much more important. Moving the gooseneck back in heavy air is like night and day. Take Cor van Aanholt, for example. He's the best at going in a blow and he puts his gooseneck back behind the second grommet. We practiced in Sardinia one day when it was blowing 35 knots. We had the goosenecks way back and we were about the two fastest guys out there, especially for our weight. This was the first time I had moved my gooseneck back

Interviews with the Champions • 1981-1982

that far and I found that the boat laid off and almost sailed itself. You don't have to fight it as much.

W: *Do you worry about the weight and stiffness of the boat?*

D: I think the weight is important and I prefer a light boat. I think they're all quite weak and I don't think stiffness matters much.

W: *How about your own personal preparation? Do you have any exercises that you like to do to keep fit?*

D: I just like to sail. It's good to sail a lot before you go to a regatta. I don't do sit-ups or anything like that. The first thing that happens when you get tired in a race is that you lose your wind, so it's a good idea to play basketball or do something that will keep your wind up. If you want to get used to hiking out, you should go out and sail a Laser or something comparable. They will really work you out, and then when you get into a Sunfish, it will feel like nothing. I think sailing a Laser helped me a lot. My arms may get tired sometimes, but never my legs.

W: *I noticed in Medemblik, Holland, that you were sailing with bare arms. Is that just to give you more maneuverability?*

D: Yes, I don't like putting anything on my arms. I think it is the worst thing you can do, because your arms get tired - especially if you don't have cleats on your boat.

W: *You weren't bothered by the cold?*

D: Well, I don't think about it in the middle of a race, if I'm doing well. If I'm not doing well... I always get cold between races. I have to wear a lot of clothing on my torso, so I don't get really cold.

W: *Do you carry weight?*

D: Yes, I carry 10 pounds, 15 maybe if it's blowing hard. I wear water bottles on the shoulders - they're much safer than sweat shirts. You can get rid of them quickly. I don't know what would happen if I got hit in the head with a boom and tossed into the water with sweat shirts on. If I were dazed, I'm not sure I could get them off.

W: *Thanks, Dave.*

Interviews with the Champions • 1981-1982

● Derrick Fries

Derrick Fries, of Pontiac, Michigan, won his first Worlds at Miami in 1975, in relatively light air. He had been the top finisher among the Americans the previous two years and had finished well in several North Americans. Then, in 1978, he walked off with another World title. This series included one heavy-air race that knocked out half the fleet. In 1983 at Wilmette, Illinois, he won his first North Americans, followed by another at Brant Beach, New Jersey in 1985, and a third at Tawas, Michigan, in 1989. He's a former sailing Intercollegiate All-American. His book *Successful Sunfish Racing* was published in 1984 and is reprinted starting on page 191.

Will: How do you make a Sunfish go to windward?

Derrick: In heavy air - because the daggerboard is so small - I feel that I am always in a continuous process of depowerizing the rig to make the boat go through waves without stalling. I start by using a vang, then I tighten the outhauls, and gradually go to a Jens rig - from small Jens to medium to a big Jens.

W: *What is a big Jens?*

D: A big Jens for someone my size - 175 pounds and six feet one inch tall - is about 16 inches of mast exposed. For someone 130 or 140 pounds, it should be about 20 to 25 inches of exposed mast. The gooseneck has to move foreward as you use a bigger and bigger Jens, as close as 15 inches to the tack. At first I was reluctant to use the Jens, thinking I was big enough and strong enough to do without it. Chapin was the one who exploited it well and showed that it is effective.

Going back to the initial question of how I make the boat go to windward, I think what I do is try to stay fluid. I use my body a fair amount and sheet very hard. Usually, as I go through a wave, I head up into it and then head off as I go down the back side. I don't know if I do it more than other people, but I like to sail a boat in waves on a little bit of a heel so that I'm not plunging the boat through the waves. You never want to sail a Sunfish through a wave, because it is so small and light. It has to go up and over. I try to knife it over the wave. I sheet in and semi-pinch, but not too much, because then the boat goes dead. I try to keep it right on the edge.

W: *You say you heel the boat somewhat. So half the bottom is flat?*

D: Yes. If the water is really flat, I don't heel it. But if it is really blowing, on an inland lake or small body of water, so there are small waves, I'll heel the boat so half the bottom is flat. In bigger waves, I heel it more, to slice through them better. Maybe it's only psychological, but I feel that if you sail the boat on a slight heel, less of the boat is in the water, so you have reduced the wetted

Interviews with the Champions • 1981-1982

surface. I feel that, as in a Hobie cat, I'm using the chine as an extra daggerboard to reduce slippage. Pierre Siegenthaler is one who does this very well, as far as I'm concerned, in all types of conditions with a great deal of heel.

W: *Let's talk about kinetics. What do you do upwind, if anything?*

D: There is an obvious variation in techniques between sailors, and there are a number of techniques that work. I think there is a parallel between kinetics and boatspeed. The more you use kinetics, the faster you are going to go. But at some point it becomes a question of legality. I feel that I use my body for steering, as opposed to just transforming energy to shoot the boat forward. At some point as I come up a wave, I swing my upper torso forward a little bit to help punch the boat through the wave. I do that in a very subtle motion.

Kinetics is a grey area. As I see it, you can use them "as much as the market will bear." Each fleet has its own definition of what's acceptable behavior and I try to be sensitive to that. You can usually analyze this sort of thing after the first race and sometimes even before it, by talking to racers on shore.

W: *What do you do with your bridle?*

D: I use the rope bridle now and try to gear it just like the wire one. In light air, I actually try to keep the mainsheet centered. Then as the air increases I let the sheet slide off to port when I am on starboard tack. In medium air, I like to put a knot in the rope so the sheet doesn't slide off to port. As the wind picks up more, I let the sheet slide freely in both directions. It's important to let the sheet off on both tacks in heavy air, not just on starboard tack. The key thing that affects leech tension is not necessarily the bridle but the degree of poundage you apply when you pull in the sheet. That's probably more important than the actual location of the bridle, at times.

W: *How about your gooseneck? Do you move it around a lot?*

D: Yes, I feel this is one of the most critical adjustments on the boat. If it's a light-air day, I set the gooseneck at about 17 $^{1}/_{2}$ inches from the tack, but I don't set it tight. For downwind and all other kinds of conditions, I slide it back to around 20 inches. I adjust the gooseneck on the water. As I round the weather mark with the gooseneck at 17 $^{1}/_{2}$ inches, I simply lean forward, stretch my long arm out, grab the gooseneck with my two forefingers, and then with my thumb and little finger I slide the boom forward through the gooseneck so the whole rig goes forward. I think this helps speed and steering downwind.

As I round the leeward mark, I slide the gooseneck back, doing the same thing in reverse. It takes me about five seconds. Once in a while it will get hung up. I try to make sure it doesn't by wrapping light duct tape around the boom and then peeling it off so it leaves a gummy residue that seems to hold the gooseneck in place.

If I am sailing in light air and the velocity of the wind increases dramatically, I adjust the gooseneck as I sail upwind. I find it easier to adjust on the port tack when the gooseneck appears to be close to me. I may lose half a boat length in the process, but in the end I gain a lot of speed.

W: *Do you adjust your foot and luff?*

D: As an experiment and to prove a point to myself I never adjusted my outhauls for the whole summer of 1981. I set them loosely for about eight knots of wind, and when it blew harder, I just left them. I was trying to prove that those kinds of thing aren't that important and that sailing wind shifts is much more

Interviews with the Champions • 1981-1982

important. My boatspeed seemed fine.

Generally, if I want to make adjustments, I start by adjusting the upper outhaul first. I'd say in medium air, maybe 10 to 12 knots, probably the upper outhaul is taut and the lower outhaul is loose. As the wind increases, I make the upper outhaul tight and the lower outhaul taut. Then, as the air gets up to around 20 knots, I make both outhauls tight.

W: *You talked about steering in waves, saying you head up a little as you go up the wave and then bear off and foot down as it goes past. Anything else that you do when you're steering in waves?*

D: There are a couple of things that I keep aware of. I like to look ahead. When I'm sailing upwind in heavy air, I'm spending probably close to 60 or 70 percent of my time not looking at the sail but looking at the wind. I watch what's happening 300 yards ahead of me. I'm not really looking at the sail; I'm sailing by feel.

When I'm sailing through waves, I'm dealing with the wave I'm on, but I'm also looking four or five waves ahead. If I see a really big wave coming and it's compact, I will attempt to steer around it. I would say I'm only successful steering around a wave about half the time because often the wave is so large it would not be beneficial to sail around it. If I can't go around a wave, I try to bear off maybe a degree, gain a bunch of speed and as I come up into a big wave, I tip the boat to leeward and slice through it. I also scoot my torso back, which propels the boat forward somewhat. I don't move very much, just a little bit.

If I'm constantly taking some waves over the bow even with a slight heel, I generally move farther aft. Generally, I hike out spread-eagle style, which is very comfortable for me. In heavy air and big waves, I keep my weight about in the center of the cockpit. If the waves are still a problem, then I end up sitting more toward the back of the cockpit and hiking off my aft leg, which is wedged in between the storage compartment and the top of the deck. My legs are usually long enough that I usually hike off both legs. Only in the most severe conditions do I find myself scooting back farther than the center of the cockpit.

W: *Can you keep it from getting mushy? I find that when I'm that far back, the wind seems to catch the bow.*

D: Yes, I have the same problem, but I think having the wind catch your bow is better than having the bow submarining and taking in water over the splashboards. For the last couple of years, I've been sailing without clam cleats. I just sail with the center ratchet and never cleat the main, because it's always being trimmed and adjusted. Some people ask, "When do you rest?" I say, "If you're resting, you're not going fast."

There are many times sailing downwind when I want to slide my body weight farther forward than the clam cleats. If they're there, I have to hump over them, and it's an awkward body movement. Without the clam cleats, I can slide my buttocks very easily and help plunge the boat over the top of the wave.

W: *One more thing about going to windward - telltales. You don't use the woollies on the sail?*

D: I feel that telltales are extra windage and usually give you a false reading. They certainly give you a false reading on port tack, when you not only have the upper and lower spars distorting the wind, but you also have the sail against the mast, and the scallops as well. I'd be very interested to watch the Sunfish sail in a wind tunnel and see how the wind actually crosses it. I would imagine it would not get flowing smoothly until the last third of the sail because there are so

Interviews with the Champions • 1981-1982

many things to interfere with it.

I just feel that telltales give me a false reading and I don't want to spend time looking at them. I feel I've sailed the boat long enough so I can feel if it's being trimmed optimally. I can spend more beneficial time looking at the waves, and the wind coming across the water. They help me plan my strategy as I go. I feel that I should be reacting to something that is about to happen, not something that has already happened. I'd rather be three or four steps ahead. Then I feel I have better insight, a psychological edge or something. I think there are many absolutely terrific sailors worldwide who use telltales successfully, but they just don't seem to fit my particular style.

W: *Anything about sailing to windward in light air?*

D: Yes, I think it's important to be in harmony with your boat. Your body and the boat must act together. You never want to go through any motions in steering, body adjustments or trim that are rigid or jerky, because they could disturb the flow around the boat. When a puff comes and I have to get up out of the cockpit, I sit up very slowly and stretch my legs slowly so I'm doing it in a very fluid manner. I don't ever sit up and jerk the boat down flat - I try to be graceful. That's part of my philosophy of reacting to that small board. If you jerk the boat, you will interrupt the flow around that small precious board and you will end up inhibiting your speed. Also, when I roll tack, I never jerk the boat around or flap the sails - I use very fluid motion. It's all one big movement in a series of steps.

W: *Let's talk about rounding the weather mark.*

D: After rounding the weather mark, many people automatically start pulling up the daggerboard, adjusting the gooseneck, trying to get water out of the cockpit, untangling the main sheet, whatever. They're not concentrating and they begin to lose speed. Then the guys from behind catch up.

When I round the weather mark, right away I examine the situation and get the boat moving well without making adjustments. I get myself positioned in the fleet where I want to be, high or low. Once I feel I've got my position solidified, I go ahead and raise the daggerboard, move the gooseneck, usually from about 18 inches to 20 inches, and make sure the sail is set right. Then I concentrate on speed.

Downwind in medium to heavy air, I like to put myself in the position where I'm not antagonistic. I feel that if you are going to pass someone, you should not pass right next to him. You should get far enough away from him, get in the passing lane, and go by. Many sailors, if they're going to pass someone to weather, come right up behind him and antagonize him. Then they've got a luffing match on their hands. When I'm going to pass, I get up to four or five boatlengths to weather of everybody; I get clear water and air and by the time they see me coming I'm too far to weather for them to do anything.

Many young people have the philosophy that as soon as you round the weather mark you can relax a little bit and reach. That's not the case for me. I probably work harder on the reaches than I do sailing upwind. I feel I have very good control and that everything anyone else is going to do is very predictable. They're sailing from Point A to Point B, basically in a straight line. All I have to do is make my boat go fast and I'm going to pass people. On reaches, all I have to do is make sure I have free wind and air and then concentrate on sailing my boat right and surfing properly and I can make up a lot of ground.

On the reach, I concentrate on steering with my body by heeling the boat a lot. I try to make as few rudder movements as possible.

It takes energy to turn the rudder, and that has a slowing effect. I concentrate on watching the wind and water, anticipating puffs and lulls and balancing the helm so there is little rudder movement. There are situations when you have to pass someone or get up around the mark - then you have to ignore these things. But for 70 percent of the reach, that's what I try to concentrate on. In my view of a race, there is no place to rest. Even if the whole race takes an hour and a half, I use 100 percent concentration.

W: *You like to drop low in light air, but you go high if it picks up?*

D: Yes, I think it's much more difficult to get yourself in a passing lane in light air. It's harder to get up above the fleet and blow by them, because the variations in speed are so much smaller. The difference between a good light-air sailor and a very good light-air sailor on a reach is not very much. It becomes more of a strategic game in light air, as opposed to a technique-type situation in heavy air. You have to evaluate each situation. If a whole series of boats is going high on a wild reach and you can get some clean waves below them, go for it.

Although there is so much to do as I round the weather mark, I try to anticipate where I want to be in the fleet, if I'm going to go high or low. Many times this is not possible because there's a big mess at the weather mark. It's one of those things you have to play by the moment, but if I can, I try to plan my attack way ahead of time. I also do try to do this as I come down to the leeward mark. I try to determine where I am going to tack and which side I will try to get on. Usually when you round the leeward mark, you're busy getting your boat ready. There are other boats around, and there may be boats coming across on the starboard tack. There may be so much to do that many times you lose the flow. But if you have given some thought to where you want to be, you may be in a better position to handle these things.

W: *Do you feel pumping works well with a Sunfish?*

D: Absolutely. Pumping, as far as I'm concerned, is rhythmic sheeting of the mainsheet, which is in direct violation of the rules. But if there are five other guys who are pumping like heck and it seems to be acceptable behavior, I'm going to pump. Pumping works very well on a Sunfish because of its surfboard-type hull.

W: *What about ooching and sculling?*

D: I'm not an oocher at all, I don't think, and I'm not a sculler. There are some incredible oochers in the Sunfish fleet who have made incredible breakthroughs in sailing the boat off the wind. I think one person who has done it remarkably well is Mike Catalano. He wedges his forward leg between the cockpit and the deck of the boat and flexes his thigh and pushes off the floor in every little wave. It's such a subtle movement I don't even know if you can define it as ooching. He's incredibly fast off the wind, and the way he does it is truly unique.

W: *I've found that when a wave comes up under me, I want to get moving with a scull, an ooch, and a pump, all together. The pump is more to get the sail adjusted to the apparent wind as it moves forward. It seems to work for me. Other guys say they don't do any of that. They just head downhill, as you were describing earlier.*

D: To me, the pump is the main ingredient in getting the boat moving. An ooch may be a secondary movement and a scull I don't think I use very much.

W: *How do you sail the run?*

D: The Sunfish sails by the lee pretty well, so I don't worry about sailing laterally, off to one

Interviews with the Champions • 1981-1982

side or the other. I can concentrate on keeping the bow low and heading downhill into a trough. The Sunfish doesn't want to plane as easily downwind as it does on a reach; you have to do a lot of steering to keep the boat going downhill as much as possible. If that makes you sail by the lee part of the time, don't worry about it. It goes just as fast that way.

I also make sure that I have a long enough mainsheet and that the sail is out all the way, at 90 degrees to the center line of the boat. I heel the boat constantly to weather, even in heavy air, to balance it so I have very little rudder movement. In lighter air, with flat seas, I have the rudder almost glued to the center of the boat. If I want to head up, I flatten the boat a little bit. If I want to go to leeward, I heel the boat a little farther to windward. It's like sailing a sailboard. In fact, one of the best ways to learn to increase your speed downwind in light air in a Sunfish is to start sailing a sailboard because it teaches you how to sail a boat without a rudder.

W: *How do you keep your bow from burying?*

D: If I see myself coming into the backside of a wave, I automatically give a trim to the mainsheet, which has a tendency to lift the bow somewhat, and at the same time I move back in the boat. Sometimes I even try to hike back and lift the boat up with my leg, under the cockpit lip. If you can steer around a wave, fine. But it's inevitable that sometime during the downwind leg, you're going up the backside of a wave.

W: *What is your favorite start?*

D: I like to get a front-row seat and hold my station. If I can hold off the boats to weather, I will automatically develop a hole for myself to leeward. This is what I try to key on, so when I get down to four or five seconds, I can sheet in, peel off a little bit, and have enough room to leeward to really jet out in front of the fleet. The Sunfish's long boom helps because if someone wants to luff you up, he is going to have to go way around your boom. It also helps create your hole to leeward, if you have the boom way out. I think it's very important to be able to hold your boat on station at the starting line. But it's difficult, because the boat is so light, the sail is so big and the daggerboard is so small. The boat tends to skitter around a lot. It takes a lot of practice to keep it hovering in one place. One good exercise is to set up an imaginary starting line and have someone on shore watch and comment on your success as you practice.

W: *Do you have any tuning tips?*

D: One of the things I find inherent in the Sunfish is that the bolt that goes through the tiller and head of the rudder wiggles itself loose and you end up with the cheeks of the rudder fitting loosely. I tighten this up; it's important. Also, when I buy a new boat I tip it over and make sure that the rudder brackets are aligned properly. I pretty much do this visually and if I think they're crooked, I take measurements in relation to the daggerboard and front of the boat. Another important thing I do is install inspection ports on the front vertical wall of the cockpit. I use the kind with O-rings so there is a watertight seal and I install one on each side of the daggerboard. They provide a good view to inspect the inner hull and if I get any water inside I can pull one of these off and sponge out any water in there. This way I can make sure there is absolutely no absorption in the foam or fiberglass.

When the boat comes from the factory, the splashboards are very ridged and burred. I sand them, not to reduce weight but to make sure they're smooth. A great deal of wind comes across the forward side of them and I feel if the wind is deflected by a smooth surface it helps the speed. Also when you get water up there, if it can deflect off a smooth surface, there's less friction slowing you down. Another thing I do with a new boat, and at the beginning of every season, is take off the fittings and bed each one with silicone to make sure it's airtight. That's very critical.

W: *What kind of an end do you put on your stick?*

D: I use a plastic ring but I'm thinking of going to a metal one because I've been breaking the plastic rings every once in a while and that's no fun. Obviously, I use the universal. I also try to make sure I get a tiller with an angle going up, not parallel to the deck. I mark the spars for adjustment purposes and I put a tie around the boom, under the mainsheet, so the boom doesn't get hung up on my life jacket when I tack.

One thing I do is use several different thickness of mainsheet for different wind velocities. I find them helpful. Three-eighths of an inch is the biggest I use and then I go down to ¹/₄ inch line for light air. For the halyard and all the lines I get pre-stretched line so I don't get any lag at all. Whenever I get a new mainsheet, even the pre-stretched variety, I tie it to a tree, hook it up to my car, and stretch that baby out. Then, when I put it on the boat, I get .001 percent of stretch.

W: *That seems like a delicate adjustment.*

D: It works well. It's amazing how much they will stretch, and you want that energy right away when you sheet in.

W: *What about the shape of the edge of the board and rudder? Do you worry about them?*

D: The rudder I don't worry about at all. I do pay attention to the smoothness and actual size of the daggerboard. I always sail with the old-type board and try to have the biggest size the rules permit. I file the leading edge andmake it as blunt as possible, like a semi-circle. I make the trailing edge somewhat tapered, but you can't taper much because of the rules.

W: *What about physical fitness?*

D: I'm into that a lot; I think it's a big help. I do a combination of weights, for upper-body strengthening, and running. In the book I'm doing I talk a lot about being able to simulate sailing off the hiking bench. I don't like working on a hiking bench, but I force myself to do so.

A typical workout for me is running three miles on Tuesday, Thursday and Saturday. On Monday, Wednesday and Friday I work with weights - bench and military presses, foreleg and reverse leg curls, some isometrics on the arms, then maybe about 20 minutes of sit-ups with weights on the hiking bench. As April comes along and the lake opens up, I sail as much as I can and on days I sail, I don't exercise.

The areas I work on for strength are thigh muscles and muscles for hiking. Because I don't use clam cleats, I try to work a lot on forearm strength. I have to be able to hold on to the mainsheet for an hour and a half, so I do a lot of forearm curls and reverse arm curls. In about a year, I've put on a lot of weight and strength. I've been working on upper body strength, which will help in hiking and is also important for carrying weight without fatigue. The minute lactic acid builds up or the minute you have fatigue in your body, your chances of making sound, rational tactical decisions are reduced. If you could sail a fatigue-free race, your chances of thinking clearly are greatly increased. That to me is half of racing, being in shape.

W: *Do you believe in getting out on the course early?*

D: I definitely believe in it, but often I don't live up to my beliefs. I think it's important to get out there early to examine the starting line and the windward leg.

W: *What about clothing?*

Interviews with the Champions • 1981-1982

D: I think it's important to dress properly. I mean not only warmly but so that your clothing does not restrict any blood flow. Some people just wear a couple of pairs of sweat pants. On a Sunfish this may not be a good idea because when you hike out, the metal chroming on the edge will restrict the blood flow into the lower ends of your legs. If you restrict blood flow you have a bigger chance of lactic acid build-up. I wear hiking pants. They have pads in them that make it much more comfortable to hike out and keep the blood flowing.

I also think it's important, when you're doing a lot of trimming on the mainsheet and pumping off the wind, that the upper body has a lot of free movement, especially if you carry weight. That's why I like to wear sweat shirts and warm clothing. But I wear the sleeveless types so they don't restrict my movement. I don't sail with a life jacket as the last layer of clothing. It's good to wear a tee shirt or something over it because it is inevitable that when you tack with the Jens rig or whatever, the mainsheet or the boom is going to get caught on top of the life jacket as you tack. I also wear suspenders because they keep my shoulders rolled in as well as holding up my hiking shorts. Wearing the right kind of clothing is essential.

W: *What do you wear on your feet?*

D: I don't wear those silly boat shoes. I put on a long pair of knee socks and wear a pair of tennis shoes, hightops. I get plenty of ankle support and it seems like the rubber on the bottom of those is very good when it's wet. You get lots of traction. You know the drainage groove off the storage area? I wedge my foot in there so when I hike out I can help pull the boat flat. When I torque my body, I flex off that leg. It's like wearing a ski boot. If your leg is wedged there tight, whatever movement you make with your upper muscles is going to be transferred right into the ski. When I jerk my leg up, I automatically transfer my energy into the boat. I do that constantly when I'm sailing in heavy air.

W: *Who do you think are the best sailors in the Class?*

D: Dave Chapin is absolutely a superior sailor. Remarkable. He is a very, very smart tactical sailor with a keen nose for the wind shifts. Another person who is consistently up there is Paul Odegaard; I was delighted to hear he won the North Americans. Mike Catalano's good and also Paul Fendler, but Paul hasn't sailed Sunfish much lately. Cor van Aanholt is good as well.

I like the Sunfish Class because it is one of the few classes that is transitional, old-to-young. The Laser Class is all young people. The Sunfish Class has a universal spread of people and sexes, which I think is a big benefit to the class.

W: *What about women? Can they compete with the best men sailors?*

D: They don't have the upper-body strength that men have. I think that when they compete against men in heavy air, they're at a disadvantage for that reason alone. In light air, I think they should be just as good. Traditionally sailing has been a man's sport, but I'd like to see many more women in it. They should be superior to men because physiologically their bodies are much more fluid. They are more flexible and agile, so in light air they should be able to excel. One who has excelled in the Laser is Suzie Pegel. She's phenomenal. I hope and I think that the number of women in sailing will continue to increase. They need to organize well and they need to get out there and do it - they cannot be shy. Women's sailing is still in the embryonic stages, and it needs a few more years before it takes off.

W: *Thank for all the tips, Derrick.*

● Joel Furman

Joel Furman is a light-air ace who walked away with the North American Championship in 1975 on Indian Lake in Ohio. That was mostly a series of drifters, except for one horrendous thunderstorm that scattered the fleet. He's done well in Worlds competition, winning a couple of light-air races. His dad, George, was also a perennial winner in Senior Olympic Sunfish competitions. Joel, at this writing, is Class Measurer for both USSCA and ISCA (which also puts him on the International Class Advisory Council and the Rules Committee for USSCA) as well as the Regional Representative for the New York Region. My hat's off to Joel. Chief Measurer is the toughest job in the Class in terms of psychic wear and tear. No one likes to be told his boat doesn't measure in. To do that on top of handling the New York Region's affairs is rare dedication.

Will: You're a demon in light air. How do you make a Sunfish go to windward in light air?

Joel: I don't know whether weight has much to do with it or not. It's kind of a compromise between pinching the boat as much as possible and keeping the windward chine in the water, heeling the boat to windward. I found this most successful when the wind is blowing between five and ten miles per hour. I know whether it's the right time to position the boat that way from a typical coat hanger telltale. When the string is blowing about 45 degrees from vertical, that's the right time. In wind above 10 to 12 miles per hour, I sail pretty much on an even plane, like everyone else.

W: *For telltales you just use a coat hanger with a piece of string sticking straight up front?*

J: No, the coat hanger wire I usually use is about 14 inches long and runs in a straight plane

Interviews with the Champions • 1981-1982

about three feet up on the gaff, right across the front of the boat. The piece of string is about six inches long and I usually get it by pulling a canvas string out of the sail bag. For windward work on starboard tack, if you find yourself pointing the string towards the mast, you're about right. On port tack, if you point the string toward the back edge of the sail, the leech, that's about right.

W: *And you say you actually heel to windward?*

J: Yes. I'm not sure how to describe it. When you get enough air to feel a little resistance on the tiller or the rudder, then you can heel the boat to windward. As soon as that resistance comes off the tiller, you know that the boat is no longer sliding sideways, but is going straight ahead. That's the best I can do to describe it. It seems to be very successful, especially with the lanyard system on the old sail. I found that with lace lines instead of the plastic clips, you could move the draft of the sail around.

W: *I gather that, at least in light air, you're a pincher rather than a footer?*

J: Yes, as much as possible. The idea is to get the boat footing and then pinch it up. There is kind of a break point between footing and pinching, about halfway between the two. I think most people fall off and start to foot when they feel themselves start to slide sideways. I think if you go up higher, you can go through that break point, and if you heel the boat to windward, it makes it easier. Then you lose all resistance on the tiller, so you know you're not stalled, not sideslipping. That's when you know you're going. It works. It's critical to position your weight right.

W: *What do you do when the wind picks up?*

J: The more wind there is, the farther aft I move my weight. I move to the middle of the cockpit and hike out with my legs spread in the cockpit. It feels more like working with a surfboard than a boat.

W: *What about the bridle?*

J: I let it slide on the starboard tack and I keep it in the middle on the port tack.

W: *No matter what the wind?*

J: No matter what the wind. With the new sail most people let it go on both sides. How do you do it?

W: *I really haven't learned the new sail either, but I've been tying knots in the bridle so I can vary the distance the sheet will slide. I keep it in closer in lighter air and let it go farther and farther out as the wind picks up. But I find that I'm not particularly faster that way. I like the new sail in heavy air, but I don't like it in light air.*

J: The best success I ever had with the new sail was when I bought one of the brand-new ones down in Gulfport for the North Americans. Catalano was picking on me as I was putting the new sail on the spars and because I was talking to him I made a mistake and put the sail on upside down. I didn't know I'd done it until I got out on the water and hoisted the sail. As usual I was the last one to leave the beach - I can't break precedent. I had to keep going to the starting line, which was three or four miles out. I couldn't believe how I was going by boats all the way out there. It was incredible, with the numbers upside down and the window going vertically. Before the start I had time to turn it around and I was sorry I did. I no longer had the same speed.

W: *Did you ever try it again?*

J: No, I've never done it again. I don't know if there is a variance to the draft of the sail or what, but I sure would like to try it. It probably wouldn't be legal since the Sunfish would be in the wrong position and the numbers would also be improperly positioned.

W: *Mike Catalano still doesn't think the new sails are any better. He still likes his old sail.*

Interviews with the Champions • 1981-1982

J: Really? Well, I feel the same way as far as light air is concerned. I like my old sails. But when it gets above - actually, I'm not sure the velocity of the wind matters. I think the difference comes about when there is a chop. The newer sail definitely puts you through the chop, compared with the old sail. So that's the advantage.

W: *How do you carry the foot and the luff?*

J: It's hard for me to get over the old ways. I keep going back to them and that's probably why I haven't been as successful lately. I carry both the foot and luff quite tight. I don't have them as loose as everyone else usually does. Anything to keep the darts out of the sail. With my lanyard system, I'm always working to keep the darts out. I like to have a clean-looking sail. The lanyards control the leech. In light air, I tighten down on the last grommet on both the gaff and on the end of the boom. That gives the leech a bit of a curl. That curl pushes you to windward, especially if you are working in light air. It makes it easier to pinch. When it blows hard, I loosen the leech by loosening the last strings on the two grommets on the end.

W: *Do you have any particular steering techniques in light air?*

J: In light air I don't move the tiller at all. In fact, I try to arrange it so that the boat will sail itself without my moving the tiller for at least three to five seconds. If you can get it up to about 10 seconds, you've got it. You're steering with just your weight. That's when it's right. As little movement as possible with the tiller makes a big difference. If anything, I think I try to stay with the tiller to leeward a little bit.

W: *Let's get on to reaching. What do you do?*

J: I try to steer a straight course from one mark to the next. Generally, as you round the first windward mark, everyone goes to windward right away. I usually sail on the straight course for the first 15 to 25 yards and then I try to slide off to leeward as much as possible. That way I'm clear of everyone. They think they're going like bandits, but nine times out of ten they're not sailing a true course to the next mark. Since the majority of people go to windward together, they're fighting for the same air. After you sacrifice the first 20 to 30 yards, you'll find you have clear air; unless Will White decides to contend with you. It's lonely there.
Nine times out of ten you are eliminating yourself from the typical fight at the gybe mark. When you arrive there you have the advantage of being the inside boat on the gybe and you also have the best speed toward the mark, as opposed to those who went to windward early. You can also pick your wave and go wherever you want to go when you are down to leeward. Coming into the mark on a collision course with the other boats, you have the right of way. You still have air coming in at the very last minute at the mark, as opposed to the boats that are dropping down. They're still fighting for air. You also have the advantage of being able to keep your boat moving.

W: *How about the second reaching leg?*

J: The second leg usually turns out to be a broad reach. Like everyone else, I find myself heeling the boat to windward, keeping the sail up in the air as much as possible. Again, I usually try to drop off to leeward to get away from the crowd. I find the boat actually goes faster if you're sailing below the line. For some reason, Sunfish seem to go faster when you're sailing by the lee. It gives you better opportunity to take advantage of the waves and it gives you better boatspeed.

W: *What about kinetics?*

J: On a reaching leg, I mentally visualize myself

Interviews with the Champions • 1981-1982

as being on a surfboard rather than a sailboat. You can actually gain about half a knot if you scoot forward in waves and then scoot back at the end of a series of waves. It pays to move your weight in a Sunfish. Even moving three or four inches makes a difference. The harder it blows, the less time you have to move your rear end. But just by leaning forward and back with your upper torso you can have a tremendous amount of modulation.

W: *How do you keep your bow from burying?*

J: I pray a lot. Sometimes it's so bad you literally have to almost hang tail off the stern of the boat.

W: *You have to do a lot of steering?*

J: Yes, the harder it's blowing, the more you have to steer. You can't make any mistakes. If you do, you're going to find your boat under water. Then it's all over. I think you have to do a lot with the centerboard too. Just a couple of inches of board in the water can make a big difference.

W: *How about the start?*

J: I like to start by myself. I think probably the bigger the regatta, the more important it is to get an excellent start. I think it's absolutely necessary to be aggressive. It's so amazing that the majority of Sunfish sailors are so intent on concentrating on their watches that they lose sight of the boats around them. You've got to be totally aware of all four directions around you and at the same time you have to computerize yourself with the time sequence. You can't be preoccupied with worrying about how much time you have left. You have to stay aware of what the situation is around you. A tremendous number of openings are going to materialize even though you see boats all around you and it seems there's nowhere for you to go. You'll find that there will be room, there will be places for you to duck into, but you must stay alert and take advantage of them to get a good start.

W: *When one end of the line is favored, do you fight it out there?*

J: No. Unless I'm absolutely sure that I can get the number one spot, I won't fight for it. Especially when I know that some sailors, particularly in the Sunfish league, are always there. I won't get into a fight because I have found that it's better to sacrifice proper positioning to gain that clear air spot.

W: *What about weight? Do you worry about weight?*

J: If it's going to blow more than 15 miles per hour, I might just as well stand on the shore and knock my knees to the wind. I feel that you have to be in about the 160- to 170-pound range to do well when it's blowing hard.

W: *Have you tried wearing weight?*

J: Yes, I've tried wearing a water jacket for the past three years. Anytime it blows hard, I have to put it on. It helps me, and it does make a difference. I find that I'm at least within shooting or knocking distance of the front door when I get to the windward mark, as compared to when I don't wear weight. It also makes me work a lot harder to windward when I know I have the weight on me, so there's a psychological effect. It's a lot easier handling the puffs. I don't have to wear the sheet out when I get hit by them. I know I'm going to get immediate response from the boat by shifting my weight, instead of having to wait for the response after I make an alteration to the sail. The more weight you have, the better off you are. I wish my father could transfer his gut to mine.

W: *How about the Jens rig? I'm sure you use it.*

J: Yes. Remember the *Yacht Racing/Cruising* magazine edition from the Netherlands? I was the example of the Jens that they pictured and that really surprised me because I think

I was probably the one candidate who never did really figure out how to set up that arrangement right. It never worked for me there.

I guess it was in Aruba that I finally was able to find the fine points of the rig. I learned that it is critical to keep the sail adjusted exactly right. I found that if I moved it even about half-an-inch to an inch, then I lost balance control - which made a terrific difference in my ability to go to windward. To me, the sacrifice in using the Jens was not worth it unless I needed it to survive. Even then I was sorry to use it. I think I would have done a lot better if I had not used it in the first four races in the Netherlands.

W: *I didn't use it in the Netherlands and wished I had. I guess we find our excuses where we can.*

J: In Aruba, it was necessary to use the Jens. My problem was that I would beat my brains out to get into about the top 15 boats to windward and then I would end up capsizing because my water jacket wouldn't clear the boom.

W: *What about your board?*

J: I've stayed with the original board. It still has the original shape from the factory. I use the sander and take off the varnish that they put on and then brush on fiberglass resin. I don't brush it on like everyone else does, though - with the grain. I go from one side to the other, with the water flow. Then, I sand the same way. Usually about two or three coats of that resin does the trick. I don't put any coloration in it.

W: *You don't put any fiberglass on it?*

J: No, the glass to me is a pain in the neck. It's going to come off if it gets hit, anyway. So what's the difference? It just adds more weight to the board.

W: *Any other wrinkles or gadgets?*

J: The best I've ever done was the North American Championship in Ohio. I had two watches, both of which broke after the first race. I had two compasses, both of which I lost. I didn't have anything. I had to handmake a telltale in the middle of the series because I lost the Feathermate one. That's when I started using just a regular coat hanger and the string from the sail bag.

W: *Thanks, Joel.*

Interviews with the Champions • 1981-1982

Paul Odegaard

No one ever tried harder than Paul Odegaard and no one ever got a bigger hand at an awards ceremony than he did when he won the 1981 Sunfish North Americans in Charleston, South Carolina, at the age of 44. It was a popular win. He has also won the Northeast Regional Championship, which many feel is tougher some years than the North Americans. Paul is particularly tough upwind in heavy air and is a student of the boat. As an engineer, he applies his studies in aerodynamics and hydrodynamics to his boat tuning. In 1985, he was elected the second President of the International Sunfish Class Association, and has put in an incredible amount of time on the Advisory Council.

Will: *We're just going to go around the course, first of all. Talk to me a little bit about how you make a Sunfish go to windward.*

Paul: Well, in medium to heavy air, which I really enjoy, I think one of the most important things is the hiking. A lot of sailors don't really hike properly. You should get completely over the side hooking your feet on the main sheet as it goes through the Harken or by just barely putting a couple of toes under the cockpit lip. It makes a difference in heavy air. It's always your weight versus the boat's weight. I like to wear my weight from the waist down. Since I tend to stay wet if I'm hiking, I wear heavy sweat pants rather than weight on the shoulders. It's really tough to move around the boat with weight above the waist.

Then there's playing the waves. With the little freeboard on the bow of the Sunfish, it's very important to keep the bow up as you go through the waves. You should constantly move your body fore and aft and in and out, hiking to keep the bow from burying. You also have to really honk on the helm to keep the boat moving because there doesn't seem to be enough rudder area. I bear up as the wave approaches and then I give a good pull on the helm to get the boat to veer off down the trough. In some cases when I get a very big wave, I go almost head-to-wind and move aft, way aft, to the back of the boat, to keep the bow from being buried. I think that pinching on very big waves is even more important than trying to bear off. I've had an awful lot of success by always being a pincher rather than a footer. Even in heavy air, I try to keep the boat flat and play the waves rather than powering off.

W: *But if you're pinching and you head into a wave, how do you get speed to get over it?*

P: Well, you pinch and then veer off. You alternate the two.

W: *Are you working the sheet too?*

P: Yes, depending on how much it's blowing. As you come up the wave, sheet in; as you veer

Interviews with the Champions • 1981-1982

off, let the sheet out. Trouble is, in heavy air you get so damn tired.

W: *How do you use the bridle?*

P: I've always used the full traveler, both sides, even in medium air. I have never been able to get the boat going when the sheet was clipped in the middle. Of course, I've always had a fairly full sail. I can remember many events when the thing would catch in the middle and the boat would stop - something was wrong. I would look around and there it was, the traveler stuck in the middle. I would push it to leeward and the boat would go again.

W: *How about your gooseneck? Do you play with that?*

P: Well, in light and medium air, I always move it forward. It seems to let the boat point a lot better. With my old stretched sail, in seas and 10 to 15 knots of wind, I always kept it within two or three inches of the aft clip. With the new Fogh sail, it seems to go better with the gooseneck further aft, but it's awfully easy to get a lee helm. I had it too far back this summer and a few times I let go of the helm and instead of coming up, the boat bore off. With the old Ratsey sail I never had that situation.

W: *How tight do you keep your foot and your luff? Do you play with the outhauls?*

P: Not when I'm racing. I set them up with the classic adjustments. If it's blowing, I honk the luff down as far as I can. In very, very light air, I adjust it fairly tightly - not really tight, but so that there are no wrinkles. Then in medium air I adjust it somewhere in between. The new sail is so full that letting the outhaul loose so that there are scallops along the luff doesn't make sense anymore.
I have never played with stretching the foot. I tighten it just enough so that there are no wrinkles under sail.

W: *One more question on the beat. How do you tack?*

P: In light air, some sort of roll tack works fairly well. But in heavy air, I come around so fast it's not necessary. I try playing the waves so that I don't get stopped by one as I'm coming about. It's a question of judgement. Every third or fourth wave is a biggy, so once it's past, that's the time to tack.

W: *Do you look for a flat place in the water, or do you try to pirouette around on top of the wave?*

P: The Sunfish doesn't tack that fast. I think in a tack you're certainly going to be involved in a couple of waves. It's not the way you can turn on top of a mogul in skiing. You turn on one wave, but you're probably going to hit one or two more. After I get hit by a big wave, I try to get my speed up and then tack. I look for a flat part between waves.

W: *What about your centerboard and rudder?*

P: The Sunfish has too small a board and rudder for the sail area, so the boat tends to stall out. Once you get a high degree of water flow on the leading edge of the centerboard, the boat stalls if you have a sharp leading edge. So the blunt two-to-one ellipse leading edge of the old board makes a world of difference. Especially in situations where you are over-powered. In light air, even light to medium air, the leading edge doesn't make that much difference.
All the boards Alcort has made for the last 15 years are useless, I think. You have to use Bondo body putty, and build them up. We made a template for the leading edge. (See page 44.) With that, you can grind down the Bondo to get a perfect ellipse. I think it's very important to have a blunt leading edge, but there is an optimum airfoil shape. Of course you only have a little over an inch to play with, but a two-to-one ellipse is very close. I went to a NACA airfoil book one day and found that what we have on the board is about as close as you can get to an optimum leading

Interviews with the Champions • 1981-1982

edge for good stall resistance.

A blunt rudder is also awfully important. Unless a person has some aerodynamic engineering background, he thinks sharp is nice - it slices through the water. He doesn't realize that the boat is going to go sideways.

W: *What about kinetics? You were talking about moving around in the boat, getting the bow up and all that.*

P: I read an article on it once. I've been trying to practice it for years and still can't get it down. The classic thing is to get the boat on a plane by giving it a couple of pumps and then veering off down the wave. I have not had much luck at it, especially on reaches. To windward I do fine, but on the reaches I've always had guys go by me.

W: *I think that's as much a function of weight as anything.*

P: Well, I don't know. In Sardinia in one race I was first to the windward mark by 50 yards and the second guy was Chapin. He passed me on the reach and had 50 yards on me at the next mark. We weigh about the same. It's a very delicate thing, the right pump and you get the boat going and surf down the wave. He had it, and I didn't.

The master I've watched and marveled at is Catalano. He's all over the race course and able to veer off and keep the boat going downhill for a higher percentage of the time than anybody else. It obviously makes yards of difference. It's a real art and I think it just takes a lot of time and practice to be able to master it.

W: *Do you use the halyard end as a vang?*

P: Only to pull the gooseneck down when it blows. With the new sail being as full as it is, I think that it makes a big difference to pull the gooseneck down when it blows, to try to flatten the sail out. There aren't that many things you can do to flatten out the sail.

W: *How about on the run? What kind of things do you do?*

P: I think it is very effective to sit to windward and sail with an extreme heel, almost capsizing, without dragging your butt in the water. That delicate balance of almost going over, to reduce the wetted area and get the sail upright, make a big difference. Almost everybody does it, but not to the extreme of almost capsizing. I think the last six inches or whatever makes a difference.

W: *Do you worry about the weight of your boat?*

P: I think weight is important and very little has been written about it. It should be pointed out that the class has no hull weight limits, although there is a rule that you can't take flotation out of the hull. You can race any weight boat that you can find.

I remember one year we weighed our boats at Bolton Lake. We weighed probably 25 boats. They ranged from my boat, which was the heaviest at 159 pounds, to Major Hall's at 117 pounds. Both boats were dry, factory-built and there had been no adjustments - yet there was a 40-pound difference. If you've ever picked up a water bag weighing 15 pounds and put it on your shoulders, you know it feels like a ton of bricks. People are going around with 20, 30, 40 excess pounds in their boats. That's just dead weight.

W: *I had one super-light boat that was real loose and I couldn't go anywhere, especially in heavy air.*

P: I went through that too. One year at Madison, both my vertical foam blocks fell down. I looked in through my port and I could see the bottom of the boat flexing up and down a couple of inches. I never went so fast in my life. I did just super. There were waves, it was blowing, but the boat went tremendously. I thought it was going to break. I'd come off a wave and the whole boat would shake, but it went like hell.

I'd just like to point out that there's a variety in boat weight. Someone who's a little on the heavy side should shop around. There are a lot of light boats out there.

There are all kinds of methods for drying your boat out. People may realize that they have a leaker and think that it's tough to fix. But there's no trick. You can certainly get the weight down to where it's supposed to be. Just blow into the drain port with a vacuum cleaner, track down the leaks and plug them up. There's no reason why the thing has to leak. Once you get the thing to stop leaking, open the inspection port and leave the boat in the sun to dry out.

I've used desiccant, which absorbs about its own weight in water. You can buy these bags of silica gel and stick them in the hull and then close up the hull. Later you pick the bag up and it's twice the original size. It will suck the boat absolutely dry. It's now being sold for cruising boats to keep moisture out of lockers and things. After it soaks up the water, you stick the bag in the oven for 12 hours or something like that.

It dries out and you can use it again and again. At major events, I always dry out the hull. I put the desiccant in at night and then take it out in the morning and the boat is as dry as can be.

W: *Any other boat tuning ideas?*

P: Another thing on the centerboards. The class gives the tolerances, which are usually plus or minus a quarter of an inch. According to Alcort's Steve Baker, that really means that if you have a board cut to factory specifications, you'll find that you're a quarter-inch under the max. That quarter inch can make a big difference. So in working on the leading and trailing edges, the name of the game is to bring them up to the maximum.

I have a tip on the bailer. I've got a little gismo in there that really works well. The standard plastic bailer with the cap on the top doesn't fit well. It leaks and is very difficult to undo when you are on a plane. I've hooked up a plumber's half-inch faucet washer on the end of a string and it fits in the hole exactly. So you can go to windward without the bailer open. As you veer off on the reach, even when you are hiking, you can just reach over, pull the string and your bailer is open.

W: *You don't kick it loose when you tack?*

P: No, I haven't had any problems. I drilled a hole in the back of the cockpit and the line is long enough to hang back into the storage well.

W: *How do you like to start?*

P: In the big regattas, a start I've been able to get away with is a late start at the committee boat. It seems that at big events, like the North Americans and the Worlds, people are a little nervous and tend to get up to the line early. They usually go for the middle of the line or try to be up on it. I just kind of hold back, stay in a barging position at the committee boat end of the line, and come in late. I've got speed. Chances are a hole will develop and I can go on to port tack. I might sacrifice five to ten seconds, but within about 30 seconds after the start, I have free air and can tack. That's the tactic I usually use and I've had tremendous luck with it.

W: *Thanks for your help, Paul.*

Interviews with the Champions • 1981-1982

Nat Philbrick

Nat Philbrick comes from a 100-percent Sunfish family. Father Tom and mother Marianne were regular winners in Senior Olympic competition. Brother Sam has done well in the big competitions, including a ninth at the Worlds in 1979 and an 11th at the 1978 North Americans. Nat's wife Melissa was second at the Women's North Americans in 1981. Nat himself was North American Champion in 1978, and was fifth at the Worlds in 1978 and fourth in 1979. He was an Assistant Editor of *Yacht Racing/Cruising*. (Another Sunfish North American Champion, Major Hall, was Editor for several years.)

Will: Let's get into the details of how you make a Sunfish go to windward.

Nat: The primary factor in a Sunfish, compared to other boats, is the fact that it has a chine. So you want to sail it heeled a little more than you would most boats. In light air, I find that speed to weather is a function of making sure you have enough helm. If a puff lets up, you have to come in; when you anticipate a puff, you have to go out. The boat is so underpowered that if you are not attuned to what's happening with the wind, you can really stall out quickly. A lot of Sunfish sailors seem to just sit there and lose track of that aspect of sailing.

In heavy air, it's a lot like any other boat. You have to play the mainsheet and steer around the waves.

W: Talk about playing the mainsheet.

N: In light air, I usually hold it above the Harken. I pull it in if I'm trying to head up and let it out if I'm trying to come down. When in doubt, I let it out. I play with about four-inch lengths of sheet and try not to steer too much.

W: Would you consider yourself a pincher or a footer?

N: It's a fine line. I always watch how I am sailing

in relation to the rest of the fleet. At times, I'll try to pinch a little bit more, but it depends what kind of shift I'm sailing into. If I expect a header, I'll foot off. If it's a lay line situation and I want to stay above somebody, I'll pinch. I try to keep my options open. If I find myself footing all the time, it's because I can't point - and vice versa.

I keep my sail a little flatter than most people. I usually have the outhauls pretty tight, even in light to medium air. It's easier for a boat to stall out with a flatter sail, so you have to be careful.

W: *How about the bridle?*

N: I used to just clip the sheet in the middle. Now I'm using the "Hoyt effect" more and more. This means clipping the sheet to the port side of the bridle. It's named after Garry Hoyt, first World Sunfish Champion, who introduced the idea. I'm beginning to let the sheet slide when I'm on port tack, as well as on starboard tack. You know, taping the bridle so the sheet slides from side to side.

W: *How about the gooseneck?*

N: That's a very critical adjustment. In light air, I put it far forward, almost approaching the sail clip. It's a function of how much helm I have. If I'm not pointing, I move the gooseneck forward. In my sailing career, I've had a tendency to move it farther and farther forward. It seems to help pointing a lot. As conditions get heavier and I can't hold the boat down, I move the gooseneck aft. Before I used the Jens rig, I'd bring the gooseneck way back. It was just about the only way of depowering. Then, with the Jens rig, I discovered you have to move the gooseneck way forward. That was something I had to find out for myself. I think some people don't move it around as much.

W: *How do you steer through waves? Do you head up going up the wave and bear off going down?*

N: Yes, that's standard. I just make sure I have plenty of speed to do any kind of maneuver I want to do and I don't head up if I'm not going fast enough.

W: *What about tacking? Do you feel roll tacking is important?*

N: Yes, particularly in light air. In heavy air, if you don't time it right and don't use your body right, you can get in irons. It's a little more important on a Sunfish than it is on a lot of other boats, just because of that.

W: *Do you face forward or aft when you tack?*

N: I face forward.

W: *How about telltales?*

N: I usually use tape-recording tape on wires on the upper spar.

W: *How about reaches? How do you sail them?*

N: I use a lot of body movement and play the sail constantly. I always check to see how I'm steering in relation to the rhumb line, checking that I'm not getting too far to weather. I like to leave the rest of the fleet alone and go for it.

W: *Try to describe the kinetics you use. I know it's sort of like trying to tell people how to ride a bike, but give it a shot.*

N: Okay. The kinetics I use are really to help steer the boat. In a lull, when the boat goes flat and I want to initiate a move to weather, I come in. I come in and head up just to help the boat through a stagnant period, to keep the wind flow over the sails. If the wind comes up again, I go out, flatten the boat down and use the opportunity to bring myself back down towards the rhumb line.

W: *Do you do much pumping to get on a plane?*

N: It really depends on the wave conditions. If there are a lot of waves, yes, I do an awful lot of pumping. You really have to, in order to make sure the boat's jumping on every possible wave. Sometimes it can be an almost continual process, which is very exhausting.

Interviews with the Champions • 1981-1982

W: *Okay, let's get on to the run. Tell me about how you run.*

N: Particularly in heavy air and waves, you can go a lot faster than everybody else by keeping the boat right on the edge, heeling to weather. By playing that mainsail so that it's really cocked up, you can catch waves more easily and sustain a plane much better. The whole rig is more balanced when you're right on the edge.

W: *How do you keep the bow from burying?*

N: That's a tough one, because the fastest point of sail will often be just before the bow digs in. It may take a few pichpoles to discover just when you have to jump back. Sometimes, I yank hard on the sheet, bear off dramatically and come out of it. It's often easier if you just head up out of it. If it's really looking like it's a dive, you have to do something quickly.

W: *How do you like to start?*

N: Fairly conservatively. I want the ability to keep up close to the line. It's more important to me to have free air and options than going for a great start. Usually, I'm somewhere around the favored end.

W: *What about in a great big fleet, like at the Worlds?*

N: The lines are long, but they are usually pretty good. If there is a favored side, it's good to get in that area - but just make sure you're in the first row. If you're not, then it's a disaster. I like to keep my options open so I can clear my air and get to the favored side.

W: *What about your rudder and board? Do you do anything to them?*

N: Actually, I hate to say this, but my father does everything to our boards. That's his hobby and he spends all his winter just doing boards and rudders. He's a foil expert. He does amazing things to the foils. He's turned the original new-style boards, the very small ones, into the new Barrington boards. They just grow to his touch. He blunts the leading edge and has an elaborate system of gelcoating and painting. He has experimental boards that he plays with to see what happens.

W: *How about the tiller and the hiking stick?*

N: I add a little glass around the tiller where the bridle chafes. I guess it's legal to have a universal joint now, but I haven't gotten to that point yet. I use a brass ring at the end of the tiller extension.

W: *Anything special on the sheet?*

N: I just use a standard dacron line. When I was organized, I had two sheets. One for light or moderate air and a thicker one for heavier air. I think it is a mistake to have one that's too long. In heavy air, if you gybe and lose the sheet and the knot is out too far, you can dump to weather.

W: *Too short a sheet isn't good either. What about the bottom? Do you do anything with that?*

N: During the season, I'll wash it every now and then. Before a regatta, I'll sand it and fill in the dents. I sand with standard #400 or #600 wet sandpaper and use Marinetex to fill in the dents.

W: *Let's talk about sails.*

N: Okay. I think the new sails look great compared to the old ones. My first experience with a new sail was this summer and it seemed to be just as fast as the old one without doing anything dramatically different. Originally, it had a little more fullness than I wanted. I don't adjust my outhauls that much. I try to get a nice shape for what I think the conditions will be for that race. My upper spar is always a little tighter than my lower spar. I use lines instead of sail clips on the last two grommets on each spar, so I can adjust my leech.

W: *Do you worry about weight and stiffness? Which is the most important?*

N: In a Sunfish I think that stiffness is by far

the most important thing. I'm always amazed how weight doesn't seem to make that much difference. I used to have a boat that was 30 pounds heavier than the one I have now and it didn't seem much different. In heavy-air planing, the lighter boat seemed to be a bit quicker. But in anything else, I couldn't tell the difference.

W: *Do you fill in the trunk much? Do you worry about vibration?*

N: Yes. I get the trunk as smooth as possible. If there's vibration, there's usually something wrong with the board. It may just be a little ding. Or it's not absolutely straight - there's a twist in it or something.

W: *Do you do any particular exercises to get in shape?*

N: I run a little bit, but I wouldn't say it's really for sailing. The only reason I was in shape in 1978 was because I was sailing all the time. For me, arm strength is the first thing that goes. If I were going to be competitive, racing in the Worlds, I know I would have to do a lot of upper-body exercise.

W: *How about weight? Do you ever wear weight?*

N: The most I would put on is four sweat shirts. I'm morally against water jackets and things like that. They hurt my back - I think that's where my morals come from. I don't get mad if somebody else uses them. More power to them. I just don't think it's worth it.

W: *How about clothing? Do you wear padding under those thighs?*

N: I would now if I had to do a lot of racing. When I'm sailing a lot in the Sunfish, I guess the calluses are there. I'll maybe wear an extra pair of shorts. I find what is really important is the texture of what you have on your rear end. You want something you are able to push against. You don't want something too slippery and you don't want something that's like sandpaper.

W: *Thanks, Nat.*

Interviews with the Champions • 1981-1982

Cor van Aanholt

Cor van Aanholt, 1980 Sunfish World Champion, started sailing in 1971 at the age of 12. He and his brother began racing in the Flits class (an 11½ foot wooden two-man boat popular in the northern Netherlands for juniors up to age 18). They won the Flits Nationals twice in a row when Cor was 13 and 14. The next year, Cor crewed for his older brother Peter in a Flying Junior. Cor was tactician and Peter handled the helm and kept the boat moving.

Cor was impatient crewing, so he looked around for a good single-hander. He said that although he didn't particularly like the looks of the Laser, he sailed one anyway because they were popular. At age 17, he won the famous Kielwoche in Kiel, West Germany (Kiel Week was used in 1980 by the nations boycotting the Olympics as a substitute event). This qualified him for the 1976 Laser Worlds, in which he finished sixth. He placed very well in several major Laser championships and placed second in the 1979 Sunfish Worlds in Medemblik, Holland.

He arrived in Aruba for the 1980 Sunfish Worlds two-and-a-half weeks prior to the event. He said that he often does this to acclimatize himself to the differences in time, weather and food. He sailed only three times on a borrowed Sunfish - he said that he doesn't think sailing is the best way to psych up for a regatta. He prefers to see the area or country he is visiting. This sightseeing gives him plenty of time for relaxation, which he considers essential to good sailing. Like most good sailors, Cor always arrives at the starting line at least 10 minutes before the start. He checks the wind and wave conditions and makes last-minute adjustments to his rig. Cor continued sailing the boat for several years, especially since he was a Sunfish dealer.

Will: How did you get interested in Sunfish?

Cor: The Dutch Sunfish Association invited me to the World Championships in Medemblik in 1979. I thought it was very interesting to start sailing Sunfish, because they are quite similar to the Lasers. I went to this championship and was amazed at how nice a class it was. The boat is easy to sail and still nice with tactics and things like that.

W: *Let's talk about how you sail. How do you make the Sunfish go to windward?*

C: It's very hard for me to go to windward in light wind, because it is so important to know exactly the correct trim of the boat. For that you need a lot of practice. When there is a lot of wind, there is a lot of fighting to it. I think it's easier to sail a boat you've never sailed before when there is a lot of wind, because trimming the sail is much easier. You can flatten it out, you can use the vang and other things that are quite similar in all boats. That's why it was so easy for me in my first

World Championship. We had four of the six races with a lot of wind and in those four races, I had very nice results.

W: *Do you point or foot?*

C: I think I foot. I veer off more than the others do. That was very apparent at the first Worlds I sailed in Medemblik. I went very, very low compared with Fries and Chapin. They sailed much higher, but because I went faster, I could take the shifts faster. That was quite an advantage because the wind was shifting a lot.

W: *Did you use the compass a lot? Or were you able to tell by the shore?*

C: I never sail with a compass. Never. I haven't even got one. I think it's better to look at the other competitors because they can give you an indication of all the wind shifts even better than a compass can. You're not sailing against the wind; you're sailing against other competitors. I think if you look at the other competitors, you can observe two things at once: the wind shifts and the tactics.

W: *How do you set up your bridle? How do you put your sheet on the bridle? Do you use the rope bridle?*

C: For me it's very difficult because I hardly know the class. I know quite a bit about tactics, but the Sunfish itself is pretty new to me. I prefer the rope bridle because I want to put the traveler pretty low, so tight that when there is not much wind it works a little bit as a downhaul.

W: *How tight do you have your foot and your luff?*

C: That's difficult - I think not that loose. If you put it too loose you get wrinkles in your sail and I don't like that. The more wind I get, the tighter I make my outhaul.

W: *How about kinetics to windward?*

C: I think they're very important in Sunfish and Lasers and all these very light boats. Compared to the total weight of the boat, the sailor is about 50 percent of it, and that's quite a lot. So I think it's very important to move your body. As you go up a wave, you have to put your body to the front of the boat, and when you're on the top, you move your body back again. I go forward and backward, in and out, and I don't know exactly how I do it. I think I make a circle with my shoulders. If I am going up the wave, I am hiking out a little bit and I'm going forward with my shoulders. As I go down the wave I go back and in again. I think it turns out to be a circle.

W: *How do you tack in waves? How do you pick the time to tack?*

C: I try to start tacking when the wave is coming and finish my tack when I am sailing down the wave.

W: *You're tacking across the crest of the wave?*

C: Yes, on top of the wave. I try to make something like a roll tack, but it's hard to do. If the waves are different sizes, you should try to tack on the flattest possible spot. But if you have to tack, well, tack on top of the wave. It's better to have a good technique for tacking on waves than waiting to tack for 20 meters and losing your position.

W: *Do you use telltales at all?*

C: No, never. They mix me up too much. They might be very good for training, but I wouldn't use them in a regatta.

W: *Let's get on the next point of sailing. Tell me about your reaching technique and tactics.*

C: Usually I try to make a straight line from one mark to the other. I remember I once read something by a guy who won the Sunfish Worlds. He wrote about surfing on a wave on a normal surfboard, and actually that's the same way you have to sail a Sunfish. It was very helpful.

W: *Was that Garry Hoyt's* Go for the Gold?

C: Yes! That's the only book I've ever read about sailing. It was a good book and I learned a lot

Interviews with the Champions • 1981-1982

about surfing on waves in small boats.

W: *You're going downhill all the time?*

C: Yes. If you really work on it, I think you can surf down the whole reach. You need a lot of training for that or else all the waves would look the same. If you're working on it and if you've been training on the waves for a while, then you see the differences. Then you can take the waves you like.

W: *Do you find it helps to pump the sail?*

C: It's harder than the Lasers because when you pump, you have the forward part of the sail, the part in front of the mast, working against you. You do need the help of a good pump to get planing. It's hard for me to pump in the right way, but that's lack of training. I never trained in Sunfish at all. The only times I sailed the Sunfish was in the regattas. I think altogether I've sailed Sunfish about 28 times.

W: *How about on the run? Do you do anything different on the run than on the reach?*

C: I don't think so. I like to sail by the lee. I think you can get a lot of advantage out of that. If you sail a little bit by the lee, it seems to be easier to catch a wave and to keep on surfing.

W: *Do you try to gybe on shifts?*

C: Yes, I try. I also try to get a little bit away from the field of boats. Fifty percent of the time I do it, it turns out to be equal. But the other 50 percent of the time, I think I have a small advantage. I try to keep a clear wind.

W: *How about kinetics on the reach and the run?*

C: Again, very important. As I said, it's very important to move your body forward and backward as you go upwind. It's also very important when you're on a run or a reach. As I read in the book, *Go for the Gold*, it's just as if you're surfing down a wave on a surfboard. If you want to catch a wave, you must be in the front of the boat at the moment you catch it. Then you have to move backward. It's not a quick jump in the boat - it's just a changing of weight.

W: *How about starting tactics? How do you like to start?*

C: Actually I don't care about other people. I just try to take the best place and go off. I think you need good boat handling and you must be sure of yourself. I prefer to start on the left side of the line. At Medemblik I was always to the left, but this was because I had a lot of speed when I footed. I found that at the right side of the line, I would be in everybody's wind. I also had to tack immediately if I started at the right side of the line and that was not always possible. If I started at the lowest end I could make good speed, take a nice shift and pass in front of the fleet.

W: *Do you do any training - physical exercises?*

C: At the moment I do too little, but usually I do a lot of running. When I'm really trying hard to win something, I run three or four times a week, about 10 kilometers. After that I do some physical fitness things like push-ups and sit-ups. I also do something like a meditation where I am moving my body and stretching it. Altogether, it takes about one-and-a-quarter hours. I play a lot of squash and do other sports like water skiing and surfing. I sailed the Dutch windsurfing championships and won.

If you do a lot of sports and are doing extra work on your muscles, I think that's enough. You have to be very, very fit to sail the Sunfish in heavy wind. It's very important in all classes where the boat is pretty light compared to the body. You really have to work hard.

W: *Do you wear weight?*

C: A bit. I only wear wet sweat shirts - about three or four kilos (six-and-a-half to nine pounds).

W: *Many thanks, Cor.*

Interviews with the Champions • 1995-1996 10

These interviews were conducted by phone in the winter of 1995-96. Two of them, the ones with Eduardo Cordero and Donnie Martinborough, I messed up. The new tape recorder I had just bought specifically for the interviews baffled me. Both of them were very gracious about it, and went through the whole interview procedure with me a second time. The interviews were the better for it; we mostly remembered what was said the first time around, and they both had thought of interesting things to add by the time we did it again. The second interview with Eduardo was in person, the last day of the howling '96 Midwinters. He used a number of examples from the two days' racing, and that material, fresh in his mind, also added to the interest. I am particularly grateful to both Eduardo and Donnie, although all the sailors in this chapter and the last were happy to oblige. Like most of us, they love to talk about sailing, especially Sunfish.

Here are the World and North American Champions from the first regatta to publication date. The names of those interviewed in this book are printed in bold. Jean and Don Bergman and Mike Catalano never made the lists, but they came so close so often and are so revered by the Class that their comments are important. I did not interview Scott Kyle because his article in Sailing World, *reprinted on page 350, covers most of the questions asked of the others.*

SUNFISH WORLD CHAMPIONSHIPS

Year	Location	Champion	Home
1970	St. Thomas, USVI	Gary Hoyt	USVI
1971	Venezuela	Ted Moore	MA
1972	Bermuda	Bob Bowles	NY
1973	Martinique	Pierre Siegenthaler	Bahamas
1974	Aruba, N.A.	Serge Marsolle	Guadeloupe
1975	Miami, FL	**Derrick Fries**	MI
1976	Venezuela	Paul Fendler	NY
1977	Bahamas	Pierre Siegenthaler	Bahamas
1978	Puerto Rico	**Derrick Fries**	MI
1979	Holland	**Dave Chapin**	IL
1980	Aruba, N.A.	**Cor van Aanholt**	Holland
1981	Italy	**Dave Chapin**	IL
1982	San Francisco, CA	John Kostecki	CA
1983	Colombia	**Donnie Martinborough**	Bahamas
1984	Ontario, Canada	Andy Pimental	RI
1985	Italy	**Donnie Martinborough**	Bahamas
1986	Barrington, RI	Scott Kyle	IL
1987	Aruba, N.A.	Bruce Sutphen	RI
1988	Bahamas	**Donnie Martinborough**	Bahamas
1989 1990	Orlando, FL	Scott Kyle	IL
1991	Curaçao, N.A.	Steven Smeulders	Curaçao
1992	Houston, TX	Paul-Jon Patin	NY
1993	Virgin Gorda, BVI	**Eduardo Cordero**	Venezuela
1994	Bermuda	**Malcolm Smith**	Bermuda
1995	Bahamas	David Loring	SC

SUNFISH NORTH AMERICAN CHAMPIONSHIPS

Year	Location	Champion	Home
1963	Candlewood Lake, CT	Scott Stokes	IL
1964	Wequaquet Lake, MA	Dave Davies	CT
1965	Indian Lake, MI	Scott Stokes	IL
1966	Cazenovia Lake, NY	Will White	CT
1967	Ganonoque, Quebec	Henry Post	NY
1968	Devil's Lake, MI	Will White	CT
1969	Cazenovia Lake, NY	Carl Knight	NJ
1970	Winnetka, IL	Dick Griffin	USVI
1971	Sayville, NY	Jack Evans	CT
1972	Devil's Lake, MI	Major Hall	IL
1973	Fort Monroe, VA	Carl Knight	NJ
1974	Association Island, NY	Carl Knight	NJ
1975	Russells Point, OH	**Joel Furman**	NY
1976	Association Island, NY	Jens Hookanson	USVI
1977	Seabrook, TX	Buddy Brown	TX
1978	Barrington, RI	**Nat Philbrick**	PA
1979	Springfield, IL	Alan Beckwith	MA
1980	Gulfport, MS	Joe Blouin	LA
1981	Charleston, SC	**Paul Odegaard**	CT
1982	Ridgeway, Ontario	Leonard Ruby	MA
1983	Wilmette, IL	**Derrick Fries**	MI
1984	Houston, TX	Lawrence Maher	TX
1985	Brant Beach, NJ	**Derrick Fries**	MI
1986	Corpus Christi, TX	Lawrence Maher	TX
1987	Charleston, SC	Scott Kyle	IL
1988	Rohoboth Bay, DE	Bob Findlay	IL
1989	Tawas, MI	**Derrick Fries**	MI
1990	Sayville, NY	Scott Kyle	IL
1991	Bay Waveland, MS	Bob Findlay	IL
1992	Barrington, RI	Rod Koch	FL
1993	Spingfield, IL	**Jeff Linton**	FL
1994	Charleston, SC	**Jeff Linton**	FL
1995	Lewes, DE	**Jeff Linton**	FL

Interviews with the Champions • 1995-1996

Don and Jean Bergman

Don and Jean Bergman have been racing Sunfish for close to 30 years - at least Don has. It's the second marriage for both; together, they have 10 children, six years between youngest and oldest (each had a set of twins) plus eleven grandchildren "and counting." Many of the kids have been Sunfish racers, as well as crew on the family's S2 7.9 midget ocean racer. They've done well in the 7.9; even better since Jean took over the helm ("I shut up and steer.") Now Don concentrates on tuning and tactics ("I nag Jean.") At the S2 7.9 Internationals in '95, they finished third, two points out of first, behind a couple of "pro" sailmaker teams.

In Sunfish racing, Jean has won four Women's North Americans, was in the top 10 twice at North Americans, and was leading the '90 Worlds in Orlando until the heavy-air last day. She was Class Secretary for many years, and at this writing is President of the International Sunfish Class Association.

Don has raced in 24 North Americans, and has taken every place in the top 10 except first. They have been to 19 Worlds together; Don's best finish was sixth in '84 in Kingston, Ontario. He has won a Midwinters, and innumerable Regional and Masters championships.

Their son-in-law Bobby Findlay was North American Champion in '88 and '91.

Will: *What's your technique, Don, for going to weather?*

Don: When it's shallow and the waves are close together, it seems to help to heel a little bit, even in light air. It doesn't bang quite so hard. You're not going up and down in those little short waves. Otherwise, as the wind picks up, the flatter you can keep it the better. And I try to keep my tacks to a minimum unless it's shifting quite a bit. I used to pay more attention to keeping clear air. I used to give that number one priority, but I'm leaning toward doing what I see the best sailors doing - sailing on the lifted tack whether they're taking bad air or not. And I think they're right. I think it's more important to sail the lifted tack. It's better to sail in the dirty air than to sail a little further on the headed tack and maybe miss the shift.

W: *What about when it's more puffy than shifty, when it's more important to find the puffs and avoid the holes?*

D: I don't worry about that so much, except in real light air on small waters. But in the larger courses, where you have plenty of water, there aren't that many holes. I don't pay much attention to that, although it may be more important than I give it credit for.

W: *Do you think you're a pincher or a footer?*

D: I think I'm a footer, although it depends on how the boat is behaving. Depends on how you've got it rigged. Sometimes you'll have quite a bit of weather helm, and then you're fighting that, and doing more pinching than anything, and feathering. If you have the boat balanced pretty well, I think you're better off if you foot.

W: *Even with the new board?*

D: Even with the new board.

W: *Have you found the new board has changed your technique at all?*

D: Yes. It allows you to point higher. It doesn't stall. It's been excellent, because it's equalized the fleet quite a bit - that and the new sail. Jean says it's taken away her only advantage.

W: *I remember, every time I'd see you, you'd have a new sail, both of you.*

D: Yes, but now the new sails seem to hold up better.

W: *How do you adjust that sail for different conditions?*

D: I don't. I used to loosen it up a bit in lighter air and tighten it up in the heavier air. But I've had quite a few good races in light air with the outhauls moderately tight, so I don't sail with them loose any more. Moderately snug, with just a very slight scallop. The gooseneck I don't move, although most people do. I keep it around 18, which is a little back of the desired spot in light air and ahead of the desired spot in heavy air, but it seems to be about right for me in 80 percent of the conditions, so I don't fool with it.

W: *Do you do any adjustments after you've gone around the weather mark?*

D: No I don't. I don't even have adjustable outhauls.

W: *You don't?*

D: No, I just tie 'em out there. I found when I was fooling with those things I made little mistakes when I was sailing, tugging on one thing or another, and it didn't seem to make that much difference. I think I'm sailing a little bit better by avoiding those things.

W: *Jean, you're awfully fast in medium and light air. What do you do?*

Jean: Well, in light air I normally have the gooseneck around 17. And I do change my gooseneck. I go from 17 to as much as 24 in the heavy stuff. I have an adjustable gooseneck, which helps a lot. And I do change my outhauls. I use the Cunningham if it's heavy and loosen if it's not. And I do have an adjustable outhaul on the boom. I can change those even in the middle of a race if conditions really change. I don't do it if things change just a little bit, and I don't change it for the different legs. Upwind I think the shifts are the key thing. Get out there and get in sync with the shifts, particularly in light air. Finding the air is the other thing, and not getting in the holes. It seems very often on a large course that the middle isn't good. If you go up the course ahead of time and figure out where the winds seem to be coming from, in light air, more often than not, it seems to be the edges. The wind doesn't seem to fill in all the way in the middle. Not always, but often. So the most important thing is finding the wind and playing the shifts. In heavier air, I'm not a good one to ask. I always seem to get ridden over, so I'm always in someone's bad air.

W: *I know the feeling. Don, you said earlier that you used to think clear air was all-important but now you think staying on the favored tack is more important. Anything else?*

D: I don't mind following a good sailor. If I happen to see Eduardo or Donnie or Malcolm somewhere near me, I'll copy 'em. If they tack, I'll tack, because I know they're going to be up there in the first three or four boats, and if I can be within five of them it's about as good as you can hope for.

W: *So you obviously believe in consistency. You're one of the most consistent sailors around.*

D: I always finish 22nd, yes.

W: *Oh sure. On the other hand, you've always just missed at the top regattas. Maybe that's part of the problem? Sometimes you've got to figure you're smarter than the other guy?*

D: No, I don't think I am. In fact, I'm not sure I even detect the wind shifts as well as many

Interviews with the Champions • 1995-1996

of the sailors do. I always used to kind of rely on boatspeed rather than being a good tactician or a good wind shift detector. I have to work harder on my tactics, I think.

W: *Do you roll tack?*

D: No, I don't.

W: *Not many of us old guys can.*

D: No, I tip over. In light air I delay moving over to the new side, so actually I do do a bit of a roll tack. But nothing like the dramatic ones that you see the kids do.

W: *Let's go on to the weather mark rounding. How do you like to approach it?*

D: In a big fleet I prefer to come in closer to the port tack layline, because you have a little better air. You've got to be awful careful of the starboard tack boats, though. A 720 there can be a disaster. And if you try to duck in low, under the starboard tackers, you don't make that mark. Usually you have to find a hole and poke your nose through, and then flop in clean air and come down on starboard. The other thing is you've got to be careful...

J: The current.

D: Well, the current, but more so the buoy anchor line. It will snag, so you often have to give the buoy six or seven feet clearance, especially with the new board, because it's pretty lengthy.

W: *When you come in on port, about how many boat lengths from the mark?*

D: It depends. You've got to tack with the shifts. Sometimes you may be pretty close to the buoy, and sometimes you may be 15 or 20 boat lengths from it. But I think ideally, five or six boat lengths, so you're coming in pretty close on port.

W: *And after you round, what order of things?*

D: Well, first you have to head in the right direction. And then let out your sail to the right position, and try to get surfing if you have a chance. If you're in heavy air, you try to get on a surf even before fooling with your daggerboard. That's the last thing I think about, getting the board up. But the quicker you can get surfing, the better off you are.

W: *Do you use the JC strap to hold up the board, or some other way?*

D: No JC...Well, I do, actually, when it's light.

W: *Jean, how do you round?*

J: Coming up to the windward mark, I want to stay away from the layline on the right side, pretty much the way Don said. I try to come in early towards the port layline, because I don't want to get in that starboard layline early. When you do that, you get so far outside if you come in with a whole group of boats. If you tack on what should be the lay line, you'll never get there because there's no wind with all those boats coming down. So I try to get into the starboard line maybe 10 or 15 boat lengths from the pin. Once you get around, the first thing you've got to decide is whether you want to go high or low. And that all depends on what I see immediately ahead of me. If there are a lot of people fighting to go high, my tendency will be to go low, and go very low. You've got to do it one way or the other - going down the middle is not very good, I don't think. Either go very low, or fight for high. In enough air, I will fight for high because...well, I used to be able to go over everybody and get back down again. But with the new sail, the bigger guys do just as well. So my tendency now is not to go as high. Going back to the windward leg...in heavy air I raise my board about four inches. If you're doing chop, it keeps you from stalling as much, when you're light. You can kind of scallop up. The thing I have trouble doing, which you have to do in waves, is to let off on the sheet a little bit and then come up, let off and come up, and I have trouble with strength, to be able to haul the sail in and out like that. But with the board up I don't have as much trouble. It doesn't stall as fast.

W: *Zeestraten (fastest man at the '73 Worlds) told me that he actually switched his ratchet off so*

Not all champions are men. Jean Bergman has won four Women's North American Championships, and was leading at the 1990 Worlds until the wind piped up on the last day. She often beats the best of the men, including husband Don and all 10 of their children.

he could work the sails in and out faster.

J: Oh, for that strength! OK, back to off the wind...the decision whether to go high or low depends on what those immediately ahead of me are doing. If they're going pretty much straight or low then I'm going to go high. If the ones right ahead of me look as if they're going to fight it out to go high then I'll go low. On the second reach I'll almost always go high, because then you're inside at the mark. Even if everyone is fighting to get high, I don't like to go low on that second one.

W: *What techniques do you use on the reaches?*

J: Mainly trying to surf, if there is anything to surf. Being light, even in 10 knots I can do really well, because the guys can't get on a plane and I can. Don says he can. You know, you can give one big pump, but you have to be careful, because the jury's always watching at big regattas. Here's Don again.

D: If it's a close reach, I'll try to stay on the high side. If it's a broad reach I'll try to stay on the low side. Otherwise, I'll go wherever I can go and stay surfing. If I get on a surf I'll go wherever the wave takes me, whether it's high or low, because I think the surfing is so important. Holding that wave...You know, you pick up an extra 50 percent of speed, so you don't care where you go, as long as you can keep surfing.

W: *What do you do to catch a wave and then stay on it?*

D: Well, as you feel the wave start to lift the stern of the boat, you'll hike a bit and pull your mainsheet, and stay hiked, with the sail trimmed to get it going. Then, once you get it going, then you'll bear off on the wave, and then just try to hold the wave. In lighter air, you can bear off to a straight downwind situation, which gets you low, which is desirable. In heavy air, you can't go straight downwind, because you'll go faster than the wave, so you'll generally have to sail high to stay on that wave. You can't go in the direction you want to go. So in heavy air, you'll have to go high, and then switch around and go by the lee, even...just to stay on the wave. Because if you go straight down, you'll catch up to the wave in front of you, and just get stopped. Quite a bit of up-and-downing, even on the reach. You pay a little bit of attention to the boats around you, keep out of their wind, but it's not as important, particularly when you're surfing. The wind isn't as important as being on the wave.

Interviews with the Champions • 1995-1996

W: *And you said you like to go high most of the time?*

D: No, I will lean toward going low, particularly on the second reach. I find that the boats are fighting to get up high. Even the leaders are up there pretty high. They're all up there following the leaders or going even higher. If you go low, you can pass a lot of boats, especially if there's surfing conditions.

W: *What do you do when you get to the leeward mark?*

D: You have to see how you're going to set up with the other boats, because you're coming in from the outside. Hopefully you've passed several of those boats, and you're looking for your niche to get into. It's good to talk it over with the boats around you before you get there. You might say, "I think I've got to give room to so-and-so, and I don't think you have an overlap, and I think Joe and Bill have overlaps and Pete doesn't." So everyone is in agreement as to how you're going to go around that leeward mark. If everybody is working together you can eliminate the crashes and the fouls. Usually people will work those things out with you. Most people are willing to get around as best they can, too, just to survive those leeward mark roundings. Coming around the mark, you want to be able to round it right at the mark. You can't take the pinwheel outside, or everyone just sits on you and you go further and further downwind. You can't point, you can't tack, you can't do anything. So often you're better off to delay than to come in close with the other boats, and then come in tight to the mark. You don't have any trouble with ground tackle because it's going upwind, so you can cut that one pretty close.

W: *The next item is kinetics, which is the bad word. Do you move your body a lot to steer?*

D: I...well, I scull, as a matter of fact. That's a bad word. It isn't really sculling, but in heavy air I am moving the tiller quite a bit to get through the waves. Probably more so than is effective. I think sometimes that I slow the boat down with all that steering. But I do a lot of steering upwind. Off the wind, only when you're altering your course to hold the wave. But other than that I don't do much in terms of steering. On a wave, I make kind of radical tiller adjustments.

W: *How about swinging your body and that sort of thing?*

D: Well, yes. When you surf, when you're just getting on the wave, you have to move your body forward, so the bow is down. And when you're avoiding getting your nose into a wave in front of you, you've got to get your weight back. So your weight has to move from that standpoint.

W: *Then you're more concerned with fore and aft than side to side?*

D: Well, yes, but the side-to-side is important when you're trying to get on the wave, because that one hike and that one yank on the mainsheet really does give you a little more impetus, you know.

W: *So you're steering down the wave; the heeling helps to get you down the wave along with the pull on the sheet?*

D: Yeah.

W: *Anything more about leeward mark roundings?*

D: Well, that "slow-down-and-win" tactic I mentioned is important sometimes to get close to the pin, and then once I round the mark, I tend to pinch a little bit at first, because there's usually a boat in front of me. If you can pinch up above him a little bit, you can get better air. If you foot, it doesn't work. All you're doing is setting yourself up for a tack. Otherwise you'll just be in bad air.

W: *Jean?*

J: Well the main thing is not to get on the outside of that pinwheel, as Don said. I normally come in high at that mark. In lighter air I'm usually faster and I don't have trouble staying on the inside. In heavier air I will often go low, but you have to pick your point to come up so you're not outside when you get to the mark. When you pick your time and a couple of boats decide you won't get inside them, you're better off to slow down a bit. Just take your place behind them and ahead of the next guys. Just get on the inside, because if you have to drop down three or four boat lengths, everyone is just going to pour through there. You're not inside the two-boat-length circle any more. And then too many boats get in there, and I really hate that. Everybody's got your air and you can't tack because you'd be tacking too close and it's just very hard to get out of there. So I'll do almost anything to make sure I get a close inside rounding. And then pinch up as Don said to try to get a little clear air once you get around. Then decide immediately whether you want to tack. There's usually a space where you do have a chance to tack right after you've rounded the mark.

W: *On a run: anything different there?*

J: I've never been that good on a run. I'm much better on the reaches than the run. I tend to want to go left for some reason.

W: *To make sure you get your overlap?*

J: Yes, I suppose, at the other end. I tend to slip over there, by the lee. I don't know why. My tactics aren't that good downwind. Let's see if Don has anything more to say about that.

D: I try to imitate Nancy Haberland and David van Cleef (4th and 2nd at '95 NAs.) No one goes downwind the way they do. They're all over the course. Right, left, all over the place, anything to stay on that wave. Once they get on that wave they'll sail by the lee dramatically, they'll sail up dramatically, not to lose the wave. And I've been trying to do that, too. Concentrating, spending my whole time trying to stay on the wave. They're right, left, right, left, and picking up 100 yards on the fleet, they do it so well.

W: *And at the leeward mark, the same sort of tactics to get inside?*

D: I do try to get to the left, because that's important. But I don't do that until right at the end of the run. The rest of the time it's the waves; the waves are so critical.

W: *Anything more about setting up the boat?*

D: We don't do much setting up before a race. I try to keep my halyard position so that the tack is about three inches above the deck. In heavier air I put a little vang on. And I also like to use the Bill Haberland slip knot - a trucker's hitch - to snug up the halyard. And I use like a triple clove hitch to tie the halyard to the spar - a clove hitch with an extra turn - to keep it from slipping. I haven't had any trouble with the halyard slipping.

W: *You don't use tape up there?*

D: No, I don't use the tape. On my own boat, I put cross-scratches on the upper spar, not very heavy ones...just enough so the rope grips a little better, doesn't slip. Can't do that with the Worlds boats, though.

W: *Let's talk a bit about how you stay in shape. I know you do more than most people.*

D: I used to jog; now I shuffle. They say, "There goes Don; he's out shuffling again." I try to get out and shuffle every day. I think the thing that sets us up best is our canoe race training. We work. Every other day, Jean and I are out in the canoe in the spring. We put in a couple of hours of heavy duty paddling. We're really into the canoe racing. That's probably our best conditioner. Oh, I do some sit-ups, but I don't do calisthenics, no, or weights.

W: *How about Jean?*

D: She does the same things. We do cross-country skiing, which is good exercise in the winter. And we have a cross-country machine, which we use. She doesn't shuffle.

J: I hate running. That I can't do, because my knees are no good. I do the cross-country ski machine, which is smooth and good for endurance. And we do a lot of cross-country

Interviews with the Champions • 1995-1996

skiing in the winter. I did manage pretty well at the Worlds, and that was only two months after a bilateral mastectomy.

D: She steered the S-2 a week after the operation!

J: I was on board but I wasn't really steering. Oh, and I use the Jens. I'm the wimp. As soon as there's whitecaps I put the Jens in. It helps. If I were heavier and stronger I'd do a lot better, but it does make it easier to control the boat. I like the one with a long line and a loop around the halyard that pulls it into the mast, pulled very, very tight. I don't like the short one tied-to the mast cap, because I think it tends to pull the mast cap off.

W: *How about mental prep - mind games or sailing races in your head?*

J: No. But I do try calming things. Otherwise I can tend to get frantic in the head. That happened to me when I was winning the Worlds. When the wind got heavy it really played havoc with my mind, because I thought, "Oh, no, I can't do it." If I had been able to go off and not worry about it I probably could have been in the right place and, when the wind died down, been able to keep the lead. But that's long past.

W: *Do you have any secrets for keeping calm? Do you meditate?*

J: I have to keep telling myself that it's not that important in life. That's the opposite of what they tell you to do, but I tell myself, "Just go out and do the best you can. Don't make a big deal out of it." I try to think calming ways of being. Once I'm out on the course, I'm a lot better. I can start thinking, "OK, what do I need to know? What's the wind doing out here? What kinds of shifts are there?" If you're concentrating on exactly what you're going to do, you're not worried about things.

W: *You like to get out there early and scope those things out?*

J: I would like to do that, but my tendency is not to get there. My tendency is to be a little bit late. I almost always can go about halfway up the course, anyway. And standing up for a while and watching how the puffs are coming in, which you can see on the water. And I try to be up above the line between five minutes and go, looking upwind to see where the next shift is coming from. It's sometimes hard to judge. And if you're on the wrong end, if it shifts at the very last minute, then you've got to get back over to the other side as soon as you can to get back in sync again. Here's Don again.

D: I don't think I play mind games or anything like that. I'm always excited beforehand. I try to get there on time or early. My biggest concern is not to be late. And keeping Jean moving, to get her there. I used to get real nervous. At the 10-minute gun, you'd feel that adrenaline pumping inside you, you know. But that kind of went away about 15 years ago. Now, I think I'm fairly calm out there. It's probably because you're not fighting for first place any more. When you thought you had a chance, getting that best start seemed so critical at the time. But now, even at the start, I feel fairly relaxed. But now I'm just enjoying it. It's been fun.

W: *Do you and Jean compare notes after a regatta?*

D: We talk about why we did or didn't do well. At the Worlds it's hard to keep track of each other, there are so many boats scattered all over the course. And you don't know the numbers. At the North Americans we keep track of each other, and we know the other boats. It's important to each of us to beat the other, you know. That's kind of a goal for each of us. So after the race the winner is a little careful of what he says, so that the loser doesn't get huffy about things. We do have a good time racing against each other, but it's always competitive between us.

W: *Thanks to you both. See you at the Midwinters?*

J: Right. See you there!

Interviews with the Champions • 1995-1996

● Eduardo Cordero

Eduardo Cordero of Puerto la Cruz, Venezuela, has been the offwind scourge of the fleet since he first appeared in major Sunfish regattas a few years ago. He has always finished well, and won the Worlds at Virgin Gorda in '93. He has won at least two Midwinter Championships, including the one at Sarasota, FL, in 1996. The following interview took place there on Saturday evening, and Eduardo had won all three races, two of them in winds with gusts well into the thirties. Sunday was even colder, with even higher winds, so the racing was cancelled. Eduardo had scored a perfect blackout.

Will: How do you like to start?

Eduardo: First thing I do, before the start, is to check the wind, and I like to know which end of the line is favored. But I also like to know which side of the course is favored. Most of the time, I try to start with the fast boats, because I know I can get away easier from the pack than if I was starting with the slow boats. If I'm with the gun, for example, and I'm in the middle of the pack, sometimes I can't get out there in front. If I tack, and they tack, they may be covering me, and I've lost a lot of boats. So I go with the fast boats. It helps a lot.

W: *You mean you'd rather start with the fast boats than at the favored end?*

E: Yes. Well, I try to do everything. The fast boats usually know the favored end. If I'm with the fast boats, I'm usually at the favored end. And I don't like to have anyone close to me on the windward side. So what I like to do is make a big hole on the leeward side - sometimes someone will get in there at the last second - but I like to make a big hole so that right after the gun I can foot for a while to get up speed and then point.

Interviews with the Champions • 1995-1996

W: *And you like to start with the fast boats? Tell me again why?*

E: You can separate from the pack easier. Then you can do what you want, tack when you want. But the most important thing for me is to get to the favored side early.

W: *So you like to get out there early to check that out.*

E: Yes, it helps a lot. I check out the wind.

W: *How about current?*

E: Current is not so important when it is coming from behind on the beat. The problem with current is when it is against you.

W: *Can you tell us how you make a boat go fast to windward?*

E: I'm always looking for speed. I'm not a pointer; I'm not a footer; I'm middle. I look more for speed. More speed and probably more pointing than footing. I concentrate a lot on the boat. I adjust my boat until I feel I have a lot of power in my sail. Yesterday (first day of the '96 Midwinters), it was blowing very hard. I had set my gooseneck at 22 inches and I was feeling powerless. So today I moved it forward to 18 inches. I like to feel power all the time on my sail. Another thing I keep in mind - I know how aerodynamics of sails works - is the adjustment, the position of the draft. I always tune my sail very well with the outhaul.

W: *Just the outhaul?*

E: Yes. I don't pull the Cunningham until it's blowing like 20. For example yesterday I had very slight Cunningham tension. Not very much. The waves were not very big. They weren't going to stall you. So I didn't need power. If you pull the Cunningham, that moves the draft forward; that's for power. I didn't need any more power. The outhaul, when the water is flat and it's blowing, I like to pull it. But today - winds of 15 knots, wouldn't you say? - I didn't pull it much. There were little scallops on the foot. I had some vang tension, in order to bend the boom. But I also like to have a good twist on the reaches. Not too much.

W: *So you keep some vang tension?*

E: Yes. Around the windward mark, I always approach on starboard. Although today, in both races, I approached on port. It depends on the wind. As I said, I have to know which is the favored side. Today, it was the left side, so of course I approached on port tack. What I always keep in mind is the favored side.

W: *So when you come in on starboard, you're usually well up in front and don't worry about other boats coming in later and sitting on your wind?*

E: Well, today, at the first mark in the first race, I went up high, and two boats tacked under me. I lost two boats. About approaching the mark: when it's shifty, I like to stay in the middle. I don't like to go to the corners. Today, in the second race, it was shifty, and I stayed in the middle. I did all right - I rounded in the top four - but I would have done better if I had gone left more. There was more wind over there. The three boats in front of me all went to the left side.

W: *OK, let's talk about the reaches. Everyone says you're unbelievably fast on the reaches.*

E: The first thing for reaches is to have power in the sail. I like a powerful sail until about 20 knots. I loose all the outhauls, all the Cunningham. And the other thing is to concentrate on the boat. I practice the reaches at home. I think I have a good feeling for the boat - just that. I think that I don't pump too much. I watch for the puffs, and I don't like anyone to windward.

W: *So you go high?*

E: Yes, I go high. I like clear air. If I want to pass someone, and his boat is slow, I can pass him low or windward; it doesn't matter. If I'm going to do it lower, I stay away three boat lengths or more, in order that the turbulence doesn't affect me.

W: *How do you catch a wave?*

E: I watch the waves, all the time.

W: *In front of you, beside you, all around...?*

E: Oh, let's say 30 degrees off my course. I don't look at the waves behind. Just in front of me, and a little bit off, a little bit to windward, so I know what's going on with the waves. Today there weren't big waves. It was more planing than surfing.

W: *Without waves, how do you manage to be so fast?*

E: Well, I have a feeling for the boat. I don't know why. I see people who are lighter that don't go that fast. I think that telltales - I use telltales on the reaches.

W: *Woollies, telltales right on the sail?*

E: Yes. I never liked telltales, but then I started racing Lasers, and in Lasers you need telltales for pointing. So when I came back to the Sunfish, I was missing something for the reaches, so I tried telltales, and they tell me a lot.

W: *Just on the reaches? Not to windward?*

E: No. I don't use them to windward. I like to have the windward one a little up. Then I know I have my sail well trimmed.

W: *Do you use any on the leach?*

E: No.

W: *OK, we're coming down to the gybe mark, and you're usually going high, do you duck down and try to get room at the mark?*

E: Yes, definitely. And I want to know the course to the next mark. Today, for instance, I knew that the course to the leeward mark was essentially downwind. The first reach was very close. So I stayed on starboard. Everyone ahead of me gybed. They were luffing each other up and sailing in turbulent wind. I took advantage of that and sailed my own race. I didn't care if I was an inside or an outside boat. But usually I want to be the inside boat.

W: *Especially at the leeward mark...*

E: Yes, always.

W: *OK, we're rounding the leeward mark, and setting up for the next beat. Anything special about that?*

E: At the bottom mark, if someone is behind me, I want to stop the boat to make them pass to my leeward so they get bad air. Then I may foot a little bit so they get more, until I'm out of trouble with them. I don't want to worry about them for a while. When I round the bottom mark, I have to adjust my outhaul. I'm not quite ready to go upwind, because I have to tune my boat. So I want the boats behind me to tack, or go down to leeward.

W: *You play both the outhaul and the Cunningham?*

E: Not the Cunningham. On the reaches I have the outhaul loose - too loose for going to windward, so I have to pull it in a little bit. If it's light wind, I always like to have a baggy sail.

W: *You adjust the outhaul but not the Cunningham; Jeff Linton apparently does just the opposite.*

E: It depends on the way you like to sail. If it's chop, I like to pull the Cunningham. But it has to be blowing very hard. And it depends what kind of sail you have. I think the sails we have now are not as good as the original North racing sail. The cloth we have now I think is soft, and stretches easier. Here at the Midwinters, I was able to bring a sail that was almost new. It's a '92 model, and it's working very good. Nice shape. But with my sail at home, which is newer, I have to pull the Cunningham. I don't have to do that with the sail I have here. I can tell from the shape of the sail. If it's too far forward, no Cunningham. You want the draft at 50

Interviews with the Champions • 1995-1996

percent of the sail.

W: *You like your draft right in the middle of the sail?*

E: Yes. I sail J-24s and I always look for that. I concentrate on the foresail. I know how to do that. I know how to play the backstay, and the main...I know how all that works.

W: *We haven't talked about finishing. You figure out the favored end of the line and head for that?*

E: On the finish, I always like to cover the boat that's next to me. When I know I can't catch the boat ahead of me, I don't care about that. I just don't want to lose position. But I try to stay on the favored side...always. Sometimes I look for advantage in the corners but I shouldn't. It almost never pays. At Abaco in the Worlds, I was sixth in one race and I went to the left corner. I finished 21st. If I'd kept going with the fleet I would have been better than sixth. I would probably have won the regatta. I went for a shift that never came. You have to go with what you know for sure. Another thing I think is important, especially in heavy air: conserve your energy. In the first race here, in very heavy air, I was fourth at the first mark. Downwind, I pass everybody. So on the second beat, I conserve energy. I don't care if somebody passes me. I know I can pass them on the run. I save my energy for the last beat. Then I work really hard to stay in front, to win.

W: *But on that second beat, you keep a lose cover on the fleet?*

E: Yes, of course, always. In that race, Dave Van Cleef was right behind me, and I tacked when he did. I let him sail in clear air. I don't want a tacking duel.

W: *How about the daggerboard? Do you always sail with it full down going to windward?*

E: Yes. I never lift it then.

W: *How about on the reaches. Do you lift it a lot? Do you mind a little side-slipping?*

E: I move the centerboard a lot on the reaches. I have a good feel for the boat. I can feel when I'm going sideways a little; I can feel when it slows because I have the daggerboard too low. Maybe I play with it too much, I don't know. I'm looking for puffs, or for when the wind dies. When it dies, and I go up, I lower the board. Then the puff comes, and I bring the board up and go with it. So I play with the daggerboard a lot.

W: *In Venezuela, the second time the Worlds were there, the two who finished on top sailed even the reaches with the boards all the way up. They sometimes seemed to go up and over waves sideways. Have you ever seen that? Have you ever done that?*

E: Who were they?

W: *Paul Fendler and Mike Catalano.*

E: Paul is fast downwind. Absolutely.

W: *You've sailed against him?*

E: Yes, I had a chance to sail against him in Springfield at the '93 North Americans. He has been the only guy in my life who has been able to pass me downwind. He passed me on a reach to leeward, like a bullet, and I was surprised. You've sailed off Puerto Azul. Big swells. Where I sail (Puerto la Cruz) it's mostly like this (Sarasota Bay.) That's why I did excellent here. I felt like I was at home.

W: *How do you feel about the idea of a new rudder?*

E: Definitely, I am against a new rudder. I think the boat is fine the way we have it now. I think there is no need for new changes. If we change it, everyone is going to have to have it to stay competitive, so we're going to spend more money. The boats are even now. More changes are going to get people upset. I think some people were upset with the new centerboard. But the new board was a great idea. I definitely like that.

W: *Well, both changes, the sail and the board, were to make the boat more one-design.*

E: Yes. And it's a great boat right now. I'm a member of the Advisory Council, and definitely I'm against the new rudder. A family that goes to regattas, and has three boats - they'll have to buy three new rudders. And the new plastic cheeks will break easier with a bigger and deeper blade... Last time we talked, you asked me about training? I told you that last year I had a bad year. I was feeling very weak. In the middle of January I started training again. Five days in the week, from Monday to Friday, and sometimes Saturday, I like to run in the morning and do stretching exercises. Takes me about an hour. I used to sail six days a week. When I won the Worlds I had been sailing six days a week. We have nice weather year-round. It's too much, now I have to work, so I'm sailing three days a week. It's perfect for me. The days I don't sail - Mondays, Wednesdays and Fridays - I do weight-lifting, and the other two days I ride bicycle. That makes my legs stronger. I jump rope.

W: *You spend at least an hour a day doing exercise when you can't sail?*

E: More. In the mornings I do an hour, and probably in the afternoons another hour. My mother gave me a bicycle for Christmas, and that was very good for me because I spend about an hour doing the bicycle, Tuesdays and Thursdays, about six to seven.

W: *A regular bike?*

E: A regular bike. I don't like the stationary bike. We have nice weather to go out.

W: *How about mental preparation. Do you like to get out early?*

E: Yes, definitely. About half an hour. If the weather's too rough, like today, I don't want to get out too early. But even today I was one of the first three boats. There was a lot of current from the bridge. There is no way to know what's going on unless you get to the course early. Sometimes you get out there, you check everything, and the moment you are starting there is a big shift. But that's unusual. I like to go out early, always.

W: *Do you use a Jens in heavy air?*

E: Never used it. At the Worlds this year, on the very heavy air day, I decided to try it, and I had very bad results. Never again.

W: *Well, you sure proved here you don't need it. Many thanks, Eduardo.*

E: You're welcome!

Interviews with the Champions • 1995-1996

● Jeff Linton

The scourge of the North Americans the last few years has been "Team Florida," as their T-shirts proudly proclaim. It started with Rod Koch of Tampa, who won in '92 at Barrington, Rhode Island. The class act of the team since then has been Jeff Linton, who won the next three in a row, a Class first. Jeff, one of the principals at Masthead Enterprises in Tampa, is out on the water a good deal of the time, usually at the helm of an offshore racing boat or a J-24 or a Lightning or a Flying Dutchman or...

Will: At the start, what do you like to do about the favored end?

Jeff: I start at the favored end if possible.

W: *If the leeward end is favored, you'll fight it out down there?*

J: I don't like log jams, but I'll work to get within a couple of boat lengths of it, anyway.

W: *Do you come in on port and find a hole, or what?*

J: Depends on the size of the fleet. If it's a big fleet, you usually set up a little earlier. If it's a small fleet, yeah, you can get away with coming in on port.

W: *What if you have really shifty winds?*

J: Usually start near the middle, then. Take your chances.

W: *What else do you do at the start?*

J: My favorite start is to park parallel to the line, boom out about 90 degrees. That gives you about a two or three boat-length hole. Everybody's afraid to come in to you. Then at eight seconds, start going.

W: *Don't you find that leaves you vulnerable if someone comes in close-hauled?*

J: No, because they can't get inside your boom. That's a pretty good deterrent.

W: *But presumably, once they've got the overlap, you have to get out of the way, whether they're inside your boom or not.*

J: The problem is, if you trim in your boom and you hit them with it, then they're out. They didn't give you enough "room and opportunity." The "room and opportunity" thing is very key. It's a great start.

W: *Ok, let's go on to the windward leg, and let's cover technique.*

J: Technique? Hmmm...

W: *You told me once you play your Cunningham on the upwind legs...*

J: Right! Ease if off when the waves are big and tighten it up when you can point. That's pretty key.

W: *You find yourself doing that a lot, in every kind of condition?*

J: Oh yeah, that's pretty important.

W: *Interesting...I've never heard anyone else mention that. Do you know anyone else who does it?*

J: Not near as much as I do, no. But I like a real baggy luff, compared to anybody. A real baggy luff, and then when I need to point up or squeeze somebody up, I put the Cunningham on and flatten down a little bit and point a couple of degrees higher.

W: *Baggy luff...you don't mean scalloped, do you?*

J: Yes. Yes. Deep wrinkles. I like 'em. I'm more of a power person than a point person.

W: *I've known a number of people who say that, and they can usually outpoint everyone else.*

J: Well, you get a little extra speed and - especially with the new board - it works for you. Less leeway, and that means your course to windward is better.

W: *I see. OK, how about tactics to windward?*

J: Well...I'm a compass person. I try to stay on the favored tack. A lot of people do it by watching the other boats, but I usually play it by the compass. Try to gain both sides instead of just one.

W: *Sometimes, especially in bays and lakes, I've found one side or the other is favored, and you lose out playing the shifts up the middle. Have you found that?*

J: You get burned! Correct! I'm a middle person; I get burned a lot. But instead of losing the whole fleet if I go the wrong way, I only lose a couple of boats.

W: *What if you find yourself covered or backwinded when you're trying to sail the favored slant?*

J: Then I just go away. Tack, get clear air, tack back.

W: *How do you like to come in on the weather mark?*

J: Port tack. Unless I'm in front.

W: *On port, how close to the pin?*

J: About two boat lengths...

W: *That close!*

J: Because the closer you are to the pin, the more the options go your way. Everybody stacks up on the starboard layline, and if you come in behind...pretty ugly. The port tack entrance can be a pretty good benefit. You can usually find a way in. On starboard someone's stalled out, they're on each other's air, the only clear air is on the port side. Sometimes you have the reachers coming down on top of you, but it doesn't seem to be near as bad.

W: *OK... How about that first reach?*

J: That's beyond me. That's why I can't win a World Championship. I just kind of go with the flow.

W: *High or low?*

J: Oh, I'm a passing lane person.

W: *So if you're going as fast as the rest, you'll get a puff and start hauling some boats?*

J: Right.

W: *What happens at the gybe mark?*

J: You just have to wriggle your way through it. Going high and trying to sail fast is a little bit better, I think, than digging way down. You'll

Interviews with the Champions • 1995-1996

get burned sometimes but I think in the long run a puff will come up from behind, from above...

W: *And then ride it down...*

J: Right. But sailing against Eduardo (Cordero) and those guys, there's not much you can do. They go right by you anyway.

W: *And then the second leg...I take it you go high there, too?*

J: Yeah, that's when it pays to go high. You're setting up to be inside at the leeward mark.

W: *How do you get as much surfing and planing going as you can?*

J: I'm a body weight person. Coming up the backside of a wave, body aft, then, as you try to rock over a wave, body forward. You're not really ooching. You're not hitting anything. Just rocking your body back and forth.

W: *Steering with your body.*

J: Exactly.

W: *Downwind, do you let the sail out as far ...*

J: I use telltales. That's the only time it really works.

W: *You mean woollies on the sail?*

J: Right. They don't seem to tell you much upwind, but on the reaches they give you a pretty good line on when you're close to optimum.

W: *Do you use trailers on your leach?*

J: No, I don't.

W: *How about the woollies on your sail - how far back do you put them from the mast?*

J: Let's see...on starboard tack, about a foot from the mast, and...two or three feet above the window, starboard tack closer to the mast; port tack a little further from the mast.

W: *You have a set for each tack?*

J: Right.

W: *OK, we're at the leeward mark. How do you set up for that?*

J: Make sure you're inside, and try to sail in clear air as much as possible. And if you have to tack away, make two quick tacks. Try not to sail under the reachers.

W: *So even if the port side is favored on the second beat, you don't want to sail through the fleet to reach it?*

J: I try not to. It's pretty slow going through there. Unless it's really favored.

W: *Anything special about that second beat?*

J: Just stay in phase and stay in front.

W: *How about the run?*

J: That's another problem. I don't run very well, either. Downwind's just not my forte. But sail by the lee. My first inclination in lighter air with not much chop is to stay on starboard tack, get her powered up, get the bailer out of the water (by heeling to windward). In waves, take the gybe where the waves are best...the best angle to get you towards the mark.

W: *And how do you figure that?*

J: Check right after going around the windward mark. If the waves are going left, you're on the wrong gybe. Or if you're pointing at the mark and the waves are going right, you're probably on the wrong gybe, too.

W: *You mean if the waves are going right, you should be on port tack?*

J: Right. If you're sailing by the lee. Then that will drive you down toward the mark.

W: *Now tell me how you set up your boat, how you tune it.*

J: Gooseneck as far forward as you can.

W: *What's the farthest forward you carry it?*

J: Fourteen...fourteen and a half...fifteen.

W: *And that's for light air?*

J: Light air until you can't hold it down any more. Up to the 12- or 14-mile-an-hour range. Don't move the gooseneck aft until you can't steer any more. It really seems to do well on port tack that way.

W: *How about your outhauls?*

J: Pretty snug all the time.

W: *When you have that Cunningham loose, you really don't have a scalloped edge, do you?*

J: Not too bad. I keep my tack real tight, so the Cunningham doesn't affect the outhaul much. I never have any wrinkles in the foot even in light or moderate winds. I power the luff up and keep the foot pretty tight.

W: *Going to windward, do you keep that board down all the way, all the time?*

J: All the time.

W: *I've had people tell me they've been experimenting with it a bit.*

J: It's probably not a bad thing to do, but even the new board is still pretty underpowered compared with the sail. In light air you could lift it, up to three inches, to reduce wetted surface, or in heavy air the same thing to depower a bit, but I've never done it.

W: *Do you use a Jens?*

J: Yup. Sometimes I use it. I go both ways. Two years ago I used it pretty much religiously in 22, 23 knots of breeze, and put the gooseneck at 16.

W: *You're relatively light.*

J: 165, 170.

W: *Well, that's not that light. Do you do any working out?*

J: Not as much as I need to.

W: *But you do a lot of sailing. That's probably the best kind of working out.*

J: A lot of cross training.

W: *What other classes have you been sailing?*

J: Snipes. Flying Dutchmen. Lightnings.

W: *How about mental preparation?*

J: Get out on the course early. Get to the race early...a couple of days early at major regattas.

W: *You sail the qualification series at the NAs even though you don't have to?*

J: Right. Always. It's too good a practice not to. I may not finish all the races, but it's good starting practice, and you learn the area.

W: *Anything else about racing Sunfish that's worth mentioning?*

J: I think one thing I do more than anybody is really heel the boat over. In light air chop. Going to weather. Let it heel over and it doesn't slam the chop that bad. And when you roll tack, do rail-to-rail roll tacks.

W: *Someone said you don't think you've done it right unless you get some water in the cockpit.*

J: That's it! The main thing is, on the way back down, you don't slam the chine. That's where a lot of people make a mistake. On the roll, when you're standing up on the way down, you just kind of drop into the cockpit. That way, the momentum of your body kind of hits down in the bottom of the boat instead of hitting the chine. Since you're rocking all the way over, the chine will just slap.

W: *I'm not sure I can visualize what you're saying.*

J: Just come down really slow, that's the hard part.

W: *So when you're rolling way over on the second part of the tack, you want to do it slowly.*

J: Very slowly.

W: *Anything else?*

J: I guess that's it. But you want to get Eduardo on the phone and find out how he goes downwind.

W: *You bet. I've got his phone number. One more thing...Do you hold your hiking stick and all that the way Bobby Findlay and James Liebl teach?*

J: Pretty much. Hold the stick in front of you. I use my last three fingers to steer with, and the forefinger and thumb to work the sheet. Everybody does. A lot of things have come in from other classes since you wrote your book.

W: *So nobody uses his teeth any more.*

J: No. That's too slow.

W: *Guess I'm going to have to learn all that. OK, Jeff, many thanks.*

Interviews with the Champions • 1995-1996

Winners at 1995 Bermuda Race Week:
Left to right: Damian Payne, junior winner; Paula Lewin, top opposite sex; and Donnie Martinborough, champ.

• Donnie Martinborough

Back in the '70s, when Pierre Siegenthaler was one of the top Sunfish sailors (he won the Worlds twice, in '73 and '77,) he used to talk about a kid name Donnie Martinborough back home in the Bahamas. "Wait until he's old enough to come to the Worlds." We didn't have long to wait, and in '83, Donnie won his first Worlds, in Columbia. He won again in '85, in Italy, and again in '88 in his home waters off Nassau in the Bahamas. He still holds the most World titles, and no one will be surprised if he breaks his own record.

Will: Let's sail a race. How do you like to start?

Donnie: I like to start about a quarter to a third of the way from the favored end, with good clear air, and with good boatspeed. But I think clear air is much more important than trying to get the best start position. You've got the whole weather leg to catch the one or two boats that may have got better position.

W: *So you pick your spot. Then what do you?*

D: I usually pick my spot a minute or so before the start and then just stay there, luffing, and keep the boats to leeward well clear, off by myself. Then, fifteen seconds or so before the gun, I'm able to bear off, build up some good boatspeed, and shoot up at the gun with full speed. Gives you a good jump on the rest of the fleet. I like to hold up the weather boats.

W: *That's the classic way, but how do you keep that hole open to leeward?*

D: I guess the trick is not to be too high up on the line...come up like two boat lengths below it. It is relatively easy just to luff along. If somebody tries to dip in, you pull up a little bit, and he realizes there's not going to be any room down below. Most of the time they tend to go to weather of you, or over the top. Either way, they're not interfering with my wind at all. The ones who want to drive over are normally too early anyway. It's a timing thing that takes a lot of practice, but I've found it to be the most effective way, especially with the one-minute rule they now use so much. It beats dipping down from windward of the line.

W: *OK, let's talk about the windward leg - what's your technique? Are you a pincher or a footer?*

D: I'm actually a pincher. I'm not as heavy as most of the other sailors, and I find it much easier for me to pinch up over the waves, especially in a strong breeze. In heavy air, I like to sail the boat with a slight heel, because it cuts through the waves a little better. Again, it takes a lot of practice to get just the right angles, the right feel. I think boatspeed is the crucial thing. As long as you have that, the rest is pretty easy.

W: *Do you like heavy air or light?*

D: I prefer medium to heavy air. I sail so much in it, here in the Bahamas.

W: *The last time I sailed against you was the first time the Worlds were in the Bahamas, and you were fast in light air - fast enough to win.*

D: Well, I went to quite a few regattas in the States, and sailed against all the Americans who are very good in light air, and tuned up against them. That helped me a great deal, so I got competitive. I was fast enough to hold my own until the breeze did come in, and then I was dominant.

W: *How do you handle waves upwind?*

D: With my light weight, in a breeze, I find that keeping the boat on a heel, it's relatively easy to work up and down on the waves. When the wave is approaching you, you let the wave hit you on the side, then luff up around the back of it. And you're always maneuvering up and down on the waves, despite what your sail is doing. It's much better than having a wave crash into you and stop you dead in your tracks. It's important to keep the boat moving, sailing through the waves, rather than trying to hold a straight direction.

W: *You say you keep a heel. About what angle do you average?*

D: I would say five, maybe 10 degrees. Depending on the wave size. The flatter it is, the better it is to keep it flat. But when the chop builds up, I find I tend to heel a lot more than the other sailors. It just feels faster. It's a groove I've gotten into that I like so much.

W: *If you stall out, do you feel it right away?*

D: It does happen in a puff. You get a big puff coming through, when it happens, I prefer pinching too much rather than footing and driving off sideways. I find I do power up a lot, especially when it's heavy. But it's a lot better to stall than to be slamming into the waves head on. You don't lose as much ground.

W: *How do you get her going again once she stalls out?*

D: Once you stall, just veer off real hard, to get a good driving force off of the wave, and get going again really quickly. The 180-pounders can drive off and foot, but I think it's important for the lighter sailor to pinch more than foot.

W: *What do you weigh?*

D: Now about 160, but in days gone by, when I was winning the Worlds, about 140, 150 pounds. But I had to put on a little weight for the Laser class.

W: *Do you like the new board?*

D: I like it a lot. I think it's made everyone more competitive. It's evened up the racing tremendously. The heavyweights have a chance against the lightweights and vice versa. The weight factor's not as crucial as it used to be.

W: *Let's switch to tactics going to windward. What do you watch out for? How do you keep out of*

Interviews with the Champions • 1995-1996

trouble?

D: Well, if you've gotten a good start, which I think is key in any big-fleet regatta, you just keep yourself clear until the first shift. Then it's important to take it, to cover the fleet. Works really well when you've got good boatspeed. You only have to stay close with the top five boats. Anything you've lost upwind you can make up going off. Siegenthaler used to do that real well. It's a lot easier sailing from the front of the pack than the back.

W: *That's for sure! What if you don't get the lift?*

D: Just ride it out... In some areas you have to be concerned with tides and currents. If the wind favors one side of the course, you need to know, from asking local sailors, if the tide will be with you or against you. The current can be crucial, as it was in Curaçao, compared with the Worlds in Orlando, on a lake, where you waited for the big shifts. It's a big difference.

W: *Right. How do you like to approach the weather mark?*

D: Pretty much on port tack, I think, towards the end. Come in 10 or 15 boat lengths below the mark. You don't want a starboard tack boat to come down on top of you. Leave room to take a little hitch. You can usually see a hole. Bear off if you have to, then take that hitch into it. That's much better than getting buried in on starboard tack, which everyone else seems to favor, where it's too easy to get caught in a bad spot. You lose too much ground.

W: *On that first reach, how do you decide, high or low?*

D: Are you ahead of me or behind me?

W: *I'm always behind you!*

D: I almost always go high, in big fleets. In a fleet of 20 or so you can usually sail down and then reach up to the mark, but a big fleet blankets so much of the air that it's important to stay to weather of everybody. I tend to ride as high as I can as long as I can. When a puff comes in I tend to bear off towards the mark. Often I stay high until I have to run down to the reaching mark...I go that high sometimes. But I find the loss is minimal, as opposed to staying low, and finding five or six boats that want your wind. They'll just stop you in your tracks, and then you'll lose everybody. But I've been going really high on the reaches, so I can come down on the puffs and get back on course.

W: *What tricks do you use, in marginal conditions, to plane as much as possible?*

D: The weight positioning is important, as long as you keep your weight aft. I find, with the new boats, it pays to get your weight as far aft as you can get.

W: *Really?*

D: Oh yes, and also with a little heel. I find it tends to ride the waves a lot better.

W: *To windward or leeward, the heel?*

D: To windward...no, leeward. I've found, with the new boats, the new sails, and I've tried different things...with the new, full sails it's really important to get the weight aft so you can get the optimum power out of them. That seems to work really well. And it's important, when you get up on a wave, because you're going faster than the normal strength of the wind, to pump that sail once or twice.

W: *Once!*

D: That's right. You know, they've gotten very strict with that rule.

W: *I understand at the last Worlds ('95) they had judges out there, and all of a sudden they started calling the leaders on it?*

D: I don't know why. This thing called pumping...which none of us do, right?...they called P.J. and Mark May and a bunch of guys. It's a hard thing to call. But the jury boats were out there, and I'm sure they can see more, see who's working harder, pumping harder than those who are not. They had binoculars! I guess it's pretty obvious from a spectator point of view. It's a hard thing for a sailor to protest another sailor for doing it. And it seems everybody is doing it.

W: *Well, the guys in front certainly are. From way in back you can see it.*

D: To a certain degree, unfortunately. It's one of the things I've always said, when you're out there training all the time, the kinetics become a part of it. You tend to naturally do it, to keep the boat moving. With the new, stricter rules, you have to be extra careful nowadays. Otherwise, they're going to disqualify you. But all the top dinghy sailors do it, a fair amount of it. I think it's just a question of who's overdoing it.

W: *Is there more done in Lasers than Sunfish?*

D: Oh, I've seen lots of pumping and ooching in Lasers. The Sunfish Class is more refined; it's not done excessively.

W: *I think you've told me that you pull your sail in more on the reaches than most people, is that right?*

D: Yes, I like to power it up. I've found that with the new sail in tighter, in heavy air, and the board up higher than normal, the boat just flies off the waves without stalling. If you get that adjusted just right it works phenomenally well. Especially now that the boards are longer. I'm not sure I've adjusted to that quite yet.

W: *How about at the gybe mark? Do you worry about getting an inside position?*

D: Well, I like to go high on the reaches, and on the second one, at the leeward mark, if you come in high they've got to let you in. If you come in low, especially with lots of boats, you're going to get buried. That's so at the gybe mark, too. I find I can come in fairly late, almost on a run, heeled well to windward, and slip in with an overlap fairly close to the mark. Then it's a simple thing to gybe and be on the high side for the second reach.

That works especially when you've got 15 or 20 boats. On the other hand, there's often someone who wants to take everyone high. Then it's good to drop low, and get out of the bad air. The most important thing is clear air.

W: *Sometimes, when you go high on that second reach, you're carried so high you have to gybe into the leeward mark. How do you handle that?*

D: You have to go with them. Go until you know you have to gybe. It's important to go first. So you have to know when to make that decision. If you wait for them to gybe, you're back to square one.

W: *How about the run? Anything different you do there compared with the reaches?*

D: Well, if there's no boats forcing you high, I do like to sail the boat to the lee. Heel to windward quite a bit. It's probably the only time I heel the boat to weather. As you ride down the wave, the further to leeward you sail, the better it is, rather than straight down the wave. I think it's a better angle, and the boat sails a little smoother that way. And I slack off the outhaul as much as I can. I don't bother on the reaches, but on the run I think it's nice to let it off as much as you can.

W: *Why is that?*

D: To get as much belly in the sail as you can get. Almost like a spinnaker. It holds a better shape, and feels a lot faster. The guys that don't do that seem to get bogged down in the waves. You want as much power as you can get.

W: *When you're scooting down a wave and about to bury in the wave in front of you...*

D: You should have been in Abaco. There were

Interviews with the Champions • 1995-1996

some serious nose dives by the best of us, you know? It's really hard in certain situations, but I think the best move is the gutsy one, where you just sail off lower than normal, sail right to the lee, which is very risky, right on the edge of capsizing, but I find it's the safest way to go. The more you sail and practice, the more comfortable you get with sailing like that, right on the edge. The same thing with gybing at the gybe mark in 30 knots of wind. The guys who've sailed every chance they get are comfortable with it. Everyone else tacks.

W: *Let's talk about how you set up your boat.*

D: I think I sail fairly tight compared with the other sailors. I sail with my outhaul snug on the boom. Going to weather, it feels better that way. I don't like to see scallops on the upper or lower boom. My gooseneck is normally around 18 inches. I've seen a lot of the others, with the new board, up at 17 or 16 inches. I've not got adjusted that far forward yet. I've found on flat water that's good, but where I sail there's always chop, so I usually leave the gooseneck alone at 18. I loosen up the outhauls offwind. Not a lot, just enough to get a bit of a scallop on the luff and foot.

W: *You say you do it more on the run than the reach.*

D: Right. Not a tremendous amount...just an inch or two at the most.

W: *Do you ever play with the luff when you're going to windward?*

D: Only when the wind picks up. I like a flat sail when I'm going to windward, because the sails now are so nice and big anyway.

W: *Do you use the Jens, or have you stopped using it, like a lot of the other guys?*

D: I never used it, you know. I've always sailed with the full rig. I though about it at Abaco, because it got up to 30 plus. One of those days it was just survival conditions. I thought it might be good to try, but I'd never raced with it, so I didn't. With the new big board and full sail, it's probably a good feature when it gets up to 20 knots. So I'm going to start to practice with it a bit. In survival conditions it probably helps a lot, especially going to weather.

W: *How about physical conditioning? What kind or exercising do you do, if any?*

D: I do a lot of jogging. And I play a lot of rugby, which keeps me in shape in the off season. Three or four days a week. My stamina's usually pretty good because of that. Here, the seasons don't overlap much, so it really works out. And I do a lot of sailing, and that keeps the hiking muscles in good shape. I find that going out two or three days a week is good. For a month or so before a big championship I try to get out five or six days a week.

W: *Do you have regular weekly races?*

D: Actually, no. We don't race here at all. We have one championship a year, which is the Nationals, for anyone who wants to qualify for the World Championship. Actually, the only racing I get is at the Worlds, or the North Americans, in a fleet of any size. That makes it difficult, you know? My first few starts are usually pretty rusty. It usually takes me a couple of races to get settled down.

W: *How about mental preparation. Do you like to get to the race early?*

D: Yes, I think it's nice to get out maybe half an hour, 45 minutes before a race. Sail to the first mark to see where the wind shifts are. So you know the difference between the lifts and the lulls. Once you get in sync with that, when the race starts I think you have a big head start on the other sailors who are not sure exactly what the wind's doing for the day yet. It gives you an advantage for that, and also to see how the current's flowing. It can

Interviews with the Champions • 1995-1996

give you a tremendous advantage, helps you with planning the race.

W: *Do you get to the venue early, a couple of days ahead?*

D: Not really. I prefer to get there the day of the event or the day before. They always say when the racing starts it's "regatta weather," not at all the usual conditions. I find in that case it's better to get out on the water the day of the event in the conditions you're going to have. An hour or two before the event is usually enough.

W: *Do you ever wear any weight - water or wet sweats?*

D: Yes, I usually carry about 10 pounds of water in heavy air. But I understand they're going to ban that this year. That's why I think the Jens is going to be used more and more by the lighter sailors.

W: *Anything else I've forgotten to ask?*

D: We've covered a lot. I think most of my boatspeed comes from time in the boat, rather than adjusting things. I don't get to race much. Just getting comfortable in the boat, maneuvering through the waves the best I can. I find that's the biggest secret. You can have all the adjustments in the world just right, but if you're slamming into the waves or diving downwind, none of that matters. Concentration is a big part of it.

W: *Amen to that. Anything else you'd like to say?*

D: In general, I think the Sunfish Class has excelled so much in the last three to five years. I think the level of skill has come up a tremendous amount. It's a good thing to see because the Class is a competitive class. With all the changes to the boat, it's been a big benefit to all Sunfish sailors. The boats are so even now the test is truly between the sailors.

W: *There's some talk about a new rudder. What do you think of that?*

D: I've got mixed feelings about that. But if the design is right, and everybody has the same rudders, and they can control that even better, then it might not be a bad move. It's one of the few changes left to make to improve the boat. But I think they need to be careful, because there have been a lot of changes in the last few years. Maybe it's best to let the sailors settle in with what they have. The rudder might be a little too soon. It might be a good time to start designing one. The new plastic board is certainly nice, and has made things more even. I guess it's inevitable that we get a plastic rudder, to cut out any tampering with the rudder style or shape. I suppose it's inevitable in the next couple of years.

W: *Well, it took us more than five years to get the board done...*

D: Yeah, but you did it right. It's important, when you do do it, to make sure everything is perfect, and that it's tested properly...in all conditions. I have confidence in Sunfish Laser to do it right.

W: *OK, Donny, I sure appreciate your help.*

D: Always nice talking with you, you know? Take care.

● Malcolm Smith

Malcolm Smith has attended more Sunfish World Championships than he can remember offhand. He is always a threat, and is considered by most experienced Sunfish racers to be one of the all-time greats, judging by the number of times his name comes up in the reminiscing that goes on at all Sunfish regattas. He is also one of the great hosts among many at Bermuda Race Week, where the Sunfish is well into its second decade as an invited class. For more on his sailing exploits, see the end of this interview.

Will: Let's start with the start. How do you like to start?

Malcolm: Aggressive.

W: *Meaning what?*

M: Front row. And it's important to know what the wind is going to do. You know, whether the wind's going to go right or left after the start. It's pretty important getting in phase right after the start and trying to catch the first shift. If you're on the wrong side of the shift you can lose quite a lot on a big starting line.

W: *How do you anticipate that?*

M: It's good to do upwind readings five, ten, fifteen minutes prior to the start. Maybe do one or two readings every five or ten minutes just to find out where the wind's shifting and how much. Then I guess it's important to find the favored end even though nowadays you find that most of the lines are fairly straight. But you do get shifts and you usually will get one side more favored than the other.

W: *So what do you do if one end is favored? Do you fight it out at that end?*

M: I would try to be at that end.

W: *You mean if you find out it's the pin end you fight it out and try to be right at the pin?*

M: Not necessarily. No one really wants to go for the pin. I would rather be in a position where you can tack away. Sometimes if you get caught right at the pin you get boats to windward of you and if you want to tack away you may have to duck boats - which isn't a winning situation. I probably prefer to start, when the pin's favored, anywhere from five to ten boats up from the pin.

W: *It's hard to build a hole, though, when you're that close, isn't it?*

M: I guess it just depends on how competitive the fleet is, to make your own hole within the last twenty to thirty seconds of the start. Like the Worlds we just did ('95)...I found big line sag even close to the pin, with people sitting back of the line and not getting right up on the line and being really aggressive.

W: *Did you have any PMSs - premature starts?*

M: No.

W: *Good. How did you finish, by the way?*

M: I ended up sixth. And I think that was probably because I *didn't* get good starts. I wasn't aggressive enough and I wasn't getting at the right end of the line. And it may have been not doing enough major regattas just prior to the Worlds. If you can get just to two or three big regattas it gets your starting ability up. I think that's one of the reasons I found myself behind at the first leeward mark a lot. I have been finding myself fighting back a lot to get back into the top ten or five boats. That means good second beats and fast offwind legs.

W: *Let's talk about how you like to sail to windward. How do you sail the first windward leg?*

M: Again, you want to know if the wind's going to do anything. If there are any major shifts it's probably good to do some work prior to the first beat and find out if the right side or the left side is favored.

W: *How do you do that?*

M: With another sailor. You sail for five minutes one way on starboard and the other guy can go on port. You both tack about the same time, and come together. Then you can find out if it's a bit favored on one side or if it's just equal. And usually you find that one side's more favored than the other.

W: *Do you usually get out quite early, then, to do this?*

M: Probably 45 minutes. You want to leave the shore an hour before the starting gun, if it take 15 minutes to get out to the starting area. You try and figure those things out, and then get your boat set up for the existing conditions.

W: *On the windward leg, would you say that you're a pincher or a footer?*

M: It depends on the conditions. If it's sort of flat water you can pinch a little more. If you find that it's a short steep chop you may have to foot more. Sometimes even heel the boat more so it doesn't stick the nose in so much. It really depends on the conditions and how you're setting up the rig. I find some guys sailing very tight on the lower outhaul and very loose on the upper. This helps to move the draft back and allows you to point more. So how you set up your rig affects your ability to point. Then your gooseneck comes into it as well. There's a big variation in what guys are doing now.

W: *Where do you normally have yours?*

M: Well - depending on the conditions, again - if it's anything under twelve knots then probably 17 to 17¾ inches back. I don't sail much at anything less than 17, but I know some guys sail maybe 16, Jeff Linton maybe even 14 or 15. I haven't really had anybody to train with lately. For the last Worlds, any training I had, I had to do on my own. Unless you have someone to train with you, you really

Interviews with the Champions • 1995-1996

can't check the variances.

W: *How do you like the new board?*

M: I think it's great. I think it goes upwind much cleaner and it's definitely giving everybody an equal board. With the old boards you'd get different tapers and you'd find more tendency to get warped boards. I think it's really put the boat itself in a different class.

W: *Do you ever use a Jens?*

M: Probably in anything over 20 knots.

W: *Right, when it's really honkin'.*

M: Yeah. At the last Worlds in Bermuda, where I won, we did three races on the last day. The first race I didn't have a Jens. It was blowing probably twenty to twenty-five, and I had a bad race - I ended eleventh. After that we went in and we had some time to make adjustments. I decided to throw a Jens in, and I talked to Jean Bergman, because you know she almost always uses a Jens. She showed me a very simple way - putting a running loop through the top of your mast. It worked really well. I went out there and got a first and a second. That's what probably helped me win the Worlds on that last day.

W: *Did you use any this year?*

M: I don't think so. We had one really heavy air race - it was gusting probably about 20 to 25 miles an hour, but I didn't use it. When we got out there it was about 15 to 18 and it picked up during the race. So there wasn't much chance of changing it. And I found that I could hold the boat down, so it really wasn't a problem. I think the new board helps upwind in the heavier breeze. It helps the boat drive more forward instead of sideways.

W: *Do you ever lift the board in really heavy stuff?*

M: I probably do let it come up just an inch or two. Between two and four inches at the most. It helps.

W: *How about tactics on the windward leg? Anything you do special?*

M: Basically just to try and get in phase and if there's someone you have to beat, then try not to split too much with him. If he's up in front of you then you have to try and work and get up inside him. Tactics just seem to come to you during the race.

W: *How do you like to approach the weather mark?*

M: In a really big fleet it's really dangerous coming in off port. You can lose a lot of boats. If you're anywhere from ten to fifteen boats back you can lose a lot of boats on port tack. Sometimes you can get lucky and find yourself a hole. It's dangerous, though, and the majority of times you'll find me coming in on starboard. On the other hand, if you get to the right side too early you can miss out on a shift, so it's not good to get out there too early.

W: *Let's talk about reaches. As you round the weather mark, what do you do, and in what order?*

M: It would depend on how you're situated in the race. If you have a guy directly in front of you it's kind of hard to work the waves as much. You have a choice. If you know he's slow, you can try to go up and around, over him really fast. If you have an open space, it's probably best to try and work the waves down in the puffs and work your way up in the lulls a little bit and use the waves as much as you can.

W: *How do you catch a wave?*

M: Get your boat up to speed and then sort of steer down it.

W: *You don't do much pumping?*

M: It's pretty hard nowadays with the judges there watching you. You're allowed one pump per wave. You might be able to get away with two, three small pumps to get you going. But I think steering through the waves is just as important as pumping. Big pumps aren't always good. I think short pumps and steering down the waves is probably better than trying to pump up and over waves all the time. If you work your boat up and get your speed up, you can really work back down the waves fast. You can get stuck in the troughs and you have to work your way up again. If you get to the bottom you have to steer back up and then once you get back up you try to veer back down again. A lot of people just sit there and steer straight, which is probably the worst thing you can do. The best guy I've seen off the wind is probably Eduardo (Cordero).

W: *That's what Jeff Linton says, too.*

M: He's really fast offwind. Maybe it's because of where he comes from. He sails in those kinds of conditions all the time. He's really fast offwind.

W: *Generally speaking, on that first reach do you like to go high or low?*

M: I don't like to go high. I think it's best to stay sort of in the middle and work down. Then you have the option to come back up if it gets light on you, and you can keep your speed up. So whenever you get the opportunity to drive down and still keep your speed up, you should.

W: *Anything special about the gybe mark?*

M: Just trying to do it coming down a wave is probably the best thing. When you gybe, make sure you keep your speed up right out of the gybe and try not to lose boats on the inside. It's pretty important, to get around the gybe mark, to try and get in sync with the waves again for the second reach. Watch for guys up on your wind. Sometimes they'll want to drive up over the top of you. You have to watch those guys.

W: *Do you find yourself going high more on that second leg?*

M: You probably do. Unless you're clear and don't have anyone around you. Then you can really work the waves to yourself. When you get people around you, you tend not to pay much attention to the waves and you start losing your ground. A boat might start forcing you to come up and you lose your opportunity to come down a wave or something. You have to take the opportunity. Sometimes you have to work down immediately after the gybe. If you have the space and there's no one there. Otherwise you go up, or they'll ride over the top of you.

W: *But if there's somebody behind you then you have to protect yourself and go high?*

M: Yes, unless you get some good waves. Then you can usually pull out in front of him. If you're one boat-length, two boat-lengths apart at the mark, and he wants to go up and you find that there are some good waves and enough breeze to work down, then you can do that. Because he's only going to lose out by going high.

W: *When you're coming down to the leeward mark in a crowd, how do you try to work that?*

M: Try to get in the overlap, and figure out what the wind has done before you get on the next beat. Usually, when you round the mark, you can use your compass or any landmarks, anything you can take a bearing on from the previous beat. If you know you are down five or ten degrees from the previous beat, you may not want to go too far. You may want to tack immediately to get back in phase.

W: *How about running? Anything different about that?*

M: It's a lot like reaching. You've really got to work the waves. The fastest guys are the ones who've really spent a lot of time sailing on the waves. I think it's important to sail by the lee a little bit and then work your way back up. You just keep working the waves and you can make a lot of ground on the run

Interviews with the Champions • 1995-1996

if you get in phase with everything.

W: *If you're surfing down a wave on a dead run, and you find yourself getting close to burying the bow, what do you do—bear up or bear off, or does it depend?*

M: You can go either way. A Sunfish does sail faster by the lee a little bit, but I think bearing off too hard is bad...depending on the angles of the waves. Sometimes the bigger waves will run at a different angle from the wind waves. So when you figure out what the larger waves are doing, you want to stay in phase with them. I think it's probably better to stay with a big wave and then look for an opportunity - find a hole in the wave ahead. Sometimes you find holes in the waves, and you have to work through those holes. Going back up the waves can slow you down really bad.

W: *It sure can. We've talked a little about how you set your boat up. Tell me again: how do you feel the luff should be set up for heavy air?*

M: For heavy air, with the racing sail, I think that with these sails most of the fast guys are keeping the luff still kind of slack. They're not using a lot of Cunningham. If they are, it's very little. The head of the sail is probably four to five inches from the end of the gaff. So it gives you some room down at the bottom to adjust.

W: *That's interesting. And then the outhaul on the boom: do you keep that fairly taught?*

M: Um...Not taught but flat enough to take any scallops out of the foot. I don't think that scallops in your sail down low is fast at all, except maybe offwind. You definitely need to ease the outhaul offwind, and you need to ease the Cunningham offwind and give the sail as much power as you can.

W: *Even on the run?*

M: Yes. Some guys, like P.J. Patin at the last Worlds, were really easing off a lot. I think he may have been easing off a little bit extreme. But probably you would want to ease off at least two to three, maybe four inches from what it would be set up upwind.

W: *Really that much?*

M: Really. P.J. was easing off probably five to six inches.

W: *Was he fast then?*

M: I don't think it made any difference. I think actually you're taking away from the sail area if you ease too much. So you either want, as in his case, to bag it out and get more power, or you want to ease it just minimally - just enough to give you more power, but also to keep some sail area.

W: *What kind of body conditioning do you do. Do you do any exercises? Run?*

M: Well, my dog keeps me in pretty good shape. And I like to cycle maybe two or three times a week. And I'll also go to the gym and do some upper body and leg work, sit-ups. But for keeping your stomach muscles in shape, sailing is probably 75 percent of it. If you can spend three days a week on the water, anywhere from two to three hours, I think that is probably just as important as going to the gym three days a week. I think keeping the sailing muscles in shape is more important than anything else.

W: *Right - time on the water. Do you do anything to prepare yourself mentally?*

M: Not really. Mentally, success comes from preparation, from sailing before the regatta. You can psych yourself up going out there and getting the boat going good, from brushing with someone else before a race and getting your boat in tune.

W: *That gives you the confidence you need?*

M: It does. If you know that you're going fast then you know before the race begins you should be able to sort things out.

W: *You won the Worlds last year ('94) and you've*

won any number of times at Bermuda Race Week. What other wins have you had in Sunfish?

M: I was second in '87 at the Worlds in Aruba, and I was second in '93 in Tortola and I think I was third in Houston in '92. I've had quite a few Worlds in sixth, seventh, eighth - I don't think I've ever come fourth or fifth. I've won our Bermuda National Championships twelve or thirteen times now. I was second in the Midwinters, I think in '91. That was actually the only Midwinters I've attended. I've never been to a North American. Sooner or later I'll get up there. But right now I'm campaigning for Lasers in '96 to sail for Bermuda in the Olympics. I think after that you might find me attending one or two North Americans.

W: Do you prefer the Sunfish or the Laser?

M: I think they're pretty close. The Sunfish Class is definitely a lot friendlier. You've got nice people in the Sunfish Class. You know, I've been sailing in it since I was 12 years old and I'm 37 now. It took me 19 years from my first Worlds to win one.

W: It felt good, I bet.

M: Yeah. My first Worlds was in 1975 in Miami. Derrick Fries was there. He was really someone to look up to at that point in my life. I was about 16 and thought he was the greatest. But like I said, the people in the Sunfish Class are just great people. They're always so friendly. That's why you always enjoy going back to the Worlds - not to go there and compete but to see your friends and to spend some time with them. That one week in a year that you get to see them - if you miss one it's like you're missing something in life, you know?

W: Weren't you sailing Snipes for a while?

M: I did the Western Hemispheres, two or three. I never did a Snipe Worlds. I did win Bermuda Race Week a couple of times in the Snipes, and got second twice. Last year I won Bermuda Race Week in the Lasers.

W. Great to talk with you, Malcolm.

11 River Racing

Back in 1972, when Jack Evans and I were looking for a new kind of competition for Sunfish, I remembered a cruise with my sons the previous summer from Windsor Locks, Connecticut, to Old Saybrook, a distance of 52 miles down the Connecticut River. We camped out overnight at Hurd State Park, about two-thirds of the way down. Based on that experience, Jack and I invented the Long-Distance Down-the-Connecticut-River Mixed Doubles Championship, a two-day race, and made it a series of races so boats would not get spread too far apart. The rule required that you carried your own camping equipment and lunches, but Alcort supplied dinner and breakfast. It was spur-of-the-moment, and we ran the first of these annual events three weeks later. There were six boats, and we all had a wonderful time. The next year, there were 36 boats. After that, Alcort had to limit the entries to 75 for safety's sake. One of these days, we figured, a squall would come whippping up the river, flatten everybody, and many would need help from chase boats. Every year, Alcort managed to lure five stinkpotters to bring their boats along, for safety purposes. Interestingly, most of the competitors in the Connecticut River Race were rugged outdoorsy types rather than the hotshots you will find on the regatta circuit. But every year, one or two of the good ones - real lovers of sailing - show up and, of course, clean up. Actually, racing is very informal and the winners are, with good nature, chided for trying too hard.

After the first Connecticut River Race, other point-to-point races were launched: 'Round Key West in Florida, 'Round Bermuda out there at the northern tip of *the* Triangle, and 'Round Cape Ann at the northeast corner of Massachusetts. There is also a 'Round Shelter Island race out in the crotch of Long Island, New York, even older than the Connecticut River Race, called "The World's Longest Sunfish Race." It's a day-long affair, and probably still is the longest, if you eliminate the Connecticut River Race because that's a series of races. The Connecticut River Classic, as it came to be known, died out when Pearson bought the company and moved it to Rhode Island. But, through the efforts of Paul Odegaard, it was revived in the late '80s. It is going strong again under the sponsorship of the Lions Club of Saybrook.

Even though river racing is supposed to be relaxed, and there is some social stigma to trying too hard, there are ways to make a boat sail fast down a river, and I wrote down some thoughts about them - things I've learned on the way to six victories in the early days of the Connecticut River Race. Some of those things are helpful in racing on small lakes, too.

A great deal has been written about round-the-buoys sailboat racing, meteorology, and how to predict wind shifts. Much has been written about tides and currents, as well, since many round-the-buoys courses are set in tide waters. But not too much has been written about sailing fast down a river, since river racing in small sailboats is relatively new. In fact, as far as we know, it was pioneered by the Sunfish Class on the Connecticut River.

River racing, at least so far, is a relatively low-key affair. One of the published rules of the "Great Connecticut River Race" is "Don't take it too seriously." Starts, as described by Joanne Fishman of *The New York Times*, tend to be "a floating version of bumper cars" where the rules are observed if possible, but if it's not possible...well, in the first nine years of the Connecticut River Race, there were no protests.

However, once the tangle of the start is sorted out, it becomes a challenge to sail the fastest possible course down the river. The sailor's mind must be an adaptable computer, with two major sources of input — wind and current. It is possible to get down the river just by letting the current

River Racing

The 10th Connecticut River Race was sailed in 1982. Here the vanguard of the 75-boat fleet passes Goodspeed Opera House in East Haddam.

sweep you along, with the wind helping most of the time. But the secret of getting down the river first is to find the best combination of wind and current.

This type of sailing requires a certain kind of adaptability not usually called upon in round-the-buoys racing. Every bend in the river seems to bring a brand new set of conditions. The fastest part of the current will suddenly have shifted to the other shore, and the wind will have swung 45 or 90 degrees or disappeared altogether. Actually, if there is a current, the wind never totally disappears, unless it is blowing in the same direction and at the same speed as the current. But in a flat calm, a current will sweep you along, creating a one-knot breeze if it is a one-knot current.

This phenomenon raises an interesting point. In a flat calm, is it faster just to sit in the fastest part of the current and drift downstream, or should you beat into the wind created by the current? A little reflection should provide the right answer. If you just drift, you will drift at the speed of the current. If you beat, you add the speed made good to windward to that of the current, and get there faster.

But back to the current. Where does it flow fastest? In carving out river beds, currents seem to carom from one bank to the other around the bend, carving the deepest channel on the outside of each curve. Water flows fastest in the deepest part of the river, since there is less friction from

River Racing

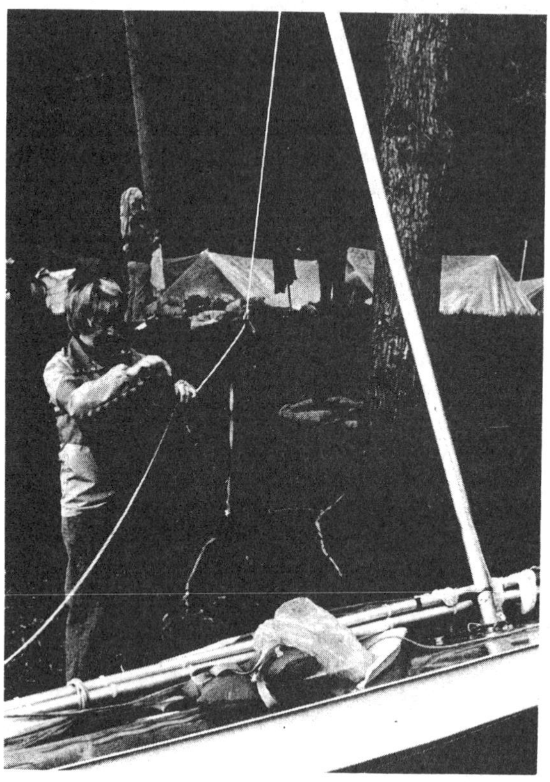

Sailors find more uses for Sunfish halyards than Indians did for birch bark. The Connecticut River Race.

The mother/daughter team of Linda and Rhoda Babcock fully rigged for the Great Long-Distance Down-the-Connecticut River Race.

the bottom. The fastest current is usually on the outside of each bend. However, this is one rule that Mother Nature sometimes likes to break. A river bottom may be formed by other than the action of the water - a shift in geological strata, for instance - and the current may hug the inside curve. This can happen in a gorge, or where there is cliff on one bank and flat land on the other. But not always. If you really want to know, study the charts of the river, if there are any. There's no guarantee that the deepest part of the channel will stay where the chartmakers put it, but it is better than guessing. Many rivers, of course, have channels dredged for commercial traffic, and you're pretty safe following these.

Sometimes bridge pilings or jetties can produce interesting effects on the current. Where a bridge piling splits the water, the current is often quite fast. There is almost a jet stream, and if you catch it, you can get a jump of several boat lengths. However, you have to catch it at the right angle, because there is often a back eddy at the downstream end, and if you get caught in that, it's like hitting a stone wall, especially if there is no wind. There are often back eddies close to shore, as well, and an occasional sailor gets caught in one if he is trying to sneak too close to shore to get a favorable wind slant.

River Racing

There is another phenomenon to watch for, this one on tidal rivers. The current may be downstream for several hours, then imperceptibly stop and start flowing upstream as the tide comes in. It is quite possible for it to flow upstream on one side of a wide river, while flowing downstream on the other. If you are racing downstream, you know where you want to be.

So you've gotten out the charts, and talked to some riverboat pilots, and you are pretty sure you know where the current will be on every stretch of the river? Don't bank on it. Watch the river. If you are in the middle, and the water seems to be flowing faster on one side or the other, you may want to get over into the faster current, even though the chart says it shouldn't be faster over there. Trust your eyes. You can tell by the action of the water, or the flotsam and jetsam that usually accompanies you downstream. Of course, if you have a nice 12-knot breeze on the beam, and you are planing down the river at an exhilarating clip, actually seeing differences in current speed becomes pretty difficult. But then, in that kind of breeze, you are probably better off playing the wind rather than the current.

And that brings in the other major factor in river sailing - the wind. Just as the current is seldom the same speed across the width of the river, so it is with the wind. Both direction and force can vary considerably from one side of the river to the other, and you can pretty well count on the current being different 200 yards downstream. So while you want to be very conscious of the current, especially in very light air, you have to try to dope out the wind simultaneously.

Every sailor knows that the shoreline does funny things with the wind sometimes. These tricks are compounded on the river. If the banks are high, or the trees are thick, the river can become a wind tunnel, bending the wind up or downstream. It is often possible to stay on one tack a lot longer than you might think possible, because the wind is bending around a curve and lifting you. It is this phenomenon that can often trap you in a back eddy, if you try to ride that lift too far inshore. On the other hand, if you don't ride in that lift to the last possible second, your competitor may - and get a jump of several boat lengths on you.

Even more than on a lake, interesting local breezes can spring up from temperature differentials between the land and the water. It pays to watch the surface of the water, not only for currents, but also for cat's paws of wind, especially in light air. Even relatively minor differences in temperature from one side of the

Lunch break the second day – the Connecticut River Race.

River Racing

river to the other, or from the water to the land, or from one stretch of river to another can cause thermal breezes to spring up. It is probably impossible to predict them. But it *is* important to watch for them.

Breezes blowing across a stretch of river can also do some interesting things. If the wind is blowing off a higher bank toward a lower bank, it is almost always best to be close to the lower bank, since the higher bank will have a blanketing effect. But cross-stream winds can give you more subtle problems. In rolling terrain, especially, the wind seems to be able to skip across the water. It may "bounce" in the middle, or close to one side or the other. Or it may skip twice, leaving a sort of dead air tunnel down the middle of the river! More troublesome still, the pattern does not remain constant, varying unpredictably as you go downstream, or even as the actual wind strength increases or decreases. You can see a boat a hundred yards ahead that seems to be right in the area where the wind is bouncing hardest, and by the time you get there, it is bouncing somewhere else. This bouncing of the wind takes place on open water, too - it is apparently the cause of localized gusts - but on the river it is confusion compounded.

Whether you are racing or not, sailing a river is a fascinating exercise in piloting. One point to remember - it is great fun to sail from a point upstream to a point downstream if there is somebody there to pick you up. But if you have to get back to your launching point, a good rule to follow is to sail against the current for the first leg. Then, if the wind quits, you will at least drift back on the current to your home port.

The Cruising Sunfish 12

Many years ago, when I had just bought my first Sailfish, I was interviewing a salesman in my office and told him about it. He said, "Oh, you'll have a ball with your Sailfish. Every summer, my son and I cruise around the Elizabeth Islands for a week on ours." Now the Elizabeth Islands are the southern boundary of Buzzards Bay, and I had sailed on Buzzards Bay. It can be a pretty wild piece of water. The idea of cruising on a Sailfish, lugging along your camping gear, sitting for hours on a bouncing board, sounds like an exercise in masochism. To do it on the stormy waters of Buzzards Bay and Vineyard Sound sounds suicidal.

I decided to cruise the Connecticut River instead and a few years later, talked two of my sons into trying it with me. They were 11 and 13, and sailed one Sunfish with just a few things on board wrapped in plastic bags - sweaters and foul-weather gear, lunch, and other thing they might need on the water. I sailed another, with most of the camping gear and clothing wrapped in plastic garbage bags and lashed on deck.

We sailed the Connecticut River from Windsor Locks to Long Island Sound, a distance of roughly 52 miles, in two days. We camped out at Hurd State Park in East Haddam. What is remarkable to me about that trip is that we had a wonderful time even though we had only one small pup tent, it was a damp and chilly April weekend, and it drizzled most of the time we were in camp. Then, on the last leg into Essex, the wind started picking up, blowing straight upriver, and the boys capsized. I fished them out of the river, along with several floating plastic bags, righted their boat, lowered the rig, tied it on the deck, and took them in tow.

Unfortunately, the Sunfish is not designed for towing things. There was a steep chop, the current was flowing upriver, and we weren't making much headway. So I lowered my sail, too, shipped the rowing rig I had devised, and rowed the last four miles with them in tow. We arrived at the ramp under the I-95 bridge in Old Saybrook in the late afternoon, tired, only a little damp, and happy. As I said, we had a good time. I was hooked, and did the trip a number of times, just for fun, in addition to the annual race.

The important thing about cruising on the Sunfish is to remember that it's very much like back-packing through water up to your neck. You want to travel light, and you want to travel waterproof. Over the years, we have found that carrying the gear between the daggerboard and the mast seems to give the boat its best balance, and leaves enough sitting room for two people to be fairly comfortable. Wrap your gear in small plastic bags - doubled up for an extra margin of safety - and then stuff all those into large heavy-walled garbage or lawn bags. I use at least two, and usually three, stuffing the first bag mouth-down into the second, and so on. Then you can strap the large bags onto the deck with two or three shock cords of the kind used to hold luggage to a car roof rack. I have capsized with this rig, and everything somehow stayed dry. Nevertheless, the plastic bags are not very strong, and can sometimes get torn, so I have taken to stuffing packed plastic bags into canvas duffel bags, just for abrasion resistance.

With this gear, of course, you have to carry the sail a little higher than you do when you are racing, but then, who's racing?

I have never heard of anybody trying to overnight on a Sunfish. I wouldn't plan it unless you don't care about sleeping. But putting into shore every night, and pitching a tent or sleeping under the stars, can be a very relaxing way to spend a week or so. In 1977, a fellow named James Lee Meadows sailed from Florida to Boston in a Sunfish, and had a wonderful time. He was in no hurry, and occasionally stayed for weeks at a time if he found a particularly hospitable spot on shore. But it's not the sort of thing you should

The Cruising Sunfish

do unless you know how to handle a Sunfish.

A few years earlier, a man and his son cruised Long Island Sound for a week in this manner, and wrote a glowing account of their trip for *Scuttlebutt*, the original Sunfish newsletter. The next year, however, they decided to continue up the coast to Buzzards Bay, and one day they found themselves out in the middle of that choppy body of water, trying to tack against a stiff wind. They finally gave up and headed back to shore downwind and wrote Alcort to let them know that cruising in the Sunfish was dangerous on open water. It certainly can be. But note that they were able to sail out of trouble, even though they were not very experienced. Just remember that two people plus sailing gear on a Sunfish is a pretty heavy load, and I can imagine that it is pretty hard to go to windward in heavy wind and open water.

If you are doing your camping/cruising on tidal waters, it's important to remember those tides. In fact, it's important to remember tides when you are sailing at regattas off the beach. More than one Sunfish has sailed away from a regatta without any skipper when the incoming tide floated it free. At a regatta, that's at most a matter of embarrassment. If you are camping/sailing on your own, you could be marooned. Being a castaway has certain romantic overtones, but I have a hunch that most people who have lived through it would just as soon not repeat the experience.

It is usually easy enough to tell where the high tide normally stops. There is usually a lot of dead or dying seaweed and flotsam drawing a line at the high tide mark. Drag the boat above that level. And, just to make sure, tie a line from the boat to something on the beach. Of course, you will want to make camp above this mark. One of the least comfortable things that can happen to you is to get your blanket roll or sleeping bag wet...especially when you are sleeping in it.

James Lee Meadows sailed from Miami to Boston. He obviously traveled light.

River current and tidal currents can often fool you. On a tidal river, the current will mostly take you downstream, but for some part of the day, the current will actually be flowing upstream. On a river, that's not likely to get you into trouble. But on coastal waters, currents can really throw you off course, especially if visibility is restricted by fog or rain. You may think you are sailing close to shore, and find that you are really so far out of line that, when visibility returns, you have lost sight of land. So it's a good idea to study a good current table before you start your trip and to know when the currents are changing and which way they flow.

One sail against a tree makes shelter (sort of) for two. Four sails interlocked tepee-fashion make shelter for six friends, or eight very good friends.

If it is at all possible that you will stray out of sight of land, make sure you take along a compass. Sometimes you will wish that you had an anchor along. The smallest Danforth is more than adequate for a Sunfish, with 3/16" nylon line. It is the most awkward gear I recommend taking along, but if you want to hold your own against the current when the wind is very light, you will be glad it's along. The alternative is a paddle, which has a lot more uses than helping you hold your own against current. It can help you get where you are going in a calm, and can serve as a crutch on which to prop the side of the boat when you drain it. And it can serve as a tent pole. So the anchor is a luxury; the paddle is not. Take a paddle.

I have heard of people navigating by road map, but it sure is a chancy way to cruise. I like to know where I am all the time, and keep an open chart close at hand. Of course, in a Sunfish, you don't have many places to keep it, and the government doesn't print its charts on waterproof paper. (In the last few years, some private publishers have reproduced government charts on plastic sheets.) One of the best wrinkles is to cut the chart up into 8 1/2" x 11" pieces, being careful to code all four sides, so you know how to find the next piece when you sail off the edge. Then you laminate these pieces in plastic, and keep them book fashion in one of those 9" x 12" clear plastic bags with a zip lock top. You can tape these to the deck. At regattas, I often do that, to hold the local chart or diagram of the race course along with race instructions.

Of course, if you are cruising a river or small lake, it's usually easy enough to get to shore and ask where you are. But if you are sailing in relatively open water, it's a lot more healthy to *know* where you are.

Most of the time, when you are camping/cruising, you will be putting up overnight on sandy beaches. In many ways, camping on sand is great. You can dig a little hole and make a fire in it and not worry that you're going to set the forest ablaze. You can dig out a bed that conforms to your body almost as comfortably as a waterbed. You can even pile it up around the edges of your tent or fly to keep out the wind.

But almost as much as water, sand loves to get into your things. It can make your clothes itchy, and even worse, make your food crunchy. If you don't like fingernails on a blackboard, just wait until you bite into a sandy sandwich. So it is important to be as vigilant against sand as against water. Keep things in plastic bags, and

The Cruising Sunfish

keep the plastic bags closed, even if they are inside a good tent.

Another potential horror is bugs. Now, you won't always have bugs. I have been camping many times and been left completely alone. But usually bugs, especially mosquitoes, seem to breed in wet places. So bring along a good bug repellent.

We have already covered the importance of keeping your things dry. But sometimes they will get wet. Plastic bags puncture. Or the ties come off. Or something that shouldn't happen does happen. Then, it seems to me, there are two routes open to you. You can dry your things out, or you can live with them. Synthetics dry faster, so you will probably want to wear mostly synthetics. And wool keeps you warm even when it is wet, as do certain synthetic pile materials like polypropylene. Your wardrobe should include both types of fabric. Then, if you can't get dry, at least you can stay warm.

In my experience, the camper/cruiser is likely to be very punctilious about keeping things dry on the water, but is likely to relax a little once he gets ashore. This is especially true if it is a nice, warm, clear day. But it's important to remember that it may rain at night. More than likely, there will be some dew. I have known people to take off their clothes and scatter them around on the ground to dry out if they are damp, or to air out if they are a little ripe. They turn in for the night, and wake up the next day to soaking wet clothing. All it takes is an average night of dew. Keep things in your tent, or in closed plastic bags outside if there is no room in the tent. Even in your tent, it might be smart to keep things in plastic. You may get a storm - even a bad enough storm to blow your tent away.

Unless I know I'm going to be sleeping on fine dry sand every night, I like to have an air mattress or an Ensolite pad to sleep on. After bouncing around on the hard deck of a Sunfish all day, I don't want to massage my bruised hip bones and spine with pebbles and sticks. A sleeping bag is lighter and more comfortable than a blanket roll. And I find that a small pillow does wonders to insure a restful night. For me, it is worth the extra space it takes up, even on a Sunfish.

For shelter, I have used the Sunfish sail, a plastic tube tent, and a two-man nylon pup tent. I was worried that I was stretching the sail when I used it as a tent. The plastic tube tent often sweated inside, and, since it doesn't breathe, it can get stuffy. The light nylon tent, I have found, is the ideal solution. Again, it takes up some room, but it's worth it.

After a long day of sailing, I have found that it is very difficult not to like almost any kind of food. I don't need a gourmet meal. And anyway, who wants to spend hours cooking after hours on water? I'm tired. So I make it as easy as possible, with things that are easy to cook and require a minimum of clean-up afterwards.

This is not a book on camping; it's a book on sailing. But most smart camping practices are smart camping/cruising practices. I mean the back-packing kind of camping, not the small house on wheels you plug in at a campsite. So I usually take along nothing but freeze-dried foods and things that come in relatively soft packages. I've been surprised at how many of these are available in the ordinary grocery store. You don't have to go and buy the super-expensive stuff at stores that sell camping equipment. Most supermarkets sell freeze-dried soups and one-step meals that you can make by pouring boiling water right into the bowl that is part of the package. There are dried fruits, nuts, and even powdered milk and lemonade. With one pot in which to boil water, and a folding sterno stove, you can have a different meal every night for a week.

I find that you can get along without canned goods and especially bottled drinks on a Sunfish cruise. They are heavy, they are uncomfortable to lie on, and they puncture plastic bags. Worst of all is bottled stuff. A cockpit full of broken glass is at best uncomfortable and at worst lethal. I find that a polyethylene gallon jug of drinking water will last me two or three days. Disposable plates, cups, forks and spoons, and a roll of paper towels completes the kitchen equipment.

Whether I'm racing or cruising, I like to take along a basic tool kit in a plastic quart bottle. This consists of a pair of pliers, a regular and a Phillips screwdriver, two open-end wrenches that fit all the nuts on the Sunfish, a couple of shackles, a roll of waterproof tape, and about a 100-foot roll of strong nylon or cotton twine. I also carry a Victorinox Swiss officer's knife-I like the one with a saw blade and the little tweezers and toothpick. I have had very good luck with the Victorinox - even after constant soakings in salt water. It will occasionally get so stiff I break a fingernail trying to open it, and then I just soak it in very hot water for a while, followed by a very, very light spritz of WD-40 in the joints. But it really is rustproof, and a lot of so-called stainless steel things aren't. Most important, the Victorinox must have a pair of scissors, the most useful tool of all. I think I use that three times for every time I use any other blade.

I like to carry a bath-size Turkish towel when I cruise. A smaller one or even paper towels would do, but a big thirsty Turkish towel rub-down after a day of damp sailing renews my faith in the world.

As the world gets more and more crowded, it becomes more and more difficult to find campsites when you are camping/cruising. It makes sense to study the areas where you might spend the night, trying to find public campsites, obviously deserted areas, or very small islands that don't get submerged at high tide. Otherwise, make landfall early in the evening so that you can arrange to camp with the landowner's permission. I have never been refused, and have even been welcomed the following morning when I have not been able to get permission the night before. James Lee Meadows was welcomed wherever he landed, and he camp-cruised from Miami to Boston. But I suppose it is possible to be sent packing in the middle of the night by an irate landowner.

In summary, the most important things to remember about camping/cruising are to keep things dry, travel light, keep things dry, be prepared for cold and wet and bugs, and keep things dry.

13 Observations and Opinions

This is a new chapter, with some observations and opinions based on more than 30 years of racing and sailing Sunfish.

• The Sailors

First, some observations on the sailors themselves. As mentioned in the introduction to the interviews with champions, the really good ones seem to love sailing for its own sake. Many sail other boats, day-sailing, cruising, or racing. Others just jump in their Sunfish whenever they can and sail. As a result they spend a lot of time on the water, and that time does more to produce good sailors than any other activity.

Some sailors just seem to be able to wring speed out of any boat; others need some time to adjust to different boats' characteristics. A number of champions have jumped into Sunfish and were fast almost instantly, from Jorge Bruder, one of the best Finn sailors who ever lived, who would have won the first Sunfish World Championship but for two disqualifications, to Tom Linskey, who sailed to a second in the '95 Masters Internationals after many years of winning national and international competitions in other hot one-designs.

On the other hand there are sailors like Dick Tillman, who won that same '95 Masters by a wide margin, after five years, by his own account, of working to master the Sunfish. Dick won three Laser championships and is still a threat in that Class in his late fifties, as well as author of three editions of the definitive Laser manual, the third titled *Laser Sailing for the 1990's*. And I remember Norm Freeman, at the last Caribbean Midwinter Championship in 1969, complaining about how different the Sunfish was. It was his first Sunfish regatta. In spite of his discomfort he finished second or third; it was just that he was used to winning in other single-handed classes.

Another marked difference among the top Sunfish sailors is their performance under different conditions. Some are unbeatable in their favorite conditions. Joel Furman in his prime was just about unbeatable in very light air, as when he won the '76 North Americans. Even today, grandmother Jean Bergman can whip most of the guys in light air. Paul Odegaard, when he was younger, whipped some of the best sailors in the Class at the heavy-air Northeast Regionals in '79. A number of Caribbean sailors have dominated World Championships - from Gerrit Zeestraten of Curaçao in the mid-'70s to Eduardo Cordero of Venezuela in '94 - because they could sail in big waves, especially off the wind.

Some top sailors seem to make certain legs of the course their specialty. Carl Knight went to windward as if he had his own wind - faster and higher than anyone on the course. At the '69 North Americans, he was always first around the windward mark; I'd pass him on the reaches, and he'd walk past me again on the last windward leg. Jeff Linton, the only three-in-a-row North American champ so far, told me wistfully that he wished he could surf the reaches the way Eduardo Cordero does - and Jeff is awfully fast on reaches. Others are just good in steady conditions, but awesome in fluky or puffy conditions. They seem to know exactly where to go to get the best combination of wind slant and speed. Jeff Linton and Dick Tillman are current examples of that innate wind sense.

Other champions seem to have mastered every conceivable condition, and are threats any time, like Derrick Fries and Scott Kyle, the winningest Sunfish sailors of all, and Don Bergman, who, at Medicare age, never grows old. If you've read this book from front to back, you've already read the secrets of many of these champs.

• The Rules

There are two basic rulebooks - the IYRU rules of sailing, under which we sail in the U.S., and the Class rules, mostly concerning what you can

Observations and Opinions

do to modify the Sunfish. If you're going to race, even just locally, I urge you to join the Class association. You'll get the Class rule book, notices of regattas, and lots of news and helpful information in the Class newsletter, *Windward Leg*. And get a copy of the current IYRU/US Sailing racing rules (they are changed a little every third year in an attempt to make them more fair.) You can buy books that reprint the official rules with commentary and interpretations at most book stores or boating supply stores. But why not join US Sailing and get the rule book free? A membership includes their publication, *American Sailor*, along with a subscription to *Sailing World*, which is full of news and articles helpful to the racing sailor.

Please note that *this* book contains my interpretations of the IYRU and Class rules. These rules may change even before this book is published, and will certainly change after that date.

• Kinetics

The most universal sailing rules infractions are in the area of kinetics, using the body to force the boat through the water a little faster than the normal action of the wind on the sails. Kinetics is a set of problems that the IYRU (International Yacht Racing Union) and US Sailing (until recently the United States Yacht Racing Union) have struggled with for years.

One problem is that some forms of kinetics are allowed. Roll tacking is OK, even though a lot of body English is needed to perform a good roll tack. Some limitations have been put into effect. You can't roll tack or gybe so that the boat is propelled faster towards the mark than if you hadn't tacked or gybed. You can't let the mast go beyond the vertical on the second half of the maneuver. But it's a tough judgement call, and very few sailors will go to a protest hearing to challenge another's technique.

Another problem is that body movement is OK to steer the boat, but not to propel it (or slow it down.) An often-repeated conversation goes like this: "You were rocking!" "No I wasn't. I was steering the boat!" As has been covered earlier in the book, steering by rolling the boat is perfectly legal. In fact, you should practice it. But where do you draw the line?

Still another tough call is with pumping off the wind. It's still OK to give the sail a sharp pull in - a pump - to get the boat planing or surfing on each wave. But, especially in light air, when is a wave a wave? Again, a judgement call. The consensus is that, as long as you don't do it rhythmically and steadily, pumping is OK...and just about necessary if you're going to stay with the leaders.

• Sunfish Special Cases

There are at least two rules situations on the race course that are greatly influenced by the long boom of the Sunfish. The boom is the same length as the boat. We sometimes forget that fact. But it creates a special geometry that doesn't apply to most other boats that race today.

Situation 1. The most obvious situation involves rounding a mark, especially a leeward mark. When approaching the leeward mark on a run, your boom will be pretty much at a 90 degree angle to your center line. Two boom lengths are an exact measure of the two-boat-length circle. When three boats are more or less parallel to each other, neck and neck, it is almost impossible for the third boat out from the mark to pierce the circle until the two inside boats have started to round. A fourth boat right behind the inner boat will pierce the circle before the third boat out does, even if it does not have an overlap. Boat Four can then round right behind One and Two, and Three must allow it room to round, because its overlap line will sweep behind Four's bow before it gets to the circle. (See sketch) This geometry is

Observations and Opinions

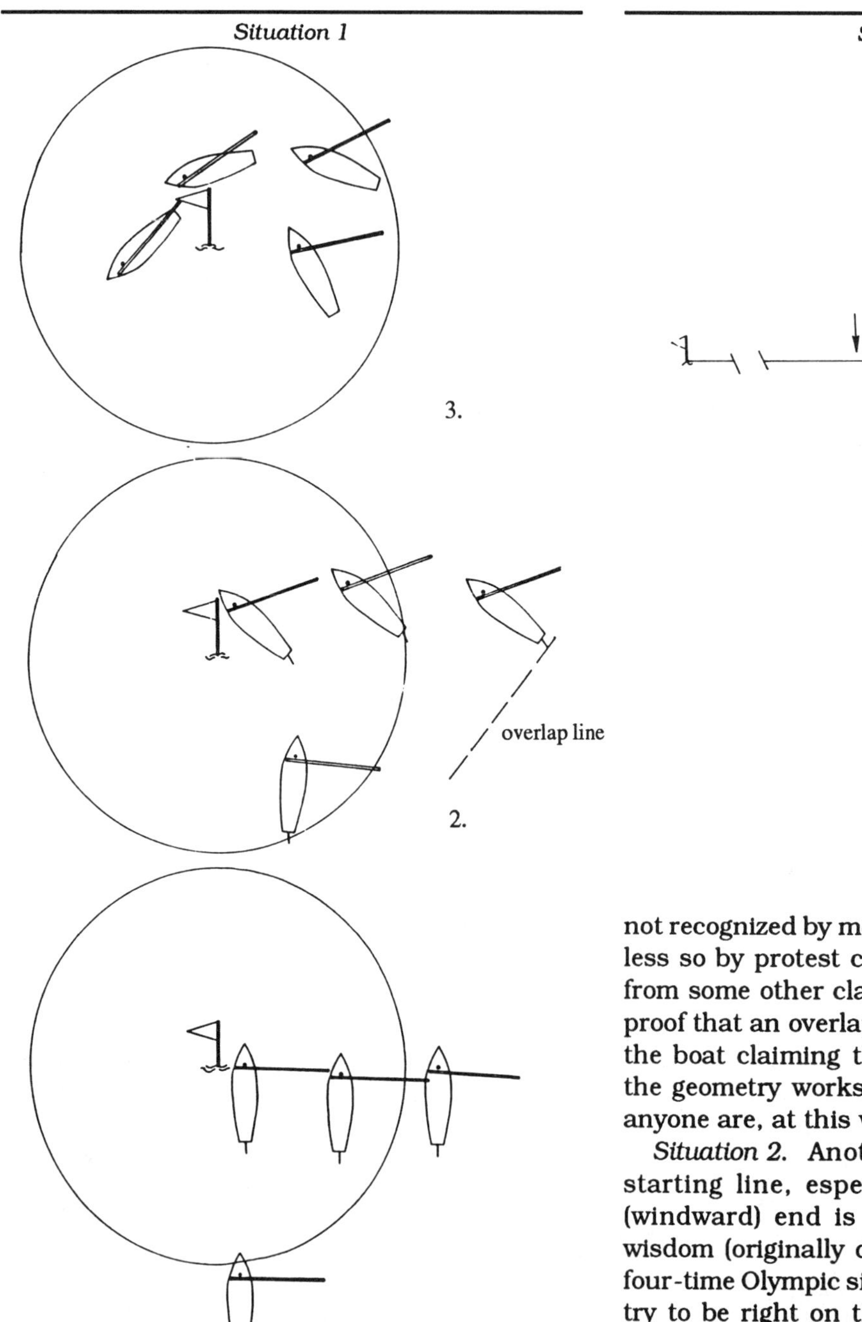

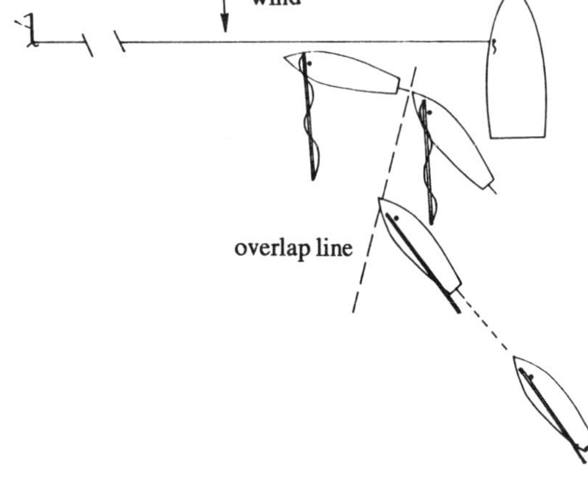

not recognized by most Sunfish sailors, and even less so by protest committees, who usually are from some other class. Moreover, the burden of proof that an overlap has been established is on the boat claiming the overlap. So even though the geometry works, the chances of convincing anyone are, at this writing, slim.

Situation 2. Another situation involves the starting line, especially when the starboard (windward) end is favored. The conventional wisdom (originally developed by Paul Elvstrom, four-time Olympic single-handed champion) is to try to be right on the line, holding position by luffing the sail, drifting as slowly as possible to leeward, opening up a hole under the lee bow into which you can accelerate four or five seconds before the start and cross the line with a full head of steam at the gun. However, a boat may find itself too close to the line, and bear off with the sail still luffing to avoid being over early. Its overlap line sweeps aft, and a boat coming up close-hauled under it will gain an overlap. The close-hauled boat now has right of way, because it is to leeward. Because of that long Sunfish boom, the leeward boat may find itself trapped between the windward boat and its boom. The rule requires that the leeward boat give the windward yacht "room and opportunity" to keep clear. In most situations, all the windward yacht has to do is pull in that long boom to allow the leeward yacht through. It doesn't have to start pulling in until the overlap is established, so the timing is tricky...and hard to prove in a protest room. Proving the overlap, and proving that the leeward boat allowed "room and opportunity" for the windward boat to get out of the way, is tough. The geometry is plain (see sketch) but the conventional wisdom is against it. And until the geometry is accepted by the Class, the windward boat is going to react with outrage, especially since sheeting in and maybe being forced over early is hard to accept by the boat that thinks it is about to pull off a perfect classic Elvstrom start.

So before you act on these two interpretations of the unique Sunfish geometry, be aware that they are my own interpretations, and, at least at this writing, not generally accepted by the Class.

• Cheaters

A word about bending the rules: I know at least two North American champs who won in illegal boats. The irony in both cases is that they didn't win because they bent the Class rules. They demonstrated that fact by winning often in perfectly legal boats. And I know for sure that neither of them felt they were cheating. They each had well articulated rationalizations for what they did. Other sailors get so competitive on the course that they bend the sailing rules. In the two rules situations above, for instance, it's easy to rationalize. "Yes, I was within the two-boat-length circle." "No, he didn't have an overlap." I've done it myself.

Occasionally sailors will compete in the Class with an attitude. They feel the rules don't really apply to them, or that it's OK to break rules if you don't get caught. Sooner or later, they *do* get caught. They lose an important regatta because someone finally gets fed up and takes them to a protest. Or they finally sense that they're not welcome in the Class. They usually drop out. Good riddance.

• Corinthians

You will have more pure pleasure from Sunfish racing if you observe the rules to the letter, to the

Eduardo Cordero of Venezuela and Jeff Linton of Florida – Friends – Competitors – Corinthians.

Observations and Opinions

best of your ability. In yacht racing, obeying the rules and acting as your own policeman and judge used to be called Corinthianism.

Sail like a Corinthian. Sail like a lady or a gentleman. Your competitors will respect you. If you bend the rules and win, and they know it, they may shrug it off. Very few of us like a confrontation.

But if you win and you've bent the rules, and nobody else knows it, *you* know it. You may have your moment of glory, but you know it's not real. Will you respect yourself?

All this is not to say that there are a lot of cheaters in the Sunfish Class. The truth is that Sunfish sailors are probably cleaner than most. Corinthians. Some sailors new to the Class are amazed at how punctilious we are about the rules. And more than one race committee chairman has told me that he or she would rather run a Sunfish regatta than any other - "They're such nice people, and they sail so clean!"

So we keep coming out year after year, long after we've lost our competitive edge. Sunfish people are, for sure, such nice people. Tough but fair competitors on the course. Friends on shore. Corinthians.

Afterwords

Kristi and the Fish Sun

by Gary Jobson

When my human alarm clock, 2 ½ year-old Kristi, woke me at 6:30 a.m. one Saturday morning, she didn't, as usual, want to have a book read to her. She wanted to play a game, and I had just the game for her.

By 8:30 a.m. we were ready to sail our Sunfish on Spa Creek. It was Kristi's first sail on our little boat, probably the best craft of all for beginning sailors. A Sunfish is a little bit less than fourteen feet long, about four feet wide, and draws about two inches of water with the centerboard up and two feet, seven inches with the board down. Kristi had been taking swimming lessons, and when we got to the dock the hardest problem was keeping her from jumping in.

With the boat alongside the dock, I put Kristi into her life jacket and then got the Sunfish ready to sail. "All set, Kristi?" I asked her. "Where is your life jacket, Daddy?" she answered with perfect logic.

I had three things in mind to teach Kristi in our first session. First was that the boat can heel. Second was that when I said "ready about" we were going to change sides and that when I said "jibe" she was to put her head down.

We sailed out into the stream. It was early and we had the stream to ourselves. The breeze was just enough to move the Sunfish along. Kristi particularly liked tacking. It was fun moving from side to side, and she was small enough to stand up without hitting her head on the bottom of the boom. When we jibed it took a little extra coaching to get her to lift her head back up after the boom had passed over. When we heeled, she kept diving to leeward to put her hands in the water. She didn't comprehend that dragging her feet or hands overboard would slow the boat down. Against all my racing instincts I said nothing.

As we passed dozens of moored boats in the creek, she asked alertly, "Where are all the people, Daddy?" Then she said, "Sooo many boats."

She particularly liked the ducks we chased from one end of the creek to the other. They would rise out of the water, fly a short distance, and then settle down in the water again. Kristi called to them. "Quack, quack," she said.

Then we sailed by some row boats, the water hissing under our bow. Kristi sang, "Row, row, row, row, down the stream."

We came about and headed back and Kristi sat quietly, taking it all in. I said, "We're going home now, Kristi." She didn't complain. "Okay, Daddy," she said, and I thought, Had we done too much? Was she still interested?

At home, she said little about the sail, even when Janice pressed her. "Maybe she's too young," I said to Janice.

On Sunday afternoon I could see ripples in the water from our back windows. The weather was clear. Kristi had been playing in her room and I was working at the kitchen table when she came to me. "Fish sun, Daddy," she said. "Fish sun?" It took me a minute to understand her name for our sailboat. Then I said, "Okay, Kristi, get your life vest."

We went down to the dock once again, rigged the Sunfish, and set sail. This time, without hesitation, Kristi decided it was time she should steer. I gave her the tiller and she wiggled it back and forth, laughing every time the boat changed course. After our first outing she obviously had thought about it and decided that she really liked sailing and she especially liked to make the boat wiggle. "Fun, Daddy," she said. "Fun fish."

Kristi has sailed on the Sunfish quite a bit with me since then. She dangles her feet in the water and she splashes and sometimes she asks to steer, and each time she does, the boat wiggles a little bit less. One day she will learn that there is a world beyond Spa Creek, just as I learned that there was a world beyond Toms River. But for now that doesn't matter. The Fish sun is enough.

Reprinted, with permission, from World Class Sailing *by Gary Jobson and Martin Luray, Hearst Marine Books, 1987.*

Afterwords

The Luffing Lassies of Sarasota

by Will White

On any Thursday morning from September through May, you can find a group of women congregating on the beach at the Sarasota Sailing Squadron to launch their Sunfish and Clearwater prams for a few hours of serious racing. Actually, most of the prams are now Optimists with a slightly smaller battenless sail, which makes them competitive with the older Clearwater prams.

They are the Luffing Lassies, and they range in age from the 20s to the 70s. The group was formed in 1972 by Lily Kaighin and some friends as the Sarasota Sailing and Sinking Society, which had five prams but a considerably larger number of women. The starting line was off the club dock because they had no committee boat and they handled their own race committee duties on a rotation basis.

Five prams would race through the moored boats of the Squadron, finish, and head for shore; then another five would jump in the boats for the next race.

"Once, the wind got a little boisterous, and most of the sailors dropped their sails," Lily Kaighin recalled. "They were getting swept towards the Gulf on the outgoing tide through New Pass. So I borrowed a rowboat and rounded them up. When I picked up the first boat, there was no place to tie a painter, so I tied it around my waist, and we picked up the others in a string. When I look back on it, it was kind of dumb, but we made it back."

After that, they negotiated the use of one of the Squadron's committee boats and talked a group of husbands and male friends into handling RC duties. They didn't have to do much arm-twisting - the women have fun, and their fun is infectious. Soon, the women began to buy their own boats, and Sunfish were added to the fleet. Now, Sunfish outnumber prams by about three to one.

All of the Lassies are now members of the Squadron, and most keep their boats there. They changed their name early on. "Sarasota Sailing and Sinking Society was just too long," Lily explains. The change was obviously not made for reasons of decorum.

The first week of the season is devoted to sailing lessons, and about a dozen women show up, drawn by the lure of sea and sun, wind and waves. Some fall by the wayside, finding the attractions outweighed by fear and ruined perms, but the rest soon become fanatics. The experienced Lassies seem to get their biggest kicks out of helping the newcomers sharpen their skills.

In 1995, school week coincided with one of the worst red tides on record. Dead fish floated all over Sarasota Bay and washed up on the shoreline a dozen deep. The stench was awful, and the bloom of red algae made everyone's eyes water.

"We thought we'd lose them," Lily said of the class, "but almost every one of them stuck it out." Ursula Olsen, this year's chief instructor, agreed. "They were a good group."

On any given Thursday, at least eight Sunfish and three to five prams turn out. The hard core of dedicated sailors is almost always on hand. The top racers are good enough to hold their own in any competition, and they do. Several of the Sunfish sailors compete in Class championships and finish well.

These top sailors have worked their way up from Luffers to Salts and then Super Salts. Season trophies are awarded in each category, so everyone has a chance at a prize, not silver but plastic: a mug with an embroidered Luffing Lassies patch molded in.

Not all the sailors are pleased when they are promoted to Super Salts. "I'm not out here to win," wails Nina McLean periodically since she made the top grade. She has blazing speed in her old red and yellow Sunfish, but she refuses to duke it out in close situations. "I'm here to sail!"

Some Lassies are determined to get good

enough to hang in there with the top three: Rita Steele, Ursula Olsen and Lily Kaighin in Sunfish; Francie Jones, Jinny Martin and Loretta Garber in prams. Others agree with Nina; they are there for the sailing and the camaraderie. They accept coaching and go-fast tips good-naturedly and keep right on doing what feels good and comfortable.

"Sit sideways at the front of the cockpit and hike out?!" one longtime Sunfish sailor replied to such a tip. "I might fall out!" All the women love to sail, but they also enjoy other Luffing Lassies activities. A group will gather after the races at the bait shack near the New Pass bridge. Was there ever a sailor who didn't love to resail each race or cruise? And there are parties, picnics, and whacky special regattas.

Racing winners somehow don't make it into the Lassies' annual handbook; those who do are winners of the Most Improved Sailor award and of the Suzanne Burt Memorial Trophy, which is given "in recognition of the person who best exemplifies the spirit and competitiveness of the Luffing Lassies."

All up and down the Florida Sun Coast are similar groups of women who love to sail. They don't take themselves too seriously, either. They have names like Bitter Ends (Venice), Broad Reachers (Pass-a-Grille), Dinghy Dames (Tampa), and Windlasses (Dunedin.) Ten of these groups are members of the Florida Women's Sailing Association. The Luffing Lassies were among the seven founding groups in 1973.

The FWSA sponsors two area-wide regattas - a Championship Regatta in the fall, usually sailed in larger keel boats with crews up to five, and a Rainbow Regatta near the end of the season, in prams and Sunfish. The Championship Regatta used to be a feeder for the Adams Cup, the original women's national championship, and Lassies crews several times made it to the quarter- or semi-finals.

One year, Lily and her crew made it to the finals in Newport, RI, sailed in Shields class boats. They came in sixth.

In 1995, at the FWSA Championship regatta on Tampa Bay, four crews sailed Sonars. "Faye Baynard of the St. Peterburg Yacht Club's Salty Sisters made a clean sweep," Lily said ruefully. "She owns a Sonar, and she had incredible boat speed. Actually, it was more like a match race; with Ursula at the helm we had three straight seconds."

"Another year, at the quarter-finals for the Adams Cup at Ft. Lauderdale, we sailed Solings," Lily reminisced. "Among the trophies we brought back were lots of black-and-blue marks, a four-stitch cut over one eye, a badly sprained ankle, and a knocked-out front tooth."

But the Lassies don't confine their sailing to racing. Many of them go out together and day-sail, after the races or on non-race days. Sometimes they just head out to the Gulf of Mexico, maybe landing at a stretch of beach for a swim. Or they head to one of the many eating spots dotting Sarasota Bay, have lunch, and sail back to the Squadron. Or they will sail under the Ringling bridge and check out the many visiting yachts anchored off downtown Sarasota. Each sail is an adventure.

I've been honored to run their races the last few years, and sometimes go with them on their adventures. They know what sailing is all about. It's FUN!

Originally published in a shorter form in Mid-Gulf Sailing, *February, 1996.*

Please note:

Some of the tuning techniques or modifications suggested in the following pages may be obsolete because of changes in equipment or may have been outlawed by subsequent Class Rules.

Some of the sailing tactics and techniques may also be outlawed today as a result of changes to the International Yacht Racing Rules as adopted (sometimes with modifications) by U.S. Sailing – particularly in the area of kinetics (pumping, sculling, ooching, rocking.)

SUCCESSFUL SUNFISH RACING

Derrick Fries

Bob Pool

Dr. Derrick Fries,
Clarkston, Michigan

High Points of his Sailing Career

1989 1st Place Sunfish North American Championship, *Tawas Bay, MI*
1985 1st Place Sunfish North American Championship, *Brant Beach, NJ*
1983 1st Place Sunfish North American Championship, *Winnetka, IL*
1983 1st Place Sunfish Canadian National, *Clinton, Ontario*
1983 2nd Place Champion of Champions, *Heath, TX*
1982 1st Place Force 5 World Championship, *Shady Side, MD*
1980 1st Place Force 5 World Championship, *Naples, FL*
1979 1st Place Force 5 World Championship, *Miami, FL*
1978 1st Place Sunfish world Championship, *Ponce, Puerto Rico*
1977 2nd Place Sunfish North American Championship, *Barrington, RI*
1977 1st Place Force 5 North American Championship, *Lake Geneva, WI*
1976 1st Place Buccaneer North American Championship, *Nashville, TN*
1976 1st Place Force 5 North American Championship, *Watertown, NY*
1976 1st Place Sunfish Champion, *Lima, Peru*
1975 1st Place Sunfish World Championship, *Miami, FL*
1973-74 Captain Michigan State University Sailing Team
1973-74 Collegiate All-American

Contents

ISBN 8286-0095-3
Library of Congress Card Number: 83-072325

Publisher: John de Graff, Inc.
Clinton Corners, NY 12514

Book and jacket design by Laura Hough

First printing

A portion of the material in Chapter 4 on Reading the Wind on the Water originally appeared in Yacht Racing/Cruising *magazine.*

Printed in the U.S.A.

Acknowledgments

Successful Sunfish Racing would not have been possible without the help of many generous people.

The friendly and kind members of Watkins Lake Yachting Association have given me much knowledge and support in the racing circuit. Their fleet is top quality with many sailors veterans of thirty years or more racing on the 250-acre lake.

My parents have been helpful in their loving and caring way in my pursuit of many personal goals. *Successful Sunfish Racing* is a small token of love and appreciation from me to them.

The Bob Pool family has been incredibly helpful in this entire project. Bob Pool, a distinguished plastic surgeon, has given me much objective insight into the overall intent of the book. He has devoted much personal time and effort developing and printing many of the photographs. I sincerely admire his fine personal character and terrific family. I dedicate this book to him, his wife Jackie, and children, John, Steve, and Marilyn.

Dave Powlison edited the manuscript for its benefit and my gratitude.

Finally, I would like to thank AMF Alcort for their cooperation and information. Jim Ronshagen and Lee Parks have helped greatly in making *Successful Sunfish Racing* a useful tool for Sunfish racers.

Happy racing,
Derrick Fries

Introduction

The Sunfish is truly an extraordinary racing craft. Its popularity is the result of its unique and simple design. Few other boats can be rigged in five minutes, carried to the beach, and raced. Sunfish racing programs have reinforced the intent of true one-design racing, and its history reflects that. The quality of Sunfish racers has made the boat a standout among single-handed classes. Great sailors such as Dave Chapin, Jeorg Bruder, Hans Fogh, Major Hall, Gary Hoyt, Gary Jobson, Carl Knight, Manton Scott, Will White, and many more emerged from success in the Sunfish class.

Another aspect of Sunfish character is longevity. A sail can last up to eight years and still be competitive. A hull, with proper maintenance, can last indefinitely, Scratches, patched holes, and color fade basically have no effect on speed. In this class, technology is blissfully ignored, and advanced equipment and continuous rig developments are games serious Sunfish sailors find irrelevant. Because the sole purpose of racing is to challenge the mind and body, there really is no evolution of the Sunfish; rather, there is an evolution of the body that sails it.

In this book, I provide insights into the advancement of modern Sunfish racing. I purposely omit in-depth discussion of tactics and rules, as other books thoroughly address these areas. This book's main purpose is the advancement of Sunfish racing.

During boat speed discussions, there are numerous references to body movement, or kinetics. Information is provided about the relationship of body kinetics to boat speed in regard to accepted body behavior in the class. No judgments are made about how the International Yacht Racing Union rules apply to these specialized movements.

The Sunfish has provided fun for thousands of families and individuals, both on the race course and off. May its success continue and prosper in the true spirit of one-design racing.

1

The Sail and Rig

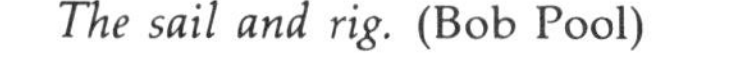

The sail and rig. (Bob Pool)

The main source of power for any sailboat is the sail, and the Sunfish is no exception. Questions about draft and fullness always arise, but in a Sunfish, differences in sail shapes and the effects of adjustments generally are overestimated. To prove this point, I raced the entire 1980 season—approximately 160 races in all types of conditions—without making a single outhaul adjustment, including racing and wave patterns. My sailing results and performance showed no changes from past years.

Such simplicity demonstrates that missing one wind shift is more costly than any minute change in speed resulting from sail adjustments. It is a mistake to become so involved in boat tuning that time is sacrificed on the water. Even the fastest boat on the course must start well and be in phase with the shifts to finish in the money.

When discussing sail trim, a problem arises when the Sunfish is compared to cat-rigged boats, such as the Laser and Force 5. This is an injustice, as the Sunfish rig and sail are unorthodox, and really only can be compared to other lateen rigs. One striking difference of lateen rigging is the incredible sail distortion created on port tack by the spars when the front sail section is pressed against the mast. In addition to this, air flow on the sail luff is greatly disturbed by the upper boom and mast, which necessitates a full entry and can leave the sail luff slightly scalloped, adding further to the distorted appearance.

When setting up the Sunfish sail, one of the first premises is that for all practical purposes, each sail is identical, although age and upkeep eventually will have some effect on shape. To understand positioning of the lateen Sunfish rig, visualize the triangle created by the sail and booms. As the wind increases, weather helm increases. To counteract this effect, the triangle must be moved forward. As the air lightens, helm decreases, and the triangle should be slid aft.

The two adjustment points for positioning the triangle are the gooseneck on the lower boom and the halyard attachment on the upper boom. Slide the halyard up and the gooseneck forward, and the triangle moves aft; slide the halyard down and the gooseneck aft, and the triangle moves forward. The tack always should remain just a few inches off the deck.

The proper range of positions for the gooseneck on the lower boom is between 17 and 21 inches aft of the tack. Position the gooseneck at 17 inches for drifters and at 21 inches for overpowering conditions. Outside that range, the boat usually is thrown off balance by excessive helm.

I never set the gooseneck bolt so tight that I can't slide the fitting on the boom. This allows me to adjust its location, even during a race, but only in light and medium winds. Offwind, the Sunfish is faster with the rig forward, so at the beginning of each offwind leg, I slide the lower boom two or three inches through the gooseneck, a maneuver that requires long arms and a fair amount of flexibility. To begin, I steer with fingertips to allow greater reach. I hold the mainsheet with my aft hand and use my forward hand to slide the boom forward. Then, to make the adjustment, I hook my two forefingers around the forward side of the gooseneck and grasp the boom with

Moving the gooseneck while under way requires agility and quickness. (Bob Pool)

my little finger and thumb. When I squeeze my hand together, the boom slides forward through the gooseneck. To ensure that the gooseneck remains positioned, duct-tape that section of the boom and then remove the tape, leaving a gum residue, which will prevent the gooseneck from sliding out of position. Taping must be repeated every ten races or so.

To slide the boom aft, for instance, when rounding leeward mark, I position two forefingers on the aft side of the gooseneck. With my thumb and little finger grasping the boom an inch or so from the gooseneck, I open my hand, pulling the boom aft through the fitting. If conditions change drastically during an upwind leg, you also may want to adjust the location, taking into account the current tactical and strategic considerations.

Tom Lihan, 1982 Laser North American champion, sails upwind with a full rig in the 1982 Championship of Champions regatta in Heath, Texas. Notice his crossed-leg hiking style, and the tape on the cockpit deck to prevent skidding. (Lee Parks)

For halyard location, the range is two to four inches, beginning at the upper end of the 10th segment and extending just into the 11th segment. (Segments are the spaces between the plastic sail clips, and are numbered from the tack up.) In light air, set the halyard at its lowest position, and as the wind increases, begin moving the halyard up the spar.

Another area of concern is the use of sail clips. In years past, it was common to see sails tied for the entire length of the upper and lower spars. Before this practice was ruled illegal, some racers even used high-poundage fishing line to tie off their grommets. However, it became difficult to assure an even distance between grommets, and today, only five grommets are tied off, replacing the standard plastic clips with one-eighth-inch, pre-stretched dacron line. Pre-stretched line virtually eliminates all stretch, so the sail can be set just as accurately as with stretchless plastic clips.

It is an absolute safety must to tie off the end grommets on the upper and lower spars. These are high-stress areas, and in heavy air, the standard clips may pop off. On the upper spar, grommets nine and ten are tied off to eliminate catching on the mast. One-eighth-inch line allows the grommets to slide freely, in contrast to the plastic clip, which must rotate around the boom with the sail.

On the lower boom, the second grommet should be fuller in front of the mast on port tack. A plastic clip pulls the sail too tight and produces distortion. By tying the sail approximately one and a half inches off the boom, air flow on port tack and the extra bag in the sail on starboard tack does not hinder air flow.

The standard metal S-hook on the sail tack also should be replaced with pre-stretched line, because in heavy air or during rapid luffing, the hook can be dislodged. To ensure adequate strength, the line must encircle the boom joint and tack grommet two or three times.

Pre-stretched line also should be used on the outhauls. For adequate purchase when adjusting the outhauls, an efficient rigging system is required. However, because there is not enough space in the last grommet for more than two one-eighth-inch lines, tie a small bowline around the clew through the grommet, and run extra purchase through that. Now the outhaul can be trimmed very

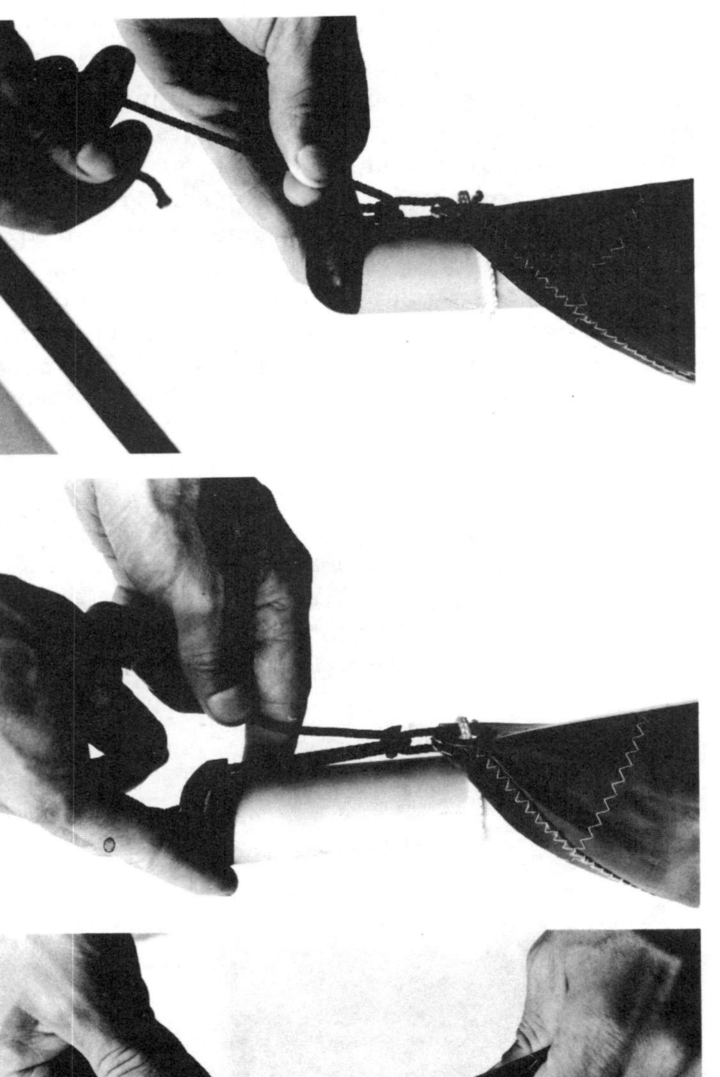

tightly, and you can be sure it will not stretch in heavy air.

Under certain conditions, you may need to make outhaul adjustments while on the water. Some sailors use an adjustable outhaul system utilizing a small cleat on the boom. But because the sail is equipped with plastic clips, clip movement along the boom is limited, and when trimming, the clips simply become caught along the boom diagonally. Because of this, adjustments are limited to one-quarter inch and only affect the last third of the sail. It is far better to adjust before or between races, when you have time to do it properly.

To adjust the outhauls on the water, you need three to five minutes and plenty of room for your boat to drift

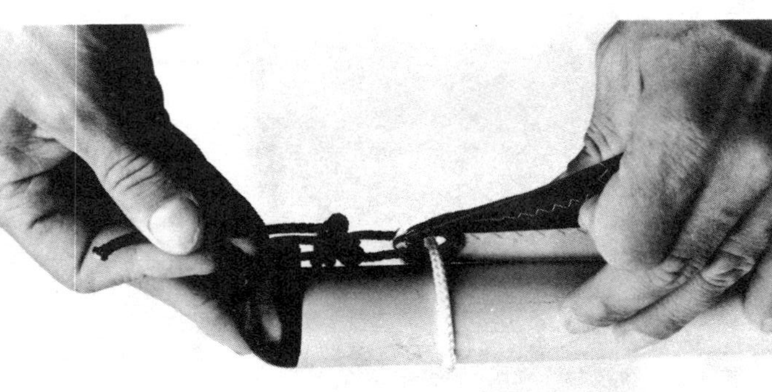

Tying the outhaul with extra purchase can be very beneficial in heavy air. Removing the plastic clips here is a must. With adjustable outhauls, the bowline and extra purchase are also needed. However, the tail is simply anchored at the tack. Using ten feet of 1/8" pre-stretch the lower outhaul can be anchored at the forward boom pulley. The upper outhaul (20 feet long) can be anchored at the tack with a small bowline for extra purchase. (Bob Pool)

leeward. The steps are simple, but a bit of balancing is required. First, go head-to-wind and drop the sail. I prefer to drop it on the port side of the boat, which gives me more room to work on the deck than if I drop it on the starboard side. Technically, it leaves me on starboard tack, so while making adjustments, I don't have to be as concerned about the situation of port-starboard.

With the sail down, the outhauls hang about twelve inches beyond the transom. Since adjustments from that position are difficult, the second step is to remove the mast from the mast-step and lay it along the deck with the two booms. Be careful not to get the sail wet or—worse—to lose the entire rig overboard. Now, slide the whole rig forward approximately four feet; you should be able to reach both outhauls easily. If you have used extra-long outhauls, adjustment can be made at the tack for the upper outhaul and forward pulley block for the lower boom. You will still have to drop the rig to ensure that no plastic clips have hung up on the boom.

When adjusting the outhauls, check each plastic clip to ensure it has not become caught diagonally. If you wish to raise or lower the rig a couple of inches with the halyard, this too becomes an easy adjustment because the halyard on the boom is now at the cockpit.

With the halyard and outhauls adjusted, you are ready to raise the sail and begin racing again. However, there are still a couple of things to keep in mind. The boat will be drifting dead downwind. Before you raise the sail entirely, the boat must be turned 180 degrees, so that it faces head-to-wind. To turn the boat, raise the sail approximately three feet. The wind will catch the sail, and the boat should spin right around. Once into the wind, quickly raise the sail the rest of the way, being careful not to catch it on the tiller or mainsheet block.

One of the best places to adjust the outhauls is near the finish line. If the race committee is relocating after the start to finish the fleet at the weather mark, simply finish and sail back to the original starting area. Stay upwind of the line, and complete the outhaul adjustment there. If the finish line is fixed and will be the next starting line, sail upwind another 100 yards, then make your adjustments.

A common difficulty with the Sunfish sail is leech control. Sailors often comment on the wide variety of leeches. The first and foremost leech control is not the outhaul, but mainsheet tension. Because there is a close correlation between leech control and boat speed, the mainsheet also can be viewed as the boat's ultimate speed control. In all wind conditions, and particularly in light air, boat speed may increase or decrease as much as 20 percent with as little as two or three inches of mainsheet trim.

Leech control is a function of general mainsheet trim. Proper mainsheet trim is the key to speed in all conditions. (Bob Pool)

Because the wind never blows in a straight line or in a constant direction, never cleat the mainsheet, but continually adjust it with each change in conditions. One sure way of keeping the sheet constantly alive is to forego mainsheet cleats. If you're accustomed to carrying cleats on the side decks, you'll find eliminating them also facilitates sliding fore and aft when surfing. On a Sunfish, as on many other single-handed boats, a good-looking leech is not necessarily synonymous with speed. During the 1978 World Championship Races in Puerto Rico, I drew a sail that looked equal to all the others, except for a leech that turned inside out whenever I sheeted hard while sailing upwind. I ignored the problem and simply concentrated on the shifts, and the sail showed no difference in speed.

Two other easily rigged controls are the JC strap and vang. The JC strap, named after its inventor John Christianson, holds the boom out when sailing offwind in light air and prevents unintentional jibes. The vang bends the lower and upper booms, pulling the draft out of the sail,

John Kostecki, 1982 Sunfish World Champion, sailing upwind in heavy air. He is using a medium-size Jens with a hard vang. Notice how flat the sail is with a proper looking leech. (Lee Parks)

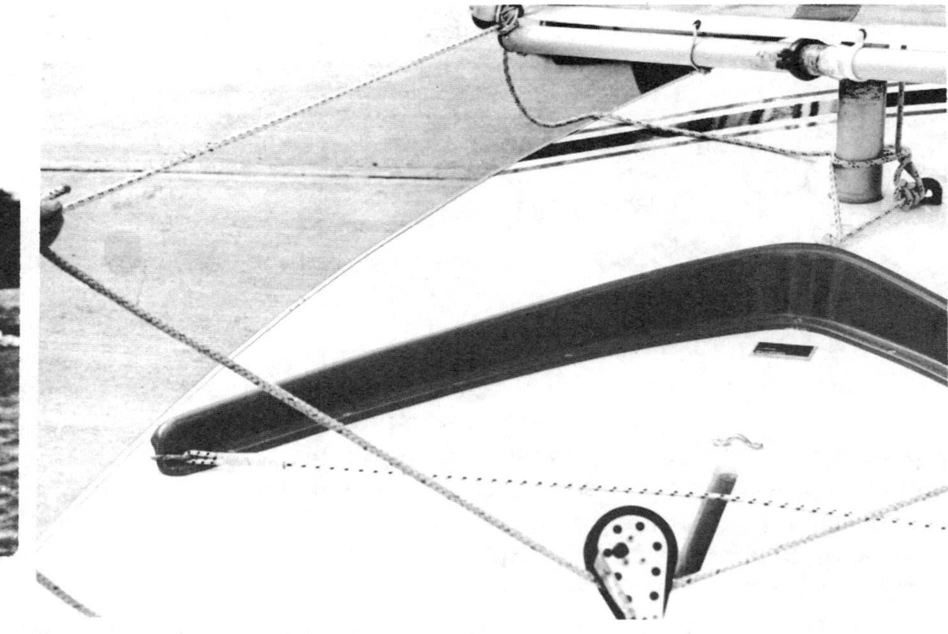

Proper use and rigging of the JC strap, used only in five knots or less. (Bob Pool)

flattening it. In addition, a tight vang makes sheeting easier. Since the JC strap and vang both require using the main halyard tail, only one control can be used at a time. Fortunately, they are used in vastly different wind conditions.

To rig the JC strap, secure the halyard around the cleat, leaving about 10 feet of halyard. Lead that line to the sail tack. With about seven feet of line remaining, tie a half hitch around the booms at the tack. Then run the rest of the line aft on the starboard side. That way, when rounding the weather mark, the strap will be positioned correctly, on the windward side. To keep the strap tail out of the water when not in use, tuck it under the daggerboard shockcord retainer.

This is the result of excess poundage from the vang. This skipper has bent the boom and torn the grommets out of the sail. Generally the maximum poundage for the vang is approximately 100 pounds of downward pressure. (Lee Parks)

The boom vang is rigged by running the halyard from the cleat to the base of the mast. Take several wraps around the mast with half hitches. The half hitches also should go around the halyard, as it comes down the mast. This keeps the halyard tight. From the half hitches, lead the line up to and over the gooseneck, between the boom and the mast, then back down through the main halyard eye and aft to the cleat. To tension the vang, push down on the bottom with one hand, just aft of where the vang

Proper tying of the vang is important. There is no need to go over the gooseneck more than once if using pre-stretch line. (Bob Pool)

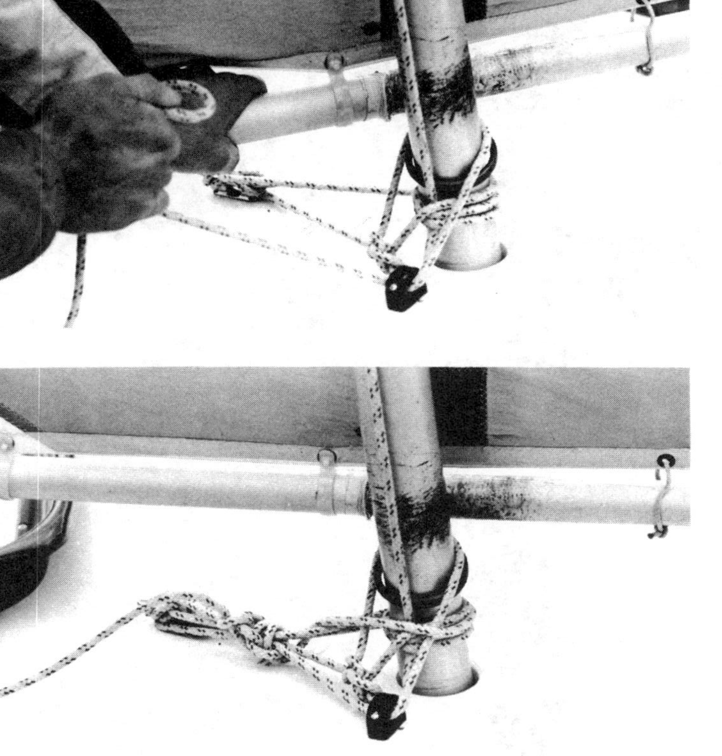

attaches. With your other hand, take up the slack created in the vang and secure the line to the halyard cleat. I've found it better to have too much vang than not enough, and when applying tension in heavy air I usually use about half my body weight.

The development of the Fogh sail has raised a question of maximum boat speed. When the new Fogh and the old standard, the Ratsey sail, are laid out on a flat surface, the Fogh is slightly larger, with a greater luff curve. Since the small tube sections of the Sunfish's upper and lower spars flex a great deal, the added luff curve is an advantage, for it better matches the spar bend. Because of its larger size, the Fogh must be sailed on both booms with more outhaul tension than does the Ratsey, but particularly on the upper boom.

Although the Fogh's fullness may be a minor disadvantage, its increased area more than compensates with better offwind performance. The Ratsey sail has grown with the class since its beginning, but the universal use of the Jens rig has demanded a sail with more luff curve. However, I still use my Ratsey regularly when sailing in very flat water.

To de-power the Fogh, the outhauls must be trimmed even tighter on the upper and lower spars. This means that very few or no scallops will develop along the upper spar. (Generally, in all wind conditions, the upper spar outhaul for a Fogh sail must be snug.) Mainsheet trim also must be slightly tighter. With a fat daggerboard and tight outhauls, the Fogh will consistently outperform the Ratsey.

2

Justifying the Jens

The Sunfish sail at its best, upwind depowerized with a mini-Jens. (Bob Pool)

The Jens rig is the newest innovation in modern Sunfish racing. Jens Hookanson pioneered the rig in the mid-1970s and proved its worth by winning the 1976 Sunfish North American Championship in medium and heavy air at Association Island, New York. Since then, the Jens has gained wide popularity at the World-racing level. Dave Chapin was second in the 1978 Worlds and won the same race in 1979 using a Jens rig.

The rig is based on a simple idea that narrows the upwind performance gap between lightweight and heavyweight sailors when the wind pipes up. In the past, a 130-pound sailor had practically no chance of matching speed with heavyweight competitors racing upwind in a breeze. A Jens rig reduces righting motion and produces a flatter, more aerodynamic sail, giving lightweight sailors an even chance in such conditions.

The efficiency of the Jens rests in its closeness to the deck, which eliminates much of the air flow under the boom. Aerodynamic tests have shown that reducing and/

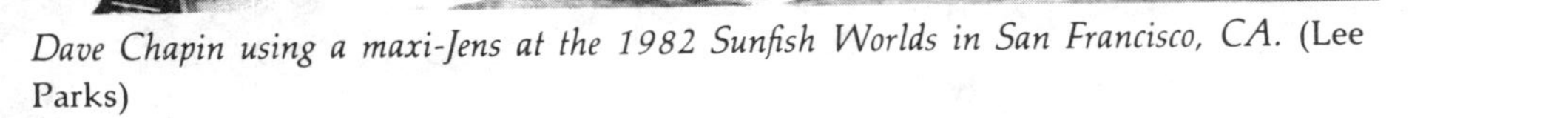

Dave Chapin using a maxi-Jens at the 1982 Sunfish Worlds in San Francisco, CA. (Lee Parks)

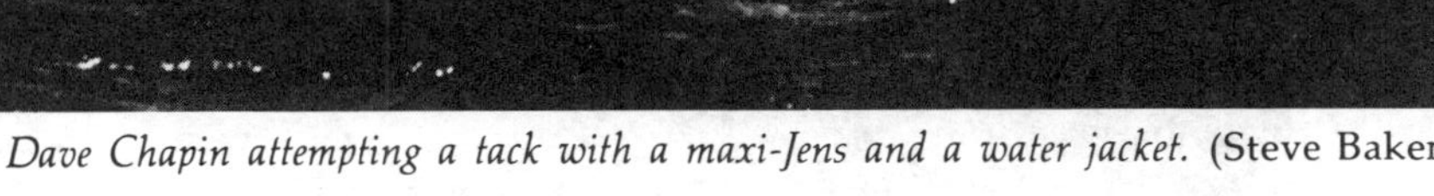

Dave Chapin attempting a tack with a maxi-Jens and a water jacket. (Steve Baker)

or eliminating air flow under the boom helps lift considerably. With the boat's small daggerboard regulating sail shape, extra lift is precisely what is needed. The sail can be de-powered further, if necessary, by raking the upper boom aft, allowing the lower boom to run parallel to the deck and thus opening the leech. The Jens is especially fast upwind on starboard tack and is a favorite of racers who like to sprint away from the fleet at the start. Finally, because the rig is lower and further forward, the Jens makes balancing the helm offwind much easier.

The disadvantage of the Jens is that it is mainly a medium- and heavy-air rig, because the sail is much closer to the water. However, especially with the new, larger Fogh sails, the competitive difference between the Jens and a full rig is not particularly great. During one race, after a heavy-air first leg, the air lightened and I was passed by a Jens-rigged boat skippered by a man only ten pounds lighter than I.

Another disadvantage of the Jens, especially for bigger sailors, becomes apparent when tacking and jibing. Because of the close proximity of the lower boom to the deck, roll-tacking and roll-jibing must be initiated earlier than is usual to allow the skipper to "kiss" the cockpit floor, thus avoiding a collision with the boom. Although tacking and jibing speed is impaired, upwind speed will compensate for the loss.

It is easy to rig the Jens. The only difficulty arises when placing the entire rig in the mast-step instead of simply hoisting the sail with the mast already in place. The job requires some upper-body strength. Follow these steps:

Step 1 Untie the halyard from the standard 10th or 11th section (sections are numbered between the plastic clips counting up from the tack). Re-tie it to the eighth or ninth section and tape the halyard in place on the boom. This is approximately 10 to 12 inches lower than the standard position. Its exact location will vary, depending on body weight and wind velocity. At 165 pounds, I have never sailed with the halyard below the ninth section. However, many smaller sailors are very fast at the seventh and eighth sections. The master of the Jens rig, Dave Chapin, usually sails with the halyard in the eighth or ninth section, and he weighs about 160 pounds. There are many variations of halyard position for different wind velocities, but here are some benchmark figures to work from. In 20 knots of wind, a 145-pound skipper probably would carry the halyard 14 inches lower than the standard location. In the same wind, a 175-pound skipper probably would carry the halyard 10 inches below the standard position.

Step 2 Lay the mast alongside the upper boom.

Step 3 Using an oversized screwdriver to avoid damaging the screw head, loosen the gooseneck fitting and slide it

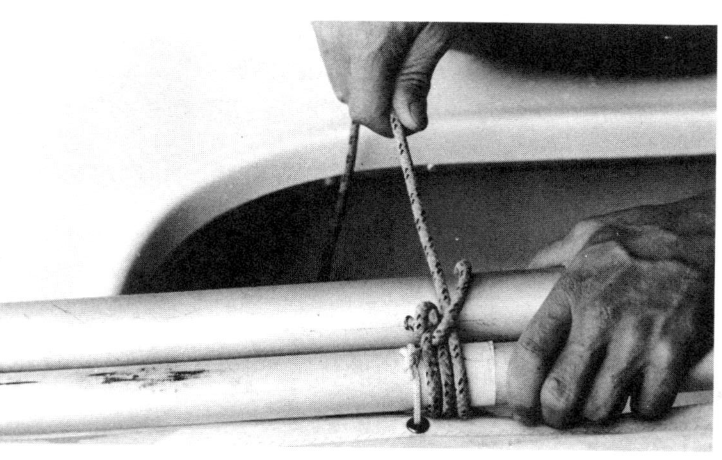

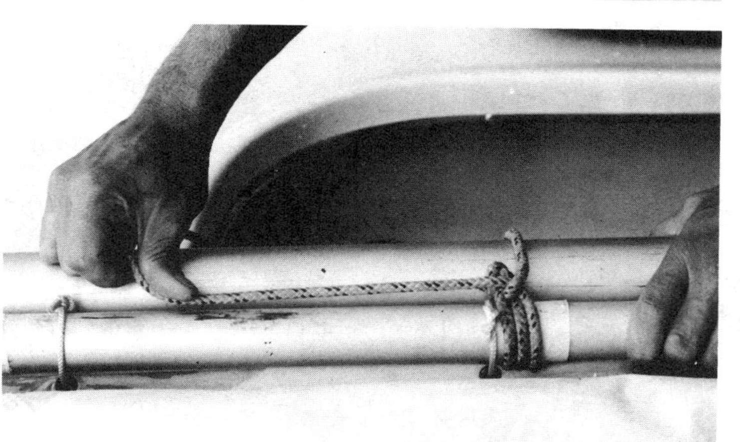

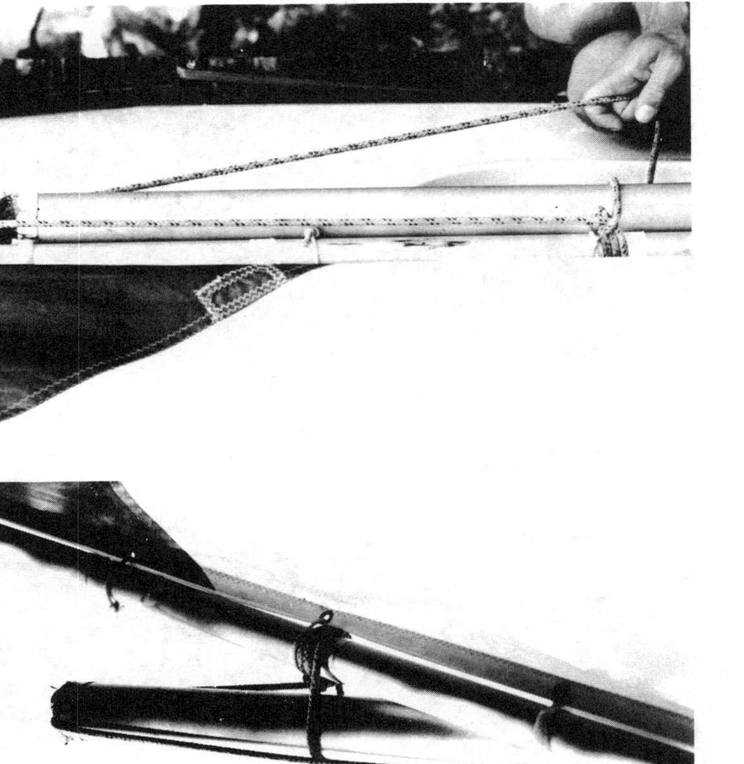

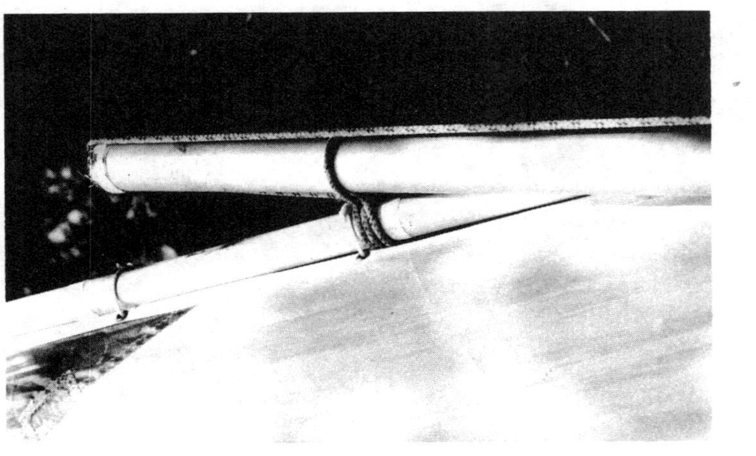

aft to a position approximately 20 inches from the tack. Like the halyard location, its exact position is relative to body weight and wind velocity, and the range is usually between 15 and 20 inches back from the tack.

Step 4 Take the halyard around both mast and spar, and then loop it through and over to make a half hitch knot.

Step 5 Put the halyard up and through the top of the mast, and bring the end back down.

Step 6 Make any final level of adjustments to the boom from the deck and pull the knot as tightly and firmly as possible around the spars.

Step 7 Grabbing both the mast and the upper spar, lift the rig into the mast-step.

Step 8 Shake the sail down to the desired level, then cleat.

Because class rules now allow an extra piece of line to be lashed to the upper spar against the mast, you may wish to modify the procedure described in Step 4. This eliminates the need for a half hitch in the halyard around the mast and upper spar.

Eventually, you may want to switch from the traditional rig to the Jens while on the water, perhaps between races. With practice, you should be able to make the change in fewer than five minutes. The most difficult step is standing the rig assembled in the boat. First, set the rig up on the deck, just as you would on land. Then lower the daggerboard all the way for stability, and make sure the wind is on the starboard beam, which will give you more room to work. To raise the rig, stand just aft of the splashboard for additional stability. Then, raise the sail as you would on land.

Rigging the Jens takes some practice. The halyard position is a key element. The halyard position here has been lowered only to a mini-Jens position. Notice the special halyard knot on the boom. The tighter the tension, the tighter it grips the spar. (Bob Pool)

Changing from a traditional rig to a Jens in the water is the single most difficult thing in Sunfish racing. One false move and you've created one horrible mess. Balance is more important than strength. At the 1978 North Americans I watched Paul Fendler, 135 pounds in three foot chop, do it with relative grace. (Bob Pool)

Learning to sail with the Jens rig is fun and easy. It is still a relatively new method and there are no universal rules about gooseneck positions or rig height. Experiment when possible, and spar with a friend. Eventually you will find the optimum settings for each wind condition, your weight, and your particular style of sailing.

The 1982 Sunfish Worlds, approaching the weather mark. The first boat is equipped with a small container hanging from the lower spar. Upon release, a protest flag will appear. (Allan Broadribb)

3

Daggerboards and Rudders

Sunfish daggerboards and rudders always have been the focus of controversy because there are several legal designs for each. Until 1972, all Sunfish featured U-shaped daggerboards and rudders. Although the daggerboard was a bit undersized, it did prove effective when sail trim and sailing technique were adjusted properly. However, the rudder had a distinct tendency to stall in heavy winds, making the boat a real handful to sail in a breeze, especially for recreational sailors.

In 1972 Alcort redesigned their daggerboards and rudders, creating the modern wing-shaped foils now found on the Sunfish. To improve heavy-air performance, rudder size was increased nearly 25 percent, but unfortunately, the already undersized daggerboards were made 12 percent smaller. The result was an immediate run on the new, larger rudders, while the old, U-shaped boards quickly became a valuable commodity among serious Sunfish racers.

Further clouding the picture, a third daggerboard was introduced by the Barrington, Rhode Island, Yacht Club. This one is three percent larger than the old, U-shaped boards and, like the old and new daggerboards, is perfectly legal.

The question of which board or rudder to use becomes even more complicated when variations in sail shape and design are introduced, since practically all adjustments made to the Sunfish are done to accommodate these underwater appendages. In addition, there are a number of fine-tuning methods that may be applied to optimize the performance of each.

DAGGERBOARDS

As more and more sailors raced and experimented with different daggerboards, it became clear that the bigger boards—the old U-shaped board and the Barrington board—had a definite edge over the new, wing-shaped boards. The logic behind this fact was brought to my attention in the summer of 1970 as I watched the legendary Carl Knight meticulously maintaining his daggerboard. He would remove it after racing to prevent the sun's ultraviolet rays from warping the wood or breaking up the hard epoxy paint. However, his rudder was sadly neglected. The rudder bottom and leading edge were not smooth, (it obviously had been scuffed hitting bottom or lying on the pavement prior to launching), and the paint was badly flaked and chipped. The contast between his rudder and daggerboard made no sense, so one day I asked Carl about this inconsistency.

"The rudder never remains in a straight line," Carl explained. "Thus, the rudder is used only in turbulent water. So smoothness there is not important. The daggerboard, on the other hand, remains fixed and flows through smooth, undisturbed water. There, the smoothness of the board serves a real purpose."

Carrying Carl's ideas about flow a bit further, I wondered if the surface of a Sunfish hull disturbs the flow of

The "New Board," "Old Board," and "Barrington Board." The Barrington has the greatest surface area and is the fastest of the three upwind. All boards are standing in the correct positions for the daggerboard trunk. The edge is placed forward (toward the bow) using the "new" and Barrington boards. The "old" board has the long edge forward for best overall performance. (Bob Pool)

water around the daggerboard. After all, sailors racing in heavy chop certainly experienced the pounding and banging of the hull on the waves, and older boats can "oilcan" in such conditions. In addition, the hull bottom between the mast-step and the daggerboard is always in motion, absorbing the shock of the waves—pushing the bow up and the stern down. Consequently, an even, or laminar, flow along the bottom of the hull hardly can be expected. Thus, the ideal board for all conditions is the one with the largest surface area—the Barrington board.

Another method of dealing with hull turbulence is to use a daggerboard of the maximum allowable thickness (2.0 centimeters). Pioneered by Carl Knight, the "fat board" allows greater speed and pointing, using a full sail for optimum power. Carl's board was so large it barely fit into his centerboard trunk. The additional thickness was achieved by wrapping the board with fiberglass cloth.

Besides making the board thicker, wrapping the board with fiberglass cloth has the distinct advantage of increasing its lateral stiffness. Such a board responds well to body kinetics, although on a much smaller scale than do boats with larger boards, such as Lasers. When done in a refined, smooth style, body movements transfer energy to the board, which, if stiff, will in turn pass accelerating energy along to the boat. Excluding body movement, a board with excessive lateral flex inhibits speed, because it stalls faster in waves, tacks, and jibes.

When applying fiberglass cloth and resin to a board, lay the cloth lengthwise to take advantage of its inherent stiffness. Use a quality resin, such as the Gougeon W.E.S.T. TM system, which is easy to apply, sand, and finish.

Assuming the Sunfish alters laminar flow when sailing through waves, a question arises as to which board shapes provide the greatest advantage. A boat going fast in the groove and steered straight benefits from a relatively sharp entry. Unfortunately, this is seldom the case with the Sunfish, which is more often than not sailed at the other end of the spectrum. As a result, a blunt leading edge with an elliptical shape and a tapered trailing edge that runs down to one quarter of an inch is as close as you can get to optimum, while remaining within class rules. This also saves the aft side of the board from damage by the daggerboard trunk.

To build up the leading edge, use quality marine filler, then glass over it to increase durability. When tapering the trailing edge remember that the maximum taper length is one and a quarter inches. Another factor critical to daggerboard effectiveness is the fit of the board in the trunk. Every sailor has sailed with a loosely fitting board and the accompanying daggerboard chatter. In addition, the board slops and twists in the trunk. All are deterrents to speed because they waste energy. The best solution is a fat board. I never have had a board chatter that was reinforced with fiberglass and resin.

To prepare the daggerboard trunk for the fat board, only minimal modifications are required. The majority of the work is preparing the board, and the main work on the trunk is ensuring that the trunk does not damage the tighter-fitting board. To be sure, vigorously sand all parts of the trunk. If you have not run the thickness of your board to the maximum, you may be able to fit in strips of anti-chafing tape, although it is decidedly preferable to build up the board instead of the trunk.

Regardless of how snugly you fit the daggerboard in the trunk, once it is wet it probably will slide up and down easily. To hold it in position, use a shockcord retainer. There are two methods of doing this. The first is to run a piece of five-sixteenths or three-eighths-inch shockcord from an eye on the upper forward corner of the board to the mast, halyard eye, or cleat. This works well, and if your board fits loosely in the trunk fore and aft, it has the advantage of cocking the board slightly aft. Another method is to rig a friction retainer. Use about two feet of shockcord with an eye at each end. Pull the shockcord across the deck to respectives sides, hooking it under the splash board. To rake the board aft simply place the shockcord on the aft-end of the board.

For years, a debate has raged about which edge should be the daggerboard's leading edge. In other words, how does this change in location of the board's center of effort affect performance? There is no exact answer to this question, because there are too many variables—wind, waves, body weight, and steering styles. But, when the results of major regattas are examined, we see that the Barrington boards perform best with the swept-back edge forward, while the old board sails best with the straight edge forward.

Often, sailors install new, untried boards prior to an important race or regatta. This can create difficulties if during the race the board suddenly begins to exhibit problems that were not experienced with the prior board. A better alternative is to use a practice board, saving the "good," thoroughly tested board for serious racing only. I have two practice boards—one for my "old" U-shaped board, and one for the Barrington board. In addition, I carry a "weed" board for inland lakes where weeds flourish. Such weeds destroy the leading edge from continuous clearing. By placing a quality marine tape on that edge, the board's life can be extended greatly. By painting the board white, I can easily view weeds.

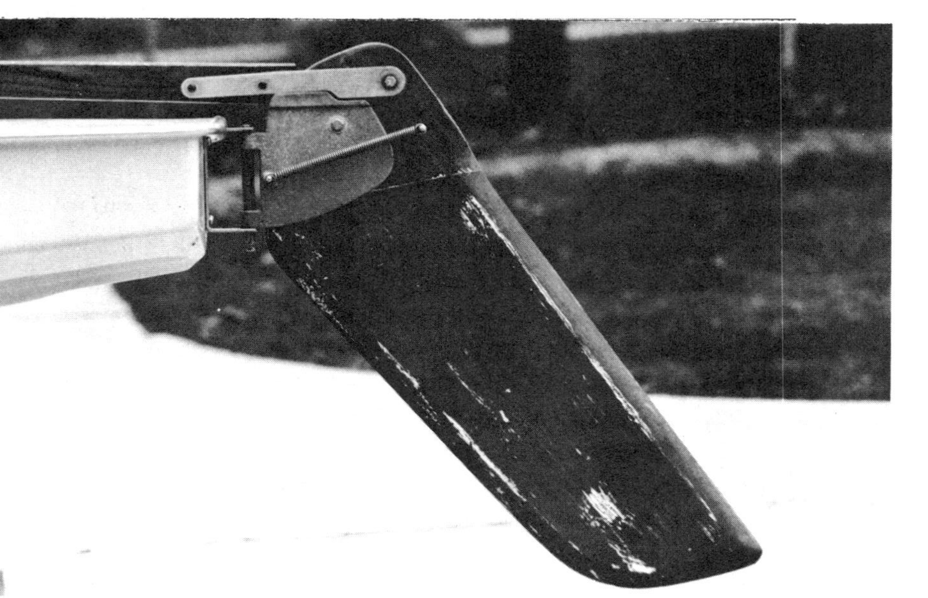

The rudder in proper alignment with the hull. Having the rudder at 120 degrees will reduce rudder stall in heavy air. The cheeks on the rudder must always be tight. (Bob Pool)

Remember, the daggerboard is the key to boat speed. A one-degree warp in the board can mean the difference between 1st and 15th place. If you continuously monitor the condition of your board, it will more than repay you for your effort.

RUDDERS

As a youngster, I recall screaming along on a wild reach and suddenly having the rudder pop up. Later, as I began sailing in regattas, I often watched someone's rudder pop up and his boat go head-to-wind, careening into two or three other unfortunate skippers in the process.

To prevent inadvertent rudder kick-up, and to facilitate boat speed, there are a few small adjustments that may be made to the rudder. First, tighten the nut and bolt holding the rudder cheeks together. Even on new boats, like those used in the World Championships, the nut and bolt can work loose after an hour or two of heavy-weather sailing. When this happens, slopping and twisting causes it to steer more like a big keelboat than a lightweight Sunfish. To prevent this, score the bolt threads with pliers or add a double locknut. In addition, tighten the rudder-head cheeks so that two hands are required to raise the rudder when beaching or docking.

Loose gudgeons and pintles are also a source of rudder slop. Looseness indicates a need to reposition these fittings by filling the old fastener holes and re-drilling holes in the proper position. Slop also may develop because of wear, especially after four or five years of hard racing, at which point the fittings should be replaced.

Don't overlook the angle of the rudder in the "down" position. This varies from boat to boat, and the further aft the rudder is angled, the greater the weather helm and subsequent slowing. Make sure your rudder is angled as far forward as the class rules allow: "The angle from the line extending from the bottom of the hull next to the keelson and the leading edge of the rudder shall not be less than 120 degrees." (Sunfish class, rule 3, section rudder, c.)

The fourth race in the 1978 Worlds, held in Ponce, Puerto Rico. With winds gusting to 50 knots, many skippers had obvious problems with rudder stall. With a boat heeled to leeward and bearing off, rudder stall may occur in winds as low as 18 knots. (Steve Baker)

Other than using one of the newer, larger rudders, there is little to be done about the rudder's shape. As with the daggerboard, round the leading edge and round off the bottom. This allows the rudder to turn with less resistance. Sand the blade smooth and apply a good coat of varnish, or apply a saturation coat of resin to provide a bit more stiffness.

One final rudder-related item: make sure you have a good, universal-type joint between the tiller and tiller extension. Illegal until 1980, universals allow more versatile tiller movements without sacrificing feel for the helm. Prior to 1980, many ingenious methods were devised to obtain universal-joint results that were not actual universal fittings.

Kerry Klinger pioneered a method utilizing a long carriage bolt that allowed up-and-down tiller action as well as athwartship movement. Unfortunately, the bolt required a loose connection, which produced inferior feel for the responses of the boat and rudder.

With the advent of the larger rudder and the legalization of universal joints on tiller extensions, the Sunfish rudder has undergone much change since the 1960s. With a little more attention to detail, as discussed here, even better feel and speed may be realized.

4

Reading the Wind on the Water

Rounding the leeward mark at the 1981 Sunfish Worlds in Sardinia, Italy. All the skippers here should be doing intense water reading to determine their upwind game plan. (Steve Baker)

Every sailor knows that the wind never blows in a straight line, even over open water. And because most racing is done within relatively close proximity to land, the problem of variations in wind direction and velocity is increased. While meteorology has provided a fairly comprehensive theory of wind movement and has greatly aided long-term forecasting of wind origins in terms of velocity patterns and directional changes, it has not helped the average sailor much with the practical, immediate problem of what the breeze is doing 300 yards upwind.

Water reading provides a sailor with data on a short-term basis. It isn't difficult to understand the tactical advantage of knowing whether the wind ahead is going to veer, back, or change in velocity. Accurate water reading enables some people to always seem to be in the right place for a wind shift or a puff.

Reading wind on the water is like looking into the future. Many sailors spend a lot of time straining their necks looking at masthead flies, which, although valuable in some instances, are of limited usefulness because they only indicate what the wind is doing at one particular point in time. Furthermore, masthead flies only show what the apparent wind is doing 25 feet or so above the water. Reading the wind on the water not only saves your neck and deals with the true surface wind, but also tells you ahead of time what the wind will be doing when it gets to you.

The key to water reading lies in the composition of groups of waves, which I refer to as "wind groups." Because waves are a function of wind, the nature of their development serves as an indicator of both wind direction and velocity. To determine wind velocity, it is necessary to discern variations in color and shape of wind groups.

COLOR

All bodies of water undergo color changes that signify changes in wind strength. It is easy to read these changes in relatively "clean" water bodies: those that are free of both motorboat slop and pollution. It is the radiant blue hue of such water that enables the sailor to read wind on the surface easily. Water bodies that are characterized by a gray hue, most often lakes and rivers near major cities, are much more difficult to read.

Typically, a puff, or what I term a "positive wind group," shows on the surface of the water as a darker area, for instance, a deeper blue. Conversely, a color change that produces a lighter hue, possibly a silver, gray-blue, should be read as a lull, or a "negative wind group."

Variations of these positive and negative color changes will depend on the base color of the water in which you are racing. For instance, lakes of a brown color, characteristic of many of the central and southern states, will exhibit a brown or mud-hue color base. Thus, a positive wind group would be indicated by a darker brown area.

While watching for color changes during a race, it is important to remember that the rate of change will be determined by the mean wind speed. Therefore, a higher mean surface wind will create numerous color changes at a fast rate. This wind condition usually exists during the first twenty-four hours of a fresh northwester. Color and shape alterations can take place at such an accelerated rate that it is often difficult to assemble them into a meaningful pattern.

In contrast, a light, morning sea breeze may produce color changes that are extremely slow and almost hueless. With such minor differences in hue, positive and negative wind groups become much harder to distinguish. But for the trained eye, perceiving these changes mean huge gains on the race course.

SHAPE

No two wind groups are identical. As with snowflakes, the outward appearance may be basically similar, but closer examination will determine that the groups are all different. For the sake of simplicity, I have divided positive wind groups into three fundamental shapes: parabolic, linear, and irregular. Familiarity with these three basic shapes furnishes a framework for the more complex variations of puffs.

The parabola is the most commonly shaped puff on the water. It is normally associated with moderate-

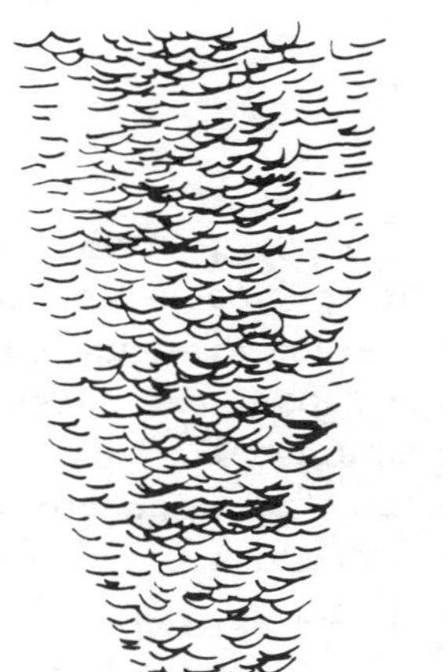

Parabolic wind group. (D. Fries)

velocity winds from the west and the south. You will notice that a greater intensity of color is found at the center of the puff, thus signifying greater velocity deeper inside the wind group. Offwind, it's a tremendous advantage to be able to spot and get into such wind groups. Within the long, narrow-shaped puffs it is possible to sail one and a half times faster than will a boat that is sailing in a negative wind group.

Linear wind group. (D. Fries)

A linear wind group, or a wind line, is most commonly associated with sea breezes. But it is also found on inland lakes when the center of a high-pressure system is sitting overhead. Usually the lake is relatively flat except for one or two linear wind groups scattered about. Linear groups are normally larger in scale than are parabolic or irregular groups, and to the racer they usually mean larger gains or losses. In most cases, the first boat to sail into a linear wind group will make substantial gains, especially upwind.

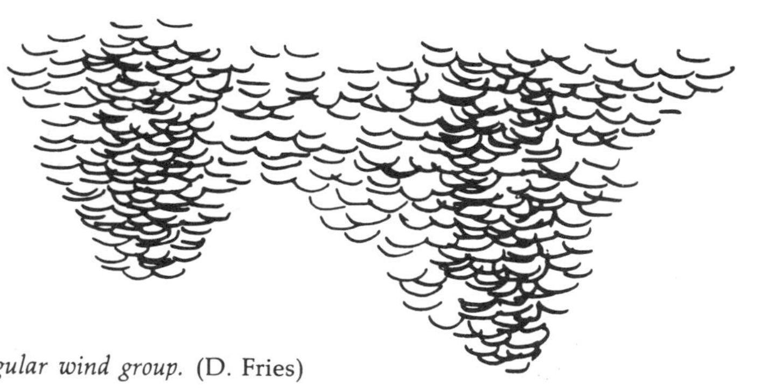

Irregular wind group. (D. Fries)

Irregular wind groups are distinguished by a basic absence of any definite, recognizable shape or pattern. In the spring and fall in North America it is not uncommon to sail a two-day series in nothing but irregular patterns. Because the puffs develop quickly, converging and diverging rapidly, a racer must be aggressive and on his toes to take advantage of such wind groups. If he fails to spot the development of these puffs soon enough, boat handling will be a considerable problem and the consequences may be disastrous.

Irregular wind group on a small inland lake. (D. Fries)

MOVEMENT

So far I have discussed only stationary identification of wind on the water. In addition to shape and color, a sailor reading wind also should be able to recognize and translate movement. For all practical purposes, the only factor that is permanent on a race course is change. When viewing a positive wind group, you must remember that its shape changes while it moves across the surface of the water. Often, after spotting a small, irregularly shaped puff, it will dissipate and become a negative wind group by the time you reach it. While this undoubtedly will be initially frustrating, with time and practice, you will be able to determine a logical, sequential pattern to wind movement and will learn to predict which wind group will be present when you reach a certain spot.

DIRECTION

With movement, all wind groups have a definable and predictable direction. Some puffs may deviate only a degree or two from the mean wind direction, while others may vary greatly. Given the proper conditions, an experienced water reader should be able to accurately identify the direction of a positive wind group, within a degree or two, up to two-thirds of a mile away. The advantages are obvious. Accurate reading of wind direction not only can help a sailor decide which side of the course to sail after rounding a leeward mark, but also helps solve the age-old dilemma of whether to tack immediately on a header or to keep going a little further, with the expectation that the wind will continue to head.

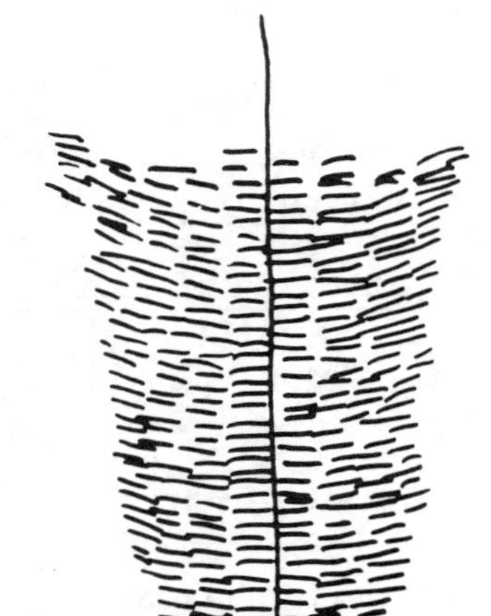

Direction in a parabolic wind group. (D. Fries)

There are two basic methods for determining wind direction in a puff. In a positive parabolic wind group, a mental line drawn vertically through the axis of the puff will indicate its direction.

Similarly, we can gain a rough approximation of wind direction, regardless of whether it's a puff or a lull, by visualizing a vertical line between wave crests. To the left and right of these directional axes, the wind should vary no more than half a degree or so. Notice in the wave group below that the wind on the right side is veered slightly and the wind on the left side slightly backed. Once a wind group is recognized and direction established, you can be reasonably assured that it will hold this direction until dissipation.

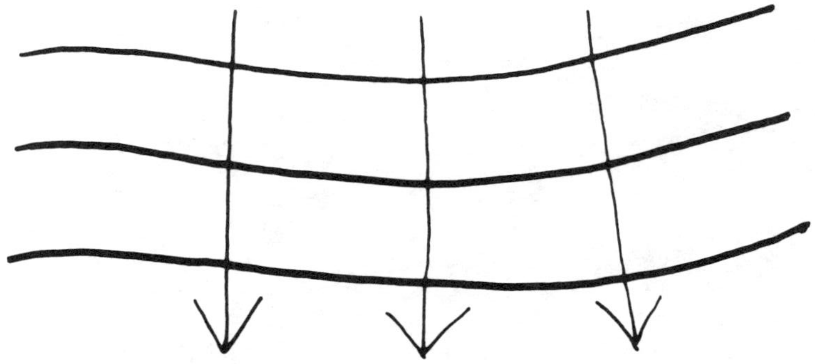

Wind direction in waves. (D. Fries)

PRACTICE

With practice, finding wind direction within a puff can become a split-second reflex. One good way to develop an eye for water reading simply is to spend some time drifting around on the water watching the wind and waves blow by. Try to spot the wind groups and forecast their strength and direction, and then wait to see if you are correct.

Another excellent method of familiarizing yourself with wind patterns is to study a body of water from an elevated vantage point such as a hill or a tall building. Even if you can't find a height to observe from, it is a good idea now and then simply to watch a race. Plant yourself a little downwind of the leeward mark and watch the proceedings. Watching other people utilize various wind groups can be tremendously educational.

OBSTACLES

Wind reading on the water, especially when determining direction, can be hindered by several factors. For instance, glare can distort wind patterns and water color and, at times, cause wind groups to appear to be positive when they actually are not. The obvious solution is to use good-quality sunglasses. A second factor that may confuse water reading is cross-chop, usually found on large bodies of water. The best way to deal with this problem is to learn to ignore the wave patterns left over from old wind systems. The new, positive wind group can be identified by watching the smaller, intermediate waves: not only will the waves be smaller, they will have a more defined shape.

RACE PREPARATION

Naturally, getting out to the race course early and checking the wind while observing the water patterns goes a long way to ensure recognition of positive wind groups during the race. To be certain, stand up in your boat before the race starts and carefully scan the water upwind to see if any changes have developed in the pattern, or if a significant wind group is coming that may affect the planning of your starting strategy.

Water reading is a little like reading a foreign language. Anyone can look at the writing, but only the person that has taken the time to learn the grammar and vocabulary can interpret and use what is written. The racing sailor who takes the time to learn the language of wind on the water will find that the skill will provide him with a tremendous advantage over the "uneducated" racer.

5

Sprinting the Start

The 1977 Sunfish Worlds in Nassau, Bahamas. One hundred boats getting ready for the start. With a line this large, there is usually a huge middle-of-the-line sag. Will boat #841 clear the anchor line? (Bob Johnstone)

The perfect start can make the rest of the race easy and fun. The real work, executing that perfect start, requires only three minutes of great concentration. A poor start, on the other hand, along with the ensuing catch-up strategies, may require up to ninety minutes of uninterrupted concentration. It's no coincidence that great racers are also great starters.

Typically, many Sunfish starts involve large fleets. Jockeying for position is challenging and exhilarating, and the boat has several atypical traits that should be considered. The boom is low and long, which means care must be taken not to get too close to another boat if you do not have right-of-way. The small Sunfish daggerboard necessitates a little extra room to leeward to get the boat going. Before the boat starts forward, it slides a bit more to leeward than boats with larger boards.

Much has been written about starting correctly. The ideas you'll find in other books have a number of general applications for Sunfish starting, but lack the necessary particulars. The variations are slight, but nonetheless important.

THE FAVORED END

One of the easiest and safest ways to determine the favored end of the starting line is the "mainsheet" technique, ideally suited for the Sunfish because of the boat's long boom and single-part mainsheet. With approximately seven to eight minutes before the start, when the fleet is large, and four to five minutes in a smaller fleet, sail down the line from the committee boat on starboard tack, steering for the pin. Keep the boat headed in a straight line. About two-thirds of the way down the line, trim the mainsheet until the sail is set just right for that point of sail. Put a mark on the sheet with a grease pencil or make a visual note about location of the sheet relative to where it exits from the mainsheet deck block.

The start of the fifth race during the 1978 Sunfish Worlds in Ponce, Peurto Rico. The right side of the course and committee boat end were favored here. (Steve Baker)

Next, round the pin and repeat the process, this time in the opposite direction. When you reach the two-thirds point, note the position of the mark you made on the first tack. If that mark is in the same location, the line is square. If it is now closer to the cockpit floor than it was on the first tack, the committee boat end is favored, and the air is to the right of the rhumb line. If the mark is between the deck block and the boom block, the pin end is favored, because the wind is to the left of the rhumb line.

Another method of checking starting line squareness suited to the Sunfish is the "friendship" start. This method requires two skippers of roughly equal boatspeed. At the eight-minute mark, both skippers start, one at the committee boat on starboard tack and the other at the pin end on port tack. Sail these tacks until it becomes obvious that one boat is clearly ahead, indicating the favored end. This usually only takes a minute or so.

In oscilliating, or shifting, breezes, caution and thought should be given prior to attempting the "mainsheet" technique or the "friendship" start in order to determine which phase of oscillation you are experiencing. To do this, watch the wind patterns on the water and take regular compass readings. A grease pencil is handy if you have a poor memory for compass numbers.

THE WARNING SIGNAL

With the ten-minute gun approaching, have two watches ready to go. Start the back-up watch at the warning, or ten-minute gun, and start the other watch at the preparatory, or five-minute gun. This way you're covered if one of the watches fails.

When the ten-minute gun is fired, you are officially racing. Focus the majority of the remaining time on strategy. Sail upwind to get a better vantage point on the weather leg. Standing up in the boat provides an even better view of the water, wind patterns, and distance to the first mark. Also watch the angles of boats sailing from the starting line, which should give you a better feel for the angle of the line and for the favored side of the course.

With seven minutes to go, make a preliminary decision about which side of the starting line is favored. Just prior to the preparatory gun, sail up to the committee boat and park next to it, sail luffing and boat motionless. If you can get there with five minutes and fifteen seconds to spare you'll have a front-row seat when the gun goes off and the flag is hoisted. You also may be able to hear the race committee counting down the five-minute gun, and make your time even more accurate. In addition, you will be in position to block others' view of the committee boat, and they will have to rely solely on the sound of the gun. Since there is a time lag between the point at which the gun is fired and when the report is heard at the other end of the starting line, the timing of your competitors may be thrown off.

PREPARATORY GUN

Now is the time to reconfirm the favored end of the starting line and to finalize your preliminary strategy. Keep a flexible attitude up to the three-minute mark in big fleets and the one-minute, thirty-second mark in small fleets. Unless you are in the final race and must defeat a specific boat, the location of the other competitors is irrelevant. Concentrate on your start. Make a final visual check upwind to identify the next wind oscillation, then sail the full extension of the line, past the pin, to help determine the line angle one more time.

As the countdown from one minute, thirty seconds begins, attention should be paid to a number of particulars. In contrast to other single-handed boats, the Sunfish's long boom facilitates good defensive strategy against luffs by other boats simply by letting the sail way out. This prevents prospective luffing boats from getting too close. Don't let the opponent even try to luff until he has an overlap. Too often, overtaking boats attempt to luff prior to an overlap. A warning usually curtails such behavior.

One move now used by many fine Sunfish sailors is the Barrett start, named after past Finn champion, Peter Barrett. This start is accomplished by obtaining a safe leeward position, which allows room to leeward to fall off and gain speed seconds before the gun. The Barrett start can be used at any location on the line, but the ideal starting spot is near the pin end. With about forty-five seconds to go in a big fleet, or with twenty-five seconds to go in a small fleet, make your final approach on port tack, cross-grain to the starboard-tack boats. Keep your eyes open for a hole to tack into. Once you have found a hole, tack into it and position your boat safely to leeward of the boats just up the line. If you tack underneath a group of luffing boats, luff right along with them without losing your access to open water to leeward. Be sure the next sailor coming up the line on port tack does not tack into your space. If this seems imminent, fall off, closing the hole, to discourage him. If you find boats up the line attempting to drive over you, fall off a little to gain speed and maintain your safe leeward position.

Often, when the fleet is large, the race committee underestimates the length of the starting line. Boats may begin lining up in rows as soon as one minute before the start. The Barrett start is not effective in such a circumstance, and the difference between a good and poor start rests in your ability to park the boat on the line. Because the Sunfish is lightweight and low freeboard, it has a tendency to drift down the line. Compensate for this and keep your boat on station, preserving a space to leeward to fall off into.

To park the boat on the line, heel it well to windward to reduce windage and place your boat in the leeward windshadow of your competitors. Luff the sail freely at all times. If a competitor attempts to luff you, make him sail out and around your long boom, a move that will put him out of luffing range. Luffing a mass of boats may be difficult. The key is vigorous verbal hailing. Hailing only the boat next to you is pointless, because the skipper must wait for the boat above him to move, and so on up the line. Instead, address the entire group, in particular, the boat farthest to windward. Demand they all come up together.

With the start nearing, prepare for your spring off the line. Often, skippers will become anxious, and a mass of boats will head over the line seconds early. When this happens, you must go with them. A general recall probably will be issued, and if not, the boats to weather of you may be called over individually. Your number may be hidden behind their sails, so cross the line with them early but inconspicuously. Keep your air clear, and your hull and sail hidden by the weather boats. If there are committee boats at both ends of the line, you may use the same screening manuever to leeward. The ideal screen is a boat that is not positioned lee-bow to you.

The race number and the number of premature starters are important to consider during a screened start. During the first races of a series, the race committee may want to set a precedent for the remainder of the event by calling as many boats over as possible and giving DNS's. However, if there are a large number of recalls, the committee may become anxious to get the race off, allowing a number of premature starters. Make sure you're among them.

With ten seconds left, cash in on your hold to leeward. Get the boat moving, gathering speed by sailing down the line, not forward across it. To do this, trim the sail and jab the rudder to windward, swinging the transom around. This maneuver places the boat perpendicular to the wind, in position for maximum acceleration.

With five seconds to go, you now have room to leeward as well as forward on the line. To ensure a maximum speed gain during this short period of time, bear off slightly, taking care not to head up before you have all the mainsheet in. At the gun, hike hard, head up, and you should squirt out in front of your competitors.

THE START

After the gun goes off and the race begins, what strategies guarantee further acceleration? In light air, some sailors nervously overtrim or, in heavy air, oversteer through the waves. Neither strategy is good, because energy always should be directed in a productive manner. To continue your spring off the line, and during the first third of the weather leg, concentration and body movements must synchronize. This skill separates the good racer from the great one. Sail by feel and observe other boats and their tacking angles. This can slow your boat, but the ability to switch from "automatic pilot" to "manual control" is a necessary skill that must be mastered.

The start of race three at the 1982 Championship of Champions, at Rush Creek, Texas, a second or two after the gun was fired. All boats are on the line and charging. Boat #1 is very close to the pin. Notice the outhaul line running down to the tack. (Lee Parks)

The use of body kinetics is crucial directly after the start. The five percent speed increase gained by utilizing body weight can mean the difference between being sandwiched in the masses or being the first boat to tack on a new wind oscillation. In light air, a smooth fluid body

The start of race two at the 1982 Championship of Champions. The committee boat has a large number of boats there; however, the left side of the windward leg proved to be favored. (Lee Parks)

move may facilitate passage through marginal lee-bow situations. In heavy air, an extra-hard hike may be necessary to blast away from a group of competitors.

Right after the start, a Sunfish competition is like a drag race. The vast majority of boats will sail on starboard tack for the first 100 yards. You must have clear air and be ready to tack if you suspect a significant oscillation has occurred. Many times, the ability to tack on the first shift can pull you right away from the fleet. As a general rule of thumb, assume that heading your boat in the right direction is more important than is clear air. This is not to say that you should sail in everyone's backwind for the first 100 yards. However, in marginal situations heading in the right direction will usually afford the greatest gain. Chances are good that many sailors are not aware of wind oscillations at the start. They will look to other boats for clues about wind direction. This often occurs at the start when an oscillation favors port tack and the left side of the course is favored.

Consolidation and clear air at the start also are important factors. Shortly after the start, you probably will want to tack onto port, especially in a substantial oscillation. Do so, but be careful not to sail too far, or more than 30 boat lengths, from the fleet. Now tack back onto starboard and stay with the fleet on the favored side of the course. This requires a fairly substantial oscillation at the start, favoring the port tack.

Inevitably, you will make a wrong decision about the favored end of the starting line. Being buried at the start is difficult, and recovering can be a chore even for the best of sailors. After a poor start, you have to beat the others at their own game. Taking a flyer is not the answer. Learning to ignore the other boats and sailing smart is. Keep your air clean and sail in the proper direction on each of the following legs, maintaining a positive and optimistic mental attitude. Your adrenaline will flow, and you will sail that much harder. The goal is to sail the remainder of the race mistake-free. You may have committed your major mistake of the regatta, but many of your competitors soon will be making mistakes, upon which you can capitalize. If one of the leaders is keeping an eye on your progress, noting the number of boats you are chewing up, you may have an added psychological edge. Your chances of regaining ground increase as the race goes on, especially on upcoming weather legs. Then, the problem of clean air lessens as the fleet spreads out.

From a race committee boat, it is possible to observe an entire series of good starts. You'll view the gamut, from light to heavy air, from aggressive to passive starts. When the fleet is large, you'll be amazed at the scope of mid-line sag and at the strategies the good racers employ to ensure a good start. Keep a note pad handy—there are so many variables it will be impossible to remember them all. Even if you remember only a few of the things you observe, your next start will be much improved.

6

Upwind

When sailing upwind, the vast majority of sailing craft are symmetrical, performing just as well on one tack as on the other. The Sunfish is an exception to this rule. On port tack, the front portion of the sail is pressed against the mast, but on starboard tack it is not. Because of this, the boat must be sailed upwind differently on each tack. It is around this difference that all discussions of upwind sailing must be centered.

Photos A and B demonstrate the correct upwind form on starboard and port tacks. The photos were taken only moments apart and the air velocity was the same in both pictures. Note that on port tack, mainsheet trim is much tighter. This is standard for all wind conditions, except light air. To make the distinctions clear between sailing in light air versus heavy air, let's examine each condition separately.

(Bob Pool)

(A,B) Port and starboard proper upwind style. (Bob Pool)

LIGHT AIR

Photo C shows the boat well balanced upwind. Note that the skipper has placed himself in the cockpit to keep the boat heeled slightly, better balancing the helm. He is not resting on the cockpit floor, but is kneeling, better prepared for a sudden roll-tack or a quick move out of the cockpit should the wind velocity increase.

(C) Light air boat balance. (Bob Pool)

Photos D and E show that upwind in 10 knots the skipper is relaxed and, most important, maintains a neutral helm. He uses his body to balance the boat and he situates himself even with the forward edge of the cockpit. There is no reason to sit any further forward, although in chop you may want to move aft a few inches to raise the bow and prevent bow plunges.

Light-air steering is very delicate. It is done with a light touch of the thumb and fingers, through which you should be able to sense the water flow around the rudder. Through his fingers, an excellent sailor instantly can detect just one small piece of seaweed caught on the rudder. Equally obvious are abnormal lee or weather helm developments. In light air, the wrist is used for minor tiller adjustments. Heel should be increased in chop to prevent waves from coming over the deck and to allow the hull to knife through the water. The Greater Detroit Sunfish Association's annual Greater Detroit Sunfish Regatta is held on Lake St. Clair, which, because it is shallow and hosts much motorboat traffic, evidences some of the choppiest seas in the world. Sailing correctly in such conditions requires continually playing the mainsheet to steer the boat. When a series of waves approaches, bear off slightly by sheeting out, and the boat will pick up speed and power. When a flat spot appears, sheet in slightly. The boat will head up and pinch, usually one or two degrees at most. During these manuevers, limit mainsheet adjustments to three to five inches, and course changes will amount only to about four degrees.

(D) Eight knots port tack. Notice that the tight sheeting provides excellent drive. Boom flex is a result of this snug sheeting. The body is compact.

(E) The Skipper has found a puff in about six knots of air. Flex the forward leg and lean out at the waist. (Bob Pool)

One common technique that increases light-air speed is capitalizing on body shape. Contrary to downwind sailing, the body acts as a speed inhibitor in lighter air. Loose clothing, such as hoods and bulky jackets, absorb increased windage and reduce speed. Although these affects are small, every element adds up. Think of your body as one tight, compact package. Keep your arms close to your torso and make mainsheet and tiller adjustments at elbow level or below rather than from the shoulders. Notice the compact body style in the light-air photos.

MEDIUM AND HEAVY AIR

In medium and heavy air, port tack is faster and provides a better angle of attack than does starboard tack. Many times, in heavy air, I have tacked from starboard to port just to increase speed and to improve my angle. In some instances, in very heavy air, I have planned my final leg to ensure that I will be on the faster, more powerful port tack as I approach the finish line. The Jens rig is an exception to this rule when used in heavy air. The Jens de-powers the sail, decreasing daggerboard stall, and equalizes speed on the two tacks.

Body movements are not as compact in heavy air as in light air. Now gross motor movements must come from the shoulders and plenty of torque is recommended when pulling in large quantities of sheet. Shoulders are curved less because weight must be moved outward to balance the boat.

Photo F shows proper form upwind in approximately 18 knots. The skipper is in a good position and has the boat trimmed perfectly. The outhauls have been tightened on both spars, with more tension on the upper spar. The gooseneck has moved aft from 18 to 21 inches, measuring from the tack of the sail. To reduce weather helm, the boat is sailed slightly flatter than it would be in light air. Mainsheet trim is increased to put the boom almost over the end of the transom.

The gentle, guiding technique used in light air is quickly replaced with aggressive and vigorous steering

(F) *Blasting upwind with a flatter sail and tighter sheet tension. The skipper, although relaxed, is hiking spread-eagle style for good boat balance.* (Bob Pool)

movements as the boat is muscled through the waves. Hold the extension firmly, with the handle between the first two fingers. Instead of steering with the wrist or elbow, use a combination of elbow and shoulder movement while trimming and easing the mainsheet with the opposite hand.

To make the boat respond to small changes in wave patterns, steer at a faster rate. To facilitate necessary meanderings through the waves, tiller and body motions must be abrupt and strong. You must place the boat on the proper position on the wave. Irregular or gross tiller movements slow the boat very little.

As you head up over the crest of a wave, trim the sail and head up slightly, swinging your upper body aft. For example, on port tack, the right arm pushes the tiller away from the body while the left arm trims the mainsheet. As you come off the back of the wave, the process is reversed. In this way, your arms and upper body move continuously, maximizing efficiency. Stay in full control; never let the boat sail you.

Hiking upwind in medium and heavy air is frequently overdone. Many sailors make the mistake of hiking 100 percent over the entire leg. Few are in adequate physical condition for this. Other legs of the course also require hiking, and speed will be sacrificed if you burn out on the weather legs.

Hiking should be done in two stages—power-on, or flat out 100-percent hiking, and power-off, which is a semi-comfortable hiked position.

The most efficient hiking method is the semi-droop, or power-off hike. This method of hiking is done from the legs not from the stomach. During a power-on hike, the

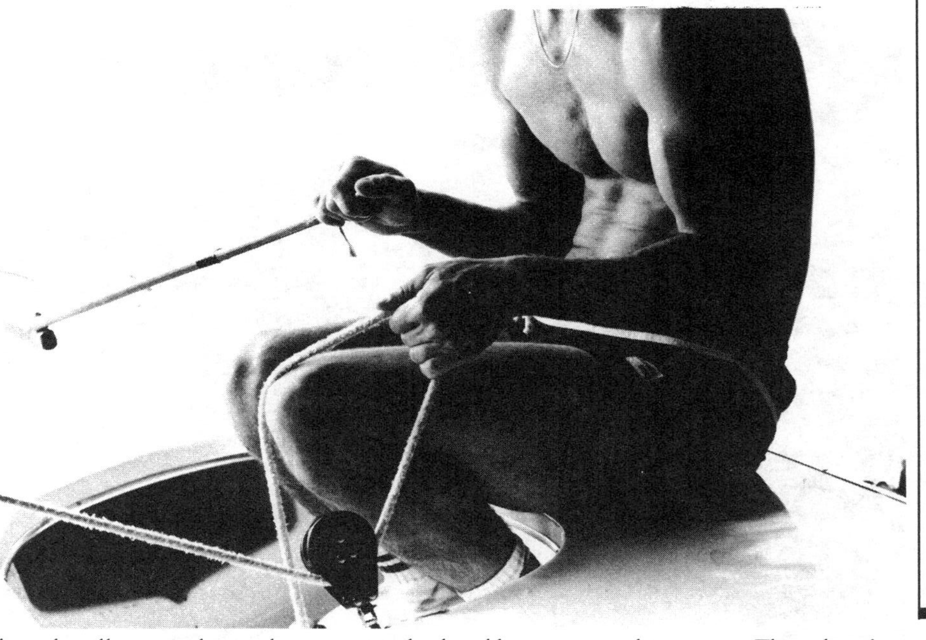

Holding the tiller properly can be very critical when blasting upwind in waves. The palm of the hand should always be facing down. (Bob Pool)

Semi-droop upwind. The mainsheet can be used for support for the upper body. Notice that in all photos, the mainsheet is never cleated. (Bob Pool)

body becomes more horizontal, transferring stress to the stomach. In power-off, the sailor is in a relaxed, semi-droop hike. Because the boat is low to the water, a full-droop will drag the skipper in the water, slowing the boat.

The photo opposite demonstrates a power hike. The skipper is wearing a water jacket, and his position makes it evident that a power hike cannot be maintained over an entire weather leg. For extra stability, I wedge my aft foot between the deck and the bottom of the storage compartment, with my heel in the drainage groove. This connects me firmly to the boat and transfers the energy of my movements directly to the hull.

Power-on hike, rounding the weather mark in 20 knots. The skipper is working to keep the boat flat and speed up. Loss of speed and excess heel will create rudder stall here. (Lee Parks)

As the tactical mind of the middle-distance runner performs 100 percent during certain points of the race, so must the mind of the power sailor perform during a number of key race points. These are the power-on stages:

1. The start. All energy is focused on producing maximum speed to power away from the fleet.
2. Tacking. In heavy air especially, each tack is followed by full hiking until boat speed is restored and flow around the board achieved.
3. Mark roundings. Because of the quantity of traffic, this area of the course requires maximum effort to pass other boats.

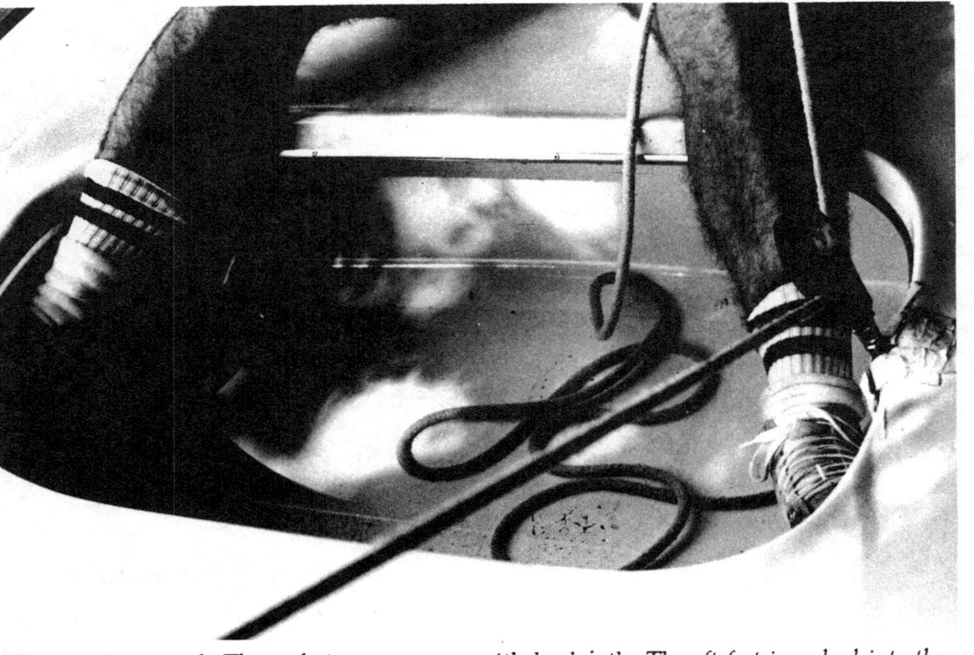

Hiking style upwind. This technique may vary with leg length. The aft foot is wedged into the cockpit storage area for better boat control and leverage. (Bob Pool)

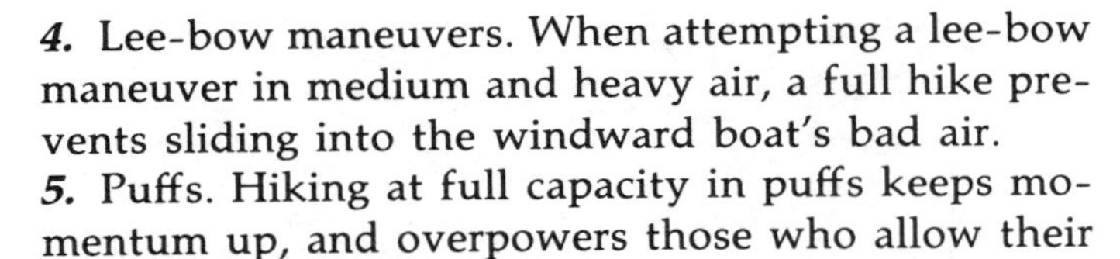

4. Lee-bow maneuvers. When attempting a lee-bow maneuver in medium and heavy air, a full hike prevents sliding into the windward boat's bad air.
5. Puffs. Hiking at full capacity in puffs keeps momentum up, and overpowers those who allow their boats to heel over or to luff excessively.
6. The finish. During the last 200 yards in any race, competition is fierce for valuable places. This is where the sailor makes his "kick" and where, when the fleet is large, the extra ounces of energy expended can bring big awards.

In heavy air, some classes of boats, such as the Laser and Force 5, benefit from raising the daggerboard a bit as wind velocity increases, reducing heeling and increasing boat speed. Unfortunately, this technique is not effective with the Sunfish. During the fourth race of the 1978 Sunfish Worlds at Ponce, Puerto Rico, a forty-five-minute squall occurred shortly after the start. With gusts approaching 50 knots, I thought the time ideal to raise the board a bit. I raised it about five inches and quickly found myself slowing and losing boats. Similarly, raising the board in drifting conditions also is ill-advised.

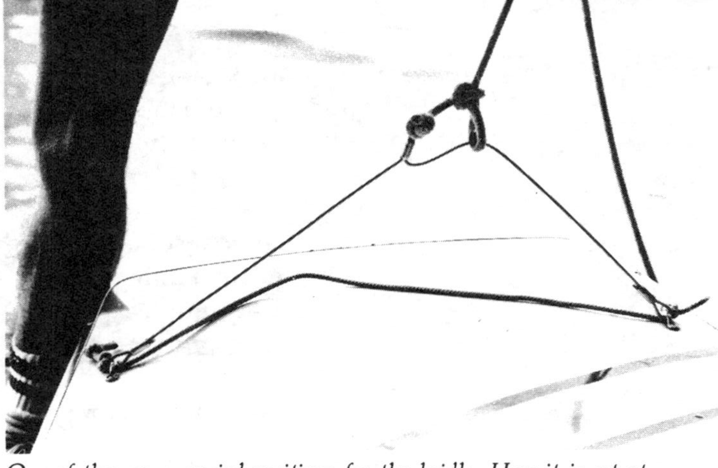

One of the many varied positions for the bridle. Here it is set at approximately eight knots. (Bob Pool)

During the 1973 Worlds competition held in Martinique, I noticed some unique sailing styles. Very distinct was the style of 140-pound Pierre Siegentheler, who compensates for daggerboard sideslipping by sailing the boat with a pronounced heel. Siegentheler's method provided several advantages. First the chine of the boat digging in the water acted like a longitudinal daggerboard, similar in principle to many boardless catamarans. Second, the reduction of wetted surface increased speed. Finally, heeling made hiking more effective because his body no longer dragged through the water. The only drawback of Siegentheler's method was its negative effect on pointing ability. Despite this, Pierre won that year's Worlds, and repeated in 1977.

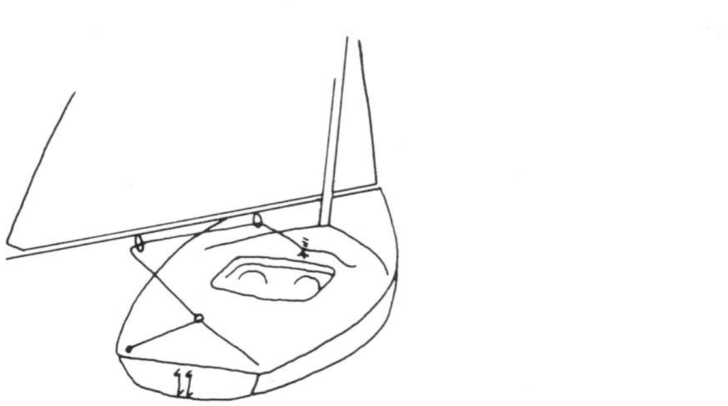

WIRE BRIDLE
0–5K

CENTERED

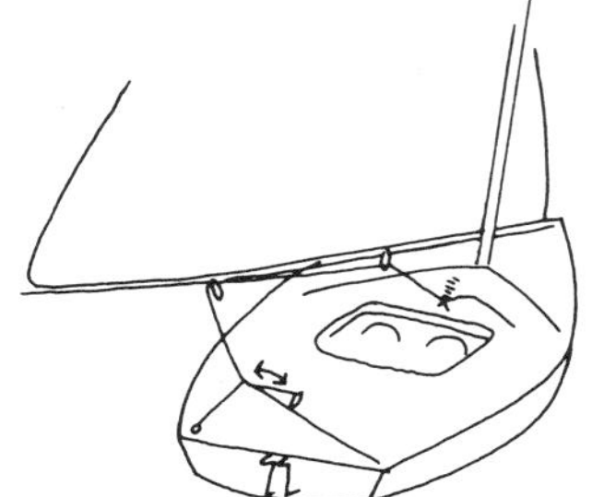

WIRE BRIDLE
5–10K

PORT SLIDE
3″

WIRE BRIDLE
10–15K

PORT SLIDE
FREELY

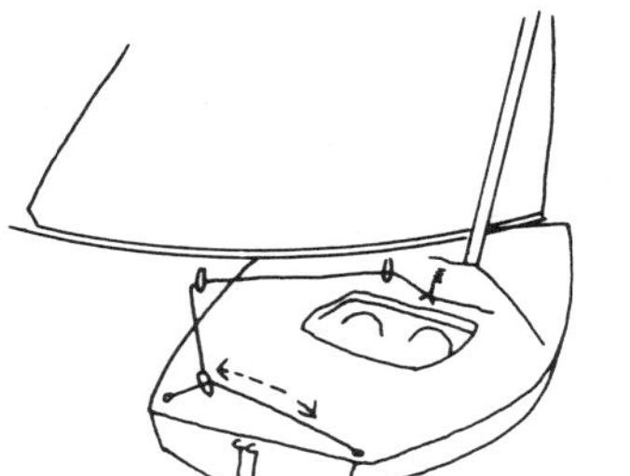

ROPE BRIDLE
15K+

PORT/STARBOARD
SLIDE FREELY

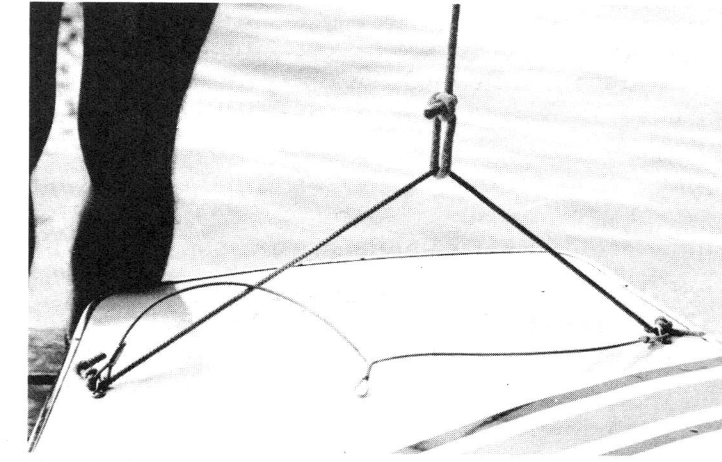

Port/Starboard heavy air position, 31″ rope, bridle sliding. (Bob Pool)

Most of the techniques mentioned here are true for both the port and starboard tack. In general, port tack allows tighter sheeting and better boat speed. Starboard tack requires extra-hard hiking and slightly less mainsheet tension. Here is a summary of upwind strategies. (See also page 143.)

THE PRINCIPLES OF UPWIND SAILING

I. LIGHT AIR

1. Boat Speed

A. Reading the water
B. Playing the shifts
C. Choosing the correct course

2. Angle of Heel

A. Eight knots or less—10-degree heel
B. Reduce heel in puffs
C. In short choppy waves, increase heel to cut through the water
D. Never sail completely flat

3. *Mainsheet Trim*

A. Slow sail-trim adjustments
B. Use thin diameter line (Ex. ¼″ 0–6 knots)
C. Use wrist and elbow to trim only
D. Use fingertips on mainsheet for better feel
E. Trim harder on port than starboard: port—over corner of transom; starboard—2–4″ past corner

4. *Proper Weight-Positioning*

A. Fluid body movements
B. Use body to aid in steerage
C. Flat water—forward leg even with forward edge of cockpit
D. Choppy conditions—forward leg 2–4″ aft of forward edge of cockpit

5. *Steerage*

A. Use your fingertips
B. Smooth precise movements
C. No more than 15 degrees tiller movement from centerline

II. MEDIUM AND HEAVY AIR

1. *Boat Speed*

A. Reading the water and waves
B. Playing the shifts
C. Choosing the correct course

2. *Angle of Heel*

A. Five-degree heel in mean wind speed
B. Reduce heel in puffs
C. Sail flat in flat water
D. Slight heel in rough water

3. *Mainsheet Trim*

A. Powerful mainsheet trims
B. Use thick diameter line (Ex. ⅜″)
C. Use shoulders and arms to make adjustments
D. Use hand on tiller for firm control
E. Trim harder on port than on starboard: port—2″ inside corner of transom; starboard—over corner of transom

4. *Proper Weight-Positioning*

A. Aggressive body movements to help power through waves
B. Center of the cockpit in all wind above 14 knots
C. Use V-hike with lower legs to better balance body
D. Semi-droop hike

5. *Steerage*

A. Use your hands and fingertips to steer
B. Jabbing tiller motions to help position the boat in the wave
C. Up to 25 degrees movement from centerline
D. Raise tiller to make jabs and gross tiller movements easier

7

The Reach

Blasting along on a good reach. Weight displacement for flat water is mid-cockpit. (Bob Pool)

Blasting along on a screaming reach can be one of the most rewarding facets of Sunfish racing, particularly when passing other boats. While on a reach you can easily predict your competitors' tactical moves and, unlike upwind sailing, boats can not split and sail in various directions. Here utilization of wind shifts is of minor importance, and making up yardage with extra speed is crucial. Maximum speed here is achieved with a combination of techniques that change with conditions.

In light air, sail the boat delicately. In most instances, rudder movement for steerage is not necessary and inhibits its speed. Good light-air reaching form is shown on page 74, where the skipper is carrying a neutral helm and the boat is heeled to windward. Besides creating a neutral helm, such heeling reduces the wetted surface and traps air, producing extra sail area. This kind of sailing requires a transition from the techniques utilized during other legs of the course. If you can think of the rudder as a fixed assembly you won't be tempted to use it to change course.

Neutral helm and plenty of windward boat heel. This reduces wetted surface and helps neutralize helm. (Bob Johnstone)

Having fun with sparring partner, John Pool. Sparring partners can be very important in determining speed and working on objective tuning techniques. (Bob Pool)

Attempting to use the rudder to change course will slow the boat.

There is a common misunderstanding about this type of steering. Body steering must be done over a long distance. Short-radius turns cannot be effective using body language without slowing the boat. To understand how much control you have without using the rudder, practice steering on a reach without touching the helm. Better still, take your rudder off, secure it in the cockpit or on the deck, and try reaching. Initial steering without the rudder may be frustrating, but with time you'll get the hang of it and your offwind speed will increase. Many college and junior sailing program use this type of exercise during routine training.

When steering with your body, all movements must be graceful and smooth, because sudden movement disturbs the flow around the rudder, daggerboard, and sail. Catlike motions are required in winds up to seven knots; in stronger winds, more pronounced movements are necessary.

To achieve maximum boatspeed in heavy air, a different approach is required. At approximately 10 knots,

1980 Sunfish Worlds in Aruba. Wild reaches are the trademark of the Caribbean. This may also mean saltwater in your eyes. (Steve Baker)

body steering becomes ineffective, and marginal planing conditions develop. When the boat begins planing, it becomes very stable, largely because of its flat bottom. Now gaining speed requires full concentration and great sensitivity because the boat cannot be muscled through the waves as on upwind legs.

Plane right away and maintain your plane for as long as possible. Involvement in tactical maneuvers with other competitors, or in housekeeping details, is a sure ticket to the back of the fleet. Keep the boat flat, give the mainsheet a couple of quick pumps when a puff hits, and you'll be off.

To help maintain planing, keep your eyes on the wind on the water behind you. Stay in the puff, bearing off as you gain speed and heading up as wind velocity decreases and the boat slows.

With increasing wind come bigger waves. In waves, the Sunfish becomes more than a sailboat—it is now a sailboat as well as a sailboard, with two power sources: the wind and the waves. The boat's flat bottom makes surfing possible on even the smallest of waves. The photos on pages 76 and 77 show the stages of catching a wave. As the wave approaches, the skipper moves forward, lifting the transom. At this point the wave is moving faster than is the boat. To increase speed, preventing the wave from passing under and by the boat, give a couple of quick pumps to the mainsheet. From this point, concentrate on keeping the bow positioned at the lowest

The skipper has moved weight forward and worked the boat to catch this wave. Notice he has trimmed the mainsheet slightly. (Bob Johnstone)

To keep the bow up, he has rotated his upper body aft. The boat is in full acceleration here. The boat is now heeled slightly to windward. (B. Johnstone)

point of the wave. Many times, this means steering across, rather than down, the wave. On a broad reach or run you can make up ground to leeward while maintaining good speed.

Getting the boat up to speed as the wave approaches is important. As mentioned, two or three quick mainsheet pumps will usually do that. Rule 60 of the International Yacht Racing Rules prohibits rhythmic pumping of the sail but allows up to three pumps to get the boat surfing down the face of a wave.

Because the Sunfish has tremendous surfing ability, the class is more permissive about kinetic interpretations than are other classes. However, knowing the exact language of Rule 60 is important, and you must be sensitive to the potential consequences of your actions.

The surf is now near its completion. The skipper should be looking for the next wave. (B. Johnstone)

Although it is wise to avoid sailing up the back of a wave, there are times when you must. Weight must be shifted aft to allow the bow to lift easily over the wave. If you pump the sail and rock aft and to windward simultaneously, a few extra ounces of forward momentum will be gained. Once through the wave, keep the bow aimed toward the low points or troughs, a strategy that should prevent having to drive through the backside of more waves.

Occasionally, you may find yourself slipping up the backside of a wave. To avoid this, plan your steering strategy in advance, always looking ahead a few waves. Your angle of attack may vary as much as 30 degrees, but the boat will continue to go fast, and you won't find yourself stopped dead by a wall of water.

To further enhance planing, particularly in marginal conditions, keep your air clean. The lack of a few grams of air may make the difference between going fast or slow. Sail in the puffs as much as possible. In lighter air, keep the boat heeled slightly to windward to reduce wetted surface and keep the helm balanced.

Mike Catalano is one of the wizards of offwind sailing. In light to medium air, he uses the smallest wave to his advantage by placing his forward knee against the forward edge of the cockpit rim. Both feet are placed firmly on the cockpit floor and his body is at the center of the cockpit. With perfect timing, he flexes his forward leg against the cockpit rim and pushes aft, a powerful flex starting in his stomach muscles and running through his entire leg. Coordinating his movements with a sail pump and slight rock to windward makes Mike an offwind terror.

In very light air, Mike adds an extra weapon to his speed arsenal. Upon approaching a boat on a reach or run, he starts a warm and friendly conversation with his opponent, usually making him laugh. This breaks the opponent's concentration and movement from the laughter disturbs air and water flow. As the opponent's boat speed diminishes, Mike quickly blankets and passes him, continuing the conversation to reduce the agony of being passed.

SAILING ON REACHES

1. If you plan to attack on the reaching leg and to pass many boats, get upwind into the passing lane. This strategy works especially well on long reaches that are 90 to 110 degrees to the wind. Avoid intruding on a skipper's "social space" when passing, or you may end up in a luffing match.
2. Except when planing, keep the boat heeled to windward to balance the helm.
3. In light air, steer the boat without moving the rudder.
4. In heavy air, significant amounts of steering help maintain a surf.
5. Slide the mainsheet to the end of the bridle on both starboard and port reaches.
6. If you have water in the cockpit, use the reaches to drain.
7. In medium to heavy air on reaches of 120 degrees or more, trim the mainsheet directly from the boom block. In light air, do this on points of sail greater than 90 degrees.
8. When rounding the windward mark, boat position and speed are more important than equipment adjustments.
9. Slide the gooseneck slightly aft for speed and helm balance. Repositioning should take less than four seconds.
10. Generally, sail up in the lulls and down in the puffs.
11. If a competitor is attempting to pass you windward, a sharp luff and a verbal hail will discourage him.
12. When demanding room at marks, always address all of the boats hindering your safe and seamanlike rounding.
13. Roll-jibes at the jibe mark or on runs are as important as roll-tacks upwind.
14. To ride waves, use fore and aft weight displacement. Move forward down the wave and aft over the top of it.
15. On the second reach, note any changes in the mean wind direction. This enables you to set your game plan for the next beat.

Chris Friend, showing excellent downwind form at the 1982 Sunfish World Championship. Chris has the boat heeled properly to weather and is holding the mainsheet from the boom block. (Allan Broadribb)

8

Downwind

Downwind sailing techniques are an extension of those used on the reaching legs. Applicable here is an aggressive attack on the wind and waves.

The Sunfish is easy to handle downwind because of the stability provided by its flat bottom. If you have doubts about the boat's stability, a short sail in a Laser or Force 5, particularly in a breeze, will prove this point. One of the best training techniques for sailing a Sunfish is to spend time on a faster and less stable boat, such as the Force 5. After the Force 5, the Sunfish will feel like a toy, both upwind and down. In fact, many of the class's finest sailors also race other boats such as Finns, Lasers, and Force 5s.

Because downwind sailing is the slowest point of sail for the Sunfish, more race time is spent on this leg than on reaches. Therefore, learning how to sail this leg well is important.

A unique attribute of the Sunfish is its ability to sail by-the-lee. Generally, sailing by-the-lee reduces the number of jibes downwind, and a properly performed jibe can be a great sailing move. Often, however, an extra jibe near the leeward mark can be costly. When sailing by-the-lee, you can go as far as 195 degrees off the wind while maintaining speed and making good your course to leeward. For this, you'll need an extra-long mainsheet, approximately 28 feet.

To attack downwind, you must use your body. Body movement turns the boat and allows it to ride across a wave. The fore and aft movements work your overgrown surfboard around to catch the finest wave. Lean windward to bear off and lean leeward to head up. As on other legs of the course, specific techniques vary from one wind condition to another. Let's take a look at the two major categories.

Jim Owen showing good light air form. Mainsheet is out approximately 90 degrees to centerline of boat. Jim crosses his legs for balance. He also is hand-holding the mainsheet for the boom block. Notice his simple dagger board retaining device, tight elastic rubber between the splashboards. (D. Fries)

LIGHT AIR

One of the few opportunities you have to attack well in light air comes when there are relatively large waves, which allow you to surf. Because of the boat's slow speed, it takes a lot of effort to get on a wave, and equally as much to maintain the ride, but if you are successful you'll be moving faster than your competition.

Another point of attack materializes when you run into large wind oscillations. Occasionally, oscillations will vary as much as 20 degrees. Jibe if you receive a significant header, but in relatively steady air, tacking downwind is not productive. Generally, tacking downwind means more than three tacks.

However, the most important attack is superior boat speed. To maximize speed in light air:

1. The sail should be 90 degrees to the centerline of the boat.

2. Sail with only as much board as needed. However, never pull the board up all the way, for that causes water to boil in the trunk opening. The board should at least fill the daggerboard trunk. A reference mark on the board helps assess its position.

3. As on reaches, balance your helm. Neutral helm keeps boat speed up. Heel the boat to weather, both in and out of waves, and use body movements to help steer and/or make minor course changes.

A = 12 BOAT LENGTHS - 0–5K
B = 8 BOAT LENGTHS - 5–10K
C = 5 BOAT LENGTHS - 10–15K
D = 3 BOAT LENGTHS - 15 + K

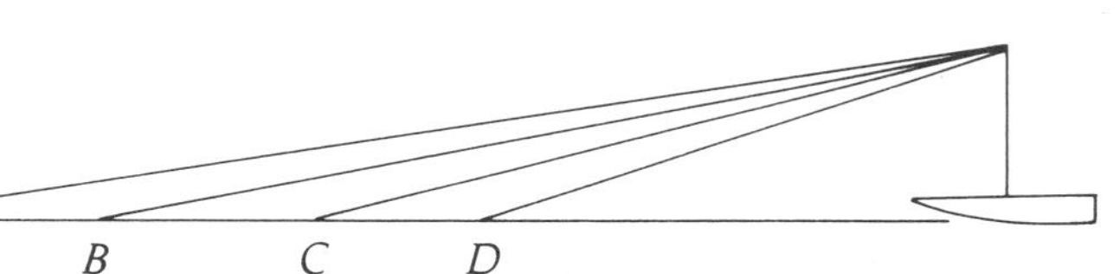

4. Move gracefully. Jerky movements inhibit speed.
5. Unless sailing a small course, avoid luffing matches.
6. In a dying breeze, when approaching the leeward mark move to the inside. This is particularly helpful if a logjam of boats develops at the mark.
7. In winds between three and seven knots, carry your vang snug. Don't use the vang in less than three knots.
8. If you require extra speed to establish or break an overlap, a slight rock to windward is usually acceptable.
9. Sailing by the lee as far as 15 degrees is allowable for short periods of time.

HEAVY AIR

In heavy air, the same principles apply as in light air, but they are modified slightly. It is critical to use waves efficiently, and more aggressive body, sheet, and helm movements are necessary to remain synchronized with the waves. To attack in heavy air:

1. Keep the bow at the lowest section of the wave and prolong the downhill ride by steering with the rudder. Steering across the wave also may be necessary.
2. When going up the backside of a wide, shift body weight aft. When going down a wave, shift it forward, near the daggerboard area.
3. Through big waves, keep the board at least one-third of the way down to assist in tracking across waves.
4. Keep the vang tight.
5. For better response and feel, trim the mainsheet directly from the boom.
6. Except when surfing down a wave, heel the boat to windward.
7. For better stability, spread your legs apart to opposite vertical cockpit walls.
8. Never intentionally sail through a wave.
9. Surf in clean water, free from other competitors' quarter waves when possible.
10. Jibe only when accelerating down a wave. Then there is less force on the rig, and the chances of capsizing are reduced.

After turning the weather mark and heading downwind, be sensitive to wind and water conditions and sail immediately for the favored side of the course. The decision to steer to the left or right of the rhumb line is determined by wind velocity and direction. However, also keep currents and water depths in mind because shallow water may mean bigger surfing waves and current may affect speed.

LEEWARD MARK ROUNDINGS

Setting up well for the leeward mark provides many opportunities. Generally, at least a 145-degree radius turn must be made, and because such a turn consumes energy and time, mistakes can occur. Learning to capitalize on others' mistakes can prove the biggest tactical advantage of the race.

In a pack of boats, an ideal leeward-mark rounding is not always possible. Then, your goal must simply be to stay inside to achieve better boat speed. In heavy air, many sailors either overshoot the mark or fail to sheet in fast enough, creating an opening between themselves and the mark. Take advantage of these situations.

In the past, much has been written about proper rounding of marks and many diverse techniques are accepted practice today. Here are some general tactical rules of thumb to remember when competing in large fleets.

1. Establish your overlap well ahead of time, as much as 7 to 10 boat-lengths from the mark. This will

Wild mark rounding leads to a great show for spectators. (Lee Parks)

cause the outside yacht to give you plenty of room to make a smooth rounding.

2. Stay to the inside and demand room.

3. When gaining on a pack of boats, swing wide in anticipation of many boats overshooting the mark. If so, chances are you'll be able to take the inside route.

4. In heavy air, do not try to establish an overlap once you reach the two-boat-length circle. At this point, things are happening too quickly for the overtaken skipper to comply.

5. In heavy air, use long sweeping motions to gather the sheet as you turn. Start trimming the sheet just prior to your course change and use your steering hand to collect the extra sheet. You'll also find that it is easier to gather the sheet when you are surfing down a wave.

6. When approaching the mark inside on port tack with a herd of boats you may be forced into a bad turn. To avoid this, counterattack by jibing onto starboard about 10 boat-lengths from the mark. Sailing by the lee if necessary, force your competitors to swing wide with you. This maneuver works best in light and medium air.

7. Prior to rounding the leeward mark, plan your strategy for the next weather leg. Preplanning enables you to round the mark prepared for your next move.

8. When rounding the mark in medium air with a clearly established inside overlap, make a safe and seamanlike rounding, gaining an extra half-boat length on your competitor and hogging a little extra room.

9. If you want to tack immediately after rounding the leeward mark and sail to the left side of the course, an absolutely tight mark-rounding is necessary. If, by chance, someone has a slight inside overlap on you, round the mark and pinch him off as you trim in on port tack. This should cause him to bear off and will free you to tack. If he instead decides to tack, immediately tack on him, taking his air and forcing him back to the right side of the course. Then sail the favored side in accordance with your game plan.

9

Roll-Tacking and Jibing

The first phase of the important roll-tack. (Bob Pool)

In light and medium winds, roll-tacking and roll-jibing a Sunfish can provide an extra squirt of speed that will pull you through the maneuvers at full speed. These techniques are a unique blend of science and art—for every action there is an equal and opposite reaction, and the ability to move through the tack or jibe fluidly and efficiently is an art.

Generally, the speed of the roll increases with wind velocity. For instance, a drifting roll-tack or jibe may take as many as five seconds, while the same maneuver might take as little as three seconds in a 15- to 18-knot wind.

Five-to-ten-knot winds and smooth water are optimum conditions for learning roll-tacking and jibing. Such conditions enable you to closely monitor which of your movements work with or against the wind. Not having to deal with waves allows you to concentrate more on your movements.

When first attempting roll-tacks and jibes, you may feel very awkward—as if you are going to fall out of the boat. However, with practice, these feelings will subside.

(Step 1) Tiller never turned more than 45 degrees. (Bob Poole)

(Step 2) Begin to heel boat with body. (Bob Poole)

ROLL-TACK

To roll-tack the Sunfish:

Step 1 With the boat heeled slightly, as it should be in light and medium winds, use your weight to gently pull the boat level.

Step 2 As soon as the boat is level, begin gradually pushing the tiller about 45 degrees to leeward, using a full arm extension.

(Step 3) Sail has now lost air, boat heel will be easier now. (Bob Poole)

(Step 4) Using the legs for support, bend at the waist. (Bob Poole)

Step 3 Utilizing your weight, heel the boat to windward, using enough force to keep the sail full. Slide out and aft to keep the bow from digging into the water.

Step 4 As the boat reaches head-to-wind, there should be about 20 degrees of windward heel. I know when I've rolled the boat far enough to windward, because the seat of my shorts takes a quick dip in the water.

(Step 5) Recovering and getting under the boom smoothly is important. (Bob Poole)

(Step 6) Sail is now driving good, boat is at greatest heel. (Bob Poole)

Step 5 With the boat just beyond head-to-wind, bend at the waist and grab the cockpit rim on the opposite side of the boat. This helps maintain balance and provides a handle with which to pull yourself to the other side of the boat.

Step 6 With the boat on the new tack, pull yourself across the cockpit, ducking the boom and pivoting on the balls of your feet. Always face forward when crossing the cockpit, as this allows a better feel for the boat's direction and keeps you aware of the position of the rest of the fleet.

(Step 7) Boat is accelerating, body movement must be smooth. (Bob Poole)

(Step 8) Hand exchange must be completed before sitting down. Can not let go of tiller or mainsheet. (Bob Pool)

Step 7 Now comes the most challenging part of the maneuver—the blind mainsheet hand exchange. Start by transferring the mainsheet to the tiller hand, so that for a moment that hand is holding both tiller and mainsheet. At this point, both hands still have a grip on the main-sheet.

Step 8 With both hands still holding the mainsheet, release the tiller hand. Then, with the hand that was holding the tiller, reposition your grip so that you take the sheet directly from the mainsheet deck block.

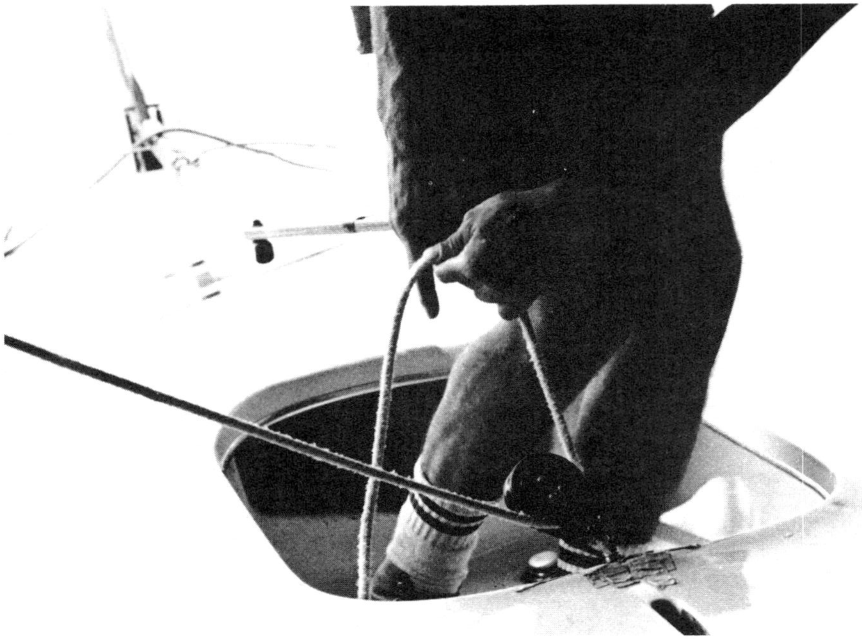

The hand exchange is quite crucial. Neither the tiller or the mainsheet should be dropped. To rotate without twisting the mainsheet in the legs, take the mainsheet to the tiller hand. This will allow a free hand. Same thing happens when adjusting gooseneck. (Bob Pool)

ROLL-JIBE

The roll-jibe is fun and exciting, and when performed with good technique it can be accomplished in strong winds. The key to success is getting through the jibe with speed equal to or better than that attained just prior to initiating the roll. Basically, the roll-jibe is a roll-tack in reverse, with less tiller motion because you steer with more boat heel.
The motion on the roll-jibe can be kept to a minimum when following these steps:

Step 1 Determine correct conditions in relation to wave and wind.

Step 2 Heel the boat to weather in a gradual motion. Down a wave and in a lull when possible.

Step 3 At approximately 20-percent heel, turn the tiller to leeward about 10 degrees.

(Step 1) Determine correct position strategically.

(Step 2) Heel boat to windward increasing speed.

(Step 3) Rudder is making a minor adjustment to lee.

(Steps 4 & 5) Maximum boat heel during jibe.

Step 4 Pull the main across in one big sweeping fashion. (Caution should be given to make sure that the daggerboard has been pushed down slightly.)

(Steps 6 & 7) Recovery, standing up to do hand exchange.

(Step 8a) Must be very smooth when sitting back down.

Step 5 Remain on the windward side of the boat until the sail has crossed the centerline. (The recovery stage, like the roll-tack, will begin.)

Step 6 Grabbing the windward cockpit rim, recover by standing up.

Step 7 Exchange the mainsheet using the blind mainsheet hand exchange and rotate on the balls of your feet, facing forward. Never rotate toward the stern of the boat.

Step 8a & b Sit down gently, neutralize the helm again by heeling the boat to weather. Caution should be given not to overturn the boat! Many skippers make tiller adjustments that are too large. This slows the boat and creates a longer sailing distance to the next mark.

The roll-jibe is a fun and exciting procedure. Boatspeed can remain constant. The speed of the roll-jibe is like that of the roll-tack. Drifting conditions will mean a slower procedure while medium conditions will mean doing things at an accelerated rate.

(Step 8b) Heel boat to leeward smoothly again, and neutralize helm. (Bob Pool)

10

Lessons Learned

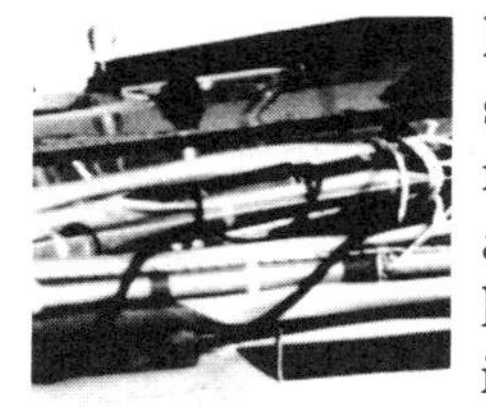

Each regatta, regardless of size, offers something to be learned. The ability to remember what went right or wrong, and why, makes these lessons particularly valuable. What follows are five important lessons I have learned on the race course.

SURVIVAL OF THE FITTEST

During the summer of 1971, the North American competition was held in Sayville, New York. The regatta was sailed in predominantly light air and at sixteen years of age, my inexperience was offset somewhat by both lightwinds and by my light weight. Because the regatta was sailed in high heat and humidity, fatigue and mental alacrity were important performance variables, although many sailors appeared undaunted by the heat and the long hours in their boats. For others, the difficult conditions created havoc, because they were unprepared for the heat and became impatient. The winner of the regatta, Jack Evans, demonstrated tremendous patience and experience under adverse conditions.

I placed seventh at the North Americans, and qualified for the 1972 Worlds, which were held in Bermuda. There, heavy air and big seas provided exciting racing—conditions quite the opposite of Sayville. During the third race, I rounded the leeward mark with a lead of about 10 boat-lengths, but when I started back upwind, I was tired. At that time, class rules allowed unlimited weight to be worn by skippers. Fatigue from carrying about 70 pounds impaired my ability to think clearly.

Bob Bowles, who won the race, passed me like a destroyer on his way up the second weather leg. As I approached the second weather mark, I was extremely tired and fell into third place. I mistook a spectator boat on the starboard side of the course for the committee boat, assumed I was on the third weather leg, and tried to finish. I was disoriented and could not believe the race continued further. I had sailed way past the weather mark and was very frustrated.

Lesson: Charles Darwin formulated the theory of survival of the fittest, and this philosophy is applicable to man's various sporting contests. The fittest, physically, emotionally, and intellectually, survive as winners. At both Sayville and Bermuda, the winner was best suited and prepared for the contest. Jack Evans showed unmatched patience and the ability to change gears readily. He adapted to difficult conditions in a smooth and natural fashion. Bob Bowles displayed intelligent sailing and used his great physical strength to excel. He had no equal in terms of the ability to adapt quickly to the conditions. Both men truly were well prepared for the environment—they had trained for the conditions, and their efforts were transformed into victory.

THE VALUE OF DETAILED NOTETAKING

During my days of collegiate sailing, I had the opportunity to travel to many sailing sites throughout North America. This experience was enjoyable and very enriching. One classic autumn racing series is the Timme Angsten Regatta, held at Chicago's Belmont Harbor. Schools from all over North America qualify to compete on the icy Lake Michigan waters, where Lehman 10s are sailed with both skipper and crew. The harbor exists next to many multi-story buildings. When the wind blows from the west, it swirls around the buildings, often diverging on the small harbor. Belmont Harbor has its own peculiar and characteristic conditions, and can seem illogical to the inexperienced sailor. Complicating the situation are the swells that come through the mouth of the harbor, creating a small current.

During my freshman year, I observed the Angsten races while other, more practiced members of our team participated. As a sophomore, my experience was bewildering—I was sailing, but could not manage consistent results, and I became confused dealing with the windshifts. As a freshman, I had compiled a series of notes on the wind's peculiarities at Belmont. These notes should have helped me as a sophomore, but I was still missing a key ingredient. Although my notes listed general conditions about the boats and about current and wind movements, I needed to make some key changes before I could be successful in my junior year.

Lesson: Shortly after leaving the harbor as a sophomore, I reflected on my experience. My boat speed was very good, near the top 20 percent. However, my ability to sail in the right direction was near the bottom 20 percent. While this was the first time I had ever had the opportunity to observe conditions thoroughly before racing, the notes from my freshman year were of little help.

During the drive home, I realized I needed to make a dramatic change in my notetaking method. I had been recording general information, not specific details, about wind conditions. What I needed was a log of every race that would detail wind velocity, current, direction, temperature, air mass, and course. I also needed to note the favored side of the starting line and every weather leg.

My sophomore year proved a good time to start making detailed notes, as the wind blew from all quadrants with varying velocity. With twenty races in three days, my log would take some time, and I needed to start right away before the memory of the race faded.

The results my junior year were tremendous. My log provided the ability to anticipate wind changes, which proved a terrific edge. In the last ten races, I finished in the top five. I rose from 16th rank in A division my sophomore year to first place as a junior.

During the course of a lifetime of sailing, the chances of sailing on the same body of water more than once are great. Often, annual events are held at the same location, so detailed notetaking can be valuable.

IMPROVING THROUGH OBSERVATION

The Winnetka, Illinois, Yacht Club hosted the 1970 Sunfish North American Championships. Many great Sunfish sailors were on hand—Carl Knight, Ted Moore, Chuck Millican, Major Hall, Will White, Larry Lewis, Tom Ehman, Bob Bowles, and others. The first day saw light air, but for the remainder of the series, winds were between 10 and 20 knots—ideal sailing conditions. At fifteen, I felt very green and had a lot to learn.

Each sailor had his own particular style. In the first race, I followed Dick Griffin up the first weather leg. I had sailed against Dick before, and considered him fast and intelligent. At 130 pounds, his upwind speed in medium air always fascinated me. He hiked hard and sailed brilliantly through waves, cutting each with grace and speed. In this qualification race, we finished first and second in what was generally light air.

As the series progressed and the wind's velocity intensified, my performance gradually faltered. During the fourth race, I examined Ted Moore's style with analytical care. He wore a large number of sweatshirts, and his aggressive upwind style and tacks made him unbeatable. I learned from observing him never to place myself in a defensive position on the first weather leg. A hard, charging offense is the key to getting to the weather mark first.

During the fifth race, I went with Carl Knight to the left side of the course in an offshore breeze of 18 knots. In his quiet manner, Carl sheeted hard and ever so slightly pinched a little further to windward. His pointing ability was unmatched. Offwind, he pumped the main, holding the sheet from the boom block to achieve better feel for the boat and sail. I was impressed with his uncanny ability to read windshifts.

Lesson: With so many great sailors on hand, it would have been foolish not to observe carefully. Although every sailor has his own style, each style has much to offer the inexperienced sailor. Many times while going upwind I would attempt their techniques. Offwind, they showed perserverance while playing the waves and keeping the boat on a plane for the longest possible time. Ashore, I would question them individually about methods they used on the water. This was informative, and they were helpful. Observing great sailors and their habits can be invaluable, and imitating their styles may be one of the quickest ways to learn how to race well.

LIGHT-AIR METHODS

During the 1973 Sunfish North Americans at Devils Lake, Michigan, there was much to be learned about sailing in light air. After the first two races in medium air, I had a small overall lead. The wind was steady and showed slow oscillations, and I adapted to this easily.

The second day brought a light, puffy wind. Consistent results would be the key to holding the lead, but it was not uncommon for sailors to gain or lose 30 boats on one leg. Wind velocity was spotty, and puffs would appear and disappear irregularly. Often I sailed toward a patch of wind, only to have it disappear by the time I arrived.

Because of my experience in regatta strategy, I began to sail defensively, but this proved to be the wrong approach. In the critical fifth race, I rounded the leeward mark 10th, and a huge starboard-tack lift came through. In the oscillating wind, it made sense to hang on, even though I was on the outside and losing boats, in the hope that the wind would swing back. As the breeze was shifting inconsistently, the oscillation back was not easy to predict, but this particular shift was strong and long. Major Hall, who eventually won the regatta, took many sterns to sail into the meat of the shift and reaped the rewards. I hung on, but the return oscillation didn't occur until after the finish line.

Lesson: My experience at Devils Lake taught me a tremendous amount about sailing in light air, and provided me with some general rules of thumb. First, patience is a big virtue, and learning to deal with heat and inconsistent conditions can be beneficial. Second, be flexible—committing yourself too soon may be a mistake, and starts should be finalized only at the last possible moment. Third, when a big shift is coming in, sail well into it before tacking. Fourth, be very still in the boat—make only graceful, catlike moves. Fifth, when there is no wind, always aim the boat toward the next mark. And sixth, when sailing upwind, do not allow yourself to stray far from the middle of the course during the first two-thirds of the weather leg.

NEVER SAY DIE

One hundred and three sailors assembled at the ninth World Championships at Ponce, Puerto Rico, for conditions that promised fresh breezes and great surfing waves. In the first race, I got caught outside of a windshift and slipped to 35th place, although I managed to scrape my way back to 11th at the finish. With six races to go, I knew consistent sailing from there on in was a must.

But just before the start of the second race, a boat ran over my transom, pushing me over the starting line early. Circling the committee boat, I had a helpless thought that this series might pose chronic problems and that perhaps I lacked intellectual preparation. But starting last made me aggressive, and I realized flawless sailing was needed. Watching the majority of the fleet go left, I went right—my initial game plan before the start. Rounding the weather mark 15th, I was aware that I had made the big play, and as the race continued, more boats fell behind me. As I sailed up the last weather leg, I thought how much fun sailing is when you are prepared.

Lesson: Winning the second race required patience and concentration, and it proved to me that giving up because of a poor start is a losing attitude.

11

Maintenance and Mothering

Twelfth Sunfish Worlds, Sardinia, Italy. (Daniel Forster)

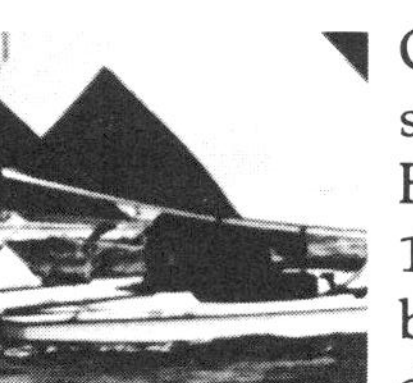

One of the fathers of the concept of simplicity in the Sunfish class was Jack Evans. As class secretary during the late 1960s and early 1970s, he was the ambassador of true one-design racing. Jack disallowed most everything a sailor might devise to circumvent the rules. The idea, he said, was to get in your boat and sail, not fuss.

During a discussion at a North American Championships, I listened to Jack talk about the Sunfish. He commented that the hull of the boat and its relatively short 14-foot length really did not develop laminar flow, particularly in waves where the boat bounces, causing the bottom flow to become very turbulent. This discussion occurred in an era when sailors dragged their boats across rocks and coral longitudinally, intentionally digging ruts they hoped would improve flow, as do the grooves in a pair of snow skis.

"Just treat the Sunfish as if it was a fourteen-foot boat," Jack said. And as if making a gesture symbolic of his back-to-basics approach, he put his sail numbers on using Roman numerals.

Most good Sunfish sailors adhere to Jack's philosophy of simplicity. Master it, and you can step into any Sunfish and do well. The Sunfish World Championships, where all boats are supplied new from the manufacturer, is a place where this philosophy is put to the test.

THE HULL

One result of the simplicity philosophy is that most boat-related work centers on maintenance rather than on squeezing out a slight edge over competitors. To keep your boat competitive, keep the inside of the hull dry. In heavy seas, or during a capsize, most boats take on some water, which can be absorbed by the fiberglass as well as by the inner foam flotation sections running fore and aft. If left damp, the foam sections can come unglued from the hull, decreasing hull stiffness. Water accumulated in the hull can increase hull weight as much as 20 percent, depending on the amount of water and the length of time it was in the hull. Ideal hull weight is approximately 130 pounds.

Recently, I checked on an old hull I sold to a neighbor. The boat had been neglected, and water had been in the hull for a couple of years as the result of a bow hole. During its prime, the hull weighed 130 pounds, but now it weighed closer to 185 pounds, due to water absorption. Drying the inside of the hull with a heat lamp, and with good air circulation through inspection ports, the boat's weight could be reduced to around 170 pounds. It will never attain its original weight.

There is a hole for hull drainage on the starboard side of the deck. However, drainage from that opening never is complete, and even a cupful of water left in the boat eventually will cause weight gain. The best solution to the problem is to install two six-inch, screw-on inspection ports, which are more watertight than are bayonet inspection ports. The ideal location for the ports is the forward vertical wall of the cockpit. A port on each side of the daggerboard trunk will allow easy access to the hull for sponging, a source of good air circulation for complete drying, and a handy storage place for any extra gear you may need.

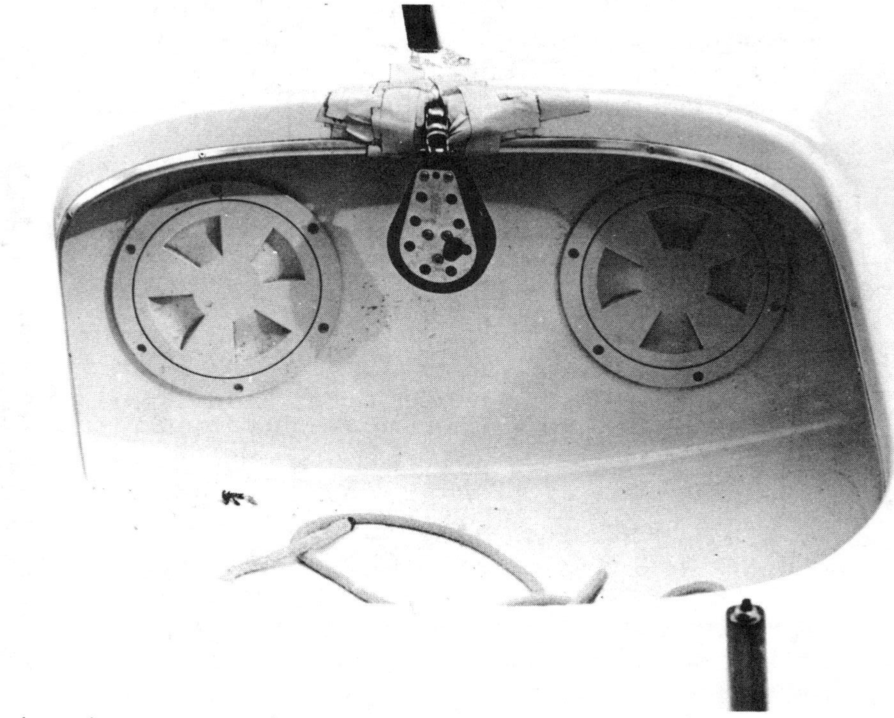

Dual 6-inch inspection ports for easy access. (Bob Pool)

When mounting inspection ports, seal the rims with silicone, to ensure they are watertight. This also adds a slight amount of stiffness to the hull. When the boat is not in use, keep the inspection ports open to allow air flow and prevent condensation from building up. Also keep the ports open when transporting the boat on your car, as the warm highway air also does a nice job of drying the hull. Once inspection ports are installed, seal the deck-mounted drain hole with silicone, and don't open it again unless checking for leaks.

To detect leaks, use a vacuum cleaner in reverse, (or a bicycle pump), and some soapy water. First, coat the hull or any suspicious areas with the soapy water. Then remove the deck-mounted drain plug, put the nozzle of the pump or vacuum over the hole and gently force air into the hull. Any leaking sections should cause the soapy water to bubble. To do this properly, you may need two people—one to operate the vacuum cleaner and the other to sponge down the boat and watch for bubbles.

For most hull fittings, the key is cleanliness and ensuring that their fasteners are secure and watertight. At the beginning of every season, take all fittings off, clean them, and put a new layer of silicone on their fasteners. One place to make sure the screws are particularly snug is the halyard cleat, since that cleat does more than one job.

Blasting around downwind can drain your cockpit quickly. Watch to be sure the mainsheet does not get sucked out the bailer. (Bob Pool)

The stock splashboard from the factory is rough and irregular. A thorough sanding will make it fast and effective, eliminating wind and water resistance to some degree. Silicone the entire splashboard and its fasteners in place. If you have an older boat with screws instead of rivets, they too should be sealed.

The bailer is also prone to leakage, so remedy that potential problem by removing it from the hull. This usually requires two people, one to hold the bailer from the bottom of the hull, and one to twist the plastic nut from the cockpit side. With the bailer removed, you might notice slight cracks in the fiberglass around the bailer hole. These can be a source of water seepage, and when reinstalling the bailer, silicone should be liberally applied to that area. To reduce water friction on the bailer, sand it lightly. So that the bailer will be as flush as possible with the bottom of the hull, take the washer that normally fits between the bailer and the hull out and disregard it. Once in place, test the bailer for leakage. If it leaks, try tightening the nut. In some cases, you may be able to solve the problem by applying more silicone.

If you have an old boat with an aluminum bailer, count yourself lucky. They are more efficient and pose less water resistance than do the new plastic bailers. Unlike plastic bailers, the plugs on aluminum bailers are threaded, which allows the plug to be slightly unscrewed, but still functional. The nut on aluminum bailers also can be tightened further than those on the plastic models, and the bailer itself can be sanded lightly to make it less resistant to water flow.

MAINSHEET BRIDLE

One fitting that has undergone a gradual evolution is the mainsheet bridle. For years, the stiff wire bridle was the foundation of all innovation at that end of the boat. In the 1960s, the mainsheet was clipped off on the port side of the bridle loop, which increased performance on starboard tack. In the 1970s, some sailors taped the loop down on the bridle wire, thus creating a "loopless" wire bridle that allowed the mainsheet clip to slide from port to starboard. One of the pioneers of the loopless bridle was Gerrit Zeestraten, who demonstrated it at the 1974 World Championships in Aruba. The only problem arose when the mainsheet clip snagged on the taped-over bridle eye, and time was lost after each tack trying to persuade the sheet to slide to leeward.

Today we have the option of using either a line for the bridle or a standard cable bridle. Most serious racers opt for the line bridle, which allows the mainsheet to slide effortlessly to leeward, as on a Snipe or Laser. However, class rules exclude you from adjusting the bridle tension while sailing. Generally, the bridle is set up tight in heavy winds, no tighter than 30 inches in length to allow the sheet to slide the maximum distance to leeward. In medium winds, the bridle should be about as long as the standard wire bridle. In light air, it should be slightly looser yet. Your tolerance for adjustment is very small. The rule says "31 inches plus or minus one inch." Nevertheless it is worth the trouble.

When rigging a line traveler, use one-quarter-inch, pre-stretched dacron line and tie each end of it to the deck eyes with a bowline. If you are going to be on the water for the entire day and expect the wind velocity to change, carry both the wire bridle and the traveler line with you just in case you want to make a change between races. Keep in mind that the mainsheet should be allowed to slide farther to leeward on starboard tack than on port tack. This will accommodate the difference between the sail's fullness and effectiveness on both tacks. To ensure that the sheet cannot go all the way to the port end of the bridle when on starboard, use the wire bridle and tie the tail to the center loop. This will allow it to slide to leeward on starboard and be centered on port. This is correct for medium winds. (See also page 68.)

Occasionally, you may want the mainsheet set at different positions on the traveler line, such as when sailing in puffy wind conditions. To keep the mainsheet in place once you have positioned it, tape the bridle line with duct tape, then remove the tape. This leaves the bridle line sticky, giving the mainsheet something to stick to. To pull the mainsheet off the area it has adhered to, push on the boom with your feet or hand, then reposition the sheet on the bridle. This gives you the option of a predetermined setting. With the rope bridle this flexibility is impossible.

Last, check the masthole for smoothness. You may have to sand it lightly. If the lip of the deck is not flush with the internal structure of the masthole, sand it flush. If sanding is not adequate, you may need to add silicone as a filler.

THE SPARS

The spars are an often-overlooked item in boat preparation. Spars create an uneven flow of air across the sail, and with the addition of burrs in the aluminum created by rough handling, tape, and unnecessary telltales, the wind flow distortion quickly increases. For that reason, I make sure any burrs are carefully filed off, keep the amount of tape and number of telltales to an absolute minimum, and give each spar a good coat of wax at the beginning of the season.

As with the hull, it is imperative to keep the spars watertight. Water in the spars increases the boat's overall weight, and also soaks into the inner wood cork at the ends of the spars, where it produces a negative effect on the boat's stability.

If you suspect water in the spars, or want to ensure that water never fills the spars, take the plastic end caps off. To do this, remove the tiny pins at the ends of the spar by punching each pin out with a center punch. This drives the pin through the spar and into the plastic cap. If this fails, carefully drill the pin out. Then remove the cap and let the spar dry. When replacing the cap, set it in place with epoxy. For added security, drill another hole on the opposite side of the present boom pin and install an extra pin.

At the 1975 Sunfish Worlds in Miami I didn't have the opportunity to pin the end cap. Winds were light, and I routinely left the halyard loose until eight or nine minutes before the start. When I started to tighten it, the mast cap pulled out and the rig came tumbling down. I was able to tape the mast cap back in place and sail back upwind just in time for the start. Had I been sailing my own boat, which has an extra pin in each cap, the problem never would have occurred.

Another spot to check is the gooseneck. Make sure the brass screw is just loose enough to allow you to slide the gooseneck on the boom. Since it is made of soft metal, use a large screwdriver to adjust it; otherwise you will strip the screw head and the resulting burrs eventually will chafe the sail. To keep the rig closer to the mast, improving pointing ability, the inner nut also should be tightened.

WIND INDICATORS

One of the most variable fittings on the Sunfish is the wind indicator. The range of types and configurations of wind indicators is infinite, and there are a number of things to consider when selecting one. When in close competition with a number of boats, one of the most important factors is durability. It is inevitable that the indicator will get knocked, bumped, hit, and banged while sailing, rigging, or just traveling. A solution is to use indicator arms made of soft aluminum, which, although easily bent, can just as easily be straightened.

In the 1960s, I used a coat hanger taped to the upper booms for a bracket, with a piece of yarn at the end of each arm. But that arrangement bent easily and was difficult to flex back. A recent innovation is the Feathermate, designed by Paul Odegard, who won the 1981 Sunfish North Americans. This design is simple, with flexible arms and relatively low aerodynamics.

The best application of wind indicators is offwind in light air. Unfortunately, under these conditions your body is generally in line with the wind indicator, making it difficult to read accurately, especially if mounted on the leading edge of the upper boom. For a better perspective on that point of sail, a masthead fly is a reasonable alternative. I use a seven-inch piece of small rod with a tiny eyelet on top, taped to the top of the upper boom on the forward side (opposite the outhaul). For the indicator, I use a lightweight strip of colored nylon material.

Like boom-mounted wind indicators, a masthead fly also has its pros and cons. A big plus is that it has only one arm, and since it is up well away from the rig, it is usually a true indicator of wind direction. Another advantage is that, apart from a capsize, it is almost impossible to damage during racing.

However, the masthead fly can be physically tough to read, as continually bending your head back a full 90 degrees is not only awkward, but time consuming. While checking it, you could slam into a wave that will stop your boat, a wave that may have been avoided had you been

'77 Sunfish Worlds in the Bahamas. (Bob Johnstone)

looking ahead rather than up. Frequent checking of the masthead fly also can be an indication to your competition that you are uncertain about your tack or sailing angle. And there are times when your competition will have a better idea about wind direction than you will, just by reading your masthead fly.

Finally, in large swells or in cross-chop, the fly moves erratically, thus becoming virtually useless. When I use a masthead fly, I carry it with me when I leave the beach. If the air is over 12 knots, I don't even attach it to the rig. But if the wind lightens between races I lower the rig and tape the fly in place.

If you decide to use a wind indicator, which the majority of Sunfish sailors do, be careful not to become a slave to it. Some sailors spend too much time watching the indicator instead of observing the wind on the water or preparing tactical decisions. Particularly in heavy air, where the apparent wind and heavy downdrafts make readings inconsistent, wind direction and velocity can just as easily be felt on the body or face. Take the time to study the wind patterns on the water, and you'll probably have a better idea about what's happening on the course than you will if you use the information gained from any one of a number of wind indicators.

When friends or an inexperienced person goes sailing on my boat, I usually take out my old rig. This is an old set of booms with an equally old sail. If the boat is capsized in mud, sand, weeds, or whatever, I have no worries about my racing equipment being damaged. In fact, I even use the old equipment when practicing, especially if I am concentrating more on tactics than on boat speed. An extra rig is a small investment compared to the advantages it provides.

TRANSPORTATION AND STORAGE

Properly transporting the Sunfish also helps ensure a long hull life. The key is never to transport the hull right-side up. Nothing is harder on the hull than the constant vibrations that occur when traveling. Carrying the boat incorrectly just once can greatly harm the stiffness of the fiberglass, and may crack the inner hull foam or cause it to become unglued. When sailing in waves, you can tell which boats have been damaged in this way, for they will pound and reverberate like big kettledrums, sending vi-

The self-sufficient single-handed sailor. (Bob Pool)

brations up through their skippers' spines. Such hulls are fine for recreational use, but will never again attain maximum heavy-air speed.

One of the biggest problems when traveling is getting the boat on a rooftop rack when you have no one to help. To do so, all you need is a stepladder and some padding, such as a towel. Turn the boat upside down, park the car next to it, and set the stepladder up near the bow of the boat. Put the padding on the fourth or fifth ladder step, and lift the bow onto that step. Now lift the stern and pivot the boat around so that you can set the stern up on the racks, being careful not to rotate the boat so far that the bow slips off the step. Then gently lift the bow off the ladder and set the bow up on the rack. This maneuver can be done in reverse to get the boat off the rack, but be careful not to pivot the boat too far, or you will tip the stepladder over.

Using a ladder to aid in car-roof transport. (Bob Pool)

Winter storage is also an important consideration. As when car-topping, store the hull upside down in a dry location. With the inspection ports left open, the boat will have good air circulation, and the hull should dry thoroughly. If you're short on space, suspend the boat from the ceiling, using wide straps (not rope) to distribute the weight evenly. Another acceptable method is to lean the boat sideways against a wall. Use padding on the floor and on the wall to prevent damage to the hull molding. While the boat is stored, don't allow anything to rest or drip on the bottom.

When storing sails, it is important to prevent wrinkling. Folding the sail produces permanent wrinkles in the cloth, as does leaving the sail on the spar for prolonged periods of time. Remove the sail from the spars and hang it from the tack and clews, if you have the space. A full basement is ideal, although an attic also can be used if the sail is folded in half and hung from the tack, head, and clew. During the summer, when the sail is used with some regularity, leave the sail on the spar and set the spars on end, allowing the sail to hang freely. To do this you need considerable headroom, such as you might have in a garage. Wherever you store your sail, make sure nothing is allowed to sit inside it—especially the family cat.

Store the rudder and daggerboard in a cool, dry place. Suspend them with a piece of line and you should prevent pressure points from developing warpage or cracks.

Adequately preparing your boat is a worthwhile endeavor. You will have accomplished preventive maintenance that will, in turn, provide hassle-free racing. More important, your boat will no longer be an excuse for a poor performance. By the same token, it will no longer be the reason for an exceptional performance, either.

The long upwind leg can take it's toll on unprepared sailors. When sailing an Olympic course the third windward leg can be excruciating. (Bob Pool)

12

The Physical Sunfish Sailor

The world's greatest singlehanded racers of the past few decades are characterized by their great strength and hiking ability. Stories about their incredible conditioning rivals their incredible accomplishments. The late Jeorg Bruder, a tough Brazilian Finn sailor who appeared at the first Sunfish World Championships, carried his Sunfish, completely rigged, to the water's edge—alone! And after a long day of racing, he took it out of the water the same way. Then there's Russian Finn sailor Valentin Mankin, winner of the 1968 Olympic Gold Medal in Finns, who reportedly does twenty-five push-ups with each arm. The stories go on, but the dedication to conditioning that Bruder and Mankin maintained, along with the likes of Paul Elvstrom, Hans Fogh, Peter Barrett, and John Bertrand, has gained them worldwide respect.

Granted, few sailors have the time or energy to devote to training as do these champions, but it is important to practice at least some conditioning. Because singlehanded boats generally sail slower than do larger dinghies and keelboats, speed differences between those at the front of the fleet and those in the middle are not that great. Some attention to conditioning can move you up quickly in the final standings.

In 1972, when I was seventeen, I sailed in the Sunfish Worlds in Bermuda. I was a little timid and anxious about the event because I knew the Bermudan winds are heavy. My suspicions proved correct—the practice race was sailed in winds between 40 and 45 knots. At 160 pounds, I felt a bit inadequate next to the class heavyweights—Bob Bowles and Hans Fogh—for I knew the conditions favored them. Being out-of-shape makes racing no fun.

In the following years, my conditioning program gradually improved, but it was not until the 1975 Worlds that I fully committed myself to a total training program. From November 1974, to April 1975, I trained six days a week. The discipline paid off, and I won that year's Worlds. Ironically, the wind conditions there were relatively light, but the confidence I gained enabled me to sail well in the hot weather.

Much has been written about correct training techniques. However, one thing all training programs seem to lack is a focus on exercises you enjoy doing. Your program should be centered around those exercises. Otherwise, unless you can focus directly on the end product rather than on the means, you'll likely become bored and end your training altogether. I enjoy running and lifting weights, so both have been incorporated into my training. Fortunately, both are great exercises for almost any type of sailing.

Once you have zeroed in on the type of exercise that appeals to you, you must consider your weaknesses. Is it arm strength? Leg strength? Flexibility? In my case, I felt that because sailing is a symmetrical body sport, and because I'm a right hander, the left side of my body needed better conditioning. So I developed a program of exercises that would help me in that area. Eventually, my work enabled me to hike on one leg, regardless of what tack I was on, allowing the other leg to rest from the previous tack. This works only in boats with hiking straps.

HIKING

Because the most physical aspect of Sunfish sailing is hiking, it is important to understand the mechanics of hiking. The favored Sunfish hiking technique is the V-hike. This is the best form for all body types—short, tall, big, small. In a Sunfish, the advantage of this technique is overwhelming because of the boat's lack of hiking straps. With legs spread into a V-shape, more body control is gained over the boat, and instead of exerting all hiking pressure on just one part of your body—such as one foot hooked under the forward edge of the cockpit—the load is now spread over two points. Paul Fendler, who stands only five feet four inches tall and weighs around 135 pounds, used this technique when he won the 1976 Worlds in Venezuela. Even when the wind piped up, he was always with the leaders, hiking hard.

Hiking bench made with less than $20 of material. Can also be used effectively with a water jacket. (Bob Pool)

The key to learning good Sunfish hiking technique is to use a hiking bench as a simulator. It's easy and inexpensive to build and, used over the winter, you'll notice big improvements in your hiking stamina the next summer.

As is true of all conditioning techniques, hiking on the bench must be done in sets—a series of repetitions done at differing time intervals. The sets I perform on the bench vary with the conditions I expect to sail in. If I'm going to be sailing on open water with onshore winds and long, moderate puffs, I'll work with a short number of repetitions in long sets. If I'll be sailing in offshore breezes or where there are short, hard puffs, as on a lake, I'll do shorter sets with a larger number of repetitions. Always, I aim first for quality, than quantity.

When working on the hiking bench, I start six months prior to a major event. Such conditioning builds up muscle groups and cardio-vascular endurance, and takes time to produce results. Before any workout, always stretch each muscle group carefully. This helps avoid injury when performing the actual exercises and increases flexibility.

During most workouts, I divide my time into three parts, running, weights, and rest. I perform flexibility and weight exercises on Mondays, Wednesdays and Fridays, and run on Tuesdays, Thursdays and Saturdays. I maintain this schedule from Thanksgiving until Easter, when I can't sail because of cold weather.

Any workout should include up to 80 percent isotonic exercises, which build cardiovascular endurance. Do exercises in sets, with a minimum of three repetitions of each set—and preferably 10 to 15 repetitions. For example, if you are doing a set of forward leg curls, your routine might be:

1. warm-ups—30 pounds: 10 repetitions
2. set 1—50 pounds: 15 repetitions
3. set 2—60 pounds: 15 repetitions
4. set 3—70 pounds: 10 repetitions
5. set 4—70 pounds: 15 repetitions

Heavy air work downwind can be physically demanding. Oftentimes more so than heavy air upwind. (Bob Pool)

Once the sets are complete, move on to an exercise that focuses on another muscle group. Rotate sets between lower and upper body muscles to allow each area of your body to rest during set breaks.

One of the best methods of ensuring quality workouts is to closely monitor your activity through predicted maximal heart rate (P.M.H.R.). This system allows adjustment for age and lets you know when you are making cardio-vascular gains. The formula is 220 minus your age equals P.M.H.R. If your age is 30, your P.M.H.R. is 190 heart beats per minute. During a workout to make cardio-vascular gains, your heartbeat should fall within 70 to 80 percent of that number, between 133 and 152 beats per minute. The best time to take your pulse is immediately after finishing a workout. As your fitness improves, you

Running on edge. (Bob Pool)

will notice it takes more effort to get your pulse up to the 70-percent minimum, and you should feel a sense of accomplishment, because you are gaining on the cardiovascular needs of your body.

There are many variations of the ideal workout program. Many people prefer to substitute a game or sporting event for workouts, such as racquetball, squash, tennis, handball, hockey, or swimming. This is acceptable as long as the exercise is undertaken for at least sixty minutes. Otherwise it will be difficult for you to make the necessary gains.

When racing, you must always be ready and able to make split-second decisions while maintaining balance and trim. Fatigue results in poor decisions that will impair these essential elements. To ensure all energy is put to optimum use, strength, flexibility, and endurance is a necessity.

13

Garments For Speed

Three contrasting sailing outfits: foul-weather gear, one-piece sailing suit, and wet suit.

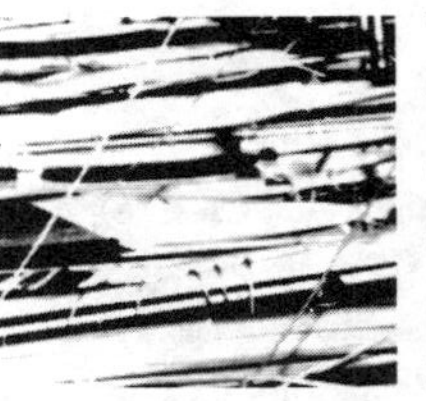

The trend in small-boat racing is to keep the body functioning at maximum efficiency at all times. Just as no high-caliber runner would consider racing in shoes not specifically tailored to his needs, no quality sailor should consider racing in clothes that prevent him from performing at peak level.

Whenever your body under- or overheats, added stress results in mental or physical mistakes. If you're not dressed appropriately for the conditions, it is likely you will falter. Other clothing factors to be considered, besides warmth and coolness, are weight, particularly when wet, and the amount of flexibility the garment affords. The choice obviously depends on the sailing conditions.

In light winds, air temperature is usually warm, if not down right hot. Select light-colored clothing that is loose fitting. If the wind is less than 10 knots and the air warm, I do not wear shoes, for feet can act as an important sensory tool. If there is enough air to allow me to sit on the deck, I place my forward foot on the cockpit floor at the point of the forward curve on the vertical cockpit wall, and place my aft foot flat in the middle of the cockpit. With both feet I can feel the flow around the board and along the bottom of the boat. Particularly after a tack, the sensations and vibrations provide me with information about my speed. I object to wearing shoes in these conditions because they tend to soak up water dripping from my pants from roll-tacking and jibing and become added weight.

One factor to consider is that offwind, when sailing at about the same speed as the wind, your body heats up considerably. For this reason, I dress on the cool side. Any body movement used upwind usually helps keep me warm there. However, if you have problems with strains or muscle pulls, dress on the warm side.

In heavy air, clothing adds important weight to your body. However, it must still allow you flexibility, comfort, and warmth. One of the best heavy-air articles of clothing is a one-piece dinghy suit. This meets all heavy-air requirements except weight, and if desired, this can be achieved by wearing wet sweatshirts or a water jacket.

Another heavy-air essential is a good pair of padded hiking pants or shorts. Hiking on the sharp deck edge reduces circulation to the lower legs. When that blood flow is restricted, lactic acid quickly builds up. This is what causes the sensation of muscle fatigue and leg cramps, destroying concentration and the ability to think rationally in difficult situations. There are many versions of padded hiking pants, but the key is to use whatever keeps you most comfortable, allows the greatest flexibility, and is not excessively heavy when wet. A simple alternative is to wear several pairs of shorts made of thick material. If you find your hiking pants tend to slide down when you hike, wear suspenders, which also help transfer strain on the hips to the shoulders.

Water jackets are one of the more controversial items in small-boat sailing. There's no question they can increase speed in a breeze, but there's concern about how they affect the back. The key to staying healthy while wearing a water jacket is to train well in advance and work slowly into it, wearing a little more weight each time. Wearing the jacket while dry-land training, either working out on a hiking bench or running, helps build your back muscles. Be sure to stretch prior to wearing the jacket so your muscles are warmed up.

One-piece spray suit over water jacket with two full bottles. (Lee Parks)

The first time you wear a water jacket, you may experience some difficulty. Water jackets do not fit well, and if you have large neck muscles or rounded shoulders, they tend to slide off. If so, have elastic bands sewn across the chest and back of the jacket by a local sailmaker or cobbler. Wearing slippery nylon jackets or shirts underneath the water jacket also causes it to shift around. A good half-sleeve sweatshirt will reduce shifting.

Another problem with water jackets is that they impair mobility, strength, and stamina. If you are just beginning to use the jacket, you may feel some numbness, along with a top-heavy sensation. If you reach that point, the jacket should be removed. Go back and train some more, or reduce the amount of weight you carry until you feel more secure and confident. With plenty of practice and common sense, using the jacket can be safe and easy.

One advantage of the water jacket is its ability to hold water of different temperatures. If it's a cold, windy day, fill the jacket with hot water, and it will act as a fine body insulator. This is especially helpful after the first race, or after lunch, when you start cooling off and your muscles begin to tighten. Remember, maximum weight for all clothing following a one-minute draining period, is, by class rules, 22 pounds (10 kilos).

Although it does not greatly help your performance, one of the most important pieces of clothing is a life jacket. It should be snug-fitting. If you have problems with the mainsheet hanging up on the back of the jacket, wear a T-shirt over it. If you are confident in your sailing and swimming ability, and if the rules permit, it may be helpful to remove the life jacket in light air, making your body less wind resistant and increasing your flexibility.

Remember, the sailing garment may be as important as any other boat-speed ingredient. Maintain a no-nonsense approach, avoiding hoods, extra pockets, and other nonessentials. Other than that, the key in clothing selection is comfort. If you're not comfortable, you're not going to perform well. It's as simple as that.

14

The Clubhouse

Sunfish racers are a unique breed of sailors. The diversity of age and personality make it a truly remarkable class. Having sailed in other popular single-handed classes, I find the Sunfish is the friendliest and most fun-loving group. It is the grass roots of single-handed board-boat sailing. To continue its success in decades to come, we must nurture that spirit and especially encourage novices in the class. Making the novice feel at home and helping him learn to race is sportsmanlike; intimidating beginners on the water is unjust and irrational. The overwhelming spirit should be that sailing involves friendly competition. We are dealing with a series of complex variables. Learning to make sense and order out of these variables is really fun. And sailing within the confines of the racing game is the ultimate in sailing enjoyment.

Fortunately for everyone, sailing can be a lifetime hobby. Sailing a boat that fits your age and ability can mean a lifelong racing career. Few sports offer this kind of extended pleasure.

The Clubhouse is where the action is put into words, and where sometimes, the words put into action. Sailors are people with many fine attributes. There is seldom a sport where information about strategy and technique flows so freely and openly. There is much to learn from each other. Ask the winners and losers to explain certain moves or adjustments made on the water. Watch them rig their boats and pack their cars and try their methods youself. If something does not work, make a note and discard it. No two people sail the boat exactly the same way, but we are all playing the same game.

15
Appendix

One of the best ways to thoroughly prepare for a regatta is to use a regatta checklist. Oftentimes sailors become rushed prior to leaving and forget something important. A list is helpful.

SAILING GEAR:

Sail
Upper and lower booms
Rudder, with extension
Daggerboards
Mast
Inspection ports
Bailer plug
Halyard
Sheets: 1 light air, 1 medium air, 1 heavy air
Telltales
Foul weather gear
Sail suit

- Hiking shorts
- Water jacket
- Life jackets
- Hiking shoes and/or boots
- Gloves
- Sponge
- Rule book and appeals books
- Sunfish class rules
- Notetaking notebook
- Hat
- Tape
- 2 starting watches
- Sandpaper of all grades
- Portable screwdriver and pliers
- Drinking bottle

SUPPORT GEAR

- Toolbox
- Rivet gun with stainless steel rivets
- Extra 1/8 inch dacron line
- Tape measure
- Oversized screwdriver
- Silicone seal
- Extra sail sets
- Screws and bolts, brass or stainless
- Marine tex or micro-balloons
- Mat or padding, to place your boat on an irregular beach
- Extra boom blocks
- Extra deck block
- Extra eye straps
- Extra bridle, rope or wire

RACING PIE GRAPH

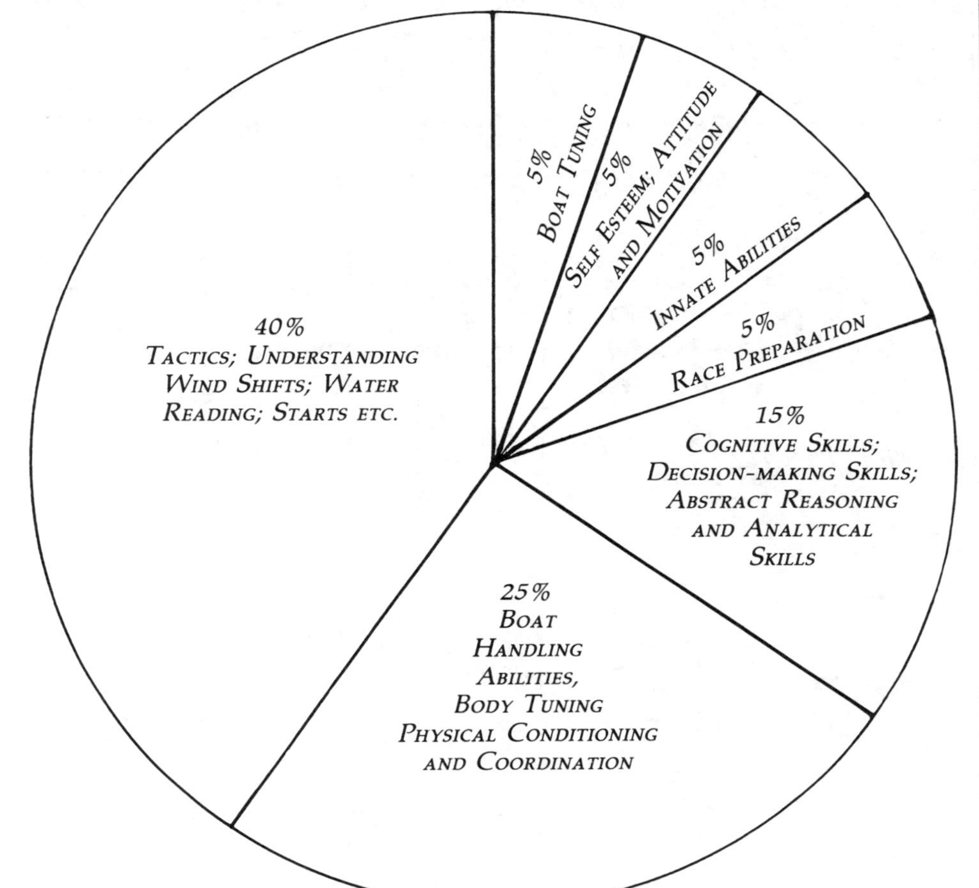

The racing pie provides a systematic breakdown of the general racing prerequisites. This is specifically designed for the Sunfish with a premium placed on physical conditioning and tactics.

Regatta Note Sheet

When a race or regatta ends, much has been learned and enjoyed. The exposure to many different techniques and situations provide experience that should not go to waste. It's not surprising, then, that some of the world's greatest sailors make a habit of jotting down notes after each event, giving them a lifelong log of information that might otherwise have been forgotten. Remembering a particular facet of a regatta site may be difficult without notes, and if you're likely to sail there again, ten minutes to fill out a note sheet is a small investment to help ensure good performance the next time you race.

Date____________

Wind Direction____________

Wind Speed____________ Boat____________

Temp.____________ Time____________

Skies____________ Waters____________

Regatta______Drill______ Current____________

Results____________

A. Positive Input:

1.
2.
3.
4.
5.
6.

B. Negative Input:

1.
2.
3.
4.
5.

Diagrams on back

Sunfish World Championship
Ponce, Puerto Rico

Date 3/4-12/78

Wind Direction S.E.

Wind Speed 10 mph to 40 mph — Boat #988

Temp. 85° - 90° — Time

Skies P. Cloudy — Waters Atlantic

Regatta ✓ Drill — Current 0 - 0+

Results 1st World Champion

Race	#1	#2	#3	#4	#5	#6
	17	0	11	3	(18)	0
	11	1st	6	2	(12)	1st

A. Positive Input:

1. Good behavior and style. Cool and Calm.
2. Good Tactics (Great Upwind): Open Seas, Steady Air
3. 75% races correct to go to semi-laylines upwind
4. Good ability to think all winter long about tactics and sailing. Previous results were clear in mind
5. Good concentrative sailing definitely worth investment.
6. Very good pre-race goals and decisions.

B. Negative Input:

1. Middle of line sag does not start until middle of line
2. Learn to compensate for wave and wind drift on starting line.
3.
4. In the 5th race when only 4.3 pts. ahead of Pierre S., made a mistake at the start. Ended up in middle
5. of the line. Should have done 1 of 2 things.
1) Either stayed much closer to Pierre S. or,
2) Gone with own Game Plan. Probably with lead, should have gone with #2, because I knew right side was favored more than left.

Diagrams on back

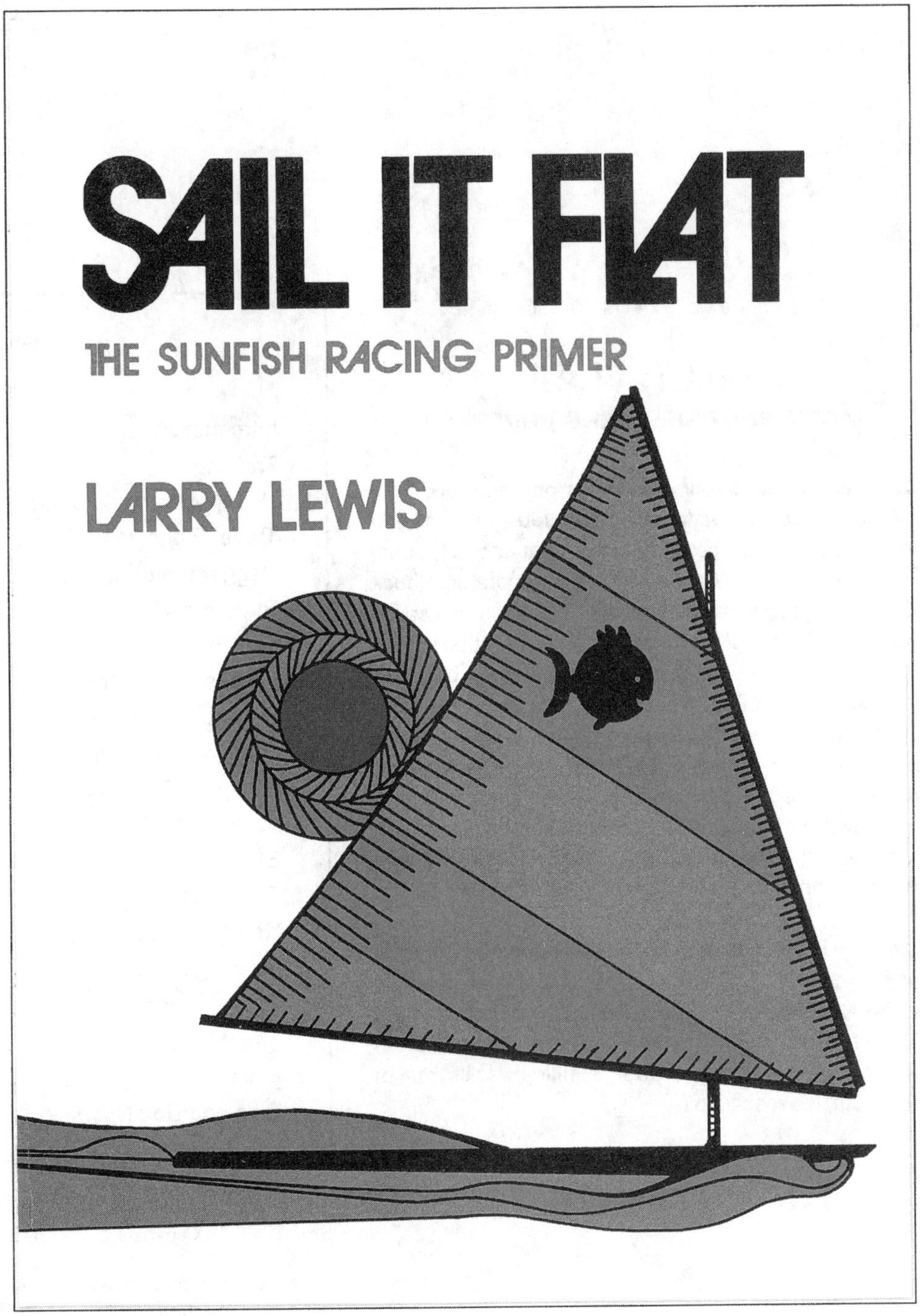

SAIL IT FLAT

THE SUNFISH RACING PRIMER

LARRY LEWIS

COVER DESIGN BY RAYMOND WELCH

Jointly published by:

One Design and Offshore Yachtsman *and*

QUADRANGLE/The New York Times Book Co.
10 East 53rd Street, New York, NY 10022

Larry Lewis, with Chuck Millican

SAIL IT FLAT

THE SUNFISH RACING PRIMER

With this book and your sails under one arm, and your 140-pound *Sunfish* under the other, you'll have all you need to compete successfully in the greatest of all sports, yacht racing. Larry Lewis and his collaborator, Chuck Millican, begin with the assumption that you have sailed around the fringes of the race course, decided that it looks like fun, and now want to get into the game – but don't quite know how. They cover the basics thoroughly and entertainingly. They have also gathered together in this one slim volume most of the really ingenious "go fast" ideas and techniques for maximum performance, developed especially for the *Sunfish* by some of the world's finest small-boat sailors. Abundantly illustrated with photographs and with detailed drawings by Mark Smith.

Larry Lewis and Chuck Millican have been runner-ups in the North American Sunfish Championship and members of the North American Team Race Champions and the World's Team Race Champions. Larry Lewis lives in Montclair, New Jersey; Chuck Millican sails out of Plymouth, Massachusetts.

CONTENTS

For information, address:
QUADRANGLE/The New York Times Book Co.,
10 East 53rd Street, New York, NY 10022.

Manufactured in the United States of America.
Published simultaneously in Canada by Fitzhenry & Whiteside, Ltd., Toronto.

Library of Congress Catalog Card Number: 78-182206
International Standard Book Number: 0-8129-0238-6

To Brownie

INTRODUCTION

Seventy five thousand Sunfish sailors can't be wrong. The AMF–Alcort Company, seller of the largest number of one-design boats in the history of the sailboat business, has developed the biggest group of nautical enthusiasts in the yachting field. This manual is for them – the novice and the salty. Hopefully we will draw the interest of other small boat sailors too.

The book is rather loosely structured although the recurrent theme is how some of us prepare for the most purely one-design regattas of them all: The Sunfish World Championships.

The point we will try to make is that with adequate preparation and plenty of practice new sailors can become competent in this highly entertaining sport.

The steps we take to get ready for a World's Championship are carefully documented here. It is often said that regattas are

Chuck Millican

won on the beach. While gadgetry is more elaborate on some other dinghies, the amount of tuning we give a Sunfish will simply astound many experienced sailors who think of the boat as a very simple plastic toy.

After some chapters on preparing ourselves and our boats, we will relate our experiences on how to make the boat go fast on certain points of sailing. Needless to say, we draw on the ideas of a number of our friends and regular competitors. While basic principles are roughly the same in all dinghies, each is different from the other in tuning and handling. We have some observations in these pages which we don't believe have been incorporated in any other "how to" sailing book.

We also offer some comments on team racing techniques. Chuck and I were privileged to sail for the 1971 Sunfish National and World team race champions and we think that out of these experiences we have some fresh ideas to offer. Team racing is more fun than any other outdoor sport and through these pages we hope to translate our enthusiasm for this exciting and exacting game.

As we write these words, the temperature is 16 above and the wind from the Northwest at 15 gusting to 29. We are not, however, hibernating for the winter. We sail tomorrow. Frostbiting has become a very popular activity, in the Northeast at least. If you dress adequately, it sure beats staying at home on a weekend doing the chores you hadn't gotten around to while you were sailing in the summer and fall. We will try to make some suggestions for frostbiting which will enhance your enjoyment of the sport; what you are going to do about the chores remains your own problems.

Finally we devote some time to the methods of repairing your boat. I don't profess to be an expert but Chuck has rebuilt so many boats that he has developed plenty of know-how. He also worked for Alcort and has had an opportunity to learn first hand how the manufacturer repairs boats. The satisfaction that arises from sailing a boat in good order which you have personally repaired gives much pleasure in itself. If you follow the advice given here, the Sunfish will last a good long time, confirming the theory that it is yachting's best investment.

The Sunfish is, after all, the vehicle which so many of us have used to perpetuate our enjoyment of sailing. Never has a sailboat created so much fun for so many people.

Larry Lewis

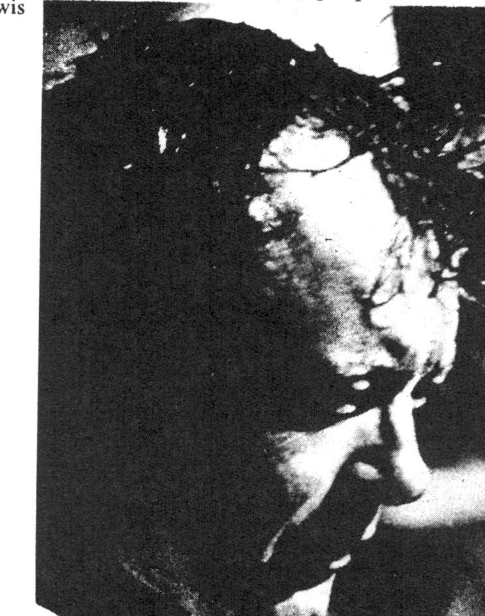

Garry Hoyt, 1970 Sunfish World's Champion

TRAINING

I have just come in from running over my 1.1 mile cross country course with my glasses steamed over and sweat pants speckled with sleet. I have been training for two months and I still stagger on the last hill. Yet this running and the forms of physical training the others will undergo is what will make us competitive.

We run because we think we achieve stamina from the activity. Normal championship courses are, as in the Olympics, triangle, windward, leeward, windward. In heavy breezes stamina is a most important factor. The great Long Island Sound light air sailors, who can't hike out flat with many pounds of wet clothes on their backs, don't have the consistent speed necessary in fresh winds.

I also run, I think, because of the smug feeling it gives me; one feels so superior when he is capable of running a mile in six minutes.

Jeorg Bruder

We hear of various training techniques others use. Valentin Mankin, of Russia, 1968 Olympic Gold Medalist in Finns, is supposed to do 25 right arm push ups and then duplicate the feat with his left arm. This usually achieves the desired effect of sending the less dedicated back to the bar from whence they came the night before.

Jeorg Bruder's feats of strength are legendary. We understand he does 100 situps with a 90 pound weight on his back as a nightly exercise. This chore is not mandatory to win a Long Island Sound club race, but we assure you that if he hadn't developed his fantastic strength, we wouldn't be including the following anecdote:

Jeorg had never won a Finn Gold Cup, but he had been runner up twice. As he approached the final leeward mark of the last race of the 1969 Gold Cup in Bermuda he had only to hold his position on the beat to maintain a third second place finish. His mainsheet block broke, which would have finished most of us, as this particular race was being sailed at the tail end of Hurricane Inga. Jeorg simply horsed the boat all the way upwind without the mechanical advantage of the series of blocks and held on against some of the world's really super athletes.

Start

Finish

We understand that after one year of Olympic training, Garry Hoyt's whole physique changed dramatically. We think Garry won the 1970 World's because of absolute physical superiority. There was no one except Jeorg Bruder who could create any competition for him on the rigorous 25-knot three race second day; and we are not deprecating the other efforts Garry goes to.

Why strength and stamina? When racing in a good breeze, you must be able to tack countless times with speed and precision. You've got to have the strength left to harden up smoothly at turning marks. You must be able to sheet in hard in a breeze. Controlling a broaching or wildly planing Sunfish off wind is physically very demanding; just look at the picture on page 14. Most important you must be mentally alert enough to concentrate on tactics rather than how tired you are.

There are many training devices used to get the champions in shape. Look at the hiking bench on the next page. This is a device popularized by Paul Elvstrom. It simulates on dry land the tortures you go through on the water when you are hiked out. Sitting on the hiking bench doing situps with weights on your back is just the trick to tone up those thigh and stomach muscles.

Plans for the hiking machine are included on page 85. The total cost of the one we made did not exceed three dollars. My leg strap is adjustable. It came off the rear seat of the family automobile. It makes a very nice place to hook the feet for all sizes and ages of hikers. Alcort should consider installing an adjustable hiking strap in the center of the cockpit of the Sunfish; at present shorter sailors are at a handicap. The fittings could be molded right into the cockpit.

A regular exercise regimen such as the Royal Canadian Air Force exercises makes a real contribution to stamina and quickness. AMF–Voit has at least three tools to help you improve the physical skills used in sailing. The Jiffy-Gym is a wide thick rubber band you stretch apart. It helps build up shoulder and chest muscles. The Exergrip helps improve your

Bob Bowles, third World Champion

The Jiffy Gym – Good for all sexes Brownie Lewis

grip, as does the hand exerciser which also strengthens the fingers and forearms.

In the final analysis, the dedication involved in sailing the boat flat in a big breeze is what training is all about. In the first minutes off the starting line, you are frequently going boat for boat with others. The sailor who can keep the boat level, concentrating on his sail and the tactical situations without coming up for a breather, will break clear.

But in a Sunfish, training becomes important for other reasons too. The Sunfish is a "weight boat". It is under-canvased, or under-Dacroned if you wish. Weight plays a tremendous part in the game. Not as an excuse mind you, but when the wind drops down and marginal planing conditions exist you would do better to put your daughter in the boat. Upwind in 20 knots the agile 200 pounder is back in the ball game. Under 15 knots and watch Herve Roche, the 135 pound South American champion, ride those waves. He will pass you to weather, to leeward or right over you.

Notice that in the picture, right, Herve has very little of his boat in the water as he is immediately accelerating into a plane upon rounding the weather mark. The reduced wetted surface he achieves because of his comparatively light weight gives him a tremendous advantage on reaching legs in particular.

Weight is a disadvantage because it keeps you from planing in marginal conditions. The biggest chunks of yardage gained or lost in racing come in off wind sailing. The boat that is planing can gain fantastic amounts on the boat that wallows. Also, acceleration after a tack or after being struck by a large wave is directly proportional to weight.

Ding Schoonmaker, multi class champion, has commented that to be competitive a Finn must be tacked in three seconds flat out to flat out. The Sunfish is no different. When you consider the narrow overlap situations that frequently determine the ultimate outcome of small boat racing, you realize the importance of seconds. The person who can gain a second a tack has that much advantage on the fleet. In the normal

Herve Roche

range of sailing conditions a weight area of 165 pounds seems ideal.

If you simply cannot take the time from whatever you are doing to don sweat clothes and work out, we have a very good exercise for you. Each morning when you are standing in the subway reading your "Times", lean casually against a door with your feet apart about 12 inches and about 18 inches out from the door. Keep your back straight. Now begin a slow descent, bending your knees and keeping your back flat against the door. When your thighs are at right angles to your calves, hold the position for a couple of subway stops. This will strengthen your hiking muscles in just the manner needed. Chances are you won't look any more peculiar than the rest of the subway riders either.

John Black Lee

HEAVY WEATHER CLOTHES

When the wind pipes up to a fresh breeze what should all of us Diet Pepsi drinkers do after getting in shape for the marginal planing conditions? The answer is simple – wear wet cotton clothes.

The 1970 World's was a convocation of teddy bears. You have never seen such a conglomerate of spindly legs overburdened with stuffed torsos. But with reason. You can always put weight on but you cannot take it off. There are a number of versions, but here is what I do to gain weight.

I wear a standard cotton T shirt. Then I put on a snug fitting Flotherchoc. Naturally, there are several other good life jackets, such as the Elvstrom and the GenTex, but I am accustomed to the Flotherchoc. This is a flexible life saving vest composed of 250 or so plastic airfilled bubbles in a nylon fabric shell. It is an easy, comfortable garment to wear and I judge it to have saved my life on at least one occasion. It is

warm in the winter and cool in the summer. The Flotherchoc is mandatory with us regardless of whether a race committee specifies one to be worn or carried aboard. We would never sail without it.

Naturally this should be covered up as explained on page 26. I next put on a cotton sweat shirt with the sleeves cut off at the shoulders. Sweat shirts should be sleeveless because when the inevitable capsize occurs, you can raise your arms out of the water unencumbered with excess weight and swim for your boat.

Next I wear a garment composed of four or five no-sleeve sweat shirts. Simply chop off the sleeves at the shoulders and the remaining shirts are put one inside the other. Cut them all straight down the front and insert three brass grommets on either side. With nylon line to secure the fronts, you have a sweat shirt jacket, relatively easy to dry, but quick to absorb water and add an additional 10 pounds or so. The garment may not be too handsome, but it is practical. (Our Sears bills for repairing the washing machine due to the nylon cords fouling the works have amounted to the original cost of 23 new sweat shirts. Don't wash them, hang them up to dry.)

Some people go to the extra trouble of neatly stitching their jacket; it is neater but the jacket does not dry as quickly. Add one more tight short sleeve shirt over the whole mess to contain any drooping cloth or lines which might serve as a drag when you are hiked full out. Now you have seven wet shirts and at least 15 pounds. Another legal method of gaining weight is to wear cotton sweat pants. Teddy Moore will wear as many as seven pairs of sweat pants. Harvey Howell, who races in Puerto Rico, cuts off his sweat pants and makes shorts of them. This makes sense as it gives freedom to his legs and keeps the weight where you really want it. Carl Knight puts pieces of carpet in the seat of his pants which not only helps him gain weight but is more comfortable. Heavy turkish towels around the shoulders are an excellent absorber of water.

Mike Shaw reckons that he adds as much as 60 pounds of wet clothes. You better not have back trouble and be engaged in this activity as this puts a real strain on the lower back.

Notice in the picture, right, that one of the competitors is wearing his life jacket on the outside. I don't know how many people have experienced the sensation of having the boom come whipping over on a tack, only to have it catch in their life vest, causing a capsize. To eliminate this problem, you wear a shirt over the jacket regardless of the breeze.

Notice that all three sailors in the foreground are wearing gloves. For someone unused to sailing in the Caribbean, gloves are recommended. The sun can burn your lily white hands so badly that it is pure torture to sheet in. Finally notice that Ken Klein, who is wearing his complement of wet sweat shirts plus beard, is holding the boat most level.

Henry Sprague and Peter Barrett staged a protest to determine the legality of wearing extra ballast in wet sweat shirt form. NAYRU Appeal decision number 109 upheld the wearer of the wet cotton cloth.

But remember, wear as little as you can possibly get away with and still hold the boat flat; the Sunfish is after all a "weight" boat.

One thing you should not skimp on is footwear. Sperry Topsider moccasins do an excellent job of helping you retain your footing. They are "de rigueur" in the evening at formal yachting parties in the islands.

In many climates hats are important. A standard white crew hat is good. Bill Gleason, former O.K. Dinghy champion of Thailand, and current Sunfish class leader from Puerto Rico, has the answer: To keep hats on in a breeze, wrinkle up your forehead and screw on the cap; sometimes it's the only way.

TRAVEL PLANNING

Those long winter nights are made warmer through the anticipation of a Caribbean regatta. The fun you can have in preparing your travel kit, training, even dieting, frequently is as enjoyable as the actual series. Here are some of the things we might do to prepare for any regatta, but particularly one in the islands.

Many regattas do not offer brand new boats. Some do not offer competitive equipment at all. These boats, however, are either loaned outright or rented at very nominal fees. Materials to repair borrowed boats are now more readily available. The dealer in Puerto Rico recently had a superb stock of parts, but the prices in the islands are high.

Make sure you bring a bailing plug, gasket and marble. I always do after an experience I had several years ago. During the opening race of the 1966 Caribbean Championships, we sailed in rather unprotected water and the sea was really working up. My bailer was corroded and did not work; the cockpit became full of water. My boat just would not tack in those big seas as water continued to slosh over the lip of the cockpit. I finally had to jibe to get onto the other tack. The Sunfish bailer is quite satisfactory only when you can unscrew it. In big seas I take the plug completely out both upwind and down.

Bring plenty of horizontal hinge pins. I hope I will not be accused of Agnewism or Hooverism if I say that you should remove every detachable part of your boat at night. Rudder pins seem to go fast. Another item that disappears quickly when there is a big sea is a Clorox bottle bailer. You should bring your own.

Bring your own sheet. New Sunfish come equipped with Dacron sheets, but many of the older boats still have the original standard cotton sheet. Cotton work gloves with plastic dots can save a significant amount of trouble with your hands. The main thing about gloves is that they should protect your hands but not restrict your dexterity or grip.

Boards, rudders and sails are not regularly supplied by the gracious lenders of the boats. Bring your own cleats – swivel variety, cam, clam or ratchet. I think it proper to leave them on the boat after the series.

Most clubs have electrical outlets, but for Sunfish purposes, a hand drill works fine and should be a part of the kit. Do not forget bits. Remember bolts and cap nuts for the rudder and tiller fittings. Also, bring plenty of tape, a screw driver, wrenches, pliers, a knife, Orlon or Nylon yarn for tell tales, outhaul line, a spun polyester halyard, a sponge and even some detergent. Caribbean beaches have oil on them too, sad to say.

We have prepared a Regatta Checklist which you will find on page 111. Reference to this will save you the embarrassment of showing up at a regatta someday without some minor piece of equipment such as the mast, a sail, etc. Don't laugh, it happens to everybody.

Don't carry knives on board the plane; check them through. You don't want to be mistaken for a hijacker. With the costumes most sailors wear, it's a wonder the airlines will carry us at all.

If you are flying get to the airport early. Even if you have a confirmed seat, Caribbean flights in the winter will go with standbys if you don't show up an hour in advance. Pan Am will now confirm and mail tickets to your home as long as you pay your phone bills on time. That's right, just call from home and they will mail and charge them to you. Other airlines probably will too.

Check the shot requirements. Most of the places where we sail Sunfish don't require shots. Venezuela does demand a smallpox vaccination. Get it early, sometimes they "take". Get a tourist card at the carrier's office in advance; it's easier than having them do it for you 10 minutes before flight time.

Most countries on the Sunfish circuit do not require passports. Venezuela does not either but definite proof of citizenship is required. A passport is simple and the best.

When you arrive at your destination, reconfirm your return reservation at the airport. Write on your ticket envelope the name of the agent who reconfirmed you. Sunday night in February in the San Juan airport is like the same night in August on the Long Island Expressway. The competitive and nefarious ways in all of us come out when Eastern, American and Pan Am are one plane short back to New York.

In all the islands accommodations in the homes of the local sailors can usually be provided. Sailors are a warm bunch and if you need a bed, they will always find one for you. Room at the mark the next day? That's another story. Some of the best friendships we have made have been as a result of the regattas we have sailed in Bermuda, Puerto Rico, St. Thomas and Venezuela. After all, the ultimate reason for racing Sunfish is fun. I am sure a lot of other classes have fine people, but it is hard to imagine a better crowd than those who campaign the Sunfish.

DAGGERBOARDS

It is highly probable that AMF–Alcort will undertake the high initial expense of creating molds from which to manufacture plastic rudders and daggerboards. While perhaps not as cosmetically appealing as the mahogany currently used, the synthetic material would be far more durable than wood. Still even if AMF–Alcort does take this step there will be 200,000 boards and rudders left around and it is for their owners that we write these next two chapters.

Your physical training is now behind you. When you open the box containing your new boat, slice off the tape holding the wooden components and feel them. Immediately you will know what one of your first tasks is going to be.

At the '70 World's we listened to runner-up Mike Shaw, Jack Evans and Dick Griffin debate the hydrodynamic aspects of the Sunfish board. The theory is that a blunted, rounded forward edge bulging out and then tapering gradually back to a sharpish after edge would produce the most even flow of water off the surface of the board.

The class rules prescribe that the boards may neither be planed or shaped, but the lively discussion we heard led us to believe that an awful lot of legal sanding is going on.

Regardless of whether the èdges should be razor sharp, blunt or rounded, unquestionably the board must be smooth. That is legal. Normal Alcort varnishing is too "mass produced" for our taste. Most of us will sand down the board and rudder, then refinish. Dick Griffin uses Helmsman Graphspeed, a polyurethane coating mixed with graphite. This surface is extremely smooth and may be the best available finish.

Bryce Suydam, the Great South Bay king, paints his board white with an epoxy paint. Bryce knows the value of detecting weed promptly after growing up on that water-covered weed patch. Against a white background it is easier to spot any foreign matter trailing from your rudder or board. Actually you really cannot see your board from a normal sailing position and the white background is only important on the rudder. However it is more aesthetically pleasing to have both wooden parts painted the same color.

I paint my board with a clear polyurethane which fills dents and then wet sand, wet sand, wet sand. When I have too deep scratches and dents I fill them with Marine Tex and resand; it does a beautiful job. And is a smooth board important? Garry Hoyt thinks so: I can remember the lunch break before the final race for the 1970 Caribbean Championship. The bulk of us were around the ice bucket gulping Cokes and other beverages. Garry was around the corner wet sanding his board; Garry won.

Alcort should provide a template for board and rudder. We are told that the board and rudder comprise about 15% of the wetted surface of the boat. This is a tremendous amount of area not to care for properly; it is also a great portion which if shaped can create dramatic improvement in speed, particularly in acceleration after tacking. While ethics are a part of the issue, what are you going to do if you crash into rocks and must sand or plane the jagged edges of a board? A template would salve everybody's conscience.

After brushing the mahogany dust out of our hair, we might as well do some more things to the board while still in the shop. Screw a small brass eye into the forward part of the cap on the daggerboard. A shock cord attached to this eye from the halyard block will hold the board in any elevated position you desire. Some people have extended a shock cord to the interlocking eyebolts on the spars – this holds the sail out on downwind legs in light air. We are sure, however, that the intent of the rule permitting shock cords is for the sole purpose of restraining the daggerboard – not for uses such as a J.C. strap.

Some people mark the board so that they know when the tip is just showing below the trunk. We think this has merit but we find that we vary the amount of immersion of the board according to the wind, sea and current conditions. The board should be up as far as it will go while still providing steerage and balance.

The subject of chattering boards is a dilemma in itself. Possibly the warp of the board determines the chatter. For sure, vibration is undesirable. We guarantee that when your speed picks up and your board begins to chatter, you are not reaching your maximum potential. To avoid a warped board keep it out of the sun when not in use.

Bob Bowles paints his board with fiberglass resin around that part contained in the trunk when the board is full down. That may be the answer. Most of us experiment with boards until we find one that doesn't chatter.

It is possible that the answer may be to load up the trunk with epoxy in a form fitting mold around the daggerboard. Skip Cook tried this with some success. Make sure you carefully wrap the board in wax paper, however, or you will never get it out. This might achieve a really stable effect. When one of our boats gets really old we may try this technique.

We know there must be people who make their boards into jibing boards. Essentially this is a board which is cocked to weather by putting a wedge at the windward trailing edge. Just a couple of degrees of angle would make a difference.

We have never seen this technique in action to our knowledge. We know it is definitely illegal. The rule which permits centerboard holding devices was designed for restraining the board, not to create a jibing board for upwind sailing.

Basically you use just as little board as possible. We even suggest that you don't need full board upwind in drifter conditions. In fluky stuff when a puff comes you should pull up the board to get motion underway. Experiment with raising the board in very heavy winds. The reduced lateral resistance created by a board a few inches up may enable you to foot faster and cancel out the pointing ability generated by a board full down.

Finally, keep the board smooth and the edges clean and free from splinters.

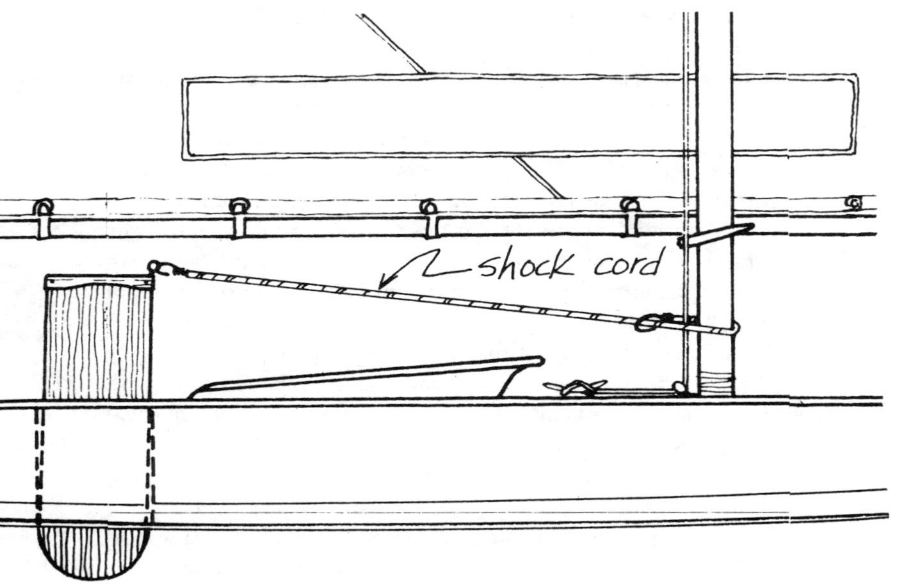

RUDDER AND TILLER

Less attention is given to the rudder than the board in most sailing books; however, one of the most significant factors in slowing the boat is poor rudder control. Most of us tend to tense up under the duress of competition and either move the tiller too much or clutch it at any angle in a death grip, intent on what's up ahead. The Sunfish rudder, smallish though it may be, still will stall when it goes beyond six or seven degrees. There are, however, some good ways to improve the contribution of the rudder.

Bob Johnstone, one of the original Sunfish leaders, suggested some additions to the latch plate which will be discussed later. We have borrowed from Bob's suggestion an idea to preserve the stiffness of the rudder/tiller combination.

The shelf of the rudder on which the tiller rests is made of more durable stuff than the tiller. Gradually the rudder eats into the tiller and the net result is that the tiller sags down onto the deck, scratching the surface as it swings. One of the best ways to control the performance of the boat is positive yet sensitive feel of the rudder by way of the tiller. Keeping the tiller up and stiff achieves this. Alcort has now put a small rubber tip on the end of the tiller to protect the deck, but the real cure lies in gluing two rubber rectangles one eighth inch thick to the shelf.

Tape the tiller where the bridle crosses it. You won't go any faster but the tiller will look prettier and the chafe will be reduced. While on tape, take a few turns at various places on the hiking stick. Some people put a little sand in some varnish and paint it. Others rough sand it. This will help in the frantic grab for the stick after a hard jibe. To come up with a handful of nothing as your sun creamed hand slips off the extension is indeed disappointing.

Alcort has now legalized the use of a tiller extension handle measuring two inches by two inches. The first I saw were really cross pieces and nice jobs of woodwork, but devilish devices for hooking pieces of clothing or life jackets when tacking or jibing.

You must use extension devices because they permit four or five more inches of effective hiking length. As the old rule permitted original equipment only, most of us took the clew outhaul sail set from the boom or the first clip back from the tack on the foot and used it as a hiking stick extension.

We drilled a hole half way into the side of the extension about one half inch back from the end. The nub of the sail set could then be forcibly inserted. We drilled a small hole in the other side of the extension and screwed in the other side of the clip. After gluing and taping we had a good ring from which we could steer while hiking by using the middle finger only.

Now that the extension is legal some people are taking the fun out of invention by making rings of brass pipe with parallel holes on flat sides. They simply bolt through. I will probably go to this method, but the heavier the ring the more powerfully you tend to handle the extension and these break. Holding a handful of hiking stick while sputtering in the water with your boat sailing merrily away teaches you to treat your extension kindly.

You should always check the cap nut on the extension. Peen it over if it looks as though it may be loose at all. Replace extensions regularly; look for signs of wear between the extension and the tiller.

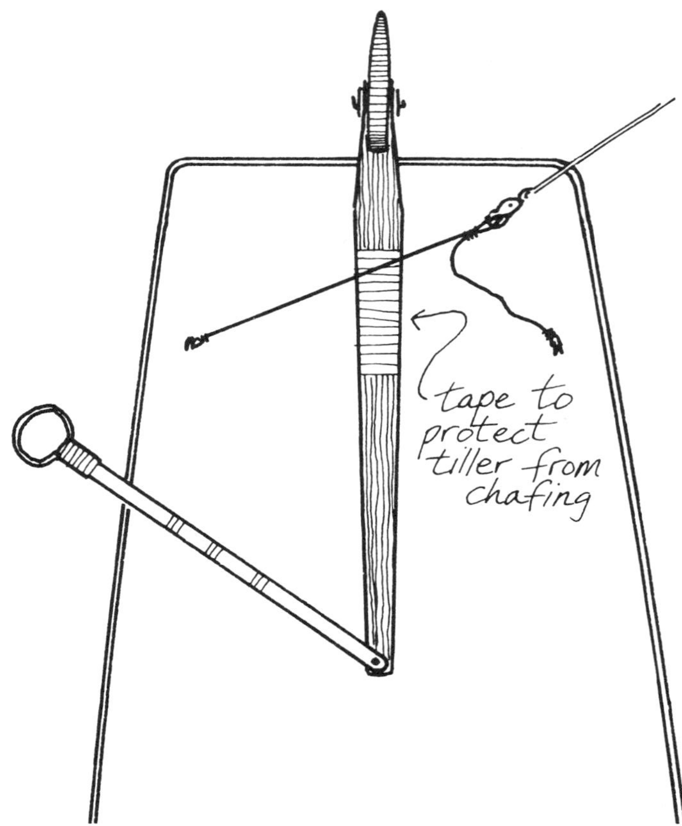

Some people go through life believing they are sailing straight only to discover to their horror that the tiller straps which connect the rudder to the tiller are slightly bent; the rudder has been at a slight angle all along.

Alcort manufactured some rudders and boards of laminated plywood at one time. I have heard that this material is not good for rudders or boards because the grain is not uniform and therefore you get excessive twist. This may be so, but I have used a rudder of this construction for two years off the rocky beaches at Darien and do not have any significant dents in the edges yet. I would use a board of laminated plywood if I could find one.

Rudders are real drags. Many fine sailors concentrate on steering by the sail, moving the rudder as little as possible. Certainly downwind in light air you will find lots of people who pop their rudder out of the water and steer by the wind and careful positioning of their weight.

For fun you might try to rig a shock cord from the bridle eye straps so that it makes a turn around the tiller and holds the tiller, and therefore the rudder, straight. Then sail with no hands on the tiller and change directions by playing the sail and shifting your weight. You will be amazed that you can not only do it but you will also go fast.

With the use of the "Hoyt Effect" on the port side bridle, increased strain on the plastic covering dictated the use of a small single block to which to affix the sheet. This reduces the friction on the bridle. You might also tie a line from eye strap to eye strap as a sort of double bridle.

THE HULL

The editors of "One-Design & Offshore Yachtsman" recently commented that the Sunfish is of generally excellent quality and uniformity of manufacture. We would certainly agree, but what can we do to improve on an already good boat?

Rudy Thompson, who has done as much as anyone to upgrade the racing image of the Sunfish, tipped me off about the hull. There are occasionally some bubbles or disfigurements caused in shipping or manufacturing. A hull just a little asymmetrical is going to cause trouble. Inspect the bottom of a new boat very carefully. Make sure the daggerboard slot is lined up with the keelson.

The Long Island Sound Interclub Dinghy sailors are as meticulous about their equipment as any sailing group. Many of them wash the bottoms of their boats in Lux or a similar detergent. They believe there is something slippery in the cleansing agent which makes the boat go faster. As long as there is a low phosphate content, we see no harm in this activity. We recommend it but not because of some magic "go fast" in Lux. A clean bottom is a faster bottom.

There is no doubt that oil spots, weed, road grime, etc., slow down the boat. The evidence is overwhelming. Admittedly a good header or a puff will put a boat further ahead than a clean bottom, but championship racing involves a lot of people who are alert enough to be in the right place at the right time. The winners take the extra care to have competitive equipment.

The deck of the Sunfish can look new for many years if you take care of it. A good fresh water rinse after every use will preserve the luster. White is the most long lasting color. I understand people have had success in getting out scratches with a regular automotive rubbing compound. The best advice is to try to avoid scratches in the first place.

Everyone uses the standard technique of tipping the boat way up to windward on runs in light air. The logic is mainly to reduce wetted surface and perhaps get the sail higher, and certainly to get the rudder out of the water and reduce weather helm. I seemed to have a particularly hard time mastering the technique. To be good at it, you must keep perfectly still. Haven't we all held our breath, locked in silent slow motion combat, not daring to breathe or, heaven forbid, even move, praying for the puff that will squirt us ahead? My trouble was that I would slide slowly and silently off the side of the boat.

My solution is to put a strip of "no slip" sand paper on either side of the cockpit. This is enough to hold me on, but not enough to tear holes in my pants. My first experiments included combining the "no slip" paper and deck lines. The virtually sanded deck certainly ruined four pairs of pants to say nothing of my modesty.

I now of course make deck lines of regular tape. The theory of the deck lines is that you can sight along them and ascertain your relative position in the fleet. As an example – you are on

a long course and you are ahead and to leeward of another boat. For one reason or another you want to tack over to his side of the course. Can you cross him? If he is behind the 135 degree line you can theoretically do so. After twice ramming Carl Knight I discovered that one had to take into consideration other factors such as the distance lost in tacking.

There are a number of people, Chuck and Carl Knight included, who do not want to be impeded in their movements about the deck. They won't use "no slip" paper. Particularly in planing conditions where they are moving back and forth on the boat, they want the deck slippery. Do what works best for you.

The aforementioned Rudy Thompson has also introduced me to some daggerboard saving devices which I believe are really vital to peace of mind, to say nothing of boat speed. I have often said that I would not put my mother-in-law in the trunk of this boat and pull her up and down – tempting but humanity would prohibit. Rudy has made the trunk habitable, at least for a daggerboard. He glues thin vinyl strips inside vertically along the fore and aft sections of the trunk. He sands and smooths the edges and fills the crevices with Marine Tex. He files and sands again. This really spoils the Sunfish board, accustomed to splintering at every insertion. Some people fill the crevices with silicone seal. This keeps the edges soft and also doubles as a restraining device for the board.

As noted, some people have glued vinyl strips to the lower aftersides of the trunk to help make a pivoting board. This is illegal.

I have often wondered about the use of "slot rubbers" – a device designed to prohibit the flow of water into the daggerboard trunk. Certainly reduced turbulence is to be desired. The other day we turned the boat over to see how much area is involved. Upwind with the board down, not much, but downwind with the board up – a whole bunch.

Carl Knight came up with an almost perfect device. He glued pieces of foam rubber pipe insulation in the trunk fore and aft. These served as a daggerboard restraining device and satisfied the legal requirements of the class thereby. They also eliminated splinters, scars, etc. Chatter was reduced as the board was snugger. As a slot rubber, however, the insulation was a failure as water came shooting up out of the trunk geyser fashion on planing legs.

If anyone can figure out a legal technique, good on all points of sail, which would reduce the flow of water into the lower trunk, we would appreciate hearing. The rooster tails spewing out of the deckside of the trunk when on a plane are enough to convince us of the need for some type of restraint on the flow of water into the slot.

In short, keep the hull clean, the daggerboard trunk smooth. Rinse the boat in fresh water at every chance. It will reward you for good care.

FITTINGS—PART ONE

When someone really wants to tee off on the boat they select the rudder fittings as their first target, and probably with reason. In every major regatta where wind has been strong, a rudder has popped up on at least one major contender. Jack Knights at the 1970 World's, John Magenheimer at a couple of his big series, Ward Young at the 1967 Nationals have all had this problem, and hundreds of others have fallen victim.

If Alcort responds to this problem, and they probably will, they will do themselves a great favor. But there will still be lots of older boats – what to do?

We mentioned Bob Johnstone before. He suggested that a small rubber gasket be fitted into the cup at the latch plate. I have done this and found that the resultant lack of rudder wiggle waggle reduced drag enough to make a difference. The rudder seems to stay put since the fit is tighter and there is less vibration. You might even file out the lip of the latch plate cup to make an even more secure fit.

Much of the cause of rudder defection is a bent deck plate. I know some people who will unscrew the plate and press it flat in a vise. I think this part is too malleable. When it bends once it will bend again, and worse. Throw it away, get a new one. Or you might try this idea: When you sail regularly in heavy winds have your deckplate bolted through to the deck as in the picture on page 31.

You might also wire the rudder to the vertical pin if you are in a position to launch regularly from a dock and do not need the pop-up feature of your rudder.

The cockpit of the Sunfish occasionally gets wet. When this happens you are probably getting a leak through the bailer. This leakage is a nuisance but it is easily corrected. Put some silicone seal around the bailer. Also a drop or two of powdered graphite on the bailer at regular intervals is all that is required to keep it in good shape. Rinse it in fresh water regularly too.

One of the items recommended in the Regatta Checklist is a pop rivet tool. The aluminum edging comes off once in a while. After hiking the molding can get loose. This is easily fixed with a drill and pop rivet tool as we will describe. The

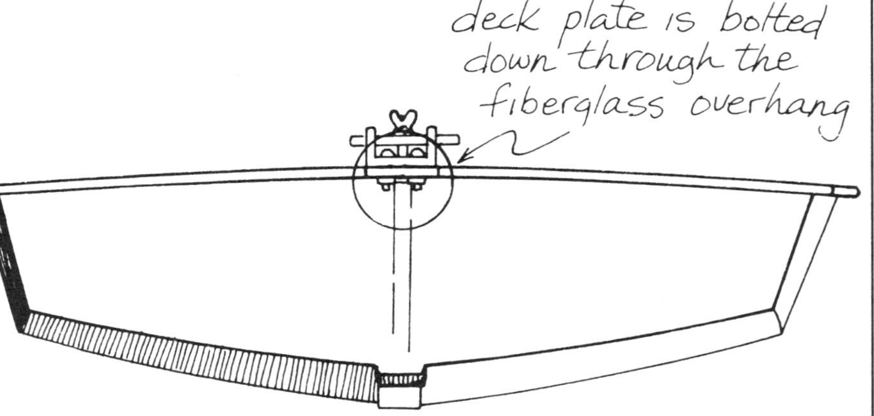

aluminum edging in the cockpit is a relatively new addition to the boat and you might have to make an adjustment to compensate for it as described below.

We still see many pictures taken in the early '60's where the boat is being sailed like a bucking bronco – the sheet leading directly to the sailors' hands with no device to flatten the sail or aid in sheeting. Alcort introduced the open fairlead or "hook" and a welcome addition it was. If you do not use the center jam swivel cleat, you must use the "hook".

If you have the least bit of trouble in getting the sheet under the hook, drop the fairlead down ¼ to ½ inch. Then the hook will be below the edging and your troubles will be over.

The other way to compensate for the edging is to bring the hook out by use of a shim. To border on legality, some have cut out a piece of sail set and inserted it between the lip of the cockpit and the hook.

Alcort does not plan for racing in extreme conditions. Indeed it is not often that you race with a cockpit full of water, but occasionally you do. If you think you might, put silicone seal around the top of the cockpit where it meets the deck.

Also, when you have purchased a new hull you now have a nice cubby hole into which you can stuff various things – sponges, gloves, etc. The best thing to put in the recess area is a pair of underinflated medium sized beach balls. Air is lighter than water and the space these balls take up displaces a much heavier amount of water should you be sailing in extreme conditions. Very clever these Sunfishers – thinking all the time. Some rudder pins do not fit the deck plate. A little filing at the hinge will take care of that problem. Don't peen over the top of the vertical pin. The wing nut almost never comes off and you do need the flexibility.

Dr. Bill Kennedy, Fish Champ from the Gulf Coast, upon his first look at the Sunfish recommended that the latch plate be rounded and smoothed. I don't believe you can legally fair this plate, but I do know you can sand it to the texture of a baby's skin. You should.

Since there are no restrictions on the type of finishes used on the bottom or the degree of smoothness, you may and should sand the bailer. The bailer is more dangerous than even the rough texture would imply however. When you take it off to sand make sure you put it back in line. It has a reasonably streamlined shape, make use of it.

When you put it back, make sure you put some silicone seal around it. The bailer is a most subversive weed catcher. You never think of this as the area causing you to slow down drastically. You can check the board and rudder but what can you do about weed streaming from the bailer anyway – other than just wait?

If you wish, remove the rubber gasket from the bottom of the bailer and put it on the cockpit side of the seal between the bailer and the deck so there is no chance of weed catching. Back up on deck you should make sure water cannot seep into the bridle, causing a break at some critical point in a regatta. I used to tape over each end but I understand that some people melt the ends, making the tube airtight.

Some people put inspection ports into the hull so they can check for water and easily bail. It is a great idea which we heartily recommend. Only do so when you suspect leaks, however; there is no sense in surgery unless it is called for. A Holt-Allen port is good; I use a clear plastic one from Nicro. Install them on the aft portion of the deck, between the bridle eye straps.

FITTINGS—PART TWO

The subject of jam cleats is one that AMF–Alcort's Bruce Connolly could write a book about. For years people had been badgering him to permit some form of jam cleat. Finally in 1968 he relented. A mainsheet jam or cam action cleat was legalized. In 1971 the rule was extended to include more than one mainsheet cleat if desired.

Alcort's objection to jam cleats was that not every boat would have one, thus spoiling the one-design nature of the class. They further felt that jam cleats were rather expensive and if they were allowed the flood gates would be opened to more expensive additions to the boat. One of the charms of the Sunfish is its relatively low price; Alcort wanted to keep it that way.

I agree with this logic but the jam cleat makes life so simple that the device is almost a necessity. The real objection to the jam cleat should have been that it is dangerous when not properly used. The center swivel variety tends to stick at just the wrong moment, usually on a jibe or a tack, and over you go. New sailors should proceed with caution when considering jam cleats. I would not prescribe one for my kids.

There are a number of types of jam cleats and there does not seem to be agreement on the best. It probably is a matter of taste and what you have become accustomed to. Bill King, one of the finest gentlemen and competitors in the sport, used my rig the other day. He hated it. He uses the center swivel cleat while I usually use two clam cleats mounted to the side decks.

From my standpoint any device which uses a closed fairlead such as the center swivel jam, restricts your ability to sheet in quickly. I think it is vital to be able to reach out and grab a lot of sheet at one time. Dinghy starting many times involves a slow luffing along the line and then a rapid trimming of the sails only seconds before the start with many other boats doing the same thing in very close proximity.

I spent many hours tinkering with other types. First I used a set of cam cleats similar to those used on the side decks of the Finn. I found that to insure that the sheet was in place I had to come in from hiking and press the sheet down. The sheet was coming up from the cockpit at such an angle that it was difficult to lay it in flat in the cleat. Then I put a half inch shim under the cleats and it was easier to secure the mainsheet. I still had trouble with this rig, however. Sand played havoc with the gears and I never seemed to get the spring tension right.

Jack Evans, one of the more imaginative Sunfish sailors, has found an Italian cam cleat which sits about two inches off its base. This looks as though it would be a good one and also might serve as a hand hold.

I finally found what was for me the right answer. I use two clam cleats. This is a plastic encased claw with nice wide jaws into which I can drop the sheet blindfolded. The cleat has no moveable parts for me to foul and it is tall enough so that it

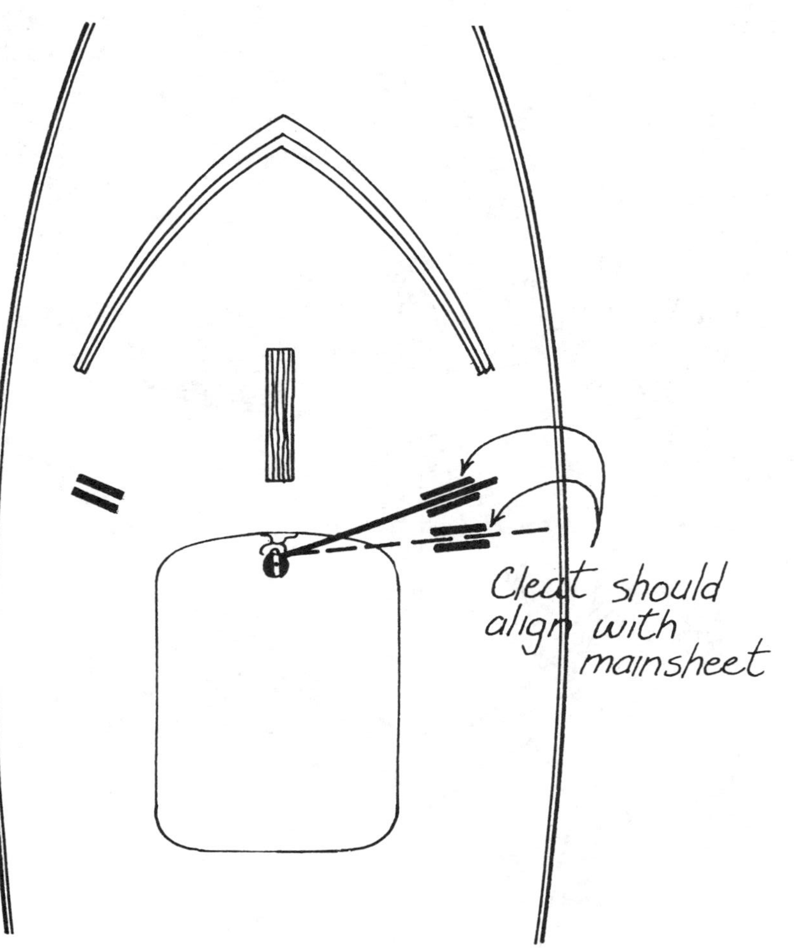

does not require a shim. I position the cleats so that they are opposite each other with the inboard end just at that section of the deck where a bolt can be used and fastened to the underside of the lip. They angle away from the cockpit to the same degree as the sheet leading from the hook. The position is a matter of taste; Chuck has his cleats perpendicular to the cockpit.

The clam cleat is a great asset. It is a third hand. I find I use it before a major move in order to get organized. I will also confess to using it when I am bushed going upwind in a breeze – but only for a moment you understand. Most of us don't really use a cleat much in a heavy breeze; you have to adjust the sail so much according to puffs and sea conditions that you cannot afford to leave the sheet cleated.

At the 1970 World's I put a standard free running block on the deck positioned just where the center jam is normally located. I did this because the courses were over six miles in length with three full beats. I reasoned that with starting lines a quarter mile long, I could find a hole someplace where sheeting in and out would not be as critical. The time saved in tacking with a block would be significant as would the ability to adjust more easily to big seas. I still believe this would have been a good device, but Larry Pratt, Sales Manager of Alcort, who had the unenviable task of enforcing the rules against a bunch of Henry Ford/Rube Goldbergs, outlawed me. Chuck independently arrived at the same conclusion as I, but his rig was upheld. Carl Knight went a step or so further. He showed up with a console. John Dane has a console in his Soling – Carl has a console in his Sunfish. Some called it a rolltop desk. It contained a pencil holder, chart holder, notebook, and stop watch holder. It was on a rotating piece of mahogany and had a block, a jam cleat and a compass. His unit was disallowed. There is just no hope for young Edisons in this class.

Chuck, however, installed a Lewmar ratchet block. This block served the same purpose as mine but it also had a cam action jam cleat which made it legal. I feel that this was stretching the rules a bit but since it was allowed you can't argue. One of the moments I will always cherish was the day Jeorg Bruder came out to sail with us in practice on Cowpet Bay. Chuck boomed out on his weather quarter, using the ratchet. Jeorg ducked, thinking some Twelve Meter was bearing down on him. The Harken ratchet has become the most popular.

In light air on relatively short courses, I still believe in the freedom of the simple clam cleats. On long Olympic type courses in a heavy sea and breeze, I think a combination ratchet plus clam cleats is desirable. Once you get used to a rig it is difficult to change, so start with the one which suits the conditions you most often will sail in.

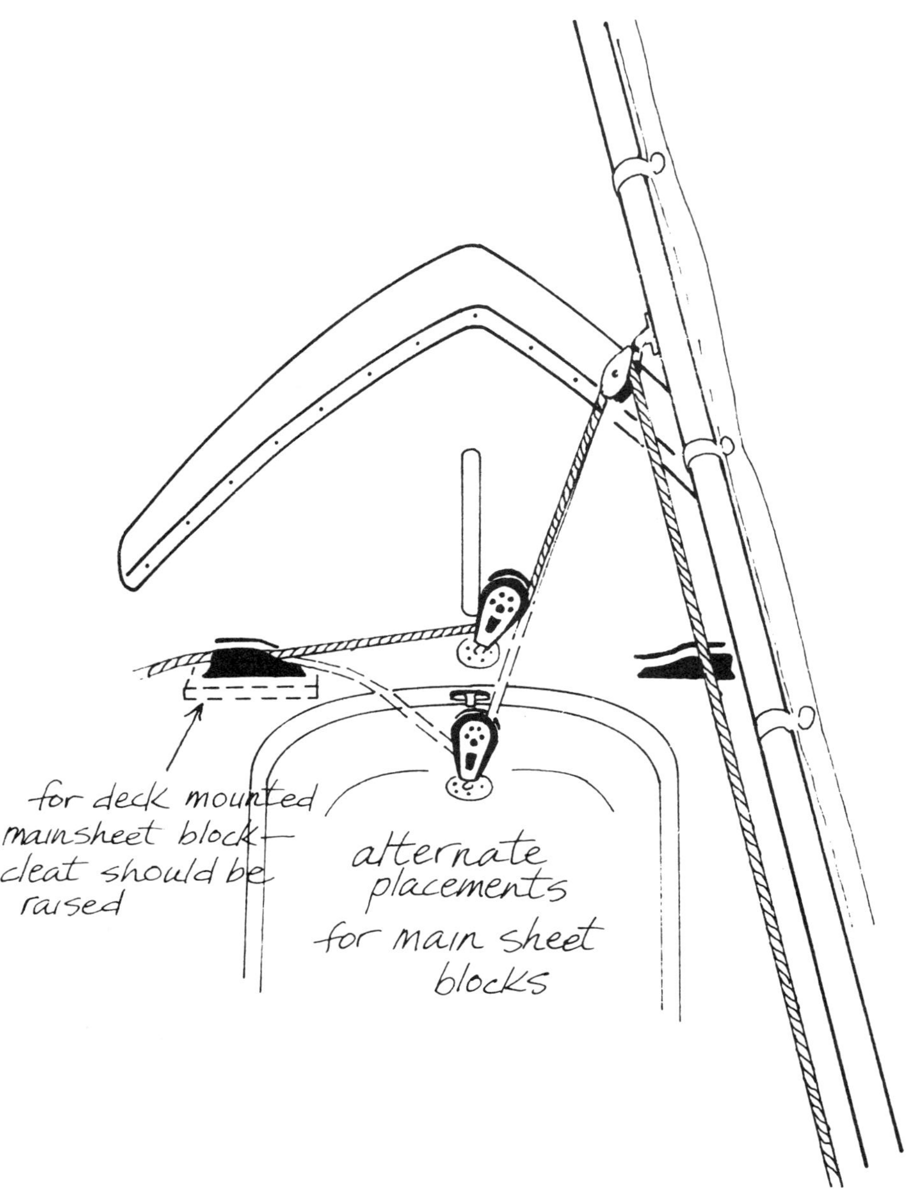

FITTINGS—PART THREE

Just forward of the jam cleats is an area which is too often overlooked: the splashboard which is secured by 12 bolts. Gradually these small holes develop leaks. Surround the board with silicone seal. Alcort may be responsive to the pleas of their overseas distributors and change the splashboard as the part is too flexible for shipping and frequently gets damaged.

The splashboard is also used by some sailors as a vang. They have filed away the outer lower ends of the board. They hook the sheet underneath on a reach. This is probably illegal as it constitutes an alteration of the boat.

AMF–Alcort replaced the old bullet shaped main halyard cleat with an adequate but less accommodating one. The purchase you got with the old one was better and quicker.

Garry Hoyt made the comment recently that for $10 worth of fittings the boat could be substantially improved. I assume he was talking about blocks but probably not the main halyard block. We have never heard this block maligned. Bob Bowles cuts the side of his deck block. He ties his halyard and sheet together to avert catastrophe in case he drops the sheet. By having the deck block open he can unrig more easily.

The halyard itself is cotton. The halyard shrinks. Even braided Dacron shrinks. You are permitted 24 feet of halyard. I cheat by using 24 feet of spun polyester. This material looks like cotton but it does not shrink. How many times between races have you had to undo your halyard and rehoist the sail because the halyard has stretched? What stretches will shrink and ultimately you will end up with 22 or so feet and this will cost you in a light air race as will be described on page 63. If you do use polyester halyards make sure you burn the ends. Also do not use braided polyester. It slips up the gaff and your rig gets so low you cannot get under the boom when you tack. The best way to insure no slippage up the gaff is to tie the halyard to a piece of no slip paper glued to the spar.

Bruce Connolly is the one who gets credit for responding to the pleas of us older gentlemen to permit Dacron sheets. I think this one move created a great many sales and retained a lot of old customers. Cotton is a great fiber but cotton sheets tear up your hands. Soft braided filament Dacron sheets are easier on us. We suggest you serve the ends of the sheet too as the sheet tends to ravel into itself. I now use a 3/8-inch Marlowe spun polyester sheet; ¼-inch in light air.

Skip Cook used to mark the sheet according to various conditions of breeze. This has real merit as long as you clip the bridle at the same point all the time, making sheet length constant. Once you get in the groove, make a mark on the sheet so that the next time you sail in those conditions you can put it into automatic pilot and away you go. I have read that people sew a black thread into the sheet to serve as a control point. This is meticulousness above and beyond the call – but I bet the people who do it are either winners or have more fun at the game.

The last area to be covered in the discussion of the sheet is just that. Please tie a knot in the end of it after passing it through the blocks on the boom.

My wife, Brownie, stood in the top 10 at the Light Corinthians in 1970 – and in a 15 knot breeze came the jibing mark and she lost the sheet. It ran through the blocks with no knot to encumber it. End of Light Corinthians. Guess whose husband had rigged the boat and had forgotten to tie the knot?

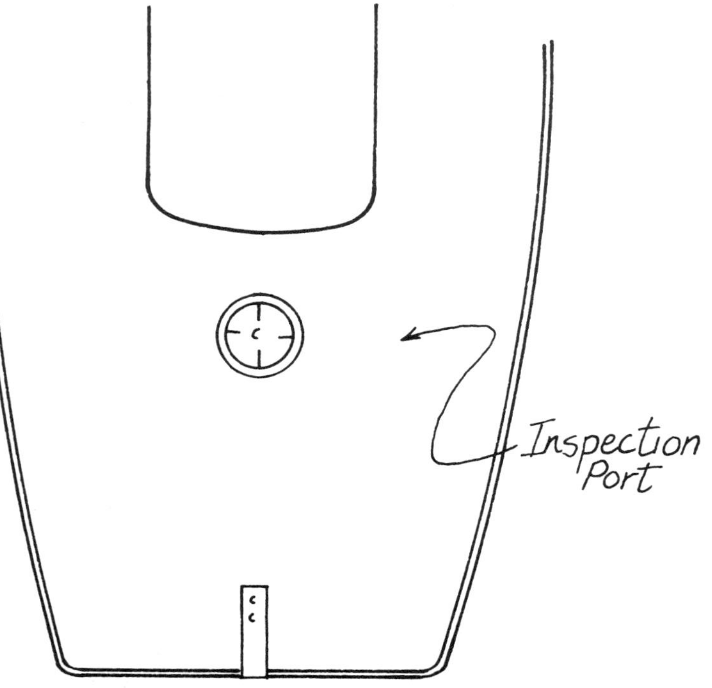

FITTINGS–PART FOUR

For many years I did not use a tell tale. And for all those years I dogged it in the lower half of the fleet in light air races. I believe that when I changed to a good tell tale system my performance improved at the same time.

You must have both a masthead fly and a lower indicator. If you don't have both you are wrong. You are losing an opportunity to increase your speed.

Everyone has his own tell tale system. Bob Bowles uses the Telo feathers. They get caked with salt, so if you use them make sure your wife or girl friend washes them out every evening. When they get wet, they don't perform too well. In light air, however, they appear to be very sensitive. They can be dried on the air conditioner of a car in two hours. In the rain, you should use magnetic recording tape – impervious to water.

Bob Bushnell, long an advocate of the "wind on your cheek" school, now uses a bullet shaped wind vane on the bow. Will White uses, as do the Finn boys, a number 10 wire with nylon yarn. He tapes the wire to the gaff. The DuPont people will be pleased to know that nylon fabric is one of the favorite tell tales. A piece of nylon stocking is an excellent fly.

I like my tell tale the best. It is a combination of ideas from Messers. Bowles, White and Ding Schoonmaker. I take an electrical clamp to which I attach pieces of number 10 wire 18 inches long on either side. I use red Orlon yarn. Nylon is o.k. too! Wool takes too long to dry. The picture of my rig is on the next page.

In big breezes tell tales lose some of their importance but not completely. When you are sailing in big seas the apparent wind changes from trough to crest; only with a masthead fly can you really correct the set of your sail. And in light stuff it really pays.

I remember one of the really horrible days of sailing in 1970. The Brookhaven Bath Bottle and Boating Society put on one of the most memorable regattas of the year. Saturday saw an awful Northwester, full of holes, and 180 degree shifts. The wind was just itching to back to the Southwest. The near reach to the finish was a study of frustration. Bryce Suydam was just ahead of me and to starboard on my weather bow. Fifty yards to the finish. He had his masthead fly; I did not. All of a sudden his fly did a 180. I let my sail out, ran up behind him, took his air, and ghosted across, just ahead of the onrushing pack. So be kind to your competitors, use a masthead fly.

One more thing about my electrical clamp. If someone hits you and bends the wire it is easy to go up, take the clamp off, fix the wire and put the clamp back up. With the taped kind you are usually done for if the wire is bent. Bob Bowles should have patented the idea.

I used to panic when I lost my tell tale. I still don't like to sail without it, but I find that when push comes to shove I sail exclusively by the luff of the sail and I can get along. When you get into a round robin series where you change boats, you will have to get used to sailing with different tell tales and sometimes with no indicator at all. You should practice for this by sailing for fun with no fly. But in an important series you must use the tell tale. You can pick up lifts on windward legs much more readily.

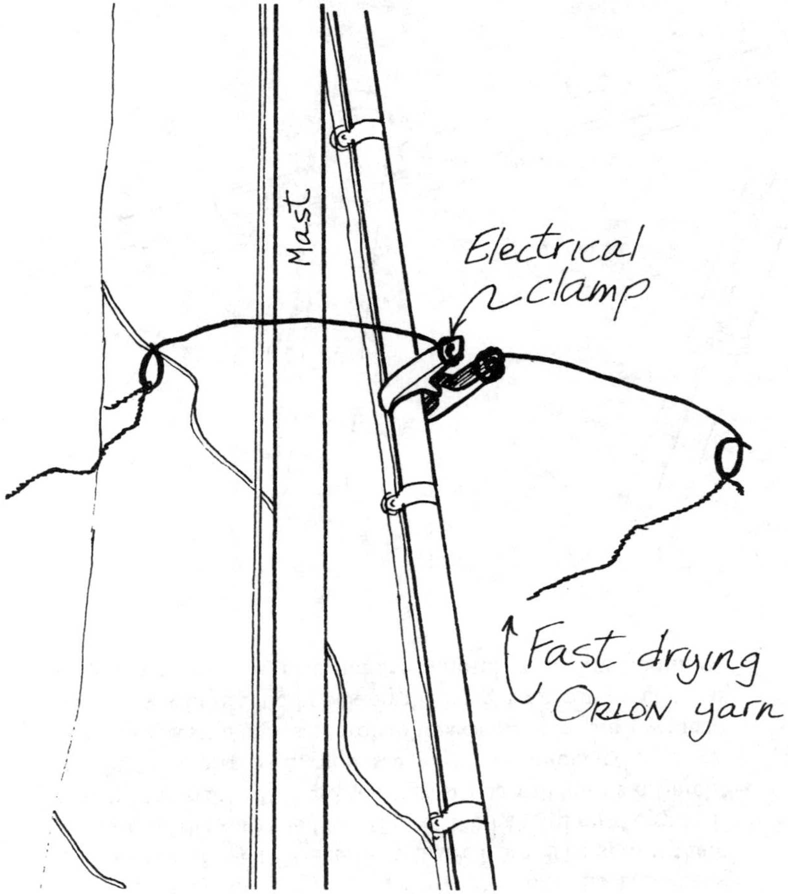

TUNING—SAILS

This last segment of the tuning portion is for us the most nebulous of all – sails. Everyone tells us this is the motor of the boat. And yet Sunfish sails which have curled leeches, look like corrugated washboards or have twisted peaks seem to do well in the hands of the better sailors. The moral in this is that the sail in the Sunfish is not nearly as important as the skipper who can adjust to the vagaries of the wind.

Don't misunderstand, you should strive to get your sail to be the best possible: free of hard spots, no sewing imperfections, a nice firm leech, full draft about 40% aft, no flutter, no twist at the peak or the foot. When you get this you have got the ultimate – you may have had to send it back to Ratsey for recutting which is perfectly proper; you may not send it to other sailmakers, however. Even so we contend that there are very narrow differences between the best and the worst of the Ratsey sails.

First, rig your sail right. Alcort positions the gooseneck 21½ inches aft of the tack on a black band. The spot is there because of the suggested location of the halyard on the spar. If you tie the halyard where we suggest you will have a different looking sail plan than you see in Alcort publicity pictures. Alcort suggests a high sail probably because they don't want to have new sailors get a knock on the noggin when they tack. As long as you want to race and are mindful of the low boom, rig

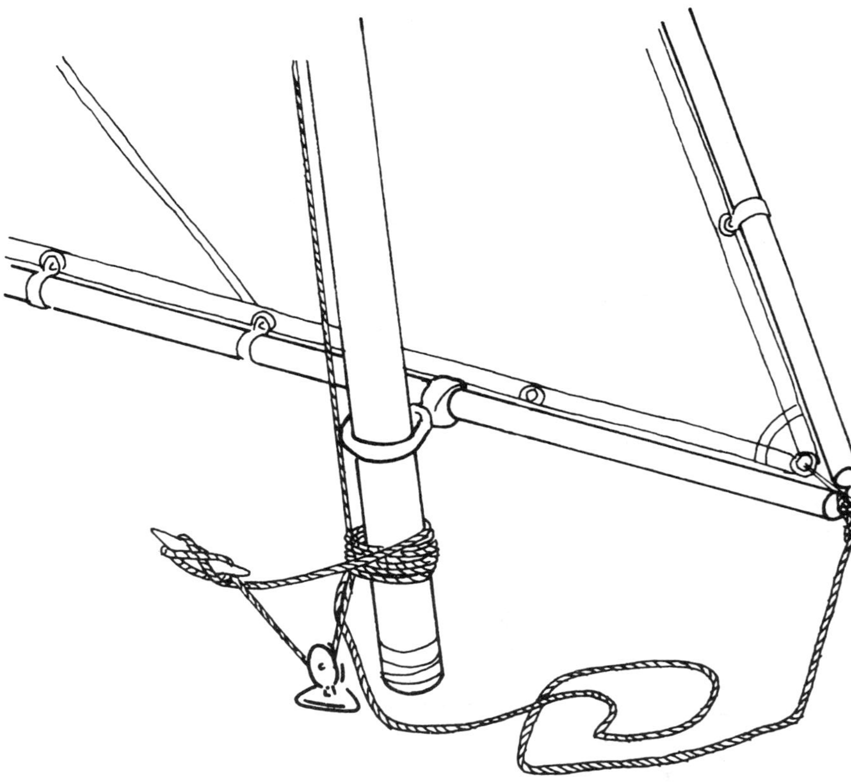

the halyard nine to 9½ grommets up from the tack. Move the gooseneck back one or two inches. There is little doubt that the resultant lower sail plan is better for speed, particularly in a breeze.

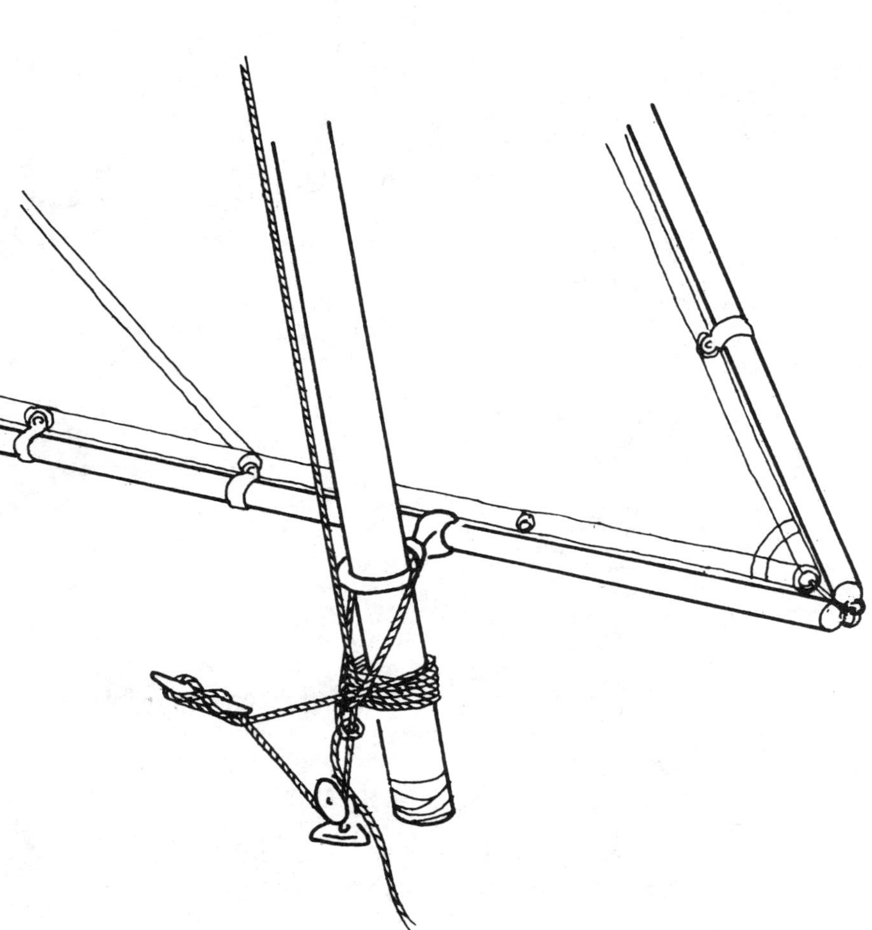

If you weigh less than 160 pounds fully clothed you can afford to put the halyard up to the 10th grommet in a breeze of 15 knots and up. And even move the gooseneck back to 24 inches from the tack. Put a line around the ninth grommet so that the mast on port tack doesn't bind the sail set and create a hard spot.

Tape the gooseneck screw. I never had a sail in which I didn't develop tiny holes at the gooseneck area until I started taping the screw. Also watch how you furl the sail; sometimes it pinches between the spars and the friction creates small holes.

When you hoist the sail, pulling the halyard through the block, cleat the line securely and then take a couple of lashes around the mast, drawing the halyard around it as in the picture, left. There is no sense in having the halyard a couple of inches away from the mast creating a separate drag. Take advantage of every opportunity to reduce wind resistance.

After lashing the halyard to the mast you can do other things with it as well. If there is a big breeze you can bring it over the goose neck as in the picture, left, and pull it down hard. This serves as a sort of vang, flattening the sail. You can also bring the halyard out on the boom as in the picture on the next page. This is the type of vang favored by most sailors.

In light air tie the end of the halyard to the interlocking eyebolts. When you are going downwind in light air and you try to tip the boat up to windward frequently there is not enough breeze to keep the sails full and then the boat inadvertently jibes. By pulling on the halyard from the windward side you can keep the sail full and drawing. This contraption is known as a J.C. Strap after its inventor John Christianson.

Some people tie the gaff to the mast. This is probably illegal but it does reduce the possibility of the halyard slipping or coming undone.

In the days of the Florida midwinters, Bob Bowles and I would slug up the weather leg and arrive in good shape at the first mark after surviving the short ugly steep seas of Biscayne

Bay. That body of water is pernicious; it literally rattles the bones. In any event, very shortly after turning to the reaching leg, zip – there would go young Doug Brown planing by. I wasn't disturbed but Bob was and is an off wind master and he couldn't believe what was happening to him.

Bob studied Doug's sail and sure enough there was a difference. Doug had a standard sail, but that year the standard had been changed without our knowledge. More draft had been

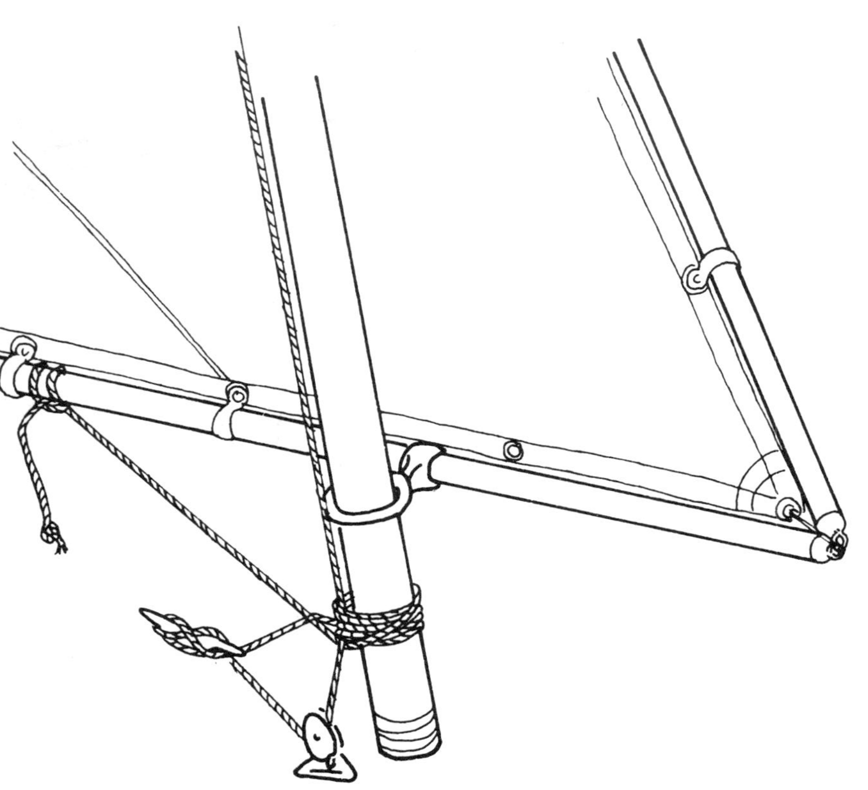

added. At the Brookhaven regatta in 1970 all sails were measured, probably to legislate against some people who had repairs done by local sailmakers and a little piece added here and there in the right place.

My sail measured 84.43 square feet. New sails out of the bag were as much as 88 square feet. The old 75 square feet days, if they ever existed, were over. All sails with a Ratsey and Lapthorn white signature patch are old and small unless they have an S or SS imprinted over the Ratsey name. We see Jim Carson, top New Jersey Lightning skipper, sailing perfect tactical races in Sunfish and losing. He has an old white patch sail. Any red patch sail is a new better sail. Don't believe people who claim there is a real difference in the area of the new sails. The shapes may be different from tuning and usage but the areas are comparable. I believe the best Ratsey sails to date have an L designator on the patch.

At Darien we hold our Bermuda Crown series. This is a 10 boat round robin event. The average position of the winning skipper this year was 3.3 – the last place sailor averaged 7.9. The average finishing position of the leading boat was 4.4 and the tail ender was 6.8. No super boats – the best averaged worse than fourth and there were no dogs – the worst averaged better than seventh. The difference in the performance of the boats is extremely narrow as you can see. We conclude that Sunfish reasonably well tuned and rigged are competitive with each other.

Methods of rigging the sail itself differ but most of us now subscribe to the Bowles/Knight method. They developed very loose rigs, restraining the clew outhaul at zero tension. The sail set which under natural rigging would fall at the forward sheet block on the boom is left either undone or drawn forward of the block. The sail set just aft of the tack is removed. Now this is a loose footed sail. It also creates a great deal of draft forward.

Make no mistake, this loose rig is not universally used. Garry Hoyt has his sail further out on the spars as does Carl

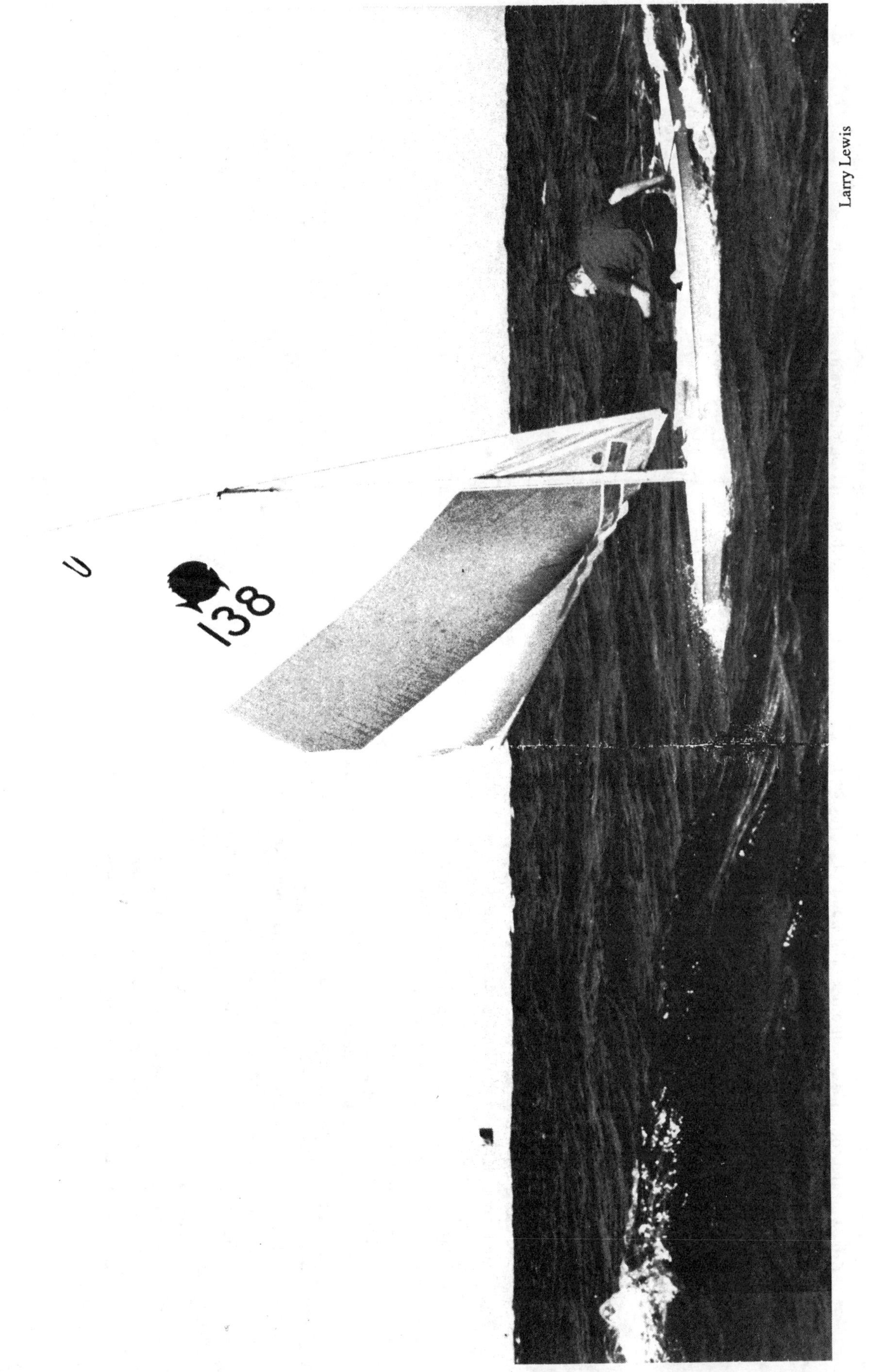

Larry Lewis

Knight, in a breeze. We think the shape of the sail is improved by loose rigging, and although scallops form along the edges the number of hard spots would be reduced in the most critical areas of sail power, and most important, the leech stays firm. Pull the foot of the sail out to the point of a firm leech in light air, and a non-cupped leech in a breeze.

In the days of smaller sails, many people used lace lines. This was in an attempt to loose foot the sail, and resulted in the Alcort rule on the sail not being more than two inches from the spar. Another reason for lacing the grommets is to change the draft in the sail for various reasons. Adjustable outhauls, however, are illegal. Notice on pages 66-67 how much draft is developed in this sail on a dead run. The sail is extremely loose footed.

Bill King has a nifty use for the lace line. He reeves his through the tack and back behind the gooseneck. He then undoes the gooseneck and it is able to slide along, restrained by the lace line. I prefer to stay simple and use sail sets only. If you use lace line I suggest you use Dacron or Nylon as cotton tends to shrink and form uneven tensions on the foot, creating hard spots.

Most of us pull the sail up taut. If hard spots form or the peak twists excessively, loosen the outhaul and you will free the sail somewhat.

Rudy Thompson introduced most of the class to one of the best developments to come along in years! The long rectangular window. Most of us were too unimaginative to take advantage of the 1x2 foot rectangular window previously authorized. All we could see was the almost box like windows that a few people had and most discarded.

Rudy put a four inch window in his sail, stretching from the tack aft about six feet. This 288 square inch window has the same area as the old one but is a lot more useful. You can see dead downwind; you can more easily judge your position relative to another boat. When you are to weather of someone right after the start you don't have to move unnecessarily to get your position; now you can watch all the way.

Some port tackers judge that if they can see a starboard tacker in their window they have to tack; if they cannot they can continue on their course assuming the starboard boat cannot reach them. Don't believe it.

You should rinse your sail in fresh water after every use in salt water. Don't iron your sail. If you are going to store the sail let it hang loose, releasing luff tension in particular. You should have a sail bag in which to carry your sail and spars. The sail stays cleaner and there is less chance of developing holes. Don't leave your sheet on the spars with the sail. Sheets pick up sand and sand abrades sails badly. Don't wind your halyard around the sail. Leave the sail loosely furled and slide it into the spar bag. Take care of your sail, it will reward you.

STARTS

It's all over now but the sailing. Tuning, exercising, rigging, the hours of meticulous preparation are through. We promise you that if you have followed all of the steps we have recommended you are ready for any World's.

The lines are usually excellent at major events. Systems are in accordance with NAYRU regulations. What techniques will we use to get out of the box, in clear air and moving to the favored side of the course? (And remember, winds shift, lines don't always stay perfect.)

Jeorg Bruder taught most of us a lesson at the '70 World's. After the first race he realized the need to get clear air right at the start. Thereafter he would start high of the line and with a few seconds to go would boom down, dipping into a hole and moving at the gun. Jeorg never had a problem upwind when he had one of those starts. There is no doubt that on big lines in huge fleets this method is successful. If you don't get caught over the line. Living life in this manner is for the hardy. Garry Hoyt did not resort to this at the '70 World's, which he won, but at the '70 Caribbean Championships he was hustling at the leeward end right on the line. So, the first recommendation on starts is get clear air. If you don't choose to achieve it by dipping or by getting the one perfect start at the favored end, get it by going a quarter way down the line from the favored side, or get it at the weather end by being the second boat past the committee boat and tacking over to the starboard side of the course immediately.

However, many races are decided today by starts governed by the locally enforced five minute rule or the IYRU one minute rule, applicable after a general recall. The five minute rule proved Jeorg Bruder's undoing at the '70 World's. What now, you dippers?

The law now gives a lot more power to the leeward yacht prior to the start. Many people find the standard technique of luffing weather yachts until the start and then diving into the hole they have carved to leeward to be even more potent under the 1969 rules. Most winning starters go with way on. What results when you stall out the boat to weather is that you stall yourself and some enterprising soul darts through to leeward with a full rap on and you are wallowing in his backwind.

So, my advice: A minute or so before the start be up to weather of the lay line at the favored end if it is to starboard. Beware of the boat approaching to leeward; if you see one and the time till the start is still adequate, bear down and discourage him from going to leeward of you. Usually he will luff up to weather of you. As long as his bow does not get ahead of yours you can usually forget him.

Now come up, keep up. If you have any more boats trying to come through to leeward, fake going down. By now enough Barrett starters have filled in below you that any boat trying to go through you to leeward has too much fiberglass ahead; they will luff up. Keep up, keep up. Now a few seconds before the start, drive, bear down on a leeward boat if you are bow to bow, luff up if not, sheet in, go!

But don't go before the gun. Use a stopwatch. Dinghy starts today at well organized clubs have two or three minute sequences with nice loudly hailed countdowns. Don't get used to this luxury. Use a watch. Carl Knight leaves nothing to chance in this regard; he uses two watches.

Normally NAYRU starting rules apply. My way of remembering the sequence which is a white flag at 10 minutes, blue flag at five and red at the start, with white and blue going down 30 seconds before the next flag is raised, is We/Better/Race – White/Blue/Red.

In the Caribbean Championships of 1970, Tito Casales ran a tight Race Committee. He started on time. When the line is downwind from the beach you cannot hear the gun sometimes. Now that is when experience pays. Look at the signal on the Race Committee launch. It's Blue – get to the line. If it is still up that means you have at least thirty seconds. I have seen two regattas blown on just this mistake. The real moral, of course, is get out early.

When I am out early I find a friend, usually Chuck. We start at opposite ends of the line on converging courses. Which end is favored? We continue on to the lay line for the mark, tack and converge again. Which side of the course was favored? Is there a drifting anchor line? Is there a current? Was the favored side of the course caused by a permanent condition or was it an oscillating wind? Then I sail to the reaching mark, I sight down from mark to mark to make sure I have the proper bearing. Once in a while I am ahead and I have gone in the wrong direction all too often.

Now I am back to the line. Incidentally, if the waves are so huge that you cannot see the marks at a distance, you had better get a good fix with a land point beforehand. I check the line again. Still one end favored? In a really oscillating wind I time the shifts; usually there is a pattern.

I determine the weather end lay line. I do it again. If I am wearing sweatshirts, I go over and get them wet. I sponge out the cockpit. I check the lines and the fittings. I'm nervous just writing about it. I fasten down the wing nut. I check for weed, pull up the board, brush off the rudder. One or two more fast sails to remember speed and then at about seven or eight minutes to go I sit down in the cockpit and relax and watch. What is Garry doing? Where are the leaders concentrating? I watch for the five minute signal, check my watch. I get up, sail around, I want to get used to speed again. Line still the same? Cockpit dry? Am I going for a port tack? If so I begin to go to that end of the line. If not I go up to the line about halfway and loaf along. I get on the line regardless of wind, but it is dramatically important in light air or against a foul current. Stay up on the bloody line!

One-and-a-half minutes – remember if seas are huge allow extra time for slow tacking. Turn, go toward the fleet. The first race syndrome may be on them all; they may be line shy. Tack to weather of a likely weaker opponent, to leeward of a stronger one. Really most important. 30 seconds. Come up just over that lay line – tell those weather boats there won't be any room. Keep moving. Don't get caught on the line with a perfect position and no speed. Keep the leeward boat well down. Last second look at the watch, sheet in and drive –––gun!

There are several other starting techniques to consider. We mentioned "Barrett starters" before. Basically, this is the crowd who approach the line on port tack and flip in front of an oncoming starboard boat. Usually this is achieved with success at the port end. It should be timed so that the tack is completed and the boat is just above the lay line to the pin with enough time remaining to hit the line with the gun.

The counter offense against the Barrett start by the starboard boat is a subtle alteration of course so that the port tack boat comes about below the lay line and cannot fetch the pin when he tacks and makes his run for it. I hold that there is no proper course before the start and that as long as the provisions of Rule 34 are satisfied you can alter course so that the port boat cannot risk tacking. The rights of the close hauled port boat under Rule 34 change only when his sails go past head to wind so he won't risk tacking too close.

Most new sailors would be well advised to go halfway down the line and find clear air rather than attack the favored end. You will find that the 20 or 30 yards you give up will be regained by the fact that you have free air. Be sure to be on the line, however. Many new sailors think they are on the line but are really several boat lengths below.

Finally there will come the day when you get the perfect start at one end or another – and the wind will shift. Have the guts to take the sterns of those on the favored side. Absorb your 50 yard loss quickly; it becomes hundreds of yards if you

don't get over to the correct side of the course in a real hurry. Remember that all those sterns you are taking are headed in the wrong direction so that when you flip back over you are being lifted up on their quarter. Regattas are won on making the fewest errors! The ability to recognize an error and rectify it promptly is what wins! In an oscillating wind, however, if it lifts behind you, hang on, it will come back.

The sequence on pages 74 through 79 tells the story graphically.

Notice that 199 and 102 are jockeying for the perfect leeward start, but they may have lost sight of the committee boat and may be too far down the line from the pin. The tide is against them.

Number 138 begins to gain speed and sail over the slowly

luffing boats ahead of him, dipping down into a hole just before the start. He may be over but there are a number of red and white sails to weather of him and it is not possible to make a really accurate determination; this is a really good example of a "Bruder" start.

All three yachts are being sailed flat but number 199 recognizes at once that he is being backwinded and drives off to leeward to get clear air. Number 102 spots the shift behind him and makes up his mind to take a number of sterns. Number 102 finished 7th in the race. Number 138 would not give up his clear air and ultimately rounded the weather mark 60th.

TO WEATHER

You're off. Clear air. Can't miss – but you can. Now comes another key point. Bob Bushnell used to clean up in this class. His technique was based on extreme effort, 100% for five minutes. He is in such good shape at that time, he can look around and sail an intelligent rather than a physical race. The moral: 100% concentration for 60 seconds – get speed, speed, speed. But then look. Do you want to get over to port?

The best sailors at Darien sometimes don't win the starts but in short order they are on their way to the favored side in clear air. Their speed takes care of the rest. If you are trapped, get out of there.

My son, Sam, started at Darien one day on a line just slightly port end favored. He had the weather start because most of the hot shots felt the port side of the course was where they wanted to be, but one thing he knew; and it is one thing no more than 10% of any fleet either knows or responds to. All those boats to leeward whose bows are slightly ahead of yours or even directly even are giving you some degree of backwind. If you start to weather on a good line, unless your bow is slightly ahead or there is some really compelling reason to get to the port side of the course, tack out of there.

Sam tacked, cleared a couple of late starters, got gradually headed and in spite of his father suggesting that he tack on the first glimpse of the header he held on until deep enough to come about and lay the weather mark. Sam won his first Darien race at age 14. He will win more.

So the first moral to weather is to get out of the parade. Take a stern or two, don't fight that leeward boat slightly ahead of you unless he is really a less experienced sailor. Tack, clear your air. Clear air is the name of the game.

Sunfish races are usually very short. Tidal current or local shifts are certainly a factor, but the wind at the time is the real key. Sail on the wind; don't sail to spots.

Sure, Rob Brooke, 20 boats behind on the reaching leg at Chelsea on the Hudson, went dead downwind along the shore holding out of the current long enough to beam reach across the fleet to beat the other boats who had held a broad reaching course to the mark.

Yes, holding to the east on a southerly at Darien usually pays in order to duck the current and maybe to pick up a land breeze. But time after time, tacking on headers, following the wind, is what pays. Go on the header. As you get in Chuck's class sometimes you can violate the rule, but usually sail on the course which is the more direct one for the mark.

How often, when we are behind, we will go off on a course on the wrong tack just to do something different in fervent hopes of catching a lucky shift. The good sailor may tack to clear his air, but he will come back, following the leader on the right course, knowing that everybody makes a mistake in a sailboat race, and the leader's time will come.

One thing has helped me in my upwind performance. For years I sailed in the ignominy of being the real tailender in gentle breezes. The cheerful Falstaffian loser. No more.

Secret number one: Lose weight. This has already been covered, of course. If you weigh 170 or less you can win in any conditions except the five to 10 knot days in a chop when the kids will tear you up. There is just no way you can go as fast as the good sailor who weighs 30 or 40 pounds less in these conditions.

In light airs I found that concentration on the sail and tacking smoothly have been important. I think you can even cleat the sheet in light flat sea days, reducing the possibility of overtrimming. In a chop you must hold the sheet in your hand adjusting the sail for the changes in apparent wind due to the waves.

Many people, Chuck included, believe in roll tacking. He teaches this method in his classes. Essentially he dips to windward before coming about, rolling the boat over. I prefer to keep the boat flat. I weigh more and feel I must move less. My rather flat tack is for light air only.

Now, upwind in a breeze. You are physically trained. You should beat seven out of 10 people in the class just because of strength. How does Garry get that little extra? First, the famous Hoyt Effect. Garry reasons that in 20 knot breezes he cannot hold the boat as flat as he would like so he simply unsnaps the sheet and moves it to the port bridle. It then looks like the picture on the next page.

Thus on starboard he creates a traveller effect – lowering the boom, moving it outboard, flattening the sail and making the boat easier to sail level. Port tack does not have as much power as starboard in the Sunfish because of the lateen rig, so there is no need to have the sheet adjust over to the starboard bridle on that tack.

Remember that the snap has a tendency to come unhooked so it is a good idea to tie a bowline in it, passing around the bridle. You may tape the snap.

Garry's technique has been overdone. It reduces pointing ability. The only conditions in which it is really effective are

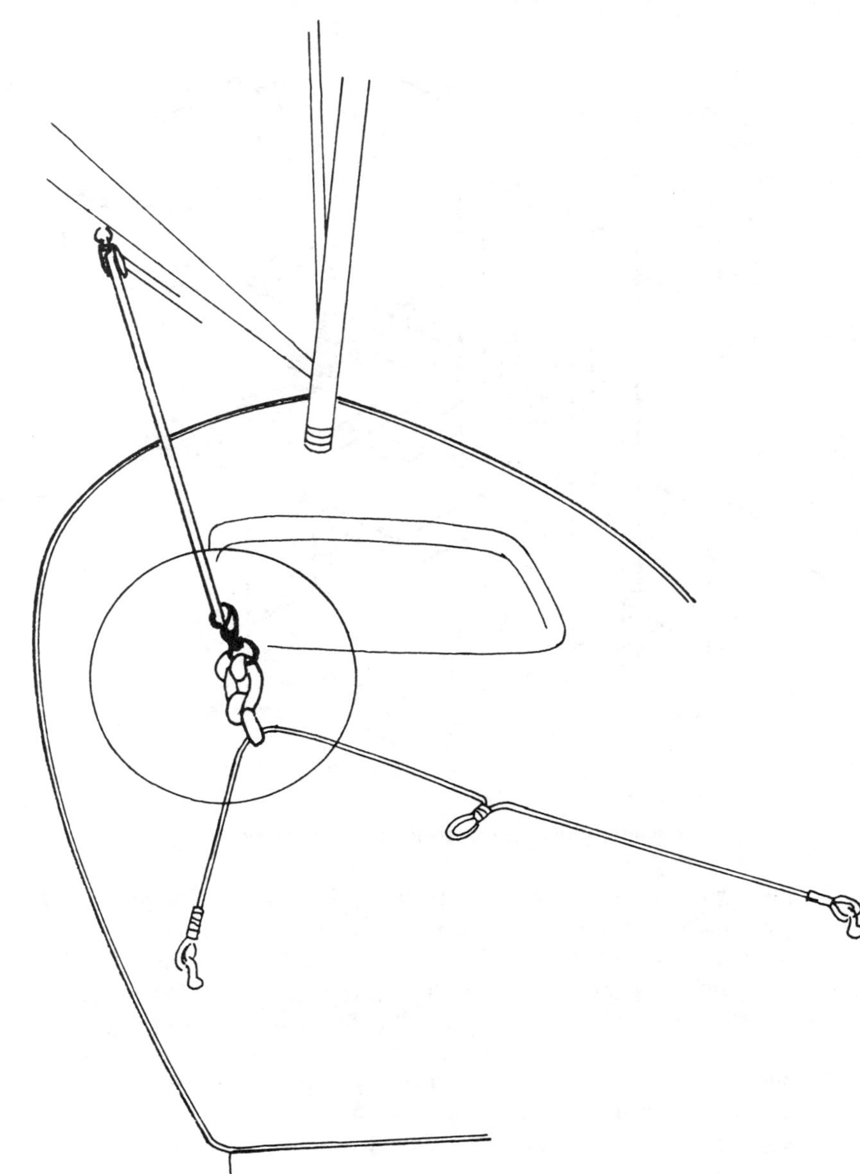

the overpowering ones. I can recall tacking to weather of Ken Klein in the '70 World's and being elated that I ate out to weather of him. All of a sudden, Ken, who used the Hoyt Effect, was footing off to leeward, holding the boat level and there he was, tacking and crossing my bow on port.

Now, regardless of gimmicks there is only one way to go upwind – flat. The Sunfish must be sailed level. Only in very light airs may you permit the boat to heel in either direction and that is only to improve the sail shape and should not be done in flat seas. My friend and son, Sam, will get increasingly tired of the cry from his father "sit forward". You should really steer this boat from the centerboard trunk. Sit forward. Sail it flat.

The main error most of us make in going to weather is holding the boat too high on the wind. Pinching is a sin. The boat wants to sail free. Particularly if you are sailing in a sea, don't pinch. My major mistake in sailing today is the naive belief that I can physically horse the boat upwind higher than anybody. All I achieve is leeway and the footer keeps the boat level, makes more forward yards and ends up ahead. Even in 10-knot breezes I am learning not to muscle the boat higher when a puff comes. I let out the sheet enough to keep the boat flat, rather than feathering up in the puff. Then I gradually pull in the sheet and sail up through the puff, the key being to keep the boat balanced flat.

When sailing in a seaway, sail up on the face of the wave, drive off the back and then up the next front. In essence sail a scalloped course keeping the boat driving.

When the breezes are really heavy, I have had superior results with raising the board a few inches, letting the sheet out and footing off.

We have mentioned tell tales before. Again, keep your eye on the fly. Most of us don't sense lifts as quickly as we should. The tell tales indicate lifts much more promptly than most of us mortals can recognize one. A header is more easily seen by the fact that the sail begins to shiver, but the lift is tougher.

While on your way upwind, watch out for wind interference. If someone comes across on port, encourage him to pass you, not tack below and give you backwind. If someone tacks on your wind, tack away immediately. Don't wait.

Don't play lay lines. You almost can never win by going out to the lay line early in the windward leg. Why? If a lifting shift occurs you have overstood. If a heading shift appears you have to tack again and the boats on the opposite tack are now coming across being lifted. If you are behind, the boats will

Plans for Hiking Bench constructed of 2x10 and 2x4 timbers

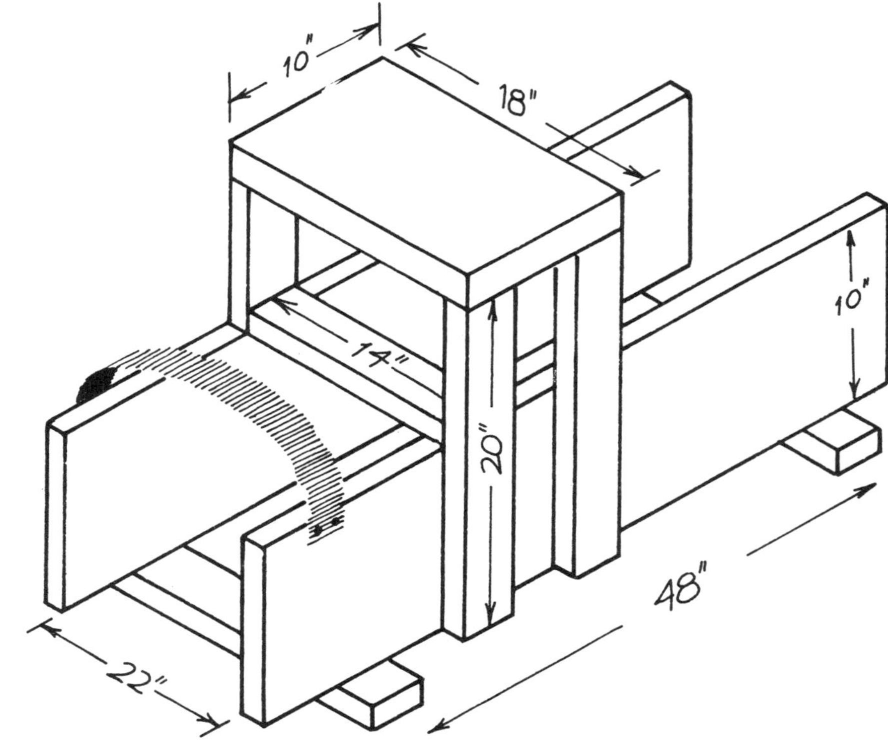

come in and tack on your air as people tend to gradually overstand the closer they get to the mark for fear of having someone else tack on their air. Only in very steady breezes can you afford to go to the lay line early. Usually you should approach a mark on port. You have clearer air. You can tack under an overstander or on top of an understander. Only with a long line of starboard boats are you in trouble and even then you can usually dart under a stern, proceed a length or two and then boom out on their quarters as they pinch for the mark.

Finally, don't overlook concentration, confidence and competitiveness. If you concentrate on the sail or tell tale and have the confidence that your boat is well tuned, you should stay right in there. What happens to me when I am sailing in Bruder/Hoyt company is that I am not awfully sure I can hold them boat for boat, even if I have tactical superiority. I split with them looking over my shoulder and gradually, after tacking on the shifts, they have worn me down.

There is no reason for this attitude. If I can sail 20 or 30 yards equally with them, I should be able to sail a whole course with them. I think this spirit should pervade everybody; the lack of it, the lack of confidence, competitiveness and then concentration when near a class hot shot, is far more damaging than a slow boat.

REACHING

If any of you wonders why the kids flock to Hawaii in quest of good surf, I can now answer the question. Sailing a Sunfish on the literally downhill reach at Puerto Azul, site of the '71 World's, was one of the most exhilarating sports activities I have ever experienced.

Even though these are extreme conditions, there are some basic principles to be learned all the same. This is the point of sail where the most yardage is to be gained or lost. Tactics are important as is a knowledge of the rules, but probably the technique of making the boat go fast is more important. Let's sail a typical reach, assuming you are entering it from a weather mark.

First, you must plan the reach as you are approaching the windward mark. If you are behind and there is a cluster of boats ahead, plan to bear off immediately upon rounding the mark to sail low on the leg. It's a good bet that boats in a group will gradually go high of the direct line to the next mark. This is the cardinal sin of this point of sail. Stay low.

Also if you do happen to have someone right on your tail, bear off immediately upon rounding the weather mark before he reaches it; discourage him from going off. Remember once you are both on the same leg of the course, Rule 39 prohibits you from bearing off if a boat within three lengths is steering a course to pass you to leeward; you bear off first, before he rounds the mark, and this keeps him high.

How many times have I rounded, pulled up the board, bailed a couple of times, adjusted the sheets and settled into the reach only to find someone has come from astern, taken my wind and pulled over me? Your first job when rounding the mark is to get on a plane; do your housekeeping later.

If you can quickly get on a plane, the course be damned. Naturally, if you can you should bear off when you have speed and come up when you are slowing; but planing gains so much yardage over other boats not on one that you can afford to carry the plane almost to where it takes you and then come back.

How do you get on the plane? Rule 60 has never been invoked in my years of sailing; at least in planing conditions. Therefore, I believe you can ooch, which is bouncing forward on the wave face and jerking the boat down the front of the wave and then moving back to keep the nose out of the water. I say you can pump, which is frequent rapid trimming of the sail. This jerks the bow out of the water and initiates the plane. And I say you can rock, which achieves the same thing, breaking surface friction. Whether once on a plane you can continue in this pumping, ooching and rocking status is a real question.

I have never seen protests lodged against people who pump, ooch or rock while on a plane because the defense is pretty easy – they were just coming off the plane and had to go to these exertions on the new set of waves to get back planing again. Awfully hard to prove someone is wrong in this circumstance.

That's how you get on the plane. Make sure you keep your bow parallel to the water; that means going forward when you are headed down the face of the wave and back when you are headed up; don't sit so far back that your nose begins to come up. This creates much more drag because of the increased wetted surface at the stern. Sit in the middle, keep the boat level, and pump like hell.

But whatever you do, when you get that puff, give your sail a little pump, maybe even come up a little to get your speed up, and then bear off and run with the new breeze. Then come back up in the lulls, off in the puffs, etc. Nowhere is the Manfred Curry maxim of up in the lulls and off in the puffs more important than in reaching in oscillating winds. As long as you keep your air clear, follow this rule all the way down the reaching leg.

If you are in very light conditions there are other techniques to employ; these will be covered in the chapter on running.

There is the type of reach which is maddening to many sailors, known as the one leg beat. The object on a close reach is to be ahead and to leeward. Then, whichever way the wind switches you gain. If the wind stays steady then occasionally the boat out on your weather quarter may fetch whatever mark you are seeking and you will have to take a short hitch; but usually, be ahead and to leeward.

Now we are almost at the end of our reach. We have held low and we are closing with the rest of the group. Size up the rounding situation. Are you going to get the inside overlap? If so, hail the outside yachts that you are overlapped and that you will require room. If they are ahead but are approaching the mark at an angle which permits you the overlap, keep going.

If, however, you are ahead of them, slow down enough to maintain the overlap certainly, but the best tactical position you can have rounding the reaching mark and heading for the leeward mark is to be slightly ahead and to weather. This is even more true when rounding the leeward mark.

If you have not achieved the overlap, keep going. Don't give up. Sometimes boats ahead slow down when they get within 10 lengths or so and do a little housekeeping preparatory to the next leg; you can occasionally get the overlap at the last legal minute.

However, if you are not going to get the room, slow down, watch the situation. Regularly in large fleets money is made on the "slow down and win" principle. In a crowd, be the first or last at the reaching mark. As many boats get involved that turning circle gets wider and wider and sometimes a lively hole appears right at the mark for the crafty opportunist to drive into.

So far we have been talking about steady breezes and planing conditions. Shifty airs present a more challenging and interesting reaching condition. First and most important, look for puffs. The Long Island Sound premise of reach to the new breeze is paramount to fast off-wind sailing. Being to weather in a shifting wind is preferable to staying low. Sometimes the wind swings forward and you are blanketing the leeward boat. Also the boat to weather gets the new breeze first.

Remember, then:

Keep your air clear.
Plan the reach ahead of time.
Stay low.
Up in the lulls, off in the puffs.
Look for opportunities at marks.
Concentrate.
Pump, ooch and rock to get on that plane.
Sail the boat flat.

RUNNING

The greatest downwind sailor in small boats today is Jeorg Bruder. Studying him in binoculars spectators say he moves about in the boat at least twice as much as most of the regular Sunfish sailors, squeezing every last inch out of the waves and puffs.

In contrast, I sail downwind in big seas and heavy winds with the basic intent of avoiding a capsize. This is not winning sailing. In a screamer, downwind work is frightening, but if you remember two principles things will become easier for you. If you sit to weather, as your normal tendency might be, you don't balance too well on this point of sail and sometimes begin the death roll. If you think you are going to capsize to weather, haul in the sheet; amazingly, you will come up level. I am convinced that the fastest course downwind in a breeze is just this – a succession of near windward capsizes. I don't have quite the courage to practice this regularly.

The other basic idea is to sail the boat level and frequently by the lee depending on the wave formation. The sail does develop a nicer shape when it is by the lee.

The slowest point of sail is dead downwind. Some sharp sailors have luck in jibing downwind. I have sailed at least 1,000 races in the last few years. I have almost never seen jibing downwind pay – mainly because Sunfish courses are so short.

Don't misunderstand, I have seen people hold low and be the last one to jibe over and ultimately gain ground, but jibing out of a fleet and jibing back? Rarely. Just stay in the parade – low if you can, playing the puffs as on a reach, watch your masthead fly, keep your air clear.

Wave riding off wind is important. Remember that wave crests are moving at as much as 20 knots, so get on the face of a wave and do everything you can to stay there. Your sail may luff but that isn't important. When the sail luffs keep playing it, this is certainly legal even though you are surfing, since you are adjusting for the natural action of the wind and waves.

Some of the best people are able to ooch the boat forward to take advantage of the last few yards of the wave face. As the boat begins to slow, through the wave running out from under you, throw yourself forward a couple of times and sometimes the stern picks up and you can get right back on the wave again and keep planing.

There are times when you go faster than the wave, usually because you are not going straight down it. If that is so, slow up by putting down the board or sitting aft a little so that you can stay on the wave. The key is to stay on the wave because if you move out ahead of it you go into a trough and it is hard to get back onto even the next wave.

Naturally, pumping, rocking and ooching are critical to promote surfing. Look behind you; when you see the wave approaching, move quickly forward, get the stern out of the water and when the wave catches you, sit as far forward as you can and not broach.

The trouble with the Sunfish downwind is that the rudder is not deep enough and the boat becomes extremely hard to

Ted Moore, second World Champion

steer dead before the wind. I try to sail across the wind as much as possible, still following the puffs down.

The Sunfish has broaching troubles. The way to eliminate them is to balance the boat so that you are precariously close to nose diving, but can shift your weight aft, even jump on the stern to keep the bow out. Sail a little by the lee too.

If you start broaching, bounce on the stern, steer up and when the bow comes out of the water like a whale, bear sharply off, otherwise you will keep coming up and substantially lose your course, and maybe capsize.

In light air it is a different game – one of patience and cunning. Really, you want to keep your sails full and driving. Remember the drawing on page 61. It shows the halyard being tied to the tack. Pulling on the halyard while sitting to windward keeps the sails cocked up, full, while still reducing wetted surface. Keep the board up as much as you can and still be able to steer. Do not pull the board out of the trunk; you are asking for increased drag due to water entering the trunk.

You might consider pulling up the rudder and trailing it at the ready but not in the water. This is particularly true and valuable when there are weedy conditions. Experiment with the tension on the rudder. You should be able to pop it free of the latch plate simply by banging the tiller down on the deck.

Make sure you are alert to conditions of tide, and current. Needless to say downwind sailing which is slow to begin with is even more deadly when you are in an adverse current. If you can, stay to the side of the course and reach over to the mark at the last minute.

Just remember that everyone is going relatively slowly downwind, and if you can take advantage of angles and sail a scalloped, reaching course, your chances of gaining distance are good.

TEAM RACING

Team racing is the most rewarding of all sailboat racing efforts. It brings out the character and quality in all of us. It requires an intimate knowledge of the rules and the most encompassing application of tactics in yacht racing. It is a sport in which old slow grey heads can excel against the young bucks with boat speed.

Basically, team racing is a contest between two groups of equal numbers of boats, usually four or five. The object is simply to place your boats across the finish line in a sequence which will give you fewer aggregate points than the other team. Twenty seven is the maximum low point total required in a five boat team race; 18 in a four boat race. On the water it is easier to add low points than to remember the combinations. We won't delve into mathematical computations here, but needless to say placing 1,2 does not insure a win in five boat racing. Team balance such as in a 3,4,5,7,8 is more important. You might tape the list of winning combinations to your boat.

It is rare that anyone agrees on starting techniques let alone regularly executes them. However, we have had astonishing success by assigning positions along the line – one man as the hatchet at the starboard end cutting off bargers and the rest spread out. If each man knows his place and sticks to it during a series, a pattern begins to form and teamwork is maximized.

Freelancing is frequently used. This theory usually implies that you are a team with superior speed. After the start you should be ahead and each man then sits on an opponent. This method is similar to man-for-man coverage in basketball as opposed to zone defense.

If the line favors the port end, one of the favorite tactics of Chuck and Teddy Moore is to luff the opponent nearest the pin to the point where Teddy can get a port tack start. In team racing a quarter point bonus is paid for a first place and it is even more important than to try to spring a fast sailor clear.

Another favorite trick against a team with two or three very strong sailors is for your slowest men to tail the hot shots of the other team away from the line or to luff them over the line prematurely.

Once out on the course the object is to stay in contact with the opponents. It is all well and good to sail fast but the wind does funny things. Leads of 100 yards evaporate quickly in a 45 degree wind shift. Generally speaking you should cover both sides of the course. Man-to-man coverage is important, but not to the point of inflexibility.

Passing an opponent from one teammate to another makes sense. As an example, teammate A is on starboard, crossing teammate B sailing on port. B is covering opponent C, also on port. C tacks to break the cover and B lets him go as A is already on the same tack.

Communication is extremely important on the water. You must talk to each other; and if you think the Venezuelans don't have an advantage when they scheme in Spanish you have one more think coming.

Upwind the most effective tactic is to blanket an opponent. The rules now permit sailing down on an enemy as long as you don't touch him. Another effective maneuver is to sail a dangerous man past the lay line. In team racing there is no proper course requirement on an upwind leg. There is therefore no requirement that a boat on another's weather quarter tack for the mark until both have overstood and it is safe to go for it. Remember, however, when you are jockeying against a boat on another leg of the course, you must sail a course considered proper for your own leg.

The weather mark presents good opportunities to help break some teammates through. As mentioned you can stay on a yacht's weather quarter until your teammates have rounded. If you are inside boat and have luffing rights, you may sail on past the required side of the mark without ever laying off for the next mark. And naturally if you are outside boat with luffing rights and hail outside two boat lengths, you can take an overlapping boat on the wrong side of the mark. This is very effective due to its surprise element. While this stipulation is a part of the regular rules of racing it is very seldom used because you usually are more concerned with the fleet rather than a single man.

Reaching and running afford many opportunities to hold opponents off to the betterment of teammates. The same mark rounding rules apply as on weather legs. Luffing head to wind is a tactic frequently used. Remember the creed, however: yacht racing is a sport of gentlemen. The object is not, and never should be, to touch another yacht out of the race. There is no fun in sailing against undermanned teams. It requires more skill to interfere legally with another yacht than it does to foul out someone.

Both upwind and downwind finishes are exciting in team racing. Always assess the point score before crossing. It is a relatively easy trick on an upwind finish to wait for an opponent and blanket him in hopes of slipping a teammate through. It is somewhat more difficult and therefore more challenging to help out on a downwind finish.

If you foul out, withdraw promptly. I have known only one sailor who felt he stayed in a race and made money even with his four point penalty. It is almost an impossibility.

Most team races which end in ties are resolved in scoring by beaten teams (if both of us lost one race but I beat you and lost to some other team which lost more than once, then I win). But sometimes they are settled by total points in the series. It is all the more important to be unselfish and sacrifice one's own position if it is to the ultimate advantage of the team.

At Darien we run off more than 75 team races a weekend during the Nationals. Identification of the boats is achieved either through colored shirts for the competitors, pennants on the leeches of the sails or decals on the Sunfish on the sail. Naturally, courses tend to get cluttered with that many boats. It is unlikely that other classes will face the complex problem, but if they do, they might consider the uniquely modified Gold Cup course which got groups off to the side for their second beat and downwind finish.

Team racing truly adds a new dimension to sailing. Lots of team races on short courses really sharpen up your techniques and tactical senses. We believe that in a few years team racing will be a part of many major singlehand regattas.

FROSTBITING

Most of my business friends are now thoroughly convinced that I am absolutely out of my mind. To give up the comforts of Sunday afternoon in front of the TV set? To miss the delights of the neighborhood saloon? Or how can your wife let you go on winter Sundays when she knows full well no work will get done around the house come spring? And then for what? To sit for two or three hours with your tail dragging in freezing water, slush forming in the cockpit and spray turning your cheeks to icicles? Oh what fun.

And I nod contentedly to myself. I have something to achieve each Sunday afternoon. I can race my boat. The pleasures of winter sailing far exceed the discomforts, and unless you capsize, the discomforts are really minimal.

Traditionally frostbite sailing is done in Interclubs, Penguins or Dyers. Only in recent years has the Sunfish gained in popularity as a frostbite boat. The objection to the boat used to be that you were so close to the water when you sat on the deck. The idea was that for a winter boat you needed a high freeboard. Now people have come to recognize that it is exactly because of the high sides that the traditional dinghies are not proper frostbite boats. How many times have you seen a capsized Dyer get up and sail the same day? Usually they are towed home half submerged, incurring some breakage along the way. Conversely the Sunfish pops right up, permitting its skipper to sail again immediately – if he hasn't congealed.

Further, the normal dinghy just doesn't sail in 20 knot breezes. I know there are some exceptions, but generally speaking the dinghies cannot go in much over 20. On the protected waters where most frostbite races are sailed, it takes 30 knots to blow out a Sunfish race. Indeed, Sunfish are even raced in conditions of 35-50 when waters are warmer. The Sunfish is a far more stable boat and has much more speed than the traditional boat. It has even made inroads as the frostbite boat used in Narragansett Bay, which is very much dinghy country.

Riverside Yacht Club in Connecticut is one of the more formal yacht clubs in the East. It was with some trepidation that the club management permitted the Sunfish to be raced with the Dyers. In deference to the seniority of the Dyer they still start the slower boat first.

Commodore Emeritus Clifton Hipkins has said repeatedly that the Sunfish has emerged as the best frostbite boat on the Sound. The numbers of dinghy sailors switching to the Sunfish are increasing each year.

Now that you are sailing the right boat you had better dress properly. If I know we are going to get a sea, I wear a one piece foul weather suit, but with sweat pants and shirt over it so that I do not slide unnecessarily. The best garment would be a wet suit. Usually, however, I wear my long underwear, pants, shirts and sweaters so that I have mobility.

I think the best gloves are rubber coated work gloves. Most people find that in the excitement of racing they don't wear gloves and just put them on in the interval between races.

Bob Bowles came up with a good idea for keeping the feet warm. He uses a thin pair of socks over which he slips a plastic sandwich bag. Another pair of socks and Topsider boots complete the outfit. I find boots cumbersome and just use a pair of Topsider moccasins.

A Navy watch cap is good headgear and a turtle neck sweater is in order when there is a good breeze.

With this gear I stay warm and find that I never have any problems with the weather.

Most well organized clubs will not go without two crash boats, which is quite important. Frequently two boats will go over under a particularly vicious puff and you need two rescue vessels. The best rule has it that should a boat capsize, the race is immediately called off and everyone goes to the scene of the accident. There is some debate about this. I have never seen a sailor who is behind in the race deliberately capsize so that his series standing won't be impaired but I really wouldn't put it past some of us.

Usually frostbite races operate under two minute starts. This works so well I wonder why we don't go this route for racing other times of the year. Frostbite courses are usually quite short and that's fun. Long races in a Sunfish test other skills but lots of short races are really more rewarding because of the greater intellectual challenge. You get much more expert in application of rules and tactics when you have so many more opportunities to practice.

People wondered at the great improvement in the American group in 1970. One of the reasons I am sure is because we race so many short courses that our starting techniques have sharpened up; we are learning to get away in clear air.

We store our boats in the open at Riverside on lovely cradles right on the dock. It is a first class situation. You should put on a boat cover. Don't leave sails, boards, rudders on the boat during the week for obvious reasons. If you do not have a cover, put a tennis ball in the mast well. Chopping out a solid tube of ice from the trunk when your competitors are milling about on the starting line is not one of the things I like about frostbiting. A cover prevents ice from forming in the cockpit. If it does, however, you can easily get it out if you are neat and a little patient. Pour some hot water around the edges and then chip with a hammer and screwdriver in a straight line away from an edge. The whole block will usually fall apart in two pieces. Make sure you drain your boat after every day. Don't let ice form inside during the week. Take the extra trouble to fresh water rinse after each sail.

Winter sailing really is glorious. You are outside in fresh air, competing fairly with decent people. You are active, stimulated by the excitement of the challenge. And after the boats are put away, you can still get a little bit of that neighborhood saloon bit in too. I think it's a lot more fun than watching Namath and his cast walking up and down the sidelines. And now there is Monday night football anyway.

MAINTENANCE

The joy of having the boat surge underneath you, literally bouncing over the waves, is something else again. And it is in recollection of the buoyancy that the knowledge that you are being both outpointed and outfooted becomes such a sickening feeling. Many times the trouble does not lie with the skipper but with the boat itself – you may be leaking. It is amazing to me that Alcort is able to mass produce so many boats and have so few that leak. But ultimately after long use, these constructions will leak.

Naturally you should regularly check for water. If any develops here is what to do.

Mix a solution of one part water to one part detergent – really sudsy. Get a couple of pieces of scotch tape. Use one to tape over the air vent in the front wall of the cockpit. Open the drain plug and blow in hard several times. When you think you have built up good pressure, tape over the drain plug.

Now slowly draw a paint brush loaded with soap suds over the danger parts of the boat:

All along the aluminum edging
The mast trunk
The daggerboard trunk
The rudder assembly

If you have a leak, the suds will bubble up. Still no bubbles? Keep going.

Inside the cockpit where the deck joins the tub
All the screw holes
Under the rudder latch
At the bow

You should have found any leak by now. But if you haven't inspect the actual bottom of the boat, sometimes hairline fractures develop which go unnoticed on a cursory inspection.

Once you have located the troubles, repairs are pretty easy, thanks to the miracles of epoxy resins. Chuck is the expert in this field. After teaching ninety kids each summer at Wequaquet Lake Yacht Club, where the main sport for the young is to sink the other kids, he learned to repair boats or he would not have had any classes the next day.

He advises the following:

Before you repair any part, make sure it is clean.

If the leak is in the mast trunk at the lip, rout around the lip and fill in with epoxy. Actually he uses Marine Tex which applies beautifully and sands better, but is expensive. Any epoxy will do.

If your problem is at the bottom of the trunk, pour a liquid epoxy, such as offered by Sears in its marine department, into the bottom of the well. Make sure the boat is level and the resin will settle evenly.

The daggerboard trunk should be treated in the same fashion, routing out the damaged area and filling with Marine Tex. A little wet sanding and you are in business.

Marine Tex the area around the trim if a leak has developed there.

The time will come when some intrepid port tacker will try to take out his frustrations on you and stick his bow through your side. If you can make it ashore you will be all right and back sailing the next day.

First, sand around the hole and remove all loose pieces of gelcoat. Make the hole large enough to work with.

Then cut out a piece of cardboard an inch larger than the hole in the boat. Also cut a matching piece of fiberglass cloth.

Put a piece of string a foot long through a hole in the center of the cardboard and fiberglass cloth. Tie a knot at the end of the line opposite the cloth.

Mix epoxy resin and paint the cloth, bonding it to the cardboard. Put the cloth and cardboard inside the hole, drawing this patch to the hull with the other end of the string. Fit the patch to the hull. Tie the string to any heavy object by the side of the boat in order to maintain pressure while the resin hardens. Once the epoxy solidifies, cut the string, and fill the depression with a filler such as Marine Tex. Paste or tape a piece of clear polyethylene tape over the entire patch and smooth it with a putty knife, wiping off the squeezings which seep under the tape. The result will be a nice smooth patch almost not requiring sanding, and one which can easily be painted over.

As mentioned, the rivets occasionally pop loose and they are easily fixed by drilling a new hole and using the pop rivet gun to insert new rivets.

Those of you who trail the boats regularly will ultimately have the problem of the cockpit lip beginning to give, showing some tell tale cracks. This can be reinforced by use of a piece of 1½ inch cardboard tube cut in half in 24 inch strips. Bond pieces of fiberglass cloth to the tube with epoxy. These pieces should be six inches wide. The boat should be placed upside down and level. Place the tube with the cloth to the underside of the lip, with the semicircle of the tube facing the lip. Let this cure and the reinforcement will work.

Just keep checking regularly for water. It must appear at some time and when it does you can rest in confidence that you can repair the leaks.

DO'S AND DON'TS

Sunfish sailors are usually relatively new to the sport. Yachting is one of the most exacting of all athletic endeavors in regard to ethics and character. Over the years we have embarrassed ourselves with foolish, ungentlemanly actions and seen other people make similar errors of judgment.

We are going to attempt in a few words to describe the type of person whom we would like to sail with, and who will be invited by all clubs to join in their activities.

Do enjoy yourself; don't make the sport so competitive that you lose sight of the fact that it is a game.

Do sail by the rules; don't violate the rules to the extent that you could not tell your son what you did on the race course.

Do protest when you have been fouled by someone trying to take deliberate advantage of the situation; don't be protest-happy and protest any and all comers regardless of the nature of the foul or the outcome of the series.

Do drop out when you have fouled; don't wait hoping that good hearted or soft hearted Joe won't protest you or that the race committee will miraculously throw out all protests.

Speak kindly to your competitors on the water; don't scream at a beginner to get out of your way and maybe lose a potential competitor forever.

DO SAIL IT FLAT.

REGATTA CHECKLIST

You must have:

Sail	Boat	Rudder	Board
Sheet	Mast	Spars	Halyard
Life jacket	Rudder pin	Bailing plug, marble gasket	

You really should not be without:

Tell tales	Bailer	Sponge	Boots
Sweat shirts	Gloves	Topsiders	Hat
Sweat pants	Detergent	Rule book	Appéals
Foul weather gear			

And in your tool box:

Pop rivet gun	Marine Tex	Extra yard	Cap nuts
S Hook	Rubber bands	Hammer	No. 10 wire
Screw driver	Tape	Pliers	Knife
Hand drill	Bits	Screws and bolts	
Wet sand paper	Silicone seal	Extra outhaul line	
Tape measure	Extra sail sets	Telephone, toll money	

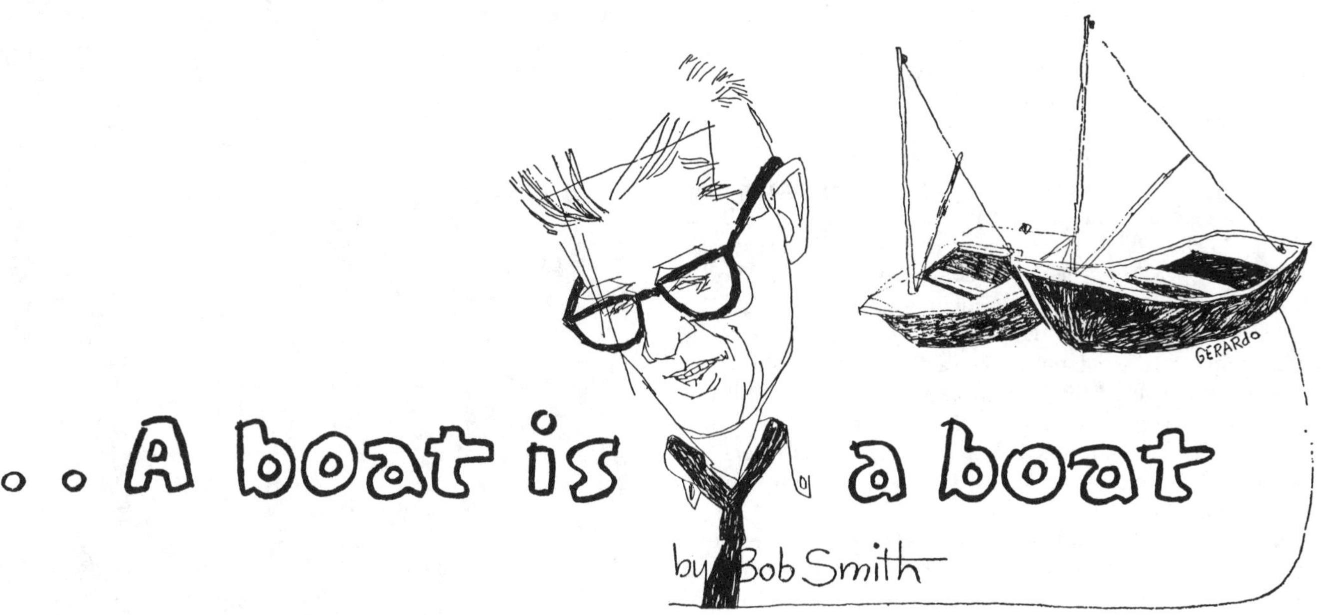

The Portable Den Father Meets the Sunfish Class

PHOTOGRAPHS BY SUE CUMMINGS

ANY sign of a new concept in yacht design in our colony scares Square-Rigged Ronald silly. Status, tradition and harbor decoration seems to be his only reason for dabbling in yachting. This shouldn't be a bother except that too many Ronalds too often are running the show. Even this wouldn't be awful if the hat-wearing admirals would make some effort to learn that yacht racing does not belong to a chosen few and that our grandfathers were not as advanced in yacht design as is our modern generation. Well, "a snap of the fingers" to them as we watch the "new" yachtsmen chew them up to weather and plane past them downwind.

The reason I feel so strongly about this right now, is because the Old Man of The Sea was plunged up to the navel into one of our new concepts, not only in yacht design, but in every facet of the sport. The following is a glowing example of the portable boat, portable yacht club, portable races and race courses that is becoming so popular—and everyone, regardless of income, age, sex, size, etc., is welcome to

The Darien Sunfish Yacht Racing Association's mobile yacht club

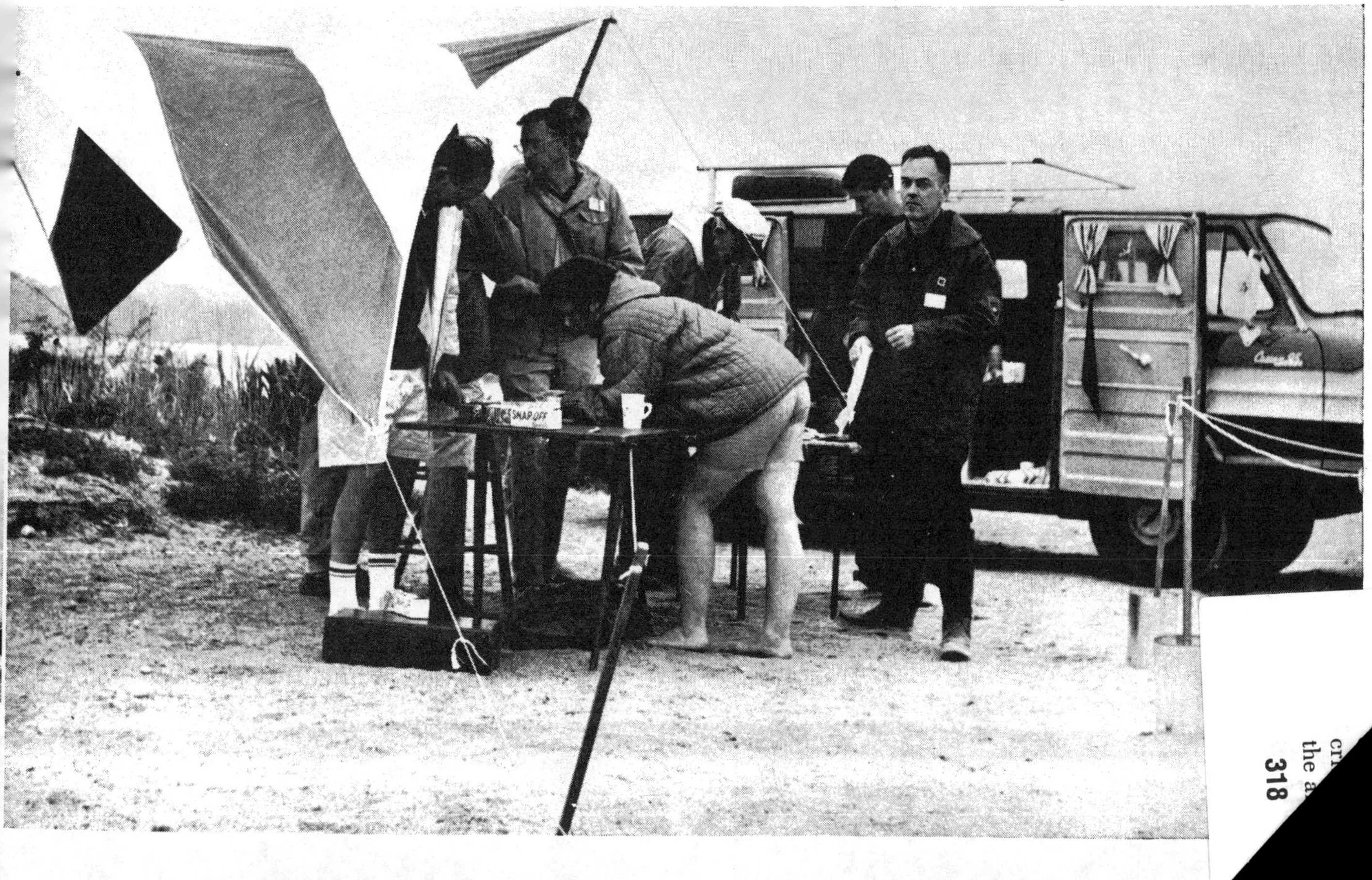

join. Most of all they have a wall to wall ball. Teenagers would say, "it's real delicatessen".

Last winter, during all those terrible days and nights escaping from the schussers, yoompers, slalomers and shivering snowy hill sliders and their expensive aboriginal fun, we were invited to participate in the Invitational *Sunfish* Team Race Matches. The regatta, sponsored by the Darien *Sunfish* Yacht Racing Association was to be held on May 22 and 23 in Noroton Bay, Connecticut.

Twelve teams of five boats each were invited from the four points of the compass. One of the invited bastions was the Noroton Yacht Club, just stuffed to the scuppers with superior tiller wigglers and of which I am a back-dues-paying-member. Needless-to-say, with my having the only real reason to sail this unique regatta, I was chosen team boss, dean, commodore, captain and baby sitter.

Realizing that I had never been aboard a *Sunfish* or a *Sailfish* before and had little hope of correcting it before the starting guns started, it appeared smart to pick an experienced team. The result of increasing the Telephone Company stock dividend by plenty, I ended up with the most talented, itinerant, motley crew of helmsmen it was possible to imagine. We had one powerful, burning thing in common—none of us had ever been aboard a *Sunfish*.

The Noroton Yacht Club team consisted of: 1-Kevin Jaffee; Sears Cup Winner, Starboater, extraverted vagabond and man-about-town. 2-Robbie Lansing; crew on anything available and a "nifty helmsman first class". 3-Jack Ritchey; big boat skipper, crew and cook with a fabulous America's Cup Defense in a *Dyer D* behind him. 4-Mark Smith, North American *Class B* Multihull Champion, a virtuoso on a tiller and a guitar and Young Man of the Sea. 5-The sheep dog of the fleet—me. Backing up this determined band of "phytin phools" was our alternate, 114 lbs. of future champion. All of 13 years old, Casey Nickerson is one of the "most" in all respects.

Howard Hill, the local Alcort dealer, supplied five brand new yachts, plus sails, plus all equipment that John Black Lee, regatta chairman, personally uncrated and rigged. Without their co-operation, our mad adventure would have been a mess.

Right now let me compliment the Alcort Company on the way in which it packs its boats. Not one piece was missing, scratched or damaged on all five boats—not even a 12 inch piece of 1/8 inch line. I wish however, the company would get rid of the cotton line that Columbus used and replace it with a soft synthetic. It shouldn't change the corporate financial structure. It is a wasteful shame to see most *Sunfish* owners throw the cotton lines away—immediately.

I did get a chance to wet my fanny. After the boats were rigged at the Noroton Y.C. we sailed them about one-half mile around the corner to the regatta location. This small sample made us realize that a night's sleep would contribute greatly toward our ability to single-hand this bomb the next day . . . particularly if the weather was hard.

BEFORE we start racing, let's first look at the area and the club. Darien, Conn., on Long Island Sound, is roughly equidistant between Milford, Conn. to the East and Bayside, N.Y. to the west. This puddle is one of the most active, most competitive yacht racing areas in the world today. With ideal deep sheltered waters of sufficient size for yachts of all breeds and a large population in the higher income brack-·ts, sailboats multiply like hamsters. The most vociferous ·'tics of Long Island Sound winds are the locals. Actually ·ea has a wide variety of weather patterns plus enough

"Storm" King—O-DY's winner of the free-for-all race

of a tidal problem to have developed some of the finest yacht racing men. The history of American yachting is well decorated with names from this area.

Back in the late 40's, in the midst of a glittering array of super tiller mechanics and posh yacht clubs, a small group of neophytes bought a few *Sailfish* in which to hack around. Racing was furthest from their collective minds. By 1958 a few *Sunfish* also made their appearance and some very casual "brushing" began to take place—something like this: *Sailfish*—"I'll race you to the girl in the Bikini." *Sunfish*—"Naw, let's race to the beer on that rock". *Sailfish*—"Chicken?"

As the beer might get warm and the girl in the Bikini might have another date next week, the ring leaders led by Dick Webb, Tom Jones and Boo Forster decided to organize. With the addition of some refugees from the *Star* Class and a few other classes in 1961, meetings were held and the racing became more formal. In late 1962 the Darien Sunfish Yacht Racing Association was chartered by Alcort.

The amazing fact about this refreshing saga of yacht racing fun was its success without a plot of ground or a club house. Headquarters is one of those Ford or Chevrolet or Volkswagon busses belonging to a member that not only houses all the racing equipment and records but plenty of coffee, doughnuts, coke and beer for participants. In addition, any light outboard acts as committee boat. For this regatta, permission was obtained to park the "Yacht Club" on

Noroton YC's "phytin phools," led by Den Father Smith

the town public beach. It works on any beach or waterfront area where small yachts can be floated. With considerate and appreciative treatment of the facilities by the competitors, this group has made itself welcome all over the neighborhood—and their "club house" goes along.

The operation is not unique as mobile clubs and yacht racing to match are springing up all over the country, on beaches, lakes, rivers, reservoirs and large rain puddles. All that is needed is a boat that is easily launched without facilities and enthusiastic interested people. The Darien *Sunfish* Club has all of the ingredients and is growing rapidly.

With the history stuff taken care of before even one beer was consumed, we prepared, as usual, for the long trek to the regatta. Loading Sue's "station wagon is a station wagon is a station wagon" with a change of clothes, a camera and sunburn lotion, we blasted off on Saturday morning and arrived 15 minutes later. We could sure use more of this.

What greeted us was a most colorful sight and most heartwarming to anyone interested in the growth of sailing as a national sport. On the beach were almost 60 *Sunfish* with multicolored sails that made a mardi-gras look drab. While signing up, etc., I was told that the entry list was illuminated with most of the top *Sunfish* skippers in the business. Among them were Dave Davies, present National Champion, Bob Bushnell, winner in Puerto Rico, John Lee, local champ, Bill King, *O-DY's* gift (not returnable) to *Sunfish* and many others breathing fire down their collective lifevests.

My limited experience with team racing consisted of two teams racing three or five races. I have never experienced a program as ambitious as this one. There were 12 teams (five boats each) that were to race against each other once during the two-day jamboree. This meant that one team would race against 11 others in individual races. Flights were set up to start six races of 10 starters each, three minutes apart, with a dinghy verbal count-down technique in force. After the 12 teams completed one flight around the course, new pairings were in effect and the next flight would start until a total of 11 flights were completed—66 races in all.

The Race Committee made up of Bob Bennett (Chairman), Jim Knight, Ted Rogers and Dick Webb (Regatta Chairman was John Lee) and Commodore Skip Cook ran the show in a really professional manner, with precision and without foul-ups. I was truly impressed by the knowledge and skill exhibited by this committee on a really difficult task. I have seen so called experts, from big yacht clubs, butcher a six boat, one race schedule.

To top it all off, sort of a one-for-the road free-for-all race (individual winner) was scheduled, making the grand total 67 races in two days.

THE RACING

Now comes the kicks. Our team decided on a racing strategy that was as imaginative as a Borgia inventing a new cocktail. We immediately eliminated man to man coverage before the race started as this method went out with corsets. Instead we figured out a loose zone defense that had the fluid mobility of an octopus. The key is to control the start and rapidly pick up the most likely opponent just thereafter. Also be prepared to switch for the benefit of the team. In a short race it works as we were able to spring one of our team into first place immediately, nine out of 11 times.

As I said, the key is to control the start and here is how we worked it. Jack Ritchey, an expert in dinghy racing and a genius at the weather end of any line, was given the job of "hatchet man" or "hammer" if you like the term better. In every race, regardless of which end of the start was favored, he was to legally drive all bargers, even slight, into the committee boat at the weather end. In one race he got two and his record of efficiency was around 11 for the regatta, not counting all the boats that had to start in a heavy dose of backwind.

Mark and Robbie were to take the center and just go-go. The skillful "tiger on the line" Jaffee and Machiavellian Smith were to hit the leeward end (coffin corner) and shut the door to all little lambs with that port tack start look in their limpid eyes—and there were plenty. It was like shooting fish in a barrel. Man, it worked like a charm all the time except once when we got too cocky with the champs and "botched" the whole job like as if we never raced before.

Our first match, fortunately, was against one of the weaker teams, so while winning, we learned a bit about how to sail this windblown shingle. The air was fairly light (0 to 10) for two days so the learning came quickly. The matches progressed until we had three wins and no losses (first four places in two races and first five in the third race) and a race with the favorites on deck. It all seemed so easy to this point that we got cocky and just simply "blew it". Both Kevin and yours truly were way over the line at the gun. We weren't forced over, we plumbered it. During our tardy return, Mark, with the best start of all, thought the committee had recalled him too—so he came back. There it was, as you can't put three of your team in last place and beat the hot team. They beat us by nine points.

At this point Jack Ritchey had to leave for home so Casey Nickerson jumped into Jack's boat, jumped into the lead and went over the horizon. Every now and then we would hear in the distance, "Is this the next mark?" He won by a mile. In fact we finished that one with 1-2-3-4-5. When the committee called it a day we stood tied for second with two other teams at four wins and one lost. The Darien Blue Team was ahead with 5 and 0.

On Sunday morning we won our opening match and had coming up, our contest with the defending champions from Greenwich—led by "Storm at Sea" Bill King, *O-DY's Sunfish* expert of note. It was a cliff-hanger but with a strong showing in the middle positions, we managed to eke them out by three points (2-3-4-8-9). The next stiff test was against the Chelsea, N.Y. team led by national champion Dave Davies. We won it handily and went on to finish the regatta with a 10 won, one lost record that landed us in second place behind the undefeated Darien Blue Team. Chelsea was third.

The free-for-all was like running a track meet in a New

York Subway during rush hour. However it was a beautiful sight of kaleidoscopic color when this mass of *Sunfish* funneled through the starting gate. The race was short, close and was decided in the last 10 inches as Bill King decided to go-for-broke on port tack to beat Bob (starboard) Bennett by millimeters right at the finish line for the prize he won last year, too. I picked my way through the mob for a satisfying fifth place and a beer won from Davies who finished sixth.

One more comment. The party at the home of Mr. and Mrs. Tom Jones on Saturday night was as nautical, as much fun and as informative, from the yachting point of view as any I have attended in many fancy yacht clubs. This is a great crew of enthusiastic yachtsmen, ranging in age from 15 to 60. I'd like to pay special tribute to all the gals who worked so hard with Mrs. Jones to feed us hungry sailors a wonderful meal and provide us with such an enjoyable evening.

Turn page

It's a "hot" colorful yacht

A BOAT'S A BOAT

Continued

THE CLASS

The *Sunfish* Class has grown to staggering proportions since its initial contact with the public in 1953. There is no question in my mind that with 30,000 units sold all over the world, and another 5,000 ordered in 1965, numerically it is the largest one-design class in existence today. As owners increase and more and more of them realize that a yacht race is more day sailing fun than just tacking around the bay, competition will continue to grow at breakneck speed. It has already achieved international status.

We have repeated many times in our examination of boats and class organizations that success can be attributed as much to the quality of a class racing association as to the qualities of the yacht itself. While there is a real need in our public yachting picture for the *Sunfish*, The Alcort Company, hierarchy of the class, has supplied the organization so necessary and stimulating to its growth.

The personal enthusiasm and foresight of Alex Bryan, Cort Heyniger and Bruce Connolly, the company brass, has resulted in an example of member communication that is a milestone in our yachting world and in the boating industry. Not only does Alcort control, with an iron hand, the one-design features of their yacht but it has come up with an additional set of rules covering the future of the boat in official competition that is so simple it fills only one typewritten sheet. In spite of their simplicity, these rules are hard to "beat". This obviously encourages the neophytes at the expense of the experts as it stimulates one's desire to sail better rather than speed up the boat on shore with knowledge that might take much longer to acquire. This is diametrically opposed to the volumes of rules and loopholes (still to be found) existing in the *Lightning*, *Star* and many other established "one-design" classes today. In fact, control of this type is only possible in a *well run* captive class (in the hands of one builder).

It is the Alcort Company that numbers and measures boats, charters fleets, makes top-level rule decisions and takes care of the gigantic job of all printed matter required to maintain close member relations. In addition to publicizing all regatta information and schedules, they supply the prizes at reduced rates, tips on how to organize a *Sunfish* regatta and a local racing organization, tips on how to sail the boat, tips on how to sail it faster, gift equipment and literally anything and everything that comes under the heading of more enjoyment and better participation for a *Sunfish* owner. Nobody "gets lost" and nobody is neglected. The job done by this company is the best I have ever seen. Other boat builders should take a good look at this operation — but remember, a *feeble* attempt at the same idea can produce a mess and nothing else.

All this costs money and takes professional help. I don't know of any more rewarding way to spend part of an advertising budget and I am yet to see better dollar return anywhere. As we all know, a *happy* boat owner is the best salesman for the builder.

It isn't free however, as a new member is charged (only once) the astronomical sum of $3.00 for the works and for the duration of his participation in the class Alcort starts the whole ball of wax from the "laying of the *Sunfish* keel" to the follow up job of seeing to it that customers enjoy them.

THE BOAT

The 13′ 10″ *Sunfish* was designed by the Alcort Company as an addition to its already popular *Sailfish* and *Super-Sailfish*. In my opinion it is much more boat than the difference in price suggests. In fact, the *Sunfish* becomes a sailboat rather than a wind propelled surf-board.

While the lateen type rig used on this yacht is open to much criticism there are enough offsetting good points to quiet them. With no wire stays or shrouds it is extremely easy to rig and de-rig. Its lower heeling moment gives the yacht more stability than its 48½″ of beam would have with a conventional cat sail.

The *Sunfish* is much drier than I would ever have believed before sailing it (I said "drier", not "dry").

There is no doubt that the boat is fast in a breeze and planes like a surf board. There is also no doubt in my mind that she is relatively not fast in light conditions. I think this is the penalty paid for the lateen rig and its low sail plan. Like playing chess, the boat is easy as pie to sail but difficult to sail well. The trim of the sail is extremely critical and the tendency to over-trim it accompanies any experienced helmsman as he tries to make the transition from another boat.

The sail always looked like it was trimmed for reaching rather than beating on the weather legs. An examination of the angle relationship of the very long (as long as the boat) boom and the thrust line of the narrow boat should correct the impression but it still *looks* wrong.

The *Sunfish* is very sensitive to the amount of weight placed aboard. There is no doubt that the lighter the weight the more the "go". Any good average size skipper single handing this flying saucer, should beat one with a crew aboard in all conditions. In fact, as the yacht becomes more and more involved in keen competition and as more helmsmen become interested, weight aboard will be the most important single contribution to winning.

There are two obvious corrections that should be made in the boat. The first and most important is to correct the vibrating chattering centerboard, evident in all of our five new boats and in most of the others. This should be done by the factory immediately if the company plans to cater to the beginner, as it should. While an experienced racing man in any centerboard class knows the brake-like effect this has on the boats' speed, the beginner does not. One of the competitors told me that he knew he was going fast when the centerboard sounded like a pneumatic hammer. He was aghast when I told him what was really happening.

The other correction involves convenient handling from shore to water and back, one of the most important selling points of the boat. In addition to the fine handle on the bow that is standard equipment, two more should be added, one on each side of the stern. If the factory doesn't do it, owners should, for their own convenience and back muscles.

This is one yacht that is famous for its self-rescuing ability. The fact that a capsize means nothing more than a wetting during a warm summer's fun is most appealing to beginners. Regardless of what it is that sells this boat, the entire yachting community of the U.S. owes the *Sunfish* and the *Sailfish* a tremendous debt. These little puddle jumpers, board boats or anything you want to call them, have led more people to the fun of sailing than any boat in the history of the sport. They will continue to do so. ◘

Severi Photos

Tuning to Win
Part I:

THE SUNFISH

BY ROBERT JOHNSTONE

With this article O-D & OY *begins a new series on the tuning of one-design racing boats. Top sailors in the major racing classes will present their current detailed knowledge of how to win the boats they know best. Each article will offer the latest in-depth knowledge regarding the nuances of "tuning to win" in top competition. This is not a series on the elements of tuning but, rather, an advanced course in honing particular boats.*

This month Robert Johnstone describes the tuning techniques that have helped him to win in the Sunfish. Mr. Johnstone, twice Sears Cup finalist (in 1950 and 1951) has won the Venezuelan Sunfish title in both 1965 and 1966.

TUNING a boat is half psychological and half "go fast" from a towing tank standpoint. The problem is to determine which half is which. I believe this is particularly true of a Sunfish which is somewhat short of sail area.

The psychological benefits result from eliminating all the factors which, by the wildest stretch of the imagination, might cause your boat to go a fraction of a knot slower. You then arrive at a freedom for concentration during a race, a feeling of being "one" with your craft, and an assurance that no one else's boat has had more TLC aimed at one purpose —*to win.*

This philosophy and work paid off in six consecutive Venezuelan national regattas during 1965 and 1966 to the degree of 24 firsts in 36 starts among fleets ranging from 20 to 40 Sunfish.

Three more firsts were lost due to momentary distractions: (a) my wife was headed for the wrong mark and I lost six boats shouting across 100 yards of ocean trying to tell her about it; (b) I thought my mainsheet was going to part in a 25-knot wind and I blew a 250-yard lead, and (c) I paused to wonder why a competitor with an odd shaped sail was doing so well and eight boats filed past.

Hull

The workmanship and quality control at Alcort is generally excellent, but the interior finish of the daggerboard trunk is rough. The deck and bottom overlap edges scratch the board. A smooth interior can be achieved, without narrowing the trunk, by filling in the rough sections with fiberglass patching compound

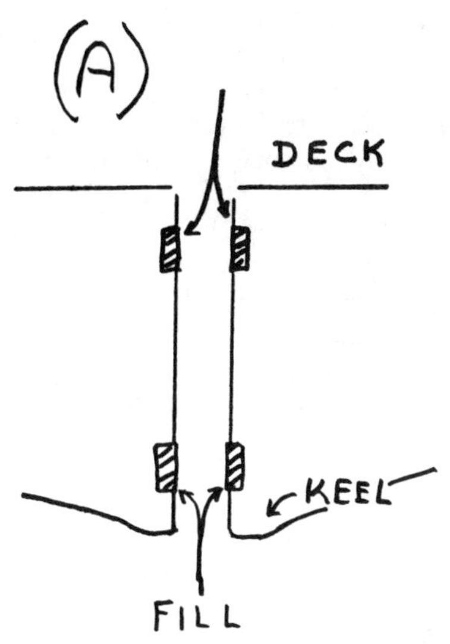

and then sanding. This seems to stop board chatter as well. See sketch (A).

Frequent simonizing of hull and deck results in a smooth bottom, more resistent to beach scuffing, preservation of original colors, and a deck which allows one to move fast.

Daggerboard and Rudder

By painting the daggerboard and rudder white one is better able to see accumulations of eel grass or lake weed without having to bend over the transom or pull up the board.

Painted lines on the daggerboard marked "Full" (up) and "½" help establish your preferred setting when off the wind. Leave the board in the slot even when dead before the wind. This displaces water, which is heavier, and reduces drag caused by water turbulence in the slot. "Full" up means there is about one inch of the tip protruding below the keel. See sketch (B). The sketch also shows the difference between fore and aft on the board, which can effect trim (lateral resistance). A painted arrow on the top of the board will aid the memory.

A useful gadget which doubles as a safety feature in the event of capsize is a quarter inch line running from a hole in the center of the splash rail to an eyestrap on top of the daggerboard. A figure eight knot is put in the end of the line so that it is long enough for the board to reach the full up position, but not long enough to permit the board to come out, or to become detached from the boat. After some capsizings in a 25-knot blow we lost one boat on a dam and had two near drownings, when, exhausted and burdened with heavy clothing, people tried to retrieve boards which floated away from their boats.

There is some doubt as to the legality of the lanyard described above or any other gear designed to aid in control of the daggerboard. In some areas a wedge is used to hold the board at the desired level, but officially this is not allowed. Also used by many class "hot shots", particularly on the U.S. east coast, is a piece of shock cord which runs from the top of the board to the mast, thus keeping a forward pressure on the board and making it stay wherever it is put.

As in any small, light boat the "feel" of the Sunfish is greatly reduced if play exists in the tiller and rudder assembly; and the tiller should never touch the deck. Lateral movement at the outboard end of the spring plate on the bottom will occur if its screw is loose or if the adjusta-

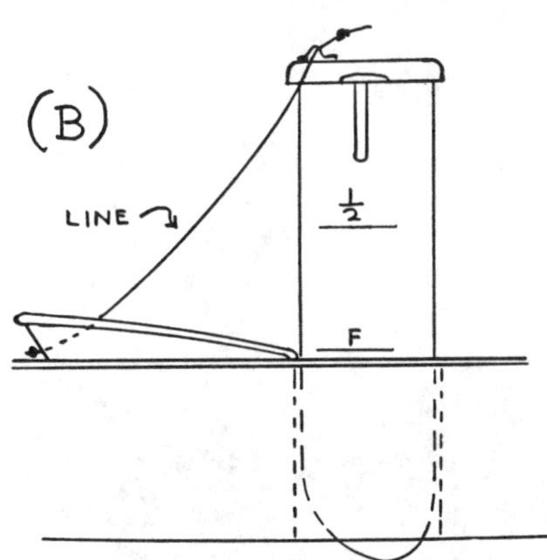

ble wing nut is not set tight. Two leather shims (old belt) placed on either side of the rudder head ahead of the poly pivot washer and under the brass plates securing the tiller, will prevent wobble there. Any play existing in the socket (located in the spring plate on the bottom) for the base of the rudder hinge is stopped by use of a one-inch square of inner tube which is put into the socket first. See sketch (C).

Foreground shows daggerboard floating away from capsized Sunfish. A simple lanyard can eliminate this hazard but is of questionable legality.

A strip of inner tube, wound tightly around the end of the hiking stick, with a whipping over it, provides non-slip, two-finger control. Some prefer an even more positive grip here, such as the standard cross end (which I find too apt to catch in pockets or loose clothing) or use of one of the plastic clips that hold the sail to the spar fastened to the end of the extension with the loop towards the helmsman.

I believe the ideal mainsheet for wear, hands (even with gloves), minimum stretch and no kinks is five-sixteenths Samson type yacht braid. Quarter inch braid on the halyard means you don't have to reset it before the start because of stretch. One-eighth inch braided nylon for the outhaul and peak ties is safer than cotton and easier to untie for adjustments. But you must be sure it is well secured as nylon, especially in smaller sizes, has a habit of untying itself.

The mainsheet snap for the bridle can fly loose in a blow. This should be taped shut or replaced by a knot at the end of the sheet.

The only weak fitting on these boats is the eye bolt holding the upper spar halyard block to the mast. This eye can open up if the boat is sailed hard. Use of a stainless steel substitute for the chromed brass one supplied, or a stainless U bolt with

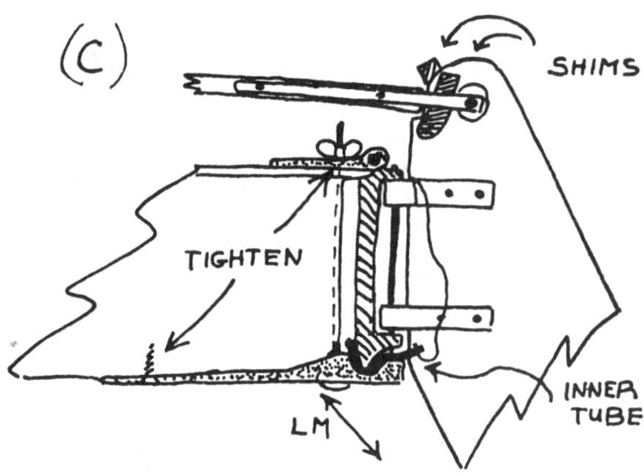

both ends going through the mast is foolproof. Alcort now has a new masthead fitting with a groove through it for the halyard and this gets away from the "opening eye", routine which has been a bother in older boats.

The black plastic tape doesn't keep the gooseneck fitting from sliding aft on the boom and (if the owner isn't careful) eventually ripping the sail. A good way to hold the fitting in place is to use a strip of inner tube wrapped with tension around the boom with the gooseneck fitting clamped over it. More inner tube or white marine tape can be used for a stop to keep the halyard clove hitch from creeping up the spar. Although I have found that the locations specified by Alcort for the gooseneck and clove hitch are just right, there are others who have had success by letting the gooseneck slide. With this method they are able to lower the sail in heavy airs by sliding the halyard up the sprit and moving the gooseneck slightly aft. The whole rig has a tendency to slide forward so a restraining line is used from the gooseneck forward to the end of the boom.

Regulations permit buffing the rough finish on the bailer and rudder spring plate to a high gloss. The base of the bailer projects about one-sixteenth inch from the bottom—an excellent weed catcher. The problem can be solved by transferring the rubber washer to the inside between cockpit floor and bailer assembly nut.

Sails

Foot adjustment seems to be the most critical factor in regulating the sail's draft for varying wind conditions. I keep the sail permanently stretched on the upper spar to the point where no forced wrinkles exist when sailing. To achieve this lash the tack grommet around the boom to ensure maximum length of luff or hoist.

Toward the outboard end of the boom I mark three locations, three, six and nine inches in from the end, for heavy, moderate and drifter winds, respectively. At all locations the foot of the sail is loose enough to scallop while sailing, but the scallops seem to work forward (if the plastic rings are used on the boom) while sailing, to create draft where it is most effective.

Some of the top sailors in the Long Island Sound area use a lacing line along the boom, which they let off to the maximum allowed by the rules (two inches). This gives an almost loose footed effect which is great in light airs or a lumpy sea. Another method often resorted to for getting draft in these basically very flat sails, is to wash them frequently in the washer, with soap. They get soft, and finally develop some draft.

The mainsheet hook on the forward edge of the cockpit should be used, especially in heavy weather. In puffs it will bend the boom and upper spar to flatten the sail, insuring that the wind drives the boat. If one uses the hand to boom method, more arm strain, a tendency to ease the sheet rather than to feather the boat, and a greater healing moment result.

There is a limit, defined by one's ability to hold the boat down and choppy seas, to how far one can go sailing with the main strapped in tight feathering the Sunfish. If wave and wind direction is such that the bow is alternately plunging under or slapping down a wave, ease the main sheet three or four inches and feather from there without change of sheet position. The added speed and driving ability will reduce the healing moment. ◘

The author goes to windward in a blow using the mainsheet hook on the forward edge of the cockpit to bend spars, thus flattening sail.

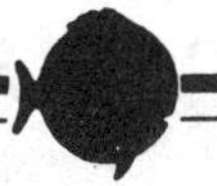

HANDICAPPED SUNFISHING?

By Jim Uroda

Have you ever thought what it would be like to sail a Sunfish using only one leg? Probably not, but, the occasion can arise and actually did happen to me.

Most of us, including myself, know little about the unseen hazards of sailing. There are small organisms called bacteria present in the waters that we sail in that can cause swift and permanent changes to ones lifestyle. The bacteria that affected me are called "Aeromonas". Being an anaerobic bacteria itself doesn't impose a serious threat unless you cut or puncture yourself while participating in salt or fresh water activities.

As an example of what could happen if you should happen to be unlucky enough to come in contact with this bacteria, I will explain what happened to me.

Since I am very active in the sport of sailing, I do many things that put me around the salt water. Last May, I was racing on Galveston Bay in a regatta where we had strong winds throughout the first day. I was wearing my wetsuit because the water is still cool at this time of year. After at least four hours in the high winds and fairly rough conditions, I removed my wetsuit and found an area behind my right knee that had some swelling. The next day, the swelling had disappeared and I thought no more about it. This day's racing was in lighter winds and I finished the regatta with no indications that I was soon to be in deep trouble. I drove the fifty miles to my home, washed up the boat and my truck, put everything away and prepared for work the next day.

Up until about 12:30 a.m. on Monday morning I had no ill effects. At this time, I developed a fever and had chills throughout the night. In the morning, I remained in bed thinking I had the flu. By the third day, I developed cramps in my legs and could barely walk when I went to the local hospital. This was Wednesday and I spent all that night being subjected to numerous tests. Seeing that this was life threatening and the local hospital was unequipped to handle the problem, the doctor sent me to a Houston hospital. On the fifty mile trip in the ambulance I remember some heavy rains, but they were not important since my right thigh had begun to swell and I was really hurting. I will personally attest to the fact that I was hurting so much during this time that I didn't care whether I lived or died from the ordeal. I again went through a number of tests and by midnight, Friday morning, I was taken into the operating room and remained there until 5 a.m. Originally, the doctors believed they could save the leg, but as time went on my vital signs diminished and my wife had to give permission for them to remove my leg. Since the infection was so high up on the leg, it was necessary to remove it to the hip to be sure of getting all of the infected area.

For the next four days, I was sent into the hyperbaric oxygen chamber twice a day to breath pure oxygen. Since this was an anaerobic bacteria, this procedure was necessary to purify my blood system. Each day they washed the area with a water pic and only then did they sew it up.

I spent three weeks in the hospital and another three weeks in a rehabilitation hospital. I was trained in "rehab" for a new way of life while the healing was taking place. It took some time to regain my strength and finish the healing process so that I could begin the process of learning to wear a prosthesis.

By the first of September, I was able to enter the water again and began racing my Sunfish again at this time. I needed this practice so that I could determine if I would be able to attend the Southwest Sunfish Regionals at the Houston Yacht Club during the middle of September. I did so and had a respectable finish. I continued to attend regattas and local events until the middle of November. I am definitely looking forward toward next season.

Now that I have reduced my weight from 195 to 160 pounds, the boat seems to be moving faster. I have been using the Jens rig in the higher winds, but hope to go back to the standard rig in 1991. I haven't had the experience of turning over since my accident, so I don't know how hard it will be to right my boat. I always wear a life jacket now. My good leg gets a little tired occasionally when the winds are high, but the only real problem I notice is that I have a tendency to roll out of the boat. I've got to hold on a little tighter now and try to avoid these conditions so I can't sail as aggressively as I use to. The "following" sea is my greatest enemy now because of this problem.

I definitely have to mention that the Sunfish sailors have been very helpful to me, putting my boat in and out of the water so that I might sail in these events. Although I am afraid that this help may diminish somewhat if I start beating them on the course.

In summary, I would like to say that the caring and help of all those involved in getting me back to a normal life has been immense. I wake up every day looking forward to whatever comes along, good or bad. Of the options that were available to me, I consider that I got the best of the deal. And for you sailors out there, please take note of the symptoms that I described. There are antibiotics that can defeat these bacteria if they can be diagnosed soon enough. Although this is only one of the bacteria present in the waters we spend time in, some don't give you much time before they can cause some serious problems. So if you are in doubt, see a doctor as soon as possible for any unexplained illness. Since my love for the Sunfish and just plain sailing is in my blood you may see this one-legged sailor in your regatta someday. If so, come over and say "hello".

As Jim Uroda's story proves, the physically challenged can and do race Sunfish.

In the early days there were a couple of deaf Sunfish sailors on Long Island Sound. They competed regularly in major regattas, and did very well. Other sailors took care to help them with the starts, giving them hand signals for the sound signals they couldn't hear. One of them was also mute; when we heard a roar and a loud thumping on the deck, we knew he was calling for room at the mark.

One of the best known of the challenged is Norm Castle of Florida, who has only one arm. He still competes regularly, and often successfully in lighter winds. He doesn't ascribe his poorer heavy-air showings to his handicap, however. Like most us old-timers, he says he is just showing his age.

At the World Championship in the Bahamas in 1988, he finished second in one of the light-air races. His joy was infectious; the competitors voted overwhelmingly to award this happy warrior the sportsmanship trophy for the regatta.

Will White

Sunfish Worlds

By Jack Knights

THERE is only one "largest sailing class" in the world. It is the Sunfish and at 75,000 now, and growing by one every 10 minutes, it is so far ahead of anything else as to be practically out of sight.

My mistake was in thinking that the Sunfish was not so much a racing boat as an adjunct to seaside holidays, rather like beachballs and suntan lotion. I was sustained in this belief by the thought that the world championship to which I was winging, on the island of St. Thomas in the Virgin Islands, in the middle of the Caribbean, was the very first to be held by the class. I wasn't at the yacht club at St. Thomas very long before the truth dawned . . . there are very many keen skippers, in both the United States and the Caribbean, who take their Sunfish racing very seriously indeed. Among the 57 entries were fanatics from Connecticut who frostbite them all year around. The trials to pick the St. Thomas team (entries were limited to eight per country) were long drawn out and hard fought. The Sunfish it appears, provides the hottest racing in Puerto Rico, Venezuela, Aruba, Martinique, Antigua and Tortola.

Rudy Thompson the yachting powerhouse of St. Thomas organized the regatta, invited the contestants, found many of them boats and competed himself with much verve. The pity of it was that the fresh SE trades proved a bit too much for his slight frame so that he missed his ambition of making the top 10—he was not alone in that. Rudy, by the way, skippered the U.S. Virgins FD at Acapulco.

There were several other Olympic skippers there and one of them, Garry Hoyt, an American advertising executive from Puerto Rico won the series with comfort. The ease of his victory was not entirely of his own making. Though his tactics and technique were as good as anybody's, there were times, particularly during the long, three race second day, when Brazil's Jeorg Bruder, that terribly strong Finn sailor, was clearly outpowering him. Bruder scored a second and two firsts on that one day. His undoing was the committees. The protest committee heaved him out of the final race at the weather mark, where they shouted he had been disqualified for an early start. Since Bruder had been surrounded by boats at this start he was unhappy that he, almost alone, had been singled out and he got the protest committee working on his problem, with the aim of forcing a resail. Though debate was long, this never came about and Bruder found himself down to 10th overall. He had scarcely had time to receive his award when it was revealed that he should have been given one more point for his disqualification, whereupon he fell to 11th and out of the prizes and his humilitation was complete. This brought certain of the Americans (not to mention their wives) a certain satisfaction, for Bruder was not a Sunfish owner but an invited expert from outside the family and there was a firm, if unspoken, resolve to show that the owners were not going to be pushovers for any "big shot" from some other class.

". . . cooled by the lukewarm deep blue sea . . . tanned by the subtropic sun . . . tempered by trade wind clouds."

Second place took these class loyalists quite by surprise. Few could have heard of the island from which he came—Tortola. And sizing up Englishman Mike Shaw, beforehand—tough, fit, sinewy, but hardly more than 145 pounds from top to toe—few gave him a chance in the hard going. But Mike Shaw is a very special person, one of a sailing family. His father is currently commodore of a leading British dinghy club. His brother sails for his university and his sister sails as well as she sews and sews so well that she made Mike the sails which drove him across the Atlantic, to Tortola (some 18 miles from St. Thomas) in the 26-foot double-ender which he built himself.

Mike once had a Tempest in which he was fourth in the worlds in the U.S. He later sold this in Puerto Rico making a singlehanded delivery trip with spinnaker at close to 10 knots. Since then he has been concentrating on his Sunfish racing, often sailing over to St. Thomas for better competition. In the worlds his best result was his opening fourth. Then followed a 10th, two fifths, a seventh and a final fifth and second place was his. He said he owed it all to the sopping heap of assorted rummage sale items he wore around his torso, but others did the same thing without such success. (It hadn't occurred to me that a 75 square footer

Garry Hoyt of Puerto Rico sailed his worst race, an eighth, right away, then had two firsts, two thirds, a second . . and the series.

Jeorg Bruder of Brazil, above, two-time U.S. national champion in Finns, was the only person with a chance to beat Hoyt by the last race. But he was declared over the line early and disqualified for the second time in the regatta. Meanwhile, Mike Shaw of Tortola, left, one of the lightest men racing, moved into second, without once finishing above fourth, or below 10th. Chuck Millican of Plymouth, Mass. was third, and the highest finisher among the sailors from the U.S. mainland.

would ever require such aids). Wh really brought him home second w. his pertinacity. Time and again I gained places on the final beats of th Olympic courses.

Third place went to the popular, up and-coming American, Chuck Millican who now works for Alcort of Water bury, Conn., makers of the Sunfish. Af ter winning the first race he tailed of unaccountably, finishing with a 13th and 12th. Then came Ken Klein, firs of the locals and the Finn representa tive for the U.S. Virgin Islands a Acapulco.

Your humble correspondent was a lowly 23rd. Not only did I make the mistake of thinking the series would be a piece of cake, but I didn't give myself enough time to acclimatize so that I shivered when others sweated and when, in the harder winds I began to find the combination, my rudder fell off, or, rather, fell up, in not one but two races. (Both times when fourth.) But by the end of the regatta I had learned a thing or two about these beguiling craft.

The Sunfish must be the strictest one-design boat of all. Not only are the hulls and sails and spars all from the same sources and the other gear too, but the only extra item of gear permitted is one jam cleat. No other rope bit or piece, save for those which come with the boat may be used. And in spite of the inefficiency of the self draining device, this too must be in position. The lug sail is an Isoceles triangle, set on a short tubular mast, the boom being linked to the mast by a figure of eight fitting of bronze, which clamps to the boom and slides over the mast.

The hull, 13 foot 10 inches long, of "cods head, mackerel tail" form broad abreast the mast and tapering to the stern, weighs something over 100 pounds. The total weight is 140 pounds. It has a flat bottom, wall topsides and generous longitudinal rocker to the keel. The hull is double skinned, surprisingly watertight (there is a small metal drain plug in one side deck) with a small foot well just aft of amidships with the slot for the dagger board just forward of it. The rudder (undersized, like the centerboard) attaches by a devilish bronze contrivance of which more anon. The simple mainsheet clips into the center of a wire bridle aft, leads over two minute blocks under the boom (which have to be used), then to hand, through most skippers fit a center jam cleat amidships just ahead of the foot well. No toe straps are fitted or allowed.

Since the sail seems to be cut completely flat and sheetlike and has no battens, it is necessary to attach it to yard and boom very slackly so that there are loose scallops between each eyelet. The sail is nowadays attached by nylon clips but some still prefer lacing. In the first race, I had my sail pulled out far too tightly, which apart from anything else, overtightens the leech.

The sail was intended to be set high up on the mast with a big clearance between deck and boom. The experts, even the heavy ones, now prefer to set it much lower, tying the halyard to the yard at least six or six and a half eyelets from the peak of the sail. Since the rig is so low to begin with I had reasoned that it would pay to set it high to get above the blanketing effect of the waves. But I was wrong. Setting it lower means that it is attached more firmly to the mast because the top of the mast is nearer the top of the sail and so there is less bend or sag to leeward at the top and less "wash out". Lowering the sail also has the effect of moving the center of effort of the sail further forward. And there is hardly a sailing boat in the world which doesn't seem to go better for having its sail plan moved a bit towards the bow.

Another thing . . . the yard was intended to be nearly vertical with the boom inclined steeply upwards towards the clew. The experts now prefer to have the boom about parallel with the deck with the yard falling back much more. To encourage this, the figure of eight clamp is loosened and moved back along the boom so that more sail pokes out ahead of the mast.

On one tack of course, the mast is the wrong side of the sail (to leeward of it) and apparently dividing the wind flow and thus ruining the proper aerofoil curve. One of the mysteries is how little this appears to affect performance. Anyway, nearly everybody appears to set the sail to port of the mast so that everybody is less efficient on the same tack—the port tack. Lighter people say that the boat is easier to hold up on the tack with the mast to leeward. It is as if the sail is reefed. Jeorg Bruder swears he went faster on this tack than the other, but this may have been a comparative matter.

It is fatally easy to oversheet the sail. The clew must always be let well off over the lee side. This is mostly because the centerboard and rudder blade are so small and the hull's underbody so flat that the leeway angle is very pronounced. If one tries to pinch up—eat out to windward like a 5.5-Meter—the board immediately stalls, the flow over its leading edge breaks down and the boat proceeds to slide off sideways in the most amazing manner. It is therefore essential to keep the little craft footing, powering down to leeward, holding it as flat as possible and easing the sheet when needed.

Current North American Champion Carl Knight, No. 14863 *has the windward start above. Below, double trouble at the mark.*

Lighter skippers will find that if, instead of clipping their mainsheets to the center loop of the wire bridle, they clip it over the port hand wire, they will go much better on starboard tack without suffering at all on port (the so-called 'reefed' tack). On port the clip will slide and stay amidships but on the more powerful starboard tack, with the mast to windward, the clip will be able to slide down to leeward and help the sail set flatter and better.

Reference was made above to the flow over the centerboard breaking down. It does seem essential to take pains to see that the leading edge of the board is as rounded and as smooth as possible. (One is not allowed to alter the cross sectional shape but one may rub down lightly with wet and dry and dress the surface with Helmsman Graphspeed or a similar preparation). Some people such as the St. Thomas expert, Dick Griffin, prefer to fit the centerboard back to front with the straighter edge leading. I would have thought it better to have the curved edge forward as intended, with the center of lateral resistance further aft.

Because the afterbody is so narrow and unbuoyant it is important to keep one's weight well forward. Most hike by tucking their feet under the lips at the front of the foot well and on the lee side. The absence of any hiking straps only benefits those who need them least, for light weight usually goes with shorter stature and shorter legs. Youngsters having dug their feet under the lee cockpit lip, find they have hardly any rump over the weather rail at all. Toe loops fitted on the centerline would make things fairer all around.

The Sunfish, because of its compactness, lightness and most of all because of its flat underbody, is a wonderful surfer. We had some marvellous wave riding in Cowpet Bay. The boat remained under much better control than

would have Finns in the same circumstances and by the same comparison, jibing was always child's play. They plane well on a beam reach too and here, of course, a light skipper begins at last to come into his own. Mike Shaw made many places on each planing leg. Strangely, heavyweights, so long as they knew the ropes, were as fast as lightweights when surfing. What is more, the heavyweights, coming to the upwind mark first, had the cleanest and best waves for surfing. Thus Bruder, Hoyt and others usually gained distance on the lighter people following on the surfing legs.

I don't think there can be a better boat in the world for the sheer fun of wave riding. The Sunfish is so "chuckable", so eager, so forgiving and so responsive.

On a square run it has one vice—a heavy helm. This is because of the broad forward sections and the slim stern and is only augmented by the smallness of the rudder blade. The best cure is to heel the hull to weather. Otherwise the 10 or more degrees of helm which is constantly needed must sap about 20 per cent of the boat's speed.

Rudy Thompson's job virtually ended by the time the regatta began. For he was the promoter. Race organization fell upon the St. Thomas YC, headed by Race Chairman John Wiggins, augmented by a small band from Alcort and their parent company, AMF, with Alex Bryan (the Al in Alcort, and one of two originators of the boat, much in evidence).

Olympic courses were laid out in the semi sheltered Cowpet Bay with an expert from St. Croix to lay the usually excellent line (he fell down badly on the final day). Race procedure was as lax as the usual American club event, which is to say that it was laxer than it should have been for a world championship. There was for instance, no signal to indicate port or starboard hand courses. John Wiggins shouted through a bullhorn instead. Races were never begun at the advertised times, neither were proper postponements signalled. Early in the six race, three day series there was no doubt that some early starters were allowed to go free with the result that some of the less scrupulous began to regularly barge the line. At last, at the start of the final race, when the committee boat had been moored too close to the shore so that the line was poorly angled there had to be two general recalls and even then some were over in the third start, not all of whom were apprehended.

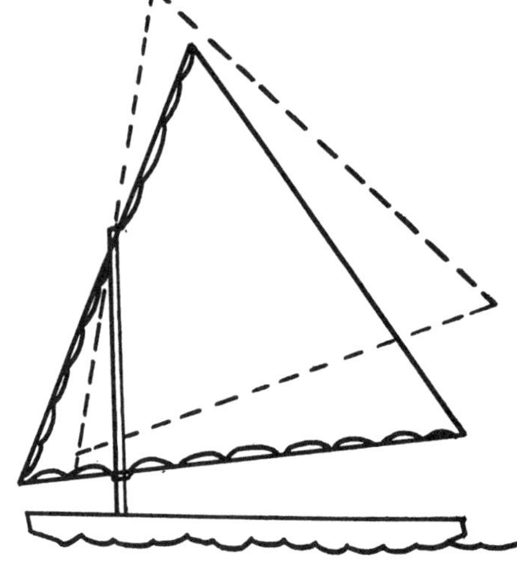

Solid line shows how sail should be set—low and well forward, and only loosely attached to the spars. Dotted line shows the old, higher set of the sail.

A spare nylon sail clip can easily be fitted to the end of the tiller to give helmsman a hand hold. The one shown is screwed into the tiller on both sides.

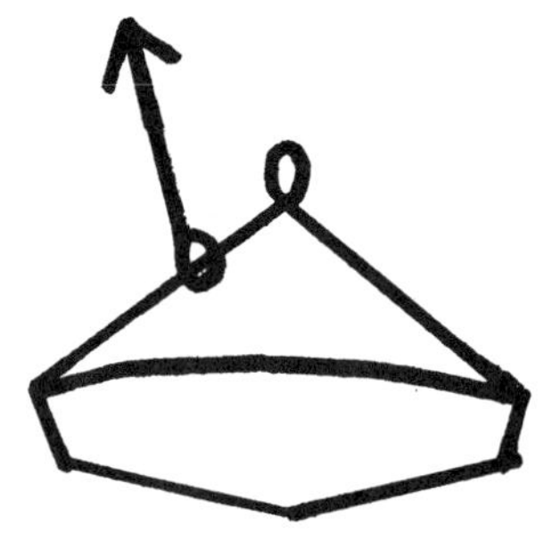

In heavy weather instead of clipping mainsheet to eye in center of bridle, clip it over port end of wire to help boom go out further on powerful starboard tack.

Some of the keener Americans, including their current champion, Carl Knight, began to murmer that the rules were not being strictly observed—and they were right. Yet with boats as small as these and with a fair proportion of the fleet not rule perfect, and others accustomed to a large measure of give and take, I think that some common sense and tolerance was necessary. Carl Knight retired from at least three races and appeared unhappy that others didn't follow his example. But most of us had come for a sail in the sunshine, not a teach-in on the rules. With boats weighing 140 pounds—less than their skippers—situations change so quickly it is exceedingly difficult to establish the facts of borderline situations. I do not believe that America's Cup style punctiliousness is either necessary, desirable, or even possible. Just as serious as rule abuses was the noisy habit of one or two Americans of shouting their way around marks, telling others how to keep clear of them.

It seems unbelievable to me that the world's largest sailing class has no properly constituted owners' association. The owners rely instead on the manufacturer.

The owners should take the initiative, and draw up their own class rules, stating in black and white what is permitted and what isn't. Corrector weights should be fitted to light boats. They should corrdinate fixture lists and get themselves recognized by national authorities. They could also bring pressure to bear for such needed reforms as a better rudder hanging than the current Bronze Age relic, a more effective self bailer, deeper, glass fiber centerboard, bigger rudder blade, hiking straps (all of which could be standard to new boats and easily fitted at small expense to existing boats).

The Sunfish offers almost infinite possibilities. As was demonstrated at St. Thomas, here is a boat so one-design and simple that skippers can fly to the venue happy in the knowledge that their hired or borrowed boat will be completely competitive. Most rented a brand new boat from the local dealer for $100. I understand that most of these were resold even before the end of the regatta.

Regatta Chairman Rudy Thompson organized ashore and raced to a 12th afloat.

I have always believed that the smaller the boat the better the sport. What matters more than the weapons, so to speak, are the location and the competition. This regatta brought together the very best sailors, from nearly all classes in the Caribbean. It was fascinating to race against big Dutchmen from Aruba, excitable Spaniards from Venezuela, philosophic Englishmen and colonials from Antigua and Tortola, insular Frenchmen from Martinique and those GO GO Americans.

And make no mistake . . . this was first and last a FUN regatta. Trade wind sailing is the best in the world. Here we were amid beautiful islands with steady Southeasters averaging about 17 knots, cooled by the lukewarm deep blue sea, tanned by the subtropic sun which was always tempered by those majestic trade wind clouds. Between and after races, Don Q came over from Puerto Rico to supply limitless Rum Daiquiries and there were parties every night. With a tidal rise and fall of 18 inches mooring meant hauling the little boats six feet up the golden beach. The Yacht Club of St. Thomas is one of those immediately likeable, open-arms institutions, buzzing with chatter and children.

After this who need a keelboat or indeed anything costing more than $600 dollars?

Alex Bryan, the 'Al' in Alcort, announced the winners

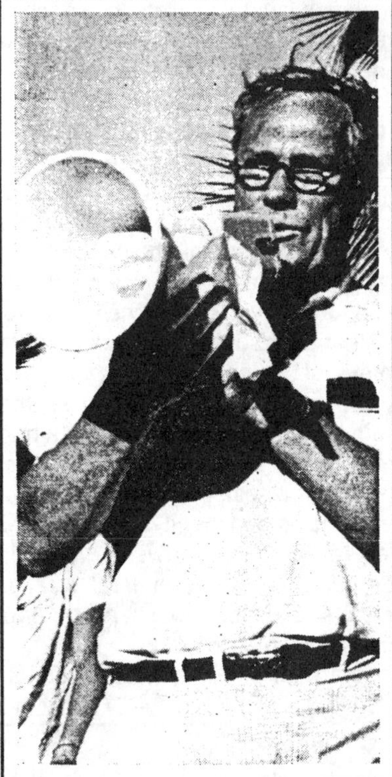

SUNFISH WORLDS
57 Entries

1.	Garry Hoyt	Puerto Rico	8-3-1-2-3-1	9½
2.	Mike Shaw	Tortola, British Virgin Islands	4-10-5-5-7-5	26
3.	Chuck Millican	U.S.	1-4-6-13-12-6	28¾
4.	Ken Klein	St. Thomas	33-9-3-3-4-12	31
5.	Larry Lewis	U.S.	7-17-8-7-5-10	37
6.	Dick Griffin	St. Thomas	14-1-12-9-24-2	37¾
7.	Bill Gleason	Puerto Rico	15-2-13-4-11-Wd	45
8.	R. Foster	St. Thomas	2-8-14-10-13-Wd	47
9.	Bill Bowles	U.S.	16-13-16-12-14-3	58
10.	A. Andrew	St. Thomas	24-15-22-11-6-14	68
11.	Jeorg Bruder	Brazil	Dsq-7-2-1-1-Dsq	68½

THE WORKBENCH

A New Column on Upkeep and Ideas

By Brian Weeks

I have found over the past few years that dry port installation is very important in the racing of Sunfish. The installation of the port is quite simple, but through the port we can provide ourselves with some key elements to upkeeping a healthy racing machine. With the dry port, we can gain access to the boats interior. There, we can restrengthen weak hardware installations, install or reinforce a hiking strap, maintain a low level of dampness and water in the hull, and repair leaking daggerboard trunks.

First you must choose a dryport or inspection port. They can be found at most marine supply stores. I recommend a flush screw in port by Beckson. Viking and Phyi also make good ones. I also recommend a six inch port to be installed just ahead of the daggerboard trunk. Here the splash rail protects it. No port is totally waterproof after a year or two of being screwed and unscrewed.

Some companies make a four inch port that a storage bag can be inserted into, to keep your lunch or gear. This is nice, but four inches is not quite big enough to enable you to reach all the critical areas.

Once you obtain a port, you need a few simple tools. If you have access to a hole saw that measures the same as the diameter of the inner port ring, you are all set, but most people don't. You will then need a drill, an electric jig saw or a hand keyhole saw, a screwdriver, a wrench, some silicone sealer and some bolts and nuts. I recommend round headed stainless steel machine screws, 8/32″x1″. Underneath you will want 8/32″ stainless hex nuts and lock washers or 8/32″ stainless nylon insert nuts.

To start, draw a centerline from the

There are three basic types of wind indicators: the masthead fly, boom mounted indicators and sail telltales. Each type has its pros and cons however, all three should be used to confirm readings taken from the water and not as the only basis for adjusting course or sail trim.

The masthead fly - as its name indicates - is mounted at the uppermost point on the boat. In a Sunfish, this point is the top of the upper boom. By being roughly 15-feet above the water, it is relatively unobstructed by other boats shadows and even stationary objects like a committee boat or land. However, as the hull of the boat makes its way through waves or chop, the pitching and yawing motion is greatly exaggerated the further away from the center of the motion you go. The top of the spar is the point of the boat which moves the most and therefore, in a light wind, the masthead fly may reflect the motion of the boat more than the direction of the wind. This problem is compounded by the fact that most sailors depend on wind indicators in light air more than in heavy air. A second drawback of the masthead fly is its position. A long afternoon of staring upwards will make for a stiff neck.

Boom mounted indicators solve the stiff neck problem. Being at eye level, they also give a good indication of what the wind is doing in the middle of the sail. Unfortunately, these indicators are fooled by even the smallest interference. Many times, particularly in very light air, skippers will try to react to an eye-level wind indicator that is spinning around in circles from interference from the rest of the fleet. Even worse is when the indicator is pointing in a steady direction that is actually quite different than the true direction.

The sailors consistently at the front of the fleet read the direction of the wind by looking at many factors. The most important and accurate is always the water. Other boats can also provide good clues about the direction of the wind—or perhaps more importantly - the direction of the wind 50 yards to windward. These sailors will use their wind indicators to confirm their other observations. It is very rare that a top sailor will make a major adjustment based on wind indicator readings alone.

A final type of indicator, which I have found to be almost completely useless on a Sunfish, are telltales. These little ribbons that hang just aft of the luff of the sail, are designed to read the air flow over the sail and thus allow the skipper to better trim the sail. However the mast of a Sunfish

in as a backing plate. We did see a number of straps pull out of the new boats last year. You can also install a hiking strap in an older boat this way also. Take a look at the last issue of the *Windward Leg's 'Q & A'*. It describes how to install hiking straps.

One last thing you can do easily with your newly installed inspection port is to install a compass. Any flush mount compass can be installed into a port cover, and other types can, too. Some sailors swear by Suunto compasses. They are good compasses. I and many others recommend Ritchie RU90 racing compass. It lists for $81.00 but if you are ready to learn to use one and think it will improve your sailing (which it will), it is worth it.

All you have to do to install the compass is to buy another dry port, the exact same one as you first purchased. Take the rim and throw it away. Draw a center line on the lid where it exactly faces forward when tightened. This is where you want North, or the center pin line of your compass to line up. Then when you screw the lid in to race, the compass faces perfectly forward.

To install the compass into the lid, use a hole saw again or a jig saw. Make sure you make a good center line and follow the same cutting instructions as you did with the hull. If after the compass is installed in the spare lid, the finger holes are still visible, fill them with a West Epoxy mixture or with silicone or some kind of filler. Pick two bolts on the compass where it gets bolted to the lid that are directly across from one another. You should be using 6/32″ x 1″ round head stainless steel machine screws. Those two bolts should have about three extra nuts wound up them under the head of the screw before they are installed. These extra high bolts can now be used as the handles to unscrew the compass from the boat, since you'll no longer have finger handles in the port. Remove the compass from the port when the boat is in transit or not in use.

These are some of the many uses of having an inspection port in your boat. You can now look for leaks, sponge the boat between races, let it air out on dry summer days, reinforce fittings and have a fail safe compass installation system. Now you are on your way with one or more ideas for making your boat into the racing machine that it should be.

To avoid foam blocks when mounting ports or compass, see Page 344 for phantom view of hull.

RACE REPORT

Sunfish North Americans

Close to 200 Sunfish sailors gathered in Rhode Island to compete for the North American Championship and a chance to qualify for the first Sunfish Worlds to be held outside the western hemisphere. Story by Major Hall and photos by Jim Curwen.

Nat Philbrick has good reason to smile. In winning the North Americans, he caps off six months of sailing in which he finished fifth in the Sunfish Worlds and was named to the Intercollegiate All-American Sailing Team.

Never before in its 17-year history had the Sunfish North American Championships produced such a large or talented field. The turnout of 178 participants was partially due to the fact that the event was held in New England, the birthplace and heart of Sunfish racing. However, it was, by no means, a regional event. There was strong representation from the rest of the Eastern Seaboard and the Midwest, as well as contingents from Texas, Florida, Louisiana, Nova Scotia, Puerto Rico, the Virgin Islands and the Bahamas.

For quality to match the quantity, the list of competitors included two world champions, three past North American champions, several Intercollegiate All-Americans and the winner of the '77 USYRU Singlehanded Championship. And to round out the requirements for an outstanding regatta, the event was held at the Barrington, R.I., YC on Narraganset Bay, which has earned considerable repute for running large and successful one-design championships.

For the first two days, a qualification series for seniors was held on one course, while the junior championship took place on another. For the final three days the top 50 seniors and the first five finishers from the junior championship raced for the North American title, while the remaining juniors and seniors raced for the Founder's Cup. Although the racing on the championship course was undoubtedly of a higher quality, nothing could match the color and excitement of 133 Sunfish on one starting line on the Founder's Cup course.

The predominantly light conditions for the first two days forced the six-race qualification series to be shortened to only four races. One of the pre-regatta favorites, past world cham-

The long lens of the camera considerably shortens the line used to start the 55 competitors in the championship division. Fourth-place finisher Kerry Klinger (42) wins the pin end while former North American Champion Will White (3158) takes advantage of a slight sag in the middle.

pion Paul Fendler, won decisively with three firsts and a third. Other top qualifiers and favorites for the championship were two-time and reigning world champion Derrick Fries (strangely enough, no world champion has ever been able to win the North Americans, a jinx which Fendler and Fries hoped to break), 1977 O'Day Singlehanded Champion Dave Chapin and Nat Philbrick, a recent Brown University graduate who had just been named to the Intercollegiate All-American Sailing Team.

The first championship race was an indication of how most of the series would be sailed. Partially because the starboard side of the course was set relatively close to shore, the port side was consistently favored with more wind and large port tack lifts. This became readily apparent on the second weather leg when some of the leaders at the first leeward mark went right and were never seen near the front again, while some of those who went left picked up as many as ten places. Fendler won, keeping up the pace he had set in the qualifying round. Yandell Rogers of Texas passed two boats on the final beat to take second. Philbrick finished fifth, but Fries and Chapin got caught to the right and started off the series with a 17th and a 35th, respectively.

In many ways, the regatta was shaping up to be an endurance contest. Each day the morning races began in moderate air, but the sea breeze quickly filled in to challenge the racers with winds of 15 knots and over and close, steep seas. Physically, the sailors had to be able to stand up to four races the first day and three races the second, a schedule that produced a lot of tired competitors in the evenings. Mentally, the sailors were faced with the possibility of as many as 10 races with no throwouts. In the highly competitive, talented and aggressive 55-boat fleet, this meant practically no margin for error, a fact that put a great deal of pressure on Fries and Chapin after their relatively poor opening races.

As the day progressed and the wind pattern became apparent to more of the sailors, the starts became a drag race from the leeward end of the starting line to the port layline. At the leeward mark, anyone who did not tack to starboard within 50 yards of the mark and sail straight to the layline was likely to lose a number of places.

Two familiar faces at the front of the fleet, O'Day Singlehanded Champion Dave Chapin (25187) and past Sunfish World Champion Paul Fendler (middle), lead Dave Blouin (37779) approaching the weather mark.

At times it even paid to overstand and close reach into the weather mark in more wind.

At the end of the day, Fendler led with a 1-4-9-6 record. In second place, with consistent top-10 finishes of 4-8-2-8, was Kerry Klinger, who also races with Fendler in a 470. Close behind these two were Rip Fisher with 7-3-12-3; Philbrick, who finished off the day with a first and a third after taking an 18th in the second race; and Fries, who recovered from his 17th with a 5-4-2.

"... Chapin sawed the jagged edges off the broken end and, racing with the mast a foot shorter, won the final race of the day."

But the fastest sailor on the race course wasn't in the top 10, or even the top 20. After his 35th in the first race, Dave Chapin came back to win the second race by a wide margin. He also held a comfortable lead at the first weather mark in the third race, when his mast broke at the deck. Forced to abandon the race and not able to find a replacement mast, Chapin sawed the jagged edges off the broken end and, racing with the mast a foot shorter, won the final race of the day. Unfortunately, the two bad races put him out of the running, for all practical purposes. The no-throwout series was already beginning to take its toll.

In the morning race the next day, Philbrick finished fourth to Fendler's 10th to move within one point of the lead. Then, in the second race, the two finished second and third, putting them in a tie for first place. The third and final race of the day proved to be a very important one. For the start, whether intentionally or by accident, the line was heavily windward-end favored, so at least everyone had an equal chance of getting to the port layline first. For Fendler, this was all academic, as his mainsheet ratchet block pulled out of the deck just before the start. He struggled through the heavy air race, using only a small fairlead to trim the mainsheet, and finished 24th, which dropped him to fourth overall, while Philbrick finished fourth in the race and took over the series lead. A little less than five points back in second was Klinger, who had improved steadily during the day with finishes of 11-5-3. Fries' consistent 6-8-2 record moved him up to third. Fisher would have stood fifth for the day, but a top-five finish in the final race was nullified when he was ruled over early at the start.

In seventh place was Dave Chapin, who won all three races the second day, giving him a record of 35-1-dnf-1-1-1-1. One of the reasons the sophomore from Southern Illinois University was able to overcome heavier opponents in the strong winds was his proficiency with a relatively new Sunfish rigging technique called the "Jens Rig." Named after its inventor, Jens Hookansen of the Virgin Islands, the 1976 North American Champion, it works on the principle that if the halyard is tied lower on the upper spar and the whole lateen rig is carried low on the mast, then the upper spar will bend more in the puffs, thus flattening the sail and easing the leech. (In essence, Chapin's cut-off mast in the fourth race accomplished the same effect as the Jens Rig.) Having superior speed and yet finding himself out of the running was an understandable disappointment for Dave, who had finished second in both the 1977 North Americans and Worlds.

So far, out of 32 weather legs in four qualifying and seven championship races, it had paid to go left on 27 of them. But for the final day of the championship, the pattern was different. Instead of the building southwesterly of the previous two days, the fleet was confronted with a spotty, up-and-down northwesterly in which more than a few sailors found themselves trapped on the outside of lifts on one side of the course or the other, while their competitors were playing oscillating shifts up the middle.

Although a number of positions changed, as many sailors had trouble shifting gears from the pattern of the first seven races, Philbrick found the conditions to his liking. He got off to a safe start, played the first beat correctly and then sailed conservatively to a second-place finish, which cemented the championship for him in what proved to be the final race. Fries came up with his seventh straight top-10 finish to place second overall. Meanwhile, Fendler and Klinger found themselves back in the 30s half way through the race. But on the second beat Fendler played the middle and pulled himself all the way up to third by the finish to take third in the series, while Klinger went left and finished 32nd to drop to fourth overall. And in fifth place in the final standings, although breaking his streak of firsts with an 11th, was Dave Chapin.

In winning, Philbrick displayed good speed (although not the best speed in the fleet), strong tactics, especially at the start and on the first weather leg, and the ability to come back from a poor position. This is a pattern that has fit a number of past Sunfish champions, who used consistency rather than brilliance to win against large, aggressive fleets. Nat has been racing Sunfish for about seven years and has improved steadily each year, last winter finishing fifth at the worlds and earlier in the summer winning the Sunfish Eastern Regionals, also held at Barrington.

Unlike many other singlehanded classes, Sunfish racing is very much a family activity. It was not uncommon to find husbands racing against wives, brothers against sisters and parents against children. The Philbricks were no exception, certainly setting some kind of a North American record with Nat's brother and father finishing 11th and 26th in the championship series and his mother racing in the Founder's Cup division. Even more interesting is the fact that Nat's intercollegiate crew at Brown, Martha Starkweather, won the first Women's Sunfish North Americans held a week earlier.

For the first 15 finishers in the championship series, the North Americans is also a stepping stone to the 1979 Sunfish World Championship. For many years now, this midwinter event has attracted top Sunfish racers to exotic Caribbean vacation spots like the Virgin Islands, Venezuela, Puerto Rico, Aruba and Martinique. And in eight world championships, U.S. sailors have won five times and usually dominated the top 10. But the U.S. qualifiers from this year's North Americans will have a special treat in that they will be the first to race in a Sunfish Worlds outside of the western hemisphere. With Sunfish scheduled to be built in Holland, the 1979 Worlds are tentatively being planned for next spring at some European site. It will be interesting to see if Philbrick, Fries, Fendler and the other top U.S. sailors will still be able to dominate world Sunfish racing the way they have in the past. ●

Juniors

Skipper	Pts.
1. David Elliot, Mountain Lakes, NJ	23.50
2. Jamie Bennett, Glencoe, IL	28.70
3. Nat Ross, Westwood, MA	34.00
4. Peter Duclos, Westport, MA	42.00
5. Andy Driver, Little Compton, RI	45.75

Championship

Skipper									Pts.
1. Nat Philbrick, Pocasset, MA	5	18	1	3	4	2	4	2	38.75
2. Derrick Fries, Drayton Plains, MI	17	5	4	2	6	8	2	6	50.00
3. Paul Fendler, Rye, NY	1	4	9	6	10	3	24	3	59.75
4. Kerry Klinger, Orangeburg, NY	4	8	2	8	11	5	3	32	74.00
5. Dave Chapin, Springfield, IL	35	1	57	1	1	1	1	11	106.75
6. Major Hall, Wilton, CT	3	13	31	10	5	7	17	23	109.00
7. Allan Scharfe, Babylon, NY	46	9	7	11	3	12	5	20	113.00
8. Rip Fisher, Suffern, NY	7	3	12	4	16	6	58	9	115.00
9. Reed Baer, Providence, RI	8	21	8	13	29	17	17	13	126.00
10. Dave Driver, Bristol, RI	10	23	20	24	19	4	14	14	128.00

Founders

Skipper								Pts.
1. Al Girard, Barrington, RI	3	5.33*	14	4	7	2	2	37.33
2. Paul Harding, Amityville, NY	10	1	1	17	2	1	23	54.25
3. Bill Draheim, Toledo, OH	2	9	23	1	1	16	5	56.50
4. Rick Stewart, Needham, MA	6	14	3	22	5	15	3	68.00
5. Pater Vessela, Providence, RI	8	6	11	27	9	9	4	74.00

*average

Women's North Americans

Skipper											Pts.
1. Martha Starkweather, Little Compton, RI	2	2	2	(3)	1	2	1	(5)	1	3	13.25
2. Pam Corwin, Mattituck, NY	1	1	1	4	2	3	2	2	(9)	(5)	15.25
3. Janice Mienke, Mattituck, NY	(3)	3	3	1	(7)	1	3	3	3	1	17.25
4. Dora Atwater, Little Compton, RI	5	4	4	(9)	5	4	5	1	2	(6)	29.75
5. Karen Robine, Croton-on-Hudson, NY	(7)	5	5	2	3	6	4	(7)	6	4	35.00

336

Sunfish Worlds

A new-world boat is introduced to the old country. Photos by Daniel Forster.

After finishing second in the worlds last year, Dave Chapin, an Illinois college student who has been racing Sunfish for almost 10 years, led from start to finish to win the first Sunfish World Championship to be held outside the Western Hemisphere. Held in Medemblik, Holland, the event was the European debut for the Sunfish, one of the most popular boats in North America.

The 88-boat fleet was made up predominantly of U.S., Caribbean and Venezuelan sailors, although there were about 20 competitors from the host country. Six out of the top 10 places were taken by U.S. sailors, while Holland made a fine showing, capturing second, fifth and seventh. Despite his convincing win, Chapin was pushed hard by defending world champion Derrick Fries from Michigan and Cor van Aanholt, a 19-year-old Dutch sailor who eventually finished second. Past Sunfish World Champion Paul Fendler finished third, North American Champion Nat Philbrick took

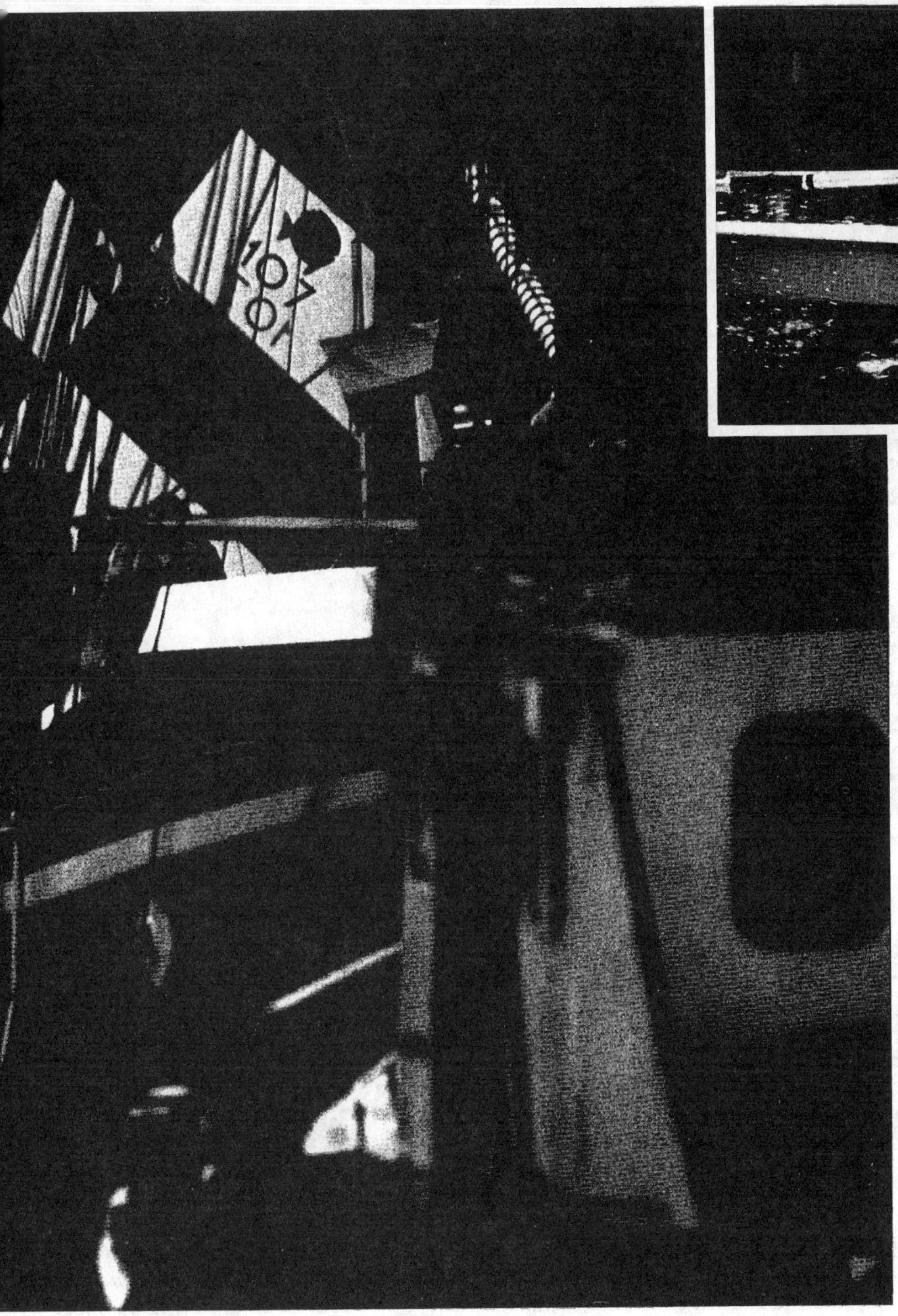

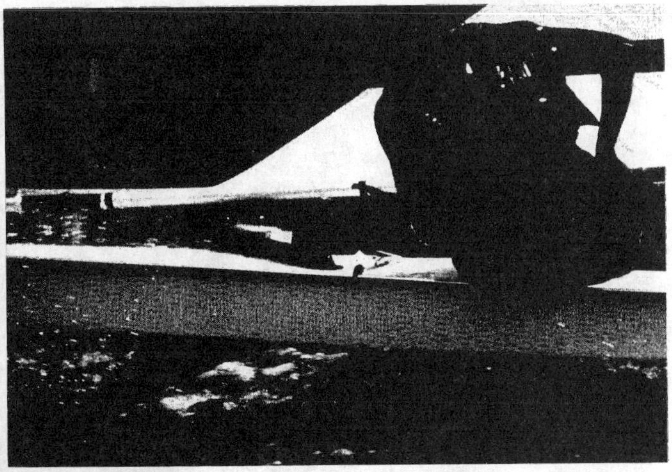

(Left) *Old world meets new. Red, white and blue Sunfish sails, a common sight across the U.S., are framed by the masts and rigging of traditional Dutch sailing yachts moored along a Medemblik canal.* (Above) *It was only a matter of time before Dave Chapin won big. In the past few years he has finished second in the Sunfish North Americans, the Sunfish Worlds and the Snipe Nationals.* (Below) *The Sunfish may have looked like a "toy boat" to many of the Europeans, but they soon found out that it is an exciting performer in a breeze.*

fourth and U.S. National Super Sunfish Champion Bill Boll was sixth.

Some of the competitors and officials at this landmark championship offer their inside views and comments:

Tom Ehman, *One-Design Director for USYRU, a top Sunfish sailor and a judge at this year's worlds.*

"It was the first I can remember that the Sunfish Worlds was not held off the beach. In Medemblik, the boats were kept on racks along a street that ran next to a canal. There was a concrete breakwater along the canal, and you had to walk down two carpeted, wooden floating ramps to put your boat in. This caused a little trouble, since you could only launch two or three boats at a time. In the fourth race, about a third of the fleet was late for the start.

"The racing area was what was formerly the Zuider Zee and now is called the Ijsselmeer. During World War II they dammed the area off from the North Sea, and now it's all fresh water. It's not terribly deep, so you get a bit of a chop. The wind always came out of the same quarter, but one time when it swung a little north of west, it blew across the diked area instead of the land, and then it really got rough.

"At first the Dutch thought that Sunfish were going to be little toy boats. But once the regatta started, they were really impressed, not only with the performance of the boat, but also with how well the boats were being sailed and how tight and aggressive the competition was.

"From the outset, it was really a three-boat regatta. Cor van Aanholt was very tough. He was OK Dinghy Champion at Kiel two years ago and Laser Champion this year. I'm sure you'll hear a lot more from him. He had been sailing the Sunfish for only a short time, but he's very strong and clearly got better as the regatta went on. He didn't have the speed that Dave Chapin did, but he hit the shifts well.

"Chapin consistently had good starts in the middle of the line, went up the middle of the course and just sailed

Second-place Cor van Aanholt was racing a Sunfish for the first time, despite having recently opened a Sunfish dealership in Holland.

Past U.S. National Champion Joel Furman uses the Jens rig in one of the heavy-air races. First introduced by Jens Hookanson of the Virgin Islands, this technique allows one to lower the sailplan while still leaving the upper spar free to bend off in the puffs. The key to the rig is the halyard wrapped around the mast and spar. Even the heavier sailors found the Jens rig a tremendous advantage in heavy air. Note also the techniques for attaching the telltales, mounting the compass and running the end of the halyard over the lower spar at the gooseneck as a combination downhaul and boom vang.

very fast. He clearly had the best overall speed, although Paul Fendler and Derrick Fries are still the fastest off the wind. There were a good number of Europeans racing but not too many of them showed much speed."

Dave Chapin, *New Sunfish World Champion.*

"The courses they set were really monsters. The starting line was set about half a mile below the leeward mark. The weather mark was 10 feet tall and you could just barely pick it out on the horizon if you stood up in your boat. You just kept going and going. Some people would get to one side of the course and actually end up going for the jibe mark by mistake.

"The pattern for the first four races was that I would be in first, with Derrick second and Cor third. Then on the last beat, Derrick would go the opposite way from Cor, trying to get me to break off my cover. In the first two races it didn't change any places, but in the third and fourth races Cor got by to beat us both. In the fifth race the wind was lighter, and Derrick was first, I was second and Cor was back around 10th.

"So going into the final race, the only way I could lose the regatta was if Cor won the race and I finished below second, or if Derrick won the race and I finished below third. After the start Cor was one of the first boats to the favored side, but he capsized and I gradually caught up with him. Approaching the second weather mark, Cor was second, I was third and Derrick had gone the wrong way on the first beat and was pretty far back. I came in on port and tacked inside Cor at the mark, but our spars touched. I thought I had completed my tack, so I kept racing.

"On the final beat I was second and Cor third, and I was forcing him toward the unfavored side of the course. Suddenly, Derrick was there covering him, too. It really surprised me, and I wasn't sure what he was doing. He had been in about 30th and probably figured that there was no way to win the regatta, but if he could get Cor below fourth, he could still get second in the series. I don't think Derrick really thought about what he was doing. Eventually we all got so far behind that none of us bothered to finish.

"At first there was no protest, but then someone from the press boat advised Cor to file one. There was some talk of Derrick and me team racing Cor, but that was disproved. What happened was that the jury disqualified Derrick from the series for cutting the last mark to cover Cor. They disqualified me for tacking too close at the second weather mark, but then they disqualified Cor for not protesting the incident. So our final finishes for the regatta went back to our positions at the end of the fifth race."

The Sunfish is basically a very stable boat, but with the long boom generally carried quite low, jibing can be tricky in heavy air. These two competitors demonstrate the right way ... and the wrong way.

Even at the end of a six-mile Olympic course, there were always a lot of close finishes in the 88-boat fleet.

Paul Fendler, *third-place finisher in Medemblik and winner of the Sunfish Worlds two years ago in Aruba.*

"Holland was quite different from what everyone was used to. It took a little adjusting to, but it was nice. The people were friendly, and Medemblik was kind of a quaint little town. Everything was within walking distance.

"The big thing was that it was colder. The water felt like it was in the 50s. You had to wear a wet suit or really good foul weather gear. I wore my frostbiting gear – wool clothes under a one-piece suit – and it worked pretty well.

"I don't know if the competition was as good as it has been in past years. It was hard to tell with Siegenthaler (two-time world champion from the Bahamas), Dunkley and some of the good sailors from Martinique missing. There were some good European sailors, though, singlehanded sailors from other classes who had been practicing in Sunfish for several weeks. They knew the area, and every time a persistent shift came through, they hit it.

"It was a big advantage for the U.S. sailors to have the Worlds this time of year, instead of in the middle of the winter. We had a chance to get in some practice ahead of time for a change. Some Sunfish sailors would rather have the Worlds coincide with a midwinter vacation, but it is a big disadvantage to have to go up cold against the Caribbean sailors who have been racing for months."

Steve Baker, *AMF Alcort Director of Class Management, for the Sunfish.*

"I think that the regatta was a good introduction to Europe for the Sunfish. The initial reaction was that the boat was a little bit old-fashioned, but after the heavy-air races, when the people saw that there were very few capsizes, the fact that the boat could be sailed in heavy weather appealed to them. They were also surprised with the quality of competition in the class.

"We hope to get over to race the worlds in Europe again in the future, maybe Kiel. But next year it looks like the first possibility would be Aruba. Second choice could be Cancun, Mexico, and third might be San Diego. We would like to have the worlds on the West Coast some year." •

	Skipper							Pts.
1.	Dave Chapin, Springfield, IL	1	1	2	2	4	(DF)	14
2.	Cor van Aanholt, Holland	3	3	1	1	14	(DF)	31.4
3.	Paul Fendler, Rye, NY	4	9	4	(10)	6	6	54.4
4.	Nathaniel Philbrick, Pittsburgh, PA	7	5	8	4	9	(11)	60
5.	Eric de Vries, Holland	5	6	18	6	(33)	2	60.4
6.	William Boll, Bolton, CT	6	(23)	17	15	15	7	89.7
7.	Wout Matthijs, Holland	10	18	7	5	(36)	25	94
8.	Quirinas Tepas, Antilles	16	11	22	(56)	20	13	112
9.	Samuel Philbrick, Pittsburgh, PA	22	17	16	19	(40)	15	119
10.	Kerry Klingler, Orangeburg, NY	17	13	20	(DF)	21	24	125

THE WORKBENCH

A Column on Ideas and Upkeep

By Brian Weeks

The avid Sunfish racer who takes to the road needs a way to transport his "racing machine" efficiently, safely and with as little wear to the boat as possible. There are a number of different ways to transport these small fourteen feet craft and I will explain a few of the different methods. First, I thought it might be fun, however, to talk about some of the more unique or humorous methods.

Of course, there is the old car top method. Simply throw a rug on the roof of your car, throw the boat on top of the car, upside down, strap down the front and the back and wait. Three things can happen now. A; The roof caves in, B; The boat cracks in half—ten miles down the interstate, C; The boat falls off the side of the car. Needless to say, I don't recommend this method, although I have seen this done. Another poor way to travel is to turn a single boat trailer into a double by throwing an old tire between the hulls. This again can cause damage to the boat, or at the very least, cover both boats with black rubber marks that have to be scrubbed off. Then there is the "Back of the Wagon" technique. I only recommend this if you live a few blocks away from the yacht club. It simply consists of throwing a boat into the back of a station wagon, after folding the seat down. It works, but half of the boat is hanging out of the car. The "Pick Up Truck" method rates equally. The club had better be close by (I started out this way!).

One of the most unique rigs I ever saw was the "Axleless Trailer". Someone went through the trouble of bolting a frame to the bottom of a small car that an aluminum "Trailex" trailer bed could be attached to, without wheels or an axle. It was stationary, non-pivoting and turned with the car. The owners reasoning for the idea was to not register it and not have to pay tolls. It did hold the boat beautifully, but I'm not too sure that I would drive to Mississippi with it or even try to convince a New York Transit Authority worker that it wasn't worth the extra fifty cents.

Now, let's talk about the options for safe transportation. With the Sunfish, unlike most other one-design yachts, you have the option of car topping as well as trailering. These, however, are the two basic models of transportation. You must decide what is more convenient for you.

Car topping is cheaper and less of a hassle in terms of maneuvering, parking, tolls and yearly paperwork with the Department of Motor Vehicles. The problem I see, however, is the constant need for assistance. At home it means asking a neighbor, wife or family member to help "play superman" often late at night or early in the morning. At the regatta site, you usually have to ask someone to take time out from their own pre-race or post-race chores to help you. There are ways of putting on or taking off the boat from the rack by yourself but is usually difficult. Most RVs that people now purchase are higher off the ground thus making it even harder.

If you do intend to cartop the boat, I recommend a couple of methods. If you have an existing roof rack on your car or truck, you can pad it with pipe insulation or a cloth of some kind and then use line to tie it down to the rack and the front and back bumpers. Some existing racks still can not accommodate the boat. You can build a simple wood rack out of 2 x 4's and screws that can then be tied to the existing rack. First you must scribe the crossing 2 x 4's to the shape of the boat. If you lay a 2 x 4 across the deck or cockpit where it will rest against the boat, you can set it up so it is sitting level. Holding it in place, take a compass and set it at a little more than the distance the 2 x 4 is away from the outer edge of the deck. Run the compass along the deck so that the pencil draws a line on the 2 x 4. Now you have the deck contours and you can cut it out and pad it. Just repeat the same procedure for the cross beam.

If you want to buy a rack, most automotive and sporting goods stores sell them. The cheap ones are okay and can be padded with carpet or pipe insulation as well. I recommend the Thule Rack System. It has many optional accessories including straps, winches, pads, etc. It's only draw back is its price tag but they are perfect for many sports outings.

Trailering is the most expensive option. The original purchase, registration, inspection, tolls, maintenance, etc. all cost money. However, the ease of the whole idea downplays all of this. Hook it up to the car in the morning; unhook it at night. If you have the right set-up, you can roll the boat off the trailer by yourself. A good trailer can be outfitted to hold as many as six boats! During the 1983 North Americans in Chicago, I saw a trailer that could hold eight Sunfish. It was a quadruple decker with two boats on their sides, overlapped on each side of the trailer. (Amazing, but I don't know if I would tow it).

Most people trailer the boats deck up but many serious Sailors believe that they should be trailered deck down to have less chafe and road damage to the bottom. After all, it is the "fast" part of the boat. Many companies make fine trailers. You'll probably be considering one of the smallest models. They should run from $200.00 to $500.00. Usually, the price will tell you how good it is made. I use a Cox trailer to trail two boats. I have put thousands of miles on it and it is still going strong. Most of the trailers are galvanized, but Trailex makes a beautiful light weight aluminum trailer, just perfect for Sunfish. Its only draw back is that it is expensive and cannot be converted into a double-decker.

Double-decker trailers are fun to design and use. Most people frame them out of 2 x 4's or 2 x 6's, nails, screws, bolts and carpeting. You can design them to hold the boat's deck facing up or down. There are many ideas you can get by looking at other people's trailers. The double-decker trailer that my father designed for our boats is a beauty and can be built in a few hours. It attaches to the trailer itself with four bolts. It is made from 2 x 6's, (scribed to the shape of the boat bottoms) steel angle iron and flat steel. The 2 x 6's are padded with carpeting and then everything is painted to protect it from weathering.

You can work out other ideas for holding your sails. You can hang them under the cradle, tie them down to the deck of the boat or tie them onto the roof of your car. One good idea I have seen is to attach 8" PVC tubing, 16' long to your trailer. You need to get some pipe plug ends for it but it's great for transporting sails. Make sure you drill some holes in the bottom so moisture doesn't stay in. 10" PVC pipe will hold two sets of sails. The PVC in not cheap, but well worth the price.

These are some of the more convenient ideas for traveling with your Sunfish. Most can be easily rigged in a few short hours. With a little time, care and thought, you can safely hit the road to take on the "hotshots" of the Sunfish racing world!!!

Editor's note: I have seen the Trailex as a double-decker. There are two in our Club.

A crazy river, an untraditional boat and a host of loyal enthusiasts make Barrington frostbiting an unforgettable experience. Story by John Burnham. Photos by Paul Mello.

11:30 The thermometer at the Barrington YC registers a chilly but tolerable 36 degrees. Beside the clubhouse, sailors are manhandling their Sunfish off the sturdy wooden racks. A colorful spectacle of knitted hats, sweatshirts and ski parkas blend with the emerging array of centerboards, ratchet blocks, pliers, screwdrivers and rolls of duct tape.

11.55 A sprinkling of sails are up and swinging in the shifty breeze. A halyard retied here, a new sail being rigged up there – all the rigging chores in progress – and the tracks of countless muddy sea boots between the parking lot and water's edge. The early arrivals are already fine-tuning their outhauls while the latecomers are hurrying down the beach from the storage shed with their sails and spars.

12:10 Al Beckwith's dusty van arrives in a whirl of parking lot gravel – another record trip down from Boston. Most of the sailors are now in the clubhouse savoring the warmth as long as possible.

12:15 Henry DeWolf enters the clubhouse, straight from church. His boat, rigged beforehand, merely awaits his quick change from Sunday suit to wetsuit.

12:28 The boats are poised at the tide line. Life jackets and last-minute sweaters are donned.

12:29 The crash boat engines are running, and the Sunfish burgee ripples from the flagstaff.

12:30 The sailors clear the beach, and another afternoon of frostbiting begins at Barrington, R.I.

It has begun this way on every Sunday afternoon between November and April since 1966. That year, eight friends founded the Barrington Frostbite Association, and after spreading the word, they usually had 10 boats on the starting line every week. It was a casual event – a bunch of friends out for some friendly, spirited competition.

Now, fourteen years later, Fred Thomas is the only one of those eight friends who still frostbites. He no longer finishes in the front every week, but he keeps returning because he finds the good spirit of his old friends still exists in the 30-boat fleet that races today.

With the growth of the fleet, the competition has become sharper, too. Today, at the head of the fleet stand the likes of John Duclos and Ed Adams, intercollegiate All-Americans who grew up honing their skills on the

Frostbiting Barrington-Style

A crooked starting line can mean a close contest for the weather end.

The quick decision: cut inside . . . or play it safe and go wide of his stern? This sailor opts to stay wide — wisely, it seems — well clear of the muddle confronting him.

Barrington River's winter waters. Sunfish North American Champ Al Beckwith is a regular, as are Bob Perry and Dave Driver, two local veterans of the summer Sunfish circuit, who, like Al, use the winter season at Barrington to stay in racing trim for the summer.

Many in the fleet sail larger boats in the summer, such as Bob Johnston, who sails his Evelyn 36 on Narragansett Bay, and Pete Lawson, a one-time 12-Meter navigator out of Newport. These "big boat" sailors look forward to the frostbiting as a chance to brush up on their tactics without the worry of crews, provisions and expensive equipment. For many, however, the challenges and the exercise available are enough to lure them down to the river.

For the developing young sailor, a Barrington winter involves a very fast learning process. In half a season, Dan Rumplik, a relative racing novice from Warren, R.I., has developed enough savvy and self-assurance in tight fleet conditions to give him a big boost when the summer season begins. For Dan, along with all the others, there are hundreds of lessons to be absorbed over and over again in an afternoon of racing.

The format of the racing lends itself to the repetition of many basic tactical lessons. With four or five races run in a two-and-a-half-hour period, that means there are five to 10 starts (counting general recalls) and up to 25 mark roundings in an afternoon.

The supervision of this busy schedule is undertaken by an efficient group of race committee regulars who are as likely to be seen working one of the Olympic Trials courses as on frostbite courses. Bill Cuthbertson has been helping with this chore since the first year the frostbiting started, and his group's experience gets the races off without long delays. Their typical courses are sometimes less than conventional, but they're never boring.

For example, against the backdrop of 36 luffing sails, you may hear Cuthbertson announce: "Start between the white flag on the dock and the red flag in the river; leave the red flag upriver to port, then sail downriver leaving N2 to port and the Obstruction buoy to starboard. Sail down past Fred Thomas' dock and leave N20 to starboard, then finish back at the Obstruction buoy."

Given courses like this one, as well as tricky currents, variable winds and obstacles such as partially submerged winter stakes, sailors who are used to winning may have a tough time at first. One must make careful pre-start calculations dependent upon the current and the wind, and it is not a simple matter of picking a side of the course. At the start the wind may be bad on the side the current favors, and then later, on the same side, the current may be bad, but the wind much better. One must predict which side will average out in your favor on any given leg. However, many conventional tactics, such as a "safe start" or "covering the fleet," often may not work as well as less orthodox, more intuitive, bolder moves.

Once the race is underway, you need to be scrappy and alert, ready to ditch all your pre-start calculations if necessary. It seems that at least half the time you have to fight your way back into the race after a big shift destroys everyone on your side of the course. You also have to be patient and relaxed to cope with the times when your perfect pin-end start finds you in a huge hole, unable to tack, with "Tailend Charlie" coming out of the second row at the weather end, tacking off and cruising to a big lead in his own private breeze. No one is immune. All-Americans, Sunfish Champions, Women's Champions and 12-Meter navigators can lose 10 boats as fast as anyone. The river can be both the great equalizer and the great educator. And one of its most often repeated lessons is humility.

Along with learning humility, one learns to develop a flexible attitude about the rules. The river gets so cramped at times that minor rule infractions are inevitable. Like when the committee sets the start in front of the club with the leeward end well-favored. Starting at the leeward end seems like a great plan to a lot of skippers, but then the left-hand bank comes up at you as soon as you clear the line. You call for sea room to the boat on your weather quarter, you both tack, and then you both tack back when the next starboard tacker comes along. Then you have to call for sea room again and the whole process is repeated. With so much tacking in such limited space and time, the opportunity for infringement of each other's rights is constantly at hand. Chain reactions of crash tacks are commonplace, and keeping track of what's going on around you and making appropriate, rational decisions is challenging, to say the least.

For those who cherish the finer points of the rules, the fact that there are no protests lodged after a leg like this would undoubtedly be blasphemous. But to keep the racing sane and tempers intact in such crowded quarters and chaotic situations, and also to keep the sport fun, it doesn't seem to hurt sometimes to give up one's right-of-way or to let the minor infractions slip by now and then. The rules purists must remember that this racing has a distinct style that occasionally bears no resemblance to any other. For example, given a surfeit of general recalls when the current is flowing upwind, the race committee will not hesitate to announce, with smiles on their faces, that the first mark will be the leeward mark. The result will be a clean start . . . followed by a horrendous jam at the leeward mark, 10 or 15 boats, gunwale-to-gunwale — a protest committee's nightmare, but just another incident to laugh about afterwards for the Barrington frostbiting veteran.

Sessions like these make one glad to be in a durable boat. Most people think of the Sunfish as merely a summer boat associated with beaches, bathing suits and barefeet rather than frostbiting. Frostbite boats are supposed to be undecked dinghies with high, dry sides that keep you as far away from the water as possible. It's true that in a Sunfish you might as well be sitting in the water sometimes — even on a relatively tame afternoon, you need a wetsuit to keep you warm.

". . . there are hundreds of lessons to be absorbed over and over again in an afternoon of racing."

On the other hand, the Sunfish has one very decided advantage as a frostbite boat — a capsize does not necessarily mean a chilly dunking, a swamped boat and an inglorious end to your day's racing. A Sunfish can be easily righted and sailed away without aid from a crash boat, and an agile skipper can recover from a capsize without even getting his feet wet.

Many of the Sunfish that appear every winter in Barrington are older boats that have been battered and patched, the gel coat cracked and the colors faded. Years of family recreation has taken the life from the sails, the numbers slapped on at the last minute with duct tape. These race side by side with Sunfish whose boards and rudders have been refinished, whose sails sprout dozens of telltales and whose decks bristle with ratchet blocks, jam cleats and compass mounts. Each of the owners has a personal philosophy about the time and money to spend on his boat, but interestingly enough, the well-seasoned family daysailer can be competitive with the fully-geared racing machine.

The warm rubber gloves go on in November . . . and don't come off until April.

Alertness on the course will more than make up for fractional differences in boat speed. It's more important to watch for that once-in-the-day shift that will give you the port startin front of the fleet. You have to keep your eyes and ears and mind open. You can't assume the leaders are going the right way or are even sailing the correct course.

No one makes all the correct moves or wins every race. Because there are so many unpredictable variables, you can't get too concerned when the wind dies as you round the weather mark and your 10-boat-length lead evaporates. Everyone has to be philosophical about the breaks — they always seem to average out eventually. Everyone, from the most heated-up hotshot, out for blood and glory, to the most laid-back old warrior, relaxing before another week in the office, must be ready to admit now and then that finishing back in the pack isn't the end of the world.

This kind of an attitude is a prerequisite for having fun racing on the Barrington River. And only if it's fun will people drive more than an hour on a Sunday morning for the privilege of chilling their fingers and toes. That's why Al Beckwith will keep coming down from Boston and Bill and Ruth Warren from even further north. Marty Billet will keep checking in every week, happy to be sailing at 50-plus years. And, of course, the senior member of the fleet, Fred Thomas, will keep sailing, fifteen years after he helped start it all.

Afterwards, with our boats on the racks, we are warmed by hot chili, soup and the hospitality of the Barrington clubhouse. The sea stories are launched back and forth, and you can feel the glow on your face. It's a nice way to end the week, and it definitely beats Sunday afternoon television. ●

SOLUTIONS FOR RUDDER PROBLEMS

By Larry Cochran

Have you ever had a rudder split during a regatta? Well, I have and it can be very frustrating. Try sailing back to shore without a rudder. You will probably have to be towed in and if you don't have a spare, you're out of the regatta. After splitting one rudder, I developed a series of refinements which have made my rudder dependable for over ten years.

Listed below are common rudder problems and recommended solutions. The letters refer to locations on the accompanying sketch.

1. **Split at X.** This most common failure is caused primarily by pulling and pushing on the tiller to raise and lower the rudder (as it is designed to be used). It can also be caused by being hit by another boat. Look at your rudder and you may already see a crack in the finish there. Install a 2″ #10 brass round head wood screw with a larger brass washer under the head at C. The exposed head will allow you to retighten the screw, if necessary, to keep this section under compression. Additional security may be obtained by installing a 1 1/2″ #8 brass flat head wood screw, countersunk, at D. If your rudder is badly cracked or broken at X, work epoxy into the crack before tightening the screws.

2. **Split at Y.** The rudder is made with a 1/4″ rod 4″ long at A, reinforcing the wood against bending but not against the tension problem described above. Unfortunately, the inner end of this rod creates a stress concentration near the center hole which can result in splitting under the bending loads from turning forces. Drill a 1/4″ hole at B, being careful to keep it centered, and drive in a 1/4″ brass or stainless steel rod 4″ long after working epoxy into the hole. Seal the depressions here and at D with grey MarineTex.

3. **Holes elongate.** When the rudder is wet, the wood softens around the two pivot holes and the holes gradually elongate under load, causing rudder control to be sloppy. Enlarge these holes around their original centers and install metal bushings. I made bushings out of brass stanchions used to raise the height of lampshades. These are 7/16″ O.D., 1″ long, with a threaded hole that can be drilled out to 1/4″. Cut and file to length, roughen the outside and epoxy the bushings squarely in place.

4. **Tiller straps gouge rudder and excessive play develops.** This wear occurs where the lower edges of the aluminum straps bear against the rudder when the tiller is moved from side to side. Use a wood rasp to remove a patch of wood from each side of the rudder about 1/16″ deep and 1 1/4″ in from the edge in the area of this contact. Fill this with grey MarineTex and file flush with the rudder surface. Obtain (from an Industrial Plastics Supply Company) some .030″ Teflon sheet etched on one side to accept adhesives. Cut pieces to fit the entire exposed inner surfaces of the tiller straps and attach the Teflon to these surfaces with contact cement. Cut the holes for the bolt to the rudder before cementing the Teflon in place. When assembling the tiller to the rudder, omit the standard nylon washers that were used between the straps and the rudder. The Teflon surface inside the straps will make contact along the entire length of the straps, eliminating all slop and wear.

5. **Bolts at pivots wear into holes.** These two bolts have short shanks so that contact with the holes is mostly from the sharp threads of the bolts, accelerating wear. Obtain from a hardware store some stainless steel bolts that have shanks long enough to contact all bearing areas but which can still be properly tightened. Install the bolts with stainless steel washers under the heads and the nuts. Put thin nylon washers under the steel washers to reduce corrosion of the aluminum parts when exposed to salt water. Be sure to account for this entire stack-up when selecting the bolts. Lock the nuts in place with LocTite or a similar anaerobic liquid and saw off excess bolt length.

6. **Aluminum rudder support wears into rudder.** The forward, lower, inner edges of the casting wear into the rudder. Teflon pads in this area help prevent this wear and also reduce slop by reducing the clearance at this point.

7. **Wear on tiller upper surface due to contact with bridle.** If you get some Teflon, use it to cure this problem, too. A piece 3″x10″ located starting about 17″ forward of the bolt hole in the tiller strap should do the trick. Before attaching it with contact cement, shape the Teflon to the tiller by heating with a hair dryer. Then cement it and hold it in place until secure.

The Chief Measurer assured me that all of these refinements are acceptable because they don't make you go faster, they just make the parts last longer. Pearson is also aware of these problems and will evaluate the cost and feasibility of improvements in these areas.

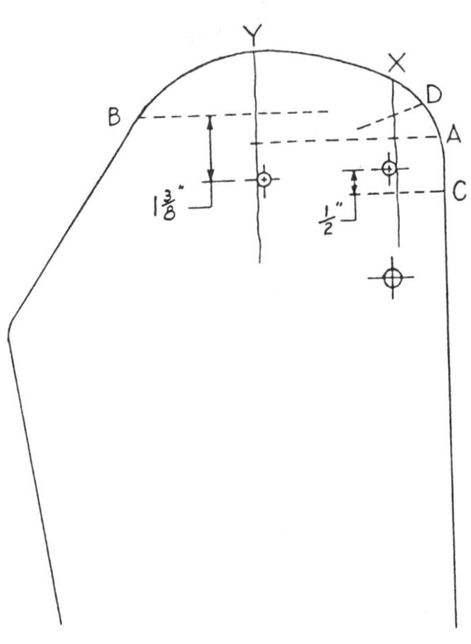

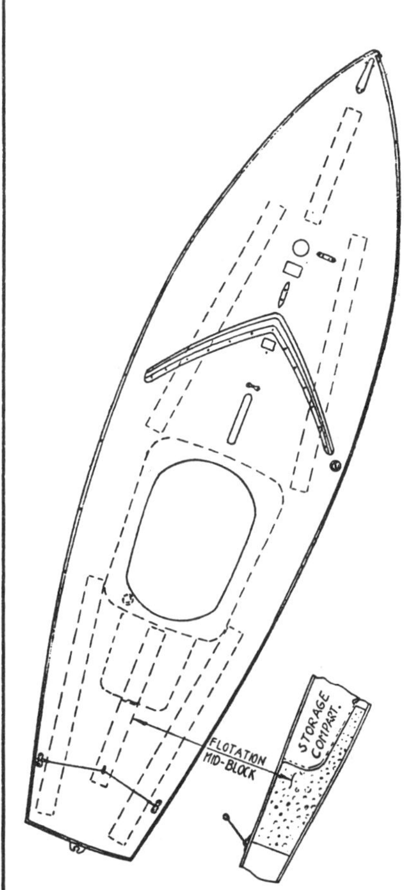

Phantom View showing placement of foam flotation blocks. Avoid these when installing ports or compass. Also shows larger cockpit opening, standard since 1988.

SUNFISH

1981 Sunfish North American champ Paul Odegard reveals the many tuning secrets that took him to the top of America's largest one-design dinghy class.

Paul Odegard (shown here displaying a worn pair of hiking pants while modeling a slightly newer pair) has attended a grand total of eight North American and seven Sunfish world championships. A 45-year-old engineer at Pratt and Whitney Aircraft with a wife and two daughters, Paul crowned his 19-year apprenticeship in the class with a popular win at last year's NAs in Charleston, S.C. Bob Heckman photo.

The AMF Alcort Sunfish is probably responsible for getting more people started in sailing than any other boat in the world. Some 200,000 boats have been produced since this 13-foot-10-inch "board" boat made her debut in 1951. While many Sunfish have been sold to strictly weekend sailors, the boat has caught on with the racing crowd in a big way. Her highly depowerable lateen rig has made her a singlehander that appeals to a wide variety of skipper sizes and ages. The racing class (58,000 strong and run by AMF Alcort with the help of an advisory board of sailors) offers hundreds of annual regattas across the country as well as North American and world championships. Graduates of the Sunfish class include such notables as Garry Hoyt, Major Hall, Derrick Fries, Dave Chapin and Chuck Millican.

Over the last 30 years, there have been many factory changes to the sails, boards and allowable racing options. Although the Sunfish remains a strict one-design class, any racer must be aware of the latest developments if he or she hopes to be competitive on the race course.

Hull

Several years ago at a local Bolton Lake Regatta in Connecticut, all the Sunfish hulls were weighed for experimental purposes. The results were a surprise to all: boats varied by more than plus or minus 10 percent from the average. The truth of the matter is that, until recently, there has been lit-

AMF Alcort photo

tle weight control of hulls at AMF Alcort, meaning that there may be thousands of overweight hulls in existence. (You're not allowed to modify a stock hull so as to lighten it.) After years of chasing used Sunfish ads and running around with a pair of bathroom scales, I finally found a 119-pound, watertight, oldie-but-goodie of 1963 vintage. If your hull falls into the "lead sled" class, I would suggest trading up — the new factory boats average a respectable 130 pounds or less.

Although new boats are now pressure-checked twice before shipping, hull leakage in older boats has always been an item of concern for Sunfish racers. However, home repair is possible. After installing a few inspection ports, blow into the hull with the pressure side of a vacuum cleaner, wet the hull and fittings with soapy water and look for leaks. Common trouble spots are the daggerboard trunk, splash rail, gunwale rubrail and rudder thru-bolts. Before sealing the leaks with silicone or Marine Tex, completely dry out the inside. Any hot-air source will do wonders (e.g. a hair dryer or a trailer ride with inspection ports open).

Hull stiffness is another top priority. The hull and deck are supported by longitudinal blocks of styrofoam held in place by urethane foam. The two blocks under the forward deck occassionally become separated from the hull by repeated wave pounding and trailering vibration. If you're a handyman and have installed inspection ports, the blocks can be reattached by applying more urethane foam along their lengths.

Because of the relatively small wetted surface area of the Sunfish hull, very few skippers go to any extremes in maintaining bottom smoothness (remember, it *is* a beach boat). My philosophy is not to worry about the gouges in the gel coat, but to remove all *protrusions* (road tar, grease, etc.) via wet sanding. Avoid wax of any kind, especially on the deck due to slipperiness and water-bead retention.

Bailer

There are several things you can do to optimize use of the plastic thru-hull bailer:

• The rubber gasket between the bailer and the bottom of the hull can be removed and placed inside the cockpit (see figure 1), enabling the bailer to sit flush against the hull.

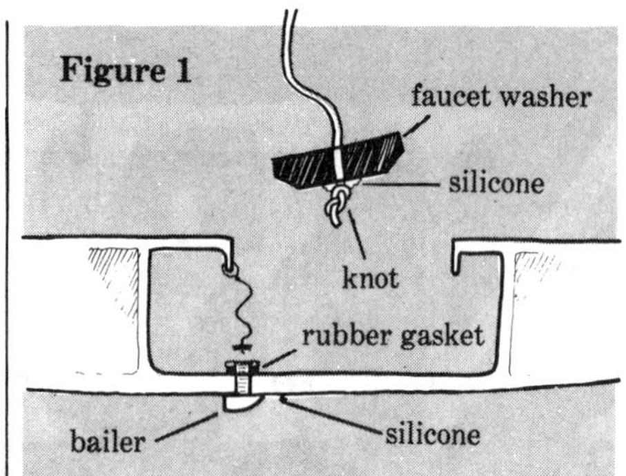

"When the breeze begins to climb over 15 mph, two depowering rig options can be employed."

Also, class rules allow sealing the edges of the bailer with silicone.

• The factory-supplied bailer plug is clumsy to remove. I have replaced it with a rubber, half-inch-diameter faucet washer attached to a pull string (see figure 1) that is easily reached while hiking.

• Although the bailer works well for normal operation, if you have a tub full of water, it is slow in doing its job. This is further complicated by the presence of an aft cubbyhole (in boats built after 1970) from which it is especially difficult to remove water. In order to reduce the volume available for water collection, I cram two child's beach balls into this cavity. This works well in screaming-plane conditions when a rooster tail of water pours out of the daggerboard trunk into the cockpit.

Foils

On a Sunfish the daggerboard is the most critical determinant of windward performance. Over the many production years no less than three board shapes (see figure 2) have been produced, all still legal and all, in varying degrees, undersized for the boat's sail area. For my money, the original "old" style board (produced until about 1970) is still the best. The "new" style board (dating from 1970-79) is completely unsatisfactory for racing because of its relatively small area. The third style — the "Barrington" board (named after an active frostbite fleet that first tested the shape out) — is a compromise configuration that has about the same area as the "old" style but is easier to manufacture in volume. Although many racers prefer the Barrington board, I still like my old, blunt-tipped antique. If you find one, grab it at any price — remember, all boards used for racing must be Alcort supplied.

Sunfish rudders have also been changed: In the early 70s Alcort replaced the original cast-bronze rudder assembly (which was prone to popping up in heavy air) with a spring-loaded system. The new assembly is a vast improvement and also features a slightly larger rudder.

Once you have the right blades, you'll probably need to modify them to get the most out of the class tolerances. Here's how to do it:

• Using a filler such as Bondo or Marine Tex, build up the leading and trailing edges to the maximum allowable width without violating the shape criteria. Contour the leading edge to an approximate elliptical shape (see figure 2) and taper the trailing edge to a thickness of about one-sixteenth of an inch. (Remember, the maximum taper length is an inch and a quarter.)

• If required, bring the board up to the maximum overall thickness (13/16ths of an inch) by wrapping it with fiberglass.

• Finish both blades off with several coats of white paint to facilitate weed-spotting while underway.

Daggerboard/Rudder Maintenance

Since the Sunfish has been around as long as it has, we know what parts

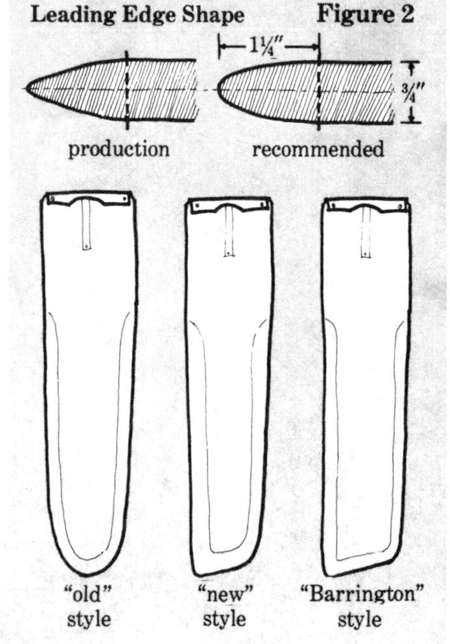

Illustrations by Brad Dellenbaugh

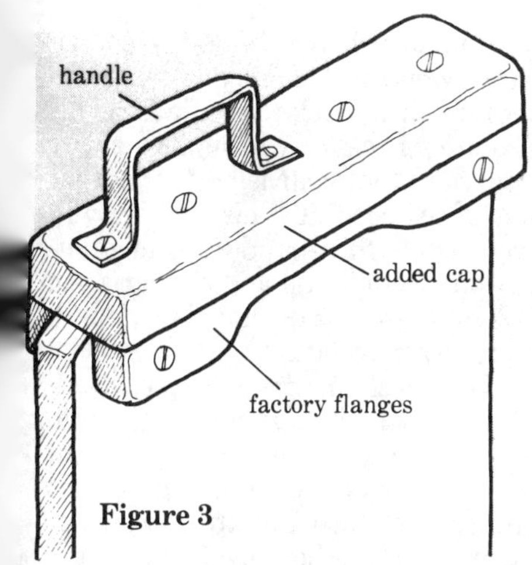

of the daggerboard and rudder/tiller assembly are failure prone and what preventative maintenance works best:

- The top of the daggerboard is assembled with side-finger flanges attached perpendicularly to the board with two to four screws per side (depending on the year). After a few seasons and repeated slamming down of the board, those screws will crack the mahogany and eventually pull out a section of wood. The fix is to put a wooden cap on top of the board (see figure 3) on which a handle or strap can be attached for easy raising.
- The bolt holes in the ends of the tiller and extension are subjected to plenty of wear and tear and can become enlarged, promoting a sloppy helm. The connecting bolt can now be legally replaced with a universal, which solves the problem and also provides the long-needed advantages of rotational flexibility. (The only joint I have found on the market designed for flat wooden tiller extensions is made by RWO Marine in England.)
- Those who prefer the stock thru-bolt assembly should be aware of another potential Sunfish failure: the old "tiller extension in the hand trick." The thru-bolt that connects the tiller extension to the tiller will eventually crack through the ends of these pieces. To prevent this, simply wrap a few layers of fiberglass around the tiller and extension ends.
- A sloppy helm can also be caused by enlargement of the holes in the cast aluminum rudder housing. The installation of two bronze bushings produces a much tighter fit.

Sail

The biggest single performance improvement to the Sunfish came in 1980 when the factory-supplied sail was redesigned by Hans Fogh. The original Ratsey sail was cut too flat for almost all conditions, requiring an extensive "breaking-in" period before it was competitive. The new sail, on the other hand, is fast right out of the bag. Besides being fuller, the Fogh sail is more durable with Dacron reinforcing in the corners, beefed up luff/foot tapes and stronger grommets. To facilitate adjusting the sail draft, the class rules have recently been changed to allow outhauls of any length mounted on the spars. My personal preference is to retain the standard fixed outhaul for the sailhead while attaching to the clew a long outhaul, which is led to a small cleat on the boom (see figure 4). At the beginning of a race day, I pull

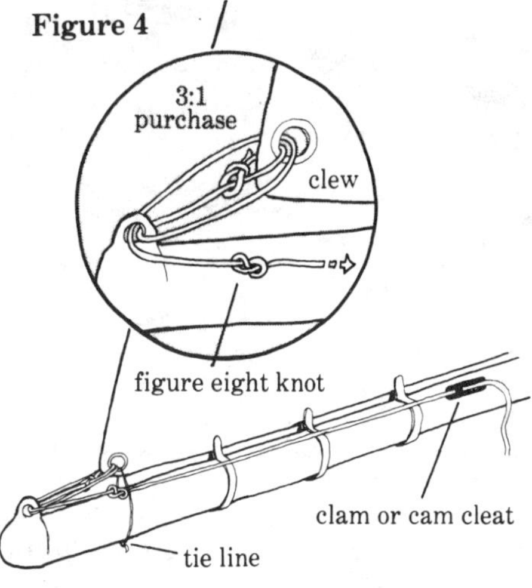

the head outhaul tight enough to remove the scallops for light/medium air and forget about it. As conditions change, I adjust the clew outhaul so that it's just snug enough to eliminate scallops along the foot in light to medium conditions, then I progressively tension it as the wind builds. A few sailors are still replacing the "sail sets" (plastic rings used to attach the sail to the spars) with tie lines (as was common practice with old, flatter Ratsey sails), but I think this is overkill. There are two areas, however, where tie lines can be beneficial: adjacent to the masthead (to prevent binding between the mast and gaff) and adjacent to the boom blocks to avoid hang-ups with clew adjustments.

Since the center of effort is further aft in the fuller Fogh sail, the gooseneck should be kept well aft on the boom (approximately 26 inches from the front cap) compared to where it was positioned when using the flatter Ratsey sail. The halyard clove hitch should be positioned just below the 10th sail clip. This puts the tack of the sail approximately two to four inches off the deck and provides added support to the upper half of the gaff (supplying more power in light to medium conditions) while keeping the center of effort low, which reduces heeling moment and leeway.

When the breeze begins to climb over 15 mph, two depowering rig options can be employed. A rig developed by Jens Hookanson in the Virgin Islands (see figure 5) allows the upper spar to bend off and open the leech while keeping the sailplan in the desired low position. Since its introduc-

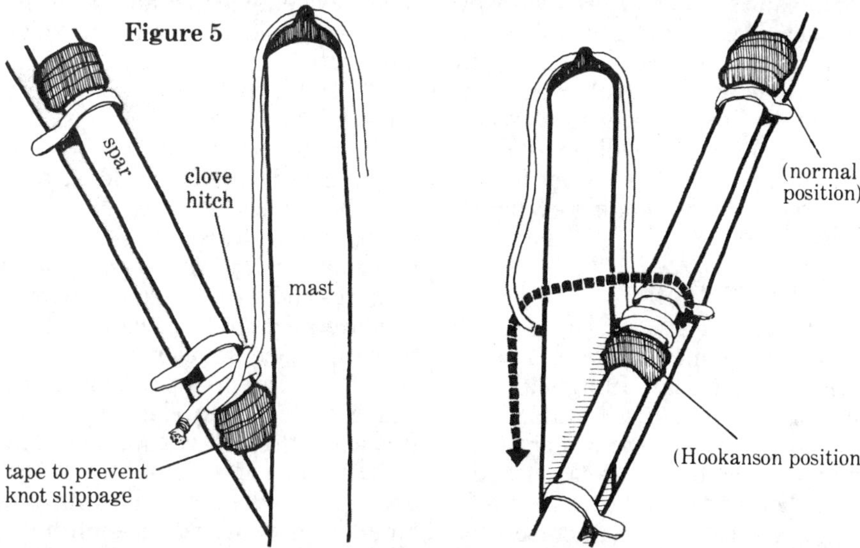

Shown above are two views of the Hookanson rig. To tie it yourself, follow this procedure: 1. Tilt the boat on its side. Tie the halyard to the upper spar 12 to 15 inches lower than its usual position. 2. Put the halyard up and through the top of the mast and bring the end back down. Instead of pulling the upper spar up to the mast tip, leave 12 to 15 inches of clearance. 3. Take the halyard around both mast and spar and tie a half hitch. 4. Make sure the boom is the correct height above the deck, then pull knot as tight as possible around the spars. 5. Tilt the boat back up and cleat the halyard on the deck.

Figure 6

The Odie rig (above) reduces sail camber on starboard tack by running the halyard down on the port side of the sail (instead of along the mast on the starboard side). Paul Odegard photo.

tion at the 1976 North Americans, the "Jens" rig has become the norm in heavy air — for lightweights and "heavies" alike. When the conditions border on survival, the last straw short of dropping the sail is a rig I developed — the "Odie" rig (see figure 6) — which utilizes the halyard to take camber out of the sail on starboard tack, the tack on which the lateen-rigged sail is not interfered with by the mast. The advantage of this rig is that it can be used in conjunction with the Jens and can be easily rigged on the water without lowering the sail. Both the Jens and Odie rigs don't seem to limit boatspeed downwind since you're on a honking plane already.

Sheet/Bridle Setups

In recent years a variety of sheet/bridle arrangements have been seen on the racing circuit. In light air it is still common practice to attach the sheet to the loop in the center of the standard bridle. However, once the breeze begins to build, this results in too full a sail shape. Remember, the Sunfish has a much fuller sail on starboard tack than it does on port due to mast interference. This requires a more vertical sheeting angle on starboard tack to flatten the extra-full sail. This can be accomplished by tying the sheet to the port side of the cable bridle

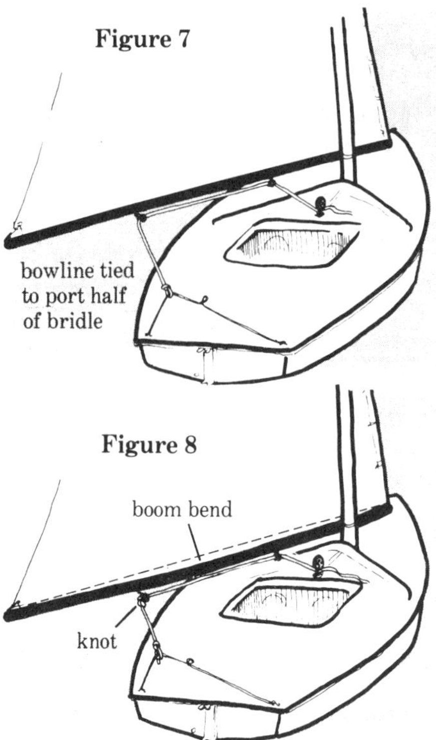

Short sheeting enables you to induce boom bend without overtrimming the sail. Simply tie a figure eight knot in the sheet between the traveler and the last block on the boom. Once the sail is sheeted to the knot, increased tension is translated into flattening the sail.

(see figure 7), which allows it to slide to leeward on the "full sail" tack and keeps it centered on the "flat sail" tack. When conditions require this flattening effect on both tacks, the sheet can be tied to a newly legalized "loopless" rope traveler, which allows it to slide from side to side across the traveler's full length.

With the new Fogh sail, the rope traveler should always be used in medium to heavy air. Its working length should be at the legal minimum of 30 inches to provide the most vertical downward force. While a free-running traveler is an improvement, I still leave the old cable bridle in place as a spare in case I should break the rope traveler.

The maximum sheet length is no longer controlled by class rules, and I find a length of approximately 28 feet to be about right. I usually carry a quarter-inch-diameter sheet for light air and a soft woven three-eighth-inch sheet for heavy air. When the breeze is up, the "short sheet" trick can be employed to flatten the sail (see figure 8).

Boathandling

Because most skippers outweigh the Sunfish hull, the boat is very sensitive to weight placement. In light to medium air in a relatively flat sea, it is absolutely necessary to sit all the way forward so that your leg hits the front edge of the cockpit. This position will level the boat fore and aft and minimize the wetted hull and rudder area. As wind and sea conditions build, gradually move aft.

Hiking styles in the strapless Sunfish are varied, but generally fall into three categories: spread eagle, straight leg and drooped. When sea conditions require some fore-and-aft "torso English" to help the boat over waves, the spread eagle position works well. Many tall skippers prefer the straight-leg/stiff-body technique, which keeps your butt out of the water, but can also be very tiring. Short to average height skippers generally droop hike and must hook their toes under the forward edge of the cockpit lip to get the necessary extension over the rail. To facilitate facing forward when droop hiking, I cross my aft ankle under my forward ankle.

Successful windward steering technique in the Sunfish requires plenty of rudder movement. Since the rudder is undersized, extreme helm motions are not detrimental to boatspeed and are in fact necessary if you are to avoid stalling out the boat's smallish daggerboard. After a day of heavy-air sailing in chop, the sorest parts of my body are my arms from horsing the tiller and mainsheet. Management of a typical "whammie" wave in heavy air goes something like this: As you enter the face of the wave, move aft and inboard to keep the bow high and pinch up directly into the wave (don't worry about luffing); at the crest, pump the helm, hike hard and ease the sheet to gather speed and foot/surf down the back side of the wave. Upwind in the heavy stuff, aggressiveness and agility within the legal limits spell SPEED.

On reaches and runs the Sunfish should always be heeled to windward to reduce wetted area, raise the sailplan and neutralize weather helm. This should be done in all conditions, even in a blow, when it's been proven repeatedly that near-capsize heeling on a run, combined with sheet pumping, results in superior speed. If the boat starts to capsize, a speed-gathering recovery can be accomplished by hauling in dramatically on the sheet. In extreme sea conditions it may sometimes be necessary to pounce onto the

Miscellaneous Tips and Accessories

Hiking Comfort — Due to the narrow gunwale rubrail and protruding cockpit lip, hiking in the Sunfish can be painful on a long beat. To pad the back of my thighs, I use homemade hiking shorts made from an old pair of jeans with rubber-backed carpet pads sewn into the seat (make sure the carpet extends down almost to the knees). To protect my calves against chafe on the cockpit lip, I wear long wrestler pads.

Sore toes are another hiking-related problem. Most hiking boots currently on the market are inadequate for the Sunfish because of their thin topsides. I prefer a basketball-type sneaker with plenty of rubber over the toes. In heavy air I insert additional pads inside the sneaker and even wrap duct tape around the tips for extra chafe protection.

Wind Indicators — Gaff-mounted wind indicators such as the AMF Alcort Feathermate (with port and starboard feathers) should always be placed low in the skipper's line of sight. Also, some sort of masthead fly, either homemade or commercial, should always be used. Wind-flow indicators on the sail are also a must, although on the lateen rig they are only useful on starboard tack. I use one placed about 30" up the gaff, just forward of the mast.

Mainsheet System — A center-mounted ratchet block is an absolute necessity for adequate mainsheet control in all wind conditions. Side-deck mounted clam cleats can be easily uncleated with a flick of the wrist. A center-mounted block and cam cleat should *not* be used since it is too easy to cleat (discouraging working the sheet) and is too difficult to uncleat from a hiking position.

Halyard Tricks — Once the sail has been raised, there are a couple of things you can do with the tail end of a Sunfish halyard. If the conditions are light, many sailors rig a "JC strap" by tying the end of the halyard to the forward tip of the boom and leading it aft to the skipper. The halyard is then used to keep the boom out, especially when heeling to weather on a broad reach or run. As the breeze builds, a downhaul should be rigged by leading the halyard from the cleat up and over the gooseneck and back down to the cleat. Since the Sunfish has no vang, this halyard setup is needed to keep the gooseneck from riding up off the wind.

Daggerboard Trunk — Class rules allow the installation of "anti-chafe" strips along the forward and aft ends of the daggerboard trunk. I have had good luck using a section of foam insulation for half-inch water pipes available at most hardware stores. These inserts should be run all the way down to the bottom of the hull, but cannot legally protrude. To further protect the leading and trailing edges of your board, attach a half-inch-wide strip of teflon sheet to the insulation with weatherstrip adhesive. A key to reducing turbulence inside the lower trunk is keeping the board vertical (not tilted) and forward when it is pulled up on a reach or run. A convenient daggerboard-retention device that accomplishes this is a bow-and-arrow, shockcord arrangement (see photo above) mounted at deck level.

Paul's bow-and-arrow daggerboard retention device consists of shockcord led to the ends of the splash rail with a section of garden hose protecting the aft edge of the board. Also note the rope traveler, mainsheet system, wind indicators and tactical compass. Paul Odegard photo.

Spar Maintenance — Mast failure due to fatigue at the mast step is an occasional problem. If you have an old mast that is showing fatigue cracks, I am told that you can swap the two plastic end-plugs and reverse the mast.

The holes for the interconnecting eyebolts that connect the boom and gaff are also subject to wear and corrosion. Old spars can be salvaged by either rotating the boom and gaff 90 degrees or by turning them end for end. Repositioning of the end plugs, sheet blocks and eyebolts are required in either case.

Old Sails — The original Ratsey & Lapthorn sails were cut far too flat for light to medium air conditions. If you can't face the "sticker shock" of a new Fogh sail, this can be remedied to some degree. To put in more shape, spread out the spars horizontally so that the sail is off the ground, and add weight to the resulting sail pocket (one third of the way back from the gaff).

With age an old sail can actually become too full (as well as porous) for most conditions. This has led many top sailors to carry around two or more sails that they swap as conditions warrant: a flat Ratsey for heavy air, a new Fogh for medium air and an old faithful bag for drifters.

Safety — The trend toward lowered sailplans in Sunfish has created a potential neck-hanging problem if the sheet is allowed to droop from the boom during a jibe or tack. To prevent the "noose" syndrome, the class allows the taping of flexible loops along the boom. Short sections of garden hose work well.

A safety retention line should always be attached to the daggerboard in case of capsize. On all new boats a line and a deck-mounted eye strap are provided for this purpose.

An absolute requirement for safe Sunfish racing is a window in the sail. The 4.5-by-64-inch window configuration is the most common.

aft deck to keep the nose from "deep sixing." The Sunfish reacts quickly to body kinetics, and when accompanied by some rudder wigglin' down the backside of the wave, the resulting ride is both exhilarating and rewarding.

Strategy and Tactics

With some 200,000 boats out there, Sunfish competition usually means big fleets. Turnouts at local regattas number 30 to 40 boats, regionals 75, and North American and world championships see 100 boats on the starting line. As you might imagine, the starts can be brutal! Therefore, your number one tactical goal in Sunfish competition should be to sharpen your starting skills and build confidence and aggressiveness on the line. In our large fleets, a good start and conservative tactics will usually buy you a respectable finish, even with only average boatspeed. Of course, the best way to practice starting is to join the regatta circuit, and since the class has always been family oriented, bring everybody along!

In the words of retired Sunfish veteran Carl Knight, "success will come if you just hang in there and don't give up." I know there are lots of Sunfish skippers out there who, with continued practice and dedication, can shorten the internship — 19 years in my case — to becoming a North American Champion. •

From the Experts SUNFISH

Sunfish champ Scott Kyle explains the keys to boatspeed for one of the world's most popular singlehanders. Illustrations by Henry Hill.

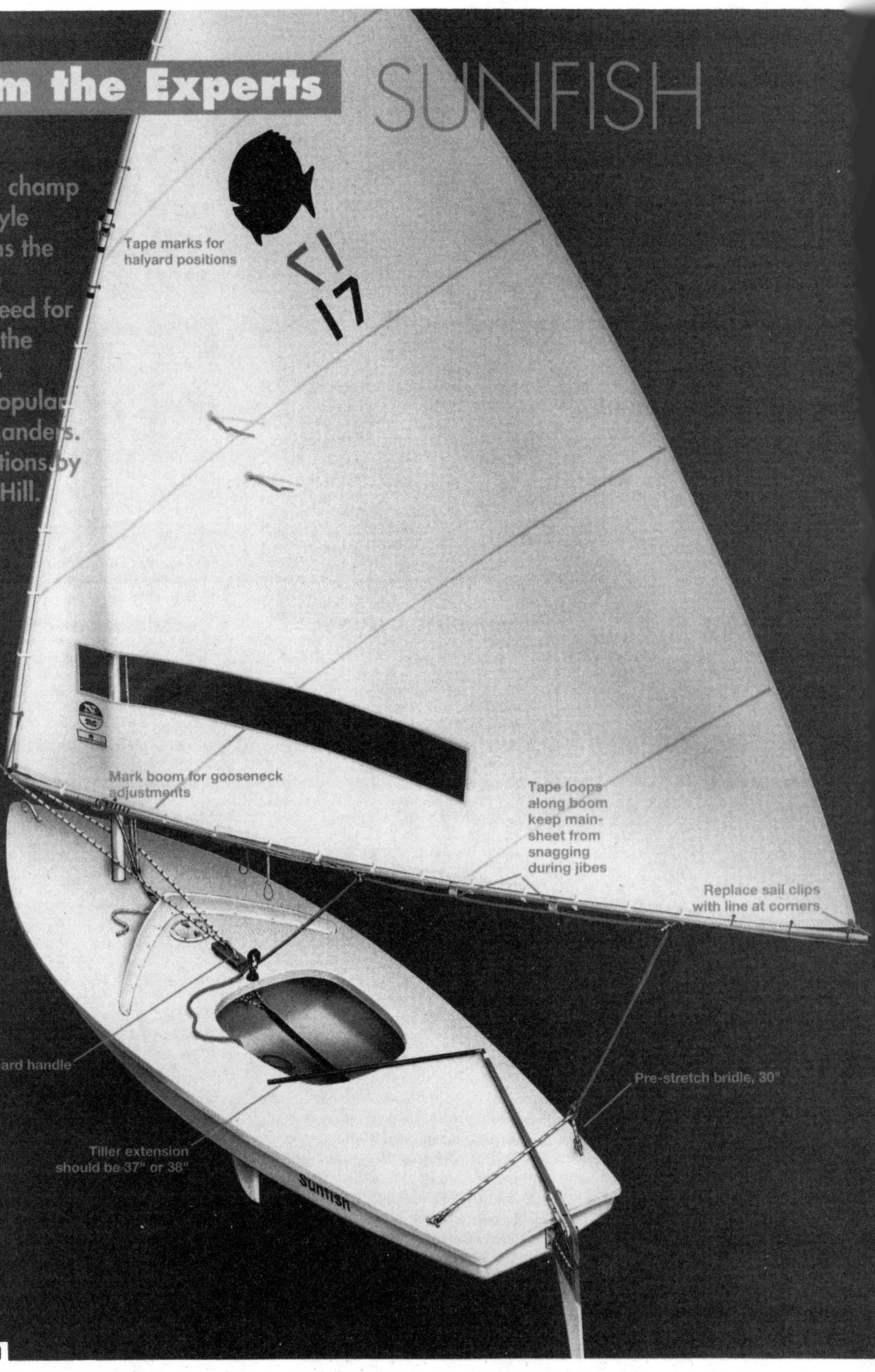

Tape marks for halyard positions

Shock cord JC strap, holds boom out and board up downwind

Mark boom for gooseneck adjustments

Tape loops along boom keep main-sheet from snagging during jibes

Replace sail clips with line at corners

Daggerboard handle

Pre-stretch bridle, 30"

Tiller extension should be 37" or 38"

Sunfish

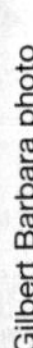
Gilbert Barbara photo

Ninety-three boats from 13 countries raced in the Sunfish World Championship last summer in Curaçao.

The Sunfish celebrated its 30th birthday in 1991 as one of the most popular one-design boats of all time. While the Sunfish has undergone many changes since its origin as an off-the-beach boat, its evolution over the past five years has been particularly astounding. The introduction of the racing sail, the hiking strap, the modernized deck layout, the aluminum tiller extension, and the cunningham system represent just some of the recent developments. These innovations have helped to make the Sunfish a more competitive, and truer, one-design class.

In the spring of 1991, Sunfish/Laser, Inc. purchased the Sunfish from Pearson Yachts, and quickly moved to implement several positive changes to the boat. While the Sunfish is still enjoyed "out of the box" by thousands of sailors around the world, today's racers must make several modifications to the hull, foils, sail, and spars in order to pick up some silver. To be sure, the rules governing the allowable changes are strict, resulting in fairer and more enjoyable racing for all Sunfish sailors. Knowing what "tinkering" is permitted, however, is essential for all racers who want to end up in the winner's circle whether they race a new or used boat.

Hull Preparation

Of primary importance is the maintenance of a light, stiff, scratch-free hull. Extensive sanding or waxing of a new boat is not necessary. Simply ensure that the hull is clean and free of gelcoat bubbles. Today, boats coming off the factory floor average around 126 pounds. If you are purchasing a used boat, try to get one in the 126- to 130-pound range. A boat as heavy as 135 pounds is OK provided that the hull is fairly stiff. If your current boat weighs between 135 and 145 pounds, rest easy. Hundreds of Sunfish regattas, including the midwinter and North American championships, have been won in 15-year-old "clunkers." Good boathandling and sound tactics can easily make up for 20 pounds of extra hull weight.

Whether your boat is brand new or a 1964 vintage, there are several things you can do to enhance its overall performance. First, add an inspection port at the first sign of leaking and find the source. Foam blocks in the hull soak up water and are the primary cause of a boat's weight gain. A five-inch port installed to the side of the daggerboard trunk gives easy access to the most likely point of leakage — the trunk itself. If you are unable to completely stop the flow of water, bring a sponge on the water with you and dry your boat between races. This will guarantee a light boat not only for the next race, but for the seasons to come.

If your boat does not already have a hiking strap, consider installing one for more effective hiking in medium and heavy air. Use your inspection port to through-bolt two eye straps, approximately three inches apart, at the desired height on the front side of the cockpit. For the aft end of the strap, through-bolt two more eye-straps on the lip of the cubby hole, with the ends of the bolts going through the lip and into the cubby hole, not the hull itself. Finally, tie off your strap using line and shock cord for proper height and tension. This system spreads the load out over eight bolts, and stays very secure even for sailors over 180 pounds.

More damage is done to a Sunfish hull while being transported to a regatta than on the water, even in heavy air. Trailering your boat upside down will add years to its competitive life. I've seen too many people polish the bottom of their boats only to toss them on a trailer right side up and bounce the boat's stiffness right out.

Two operations should be performed to the daggerboard trunk to ensure a scratch- and vibration-free board. First, sand the sides of the trunk, both top and bottom, until any sharp ridge is eliminated. Secondly, add 13-inch by 1-inch carpet or other protective strips to the fore and aft walls of the trunk. Silicone glue or contact cement works well in applying the strips. Before installing the strips, insert your board into the trunk and determine the amount of extra space. Use enough glue to eliminate this play.

Replace the standard wire bridle traveler with a 30-inch piece of pre-stretch line, the minimum length allowed by the rules. Some sailors like to tie off-set knots in the traveler to account for the different sail shape and angle of attack on starboard versus port. I have found letting the mainsheet run the full length of the traveler to be effective in all conditions. Finally, mount a ratchet block either on the deck or the lip of the cockpit. I sail without cleats which encourages continuous playing of the mainsheet. If your arms get tired in heavy air, you may want to install Clamcleats on the side of the deck for occasional use.

Blades

The tiller extension, which can be any length, should just skim the ratchet base so that the extension rests comfortably in your lap while you hike and still clears the mainsheet during tacks (37 to 38 inches). Use a rubber universal for maximum mobility and minimum play in the tiller. Concerning the daggerboard, add a handle to the top for easy raising and lowering at marks. A seven-foot piece of 1/4-inch shock cord acts as both a daggerboard retainer and a "JC strap" that holds the sail out in light air downwind. Feed the shock cord through the handle of the dag-

Halyard Position

Wind Strength	Halyard Position	Gooseneck Height*	Vang Tension
Light Air	10th Clip	3" Above Deck	Light
Medium Air	1-2" Down	4-5" Above Deck	Medium
Heavy Air	2-3" Down	5-8" Above Deck	Hard
Jens Rig	10-12" Down	5-8" Above Deck	Hard

* Gooseneck height above deck, before vang tension is applied.

gerboard, around the tack and back to itself, going around the mast and the halyard. In terms of tension, you want the cord tight enough so that the board stays up and the sail out in light air, but not so tight that you have trouble sheeting the sail properly. The seven feet gives you a little extra cord with which to fine-tune the tension.

The daggerboard is the subject of quite a bit of discussion in the class this year. In the past, sailors have gone to great lengths to modify their stock boards by building up the leading edge to produce a more parabolic shape, which helps pointing upwind, and to taper the trailing edge to reduce turbulence. In order to make the boat a stricter one-design, the class is developing a more high-performance stock racing daggerboard that will eliminate all the variations that currently exist. The new design is still being developed, but will be submitted for approval at the World Championship in Houston, Texas, in September. While we'll all be racing with our favorite boards this summer, by next year at this time many sailors will be racing with the new board, and the racing should be better than ever.

Sail and Spars

The introduction of the North racing sail in 1988 has had several favorable effects on Sunfish racing throughout the world. The primary impact has been to minimize speed differences between the boats, as seen in the past due to considerable variations in sail shape. The consistent shape and quality from one sail to the next has made for closer and fairer racing. Long gone are the days of having to decide which of your four sails you would put on the spars. Now each racer sails with confidence that his or her sail is as fast as any in the fleet. With this in mind, the following suggestions are intended to help every racer get the most out of the racing sail through optimal set-up, tuning, and trimming.

A small number of the sail clips should be replaced by 1/8-inch line to facilitate optimal sail shape. Line should be placed at the head of the sail and the last three grommets on the boom, including the clew. Having line here allows you to get rid of the wrinkles that emanate from the back quarter of the sail. The clips immediately above and below the halyard attachment to the gaff (sprit) should also be replaced with line. Clips tend to bind the sail when it hits the mast on port tack. In addition, substitute the S hook at the tack with a piece of line to ensure the tack remains close to the apex of the spars (the hook often bends, causing the tack to fall out). Finally, make two loops out of duct tape or other flexible material through which your mainsheet is fed, and attach them to the boom. This will keep the mainsheet from hooking on your life jacket during tacks and jibes.

The three most popular types of wind indicators are telltales attached directly to the sail, streamers coming off of wire attached to the gaff spar, and the masthead fly. I like to place two sets of two back-to-back telltales on my sail. I place the first set at the top of the third (middle) panel, approximately 30" from the gaff. The second set of two should be attached to the sail at the bottom of the second panel (the panel with the class insignia), approximately 26" from the gaff. This positioning is far enough back on the sail as to avoid inaccurate readings caused by disturbed air flow from the mast. Recordin tape flows well, even in light air, and wi dry quickly if the sail gets wet due to rainfa or capsizing. Gaff-mounted indicators, whic can be purchased pre-made or constructe out of yarn and a wire hanger, avoid the potential problem of inaccurate readings. These should be mounted at sight level, approximately two to three feet from the apex of the spars. The masthead fly is attached to the top of the gaff, and gives good readings on the downwind leg. It is usually the sailor who knows how to effectively read his or her masthead fly who sails the dead downwind leg on the correct jibe.

Halyard Position

The halyard should be pre-stretch or some other low-stretch line, about 24 feet in length and 1/4-inch in width. By employing a purchase system, you can keep the gaff spar snug against the mast for the entire day. You should have four halyard heights pre-marked with tape on the gaff: light air, medium air, heavy air, and Jens position. (See sidebar for explanation of the Jens Hookanson rig.) Tie the halyard using a clove-hitch just below the given piece of tape for the race's wind condition.

The light-air position, for example, allows for maximum power in the sail. Even in light air, however, use a small amount of vang to maintain leech tension downwind. After "vanging-down," your gooseneck will end up in the same height (two to three inches above the deck), regardless of the wind velocity. Placing the halyard lower on the gaff in heavy air raises the sail height, thus allowing you to vang down harder and still have the gooseneck three inches above the deck.

Outhaul Systems

The larger, more powerful North racing sail has placed a premium on effective depowering of the rig. As a result of a rule change in 1988, new outhaul and cunningham systems allow the skipper to alter easily and quickly the shape of the sail while continuing to focus on the race. Install two cleats on

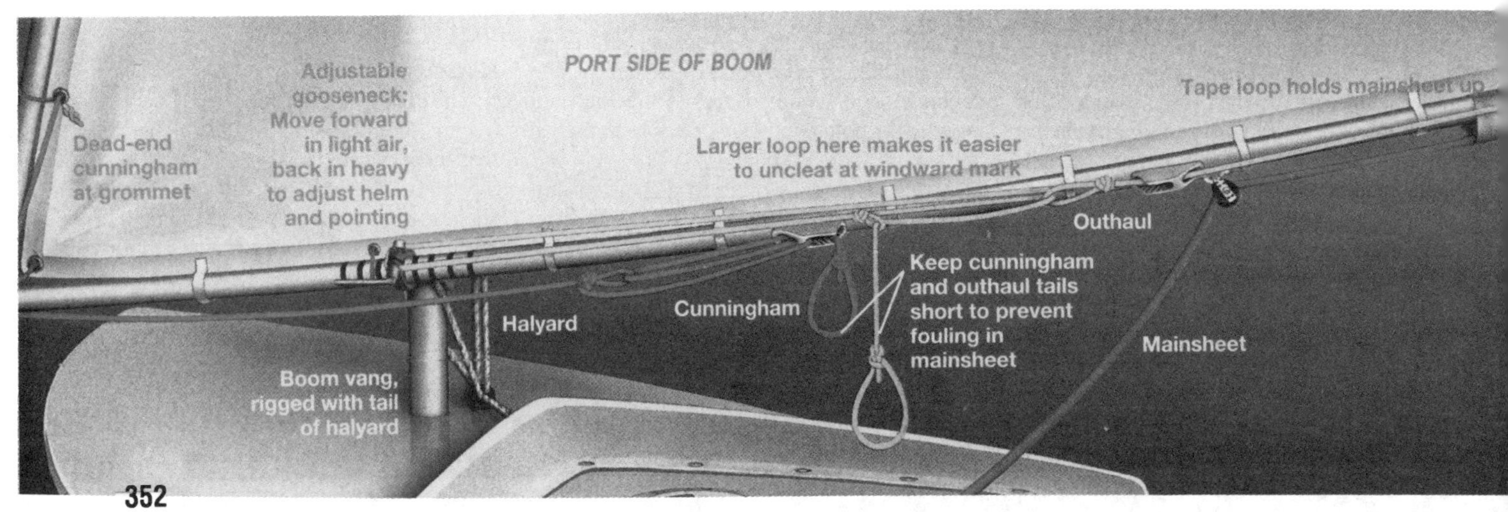

e port side of the boom, far enough forward that the tails of the lines will not get caught the mainsheet block, yet still be within each. Make certain to center the cleats between two clips so that there will be no interference as the clips slide fore and aft with the djusting of the outhaul and cunningham.

To set up the cunningham, dead-end the ine with an eight knot through the first rommet above the tack. Feed the line traight through the eye on the forward end of the boom, and tie a loop near the cleat. Pass the tail from back to front through the cleat, through the loop, and back to the cleat. Tie a loop for a handle. The head of the sail should be tied off at the "max-looseness" position, the loosest you would ever want the luff tension.

For the outhaul, attach the line to the clew, pass it through the end of the boom, and then forward through the cleat and tie a loop. Bring the tail of this same line forward around the gooseneck and then aft, and tie another loop in this section of the line. Then take the tail aft through the first loop near the cleat, and forward again to the second loop. As with the cunningham, make a loop handle for easier adjustments (see diagram). Finally, use two different color, 5/32-inch or 3/16-inch lines so that the two adjustments are easily distinguishable.

For sail tuning, ease both the outhaul and cunningham at the weather mark for increased downwind power and speed. Having the cleats on the port side serves two purposes. First, it forces the sailor to "pop" the outhaul and cunningham on his or her final port approach to the windward mark, rather than while rounding on starboard when the focus should be on making the transition to downwind. Secondly, the port-side cleats make for convenient re-tightening upon rounding the leeward mark.

The outhaul tension primarily affects the fullness of the bottom third of the sail, while the cunningham alters the draft of the sail fore and aft. In light air and flat water, the outhaul should be fairly tight, with minimal scallops along the foot. The cunningham should be set just loose enough so that the sail takes on a smooth shape on port tack. A luff that is too tight will cause a large hard spot on the luff of the sail, leading to disturbed air flow. As the wind picks up and the waves get bigger, loosen both the outhaul and cunningham for additional power to get through the chop. There should be visible scallops along both the foot and luff of the sail. As the wind increases and the boat becomes overpowered, begin to tighten both controls. In very heavy air, the outhaul should stretch to within an inch of the end of the boom. The cunningham tension should be set so that the luff of the sail is very tight and free of scallops.

Gooseneck Position

Wind Strength (knots)	Gooseneck Setting
Under 5	17 - 18
5 - 8	18 - 19
8 - 12	19 - 20
12 - 15	20 - 21
15 - 20	21 - 22
20 - 25	22 - 23
Over 25	Jens Rig, 20 - 21

Gooseneck

Today the gooseneck is recognized as one of the most important variables for optimizing upwind speed and pointing in all wind conditions. The gooseneck should be moved fore and aft as the wind changes velocity in order to neutralize the helm and place the center of effort of the sail over the daggerboard. With a permanent black pen, mark a range from 17 to 23 inches at one-inch intervals along the boom, measuring from the apex of the spars. These lines represent your seven-inch range within which you will set your gooseneck.

These numbers are approximate only, and will vary with individual weight and sailing style. In general, the lighter the wind and the flatter the water, the farther forward the gooseneck. Having the gooseneck at 17 inches in these conditions will help pointing. As the wind picks up and the waves increase in size, move the gooseneck back. A pair of wrenches or pliers and a couple of turns are all you need to loosen the bolt which keeps the gooseneck in place. For those who want to minimize the tools you bring on the water and thus the weight in the boat, invest in an "adjustable" gooseneck fitting. These are on the market and advertised in the class newsletter, the *Windward Leg*.

If the wind increases to the point where you install a Jens rig, you should move the gooseneck forward a couple of inches from your heavy air, non-Jens position. The Jens itself helps to neutralize the helm, so you need the gooseneck forward to help your pointing. Ultimately, you want to use the feel of the helm as your litmus test. If you have a great deal of weather helm, move the gooseneck back, regardless of the wind velocity. Conversely, if your pointing is poor, adjust the gooseneck forward until you reach the optimal combination of helm and pointing.

Boom Vang

The larger, fuller racing sail requires more vang tension than its predecessors. The vang is rigged with the tail of the halyard, and passes over the gooseneck and around the mast, then back down and aft to the cleat. This system is simple, effective, and easily adjusted, even during the last minutes of a starting sequence.

Because both the vang tension and gooseneck position are set for the entire race, it is important to position them for the conditions expected for the majority of the race. For example, if, at five minutes before the start, the wind is a five-knot seabreeze expected to build to 18 knots within an hour, you should set your gooseneck at around 19 to 20 inches. This setting allows for fairly good pointing off the starting line in addition to a neutral helm once the wind kicks in.

Sail Trim

A unique quality of the Sunfish is the fact that the sail is flatter on port tack than on starboard. This has several consequences when it comes to upwind sailing and tuning. In medium air (five to 15 knots), the boat is generally sailed the same on both port and starboard tacks. The "mast phenomenon" becomes a factor in light and heavy air (under five and over 15). In light air, especially if there is any chop, it is important to avoid over-sheeting on port tack. Letting the sail "breathe" helps the boat reach maximum speed, which is essential for effective pointing. The fuller sail on starboard allows for tighter sheeting without stalling.

In heavy air, the flatter sail on port tack allows you to sheet tighter without overpowering the boat. On starboard, you will need to sheet out faster when a puff hits in order to keep the boat flat and driving forward. When tacking from port to starboard in heavy air, make certain to sheet in slowly enough to keep the boat flat and to prevent the daggerboard from stalling. If you are having pointing problems, the first solution is to ease out, gain additional speed, and then slowly try to point closer to the wind. If you are still pointing poorly, it is time to consider adjusting sail shape.

While we have discussed the various components to proper sail set-up, tuning, and trimming on an individual basis, it is important to recognize that these variables must work together in harmony to achieve optimal performance. A tight outhaul and cunningham along with a loose vang in 15 knots will not combine for maximum speed. As the conditions change so must each sail adjustment, if only marginally. Think of the Sunfish as a fine instrument that must be tuned on a continual basis.

Boathandling

Good boathandling techniques, combined with proper rig set-up, can make up for body

The Jens Hookanson Rig

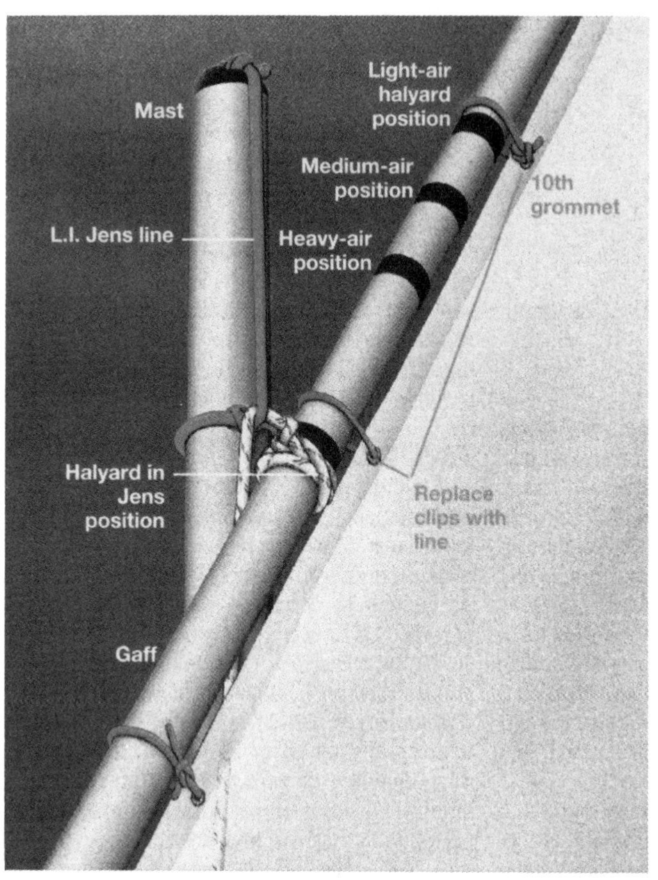

Jens Hookanson and Albert Lang developed a special way to rig the gaff on the Sunfish to allow them to keep up with the heavier sailors in windy St. Croix in the U.S. Virgin Islands. The rig has been used widely by lightweights since Jens won a couple of windy races on his way to claiming the 1976 North Americans when he was a 140-pound 16-year-old.

The introduction of the new racing sail has caused some of the class heavyweights to consider using the Jens rig as a way of effectively depowering the large sail in heavy air. The rig, known as the "Jens," helps the sailor keep the boat flat in heavy air with little risk of diminished boatspeed or pointing ability if the breeze were to lighten during the race. By exposing more gaff than the standard rig, the Jens acts as a backstay, bending the upper spar and flattening the sail. While the original method of rigging the Jens is slowly being replaced by modernized versions, the underlying purpose remains the same.

The Long Island Jens is the latest and most popular variation. With a separate four-foot piece of 1/4-inch line, tie a tight bowline around the mast. Tie the other end of the line with half hitches through the mast cap. The length of the line from the mast cap to the bowline should be around 10 to 12 inches. Move the halyard down the gaff to your "Jens position" 8 to 12 inches below your heavy-air position. Lead the halyard over the bowline, step the mast with the Jens line facing forward, and hoist the sail. Tighten the vang as needed.

As of January 1, 1992, lashing the gaff directly to the mast with a separate line became illegal. This method of rigging a Jens has proven dangerous as it is impossible to disassemble on the water without taking the entire rig out of the boat. It is for this reason that many Sunfish sailors are converting to the L.I. Jens system, with its ease of setting up and taking down.

— *S.K.*

weight disparities in virtually all wind conditions. While the optimal all-around weight for a Sunfish skipper is around 165 pounds, the heavyweights can hold their own in light air while thin can still win when the wind is over 15 knots. Given that the average skipper weighs more than the boat, each movement made is translated directly into the hull and rig. The goal, then, is to be what I call "subtly aggressive." That is, the skipper must be smooth and cat-like in the boat, but aggressively anticipating and reacting to every small change in the wind and sea conditions. In light air and flat water, sit far forward, with your legs snug against the forward edge of the cockpit. In flat water, the boat should have minimum heel, about five degrees. If the wind is light to medium and the sea choppy, or if you are approaching a set of waves, increase the heel to about 10 degrees. Given that the Sunfish has a hard chine, the boat will continue to "track" in light air, even with a fair amount of heel. When you get through the chop, however, flatten the boat back down.

Downwind in light air, sail with considerable windward heel. Sailing the boat on one chine reduces wetted surface area of the hull and neutralizes the helm, thus minimizing overall drag. You should raise the daggerboard as high as possible without losing steering ability. In breeze under 10 knots, this means about six inches of the board under water on a run, and six to 12 inches on a reach depending on the wind angle.

As the wind picks up, flatten the boat upwind, in both flat and choppy conditions. In addition, slide your weight back, especially in waves. The bow tends to plow through waves, so keeping your weight aft will help to reduce the amount of water that flows over the bow and into the cockpit.

Since the Sunfish has a small, inefficient daggerboard, it is important that you maximize its performance. This means sailing the boat very flat upwind in heavy air. You may feel as though the boat is heeling to windward, but there will likely still be some leeward heel. Anticipating puffs is an important element to upwind speed in heavy air. The sailor who waits until a puff hits, lets the boat heel, and then eases the sheet, will slip sideways for several seconds. The skipper who starts to ease the main *before the puff even hits* will maintain a flat boat, and thus a forward path. Skippers should always be active in the boat, rarely cleating the main. Downwind in medium and heavy air, heel the boat to windward slightly less than in light air. Your control of the boat should dictate the board height. If the boat becomes "squirrely," drop the board a few inches for increased stability.

With over 150 regattas a year, from the annual around Shelter Island Race to the World Championship, there is truly an event for everyone. While the Sunfish is still a family-oriented boat, attracting sailors of all ages and skill levels, the recent changes surrounding the hull and rig have made the boat a machine that can be enjoyed by hard-core racers as well.

Scott Kyle has been racing Sunfish for over 15 years, and has won every major Sunfish title including two World, three North American, one junior North American, one midwinter, and countless regional championships. He is the current U.S. Sunfish Class Association President and attends Harvard Business School. For more information on the Sunfish class: USSCA, P.O. Box 128, Drayton Plains, MI 48330; 313/673-2750, or Sunfish/Laser, Inc., P.O. Box 10, Portsmouth, RI 02871; 401/683-5900.

The Sunfish as Tender

by Will White

"Now why didn't I think of that?" the man in the Dyer Dink said as I passed him in my Sunfish on the way to the dock. We were both rowing, not sailing. And it happens all the time, both the passing and the comment.

One advantage of the Sunfish over a dinghy is that it's much faster for the same amount of rowing effort. The other advantage is the sailing. One could use a sailing pram or dinghy, but to me that's the difference between a Metro and a Miata. The first is useful; the second is fun.

The useful part: learning to sail better. You see cruising sailboats under power for just about everything except reaching in open water, and then they are usually over-trimmed. A lot of big sailboat owners, apparently, have never learned much about sailing. The Sunfish can teach them. It's so responsive that you *have* to learn fast. Once you've learned to control a Sunfish, you can control a bigger boat easily. You just have to remember that, on a big boat, everything is in slow motion, and that the boat will carry its way a lot longer, not stop on a dime the way a Sunfish does.

An example of the fun part: I was gassing up at the marina/motel in Orient, NC, last fall, on my way down the ICW, when a couple of young men in an outboard hailed me.

"Want to hang around and race your Sunfish tomorrow?" one said. "We're having an all-class regatta." It didn't take me long to decide; I could afford to lose a day.

"Sure," I said. "Any other Sunfish?" Of course there were; there always are. They handed me a race circular, and with big grins and a wave they were gone. To make the story short, I had a wonderful time, met some delightful people, and won two pounds of fresh crab meat.

A psychic benefit: a Sunfish is a great way for your crew - wife, kids, or guests - to take charge and be on their own as skipper, for a change.

If you have to travel some distance in a big harbor, or want to go gunkholing where the mother boat can't go, you can take the dink with an outboard, or sail the Sunfish. (With my little PY-23 I lashed the rig on the deck of the Sunfish; with my C&C-33 I lashed it to the big boat's stanchions.) I'll take the Sunfish any time. If you'd rather motor than sail, why own a sailboat?

A drawback to the Sunfish out of the box: its hard rubrail will chip the dickens out of the edges of your transom. I slit ordinary garden hose

lengthwise, then fitted it over the rubrail, starting at the rudder fitting and winding around the boat and back to the same place. A couple of slits fit over the rudder fitting and hold the hose in place, without interfering with the rudder itself. Later, when the hose started to wear out at the bow, I added a rubber bumper, the kind that is used at the corner of docks. It makes the Sunfish look more like a bottle-nosed dolphin, but it protects the transom beautifully.

Another drawback is that, without a skeg, the Sunfish doesn't track very well. For years, I just used the rudder, with the tiller held in place by ordinary shock cord. That works fine, except that the boat then tracks *too* well. You have to back hard with one oar and pull hard with the other to make a sharp turn. I recently built a skeg, a lot smaller than the rudder, that hangs immobile from the rudder fitting. Much better.

The rowing rig I've used is very simple, and requires two 1/4-inch holes on each side deck, over the cockpit. The holes are hardly noticeable, and help drain the cockpit when you turn the boat over. With the oarlock brackets right in the middle, between the forward and aft edges of the cockpit, and 6 1/2-foot oars, you're in just the right spot for rowing, with your bottom over the daggerboard well and your feet braced against the aft cockpit lip.

The brackets themselves fit in the storage well aft of the cockpit, and are made from scraps of 1/2-inch marine plywood, marine grade #8 screws, epoxy glue, brackets cut from 1/2-inch do-it-yourself aluminum angle, marine grade 1/4-inch by 2-inch machine screws with washers, nuts and wing nuts, and marine varnish. The first set has lasted 23 years, and, with an occasional coat of varnish, should last 'til I die.

The addition of a sliding seat would add to the fun. I've designed one, but haven't got around to making it yet.

A quick drift down the Connecticut

Story by Dom Degnon/Photographs by Dan Nerney

Paul Amelotte and Peter Darby from the vice and narcotic squad in Hartford were there. Off duty, of course. And for the third time Bob Forrest and his teenage son Dan. They won a trophy. And Gerry Gemmell and his sister-in-law Margaret Hamilton on the Sunfish he bought last summer. And Ellen Kelly and Fred Pati from New York, who had sailed their boat at the Tall Ships celebration last year.

And Peggy Wagner and Russ Jessop from the Monmouth Boat Club in Red Bank, New Jersey, on their fourth outing. "We have a good time. It's fun." And Will White, one of the founders of the race, with son number five, and Lee Parks, One-Design Director of the United States Yacht Racing Union and a friend, and four brothers from Lyme, Connecticut, on four different boats with four friends, and a large contingent of the Traub family from Torrington, Connecticut. And fathers and sons, mothers and daughters, fathers and daughters, mothers and sons—and friends. Every possible combination of relationship was represented among the 70-odd boats in the fifteenth annual Sunfish Connecticut River Classic.

The two-day annual fun race in May follows the lower Connecticut River from Hartford downstream to Essex, with an overnight camp-out at Hurd State Park. The river at Hartford reflects the high-rise buildings, and

Over 70 boats turned out for the Hartford start of the Sunfish Classic

its banks are lined with industry and highways. But soon you are sailing past meadowlands and wetlands. You meander to Middletown, once a leading eighteenth-century seaport, now linked by bridge to Portland, famous for its brownstone quarries. Then the river narrows, the terrain becomes steep and tree-covered, punctuated by a nuclear power plant and occasional houses. From the elegantly restored nineteenth-century Goodspeed Opera House in the settlement of East Haddam to the finish at the Pettipaug Yacht Club, the steep banks drop off, the river widens and narrows, curves and bends as it finds its way to the sea just beyond Essex.

Two people sailed per boat, carrying on board the necessary camping gear (tents, sleeping bags), life jackets, clothing and foul-weather gear, lunch and drinks for two days. The folks at Alcort, builders of the Sunfish, provided the food, drink, and staff for the Saturday night cookout and a complete breakfast Sunday, as well as a postrace party.

The big question for me and fellow cruiser Paul Banks from England was just how serious a "fun race" was. Experienced in provisioning for ocean passages, we found the idea of cramming everything we needed onto a Sunfish daunting. Discrete prerace inquiries to former participants all yielded the same basic responses. "You'll have a great time." "Take lots of garbage bags to wrap things in." There wasn't much in the way of technical advice or suggestions for gear.

Arriving at the starting site, we

On the water and ashore, the prevailing mood was one of lighthearted fun and camaraderie, though there were a competitive few who kept a sharp eye on breeze, windshifts, and gear

discovered a blaze of color. Sails of all hues hung quietly in the absolute brilliance of the blue-sky windless May day. The racers went about preparing their boats, strapping down their equipment, visiting with old friends and making new ones. I was surprised that our big pile of stuff was no bigger than most and in some cases smaller. We wrapped our gear and secured it to the boat with shock-cord as we saw others doing. Then we hoisted the sail. As Paul and I puzzled as to why our boat had no mainsheet but did have a peak halyard, a passing entrant muttered, "Upside down!" and went on his way. This was quickly remedied.

The race rules were laid out at a brief meeting, the most important directive being that all boats were required to aid anyone who capsized or risk disqualification. There were three races planned for Saturday and two for Sunday. Without fuss, 70 boats were launched. I was impressed by the camaraderie, the goodwill, the general spirit of fun and cooperation. The boats milled about on the river, the warning horns went, and we were off—floating on the placid surface with the current, propelled by an occasional barely discernible zephyr.

Instead of shouts of "starboard," there were greetings. "How are you? How have you been?" The fleet divided into groups, the serious racers playing the puffs and currents, while the less serious contented themselves with what progress could be made just by being there. Paul and I found ourselves between the two groups.

"We seem to be in a no-man's land," Paul said. Some of those behind had already broken out the water balloons, and some had even slipped over the side for a quick swim.

"Maybe it's because we haven't really made up our minds what our intentions are," I replied.

We drifted, sailed when we could, and exchanged conversation with neighboring boats. Crossing tacks with Bill and Dawn Morton from Rye, New York, for about the tenth time, we were offered chocolate chip cookies as well as right-of-way. We elected to take the cookies. The wind never filled in. The second race was shortened and the third called after 1700. All the boats were towed like ducklings to the state park by the faithful group of escort boats that stayed with us for two days.

Tents sprang up everywhere. Clothes and bedrolls were unpacked. Then there was food and drink and friendship and stories of other years on the Connecticut. A bonfire was built and many stayed up and talked as the stars and a new sliver of a moon appeared, while the rest drifted off to sleep, tired, sunburned, but relaxed.

Sunday was also windless. By 0830 breakfast (including 50 dozen eggs) had been served, camp struck, and the boats reloaded. I marveled at the order of it all. After the early start, people began to paddle leisurely. One man inflated an air mattress and, tethering it to his Sunfish, lay on his back and drifted with the current. Others swam by their boats, pushing them or pulling them along in the hot, still day. One woman stood by her mast reading a book while her partner steered.

The final race started around 1300, and with it came the wind. The brightly colored sails skimmed across the water. The pack spread out, and everyone enjoyed a delicious sail on the final leg. In Essex boats were packed up; trophies were awarded, in the end, the winners determined by who had drifted fastest. In the mixed doubles division (one male, one female per boat) the husband-and-wife team of Bob and Sharon Heckman were victorious for the second year in a row, while in the odd-couples division (two of the same sex per boat) Dan and Mark Newey, father and son, claimed the honors.

Paul and I unrigged our boat. New friends came by to say farewell. I waved goodbye to Fred Pati. "Did you have a good time, Fred?" I shouted.

His gear stowed, his white hair neatly combed, the afternoon sun reflecting in his glasses, Fred hardly looked like he had spent two days on the river. "Well, if you consider tips and everything," he called back, his face opening with a dazzling smile, "it was fantastic!" And so it was. □

MASTERS JUST WANNA HAVE FUN

Story by Tom Linskey; photographs by Peter McGowan

A wave hops over my bow, explodes onto the splashrail and into my face. But it's only a 6-inch wave, another dollop of Sarasota Bay's warm cream frosting, and when my eyes clear I'm still sailing side by side with the same bunch. To windward is Dick Tillman, 58, tough competitor and nice guy, but suspiciously well muscled—a Laser champ from way back. To leeward is Rita Steele, 46, blonde, attractive, and one of the few women in this fleet who *isn't* a grandmother. Back a little ways but hanging tough is Earl Gerloff, 79 years young, a boot-tough Texan. All of us are hiking, playing the mainsheet and feathering our Sunfish through gusts, our eyes on the wind on the water, the flock of port-tack boats converging in our mainsail windows, the 30 or so boats on starboard tack riding a lift behind our backs.

Such was the racing at the three-day Sunfish International Masters in mid-March, a seven-race, one-throwout championship for over-40 sailors who are more bent on fun than fratricide, who get their kicks out of racing a boat that's low on hassle and hype and high on spray and speed. The event was hosted by Florida's Sarasota Sailing Squadron, the perfect venue for sandy-footed Sunfishers: tents, picnic tables, a knack for running regattas. The fleet is scored together and by age division—age 40–48, Apprentice; 49–59, Master; 60–67, Grand Master; over 68, Great Grand Master.

Did you say *over* 68? What are

The Sunfish delivers low-cost, low-hassle water fun for the young and not-young. Here, author Linskey gets creamed

In Masters racing, "old guys" finish first. The Sunfish, a 13-foot, 10-inch hot rod, puts smiles on their faces. Join 55 Sunfish sailors on the sundown side of 40 in a championship where the vibes are sunny, the water is warm, and bald spots are fast

senior citizens doing hot-rodding around in off-the-beach boardboats that weigh less than last month's groceries? Such audacity may be possible only in the Sunfish, at 250,000 strong an icon of small-boatdom and that rarest of crossover boats—forgiving enough for beginners, yet challenging enough for experts.

Compared to more results-oriented one-design regattas, the tone at the Masters championship is a blast of fresh air: no pros, no big budgets, no exotic materials, no two-boat testing programs—just racing. And good vibes. The Sunfish experience engenders both class legends and abiding loyalty in equal measure. "I sail J/24s, PHRF, lots of other boats, but I keep coming back to the Sunfish. It's the people," says Charlie Clifton, a class stalwart since 1962. If the Masters here aren't family, they're close: the joshing, the story-swapping, the Tupperware picnics on tailgates. In 30 years of regattas I've never witnessed so many backslaps and bear hugs.

On the water, things get exacting. During the first half of the series, sailed on Olympic and windward-leeward courses, the wind is 12 to 15 knots and gusty, and the racecourse is a patchwork of short sharp wind lines and near-windless holes. In these heads-up conditions, Dick Tillman gets off the starting line clean, doesn't miss a major shift, and handles his boat with aplomb. Beautiful to watch, as he waltzes by. For the rest of us, fortunes come and go, throwing a pack of former champs, such as four-time Masters winner Don Bergman, 64, into a scrap for second overall.

The racing is close, hard fought, but civilized; there's a little yelling during the logjams at marks, but no bloody-murder screams. In close crossings, people seem as apt to trade verbal sallies as to holler "Starboard!" There's a sense of perspective about life's inevitable ups and downs; in one race, as a magnificent elevator puff lifted Andy Hodgson into first-place glory, I distinctly heard him *singing*.

MAYBE IT'S THE WISDOM OF AGE, OR maybe everyone is just too preoccupied sailing their boats to project the racer's requisite aggro. Racing the Sunfish is an exercise in feel, and the lessons apply to every type of boat. In a hiking breeze the Sunfish rudder, small and heavily raked, is easily overpowered by the sail. First get the hull

Hotshot grandmother Jean Bergman, above, explodes through the chop. Masters champ Dick Tillman, rigged and ready, is about to prove that nice guys finish fast

trimmed right (both heel and fore and aft), then the sail trimmed right, and the rudder will follow. Reaching, the shallow-V Sunfish hull planes with scowlike ease and giddy speed, the chines reeling off a firehose of spray.

On windy runs, if you do it just right, you'll peg the thrill meter. The fastest, most on-edge technique is to heel the boat over to windward on top of yourself, ease the sail well out in front of the bow, and steer deeply by the lee. When a gust hits you're suddenly on a full plane on the windward chine, the daggerboard is too high, the sail is out too far, the boat is launched off the chop and coming in for a landing—but you're traveling incredibly fast directly toward the leeward mark. The two ways to submarine a Sunfish—the crowd-pleasing catapult and the slow, certain submerge—share the same soggy denouement. You learn to move back. Fast.

There's mystique, if not a touch of mysticism, surrounding the Sunfish's rig. "I've been in the class five years now, and I'm just starting to figure out the tuning," says Dick Tillman. "There's some subtle things going on." Seemingly an anachronism, the Sunfish's lateen rig is clever in its adjustability; by sliding the gooseneck forward or aft along the boom, or by tying the main halyard higher or lower on the gaff spar, sailors can shift the sail's center of effort aft for light air, forward for heavy air, to balance the helm.

To depower the generous-size sail in heavy air, lightweight (under 150 pounds) sailors go to the "Jens" rig, first used in 1976 by Jens Hookanson to win a windy North Americans. The main halyard's clove hitch is retied lower on the gaff spar, and the halyard's hoist point is moved down on the mast; in puffs, the gaff bends off to leeward, spilling wind and keeping flyweights on their feet. On the beach before a windy race, the buzz is Jens, Jens, Jens.

I'M ALWAYS THE FIRST TO JENS. I'M A wimp," quips Jean Bergman, the hotshot grandmother who, in 1990, came within a race of winning the Sunfish world title. That's the *open* Sunfish Worlds—all ages. How to console your tanned, toned, and well-hormoned teenager after he's been politely but firmly rolled by a gray-haired grandmother? Masters regattas are not kid stuff.

Well—somebody should tell *them* that. Sometime between Saturday night's shrimp peel, the Jimmy Buffett–style live entertainment, and the last skirl of Bermudian sailor David Firth's bagpipes, a posse of Masters, Grand and Great Grand, carried out some midnight skullduggery. I arrived Sunday morning to find my Sunfish parked in the yacht club bar, a beer crate with a sign on the foredeck: *Raffle! Win a Sunfish!* As hazings go, I got off easy; other freshmen Masters have found their vessels perched on yacht club roofs or floating fully rigged in the hotel pool. "It means we like you," Don Bergman explained kindly, "and, you're in the Masters now."

What kind of folks sail in the Masters? Some beginning sailors, sure, but most Masters are converts from other classes. "Usually I've got three people sitting in front of me on my Pearson 26, so I don't catch a wave in the face, but not on a Sunfish. It's fun, though," says Ray Cash of Okeechobee, Florida, a first-year Sunfish racer.

"A bunch of us got tired of calling up crew and having them not show up," says Pat Manning, who with husband Vic started a fleet on Lake Travis in Austin, Texas. Now it boasts 70 boats and 10 skippers who sail nationally, and Pat has acquired one hell of a tattoo (she showed me) on her upper right thigh: a rainbow, a tropical island, and a Sunfish.

Much of the Sunfish's appeal lies in the fact that everyone gets to be the skipper. "I always get last," says New Jersey's Ellen Rowen, rather unfairly. "But it doesn't matter. I'm sailing my own boat, that's the point."

For the more hard-edged racing types, there's an immediacy to a small boat—a really small boat, with only one sail and one string to pull—that feels a lot like liberation. A quick tack

One sail, one string, one skipper—and 54 other boats on the starting line

Reaching, the generous-size sail and shallow-V hull make the Sunfish take off. Hike out, enjoy the ride

on a header, then a flip back, and you can ride the skirts of a gust that would amount to only a passing frustration in a bigger boat. And the challenge of the Sunfish to the sailor who's done it all is this: Do you still have what it takes to make a little boat go? No instruments, no Mylar/Kevlar, no ratings, no excuses; just your butt on the rail, the spray and wind in your face, the tug of mainsheet and tiller, the flutter of the sail—racing at its purest.

THE SECOND HALF OF THE CHAMPIONship belongs to Dick Tillman, who knocks off more bullets to win the title. The battle for second is a dogfight between Don Bergman, Charlie Clifton, New York's Bruce Kennedy, former North American champ Joe Blouin, Floridians Steve Honour and "Big Al" Thompson, and me, the new kid who's getting some breaks. Roll the puff dice, hit the shifts, hike, hike, hike! But where are the ladies?

It's getting breezier by the race, and the series is turning into a grind for small, lightweight people. In the end, local sailor Rita Steele will nose out favorite Jean Bergman by a mere point, both of them just out of the top-10 overall. But off the wind, lightweights extract their revenge; on one planing reach, Linda Tillman, two boatlengths ahead of me, finesses the bejeezus out of a black gust and puts a quick 75 yards on me as my jaw drops. It's almost as if she pops a secret clutch and roars away in a gear I don't have. Worse, she doesn't even wave goodbye.

The regatta is getting to be a tough one for Great Grand Masters, too. "I can't hike as hard or as long as the 40s [age group], but I'm fighting it out with the 60s," says Earl Gerloff, who'll have to console himself with sailing 20, but not 40, years faster than his classification. But everyone's stomach muscles, leg muscles, arm muscles are giving out. This is not a class of jocks, of Jack LaLannes, after all. A familiar postrace refrain on the beach: "Are we having fun yet?" Creak. Groan. And another: "Ahhhh," as body after body sinks into the yacht club couch.

The last race is a honker, real hang-on-tight-and-wipe-the-sunscreen-out-of-your-eyes-with-a-sailing-gloved-knuckle kind of stuff. Survival of the grittiest. Tillman wins yet again—all right, already!—and second place in the series comes down to who beats whom between Don Bergman and me. Then it comes down to the last beat, the last *tack* into the finish line. Don is to windward of me on starboard tack, and I need to cross his bow to make the finish. I slam the boat onto port right at the finish buoy. Hike out, sheet in, a glimpse through the sail window: I can't make it. No way can I cross him. He's got me nailed. *Starboard!!* A puff—I clear him by one foot. Whoa! Second place! It doesn't get any closer.

Not all Masters events are this windy, but after such a black-and-blue series (the fleet's collective bruises will go uncounted; Jean Bergman, clocked by the boom, posted the week's most impressive black eye), you wonder: Why don't these folks give it up, start acting their age? Why don't they settle into some sedate keelboat with cockpit cushions and teak backrests, or for heaven's sake, into a slow and stately Beetlecat that won't upset their chardonnay?

"We're having too much fun," says Vic Manning, massaging sore legs. "Ohhh, yeah, *way* too much fun."

For information about the Sunfish and Masters races, contact Peg and Terry Beadle, U.S. Sunfish Class, P.O. Box 300128, Drayton Plains, MI 48330-0128; tel./fax 810-673-2750.

Results

Overall: (1) Dick Tillman, Merritt Island, FL, 6.75; (2) Tom Linskey, Boston, MA, 23.0; (3) Don Bergman, Holland, MI, 26.0; (4) Charlie Clifton, Sarasota, FL, 30.0; (5) Bruce Kennedy, Amityville, NY, 35.0; (6) Joe Blouin, Tampa, FL, 36.75; (7) Steve Honour, Seminole, FL, 36.75; (8) "Big Al" Thompson, Lithium, FL, 46.0; (9) Andy Hodgson, Sarasota, FL, 57.0; (10) Tom Katterheinrich, New Knoxville, OH, 65.0

Apprentice, Tom Linskey; Master, Dick Tillman; Grand Master, Don Bergman; Great Grand Master, Larry Cochran, Manchester, CT

Notes

Notes

more 

Young or old, male or female...

GET IN ON THE FUN - SAIL A SUNFISH!

Used Sunfish

Many sailors start with a used Sunfish. Here is what to look for.

A Sunfish hull, even one that has been sitting out in a pasture for years, if it is dry inside can usually be brought back to life with a good scrubbing and a little wet sanding.

The weak point in the spars is under the gooseneck, if the tape between gooseneck and boom has worn away. If the bronze gooseneck and the aluminum boom have been touching, especially in a seaside environment, the aluminum can be eaten away.

The same is true between the gooseneck and the mast, if they have been stored linked together. Check both spots, and the holes where boom and upper spar are linked together by eye bolts.

The wood parts, of course, can lose their varnish and become weathered, and may even rot. The sail, if it has been left exposed to the sun, will also weaken and eventually disintegrate, as will the plastic parts. They can all be replaced at relatively low cost.

But few boats can stand neglect the way a Sunfish can. More than one decrepit-looking Sunfish has raced, in the hands of a good sailor, and won some silver. That's why *Fortune* magazine, back in the '70s, named it one of the 25 best-built products in America. And that's also one reason Sunfish hold their value over the years - that and the strong Class organization.

Check the boating want ads in the paper, and the classified boating flyers found in many sailing areas of the country. Or check the yacht clubs and boating groups near you. Many boat dealers have Sunfish on hand, of course. There are a lot of Sunfish out there.

New Sunfish

Nothing can gladden the heart like a new boat. There are many Sunfish dealers across the United States. Check your Yellow Pages, or call

Sunfish Laser, Inc.
200 High Point Avenue
Portsmouth, RI 02871
Phone (401) 683-5900
FAX (401) 683-9640

The Sunfish Clan

The head office of both the International Sunfish Class Association (ISCA) and the United States Sunfish Class Association (USSCA) is run, at this writing, by Peg and Terry Beadle, and has been for many years. Whether you are looking for a Sunfish, or already own one, they can put you in touch with a fleet near you. Join a fleet if you can. You'll make great friends, and learn a lot. If you're an experienced sailor, they'll be glad to learn from you, as well.

Even if you aren't interested in racing, it's worth the small dues to join the Class organization in your country if there is one, or ISCA if there isn't. You will get an official racing number to put on your sail, the Class yearbook (first published in 1996), the regatta schedule, the Class rules, constitution and by-laws, and most important, the Class newsletter, *Windward Leg*. It's full of regatta news, of course, but it also has many articles on boat maintenance and repair, sailing and safety tips, gadget ideas you can make or buy, and more. A number of important articles and reprints from *Windward Leg* are available from the Class office, as well as videos, including Bob Johnstone's dynamite production, *Sail to Freedom*. It came out in 1976, but it's still one of the best sailing videos ever made.

Sunfish Class Office
Peg and Terry Beadle
P.O. Box 300128
Drayton Plains, MI 48330-0128
Phone/FAX (810) 673-2750

For the net surfers, there's a Sunfish Class home page on the World Wide Web.

To join US Sailing, the national organization for sailboat racing:

United States Sailing Association
P.O. Box 1260
15 Maritime Dr.
Portsmouth, RI 02871-6015
Phone (401) 683-0800
FAX (401) 683-0840
CompuServe # 75530,502